INTEREST RATE FUTURES: CONCEPTS AND ISSUES

Gerald D. Gay
Georgia State University

Robert W. Kolb
Emory University

Robert F. Dame, Inc.
1905 Huguenot Road
Richmond, Virginia 23235

To Mary and Gabi

© Robert F. Dame, Inc. 1982

All rights reserved. No part of this publication
may be reproduced, stored in a retrieval system,
or transmitted, in any form or by any means,
electronic, mechanical, photocopying, recording,
or otherwise, without prior written permission of
the publisher.

ISBN 0-936-328-19-3
Library of Congress Catalog No. 81-68697

PRINTED IN THE UNITED STATES OF AMERICA

Designed and typeset by Publications Development Co. of
Crockett, Texas, Developmental Editor: Nancy Marcus Land,
Production Editor: Bessie Graham

PREFACE

Since the first interest rate futures contract was traded on October 20, 1975, the interest rate futures market has experienced phenomenal growth. Never before has any financial market grown so quickly to reach such a prominent place in the economy. That first day 815 GNMA contracts were traded, and the open interest was 244 contracts. By year-end 1980 the open interest had grown to 115,000. In addition, other contracts, both on the Chicago Board of Trade and other exchanges, have begun trading as well. Today contracts exist on U.S. T-bills, notes, and bonds, on commercial paper (30 and 90 day contracts), on two different GNMA instruments, and on domestic certificates of deposit.

Currently, various exchanges are vying for regulatory permission to trade other contracts as well. Today the total open interest for all interest rate futures contracts represents almost $100 billion dollars worth of deliverable instruments. This market has become so large that some observers fear it may come to dominate the primary markets, and even interfere with Federal Reserve monetary policy.

One consequence of this rapid development is that the market's growth in size may have outstripped the growth in knowledge about the market. While much has been written in the popular press and in trade publications about the interest rate futures market, it is often the same article that is being written and rewritten. Further, it is not unusual to find such articles filled with mythic lore about the market, or even with error. By contrast, the academic literature has been relatively scarce until recently, and the little that has appeared has focused largely on a few narrow areas. One reason for the scarcity of articles is the long lag between submission and publication of an article in an academic journal. The respective difficulties of the trade and academic journals have both contributed to the present unsatisfactory state of knowledge about the interest rate futures market.

Interest Rate Futures: Concepts and Issues attempts to promote the development of knowledge regarding interest rate futures by bringing together for the first time a collection of the best that has been written in the field. The available pool of worthwhile articles is already too large to make possible the inclusion of everything, yet it is not so large that the anthology fails to be comprehensive. In addition to being comprehensive of present knowledge, the anthology was designed to advance the state of knowledge as well. Consequently, a number of articles appear here for the first time, while others appear roughly concurrently with their publication elsewhere. This effort to be current is particularly important in a field of such rapid growth and change.

The book is arranged into five sections:

I. Introduction to Futures Market
II. The Efficiency of the Interest Rate Futures Market
III. Hedging with Interest Rate Futures
IV. The Institutional Environment
V. Bibliography

Each section is preceded by a short introduction. The first section is designed to acquaint the reader with some of the seminal articles about futures markets as a whole that have particular relevance to interest rate futures markets. The topic of market efficiency, which has been the issue of greatest academic interest, is explored in Section II. If the market is efficient, then speculative opportunities do not offer much attraction, and the social justification for the existence of the market devolves upon the issue of hedging—the subject matter of Section III. Until recently, a number of features of the institutional environment surrounding the interest rate futures market have been neglected. Specifically, Section IV addresses the relationship between spot and future prices, tax and legal issues, the accounting treatment of futures transactions, and the regulatory environment within which financial institutions participate in the interest rate futures markets. Additionally, Section IV addresses further pending innovations in financial futures such as stock index futures contracts and inflation sensitive contracts as well. The book concludes with an extensive bibliography that includes other articles on interest rate futures as well as related articles on bond valuation. While it cannot be claimed that the bibliography is complete, it is at least, like the book itself, comprehensive.

We wish to express our gratitude to the many authors and friends who permitted their work to be included here. A special note of thanks goes to those authors who allowed their work to appear here first. Fi-

Preface

nally, we wish to thank the publisher, Bob Dame, for his support of an unproven entry into the financial publishing field. Any stimulation to the advancement of knowledge that this book provides derives in large part from Bob's commitment to the encouragement of research.

> Gerald D. Gay
> Georgia State University
> Atlanta, Georgia
>
> Robert W. Kolb
> Emory University
> Atlanta, Georgia
>
> November 1981

ABOUT THE AUTHORS

Currently serving as an Assistant Professor at Georgia State University, **Dr. Gerald D. Gay's** current research interests focus on interest rate futures and bond portfolio management. An author of papers testing the effectiveness of alternative hedging strategies using interest rate futures, Dr. Gay has also developed a technique for immunizing a bond portfolio against interest rate changes by using interest rate futures. In addition to having participated in seminars at the Chicago Board of Trade, Dr. Gay's research findings have been presented at recent conferences in the United States and abroad.

Now an Assistant Professor at Emory University, **Dr. Robert W. Kolb** is an author of several papers on interest rate futures, two of which appear in this volume. Additionally, Dr. Kolb's book, *Interest Rate Futures: A Comprehensive Introduction*, is soon to be released by Robert F. Dame, Inc. Currently conducting a series of two-day seminars on interest rate futures at major U.S. cities, Dr. Kolb is also a partner in the firm Kolb and Gay Associates, which specializes in interest rate risk management.

CONTENTS

PREFACE   iii

I. INTRODUCTION TO FUTURES MARKETS   1

   1. The Simultaneous Determination of Spot and Futures Prices   5
Jerome L. Stein

   2. Futures Trading and Investor Returns: An Investigation of Commodity Market Risk Premiums   21
Katherine Dusak

   3. The Pricing of Commodity Contracts   41
Fischer Black

   4. Interest Rate Futures   55
Marcelle Arak and Christopher J. McCurdy

II. THE EFFICIENCY OF THE INTEREST RATE FUTURES MARKET   81

vii

5.	Using T-Bill Futures to Gauge Interest-Rate Expectations *William Poole*	85
6.	Is the Futures Market for Treasury Bills Efficient? *Donald J. Puglisi*	107
7.	Is the Futures Market for Treasury Bills Efficient? *Anthony J. Vignola and Charles J. Dale*	115
8.	A Comparison of Yields on Futures Contracts and Implied Forward Rates *Richard W. Lang and Robert H. Rasche*	123
9.	Testing the Unbiased Expectations Theory of Interest Rates *Ben Branch*	143
10.	The U.S. Treasury Bill Futures Market and Hypotheses Regarding the Term Structure of Interest Rates *Brian G. Chow and David J. Brophy*	159
11.	Treasury Bill Pricing in the Spot and Futures Markets *Dennis R. Capozza and Bradford Cornell*	175
12.	The Efficiency of the Treasury Bill Futures Market *Richard J. Rendleman, Jr. and Christopher E. Carabini*	191
13.	The Efficiency of the Treasury Bill Futures Market: An Analysis of Alternative Specifications *Anthony J. Vignola and Charles Dale*	213
III.	**HEDGING WITH INTEREST RATE FUTURES**	**237**
14.	Interest Rate Futures: New Tool for the Financial Manager *Peter W. Bacon and Richard E. Williams*	241

Contents

15. Hedging for Better Spread Management 255
    Robert W. McLeod and George M. McCabe

16. Hedging Possibilities in the Flotation of Debt Securities 265
    Richard W. McEnally and Michael L. Rice

17. The Hedging Performance of the New Futures Markets 279
    Louis H. Ederington

18. The Hedging Performance of the New Futures Markets: Comment 297
    Charles T. Franckle

19. Risk Reduction Potential of Financial Futures 307
    Joanne Hill and Thomas Schneeweis

20. The Error Learning Model and the Financial Futures Market 325
    George Emir Morgan and Charles T. Franckle

21. Improving Hedging Performance Using Interest Rate Futures 339
    Robert W. Kolb and Raymond Chiang

22. Duration, Immunization, and Hedging with Interest Rate Futures 353
    Robert W. Kolb and Raymond Chiang

IV. THE INSTITUTIONAL ENVIRONMENT 365

23. Market Incompleteness and Divergences Between Forward and Futures Interest Rates 369
    Edward J. Kane

24. Forward and Futures Pricing of Treasury Bills 387
    George Emir Morgan

25. Tax-Induced Bias in Markets for Futures Contracts 401
    Edward Miller

26.	Tax Topics: Interest Rates Futures—Commercial Banks *James G. O'Brien*	405
27.	Bank Regulations for Futures Accounting *James Kurt Dew*	413
28.	Futures Trading by National Banks *Robert C. Lower and Scott W. Ryan*	421
29.	Financial Futures Markets: Is More Regulation Needed? *Phillip Cagan*	437
30.	Living with Inflation: A Proposal for New Futures and Options Markets *Louis H. Ederington*	463
31.	Market Index Futures Contracts *Victor Niederhoffer and Richard Zeckhauser*	477

V. **BIBLIOGRAPHY** 491

PART I

INTRODUCTION TO FUTURES MARKETS

Part I consists of four articles, three treating issues of the general futures market, the fourth providing an introduction to interest rate futures. The first article, by Jerome L. Stein, The Simultaneous Determination of Spot and Futures Prices, argues that a market participant should take a portfolio approach, regarding the futures and spot positions as being jointly determined. Then, with the spot position held constant, it is possible to find the optimal holding of the futures contract to secure a hedge with certain desirable risk properties. The approach to hedging advocated by Stein for commodity contracts has been very important to the interest rate futures market by providing an impetus for several of the hedging studies included in Part II. For this sequence of articles, the goal is to find the risk minimizing futures positions for a given spot position by the use of regression analysis.

Katherine Dusak's article, Futures Trading and Investor Returns: An Investigation of Commodity Market Risk Premiums, examines two key questions concerning commodity futures markets. First, Dusak seeks to determine whether a position in a commodity futures contract embodies an exposure to systematic risk, and second, whether the systematic risk (if any) is properly compensated by investor returns. By applying a variant of the traditional capital asset pricing model, Dusak specifies a model that allows her to test for the presence of systematic risk. According to capital market theory, investors' returns should compensate investors for all, and only, the systematic, or nondiversifiable, risk they bear. In the absence of systematic *risk an investor should merely expect to earn the risk-free rate of interest on invested capital. Dusak concludes that commodity futures contracts embody no systematic risk. Consequently, the holders of such futures contracts should expect to earn only the risk-free rate on their invested capital. However, since futures contracts do not require investment the expected return from holding a futures contract should be zero. For the time period and the commodities she analyzes, Dusak finds that the realized returns are near zero, in accordance with capital market theory. Although Dusak did not address the interest rate futures market, which did not exist when she wrote, her research has clear implications for the interest rate futures market. Since interest rate futures require no investment, it is quite likely that their normal return is zero as well. Since the futures market is a zero-sum game in the absence of transaction costs, it is necessary that a sufficiently large random sample of returns would show a zero net return. These considerations regarding the level of systematic risk and expected returns have important consequences for the role of speculation in the interest rate futures market.*

One of the creators of the famous Black-Scholes option pricing model, Fischer Black, applies the option pricing model to commodity contracts in his article, The Pricing of Commodity Contracts. *One important point made by Black is to distinguish forward and futures contracts, since there are important institutional and economic differences between the two types of contracts. This accomplished, Black points out that his model pertains directly to forward contracts, although there are implications for futures contracts as well. This is particularly clear since Black is able to conclude that the value of the forward contract is a function of the difference in price between the forward and futures contract, and the risk-free rate of interest. Additionally Black discusses the relationship between futures prices and expected spot prices, and argues that futures markets serve their primary social function by providing a source of information to all market observers regarding the future spot prices. In terms of the interest rate futures markets, the futures prices reveal the market's expectation of future spot prices of the bonds deliverable against the futures contracts.*

The final paper of Part I, Interest Rate Futures, *by Marcelle Arak and Christopher J. McCurdy, provides a useful introduction* to the specific area of interest rate futures. The paper covers the operation of the market, the nature of the participants, contract specifications, and the societal function of the market. In addition, Arak and McCurdy discuss the role of speculation and its technique. Some of the tax consequences are considered also, and the relationship between the cash and futures market is explored. While Arak and McCurdy perform commendably in providing an orientation to the interest rate futures market, the reader might find some of the pamphlets of the Chicago Board of Trade useful as well. These, and some books specifically concerned with the interest rate futures market, such as those by Kolb, Loosigian, Powers and Vogel, and Schwartz, are listed in the Bibliography.

The Simultaneous Determination of Spot and Futures Prices[*]

Jerome L. Stein[†]

    This paper develops a simple geometric technique for the simultaneous determination of spot and futures prices in commodity markets; and it explains the allocation between hedged and unhedged holdings of stocks. On the basis of this analysis, it is possible to determine whether changes in spot and futures prices have occurred as a result of (a) changes in the excess supply of current production, or (b) changes in price expectations.
    The possessor of stocks has two alternatives. He may contract to sell a given physical entity at a stated price, or he may hold stocks for sale at a later date at an uncertain price. If the first alternative is chosen, he may sell either *spot* or *forward*. A forward sale involves delivery at a later date; any storage that the seller is performing is merely a service to his customer.
    If the second alternative is chosen, he may hold his stocks either hedged (be selling a *futures* contract) or unhedged; but this form of stockholding involves an uncertain expected return and a probability of a capital loss. Consequently, the owner of stocks will allocate his stocks between hedged and unhedged holdings to maximize his expected utility.
    This paper is concerned with both alternatives: the spot sale and the holding of stocks for sale at a later date. Part I develops a theory of

---

[*]Reprinted from *The American Economic Review*, Vol. 51, No. 5, (December 1961). Reprinted by permission of the publisher and author.
  [†]The author is associate professor of economics at Brown University. He is indebted to M. J. Brennan for stimulating comments on an earlier draft of this paper.

holding stocks. It is shown how the possessor of a given quantity of stocks allocates his holdings between hedged and unhedged stocks. Thereby, the supply of hedged and unhedged storage is derived.

Part II discusses the spot and futures markets. Two curves are developed to determine simultaneously the spot and futures prices. One curve gives the pair of spot and futures prices which equilibrate the supply and demand for storage. The other curve gives the pair of spot and futures prices which equilibrate the supply and demand for futures contracts. Equilibrium exists where the two curves intersect.

Part III indicates how these prices are affected by (1) variations in the supply and demand for current production, and (2) changes in the prices expected to prevail at a later date.

Throughout this paper, pure competition is assumed to prevail.

I. THE DECISIONS TO HOLD HEDGED AND UNHEDGED STOCKS UNDER PURE COMPETITION

A. Unhedged Holding of Stocks

The expected gain from holding unhedged stocks (u) is equal to the spot price expected to prevail at a later date (p^*) minus the current spot price (p) minus the marginal net carrying costs (m). There are two components of the marginal net carrying costs: the marginal costs of storage and the marginal convenience yield, the latter a negative element in carrying cost. The concept of the marginal convenience yield has been developed by Brennan [1, pp. 53-56] and Tesler [4, pp. 235-37]. Since the convenience yield is a measure of the advantage (to the producer, processor, or wholesaler) of having stocks readily available, it depends upon the total quantity of stocks carried—hedged and unhedged. Since the marginal convenience yield is negatively related to the total quantity of stocks carried, the marginal net carrying costs rise with the total quantity of stocks held [1] [4].

The variable p^* is a stochastic variable. There is a probability that a capital loss will be made on the holdings of unhedged stocks: i.e., that $p^* - p - m$ will be negative.

B. The Holding of Hedged Stocks

When stocks are hedged, the owner incurs a liability to offset his holding of assets (stocks). His liability is the sale of a futures contract, for the delivery of one of several grades of a commodity sometime within the period of the futures contract. The owner of hedged stocks does not intend to deliver a physical commodity in fulfillment of his futures contract, but intends to repurchase a futures contract at the time that he sells his inventory of stocks [2, Ch. 12-14] [3, p. 153] [6]. The expected gain from holding hedged stocks is equal to the expected gain from holding unhedged stocks minus the expected loss involved in the sale and purchase of a futures contract. At worst, the holder of hedged stocks can deliver one of several grades of a physical commodity in fulfillment of the futures contract, at a premium or a discount to the contract price [2, pp. 33-34].

Let q be the current price of a futures contract and q* be the price of the futures contract expected at a later date. Then, the expected gain from holding hedged stocks is h,

$$h = (p^* - p) - (q^* - q) - m. \qquad (1)$$

The firm buys stock at p and sells a futures contract for q. The marginal net carrying costs are m. The firm expects to sell the stock at p* and repurchase its futures contract for q*. In the event that it costs more to repurchase the futures contract than can be received from the sale of the unit of stock, it is cheaper to make delivery on the futures contract than to repurchase it, provided that the futures contract permits the delivery of the commodity which is held in storage. In this way, hedging may bound the possible losses that can be suffered in connection with holding stocks. The expected gain from holding *hedged* stock, h, can be written:

$$h = u - (q^* - q) \geqslant q - p - m. \qquad (2)$$

The term $q - p - m$ is the cost of delivering the basic grade on the futures contract.

There are two stochastic variables involved in h: p*, the expected commodity price, and q*, the expected price of the futures contract. Inventory losses can be made on hedged inventory, despite the fact that the loss is bounded at $q - p - m$.

C. The Optimum Combination of Hedged and Unhedged Stocks

An owner of stocks, for sale at an uncertain price, is assumed to allocate his holdings between hedged and unhedged stocks so as to maximize his expected utility. The method of optimizing developed here is based upon James Tobin's theory of liquidity preference [5, pp. 71-77].

As the proportion of unhedged stock varies between zero and 100 per cent, the expected return per unit of stock varies from h to u. Risk is inherent in each form of stockholding, where risk is defined as the situation whereby the owner may fail to receive his expected return. Many different measures of risk are possible. Tobin [5, p. 72] used the standard deviation of the expected return as his measure of risk. Since he assumed that the probability density functions are symmetrical, a high standard deviation or variance means a high probability of both negative and positive deviations from the mean. Other reasonable measures of risk, which emphasize the disutility aspects of uncertainty, are the probability of loss or the expected value of the loss. These two measures of risk do not presuppose symmetrical density functions. For expositional convenience I shall use the variance of the expected return as a measure of risk, with the assumption that the density functions are symmetrical.

An owner of a unit of unhedged stock has a risk equal to the variance of u. Given p and m, the variance of u is equal to the variance of p^*. The possessor of a unit of hedged stock has a risk equal to the variance of h. Given p, m and q, this is equal to: $\text{var } p^* + \text{var } q^* - 2 \text{ cov } p^*q^*$. As the proportion of unhedged stocks varies from zero to 100 per cent, the risk varies from $\text{var } p^* + \text{var } q^* - 2 \text{ cov } p^*q^*$ to $\text{var } p^*$.

An opportunity locus for expected return and risk, facing the owner of 100 units of stock, is given by line HU in Figure 1. At point H all of the stocks are hedged, giving an expected return of h and a risk of var h. At point U all of the stocks are unhedged, giving an expected return of u, and a risk of var u. As the ratio of unhedged to total stocks rises (see the scale at the top of Figure 1), the combination of expected return and risk is given by opportunity locus HU. In this diagram it is assumed that unhedged stocks are both riskier and carry a higher expected return than hedged stocks, thereby making line HU positively sloped. There is no reason why line HU could not be negatively sloped. In such a case (as will be apparent from the argument below) no unhedged stocks would be carried. Points H and U are based upon given price expectations and risks. As price expectations change, points H and U will move accordingly.

The indifference curve between expected return and risk will be convex—rising at an increasing rate—if the individual has a declining marginal utility of income and a total utility function which can be approximated by a quadratic. The proof of this proposition is given by Tobin [5, pp. 76-77].[1] A family of such indifference curves is given in Figure 1. Given the risk—a point on the abscissa—a higher expected return implies a higher expected utility of income; the utility expected from the ownership of 100 units of stock rises as we rise vertically in Figure 1. Curve I_2 is preferred to curve I_1 because expected utility is greater along curve I_2 than along curve I_1.

---

[1] Tobin also considers individuals with constant and rising marginal utility of incomes, i.e., individuals with indifference curves which do not rise at increasing rates. I shall restrict the present analysis to individuals with declining marginal utility schedules.

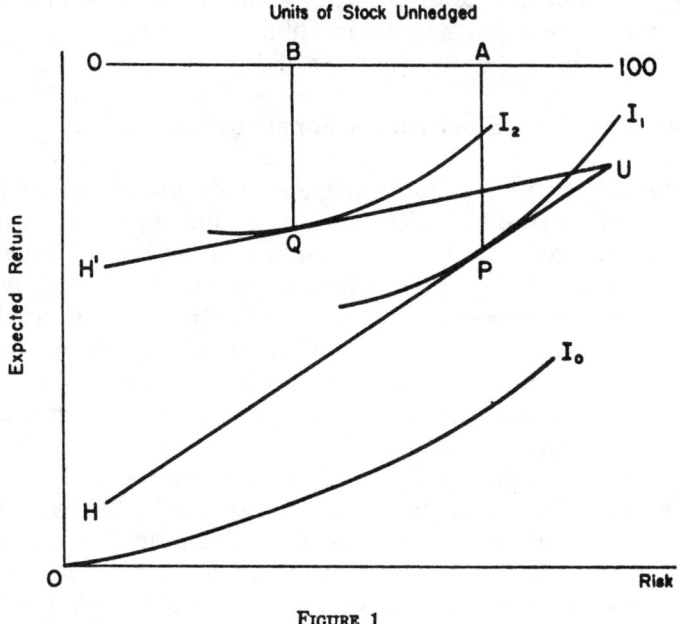

FIGURE 1

Point P represents the optimum combination of hedged and unhedged stock, given opportunity locus HU and the indifference map, since expected utility from 100 units of stock is maximized at this point. The individual will hold OA units unhedged and 100−OA units hedged.

Suppose that the price of a futures contract rises, other things remaining unchanged; then the expected return from hedged stock rises to H'; but the expected return (and risk) on unhedged stock does not change. The new opportunity locus is H'U.

The new equilibrium combination of hedged and unhedged stock is given by point Q. As the slope of the transformation line, or opportunity locus, is decreased there is a substitution effect. The ratio of unhedged to total stock will be decreased as the hedging of stock becomes relatively more attractive. Tending to offset this substitution effect is an income effect. The higher expected utility, made possible by the rise in the price of a futures contract, may affect the individual's aversion to risk. In so far as he is more willing to take an additional unit of risk per increment of expected return, when his expected utility is increased, the income effect will induce him to increase the ratio of unhedged to total stock. The crucial question is which effect will dominate? Will the greater attractiveness of holding hedged stock be offset by a greater willingness to assume risk? The substitution effect will be dominant, so that the ratio of unhedged stocks will be decreased as hedging becomes more profitable, given the utility function described above and the occurrence of tangency solutions. *Mutatis mutandis*, the proof of this proposition is found in Tobin [5, p. 79].

D. The Demand for Stocks or the Supply of Storage

The total quantity of stocks demanded by owners of stocks (i.e., the supply of storage) is assumed to be an increasing function of the maximum expected utility derived from holding stocks. Initially, the maximum expected utility from holding 100 units of stock was given by I_1. When the expected return from holding hedged stocks is increased, the maximum expected utility from holding 100 units of stock is given by I_2, which is preferred to I_1. As the expected utility from stockholding is increased, the total quantity of stocks demanded (i.e., storage supplied) will also increase.

Storage will only be supplied if the maximum expected utility from storage exceeds the utility derived from a spot sale. Consider an indifference curve I_0 (in Figure 1) passing through a point 0 (= 0, 0) with an expected return of 0 and a risk of zero. This curve will be convex, under the assumptions made above. No stocks will be held for later sale at an uncertain price unless the opportunity locus is tangent to an indifference curve which is preferred to I_0. In the event of a corner solution, stocks will be held only if the highest attainable indifference curve is preferred to I_0.

A rise in the maximum expected utility will also occur if the opportunity locus HU, fixed at H, rotates in a counterclockwise direction. For example, suppose that p* and q* rose by equal amounts; then, all other things remaining the same, the expected return from unhedged storage rises relative to the expected return from hedged storage—risk remaining constant. The ratio of unhedged to the total stocks will rise; and there will be an increase in the total quantity of stocks demanded. Both income and substitution effects operate in the same direction in this case.

The demand for stocks (i.e., the supply of storage) then depends upon points H and U. Given the risks (var h, var u), the demand for stocks rises with (1) p* − p − m, and with (2) (p* − q*) + (q − p) − m. The first term is the expected return derived from holding unhedged stock; the second term is the expected return derived from holding hedged stock. The demand for stocks in the market (S_D) is given by equation (3):[2]

$$S_D = U(p^* - p - m) + H[(p^* - q^*) + b - m]; \quad U' > 0, H' > 0, \qquad (3)$$

[2] The process of aggregation is difficult in so far as expectations of individuals differ. Let p* and q* refer to the "average" expectations, appropriately weighed, of those who are in the business of supplying storage. See Telser [4, pp. 239-40] on this point.

where $b = q - p$, the spread, U is the market demand for unhedged stock, and H is the market demand for hedged stock. That is, U is the supply of unhedged storage and H is the supply of hedged storage.

E. The Duality of Long and Short Hedging

There are people, such as millers, who have contracted to sell a certain number of units forward at a fixed price. A miller contracts to sell x units of flour for p dollars, to be delivered in (say) 90 days. His stock of flour is $-x$ units, just as the stock of the individual in Figure 1 was $+100$ units. The miller does not know the exact price at which he will be able to purchase his wheat. His gross profit will be $p - p^*$, where p^* is the price at which he expects to purchase the wheat. A miller can hedge by purchasing a wheat future contract at price q, at the time that the flour is sold forward. His expected return is $(p - q) + (q^* - p^*)$, where q^* is the price at which he expects to sell the wheat futures contract.

The miller, i.e., the potential long hedger, holds a negative quantity of stock. Moreover, the expected return from his hedged or unhedged position is the negative of the short hedger discussed in the sections above (excluding the marginal net carrying costs).

On the basis of the analysis described in Figure 1, the potential long hedger (e.g., miller) can determine (1) how much of his short position should be covered by the purchase of a wheat futures contract and (2) how many units of flour he should sell short. The first problem is solved by hedging that proportion which will maximize his expected utility—exactly as described above. The second problem is solved by varying his short sales on the basis of the maximum expected utility that he can derive from a short position, where he hedges the proportion called for in the answer to the first problem. The position of the long hedger is the negative of the position of the short hedger, and the same method of analysis is applicable in both cases.

II. MARKET EQUILIBRIUM

Market equilibrium prevails when (1) the quantity of stocks demanded (i.e., the supply of storage) is equal to the quantity of stocks in existence (i.e., the demand for storage) and (2) the supply of futures contracts is equal to the demand for futures contracts. An SS curve will be derived which equilibrates the market for stocks and an FF curve will be derived which equilibrates the market for futures contracts (see Figure 2). Market equilibrium exists when these curves intersect.

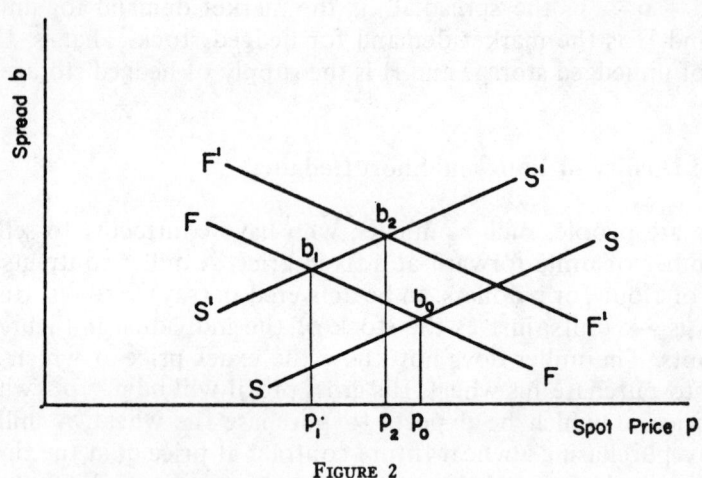

FIGURE 2

A. The Supply and Demand for Stocks

The demand for stocks has been given in equation (3). The quantity of stocks in existence is equal to the initial quantity of stocks, S_{-1}, plus the difference between current production and current consumption $X(p,a)$. The quantity $X(p,a)$ is the excess supply of current production, p is the spot price and a is a parameter. An increase in a means a rightward shift of the excess supply curve of current production. This curve is upward-sloping since a rise in the spot price increases the quantity supplied, and decreases the quantity demanded, of current output.

In equilibrium, equation (4) must be satisfied:

$$U(p^* - p - m) + H[(p^* - q^*) + b - m] = S_{-1} + X(p,a). \tag{4}$$

The total quantity of stocks demanded, $U + H$, must equal the total quantity of stocks available, $S_{-1} + X$. The two dependent variables are p, the spot price and b, the spread between the futures price and the spot price. Once p and b are known, $q \equiv b + p$ is also known. The variable b can be negative; but p must be nonnegative.

Differentiate (4) with respect to p and solve for $\partial b/\partial p$. This is described in equation (5) below.[3]

$$\frac{\partial b}{\partial p} = \frac{X_p + U'}{H'} > 0; \tag{5}$$

[3] The marginal net carrying cost has been treated as a constant. This is not necessary. Let (4′) $m = m(S)$; $m' > 0$. That is, the marginal net carrying cost rises with the size of the stocks. $S = S_{-1} + X(p, a)$. When we solve for $\partial p/\partial p$, given equations (4) and (4′), we again obtain a rising SS curve. The slope of the SS curve, with a rising m, is steeper than the slope of the curve in Figure 2.

$$X_p = \partial X/\partial p > 0,$$

$$U' = \partial U/\partial (p^* - p - m) > 0,$$

$$H' = \partial H/\partial [(p^* - q^*) + b - m] > 0.$$

For equilibrium to prevail b and p must move in the same direction, and this is described by the SS curve in Figure 2 below. The SS curve is the pair of p and b that must prevail if the supply and demand for stocks (i.e., storage) are to be equal.[4]

The logic of a rising SS curve can be expressed in literary terms, to correspond with equation (5). Given price expectations, a higher spot price will increase the quantity of stocks in existence by increasing production and decreasing consumption. What must happen to the spread b to increase the quantity of stocks demanded by those who hold stocks? The spread b must change in such a way as to increase the quantity of stocks that people want to hold. Since a rise in the spread will achieve this end, by increasing the expected utility of holding hedged stocks, b must rise with p to equilibrate the supply and demand for stocks. This establishes the rising SS curve.

B. The Supply and Demand for Futures Contracts

Whenever a unit of stock is hedged, there is a forward contract supplied. The demand for hedged stock (i.e., the supply of hedged storage) is equal to the supply of futures contracts. Hence, the quantity of futures contracts supplied is $H[(p^* - q^*) + b - m]$.

Speculators demand futures contracts and expect to profit from an anticipated rise in the price of futures contracts.[5] The price q^* expected by hedgers need not be the same as q', the price of futures contracts that speculators think will prevail in a subsequent period. Speculators expect to make a profit of $(q' - q)$ on each futures contract purchased.[6]

---

[4] The excess supply of current production could be written as X(b,a), $X_b < 0$ and $X_a > 0$. The rationale for this formulation is that: as the spot price rises relative to the futures price (i.e., b falls) producers speed up production and consumers tend to postpone consumption. The slope of the SS curve obtained thereby is: $\partial b/\partial p = U'/(H' - X_b)$, which is strictly positive. No essential change is introduced into the analysis of the text by altering the excess supply curve of current production in this manner.

[5] For purposes of exposition, the term speculator is reserved for those who are solely in the futures market. I do not refer to an individual who is entirely unhedged in the spot market, on the basis of maximizing expected utility, as a speculator. The only justification for this usage is expositional convenience.

Speculators (as defined above) can be either buyers or sellers of futures contracts depending upon the value of $(q' - q)$. In a market where long hedging dominates short hedging $(q' - q)$ will be negative; and speculators will be short futures.

[6] Individual speculators take q as a datum and adjust their positions on the basis of $(q' - q)$.

The quantity of futures contracts demanded by speculators is $G(q' - q)$, $G' > 0$. The greater the anticipated profit the greater the quantity of futures contracts demanded. Equilibrium prevails in the market for futures when the supply and demand for futures contracts are equal. This is described by equations (6):

$$H[(p^* - q^*) + b - m] = G(q' - q). \tag{6'}$$

Since $q = b + p$

$$H[(p^* - q^*) + b - m] = G(q' - b - p). \tag{6}$$

An FF curve is drawn in Figure 2, based upon equation (6). It describes the relation between b and p that must exist if the supply and demand for futures are to be equal. Differentiate equation (6) with respect to p, and solve for $\partial b/\partial p$. This yields equation (7), the slope of the FF curve:

$$\frac{\partial b}{\partial p} = \frac{-G'}{H' + G'} < 0. \tag{7}$$

It follows that FF is negatively sloped.[7]

A literary explanation of the negatively sloped FF curve can be given. Suppose that the spot price p rises, but the spread b is unchanged (i.e., both p and q rise by the same amount). What will occur? The rise in the price of futures will increase the quantity of futures contracts demanded by speculators, since $q' - q$ is reduced. On the other hand, the quantity of futures contracts supplied will be unchanged, since the expected profit from holding hedged stocks: $b + (p^* - q^*) - m$, is unchanged. The excess supply of futures contracts lowers the futures price q; and hence b must decline. When the spot price rises, the supply and demand for futures will be in equilibrium if b is lowered. Hence the negatively sloped FF curve.

Equilibrium exists when (1) the supply and demand for stocks are equal—the economy is on the SS curve—and (2) when the supply and demand for futures contracts are equal—the economy is on the FF

---

[7] If m is a rising function of the stocks held, then:

$$H[b + (p^* - q^*) - m] = G(q' - b - p);$$

$$m = M(S_{-1} + X), \quad M' > 0,$$

$$\frac{\partial b}{\partial p} = \frac{-G' + H'M'X_p}{H' + G'}.$$

The term $H'M'X_p$ is positive. The slope of the FF curve will be negative if $-G' + H'M'X_p$ is negative. Assume that this term is negative.

curve. This equilibrium exists at (p_0, b_0) in Figure 2. At this point the future price $q_0 = b_0 + p_0$. The simultaneous determination of spot and futures prices has been demonstrated.

III. COMPARATIVE STATICS

With the aid of the graphic technique developed above,[8] we show the effects upon the spot price (p) and the spread (b) of (1) a change in the excess supply of current production and (2) changes in price expectations.

A. A Change in the Excess Supply of Current Production

An increase in the excess supply curve of current production shifts the SS curve upward to the left to S'S' and leaves the FF curve unchanged, as shown in Figure 2.[9] In the new equilibrium, the spot price is lower ($p_1 < p_0$) and the spread is higher ($b_1 > b_0$).[10]

The upward shift in the SS curve to S'S' can be explained in the following way: Given the spot price p and the expected prices p*, q* and q', an excess supply of current production increases the total quantity of stocks available. This increase must all be held hedged, since the unhedged quantity demanded is given as U (p* − p − m). Hedged stock-

---

[8] For simplicity, m is assumed to be constant. A variable m does not change the results if the assumption of the previous note is made.

[9] The shift of the SS curve, upward and to the left, as a result of a rise in a is derived. Differentiate (4) with respect to a.

$$H' \frac{\partial b}{\partial a} - (U' + X_p) \frac{\partial p}{\partial a} = X_a.$$

Given p, $\frac{\partial b}{\partial a}$ is positive. Given b, $\frac{\partial p}{\partial a}$ is negative.

[10] The changes in p and b, resulting from a change in a, are seen by differentiating (4) and (6) with respect to a, and solving for

$$\frac{\partial b}{\partial a} \text{ and } \frac{\partial p}{\partial a}.$$

$$H' \frac{\partial b}{\partial a} - (U' + X_p) \frac{\partial p}{\partial a} = X_a$$

$$(G' + H') \frac{\partial b}{\partial a} + G' \frac{\partial p}{\partial a} = 0.$$

$\frac{\partial b}{\partial a}$ is positive and $\frac{\partial p}{\partial a}$ is negative.

holding will only increase if b is raised. Hence, the SS curve shifts upward: i.e., given p, b must rise when a is increased.

The equilibrium process shown in Figure 2 can be described as follows: The increase in the available stocks tends to depress the spot price and encourages present consumption. By the same token, storage becomes more profitable. The quantity of unhedged stocks increases since (p* − p) is increased. Given the price of futures, hedged stock holding also becomes more profitable since (q − p) rises. But the increase in the holdings of hedged stocks produces a greater supply of futures contracts. This tends to reduce the price of futures. In the final equilibrium, q falls by less than p, i.e., the spread b increases. The quantity of unhedged stocks increases because p has fallen relative to p*; and the quantity of hedged stocks increases because b rises relative to (p* − q*).

This analysis implies that, whenever there is a variation in the excess supply of current production, (1) Δb and Δp will be negatively correlated, and (2) Δp will be negatively correlated with ΔS, the change in the quantity of stocks held in storage.

B. Changes in the Expected Spot Price

When the expected spot price p* is increased, other things remaining unchanged, the SS curve will shift to the right and the FF curve will shift to the left. If the initial equilibrium was at (p_2, b_2) in Figure 2, the new equilibrium will be at (p_0, b_0). The spot price will rise from p_2 to p_0; the spread will fall from b_2 to b_0.

The SS curve shifts from S'S' to SS because the rise in expected price makes both hedged and unhedged stockholding more profitable, given b. The excess demand for stocks cannot be satisfied, at the given b, unless the spot price p rises. Hence, the curve shifts to SS.[11]

The FF curve will shift from F'F' to FF as a result of the increase in expected price. Given b, a rise in p* makes hedged stockholding more profitable. This increases the supply of futures contracts. Speculators will only increase their demand for futures contracts if q, the futures

---

[11] Differentiate equation (4) with respect to p*, given p. Then,

$$\frac{\partial b}{\partial p^*} = \frac{-(U' + H')}{H'} < 0.$$

This means that the SS curve falls with a given p. Similarly,

$$\frac{\partial p}{\partial p^*}$$

rises for a given b.

price falls. Given $b = q - p$, p must fall. Hence, the FF curve shifts to the left.[12]

In the final equilibrium, b falls from b_2 to b_0, and p rises from p_2 to p_0, as shown in Figure 2.[13] A rise in the spot price is required to satisfy the increased demand for stocks.

When there has been a change in the price p* expected to prevail in the future, it follows from this analysis that: (1) Δb and Δp will be negatively correlated, (2) Δp and ΔS (the change in the quantity of stocks held in storage) will be positively correlated.

On the basis of observed price and quantity behavior, we can infer whether there has been a change in the excess supply of current production or in expectations concerning the price p*.

C. An Expectation of Price Rises in Spot and Futures Markets

Suppose that p*, q* and q' rise by equal amounts. What will be the effects of this change in expectations upon the current spot price p and the spread b?

On the basis of equation (4) the demand for unhedged stocks will rise, as $p^* - p - m$ is increased. The demand for hedged stocks will be unchanged since $p^* - q^*$ has not increased, and m is assumed to be constant. The excess demand for stocks, given b, can only be satisfied if p rises and induces a greater excess supply of current production. Consequently the SS curve shifts to the right.

On the basis of equation (5) the supply of futures contracts does not increase, because the demand for hedged stocks is unchanged. However, the demand for futures contracts has increased as a result of the rise in q'. This excess demand for futures contracts can be eliminated, given b, by a rise in p. Consequently, the FF curve also shifts to the right.

It is clear that the spot price p must rise. That the spread, $q - p$, must also rise can be explained as follows: The excess demand for fu-

---

[12] Differentiate equation (6) with respect to p*, holding p constant.

$$\frac{\partial b}{\partial p^*} = \frac{-H'}{H' + G'} < 0.$$

This means that the FF curve shifts down for a given p, or shifts to the left for a given b.

[13] Differentiate (4) and (6) with respect to p*.

$$-(X_p + U')\frac{\partial p}{\partial p^*} + H'\frac{\partial b}{\partial p^*} = -(U' + H')$$

$$G'\frac{\partial p}{\partial p^*} + (H' + G')\frac{\partial b}{\partial p^*} = -H'.$$

$$\frac{\partial p}{\partial p^*} > 0 \text{ and } \frac{\partial b}{\partial p^*} < 0.$$

tures contracts tends to raise the spread and thereby induces an increase in the quantity of hedged storage.[14]

In the case where spot and futures prices are expected to rise: (1) Δp and Δb are positively correlated, (2) Δp and ΔS are positively correlated and (3) Δp and Δq are positively correlated.

D. Conclusions

In so far as the above model (summarized by equations 4 and 6) is a realistic one, it is possible to infer the nature of the forces which produce changes in spot and futures prices.

A positive correlation between Δb and Δp suggests that the market has expected spot and futures prices to move together.

A negative correlation between Δb and Δp, by itself, is not too revealing. If, in addition Δp and ΔS are negatively correlated then there has been a change in the excess supply of current production: for example, an unexpected dumping of Soviet commodities on the world market.

On the other hand if Δp and Δb are negatively correlated, but Δp and ΔS are positively correlated—then there has been a change in the expected spot price but no change in the expected futures price.

THE OPPORTUNITY LOCUS IN A HEDGING DECISION: A CORRECTION[15]

In my 1961 *AER* article on spot and futures prices,[16] I drew the opportunity locus between expected return (E) and risk (R) as a straight ling. This is incorrect; it should be a concave function (negative second derivative). All the other results of that paper are unchanged.

The risk on a linear combination of hedged and unhedged stock is equation (1), where x refers to the fraction unhedged.

---

[14] These conclusions are derived as follows:

Let $p^* = p_0^* + k$, $q^* = q_0^* + k$ and $q' = q_0{}' + k$.

Equations (4) and (6) become:

$$U(p_0^* + k - p - m) + H[(p_0^* - q_0^*) + b - m] = s_1 + X(p,a)$$
$$H[(p_0^* - q_0^*) + b - m] = G(q_0{}' + k - p - b).$$

Solve for $\frac{\partial p}{\partial k}$ and $\frac{\partial b}{\partial k}$. They are both positive.

[15] Reprinted from *The American Economic Review*, Vol. 54, No. 5, (September 1964). Reprinted by permission of the publisher and author.

[16] J. L. Stein, "The Simultaneous Determination of Spot and Futures Prices," *Am. Econ. Rev.*, Dec. 1961, *51*, 1012-25.

$$R = \text{var}[xu + (1-x)h]. \tag{1}$$

Variables u and h are the returns derived from unhedged and hedged stock, respectively.

(a) u = p* − p − m where p* is the expected price, p is the current price, and m is the marginal net carrying costs.

(b) h = (p* − p) − (q* − q) − m where q is the futures price, and q* is the expected futures price at the time the contract will be liquidated.

Solving for R, we obtain equation (2). σ_p^2 is the variance of p*; σ_q^2 is the variance of q*, and r is the correlation coefficient between p* and q*.

$$R(x) = \sigma_p^2 + (1-x)^2 \sigma_q^2 - 2r(1-x)\sigma_p \sigma_q. \tag{2}$$

(a) $R(0) = \sigma_p^2 + \sigma_q^2 - 2r\sigma_p \sigma_q$

(b) $R(1) = \sigma_p^2$

The slope of the opportunity locus is dE/dR, where E = xu + (1 − x) h, and is equation (3).

$$\frac{dE}{dR} = \frac{dE/dx}{dR/dx} = \frac{(u-h)/2}{(r\sigma_p\sigma_q - \sigma_q^2) + x\sigma_q^2} = f(x). \tag{3}$$

(a) $f(0) = \dfrac{(u-h)/2}{r\sigma_p\sigma_q - \sigma_q^2}$,

(b) $f(1) = \dfrac{(u-h)/2}{r\sigma_p\sigma_q}$.

The slope of the opportunity locus is positive at x = 1 if the expected return on unhedged stock exceeds that on hedged stock. When x = 0, the slope will be negative if the variance of q* exceeds that of p*. There would exist an x between zero and unity where a vertical tangent occurs.

Since f′(x) is negative, the general concavity is proved.

No change is required in the rest of the paper.

References

1. M. J. Brennan, "The Supply of Storage," *Am. Econ. Rev.*, Mar. 1958, *48*, 50-72.
2. Gerald Gold, *Modern Commodity Futures Trading*. New York 1959.
3. H. S. Houthakker, "The Scope and Limits of Futures Trading," *The Allocation of Economic Resources*, Moses Abramovitz et al. Stanford 1959, pp. 134-59.
4. L. G. Telser, "Futures Trading and the Storage of Cotton and Wheat," *Jour. Pol. Econ.*, June 1958, *66*, 233-55.
5. James Tobin, "Liquidity Preference as Behavior Toward Risk," *Rev. Econ. Stud.*, Feb. 1958, *67*, 65-86.
6. Holbrook Working, "Futures Trading and Hedging," *Am. Econ. Rev.*, June 1953, *43*, 314-43.

Futures Trading and Investor Returns: An Investigation of Commodity Market Risk Premiums*

Katherine Dusak[†]

The long-standing controversy over whether speculators in a futures market can earn a risk premium is analyzed within the context of the capital asset pricing model recently developed by Sharpe, Lintner, and others. Under that approach the risk premium required on a futures contract should depend not on the variability of prices but on the extent to which the variations in prices are systematically related to variations in the return on total wealth. The systematic risk was estimated for a sample of wheat, corn, and soybean futures contracts over the period 1952 to 1967 and found to be close to zero in all three cases. Average realized holding period returns on the contracts over the same period were close to zero.

I. INTRODUCTION

Considerable controversy exists over the amount and the nature of the returns earned by speculators in commodity futures markets. At one extreme is the position first set forth by J. M. Keynes in his *Treatise*

*Reprinted from the *Journal of Political Economy*. Vol. 81, No. 6, (December 1973). Reprinted by permission of The University of Chicago Press. Copyright © 1973 by The University of Chicago. All rights reserved.
†I am indebted to Eugene Fama, Charles Nelson, Harry Roberts, and especially Merton H. Miller for many helpful comments and suggestions.

on Money (1930, pp. 135-44) that a futures market is an insurance scheme in which the speculators underwrite the risks of price fluctuation of the spot commodity. The nonspeculators or "hedgers" on the other side of the market must expect to pay and, according to Keynes, they do in fact pay, on the average a significant premium to the speculator-insurers for this service. At the other extreme have been those such as C. O. Hardy (1940) who argue that for many speculators a futures market is a gambling casino. Far from demanding and receiving compensation for taking over the risks of price fluctuation from the hedgers, speculators, as a class, are willing to pay for the privilege of gambling in this socially acceptable form (with the losers continually being replaced at the tables by new arrivals). Despite many empirical studies, the conflict between the insurance interpretation and the gambling interpretation of returns to speculators in futures markets remains unresolved.[1]

This paper offers another and quite different interpretation of the returns to speculators in futures markets. It is argued that futures markets are no different in principle from the markets for any other risky portfolio assets. Futures markets are perhaps more colorful than many other subsegments of the capital market such as the New York Stock Exchange or the bond market, and the terminology of futures markets is perhaps more arcane, but these differences in form should not obscure the fundamental properties that futures market assets share with other investments instruments: in particular, they are all candidates for inclusion in the investor's portfolio.

The portfolio approach, by itself, makes no presumption as to whether returns to speculators are positive, as Keynes hypothesized, or zeroish to negative, as Hardy believed. It says, rather, that returns on any risky capital asset, including futures market assets, are governed by that asset's contribution, positive, negative, or zero, to the risk of a large and well-diversified portfolio of assets (in fact, all assets, in principle). In contrast to this portfolio measure of risk, Keynes and his later followers identify the risk of a futures market asset solely with its price variability.[2] These difference in the proposed measures of risk make it possible to test the portfolio and Keynesian interpretations of futures

---

[1] Among the most influential papers devoted to the Keynes-Hardy controversy have been those of Telser (1958, 1960, 1967) and Cootner (1960a, 1960b). Other studies of the returns to speculation in futures markets include Houthakker (1957), Gray (1961), Smidt (1965), Rockwell (1967), and Stevenson and Bear (1970).

[2] This is at least the conventional interpretation of the Keynesian position as suggested by the following quotation: "It will be seen that, under the present regime of very widely fluctuating prices for individual commodities, the cost of insurance against price changes—which is additional to any charges for interest or warehousing—is very high" (Keynes 1930, p. 144). A somewhat broader interpretation emphasizes the insurance premium and tries to relate the size and sign of this premium to variations in the stocks of the commodity over the production cycle (see Cootner 1960a, 1960b).

markets against each other and, in principle, also against the Hardy gambling casino view.

It turns out that for each of the commodity futures studied (wheat, corn, and soybeans) returns and portfolio risk are both close to zero during the sample period even though variability or risk in the Keynesian sense is high. Hence, as far as this set of observations is concerned, the data conform better to the portfolio point of view than to the Keynesian insurance interpretation. The sample did not permit any direct confrontation between the portfolio interpretation and the Hardy view, but some indirect light is thrown on this part of the controversy and some suggestions for further tests are offered.

In the next section the salient points of the equilibrium pricing of portfolio assets are noted, and futures contracts are analyzed within this context. Measures of Keynesian and portfolio asset risk are then developed and interpreted in the light of the returns observed.

II. CAPITAL ASSET PRICING: THE DETERMINATION OF AN EQUILIBRIUM RISK-RETURN RELATION

A model of the equilibrium pricing of portfolio assets was proposed originally by Sharpe (1964) and extended by Lintner (1965), Mossin (1966), and Fama (1971).[3] Sharpe showed that conditions exist under which the equilibrium risk-return relation for any capital asset i can be represented as

$$E(\tilde{R}_i) = R_f + \left[\frac{E(\tilde{R}_w) - R_f}{\sigma(\tilde{R}_w)}\right] \frac{\partial \sigma(\tilde{R}_w)}{\partial x_i}, \qquad (1)$$

where $\tilde{R}_i$ is the random rate of return on asset i, $E(\tilde{R}_i)$ is its mathematical expectation, and R_f is the pure time return to capital or the so-called riskless rate of interest; $\tilde{R}_w$ is the random rate of return on a representative dollar of total wealth or, equivalently, the return on a portfolio containing all existing assets in the proportions, x_i, in which they are actually outstanding: $E(\tilde{R}_w)$ is the expected rate of return on total wealth, and $\sigma(\tilde{R}_w)$, the standard deviation of the return on total wealth, is a measure of the risk involved in holding a representative dollar of total wealth. The term $[\partial \sigma(\tilde{R}_w)]/\partial x_i$ is the marginal contribution of asset i to the risk of the return on total wealth, $\sigma(\tilde{R}_w)$. Thus expression (1) says that, in equilibrium, the expected rate of return on any asset i will be equal to the riskless rate of interest plus a risk premium propor-

---
[3] The description of the equilibrium pricing model presented here assumes some familiarity on the part of the reader. For a more complete discussion, see Sharpe (1964) or Lintner (1965). A detailed exposition of the model is also given in Fama and Miller (1972, chap. 7).

tional to the contribution of the asset to the risk of the return on total wealth.

To see some of the broader implications of this proposition and especially to highlight its fundamental difference from the simple Keynesian approach to risk, note that since

$$\sigma(\tilde{R}_w) = \left[\sum_{i=1}^{N}\sum_{j=1}^{N} x_i x_j \operatorname{Cov}(\tilde{R}_i, \tilde{R}_j)\right],$$

it follows that

$$\frac{\partial \sigma(\tilde{R}_w)}{\partial x_i} = \frac{1}{\sigma(\tilde{R}_w)}\left[\sum_{j=1}^{N} x_j \operatorname{Cov}(\tilde{R}_i, \tilde{R}_j)\right]$$

$$= \frac{1}{\sigma(\tilde{R}_w)}\left[x_i \sigma^2(\tilde{R}_i) + \sum_{j \neq i}^{N} x_j \operatorname{Cov}(\tilde{R}_i, \tilde{R}_j)\right].$$

Thus what governs the riskiness of any asset i is not merely its own variance $\sigma^2(\tilde{R}_i)$ but its weighted covariance with all the other assets making up total wealth. Normally the latter terms can be expected to swamp the former, since there are $N - 1$ terms making up the covariance portion and only one in the variance portion, and that one, moreover, weighted by a very small number, x_i.

Additional insight into the equilibrium risk-return relation is gained by noting that the expression

$$\sum_{j=1}^{N} x_j \operatorname{Cov}(\tilde{R}_i, \tilde{R}_j)$$

can be rewritten as $\operatorname{Cov}(\tilde{R}_i, \tilde{R}_w)$, the covariance of return on asset i with that of total wealth. Hence we can rewrite (1) as

$$E(\tilde{R}_i) = R_f + \left[\frac{E(\tilde{R}_w) - R_f}{\sigma(\tilde{R}_w)}\right]\frac{\operatorname{Cov}(\tilde{R}_i, \tilde{R}_w)}{\sigma(\tilde{R}_w)}, \qquad (2)$$

or equivalently as

$$E(\tilde{R}_i) - R_f = [E(\tilde{R}_w) - R_f]\beta_i, \qquad (3)$$

where $\beta_i \equiv [\operatorname{Cov}(\tilde{R}_i, \tilde{R}_w)]/\sigma^2(\tilde{R}_w)$. The coefficient β_i can be interpreted as the relative risk of asset i, since it measures the risk of asset i relative to that of total wealth. Equation (3) then says that the risk premium expected on asset i is proportional, in equilibrium, to its systematic risk β_i, the factor of proportionality being the risk premium expected on a representative dollar of total wealth.

Needless to say, the capital asset pricing model rests on a set of fairly strong assumptions. Nevertheless, it has proven to be remarkably robust empirically. Studies by Miller and Scholes (1972), Black, Jensen, and Scholes (1972), and Fama and MacBeth (1972) indicate that while simple expressions such as equations (2) and (3) may not be entirely satisfactory descriptions of the relations between return and relative risk, there is a strong connection between them, whereas there seems to be virtually none between the risk premium and measures of non-portfolio risk.[4]

III. APPLICATION OF THE CAPITAL ASSET PRICING MODEL TO FUTURES CONTRACTS

One difficulty in applying the Sharpe model of capital asset pricing to the risk-return relation on futures contracts is that of defining the appropriate capital asset and its rate of return. Since virtually all futures contracts are bought (and sold short) on margins that typically range from 5 to 10 percent of the face value of the contract, it might seem at first sight that we can treat the margin as the capital investment and treat the ratio of the net profit at closeout to the initial margin as the rate of return on investment. In fact, one theoretical study, that of Schrock (1971), takes this point of view and makes it the basis of a standard mean-variance portfolio analysis, à la Markowitz (1959), though restricting attention only to futures market assets.

This appealing procedure for computing futures market returns breaks down, however, as soon as we trace the subsequent history of the payment that is turned over to the broker. Unlike other capital assets such as common stocks where the margin is transferred from buyer to seller, the margin on a futures contract is kept in escrow by the broker. Not only does the seller of the futures contract not receive the capital transfer from the buyers, but he actually has to deposit an equivalent amount of his own funds in the broker's escrow account. At closeout, the broker returns the escrowed margin plus or minus any profits or losses (net of commissions in the case of profits and inclusive of commissions in the event of losses) that occurred over the period.

The margin, despite surface appearances, is thus not a portfolio asset in the sense of the Sharpe general-equilibrium model, but merely a good-faith deposit to guarantee performance by the parties to the contract. If the brokers had other ways of ensuring that traders did not make commitments beyond their resources, then no such performance bonds would be required. For example, forward foreign exchange markets, where firms deal through their own banking connections, typically

---

[4] Recently Black (1972) has generalized the Sharpe model by replacing the riskless asset having return R_f with another asset whose return is a random variable but whose covariance with total wealth is zero. Empirical tests by Black, Jensen, and Scholes (1972) and Fama and MacBeth (1972) seem to indicate that the generalized model fits the data somewhat better than the Sharpe version.

operate without any explicit margins, whereas participants in public futures currency markets are required to post margins.[5]

Although the rate of return on the margin is not a meaningful number from a general-equilibrium point of view, and need not even exist if other types of guarantees could serve, there is another natural candidate which can always be computed: namely, the percentage change in the futures price. We cannot interpret this percentage change as a rate of return comparable to the $\tilde{R}_i$, in equation (2) above, since the holder invests no current resources in the contract. But we can interpret it as essentially the risk premium, $\tilde{R}_i - R_f$, on the spot commodity.[6]

What corresponds to the full return $\tilde{R}_i$ is the return (net of storage costs) that would accrue to the holder of an unhedged spot commodity.[7] That return consists of interest on the capital invested in the commodity plus any return, positive or negative, over and above pure interest due to the unanticipated change in the price of the commodity. If the spot holder chooses to hedge his holding, he thereby converts it to a riskless asset on which he earns only the riskless rate, R_f. The purchaser of the futures contract who takes over the risk has no capital of his own invested and hence earns no interest or pure time return on capital. He receives only the return over and above interest, which is to say, $\tilde{R}_i - R_f$.

This argument can be formalized by restating the Sharpe equilibrium

[5] That entering into a future contract need involve no margin or other specific payment that could be interpreted as an "investment" (and hence that could serve as the basis for computing a "rate of return") does not mean that the mean-variance portfolio model cannot be applied at the microlevel to analyze an investor's decision process. The price changes on the contracts held will affect *terminal* wealth, just as in the case of any other asset; but the contracts do not appear in the *initial* wealth constraint. For a rigorous treatment in the context of forward foreign exchange, see Leland (1971). A study by Johnson (1960) of futures spot commodity holdings also proceeds in this way. That is, the entire analysis is conducted in terms of price changes and not in terms of rates of return. The fact that the margin does not really represent capital invested in futures contracts, even in those markets where margin is required, might perhaps have been appreciated earlier by analysis of futures markets trading if brokers paid interest on the escrowed funds (or, what amounts to the same thing, if they allowed all traders to deposit or to hypothecate income-earning assets rather than cash). In practice, of course, the brokers presumably do pay interest on the escrowed funds, but only in the hard-to-see form of lower commissions or higher levels of "free" services than would otherwise be the case.

[6] I abstract from such complications as transaction costs, basis risk, the business risk of the storage and processing industries, limitations on borrowing, and so on. Or, what amounts to the same thing, I assume that differences in the returns on spot and futures market assets from these sources are so small and so unsystematic relative to the variations in returns on both assets as a consequence of price fluctuations that they can safely be ignored in a first approximation. Some of the main second-order qualifications are indicated at various points in the text and in footnotes in the course of the discussion.

[7] Actually total return to the spot commodity holder can be decomposed into three components: a pure time return to capital, a risk premium, and remuneration for storage costs, defined in this context as insurance charges, spoilage, and warehousing and administrative costs. Since we are concerned only with the return to capital embodied in the spot commodity, $\tilde{R}_i$, the "full" return on the spot commodity is to be understood as net of storage costs.

conditions in present-value form. We say that the expected return on any asset i can be expressed as

$$E(\tilde{R}_i) = (1 - \beta_i)R_f + \beta_i E(\tilde{R}_w), \qquad (4)$$

where $\beta_i = \text{Cov}(\tilde{R}_i, \tilde{R}_w)/\sigma^2(\tilde{R}_w)$. Equivalently, since we can represent $E(\tilde{R}_i)$ in terms of period 0 and period 1 prices for the asset as $[E(\tilde{P}_{i,1}) - P_{i,0}]/P_{i,0}$, the equilibrium risk-return relation on asset i can be expressed as

$$P_{i,0} = \frac{E(\tilde{P}_{i,1}) - [E(\tilde{R}_w) - R_f]P_{i,0}\beta_i}{(1 + R_f)}. \qquad (5)$$

Expression (5) says that the current price of any asset i is the discounted value (at the riskless rate) of its expected period 1 price, adjusted downward for risk by the factor $[E(\tilde{R}_w) - R_f]P_{i,0}\beta_i$.

Now suppose one were interested in knowing the price of asset i under a contractual agreement to purchase the asset at time 0 but with payment deferred a period to time 1. Clearly the current price for the asset under such an agreement must be given by $P_{i,0}(1 + R_f)$. That is, since the transaction is made at time 0 but consummated at time 1, the purchaser must pay a one-period credit, or borrowing charge of $P_{i,0}R_f$ in addition to the current price $P_{i,0}$. Multiplying both sides of equation (5) by $(1 + R_f)$ we see that

$$P_{i,0}(1 + R_f) = E(\tilde{P}_{i,1}) - [E(\tilde{R}_w) - R_f]P_{i,0}\beta_i. \qquad (6)$$

But the contractual agreement just described is a futures contract where asset i refers to the spot commodity. Hence the expression $P_{i,0}(1 + R_f)$ can be interpreted as the current futures price for delivery and payment of the spot commodity one period later, and $E(\tilde{P}_{i,1})$ can be interpreted as the spot price expected to prevail at time 1. The essential point is that buying a futures contract is like buying a capital asset on credit where the capital asset in this case happens to be the spot commodity.[8] The only issue is what is the "discount for cash" or, equivalently, the financing charge. Since the financing is assumed to be riskless, the correct charge is clearly R_f. That is, if $P_{i,0}$ is the current price for immediate payment, $P_{i,0}(1 + R_f)$ must be the price if the buyer buys on one-period credit terms.

[8] It does not really matter whether there is a spot commodity in existence yet. That is, just as I can order a car not yet produced, so I can agree to accept delivery next period at a specified price of a commodity still unproduced. The "implicit" spot price, which always exists, is then simply the futures price minus a discount for payment in advance, i.e., $P_i = P_f/(1 + R_f)$. Note also that the seller need not actually contemplate producing the spot commodity; i.e., he can be a pure short speculator. He merely offers to make delivery to you next period, intending, if necessary to go out and buy the spot commodity then, if you insist on delivery rather than settlement.

Setting $P_{f,0} = P_{i,0}(1 + R_f)$ and rearranging terms, we get

$$\frac{E(\tilde{P}_{i,1}) - P_{f,0}}{P_{i,0}} = \beta_i[E(\tilde{R}_w) - R_f]. \qquad (7)$$

Equation (7) can be interpreted as expressing the risk premium on the spot commodity as the change in the futures price divided by the period 0 spot price. Thus once again we see that futures contracts, properly interpreted, pose no problem for capital market theory.

One implication of this analysis is that there are two essentially equivalent ways of calculating the risk premium. On the one hand, we can try to measure the risk premium by taking the percentage change in spot prices (net of storage) over a given interval minus the riskless rate. Alternatively, we can approximate the risk premium as the percentage change in the futures price over the same interval.[9] Of these two approaches, it is the latter that will be adopted here. Data on futures prices are more accessible than spot price data and, of course, use of futures prices also avoids the necessity of having to estimate the storage costs directly. It is important to remember, however, that this choice of measurement is essentially a matter of computational convenience; and that the relevant risk from the general-equilibrium point of view remains the risk inherent in the ownership of the spot commodity itself, regardless of who actually chooses to bear it or what measurement strategy we choose to employ.[10]

IV. THE EMPIRICAL PROPERTIES OF FUTURES MARKET RETURNS

Tests of the risk-return relationship in the futures market are based on a sample of three heavily traded agricultural commodities: wheat,

---

[9] I have argued that in equilibrium $P_{f,t} = P_{i,t}(1 + R_f)$, where i refers to the spot commodity. Thus the percentage change in the futures price underestimates the risk premium on the spot commodity by the factor $1/(1 + R_f)$. Given the intervals over which I will be computing returns, the factor $1/(1 + R_f)$ is likely to be very small. Hence for simplicity of exposition I shall refer (somewhat loosely) to the percentage change in the futures price as representing the risk premium on the spot commodity.

[10] I have assumed that unanticipated changes in the spot and futures prices are perfectly correlated. (For some evidence on the high degree of correlation between spot and futures prices, see Houthakker [1968]). Where this correlation is not perfect, the spot commodity holder will bear some risk even though hedged, and some compensation for this risk may be impounded in his return. Working (1953) has made this type of risk central to his analysis of futures markets. He regards spot commodity holders not as passive short hedgers but as speculators on the movement of the spot-future price differential, or basis, over time. He argues that professional commodity dealers are better able to predict differentials or relative prices than price levels. Thus they assume a position in both the spot and futures markets in response to expected changes in the basis. Since Working's hypothesis appears to have no testable implications with respect to the risk-return relation in futures markets of the kind that are of main concern in this paper, I will not pursue it further here.

corn, and soybeans. There are five different contracts per year for wheat and corn and six for soybeans. For all contracts, semimonthly price quotations were obtained for a 15-year period from May 15, 1952 through November 15, 1967—resulting in an approximate sample size of 300 observations per contract.[11] In all cases returns were computed as a simple 2-week holding period yield with no allowance made for transaction costs. Following universal practice, returns have been computed separately for each commodity contract (e.g., May wheat or September corn).[12] It should be noted that the return series computed in this way is discontinuous, since published price quotations on any one contract are typically available over a 9- or 10-month span.

Since the procedures for computing all subsequent statistical measures assume serial independence of returns, serial correlation coefficients of orders 1-10 have been computed for each contract return series.[13] The results are presented in table 1. As can be seen, the coefficients fluctuate about zero. Out of a total of 160 correlation coefficients, 132 are less than .10, and only 11 coefficients are more than two standard deviations away from zero. Even the largest in absolute value, moreover, is only .22 and hence accounts for only a trivial portion of the variation in returns on the particular contract. There are about the same number of negative as positive coefficients, with no particular pattern in the signs.[14]

---

[11] Price quotations were taken from U.S., Department of Agriculture (1952-67). Lester Telser kindly supplied price data for 1952-64. The rest were collected independently from the same source. The terminal date of 1967 was the last year for which price data were available at the time this study was started. The initial date of 1952 was chosen to minimize wartime and postwar controls on commodity prices and futures trading.

[12] Another possible principle for computing returns would be on the basis of time to contract expiration (e.g., wheat contracts with exactly 4 months to run or corn contracts with 2½ months to run). In a later paper I shall show that the theoretical and empirical justification for looking at returns in this way is weaker than certain treatments of the matter, notably Samuelson's (1965), would suggest.

[13] The sample serial correlation coefficient is defined as $\hat{r}_t = \text{cov}(\tilde{u}_t, \tilde{u}_{t-\tau})/\text{var}\,\tilde{u}_t$, where in this case $\tau = 1, \ldots, 10$ and u_t is the 2-week rate of return. Even in the case where $\tilde{u}_t$ belongs to the family of distributions for which variance does not exist, it has been shown that $\hat{r}_\tau$ is an adequate descriptive measure of the serial correlation in the population in the sense that it behaves much the same as its counterpart from a normally distributed sample of observations (see Fama and Babiak 1968, p. 1146). Under the hypothesis that the true serial correlation is zero, the standard error of the sample serial correlation coefficient is given by $\sigma(\hat{r}_t) = \sqrt{1/(N-\tau)}$, where N is the sample size and $\tau = 1, \ldots, 10$.

[14] These results are consistent with previous studies of the time series properties of future prices. Studies by Larson (1960), Houthakker (1961), Smidt (1965), and Stevenson and Bear (1970) tend to show that although there are occasions when futures prices appear to have exhibited some degree of dependence, there have been no striking cases of large and pervasive price trends or patterns. Computed measures of statistical dependence have usually been small, and the profitability of trading rules has typically been less than that obtained by following a policy of buy and hold.

TABLE 1
Semimonthly Serial Correlation Coefficients for Wheat, Corn, Soybeans
($\tau = 1, 10$)

Contract	1	2	3	4	5	6	7	8	9	10
Wheat:										
July	.14*	.01	−.15*	−.07	.10	−.07	−.02	.03	.12	−.03
Mar.	.07	−.07	−.03	.05	.03	.11	.12	−.11	.06	−.22*
May	.17*	.03	−.09	−.11	.06	.10	.10	.06	−.05	−.18*
Sept.	.15*	.07	−.02	−.03	.07	−.01	−.10	.09	.15	.05
Dec.	.14*	.10	.04	−.01	.04	−.14*	−.08	−.01	.03	−.11
$\bar{p}$	.13	.03	−.05	−.03	.06	−.00	.00	.01	.06	−.10
Corn:										
July	−.02	−.04	.03	.03	−.05	−.02	.01	−.03	.08	−.06
Mar.	.01	.08	−.09	−.00	−.03	.10	.04	.17*	−.07	−.03
May	.02	.08	.00	−.03	−.04	−.02	.00	.05	.05	.05
Sept.	.10	.10	.02	−.02	−.04	.03	.08	−.04	.03	−.03
Dec.	.02	.06	.02	−.04	−.07	.05	−.07	−.06	−.01	−.04
$\bar{p}$	.03	.06	−.00	−.01	−.05	.03	.01	.02	.02	−.02
Soybeans:										
Jan.	.02	.05	−.04	−.04	−.11	.09	.03	−.10	−.03	.01
Mar.	.03	.18*	.02	.07	−.05	.13	−.05	.05	−.07	.10
May	.09	.17*	.16*	.11	.06	.10	.09	.19*	.06	.10
July	.09	.15*	−.07	.16*	.02	.06	−.02	−.01	.07	−.05
Sept.	.06	−.03	.07	.00	−.03	.04	.20*	−.11	−.08	.09
Nov.	.03	.06	−.07	−.08	−.09	.01	.13	−.09	.04	−.03
$\bar{p}$	.05	.10	.01	.04	−.03	.07	.06	−.03	−.00	.04
SE ($\hat{r}_t$) for $N = 300$	.058	.058	.058	.058	.058	.058	.058	.059	.059	.059

* Coefficient is twice its computed standard error.

V. CONSTRUCTION AND INTERPRETATION OF A KEYNESIAN RISK MEASURE

There is nothing in Keyne's essentially heuristic discussion of futures market risk to suggest the use of any one measure of simple variability over another. Subsequent writers have adapted the Keynesian argument to the Markowitz mean-variance framework (e.g., Johnson 1960; Schrock 1971). The use of sample variances to measure risk is open to objection, however, if the distribution of returns is stable non-Gaussian, as some have suspected may be true for futures market returns. For such distributions the second and higher-order moments of the distributions do not exist. The variances and standard deviations in any particular sample are always finite, but their behavior will be erratic and affected by outliers.[15]

---

[15] See Fama and Roll (1971, p. 332) for evidence on the sampling variability of the standard deviation when the sample values come from a non-Gaussian distribution.

Evidence of nonnormality is indicated by the normal probability plots of the cumulative distributions of sample returns in figures 1-3. To facilitate comparisons among the distributions of contract returns, the normal probability plots have been grouped by commodity. Five observations in the critical upper and lower tails of the distributions have been plotted and every twenty-fifth observation in the less revealing middle range. If the distributions were normal, the plots would closely approximate a straight line with slope $1/s$ and intercept $\bar{x}/s$, where s is the sample standard deviation and $\bar{x}$ is the sample mean (Roberts 1964, chap. 7, p. 13). As can be seen, there are substantial departures from linearity, not only in the tail areas but in the middle ranges as well, in every graph. The departure from normality in the tails is particularly marked in the case of the six soybean contracts.[16]

It can be shown that any symmetric stable distribution is characterized by three parameters: a shape parameter, a; a location parameter; and a scale or dispersion parameter. For the normal distribution a has the value 2; the first moment or mean serves as a measure of the location parameter, and the standard deviation (divided by $\sqrt{2}$) defines the scale. The fat-tailed distributions encountered in studies of asset pricing have shape parameter a less than 2. For such distributions, the mean can still serve as the location parameter, provided a is greater than one (the case of $a = 1$ being the Cauchy distribution), although it has been shown that a truncated mean has smaller sampling dispersion than the

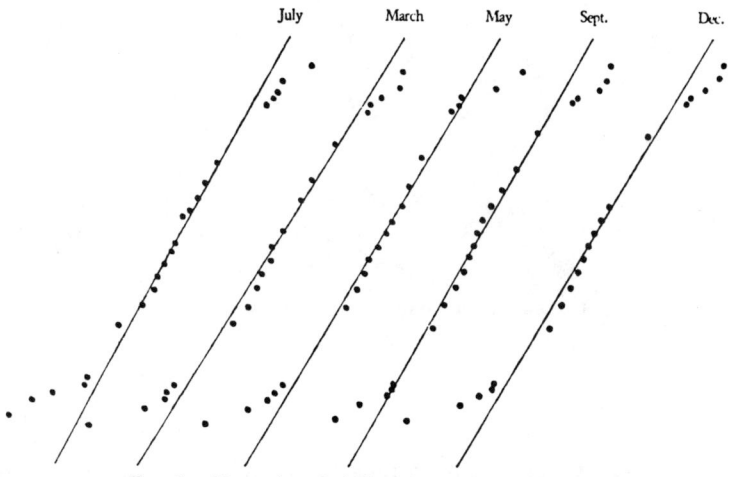

Fig. 1.—Normal probability plots: wheat contracts

---

[16] The phenomenon of fat tails (i.e., more probability in the tail area of the distribution than in the Gaussian distribution) for distributions of futures returns has previously been noted, but not rigorously investigated, by Smidt (1965), Stevenson and Bear (1970), and Houthakker (1961).

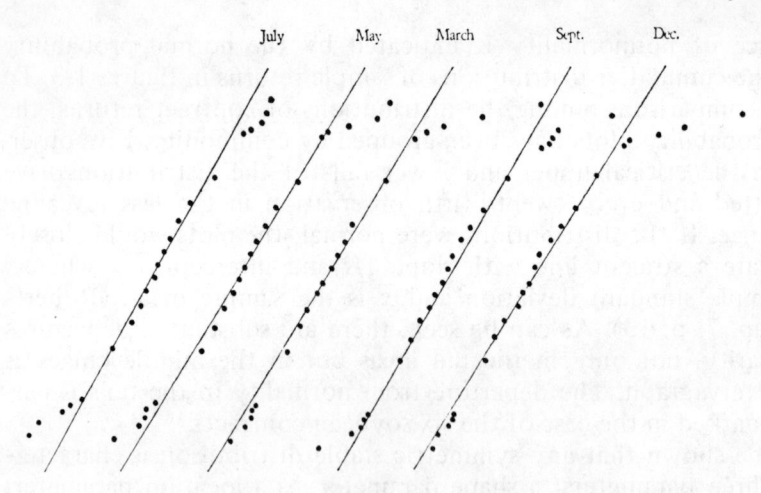

FIG. 2.—Normal probability plots: corn contracts

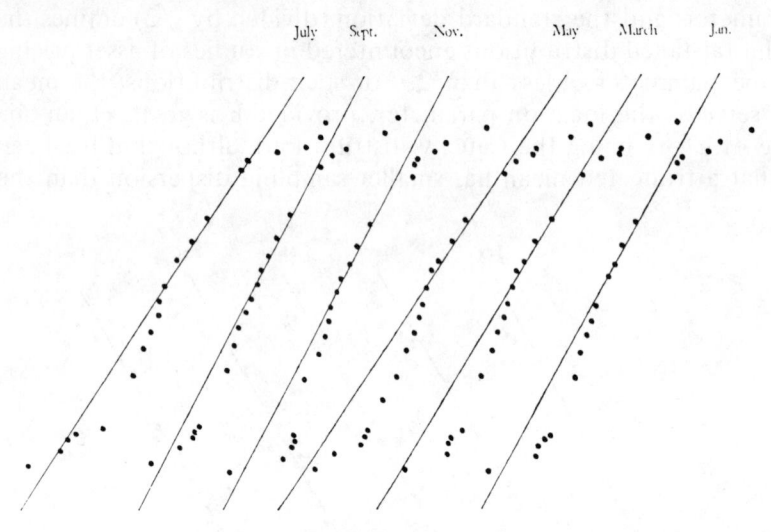

FIG. 3.—Normal probability plots: soybean contracts

sample mean and thus is a better estimator of the location parameter.[17] But, as noted above, the second and higher-order moments, and hence also the standard deviation, are not finite. Interfractile ranges do exist,

[17] "The g truncated sample mean is the average of the middle 100g percent of the ordered observations in the sample. That is, in computing the mean, 100(1 − g)/2 percent of the observations in each tail of the data distribution are discarded" (Fama and Roll 1968, p. 826). The optimum degree of truncation depends on the size of a. The lower the value of a, the greater

TABLE 2
ESTIMATES OF STABLE PARETIAN PARAMETERS FOR WHEAT, CORN, AND SOYBEANS

Contract*	a† (1)	Scale Factor (2)	SE‡ of Scale Factor (3)	Truncated Mean Return (4)	SE§ of Truncated Mean (5)
Wheat:					
July (302)	1.55	.01111	.00085	−.00164	.00126
Mar. (302)	1.75	.01228	.00091	.00060	.00139
May (302)	1.70	.01259	.00094	.00096	.00142
Sept. (319)	1.56	.01127	.00086	−.00194	.00127
Dec. (319)	1.74	.01184	.00088	.00044	.00134
Corn:					
July (301)	1.52	.01027	.00079	−.00158	.00116
Mar. (301)	1.65	.01222	.00092	−.00381	.00138
May (301)	1.49	.01062	.00082	−.00268	.00120
Sept. (320)	1.65	.01136	.00086	−.00243	.00128
Dec. (320)	1.84	.01304	.00092	−.00212	.00147
Soybeans:					
Jan. (287)	1.49	.01293	.00100	−.00025	.00146
Mar. (287)	1.47	.01347	.00105	−.00029	.00152
May (287)	1.44	.01309	.00102	.00038	.00148
July (287)	1.44	.01399	.00109	.00006	.00158
Sept. (287)	1.66	.01391	.00105	−.00105	.00157
Nov. (287)	1.50	.01212	.00093	−.00071	.00137

* Numbers of observations are given in parentheses.
† No exact methods have been derived for computing the standard error of $\alpha_{.95}$ or its bias. Using Monte Carlo techniques, Fama and Roll (1971), p. 333) report that for samples of 299 observations the standard deviation of the values of $\hat{\alpha}_{.95}$ in 199 separate replications was about 0.13 when the true value of α was 1.5, about 0.15 when the true value of α was 1.7, and about 0.12 when the true value was 2.0. The mean value of $\hat{\alpha}_{.95}$ was slightly less than true of α when that value was very close to two; the apparent bias was only 0.04 when α was 1.9 and was beyond detection at a value for α of 1.7.
‡ An expression for the variance of the scale factor is given in Fama and Roll (1971, p. 331). Standard errors have been computed from estimates of $\sigma(s)$ for standardized symmetric stable distributions. See Fama and Roll (1971, table 1, p. 332).
§ The standard error of the truncated mean has been computed as: $s\sigma(\bar{\bar{x}}_{.5,N})$ where s is the scale factor from the underlying distribution of returns and $s\sigma(\bar{\bar{x}}_{.5,N})$ is the standard deviation of the .5 truncated mean from a standardized normal distribution. For a discussion of this estimator see Roll (1968, chap. 6, p. 30).

however, and have been found to serve quite adequately as measures of scale or dispersion.

Estimates of a, the scale factor, the .5 truncated mean, and standard errors for the last two estimators are presented in table 2.[18] Following Fama and Roll (1968, 1971) the .28-.72 interfractile range was used to estimate the scale factor, and a fractile matching procedure (in this case the .95) was used to estimate a.

From column 1 of table 2, it would seem safe to conclude that the distributions of returns on futures contracts conform better to the stable non-Gaussian family than to the normal distribution. The values of a range from 1.44 to 1.84, with half of the estimates below 1.56.

The scale factors, which I shall interpret as measures of Keynesian

the optimum degree of truncation, reflecting the fact that the more outliers there are in a sample, the greater the number of observations that must be deleted before an efficient estimate of location is obtained. Fama and Roll (1968, p. 832) conclude that "an estimator which performs very well for most values of alpha and N (sample size) is the .5 truncated mean."

[18] The procedure for estimating a assumes that successive returns are independent—a hypothesis that has already been tested.

risk, and their standard errors of estimate are shown in columns 2 and 3 of table 2.[19] To judge how large these scale factors are, we can compare them to the corresponding dispersion parameter for some other more familiar capital asset such as common stock. The most convenient measure of common stock returns for our purposes is the Standard and Poor Composite Index of 500 industrial common stocks. The estimated dispersion parameter for that index taken semimonthly over the sample period 1952-67 is .0170, which is the same order or magnitude as the scale factors for the commodities. Since the Standard and Poor Index is in effect a well-diversified portfolio, we know that the variability of the average stock return will be two or three times as large (see King 1966; Blume 1968) and hence also two or three times that of returns on futures market assets.

These comparisons may surprise those accustomed to thinking of futures markets as especially volatile, and the futures contract as one of the riskiest of capital assets.[20] The impression of substantial return volatility probably arises from the practice of calculating percentage returns on the margin. It should be remembered, though, that the margin is not a capital asset within the economic meaning of that term. Hence in the general-equilibrium context the variability of rates of return on the margin is not a relevant measure of risk.

Since the variability of futures returns is about as great as that of a diversified portfolio of common stock, we should expect that if Keynes was correct in identifying asset risk with simple variability, then the mean return over and above the riskless rate should be about the same for both assets. The mean rate of return (over and above the riskless rate) on the Standard and Poor Index over the period 1952-67 on a semimonthly basis was approximately .0029 (with a standard error of .0012) without allowing for dividends.[21] Had dividends been included, they would probably have added another .0017 to bring the total return to .0046. This figure is in striking contrast to the point estimates of the truncated means for the commodity returns (table 2, col. 4). All of the truncated means for corn returns are negative and of roughly the same magnitude. In the case of soybeans, four of the six truncated means are negative but the range between the smallest and largest values is only .00143, which is the same order of magnitude as the standard errors of the estimates. The truncated means for wheat returns exhibit

[19] In principle, any number of interfractile ranges might serve as a measure of risk. For reasons of simplicity and economy we have chosen the same interfractile range used to estimate the dispersion parameter of the distribution.

[20] Some indirect evidence on this point is afforded by the refusal of Merrill Lynch, Pierce, Fenner, and Smith to sell futures contracts to women on the grounds that they do not have the psychological stamina to withstand futures market price fluctuations.

[21] An ordinary sample mean has been computed for the return on the Standard and Poor Index, since the distribution of stock returns more closely approaches normality than do the distributions of commodity returns (Officer 1971).

somewhat greater variation. The mean returns for the July and September contracts are large and negative whereas the mean returns for the March, May, and December contracts are slightly positive. For all but two of the 16 contracts, however, the mean returns are within two standard errors of zero.

These results are a serious blow to the theory of normal backwardation. Using Keynes's definition of asset risk, anyone who invested (i.e., sold insurance) in wheat, corn, and soybean futures in the period 1952-67 incurred risk for which he received on average a return very close to zero, if not actually negative. What is even more damaging to the Keynesian theory is the fact that for the same amount of risk (defined as simple return variability) an investment in a diversified portfolio of common stocks over the same period would have yielded a substantial positive return over and above the riskless rate.[22]

VI. CONSTRUCTION AND INTERPRETATION OF THE RISK MEASURES FOR THE CAPITAL MARKET INTERPRETATION

The Sharpe model of capital asset pricing defines asset risk as the contribution the asset makes to the variability of return on a well-diversified portfolio containing, in principle, all assets in the proportions in which they are outstanding. An estimate of the relative risk can be obtained from the linear regression:

$$\tilde{R}_i = a_i + \beta_i \tilde{R}_w + \tilde{\varepsilon}_i, \qquad (8)$$

---

[22] Note that the evidence presented in table 2 does not constitute 16 different tests of the Keynesian hypothesis. The similarity in the distribution parameters (and indeed, of the entire distributions, as a glance at figs 1-3 will testify) suggests that within any commodity group the distribution of returns has the same parameters and that such slight differences as do exist represent only sampling fluctuations. Correlation coefficients between the returns on different contracts of the same commodity have been computed. Out of 35 coefficients, 12 were .90 or higher; another 17 were between .80 and .89; and only six were below .79, the lowest being .72. In some cases, as, for example, the adjacent July and September wheat contracts or the adjacent March and May contracts for corn, the correlation was virtually perfect. As a group, wheat contracts seemed to exhibit the most interdependence, and soybeans the least. This high correlation between returns on different contracts is especially striking in light of the insistence on contract uniqueness in much of the traditional literature on futures markets. The contemporaneous coefficients of correlation between returns for the same contract but different commodities have also been computed. Out of 13 correlation coefficients only two are even as high as .5, and even the highest of these coefficients (.67) is lower than the lowest correlation for returns on the same commodity (.72). Under these circumstances, then, there would appear to be little objection to maintaining a distinction among the three commodities.

where the usual assumptions of the linear regression model are assumed to hold.

Although equation (8) implies that the independent variable is the return on total wealth, such a variable is virtually impossible to construct, and instead some proxy measure must be utilized. In this study the return on the value-weighted Standard and Poor Index of 500 Common Stocks is used as a proxy for the return on total wealth. Common stocks, after all, represent an important fraction of total wealth, so that even in a more comprehensive index they would be heavily weighted. This has been, moreover, the standard approach followed in most studies of the pricing model.

The selection of the Standard and Poor Index to represent common stocks was dictated by the fact that the leading alternative, the Fisher index (1966), is available on a monthly basis, whereas the futures market returns are computed on a semimonthly basis. The main drawback of the Standard and Poor index is that it does not include the dividend component of returns on common stock. Dividends, however, are not highly variable in the short run, and their omission is not likely to have any noticeable effects on the regression coefficients that I will be using as measures of risk.[23]

Consistent with the interpretation of the futures return as a risk premium, that is, as a return over and above interest, the market index variable is also stated in risk premium form. As a measure of the riskless rate of interest, I used the 15-day Treasury bill rate.[24]

The estimates of a_i' (where a' denotes regression variables expressed in risk premium form) and β_i from equation (8), their standard errors, the R^2s, and the first-order serial correlation coefficients of the residuals for the sample period 1952-67 are presented in table 3 for each of the 16 commodity contracts. The most striking feature of table 3 is the small size of the regression coefficients, which range from .007 to .119. With few exceptions the standard errors are approximately the same size, if not somewhat larger, than the regression coefficients. Furthermore, the standard errors in table 3 may be understated because ordinary least squares is not efficient if the underlying returns are non-Gaussian (see Fama and Babiak [1968] for a discussion of this point).

---

[23] There are problems posed by the fact that the underlying distributions conform better to stable non-Gaussian than to normal distributions. It can be shown, however, that the ordinary least-squares coefficients are consistent estimators of the corresponding population parameters, but not necessarily efficient ones; particularly as a departs further from two. However, the loss of efficiency is not likely to be of much import for samples as large as we will be using (300 observations). See Blattberg and Sargent (1971).

[24] Since the variability of the bill rate was small relative to that of the Standard and Poor Index or to that of futures returns during my sample period, the estimates turned out to be virtually identical with those obtained when the index was used in regular return form. Other specifications of the regression equation were also tested, such as the use of logarithms of the price relative, rather than percentage rates of return. There was little difference in explanatory power and no noteworthy change in the absolute or relative sizes of the coefficients.

TABLE 3
REGRESSION PARAMETERS FOR WHEAT, CORN, AND SOYBEANS

Commodity*	$\hat{\alpha}'_i$	$SE(\hat{\alpha}'_i)$	$\hat{\beta}_i$	$SE(\hat{\beta}_i)$	R^2	Autocorrelation Coefficient of Residuals
Wheat:						
July (302)	−.020	.001	.048	.051	.003	.148
March (302)	.000	.001	.098	.049	.013	.080
May (302)	−.000	.001	.028	.051	.001	.163
Sept. (319)	−.002	.001	.068	.051	.006	.149
Dec. (319)	−.000	.001	.059	.048	.005	.163
Corn:						
July (301)	−.001	.001	.038	.046	.002	−.041
March (301)	−.003	.001	−.009	.050	.000	.015
May (301)	−.002	.001	−.027	.048	.001	.032
Sept. (320)	−.002	.001	.032	.048	.001	.100
Dec. (320)	−.001	.001	.007	.047	.000	.017
Soybeans (287 all contracts):						
Jan.	.002	.001	.019	.058	.000	.015
March	.003	.002	.100	.065	.008	.018
May	.003	.002	.119	.068	.011	.071
July	.002	.002	.080	.076	.004	.083
Sept.	.001	.001	.077	.065	.005	.060
Nov.	.002	.001	.043	.058	.002	.023

* Numbers of observations are given in parentheses.

Thus the smallness of the regression coefficients relative to their standard errors is on balance even more pronounced than the figures in the table indicate. In the case of the intercept term, the standard errors are also large (in only two, possibly three, cases are they as small as half the value of the coefficient), which is consistent with expression (3) and a value of the intercept of zero. The low serial correlation of the residuals suggests that the assumption of independence upon which the calculation of the standard error is predicted is a tenable one.

It is clear from table 3 that relative risk for wheat, corn, and soybeans is very close to zero.[25] To judge how low a level of systematic risk these regression coefficients represent, it is worthwhile, perhaps, to compare them to the regression coefficients for some well-known common stocks. By construction, of course, the average stock has $\beta = 1$. For American Telephone and Telegraph, considered to be a safe "widows and orphans stock," β was .34 over our sample interval. The average

[25] It may strike some readers as paradoxical that there could exist an asset whose return is a random variable and whose β is zero. Remember, however, that a zero β asset has only zero covariance with other assets on *average*. With some assets its return will be positively correlated, and with others, negatively correlated. In fact, since the zero β assets will themselves be part of total wealth, they must be negatively correlated, on balance, with all other assets in the market portfolio. Because of this covariance with other assets, the zero β asset does make a sufficient contribution to the diversification and hence the risk reduction of the total portfolio to justify its inclusion even at a mean return (over and above interest) of zero. For a general treatment of zero β assets within the context of the Sharpe model, see Black (1972).

regression coefficient for the electric utility industry was .41, and the corresponding figure for the gas utility industry was .45.[26] Clearly, then, compared to common stocks, the systematic risk measures for wheat, corn, and soybeans are low indeed.

Since the mean returns (which are actually risk premiums) are also very close to zero, we may conclude that the data on commodity future returns during our sample period conform better to the capital markets model than to the Keynesian model. In fact, the contest is not even close.[27]

VII. SOME CONCLUDING OBSERVATIONS ON HARDY AND KEYNES

Because both mean returns and systematic risk were zero, the sample evidence permits no direct confrontation between the capital market approach and the Hardy gambling casino theory, which also predicts a mean return of zero. Had we found a commodity for which the β's were substantially and unambiguously positive while the means were zero or negative (or found a commodity with significant negative intercept terms in expression [8]), we could have concluded that for such a case the evidence was more consistent with the gambling than with the portfolio interpretation. We would also have had to conclude that risk-averse investors are apparently not shrewd enough to recognize a bargain. For the existence of a futures asset with a positive value of β when regressed on a stock index and a zero (or negative) mean would make it attractive for risk averters to become "short speculators" in that market. Selling futures short under such conditions would create an asset that was negatively correlated with the rest of the investor's portfolio and yet not reduce the mean return on the portfolio as a whole.

The possibility that other commodities besides these I studied may turn out to have nonzero β's also suggests a way of reconciling Keynesian and capital market views of risk and returns in futures markets. When Keynes wrote *The Treatise on Money* in the late 1920s, the variability that he identified with asset risk may in fact have included a siz-

[26] Information supplied by Merton H. Miller and Myron Scholes, from an unpublished manuscript. The regression coefficients have been estimated using annual rates of return over the period 1947-66.

[27] Estimates of the Keynesian risk measure, or scale factor, the truncated means, and the regression coefficients have been computed by 5-year subperiod intervals. Although there is some tendency for both the scale factor and the regression coefficient to be higher in the first 5-year period (especially for wheat), there is no systematic pattern between risk and return. More often than not, high risk, in terms of either simple variablity or systematic risk, is associated with negative means, and low risk with positive means.

able systematic risk component. In the late 1920s commodity prices were not subject to effective price support.[28] Thus prices could be expected to be more variable and also to be more strongly associated than at present with cyclical swings in the economy. It may well also have been the case that the particular commodities Keynes used as examples of futures market risk—cotton and copper—were strongly associated with the level of activity in British manufacturing in the early 1930s. If such a connection existed, share prices and the prices of raw commodities, including futures, would be related to each other. With cotton as the major input to a large sector of British manufacturers, it would hardly be surprising to observe a high correlation between the returns on cotton futures and the returns on British industrial stocks.

This reinterpretation of Keynes suggests that if my sample were broadened to include commodities more intimately associated with American manufacture, there might perhaps be cases of commodity futures having high positive β's and positive means as well. But such interesting prospects must await future research.

References

Black, Fischer. "Capital Market Equilibrium with Restricted Borrowing." *J. Bus.* 45 (July 1972): 444-55.
Black, Fischer; Jensen, Michael; and Scholes, Myron. "The Capital Asset Pricing Model: Some Empirical Results." In *Studies in the Theory of Capital Markets*, edited by Michael Jensen. New York: Praeger, 1972.
Blattberg, Robert, and Sargent, Thomas. "Regression with Non-Gaussian Disturbances: Some Sampling Results." *Econometrica* 39 (May 1971): 501-10.
Blume, Marshall E. "The Assessment of Portfolio Performance: An Application of Portfolio Theory." Ph.D. dissertation, Univ. Chicago, 1968.
Cootner, Paul. "Returns to Speculators: Telser versus Keynes." *J.P.E.* 68 (August 1960): 396-404. (*a*)
———. "Rejoinder." *J.P.E.* 68 (August 1960): 415-18. (*b*)
Fama, Eugene. "Risk, Return, and Equilibrium." *J.P.E.* 79 (January/February 1971): 30-55.
Fama, Eugene, and Babiak, Harvey. "Dividend Policy: An Empirical Analysis." *J. American Statis. Assoc.* 63 (December 1968): 1132-61.
Fama, Eugene, and MacBeth, James. "Risk, Return, and Equilibrium: Empirical Tests." Manuscript, Univ. Chicago, 1972.
Fama, Eugene, and Miller, Merton H. *The Theory of Finance*. New York: Holt, Rinehart & Winston, 1972.
Fama, Eugene, and Roll, Richard. "Some Properties of Symmetric Stable Distributions." *J. American Statis. Assoc.* 63 (September 1968): 817-36.
———. "Parameter Estimates for Symmetric Stable Distributions." *J. American Statis. Assoc.* 66 (June 1971): 331-38.
Fisher, Lawrence. "Some New Stock Market Indexes." *J. Bus.* 39 (suppl.; January 1966): 191-225.
Gray, R. W. "The Search for a Risk Premium." *J.P.E.* 69 (June 1961): 250-60.

---

[28] There were, of course, a number of price or output stabilization schemes in operation during this period, few of which were successful for any length of time.

Hardy, Charles O. *Risk and Risk Bearing.* Chicago: Univ. Chicago Press, 1940.
Houthakker, H. S. "Can Speculators Forecast Prices?" *Rev. Econ. and Statis.* 39 (May 1957): 143-51.
——. "Systematic and Random Elements in Short-Term Price Movements." *A.E.R.* 51 (May 1961): 164-72.
——. "Normal Backwardation." In *Value, Capital, and Growth: Papers in Honour of Sir John R. Hicks*, edited by J. N. Wolfe. Chicago: Aldine, 1968.
Johnson, Leland. "The Theory of Hedging and Speculation in Commodity Futures." *Rev. Econ. Studies* 27 (June 1960): 139-51.
Keynes, J. M. *A Treatise on Money.* Vol. 2. London: Macmillan, 1930.
King, Benjamin F. "Market and Industry Factors in Stock Price Behavior." *J. Bus.* 39 (January 1966): 139-90.
Larsen, Arnold. "Measurement of a Random Process in Future Prices." *Food Res. Inst. Studies* (Stanford Univ.) 1 (November 1960): 313-24.
Leland, Hayne F. "Optimal Forward Exchange Positions." *J.P.E.* 89 (March/April 1971): 257-69.
Lintner, John. "Security Prices, Risk, and Maximal Gains from Diversification." *J. Finance* 20 (December 1965): 587-615.
Markowitz, Harry M. *Portfolio Selection: Efficient Diversifications of Investments.* New York: Wiley, 1959.
Miller, Merton H., and Scholes, Myron S. "Rates of Return in Relation to Risk: A Reexamination of Some Recent Findings." In *Studies in the Theory of Capital Markets*, edited by Michael Jensen. New York: Praeger, 1972.
Mossin, Jan. "Equilibrium in a Capital Asset Market." *Econometrica* 37 (October 1966): 763-68.
Officer, Robert R. "A Time Series Examination of the Market Factor of the New York Stock Exchange." Ph.D. dissertation, Univ. Chicago, 1971.
Roberts, Harry V. *Statistical Inference and Decision.* Lithographed. Univ. Chicago, 1964.
Rockwell, Charles S. "Normal Backwardation, Forecasting, and the Returns to Commodity Futures Traders." *Food Res. Inst. Studies* (Stanford Univ.) 8 (suppl.; 1967): 107-30.
Roll, Richard. "The Efficient Market Model Applied to U.S. Treasury Bill Rates." Ph.D. dissertation, Graduate School Bus., Univ. Chicago, 1968.
Samuelson, P. A. "Proof that Properly Anticipated Prices Fluctuate Randomly." *Indus. Management Rev.* 8 (Spring 1965): 41-49.
Schrock, Nichols W. "The Theory of Asset Choice: Simultaneous Holding of Short and Long Positions in the Futures Market." *J.P.E.* 79 (March/April 1971): 270-93.
Sharpe, William. "Capital Asset Prices: A Theory of Market Equilibrium under Conditions of Risk." *J. Finance* 19 (September 1964): 425-42.
Smidt, Seymour. "A Test of Serial Independence of Price Changes in Soybean Futures." *Food Res. Inst. Studies* (Stanford Univ.) 5 (1965): 117-36.
Stevenson, Richard A., and Bear, Robert M. "Commodity Futures: Trends or Random Walks?" *J. Finance* 25 (March 1970): 65-81.
Telser, Lester. "Futures Trading and the Storage of Cotton and Wheat." *J.P.E.* 66 (June 1958): 233-55.
——. "Returns to Speculators: Telser versus Keynes: Reply." *J.P.E.* 67 (August 1960): 404-15.
——. "The Supply of Speculative Services in Wheat, Corn and Soybeans." *Food Res. Inst. Studies* (Stanford Univ.) 7 (suppl.; 1967): 131-76.
U.S., Department of Agriculture, Commodity Exchange Authority. *Commodity Futures Statistics.* Washington: Government Printing Office, 1952-67.
Working, Holbrook. "Futures Trading and Hedging." *A.E.R.* 18 (June 1953): 314-43.

The Pricing of Commodity Contracts[*]

Fischer Black[†]

The contract price on a forward contract stays fixed for the life of the contract, while a futures contract is rewritten every day. The value of a futures contract is zero at the start of each day. The expected change in the futures price satisfies a formula like the capital asset pricing model. If changes in the futures price are independent of the return on the market, the futures price is the expected spot price. The futures market is not unique in its ability to shift risk, since corporations can do that too. The futures market is unique in the guidance it provides for producers, distributors, and users of commodities. Using assumptions like those used in deriving the original option formula, we find formulas for the values of forward contracts and commodity options in terms of the futures price and other variables.

1. INTRODUCTION

The market for contracts related to commodities is not widely understood. Futures contracts and forward contracts are often thought to be identical, and many people don't know about the existence of commodity options. One of the aims of this paper is to clarify the meaning of each of these contracts.[1]

The spot price of a commodity is the price at which it can be bought or sold for immediate delivery. We will write p for the spot price, or $p(t)$ for the spot pice at time t.

---

[*]Reprinted from the *Journal of Financial Economics*, Vol. 3, No. 1, (January/March 1976). Reprinted by permission of the North-Holland Publishing Company, Amsterdam, and the author.

[†]I am grateful for comments on earlier drafts by Michael Jensen, Myron Scholes, Edward Thorp, and Joseph Williams. This work was supported in part by the Center for Research in Security Prices (sponsored by Merrill Lynch, Pierce, Fenner & Smith Inc.) at the Graduate School of Business, University of Chicago.

[1] For an introduction to commodity markets, see Chicago Board of Trade (1973).

The spot price of an agricultural commodity tends to have a seasonal pattern: it is high just before a harvest, and low just after a harvest. The spot price of a commodity such as gold, however, fluctuates more randomly.

Predictable patterns in the movement of the spot price do not generally imply profit opportunities. The spot price can rise steadily at any rate lower than the storage cost for the commodity (including interest) without giving rise to a profit opportunity for those with empty storage facilities. The spot price can fall during a harvest period without giving rise to a profit opportunity for growers, so long as it is costly to accelerate the harvest.

The futures price of a commodity is the price at which one can agree to buy or sell it at a given time in the future without putting up any money now. We will write x for the futures price, or $x(t,t^*)$ for the futures price at time t for a transaction that will occur at time t^*.

For example, suppose that it is possible today to enter into a contract to buy gold six months from now at $160 an ounce, without either party to the contract being compensated by the other. Both parties may put up collateral to guarantee their ability to fulfill the contract, but if the futures price remains at $160 an ounce for the next six months, the collateral will not be touched. If the contract is left unchanged for six months, then the gold and the money will change hands at that time. In this situation, we say that the six month futures price of gold is $160 an ounce.

The futures price is very much like the odds on a sports bet. If the odds on a particular baseball game between Boston and Chicago are 2:1 in favor of Boston, and if we ignore the bookie's profit, then a person who bets on Chicago wins $2 or loses $1. No money changes hands until after the game. The odds adjust to balance the demand for bets on Chicago and the demand for bets on Boston. At 2:1, balance occurs if twice as many bets are placed on Boston as on Chicago.

Similarly, the futures price adjusts to balance demand to buy the commodity in the future with demand to sell the commodity in the future. Whenever a contract is opened, there is someone on each side. The person who agrees to buy is long the commodity, and the person who agrees to sell is short. This means that when we add up all positions in contracts of this kind, and count short positions as negative, we always come out with zero. The total long interest in commodity contracts of any type must equal the total short interest.

When the two times that specify a futures price are equal, the futures price must equal the spot price,

$$x(t,t) \equiv p(t). \qquad (1)$$

Expression (1) holds for all times t. For example, it says that the May futures price will be equal to the May spot price in May, and the September futures price will be equal to the September spot price in September.

Now let us define the three kinds of commodity contracts: forward contracts, futures contracts, and option contracts. Roughly speaking, a forward contract is a contract to buy or sell at a price that stays fixed for the life of the contract; a futures contract is settled every day and rewritten at the new futures price; and an option contract can be exercised by the holder when it matures, if it has not been closed out earlier.

We will write v for the value of a forward contract, u for the value of a futures contract, and w for the value of an option contract. Each of these values will depend on the current futures price $x(t,t^*)$ with the same transaction time t^* as the contract, and on the current time t, as well as on other variables. So we will write $v(x,t)$, $u(x,t)$, and $w(x,t)$. The value of the short side of any contract will be just the negative of the value of the long side. So we will treat v, u, and w as the values of a forward contract to buy, a long futures contract, and an option to buy.

The value of a forward contract depends also on the price c at which the commodity will be bought, and the time t^* at which the transaction will take place. We will sometimes write $v(x,t,c,t^*)$ for the value of a long forward contract. From the discussion above, we know that the futures price is that price at which a forward contract has a current value of zero. We can write this condition as

$$v(x, t, c, t^*) \equiv 0. \tag{2}$$

In effect, eq. (2) says that the value of a forward contract when it is initiated is always zero. When it is initiated, the contract price c is always equal to the current futures price $x(t,t^*)$.

Increasing the futures price increases the value of a long forward contract, and decreasing the futures price decreases the value of the contract. Thus we have

$$\begin{aligned} v(x, t, c, t^*) &> 0, \quad x > c, \\ v(x, t, c, t^*) &< 0, \quad x < c. \end{aligned} \tag{3}$$

The value of a forward contract may be either positive or negative.

When the time comes for the transaction to take place, the value of the forward contract will be equal to the spot price minus the contract price. But by eq. (1), the futures price $x(t,t^*)$ will be equal to the spot price at that time. Thus the value of the forward contract will be the futures price minus the contract price,

$$v(x, t^*, c, t^*) = x - c. \tag{4}$$

Later we will use eq. (4) as the main boundary condition for a differential equation describing the value of a forward contract.

The difference between a futures contract and a forward contract is that the futures contract is rewritten every day with a new contract price equal to the corresponding futures price. A futures contract is like a series of forward contracts. Each day, yesterday's contract is settled, and today's contract is written with a contract price equal to the futures price with the same maturity as the futures contract.

Eq. (2) shows that the value of a forward contract with a contract price equal to the futures price is zero. Thus the value of a futures contract is reset to zero every day. If the investor has made money, he will be given his gains immediately. If he has lost money, he will have to pay his losses immediately. Thus we have

$$u(x, t) \equiv 0. \tag{5}$$

Technically, eq. (5) applies only to the end of the day, after the futures contract has been rewritten. During the day, the futures contract may have a positive or negative value, and its value will be equal to the value of the corresponding forward contract.

Note that the futures price and the value of a futures contract are not at all the same thing. The futures price refers to a transaction at times t^* and is never zero. The value of a futures contract refers to time t and is always zero (at the end of the day).

In the organized U.S. futures markets, both parties to a futures contract must post collateral with a broker. This helps to ensure that the losing party each day will have funds available to pay the winning party. The amount of collateral required varies from broker to broker.

The form in which the collateral can be posted also varies from broker to broker. Most brokers allow the collateral to take the form of Treasury Bills or marginable securities if the amount exceeds a certain minimum. The brokers encourage cash collateral, however, because they earn the interest on customers' cash balances.

The value of a futures customer's account with a broker is entirely the value of his collateral (at the end of the day). The value of his futures contracts is zero. The value of the collateral posted to ensure performance of a futures contract is not the value of the contract.

As futures contracts are settled each day, the value of each customer's collateral is adjusted. When the futures price goes up, those with long positions have money added to their collateral, and those with short positions have money taken away from their collateral. If a customer at any time has more collateral than his broker requires, he may withdraw the excess. If he has less than his broker requires, he will have to put up additional collateral immediately.

Commodity options have a bad image in the U.S., because they were recently used to defraud investors of many millions of dollars. There are no organized commodity options markets in this country. In the U.K., however, commodity options have a long and relatively respectable history.

A commodity option is an option to buy a fixed quantity of a specified commodity at a fixed time in the future and at a specified price. It differs from a security option in that it can't be exercised before the fixed future date. Thus it is a 'European option' rather than an 'American option.'

A commodity option differs from a forward contract because the holder of the option can choose whether or not he wants to buy the commodity at the specified price. With a forward contract, he has no choice: he must buy it, even if the spot price at the time of the transaction is lower than the price he pays.

At maturity, the value of a commodity option is the spot price minus the contract price, if that is positive, or zero. Writing c^* for the exercise price of the option, and noting that the futures price equals the spot price at maturity, we have

$$w(x, t^*) = x - c^*, \quad x \geq c^*, \qquad (6)$$
$$= 0, \quad x < c^*.$$

Expression (6) looks like the expression for the value of a security option at maturity as a function of the security price.

2. THE BEHAVIOR OF THE FUTURES PRICE

Changes in the futures price for a given commodity at a given maturity give risk to gains and losses for investors with long or short positions in the corresponding futures contracts. An investor with a position in the futures market is bearing risk even though the value of his position at the end of each day is zero. His position may also have a positive or negative expected dollar return, even though his investment in the position is zero.

Since his investment is zero, it is not possible to talk about the percentage or fractional return on the investor's position in the futures market. Both his risk and his expected return must be defined in dollar terms.

In deriving expressions for the behavior of the futures price, we will assume that taxes are zero. However, tax factors will generally affect the behavior of the futures price. There are two peculiarities in the tax laws that make them important.

First, the IRS assumes that a gain or loss on a futures contract is realized only when the contract is closed out. The IRS does not recognize, for tax purposes, the fact that a futures contract is effectively settled and rewritten every day. This makes possible strategies for deferring the taxation of capital gains. For example, the investor can open a number of different contracts, both long and short. The contracts that develop losses are closed out early, and are replaced with different contracts so that the long and short positions stay balanced. The contracts that develop gains are allowed to run unrealized into the next tax year. In the next year, the process can be repeated. Whether this process is likely to be profitable depends on the special factors affecting each investor, including the size of the transaction costs he pays.

Second, the IRS treats a gain or loss on a long futures position that is closed out more than six months after it is opened as a long-term capital gain or loss, while it treats a gain or loss on a short futures position as a short-term capital gain or loss no matter how long the position is left open. Thus if the investor opens both long and short contracts, and if he realizes losses on the short contracts and gains on the long contracts, he can convert short-term gains (from other transactions) into long-term gains. Again, whether this makes sense for a particular investor will depend on his transaction costs and other factors.

However, we will assume that both taxes and transaction costs are zero. We will further assume that the capital asset pricing model applies at each instant of time.[2] This means that investors will be compensated only for bearing risk that cannot be diversified away. If the risk in a futures contract is independent of the risk of changes in value of all assets taken together, then investors will not have to be paid for taking that risk. In effect, they don't have to take the risk because they can diversify it away.

The usual capital asset pricing formula is

$$E(\tilde{R}_i) - R = \beta_i [E(\tilde{R}_m) - R]. \tag{7}$$

In this expression, $\tilde{R}_i$ is the return on asset i, expressed as a fraction of its initial value; R is the return on short-term interest-bearing securities; and $\tilde{R}_m$ is the return on the market portfolio of all assets taken together. The coefficient β_i is a measure of the extent to which the risk of asset i cannot be diversified away. It is defined by

$$\beta_i = \text{cov}(\tilde{R}_i, \tilde{R}_m)/\text{var}(\tilde{R}_m). \tag{8}$$

The market portfolio referred to above includes corporate securities, personal assets such as real estate, and assets held by non-corporate businesses. To the extent that stocks of commodities are held by corporations, they are implicitly included in the market portfolio. To the extent that they are held by individuals and non-corporate businesses, they are explicitly included in the market portfolio. This market portfolio cannot be observed, of course. It is a theoretical construct.

Commodity contracts, however, are not included in the market portfolio. Commodity contracts are pure bets, in that there is a short position for every long position. So when we are taking all assets together, futures contracts, forward contracts, and commodity options all net out to zero.

[2] For an introduction to the capital asset pricing model, see Jensen (1972). The behavior of futures prices in a model of capital market equilibrium was first discussed by Dusak (1973).

Eq. (7) cannot be applied directly to a futures contract, because the initial value of the contract is zero. So we will rewrite the equation so that it applies to dollar returns rather than percentage returns.

Let us assume that asset i has no dividends or other distributions over the period. Then its fractional return is its end-of-period price minus its start-of-period price, divided by its start-of-period price. Writing P_{i0} for the start-of-period price of asset i, writing $\tilde{P}_{i1}$ for its end-of-period price, and substituting from eq. (8), we can rewrite eq. (7) as

$$E\{(\tilde{P}_{i1}-P_{i0})/P_{i0}\} - R = [\text{cov}\,\{(\tilde{P}_{i1}-P_{i0})/P_{i0}, \tilde{R}_m\}/\text{var}\,(\tilde{R}_m)] \\ \times [E(\tilde{R}_m) - R]. \qquad (9)$$

Multiplying through by P_{i0}, we get an expression for the expected dollar return on an asset,

$$E(\tilde{P}_{i1} - P_{i0}) - RP_{i0} = [\text{cov}\,(\tilde{P}_{i1}-P_{i0}, \tilde{R}_m)/\text{var}\,(\tilde{R}_m)][E(\tilde{R}_m) - R]. \qquad (10)$$

The start-of-period value of a futures contract is zero, so we set P_{i0} equal to zero. The end-of-period value of a futures contract, before the contract is rewritten and its value set to zero, is the change in the futures price over the period. In practice, commodity exchanges set daily limits which constrain the reported change in the futures price and the daily gains and losses of traders. We will assume that these limits do not exist. So we set $\tilde{P}_{i1}$ equal to $\Delta \tilde{P}$, the change in the futures price over the period,

$$E(\Delta \tilde{P}) = [\text{cov}\,(\Delta \tilde{P}, \tilde{R}_m)/\text{var}\,(\tilde{R}_m)][E(\tilde{R}_m) - R]. \qquad (11)$$

In effect, we have applied expression (10) to a futures contract, and have come up with expression (11), which refers to the change in the futures price. For the rest of this section, we can forget about futures contracts and work only with the futures price.

Writing β^* for the first factor on the right-hand side of eq. (11), we have

$$E(\Delta \tilde{P}) = \beta^*[E(\tilde{R}_m) - R]. \qquad (12)$$

Expression (12) says that the expected change in the futures price is proportional to the 'dollar beta' of the futures price. If the covariance of the change in the futures price with the return on the market portfolio is zero, then the expected change in the futures price will be zero,[3]

$$E(\Delta \tilde{P}) = 0, \quad \text{when} \quad \text{cov}\,(\Delta \tilde{P}, \tilde{R}_m) = 0. \qquad (13)$$

---

[3] In the data she analyzed on wheat, corn, and soybean futures, Dusak (1973) found covariances that were close to zero.

Expressions (12) and (13) say that the expected change in the futures price can be positive, zero, or negative. It would be very surprising if the β^* of a futures price were exactly zero, but it may be approximately zero for many commodities. For these commodities, neither those with long futures positions nor those with short futures positions have significantly positive expected dollar returns.

3. FUTURES PRICES AND SPOT PRICES

When eq. (13) holds at all points in time, the expected change in the futures price will always be zero. This means that the expected futures price at any time t' in the future, where t' is between the current time t and the transaction time t^*, will be equal to the current futures price. The mean of the distribution of possible futures prices at time t' will be the current futures price.[4]

But the futures price at time t^* is the spot price at time t^*, from expression (1). So the mean of the distribution of possible spot prices at time t^* will be the current futures price, when eq. (13) always holds.

Even when (13) doesn't hold, we may still be able to use eq. (12) to estimate the mean of the distribution of possible spot prices at time t^*. To use (12), though, we need to know β^* at each point in time between t and t^*, and we need to know $E(\tilde{R}_m) - R$.

A farmer may not want to know the mean of the distribution of possible spot prices at time t^*. He may be interested in the discounted value of the distribution of possible spot prices. In fact, it seems plausible that he can make his investment decisions as if β^* were zero, even if it is not zero. He can assume that the β^* is zero, and that the futures price is the expected spot price.

To see why this is so, note that he can hedge his investments by taking a short position in the futures market. By taking the right position in the futures market, he can make the β of his overall position zero. Assuming that the farmer is not concerned about risk that can be diversified away, he should make the same investment decisions whether or not he actually takes offsetting positions in the futures market.

In fact, futures prices provide a wealth of valuable information for those who produce, store, and use commodities. Looking at futures prices for various transaction months, participants in this market can decide on the best times to plant, harvest, buy for storage, sell from storage, or process the commodity. A change in a futures price at time t is related to changes in the anticipated distribution of spot prices at

---

[4] The question of the relation between the futures price and the expected spot price is discussed under somewhat different assumptions by Cootner (1960a, 1960b) and Telser (1960).

time t^*. It is not directly related to changes in the spot price at time t. In practice, however, changes in spot prices and changes in futures prices will often be highly correlated.

Both spot prices and futures prices are affected by general shifts in the cost of producing the commodity, and by general shifts in the demand for the commodity. These are probably the most important factors affecting commodity prices. But an event like the arrival of a prime producing season for the commodity will cause the spot price to fall, without having any predictable effect on the futures price.

Changes in commodity prices are also affected by such factors as the interest rate, the cost of storing the commodity, and the β of the commodity itself.[5] These factors may affect both the spot and the futures price, but in different ways.

Commodity holdings are assets that form part of investors' portfolios, either directly or indirectly. The returns on such assets must be defined to include such things as the saving to a user of commodities from not running out in the middle of a production run, or the benefit to anyone storing the commodity of having stocks on hand when there is an unusual surge in demand. The returns on commodity holdings must be defined net of all storage costs, including deterioration, theft, and insurance premiums. When the returns on commodity holdings are defined in this way, they should obey the capital asset pricing model, as expressed by eq. (7), like any other asset. If the β of the commodity is zero, as given in eq. (7), then we would expect the β^* of a futures contract to be approximately zero too, as given in eq. (12). And vice versa.

The notion that commodity holdings are priced like other assets means that investors who own commodities are able to diversify away that part of the risk that can be diversified away. One way this can happen is through futures markets: those who own commodities can take short positions, and those who hold diversified portfolios of assets can include long positions in commodity contracts.

But there are other ways that the risk in commodity holdings can be largely diversified away. The most common way for a risk to be spread is through a corporation. The risk of a corporation's business or assets is passed on to the holders of the corporation's liabilities, especially its stockholders. The stockholders have, or could have, well diversified portfolios of which this stock is only a small part.

Thus if stocks of a commodity are held by a corporation, there will normally be no need for the risk to be spread through the futures market. (There are special cases, however, such as where the corporation has lots of debt outstanding and the lenders insist that the commodity risk be hedged through the futures market.) There are corporations at

---

[5] Some of the factors affecting changes in the spot price are discussed by Brennan (1958) and Telser (1958).

every stage in a commodity's life cycle: production, distribution, and processing. Even agricultural commodities are generally produced by corporations these days, though the stock may be closely held. Any of these corporate entities can take title to the stocks of commodities, no matter where they are located, and thus spread the risk to those who are in the best position to bear it. For example, canners of tomatoes often buy a farmer's crop before the vines are planted. They may even supply the vines.

This means that a futures market does not have a unique role in the allocation of risk. Corporations in the commodity business play the same role. Which kind of market is best for this role depends on the specifics of such things as transaction costs and taxes in each individual case. It seems clear that corporations do a better job for most commodities, because organized futures markets don't even exist for most commodities. Where they do exist, most of the risk is still transferred through corporations rather than through futures markets.

Thus there is no reason to believe that the existence of a futures market has any predictable effect on the path of the spot price over time. It is primarily the storage of a commodity that reduces fluctuations in its price over time. Storage will occur whether or not there is any way of transferring risk. If there were no way to transfer risk, the price of a seasonal commodity might be somewhat higher before the prime production periods than it is now. But since there are good ways to transfer risk without using the futures market, even this benefit of futures markets is minimal.

I believe that futures markets exist because in some situations they provide an inexpensive way to transfer risk, and because many people both in the business and out like to gamble on commodity prices. Neither of these counts as a major benefit to society. The big benefit from futures markets is the side effect: the fact that participants in the futures markets can make production, storage, and processing decisions by looking at the pattern of futures prices, even if they don't take positions in that market.

This, of course, assumes that futures markets are efficient. It assumes that futures prices incorporate all available information about the future spot price of a commodity. It assumes that investors act quickly on any information they receive, so that the price reacts quickly to the arrival of the information. So quickly that individual traders find it very difficult to make money consistently by trading on information.

4. THE PRICING OF FORWARD CONTRACTS AND COMMODITY OPTIONS

We have already discussed the pricing of futures contracts and the behavior of futures prices. In order to derive formulas for the other kinds of commodity contracts, we must make a few more assumptions.

First, let us assume that the fractional change in the futures price over any interval is distributed log-normally, with a known variance rate s^2. The derivations would go through with little change if we assumed that the variance rate is a known function of the time between t and t^*, but we will assume that the variance rate is constant.

Second, let us assume that all of the parameters of the capital asset pricing model, including the expected return on the market, the variance of the return on the market, and the short-term interest rate, are constant through time.

Third, let us continue to assume that taxes and transaction costs are zero.

Under these assumptions, it makes sense to write the value of a commodity contract only as a function of the corresponding futures price and time. If we did not assume the parameters of the capital asset pricing model were constant, then the value of a commodity contract might also depend on those parameters. Implicitly, of course, the value of the contract still depends on the transaction price and the transaction time.

Now let us use the same procedure that led to the formula for an option on a security.[6] We can create a riskless hedge by taking a long position in the option and a short position in the futures contract with the same transaction date. Since the value of a futures contract is always zero, the equity in this position is just the value of the option.

The size of the short position in the futures contract that makes the combined position riskless is the derivative of $w(x,t)$ with respect to x, which we will write w_1. Thus the change in the value of the hedged position over the time interval Δt is

$$\Delta w - w_1 \Delta x. \tag{14}$$

Expanding Δw, and noting that the return on the hedge must be at the instantaneous riskless rate r, we have the differential equation[7]

$$w_2 = rw - \tfrac{1}{2}s^2 x^2 w_{11}. \tag{15}$$

Note that this is like the differential equation for an option on a security, but with one term missing. The term is missing because the value of a futures contract is zero, while the value of a security is positive.

The main boundary condition for this equation is expression (6).[8]

---

[6] The original option formula was derived by Black and Scholes (1973). Further results were obtained by Merton (1973).

[7] For the details of this expansion, see Black and Scholes (1973, p. 642 or p. 646).

[8] Another boundary condition and a regularity condition are needed to make the solution to (15) and (6) unique. The boundary condition is $w(0,t) = 0$. The need for these additional conditions was not noted in Black and Scholes (1973).

Using standard methods to solve eqs. (15) and (6), we obtain the following formula for the value of a commodity option:

$$w(x, t) = e^{r(t-t^*)}[xN(d_1) - c^*N(d_2)], \qquad (16)$$

$$d_1 = \left[\ln\frac{x}{c^*} + \frac{s^2}{2}(t^*-t)\right]\bigg/ s\sqrt{(t^*-t)},$$

$$d_2 = \left[\ln\frac{x}{c^*} - \frac{s^2}{2}(t^*-t)\right]\bigg/ s\sqrt{(t^*-t)}.$$

This formula can be obtained from the original option formula by substituting $xe^{r(t-t^*)}$ for x everywhere in the original formula.[9] It is the same as the value of an option on a security that pays a continuous dividend at a rate equal to the stock price times the interest rate, when the option can only be exercised at maturity.[10] Again, this happens because the investment in a futures contract is zero, so an interest rate factor drops out of the formula.

Eq. (16) applies to a 'European' commodity option, that can only be exercised at maturity. If the commodity option can be exercised before maturity, the problem of finding its value becomes much more complex.[11] Among other things, its value will depend on the spot price and on futures prices with various transaction dates before the option expires.

Eq. (16) also assumes that taxes are zero. But if commodity options are taxed like security options, then there will be substantial benefits for high tax bracket investors who write commodity options.[12] These benefits may be passed on in part or in full to buyers of commodity options in the form of lower prices. So taxes may reduce the values of commodity options.

Compared with the formula for a commodity option, the formula for the value of a forward contract is very simple. The differential equation it must satisfy is the same. Substituting $v(x,t)$ for $w(x,t)$ in eq. (15), we have

$$v_2 = rv - \tfrac{1}{2}s^2x^2v_{11}. \qquad (17)$$

---

[9] Thorp (1973) obtains the same formula for a similar problem, related to the value of a security option when an investor who sells the underlying stock short does not receive interest on the proceeds of the short sale.

[10] Merton (1973) discusses the valuation of options on dividend-paying securities. The formula he obtains (f. 62) should be eq. (16), but he forgets to substitute $xe^{r(t-t^*)}$ for x in d_1 and d_2.

[11] See Merton (1973) for a discussion of some of the complexities in finding a value for an option that can be exercised early.

[12] For a discussion of tax factors in the pricing of options, see Black (1975).

The main boundary condition is eq. (4), which we can rewrite as

$$v(x, t^*) = x - c. \tag{18}$$

The solution to (17) and (18) plus the implicit boundary conditions is

$$v(x, t) = (x - c) e^{r(t - t^*)}. \tag{19}$$

Expression (19) says that the value of a forward contract is the difference between the futures price and the forward contract price, discounted to the present at the short-term interest rate. It is independent of any measure of risk. It does not depend on the variance rate of the fractional change in the futures price or on the covariance rate between the change in the futures price and the return on the market.

References

Black, F., 1975, Fact and fantasy in the use of options, *Financial Analysts Journal*, 31, July/Aug.

Black, F. and M. Scholes, 1973, The pricing of options and corporate liabilities, *Journal of Political Economy*, 81, May/June, 637-654.

Brennan, M. J., 1958, The supply of storage, *American Economic Review*, 48, March, 50-72.

Chicago Board of Trade, 1973, Commodity trading manual (Board of Trade of the City of Chicago, Chicago, Ill.).

Cootner, P. H., 1960a, Returns to speculators: Telser versus Keynes, *Journal of Political Economy*, 68, Aug., 396-404.

Cootner, P. H., 1960b, Rejoinder, *Journal of Political Economy*, 68, Aug., 415-418.

Dusak, K., 1973, Futures trading and investor returns: An investigation of commodity market risk premiums, *Journal of Political Economy*, 81, Nov./Dec., 1387-1406.

Jensen, M. C., 1972, Capital markets: Theory and evidence, *Bell Journal of Economics and Management Science*, 3, Autumn, 357-398.

Merton, R. C., 1973, The theory of rational option pricing, *Bell Journal of Economics and Management Science*, 4, Spring, 141-183.

Telser, L., 1958, Futures trading and the storage of cotton and wheat, *Journal of Political Economy*, 66, June, 233-255.

Telser, L., 1960, Returns to speculators: Telser versus Keynes, Reply, *Journal of Political Economy*, 67, Aug., 404-415.

Thorp, E., 1973, Extensions of the Black-Scholes options model, Bulletin of the International Statistical Institute, Proceedings of the 39th Session, 522-529.

4

Interest Rate Futures*

Marcelle Arak and Christopher J. McCurdy[†]

On a typical day in 1979, futures contracts representing about $7½ billion in three-month Treasury bills changed hands in the International Monetary Market (IMM) of the Chicago Mercantile Exchange in Chicago. This market and several other new markets for interest rate futures have very quickly become active trading arenas. For example, at the Chicago Board of Trade (CBT), futures contracts representing $820 million of long-term Treasury bonds were traded on a typical day; also, at the CBT, futures contracts representing $540 million of GNMAs (Government National Mortgage Association securities) changed hands on an average day.

Besides these three well-established interest rate futures contracts several new financial futures contracts have recently received the approval of the Commodity Futures Trading Commission (CFTC) and have begun trading. Futures contracts for intermediate-term Treasury notes commenced trading in the summer of 1979; in the fall, the Comex (Commodity Exchange, Inc.), which had traded many metals contracts, inaugurated a three-month bill futures contract, and the ACE (Amex Commodities Exchange, Inc., an affiliate of the American Stock Ex-

---

*Reprinted from the *Quarterly Review* of the Federal Reserve Bank of New York, (Winter 1979-80). Reprinted by permission of the publisher.

†The authors wish to thank James Kurt Dew, Ronald Hobson, and Anthony Vignola for information and helpful comments. The foregoing do not necessarily agree with the views expressed herein, nor do they bear responsibility for any errors.

change) introduced a bond futures contract; in addition, the New York Stock Exchange is intending to start a financial futures unit.

What accounts for the rapid growth of interest rate futures? Who are the most active participants in these markets? Some businesses such as financial institutions and securities dealers use it to hedge or manage interest rate risk. By and large, however, participants are involved for other reasons and help provide much of the markets' liquidity. A large portion of the activity in these markets is speculative—people and institutions betting on which way interest rates will move and how the interest rate in one month will move relative to another. Others are involved in these interest rate futures markets for tax reasons.

Both the enormous size of these futures markets and the nature of the participants are a matter of concern for the regulatory authorities. The Treasury and the Federal Reserve System have become aware of potential problems for the functioning of markets in Government securities; these problems include the possibility of corners or squeezes on certain Treasury issues and the disruption of orderly cash markets for Treasury securities. In addition, the regulatory authorities have become concerned that the substantial numbers of small investors participating in the markets may not be fully aware of the risks involved.

WHAT IS A FUTURES MARKET?

For as long as mankind has traded goods and services, people have made contracts which specify that commodities and money will change hands at some future date, at a price stated in the contract. Such contracts are called "forward" contracts. A forward contract tailored to one's needs offers obvious advantages—one can pick the exact date and the precise commodity desired. On the other hand, there are disadvantages. It may be difficult to locate a buyer or seller with exactly opposite needs. In addition, there is a risk that the other party to the transaction will default.

A *futures* contract is a standardized forward contract that is traded on an exchange. Usually the type and grade of commodity is specified as well as the date for delivery. Once a bargain is struck, the clearinghouse of the futures exchange itself becomes the opposite party to every transaction. Thus, it is the soundness of the exchange's clearinghouse rather than the creditworthiness of the original buyer (or seller) that is of concern to the seller (or buyer) on the other side of the transaction. To ensure its viability, futures exchanges and their clearinghouses set up rules and regulations. These include the requirements that a clearing member firm and its customers put up "margin," that the contracts be marked-to-market daily, and that trading cease if daily price fluctuations move outside certain limits.

Among the oldest futures markets in the United States are those for wheat and corn which date back to the middle of the nineteenth century. Thereafter, futures markets for other farm products and raw materials gradually developed. One of the major purposes was to provide producers and processors with price insurance. Suppose a farmer expects to harvest wheat in July. Nobody knows with certainty what the price will be then; it depends upon the size of the harvest and conditions elsewhere in the world. However, by selling a futures contract for July wheat, the farmer can indirectly guarantee receiving a particular price. This is illustrated in Box 1.

Futures markets for commodities not only provide a forum for hedgers, but they also provide information. This information—about prices expected to prevail on future dates—is printed in the financial section of many daily newspapers. The farmer, for example, can use these futures prices to decide whether to plant corn or wheat. The food processor can gear up to can corn or beans depending upon the expected prices and the prospective consumer demand at those prices.

Interest rate futures are a relatively new development. In the fall of 1975, the CBT inaugurated a GNMA contract. Shortly thereafter, in early 1976, the IMM introduced a contract for ninety-day Treasury bills, and this was followed in 1977 by the CBT's Treasury bond futures contract. These three contracts—the CBT's original GNMA, the CBT's Treasury bond, and the IMM's three-month Treasury bill contract—have proved to be the most popular and heavily traded financial futures contracts. The amount of contracts outstanding, or open interest, in these markets has expanded significantly since their inception (Chart 1). Moreover, trading volume has also become quite large in relation to the underlying cash market securities. In 1979, daily average trading in the eight ninety-day Treasury bill contracts on the IMM was equivalent to about $7½ billion (at $1 million per contract), not much different from the daily volume of Treasury bills traded in the dealer market for United States Government securities.[1] Some interest rate futures contracts, however, have failed to attract much trading activity. For example, activity in the ninety-day commercial paper contract has remained quite light.[2]

---

[1] The market is described in "The Dealer Market for United States Government Securities," Christopher McCurdy in this bank's *Quarterly Review* (Winter 1977-78), pages 35-47.

[2] One of the problems with this contract has been that commercial paper issuers have at times tended to sell paper with maturities much shorter than ninety days. Also, because the paper of a large number of companies is deliverable against the contract, this generates substantial uncertainty about which paper will be delivered. In addition, the original technical specifications of the contract engendered some confusion.

Box 1

Hedge in Wheat Futures

A farmer planning to harvest wheat in July sells a July wheat futures contract at $2.98 in March.

(1) Suppose the price in July turns out to be......	$2.50	$3.00	$3.50
(2) Gain or loss from offsetting futures contract [$2.98 − row (1)] ...	.48	−.02	−.52
(3) Sales price of wheat in cash market [same as row (1)].......	2.50	3.00	3.50
(4) Total earnings per bushel [row (2) + row (3)]......	2.98	2.98	2.98

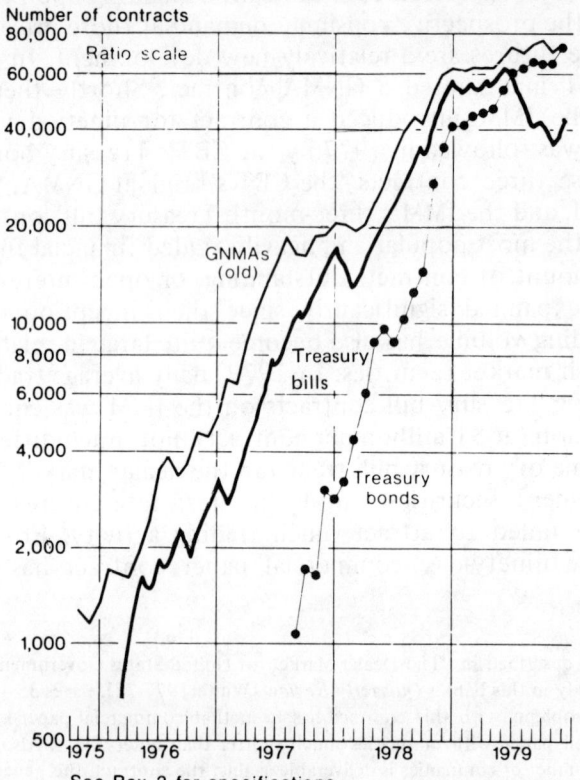

See Box 2 for specifications.
Chart 1 Sources: International Monetary Market and Chicago Board of Trade.

HOW FINANCIAL FUTURES MARKETS OPERATE

The financial futures markets operate in the same manner as other futures markets. Their terms and methods are very different from those used in the money and bond markets. One of the most active financial futures markets is that for three-month Treasury bills at the IMM. Through this exchange, a customer could, for example, buy a contract to take delivery of (and pay for) $1 million of three-month Treasury bills on March 20, 1980. In all, there are eight contract delivery months on the IMM, extending at quarterly intervals for about two years into the future.

A customer places his order with a futures commission merchant—a firm registered with the CFTC and permitted to accept orders from the public—which sends the order to the trading floor of the exchange. There, a member of the exchange enters the trading pit and announces his intention to purchase the March 1980 contract. Another member who has an order to sell that contract shouts out his offer and, if the two can agree on a price, the trade is consummated. The trading in the pit is by *open outcry*, which is typical of futures exchanges and very unlike the over-the-telephone negotiations in the cash market for Treasury Securities.

The contract's price is quoted as the difference between 100 and the discount rate on the bill in question. Thus, a contract fixing a bill rate of 8.50 percent would be quoted at 91.50. This index preserves the normal futures market relationship in which the party obligated to take (make) delivery profits when the price rises (falls). The contract quote is not the price that would actually be paid for the bill at delivery. That price is computed by using the rate of discount in the standard bill price formula.

The clearinghouse interposes itself between the buyer and the seller, so that the buyer's contract is not with the seller but with the clearinghouse. (In the same fashion, the seller's contract is with the clearinghouse and not with the original buyer.)

A key ingredient in the financial viability of the clearinghouse is the margin that the clearing member firms must post on their contracts. For each outright purchase or sale of a three-month Treasury bill contract on the IMM, the firm must post margin of $1,200 per contract, which can be in the form of cash or bank letter of credit. The clearing member firm must, in turn, impose an initial margin of at least $1,500 on the customer. This may be posted in the form of cash, selected securities, or bank letters of credit. Futures firms can and often do require higher than the minimum margins of their customers. Margins formerly were more lenient, at one point down to $800 initial margin, but were raised following the greater volatility that emerged in the financial markets in the wake of the Federal Reserve System's policy actions in October 1979.

For as long as the position is outstanding, the contract will be *marked-to-market* by the clearinghouse at the end of each business day. For example a clearing member with a long position in the March contract would have its margin account credited with a profit if the price rises, or debited with a loss if it declines. The prices used in the calculations are the *final settlement prices*, which are determined by the exchange by examining the prices attached to the trades transacted at the end of trading each day.

Profits in the margin account may be withdrawn immediately. When losses occur and reduce the firm's margin below $1,200, the firm must pay the difference to the clearinghouse in cash before trading opens the next day. It is permissible for the value of a customer's margin account to fall below the initial $1,500 but, once the margin account falls below the $1,200 maintenance margin, the account must be replenished in full—brought back up to $1,500. Since the value of a 1 basis point change in the futures bill rate is $25 per contract, relatively small changes in interest rates can result in large changes in the value of a margin account.

The exchanges impose rules that prices may not change by more than a certain maximum amount from one day to the next. At the IMM, for example, no bill futures trades may be cleared if the price is more than 50 basis points above or below the final settlement price on the previous day although, if the *daily limit* restricts trading for a few days, then wider limits may be imposed on subsequent days. Margins are often temporarily increased during such periods.

When the customer wishes to get out of his contract before maturity, he must take an offsetting position. To cancel the contract he bought, he must sell another contract. His order is forwarded to the pit and a sales contract is executed, but not necessarily with the party who sold it to him in the first place. Once again, the clearinghouse interposes itself between the two parties and the latest sale will be offset against the original purchase. The customer's overall position will be canceled, and the funds in the margin account will be returned to him.

The lion's share of all contracts traded are terminated before maturity in this fashion. Only a very small percentage of contracts traded is delivered. In the case of Treasury bills, delivery takes place on the day after trading stops. The customer who has sold the contract (the short) delivers $1 million (par value) of Treasury bills that have ninety, ninety-one, or ninety-two days to maturity, and the customer who bought the contract (the long) pays for the bills with immediately available funds. The price paid for the bills is the settlement price on the last day of trading. (With the daily marking-to-market, almost all losses and gains have been realized before the final delivery takes place.)

Variations in procedures exist on different contracts and exchanges, but they generally adhere to the same principles: open outcry trading, interposition of the clearinghouse, posting of margin, and daily marking-to-market. Box 2 delineates the key specification on financial futures contracts. Probably the most important difference among contracts is that some allow delivery of a variety of securities. The active Treasury bond contract, for example, permits delivery of bonds from a "market basket" of different bonds, all with maturity (or first call) beyond fifteen years. This has the effect of substantially increasing the deliverable supply of securities but generates some uncertainty among those taking delivery as to which bonds they might receive.

The formal organizational structure of futures trading stands in contrast to the informal nature of forward trading. Dealers in the market for United States Government securities often agree to transact trades that call for forward delivery of Treasury issues. These trades are negotiated in the same fashion as trades for immediate delivery. There is no standardized contract as in the futures market: the two parties must agree to the specific security involved, the exact delivery date, the size of trade, and the price. These terms are set according to the mutual convenience of the two Parties. Often, there is no initial margin and no marking-to-market to account for gains and losses. Thus, each participant must size up the creditworthiness of the other. Finally, these agreements, for the most part, are designed to result in delivery. (Some GNMA forward trades among a few firms can be offset through a clearinghouse arrangement.) If either side wishes to cancel the trade, it must go back to the other side and negotiate a termination.

PARTICIPANTS IN THE INTEREST RATE FUTURES MARKET

Many types of financial institutions participate in the markets for interest rate futures, but private individuals not acting in a business capacity account for the major part of interest rate futures positions in the three most active contacts (Chart 2).

According to a survey by the CFTC of positions outstanding on March 30, 1979, businesses other than the futures industry, commonly called "commercial traders," accounted for only about one quarter of open interest held in the most active contracts (ninety-day Treasury bills on the IMM, and Treasury bonds and the original GNMA contract on the CBT). In an earlier survey, such participants had held about three

Box 2
Futures Contracts on Treasury Securities (Currently Trading)

	Treasury bills			Intermediate-term Treasury coupon securities		Treasury bonds	
	ACE	COMEX	IMM	CBT	IMM	ACE	CBT
Deliverable items...	$1 million par value of Treasury bills with 90, 91, or 92 days to maturity	$1 million par value of Treasury bills with 90, 91, or 92 days to maturity	$1 million par value of Treasury bills with 90, 91, or 92 days to maturity	$250,000 par value of Treasury bills due in 52 weeks	$100,000 par value of Treasury notes and noncallable bonds with 4 to 6 years to maturity	$100,000 par value of Treasury notes maturing between 3½ years and 4½ years	$100,000 par value of Treasury bonds with at least 20 years to maturity	$100,000 par value of Treasury bonds with at least 15 years to first call or to maturity
Initial margin* (per contract).....	$800	$800	$1,500	$600	$900	$500	$2,000	$2,000†
Maintenance margin* (per contract).....	$600	$600	$1,200	$400	$600	$300	$1,500	$1,600†
Daily limits‡.....	50 basis points	60 basis points	50 basis points	50 basis points	1 point (32/32)	3/4 point (48/64)	1 point (32/32) §	2 points (64/32)
Delivery months (each year)......	January, April, July, October	February, May, August, November	March, June, September, December	March, June, September, December	March, June, September, December	February, May, August, November	February, May, August, November	March, June, September, December
Total open interest (December 31, 1979).	106	913	36,495	435	715	265	207	90,676
Date trading began..	June 26, 1979	October 2, 1979	January 6, 1979	September 11, 1978	June 25, 1979	July 10, 1979	November 14, 1979	August 22, 1977

Non-Treasury Securities Futures

Government National Mortgage Association
(modified pass-through mortgage-backed certificates)

	CBT (old)	CBT (new)	ACE	COMEX	Commercial paper CTB (30-day)	CBT (90-day)
Deliverable items	Collateralized depository receipt covering $100,000 principal balance of GNMA certificates	$100,000 principal balance of GNMA certificates	$100,000 principal balance of GNMA certificates	$100,000 principal balance of GNMA certificates	$3 million face value of prime commercial paper rated A-1 by Standard & Poor's and P-1 by Moody's	$1 million face value of prime commercial paper rated A-1 by Standard & Poor's and P-1 by Moody's
Initial margin* (per contract)	$2,000	$2,000	$2,000	$1,500	$1,500	$1,500
Maintenance margin* (per contract)	$1,500	$1,500	$1,500	$1,125	$1,200	$1,200
Daily limits‡	1½ points (48/32)	1½ points (48/32)	3/4 point (24/32) §	1 point (64/64)	50/100 point	50/100 point
Delivery months (each year)	March, June, September, December	March, June, September, December	February, May, August, November	January, April, July, October ‖	March, June, September, December	March, June, September, December
Total open interest (December 31 1979)	88,982	4,478	3,248	64	12	533
Date trading began	October 20, 1975	September 12, 1978	September 12, 1978	November 13, 1979	May 14, 1979	September 26, 1977

All specifications are as of year-end 1979.
*The speculative margin is shown where margins vary according to whether the contracts cover speculative, hedged, or spread positions.
†For all contracts but those which mature in current month. Then initial margin is increased to $2,500 and maintenance margin is raised to $2,000.
‡Exchanges frequently have rules allowing expansion of daily limits once they have been in effect for a few days (margins may change also).
§ Limits in suspension as of the year-end.
‖Principal trading months; rules allow trading for current plus two succeeding months.

63

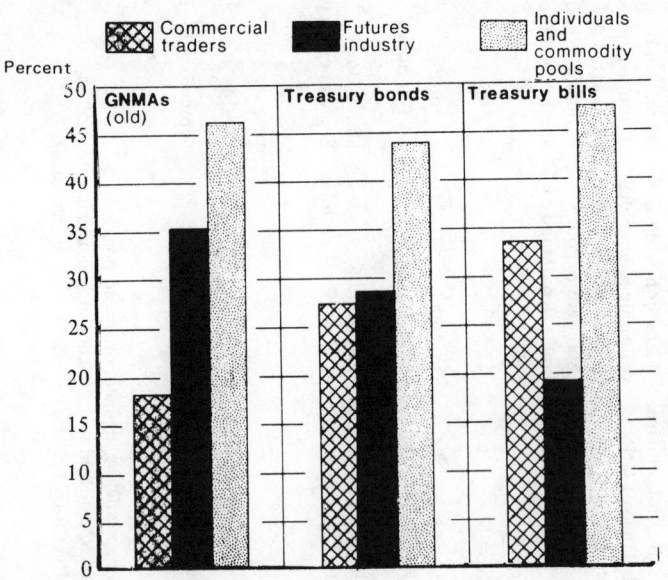

Chart 2 Futures Markets Participants, March 30, 1979. Source: Commodity Futures Trading Commission. Shares of open interest held by various groups.

eights of those contracts outstanding on November 30, 1977 (Table 1). The involvement of commercial traders is important because they are the only group that can use futures contracts for hedging cash market positions to any meaningful extent. (See next section.)

Moreover, some of the businesses who participate in these futures markets are probably not trying to eliminate risk completely. Consider securities dealers, for example, who have been very active in interest rate futures markets—they held about 7 percent of total GNMA positions and about 18 percent of total bond positions in March 1979. Securities dealers are generally risk takers, trying to benefit from interest rate change, or arbitrageurs, trying to benefit from interest rate disparities, rather than hedgers. But, in meeting customers' needs and making a market in Government securities, they do make use of interest rate futures markets to manage their risk exposure.

Among other business participants, mortgage bankers and savings and loan associations combined held about 7 percent of total positions in GNMAs. Their participation in GNMAs is to be expected in view of their involvement in generating and investing in mortgages. A total of

Table 1

Futures Markets Participants

November 30, 1977 and March 30, 1979
Average open interest; number of contracts

Type of participant	Government National Mortgage Association contract (old)				Treasury bond contract				Three-month Treasury bill contract			
	1977 amount	1977 as percentage of total	1979 amount	1979 as percentage of total	1977 amount	1977 as percentage of total	1979 amount	1979 as percentage of total	1977 amount	1977 as percentage of total	1979 amount	1979 as percentage of total
Commercial traders												
(total)	*7,226*	*36.5*	*10,899*	*18.3*	*2,025*	*67.2*	*12,393*	*27.4*	*4,950*	*32.8*	*14,992*	*33.6*
Securities dealers	3,395	17.1	4,270	7.2	1,534	50.9	8,226	18.2	2,758	18.3	5,596	12.5
Commercial banks	263	1.3	655	1.1	99	3.3	1,472	3.3	326	2.2	1,581	3.5
Savings and loan associations	494	2.5	2,500	4.2	—	—	394	0.9	56	0.4	136	0.3
Mortgage bankers	1,198	6.1	1,472	2.5	154	5.1	330	0.7	44	0.3	974	2.2
Other	1,875	9.5	2,003	3.4	238	7.9	1,971	4.4	1,767	11.7	6,706	15.0
Noncommercial traders *(total)*	*12,588*	*63.5*	*48,705*	*81.7*	*989*	*32.8*	*32,826*	*72.6*	*10,154*	*67.2*	*29,661*	*66.4*
Futures industry	7,353	37.1	21,113	35.4	477	15.8	12,924	28.6	2,765	18.3	8,434	18.9
Commodity pools	2,862	14.4	11,097	18.6	254	8.4	9,484	21.0	1,520	10.1	5,640	12.6
Individual traders	2,373	12.0	16,495	27.7	258	8.6	10,481	23.0	5,868	38.8	15,586	34.9
Total	19,814	100	59,604	100	3,014	100	45,219	100	15,104	100	44,654	100

Because of rounding, amounts and percentages may not add to totals.

Source: Commodity Futures Trading Commission Surveys. The 1977 survey covered all positions, but the 1979 survey excluded positions of fewer than five contracts.

sixty-eight of these firms held positions on March 30, 1979, not much above the number reported in the earlier survey. Few commercial banks have been active in interest rate futures—twenty-four had open positions in bill futures, and fourteen in bond futures on March 30, 1979—accounting for a small fraction of total positions in these markets. Their relatively low level of participation may have reflected regulatory restrictions on their involvement in the futures market or some confusion about the regulators' policies.

Futures industry personnel and firms held a significant fraction on the open positions. This group includes many who are speculating on rate movements in general or on the spread relations between rates on successive contracts. Or they might be operating in both the cash and futures markets, arbitraging differences between the two markets.

Individuals and commodity pools—funds which purchase futures contracts—are very important participants in financial futures markets. They held almost half of the open positions in 1979, a substantial increase from their already significant participation in the earlier survey. Indeed, the 1979 share of total positions in financial contracts was certainly higher than that because positions of less than five contracts were not included in the second survey and individuals tend to hold the vast majority of such small positions.[3]

SERVICES PROVIDED BY INTEREST RATES FUTURES MARKETS

It is commonly believed that futures markets provide certain benefits—in the main, an inexpensive way to hedge risk and generate information on expected prices. Interest rate futures markets also provide these benefits.

Several observers have noted that interest rate futures markets are not necessary to provide information on future interest rates or as a hedging mechanism. They point out that one can obtain information on future interest rates by comparing yields on outstanding securities which have different maturities. However, the interest rate futures markets do provide future interest rate information in a more convenient form.

It is also true that outstanding securities could be used to hedge market risk. Again, however, the futures market can provide a less cumber-

---

[3] Small positions in the bill futures contracts amounted to about 8,000 contracts at the end of March 1979 and thus would raise the combined share of individuals and commodity pools to a bit more than half of the bill futures market. Comparable calculations cannot be made for the CBT's bond and GNMA contracts because some small positions are posted on a net basis (*i.e.*, long positions are offset against short positions), compared with a gross basis as in the bill contracts.

some and expensive hedge. Suppose, for example, that a firm is planning to issue short-term securities three months in the future and is worried about the prospective short-term interest rate. The short sale of a Treasury bill with more than three months to maturity is one way to hedge the risk.[4] In the futures market, the interest rate risk on this prospective issue could be hedged by selling the Treasury bill contract for the month closest to the prospective issue date. If all short rates moved up, the hedger would make a gain on the futures market transaction which would offset the loss on the higher interest rate he would have to offer.

Banks, dealers, and other such financial institutions may find futures markets helpful in achieving a particular maturity structure for their portfolios while having adequate supplies of cash securities on hand. For example, a dealer may need to hold supplies of a six-month bill to be ready for customer orders. However, he may not want the risk exposure on this particular maturity because he thinks its rate is likely to rise. Or, a mortgage banker may wish to hedge the risk on rates between the time of the mortgage loan and the time of its sale as part of a large package of loans. By selling a GNMA futures contract while assembling the mortgage package, the banker can be insured against rate changes. If rates rise, the value of the mortgage portfolio will fall, but that will be offset by the profits on the short sale of the GNMA contract. If, on the other hand, rates fall, the gain on the mortgage portfolio is offset by the loss on the sale of GNMA futures. In this hedge, the banker foregoes the possibility of additional profit (or loss) and is content to profit from the origination and servicing fees associated with assembling the mortgages.

Not every financial transaction has an exact hedge in the futures market. When the cash asset is different from the security specified in the futures contract, the transaction is called a "cross hedge" and provides much less protection than an exact hedge. For example, a securities dealer might find it profitable to buy some certificates of deposit (CDs) and finance them for one month. To protect against a decline (increase) in the price (rates) of CDs over the interval, the dealer might sell Treasury bill futures contracts, assuming the movements in bill rates and CD rates will be similar over the interval. So long as the rates move in the same *direction* the dealer will be protected at least to some degree against adverse price movements. It is conceivable, however, that the rates could move in opposite directions. Thus, a cross hedge is really a speculation on the relationship between the particular cash market security held in position and the particular futures contract involved.

---

[4] The prospective issuer could borrow a six-month Treasury bill and sell it immediately; three months hence he would buy a bill with the same maturity date to return. If interest rates for that future time interval rise, the security would be purchased more cheaply three months hence than is currently expected. The gain on this transaction would then offset the loss connected with issuing securities at the higher interest rate.

In a cross hedge, the participants cannot deliver the cash security against the contract, so there is no threat of delivery that can be used to drive the prices on the two securities back into line as the expiration date approaches.

In contrast to financial businesses, nonfinancial businesses and private individuals are less likely to find a useful hedge in the interest rate futures market. Consider the typical nonfinancial business which is planning to issue securities to finance some capital purchase or inventory. If the rate of inflation accelerates, the firm will typically be able to sell its output at higher prices. Thus, its nominal profit and return from the investment will typically also rise.[5] This means that a rise in inflationary expectations, which is reflected in the nominal rate of interest, will tend to affect profits in the same direction as it does financing costs. Thus, to some extent, the firm is automatically hedged against inflation-induced changes in the interest rate.

A similar intrinsic hedge may be available to investors on any new funds they plan to invest. Presumably they want to be sure that their investment produces a certain real income or purchasing power in the future. If interest rates move down because anticipated inflation has fallen, then the return on any funds invested at the lower rate will be able to buy the same quantity of goods and services that they would have in the circumstances where inflation and interest rates were higher. (The real return on *past* savings, however will move in the opposite direction as inflation.)

Thus, to the extent that interest rate changes reflect revisions in inflationary expectations, many businesses and persons will not be in a very risky position with regard to saving or investment plans. If, as some contend, the variation in interest rates is largely connected with inflationary expectations, these groups would typically not obtain a very useful hedge in the interest rate futures market.

SPECULATION

While some participants use futures markets to hedge risk, others use them to speculate on price movements. Speculators like the high leverage obtainable and the low capital required for trades in futures markets relative to trades in cash markets. Speculation on interest rates could be accomplished in the cash markets but would typically involve

---

[5] The firm does not, however, tend to earn nominal profits in proportion to prices because the tax structure collects more in real terms during inflation. See M. Arak, "Can the Performance of the Stock Market Be Explained by Inflation Coupled with our Tax System?" (Federal Reserve Bank of New York Research Paper).

greater costs than in futures markets. For example, suppose one thinks that the three-month interest rate in the June-September period will be higher than the implicit forward rate for that time interval. The short sale of a September bill in March and its repurchase in June can produce a profit if those high rates materialize. The costs involved in these transactions include the dollar value of the bid-ask spread as well as the charges for borrowing a security. In addition, one must have sufficient capital to put up collateral equivalent in value to the securities borrowed or the credit standing to borrow the securities under a reverse repurchase agreement.

In futures markets, one does not pay for or receive money for the commodity in advance. The cost of trading in the futures market is the foregone interest on the margin deposit (if in the form of cash) plus the commission fees. Assuming a $70 commission, this would amount to about $125 on a three-month bill futures contract at current interest rates, if the contract were held for three months. A change in the discount rate on the futures contract of 5 basis points would therefore recompense the speculator for his costs (Table 2).

Besides speculating on the level of rates, some futures market participants may be speculating on the relationship among interest rates. Such speculation can take the form of a "spread" trade whereby the participant buys one contract and sells another, hoping that the rate on the contract bought will fall by more than (or rise by less than) the rate on the contract sold. Also, if participants believe that the slope of the yield curve will change in a predictable way when the level of the yield curve changes, a spread transaction (which involves a lower margin) can be a less expensive way to speculate on the level of rates.

Table 2 Change in Discount Rate on a Three-Month Treasury Bill Futures Contract Necessary to Cover Cost of a Futures Market Transaction

In basis points

Holding period	Commission (in dollars)		
	$30	$50	$70
One month........	2.0	2.8	3.6
Three months	3.4	4.2	5.0
Six months........	5.7	6.5	7.3
Twelve months	10.2	11.0	11.8

$$\text{Basis point change} = \frac{C + \frac{h(.01i)m}{12}}{25}$$

where h is the number of months the contract is held, i is the rate of interest obtainable over the period h, m is the cash margin, and C is the commission on the futures trade. The numbers shown are based upon i = 15 percent and m = $1,500.

Frequently, traders will take positions in futures contracts that are related to positions in cash market securities. A trader might think that the rate in the futures market is out of line with cash Treasury bills. If he feels the futures rate is low relative to the rates on outstanding bills, he might sell the futures contract and buy the bills in the cash market. He could then carry the bill in position until the two rates move back to their more normal relationship. Then the bills would be sold and the short bill futures contract offset. These types of trades are often called "arbitrages" by participants in the cash market although they are not arbitrages in the strict sense in which a security is bought in one market and at the same time sold in another, thereby locking in an assured return. In fact, most arbitraging activity generally reflects speculation on the relationship between cash and futures rates.

USE OF FUTURES MARKETS TO REDUCE TAX LIABILITY

Individuals and institutions have also used interest rate futures markets to reduce their taxes. One means was through spread transactions.

Until November 1978, spread transactions in the Treasury bill futures market were a popular means of postponing taxes. An individual would buy one contract and sell another, both for the next calendar year. For example, in 1976, the participant might have bought the March 1977 contract and sold the September 1977 contract. An important assumption was that interest rates on all contracts would tend to move together so that the net risk was relatively small. At some point before the end of 1976, whichever position has produced a loss would be closed out. (In the above example, the short position or the sale of the September 1977 contract was the item that showed a loss during the latter part of 1976.) That loss could then be deducted from other income for 1976, reducing the 1976 tax bill. The contract for March 1977, on which the gain had accrued, was not closed out until 1977 when it no longer affected the 1976 tax liability.[6]

What made Treasury bill futures particularly attractive for such spreads was the belief of many taxpayers that, just like actual Treasury bills, they were not capital assets. In contrast, it was clear that other types of futures contracts, not held exclusively for business purposes, were capital assets.[7] If Treasury bill futures were not capital assets,

---

[6] After the September 1977 contract was offset, another contract for 1977 would be sold to maintain a balanced position. In our example, the June 1977 contract would be sold to counterbalance the March 1977 contract that was still being held. Then sometime in early 1977, these two contracts would be closed out.

[7] *E.g.*, Faroll v. Jarecki, 231 F.2d 281 (7th Cir. 1956).

then losses on them could be fully subtracted from other ordinary income (providing that *net* ordinary income did not become negative). Capital losses, in contrast, could be subtracted from ordinary income to a very limited extent.[8]

This attraction of the Treasury bill futures market for tax postponement was eliminated in November 1978 when the IRS declared that a futures contract for Treasury bills is a capital asset if neither held primarily for sale to customers in the ordinary course of business nor purchased as a hedge.[9] Further, the IRS, amplifying on an earlier ruling,[10] stated that the maintenance of a "spread" position, in transactions involving futures contracts for Treasury bills, may not result in allowance of deductions where no real economic loss is incurred.

A way that individuals can reduce taxes through the futures market is by indirectly converting part of the interest income on Treasury bills into long-term capital gains. Suppose that the discount rate on a bill is expected to fall as it matures. Since the market usually regards longer dated bills as less liquid (or as having more interest rate risk), an investor would typically expect that a bill maturing in, say, March 1981 would offer a higher annual discount rate in June 1980 than it would in February 1981. Similarly, the interest rate on futures contracts would tend to fall as they approach expiration (their price would rise). Pursuant to the November 1978 IRS ruling, the price increase in a Treasury bill futures contract should, in nonbusiness circumstances, be treated as a capital gain for an investor. In contrast, since a Treasury bill itself is not a capital asset, all the price appreciation on it—from date of purchase to date of sale—would be treated as ordinary income for tax purposes.

An investor would clearly prefer to have the price appreciation treated as a long-term gain rather than as ordinary income, since the long-term capital gains tax rate is only 40 percent of that for ordinary income. If a long position in a bill futures contract were held for more than six months, the profit would be a long-term capital gain. (Gains and losses on short positions in futures are always treated as short-term regardless of the holding period.) Consequently, some investors who might normally purchase 52-week bills would have an incentive to purchase distant futures contracts and, as those contracts matured, sell them off to take their capital gains. They could then invest their funds in three-month bills. These activities would tend to raise the discount rate on the 52-week bill. It would also tend to reduce the required discount rate on distant futures contracts. Thus, the discount rates on futures

---

[8] Capital losses can be offset against capital gains with no limitation, but the excess of loss over gains that may be deducted from ordinary income in a single year is currently limited to $3,000.
[9] Rev. Rul. 78-414, 1978-2 C.B. 213.
[10] Rev. Rul. 77-185, 1977-1 C.B. 48.

contracts would be pushed below the implicit forward discount rate on cash bills.

There are, of course, limits on the size of the wedge that can be driven between the forward rate on cash securities and the rate on futures contracts. Financial businesses cannot treat profits in bill futures as capital gains. For them, the futures contract has no tax advantage over a cash bill. When the wedge produced by investors exceeds the cost of arbitrage, these financial businesses will buy long-term bills and sell futures contracts to profit from disparities in rates.

RELATIONSHIP BETWEEN THE CASH AND FUTURES MARKETS

For many commodities, the spot price and the futures price are very closely related. Part of the explanation is that, if a commodity is storable, it can be bought today, stored, and sold at a future date. If the futures price were to exceed the spot price by more than the costs involved, arbitrageurs would buy the commodity in the spot market—raising the spot price—and would sell it in the futures market, lowering the futures price. These activities would reduce the disparity between the future price and the current price.

The relationship between cash and futures markets for bills is somewhat different from that for other commodities. A three-month Treasury bill cannot be stored for more than three months; it matures. However, a longer term bill could be "stored" until it has three months left to run. It is the cash market for that *longer term bill* which bears a relationship to the futures market that is typical of agricultural and industrial commodities. In the case of note and bond contracts, the deliverable item exists throughout the life of the contract.

For example, consider what cash market securities correspond to the IMM's June 1980 three-month Treasury bill contract. This contract calls for delivery of bills which have ninety-one days to run on June 19, 1980. Treasury bills having this maturity date will be sold by the Treasury in two auctions—as six-month bills on March 17, 1980 and as three-month bills on June 16, 1980. During the first three months of its life, the six-month bill issued on March 20, 1980 is the commodity that could be "stored" for delivery on the futures contract.

The funds used to purchase the six-month bill when it is initially issued could have been invested in three-month bills which mature on the contract expiration date. One measure of the interest cost involved in storage is therefore the foregone interest on the shorter bill—this is the "opportunity cost" of the decision to invest in the longer bill which is deliverable on the futures contract. It is common to subtract that opportunity cost from the bill price to get the "forward" price and the corresponding "forward" rate; this rate can then be compared with the discount rate on the futures contract.

Because in the past only three-month and six-month bills matured on Thursdays, only bills originally issued as three-month or six-month bills could be delivered on a ninety-day bill futures contract.[11] In fact, at any date, there was only one bill issue in existence that could be delivered on an IMM bill futures contract. That particular bill had between three and six months to maturity and could be delivered on the closest three-month bill futures contract. For longer bill futures contracts, there was usually no exact correspondence. There is no cash bill in existence today that could be delivered on the September 1980, December 1980, March 1981, and subsequent contracts traded on the IMM. However, there are bills which have a maturity date that may be quite close. For example, the 52-week bill maturing on September 16, 1980 will have eighty-nine days to run on June 19, 1980, while the June futures contract calls for bills which have ninety to ninety-two days to run on that date. By comparing the rate on this 52-week bill with the rate on the 52-week bill which matures twelve weeks earlier, a forward rate which covers an interval close to that of the futures contract bill can be calculated. Through this method, a rough forward rate in the period nine months prior to the contract's expiration can be obtained.

How does the rate on a three-month Treasury bill futures contract compare with the implicit forward rate in the cash market? The futures rate on the June 1979 contract and the "forward" rate on the corresponding cash bill (which matured September 21, 1979) moved very similarly in the last ninety-one days before the futures contract expired (Chart 3). Typically, the spread between the two rates was less than 25 basis points, with the forward rate somewhat higher than the futures rate. On most other futures contracts for three-month Treasury bills as well, the futures and forward rates were fairly close in the last ninety-one days or so before expiration.

When the contract's expiration date was far in the future, however, the link between its rate and the comparable forward rate was much weaker. In fact, spreads between forward and futures rates have at times been over 100 basis points in the three to nine months before the contract expired. Generally, in recent contracts, futures rates have been substantially below forward rates, and the spread between the two appears to have been wider than it was in earlier contracts.

Within three months of the expiration of the futures contracts, fu-

---

[11] Now that the Treasury has begun to issue 52-week bills maturing on Thursdays, there will be some occasions on which bills issued as 52-week bills will be deliverable against the three-month bill contracts.

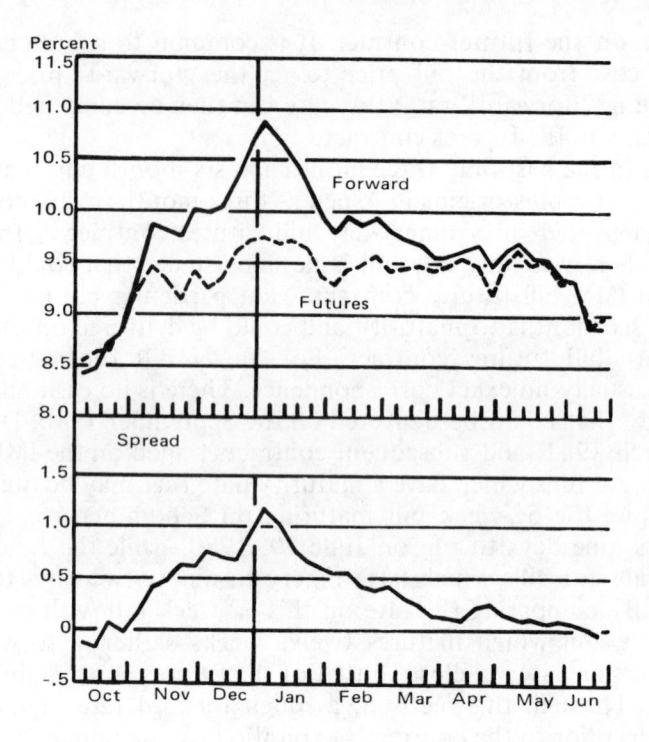

Chart 3 Discount rate on the June 1979 Treasury Bill futures contract (IMM) and the forward rate in the cash market. Spread equals forward rate minus futures rate.

tures and forward rates appear to be kept in reasonable alignment by investors and arbitrageurs. An investor, for example, can on the one hand hold a six-month bill, or, on the other hand, hold a three-month bill plus the futures contract for the month in which the three-month cash bill matures. If the six-month bill is yielding more than the other combination, investors will tend to prefer six-month bills. And their demand will tend to reduce its discount rate, bringing the forward rate down toward the futures rate. Similarly, if investors find the three-month cash bill plus the futures contract more profitable, their buying pressure on the futures contract will tend to reduce its discount rate, bringing it down closer to the forward rate.

Another group of market participants who help keep rates in line are arbitrageurs. If they observe that the six-month bill provides a forward rate which is high relative to the futures rate, they could buy six-month bills and sell them under a repurchase agreement for thee months,[12] at the same time, they would sell a futures contract. They would then

---

[12] A repurchase agreement specifies that the seller will rebuy at a prespecified date and price.

Interest Rate Futures

have no net investment position: the bill returned to them in three months corresponds to the commitment to sell in the futures market. But they would earn a profit equal to the futures price minus the six-month bill price, the transaction cost, and the financing cost. As arbitrageurs conduct these activities, they put upward pressure on the six-month bill's price by buying it and put downward pressure on the futures price by selling the futures contract. These activities of the arbitrageur usually tend to keep the forward and futures rates within certain bounds.

On contracts other than the nearest, however, there is no deliverable bill as yet outstanding—that is, no security exists that can be purchased, stored, and delivered against the contract. Consequently, arbitrageurs cannot lock in a profit by taking exactly offsetting positions in the two markets. If there is an order flow in the futures market that is persistent, sizable, and at variance with the prevailing view in the cash market, it is possible for speculators to drive a wedge between the rates on futures contracts and the implicit forward rates in the cash market.

One notable example occurred in the spring of 1979. Apparently, many small speculators purchased bill futures contracts due in mid-1980, in the belief that short-term interest rates had reached a cyclical peak and would begin to fall sometime within a year or so. From the end of April to the end of June, their holdings rose from about 25 percent to 35 percent of the total open interest and their net long positions expanded sharply. As a result of this buying pressure and purchases by those trying to get out of large short positions, rates dropped sharply, with the March 1980 and June 1980 contract rates falling by nearly 1¾ percentage points from mid-May to the end of June. Rates also fell on contracts with shorter maturities—those due in the latter half of 1979.

Many other participants were net short, and some of these were firms that felt they were arbitraging between the cash and futures market, holding in this case long positions in the cash bill market against short positions in futures contracts. One of the several cash futures operations they engaged in was a long position in bills in the six-month area (*i.e.*, due in November for the most part) versus a short in the September contract (calling for delivery of the bill to mature on December 20 which had not been auctioned yet). As the rates on futures contracts fell, those with short positions faced sizable margin calls. To the extent that they then bought futures contracts to offset their short positions and also sold their cash bills, they greatly enlarged the wedge that was being driven between the rates in these two markets in late May and early June (Chart 4).

The widening wedge between the forward and futures rates made arbitrage involving futures contract sales even more profitable. But, after the shock of seeing large losses mount on short positions and show

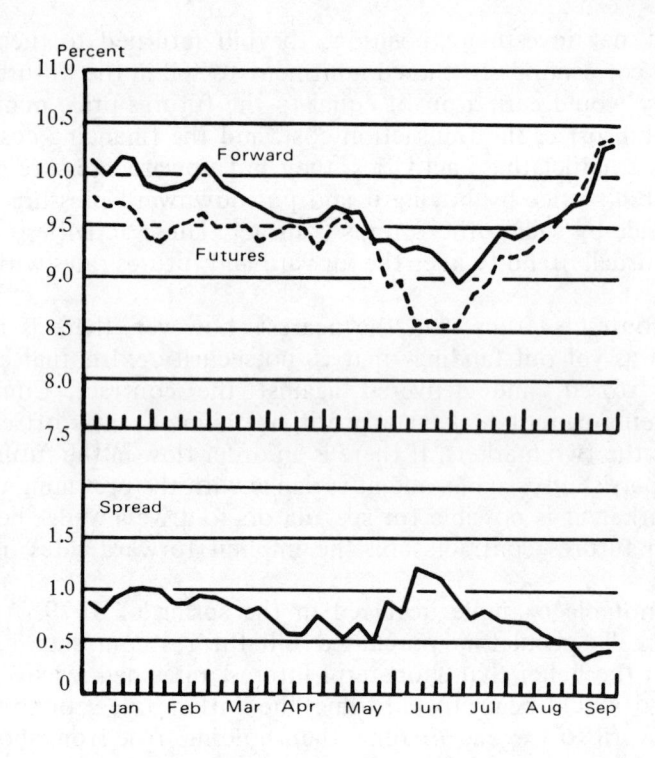

Chart 4 Discount rate on the September 1979 Treasury Bill futures contract (IMM) and the forward rate in the cash market. Spread equals forward rate minus futures rate.

up in quarterly income statements, financial businesses were reluctant to expand their short positions. The futures and forward rates did not come back into alignment until late in the summer when interest rates started rising again.

PROS AND CONS OF INTEREST RATE FUTURES MARKETS

Many observers of the new financial futures markets argue that these markets permit investors to obtain flexibility in ownership of securities at a very low cost. Someone who expects to have funds to invest in the period from mid-June to mid-September 1980, for example, can lock in an interest rate by purchasing a June Treasury bill futures contract. (For those who plan to purchase or issue other securities such as commercial paper or CDs, the links between the movements of rates in the bill futures market and the rates that obtain on these other instruments can be weak.)

By transferring the interest rate risk to those most willing to assume it, interest rate futures may increase the commitment of funds for some future time intervals. This could reduce the premium attached to funds committed for that future interval relative to funds committed for the nearer term. For example, the yield on 52-week and nine-month bills might fall. The resulting greater liquidity represents a gain to investors, while the lower interest rate on Government debt reduces the taxes necessary to service that debt.

While the provision of hedging facilities is a desirable aspect of interest rate futures markets, much of the activity appears to be speculative, and this has created some concern. One such concern is that speculation in the futures markets might push the prices of certain Treasury bills out of line with the prices of other securities. Because speculation is very inexpensive, entry into the futures market could be much more massive than entry into the cash market. Heavy demand in the futures market could be transmitted to the cash market by arbitrageurs. According to some analysts, the bill deliverable on the June 1979 contract was influenced by activities in the futures market. The June contract specified delivery on the Treasury bill due September 20 and only that bill. While the Treasury had sold $5.9 billion of bills with that maturity date, the Federal Reserve, foreign official accounts, and small investors held about one half. Thus, it appeared likely that the available trading supplies would amount to about $2 billion to $2½ billion.

However, open interest in the June 1979 contract stood at about 4,300 contracts, the equivalent of about $4.3 billion of bills at the end of May (Chart 5). This substantially exceeded the prospective trading supplies. During the spring, dealers reported that trading supplies in the September 20 bill were very thin and that it traded at a rate that was out of line with other bills. For example, it averaged about 4 basis points below the rate on the bill that was due a week earlier. Since investors usually require a higher rate when extending the maturity of their bill holdings, the 4 basis point difference provides a rough lower limit on the pressure that was exerted on the June contract and its spillover on the cash market.

Some observers argued that some investors were desirous of taking delivery because they thought there would be further declines in interest rates. Others pointed out that some people who had booked gains on long positions wanted to qualify for long-term capital gains. In any event, about a week before the contract expiration there was news of large increases in the money supply and industrial production which the market interpreted as indicating that a recession was not imminent and that interest rates would not fall immediately. This view probably contributed toward reducing pressure on the contract, and it was liquidated

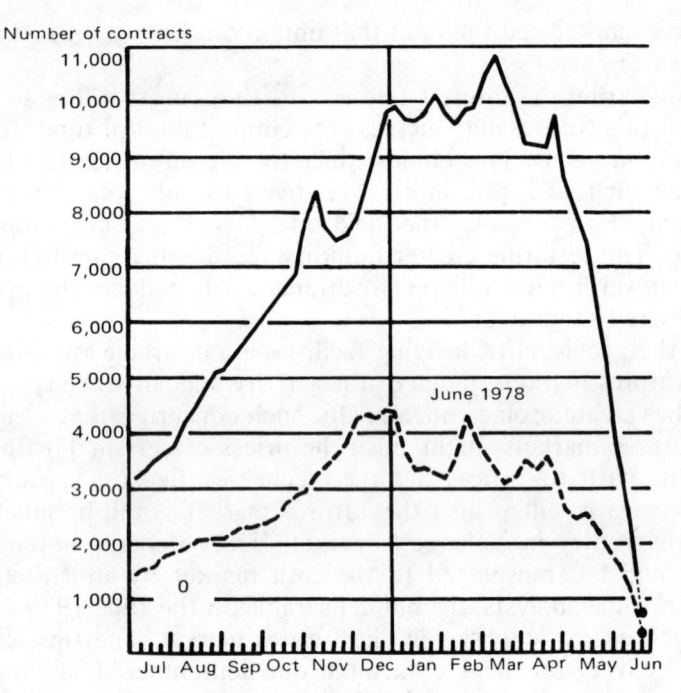

Chart 5 Open interest in Treasury bill futures contracts for June 1978 and June 1979. Weekly averages, week ending each Wednesday. Total open interest as of last trading day is indicated by dots. Source: International Monetary Market.

in an orderly fashion. Deliveries turned out to be a then record high of $706 million of bills due September 20, 1979, about a third of the available trading supplies of that bill. Deliveries on the September contract were somewhat lower, although still sizable (Chart 6), and deliveries on the December contract amounted to $1 billion.[13] Over the last month before delivery, the rate on the bill deliverable on the December contract averaged 8 basis points below the rate on the bill due one week earlier. As a result of these events, the question arises whether supplies of the deliverable bill are sufficient to prevent pricing dislocations.

In contrast to bill futures, other future contracts, notably in notes and bonds, have adopted a market basket approach to deliverable supplies. By allowing a variety of issues to be delivered, the contracts greatly reduce the possibility of a squeeze. If, for example, the September 13 bill had also been deliverable against the June contract, then traders

---

[13] A part of the large amount of deliveries on the three 1979 contracts may reflect investor's preference for ordinary income losses instead of capital losses, a transformation that can be achieved by taking delivery on a contract on which one has booked a loss. See Arak, "Taxes, Treasury Bills, and Treasury Bill Futures."

Interest Rate Futures

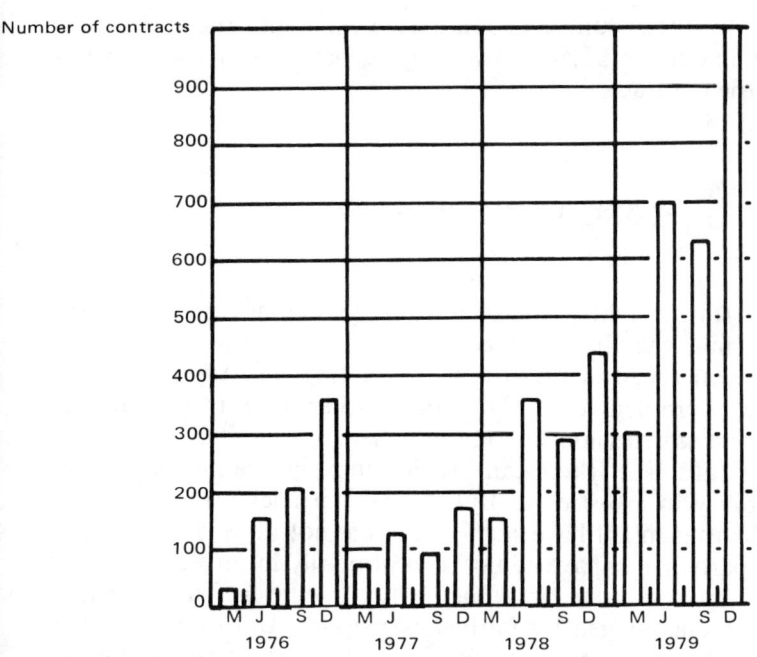

Chart 6 Deliveries on three-month bill futures contracts. Source: International Monetary Market. where M=March, J=June, S=September, and D=December.

would have had no incentive to deliver the September 20 bill at a rate that was below that on the September 13 bill. The mere availability of the other bill would therefore have provided a floor for the rate on the September 20 bill.

This analysis of bill futures has led some to suggest that, instead of a single deliverable issue, the deliverable security should be any one of a "basket" of Treasury bills with different maturity dates. However, others see disadvantages with the "basket" approach. In any event, the CFTC has authorized the new exchanges such as the ACE and the Comex to trade futures which involve bills maturing in a different week of the quarter than the IMM bill contracts. If these markets grow and become more active, there should be less likelihood of pressure on the one particular March, June, September, or December bill whose futures contract is traded on the IMM.

Finally, to many of the regulators, the size of the required margin deposit is a key issue. Larger margins would help insure the exchanges against possible defaults as well as discourage excessive speculation with little capital. Moreover, they might make participants more aware of the possibilities of loss inherent in trading in interest rate futures. In early October 1979, the minimum initial margin on Treasury bill futures contracts at the IMM was only $800, and a 32 basis point move in the rate on one of those contracts could have wiped out the entire margin. Now that margin is $1,500, which gives better protection to the exchange and the contract.

CONCLUDING REMARKS

Interest rate futures markets have generated much new activity within a very short time; they have also generated some apprehension on the part of those concerned with orderly marketing and trading of the United States Government debt. Thus far, neither the extreme enthusiasm nor the worst worries appear to be justified.

Interest rate futures markets can provide inexpensive hedging facilities and flexibility in investment. But, to date, participation by financial institutions that might have such a need has not been large. Rather, it appears that participants have so far been primarily interested in either speculating on interest rates or reducing tax liabilities. These participants have been encouraged by fairly low margins. Until recently, the exchanges had shown a penchant for reducing these margins, but in October 1979 when interest rates fluctuated widely following the Federal Reserve System's adoption of new operating procedures, several exchanges raised margins substantially.

Most of the time, the financial futures markets have operated fairly smoothly. In general, there has been no greater volatility in the prices of bills which are deliverable on futures contracts than in the prices of other bills. And despite the huge run-up in open interest in some of the bill futures contracts, actual deliveries have not been large enough to disrupt the operation of the cash market. However, on several bill futures contracts, the price of the deliverable bill was pushed slightly out of line with prices on other issues with adjacent maturities. The CFTC, the Treasury, the Federal Reserve, and market participants themselves will have to continue to observe futures market activites to assure that significant problems are not building up.

Interest rate futures markets have already provided an arena for some institutions to manage interest rate risk. And, as these markets mature, their economic usefulness may come to be more widely appreciated.

PART II

THE EFFICIENCY OF THE INTEREST RATE FUTURES MARKET

 A financial market is said to be "efficient" with respect to a given information set if the prices in that market at all times fully reflect the information in that set. One important consequence of this definition of market efficiency is that the market is efficient relative to some body of information. If that is so, then different forms of market efficiency can be specified in relation to different information sets. Three forms of the efficient markets hypothesis have been distinguished traditionally: the weak, the semi-strong, and the strong form. These three forms are distinguished by being stated in reference to increasingly more inclusive information sets. The weak form of the efficient market hypothesis states that a market fully reflects all publicly available price and volume trading data. From this it would follow that it is not possible to derive a strategy that would yield super-normal returns that was based on such an information set. A market is semi-strong efficient if prices in that market at all times fully reflect all public information. In addition to price and volume data, this information set would include news reports, economic forecasts, weather reports, and the like. Finally, the strong form of the efficient markets hypothesis maintains that a market's prices fully reflect all information, public and private. Private information includes the information possessed by corporate "insiders" (e.g., top management), attorneys to corporations, and government regulators. The strong form of the efficient markets hypothesis would maintain that even this private information is already fully reflected by security prices, and therefore could be of no use for developing a profitable trading strategy.

One of the worst kinds of inefficiency that a market can exemplify is the existence of arbitrage opportunities. An arbitrage opportunity exists when one can transact to guarantee a profit with no investment. In other words, the same good trades for two different prices, perhaps in two different markets. To take advantage of such an opportunity one buys the good at the lower price, pays any necessary transaction costs to get the cheaper good to the market of the more expensive good, and sells the more expensive, but equivalent, good. Given that the transaction involves no risk of a loss, and no investment, then an arbitrage opportunity exists. The existence of a straightforward arbitrage opportunity constitutes a blatant violation of weak-form market efficiency.

The papers of Part II all deal with the possible existence of arbitrage opportunities. As such, these tests are best thought of as tests of the weak form of the efficient markets hypothesis. But if the weak form hypothesis is rejected, then the semi-strong and strong also fail, since they are even more inclusive than the weak form.

To test for the existence of arbitrage opportunities, the authors of this part consider a futures position and then attempt to mimic the futures position by trading the appropriate combination of long and short positions in the spot market. Under certain circumstances, the prices (or yields) of the two positions should be equal. Departure from equality, in excess of transaction costs, constitutes an arbitrage opportunity, and a counterexample to the claim of market efficiency. The results of early studies in this area reached strikingly different conclusions. William Poole, in Using T-Bill Futures to Gauge Interest-Rate Expectation, concludes that the market is generally efficient. By contrast Donald J. Puglisi titles his paper with the question, Is the Futures Market for Treasury Bills Efficient? and answers, "No, arbitrage between bills-futures and bills-only offers profitable trading strategies." Likewise, Anthony J. Vignola and Charles J. Dale also find frequent arbitrage opportunities in their paper identically titled, Is the Futures Market for Treasury Bills Efficient?, which is a comment on the Puglisi paper. The work of Richard W. Lang and Robert H. Rasche, A Comparison of Yields on Futures Contracts and Implied Forward Rates, corroborates the existence of apparent arbitrage opportunities.

However, Lang and Rasche maintain that these apparent yield differences between the futures and spot markets may be due to a default-risk premium on the futures contracts that does not pertain to the spot T-bills.

The idea that futures may be a close, but not perfect, substitute for similar spot positions leads naturally to a consideration of alternative theories of the term structure, particularly the unbiased (or pure) expectations theory, the liquidity premium theory, and the market segmentation theory. Ben Branch examines the futures rates and the forward rates derived from the yield curve in Testing the Unbiased Expectations Theory of Interest Rates. *Noting strong divergences between futures and forward rates, Branch concludes that the futures and spot T-bill markets are not fully integrated, but rather segmented. If market participants are unwilling to trade between the futures and spot markets, then price differences, consistent with the presence of arbitrage opportunities, may continue to exist. If the markets were not effectively segmented, then profit seekers would take advantage of the arbitrage opportunities and they would soon disappear. The continued presence of arbitrage opportunities that Branch finds, he regards as a strong evidence of market segmentation.*

Brian G. Chow and David J. Brophy adopt a different methodology in their paper, The U.S. Treasury Bill Futures Market and Hypotheses Regarding the Term Structure of Interest Rates. *If one assumes that both the futures and spot T-bill markets are efficient, Chow and Brophy's results suggest that, of the traditional theories of the term structure (pure expectations, liquidity premium, and market segmentation), none is consistent with the data. Dennis R. Capozza and Bradford Cornell also find yield differentials in their article,* Treasury Bill Pricing in the Spot and Futures Markets. *However, these authors maintain that the differential can be explained by the existence of transaction costs, by institutional reluctance to incur the start-up costs necessary to enter the market and eradicate the unwarranted yield differentials, and by the risk premia due to the inherently riskier character of futures or shorted T-bills in comparison to T-bills themselves.*

In light of the seven articles just mentioned, Richard Rendleman and Christopher Carabini attempt once more to test The Efficiency of the Treasury Bill Futures Market. *They point out that earlier studies often proceeded even when the T-bills that* would have to be used to make delivery against distant T-bill futures contracts did not exist. Often these rates for nonexistent T-bills were estimated using other instruments with coupons, thereby creating estimation bias. Rendleman and Carabini also note that transaction costs have been treated differently by various authors and that this may account for some of the divergent results. Using bid-ask spreads and a careful treatment of transaction costs, Rendleman and Carabini conclude that no arbitrage opportunities existed in their sample period for a trader without an initial portfolio of T-bills. In their terminology, they find no pure arbitrage opportunities. However, Rendleman and Carabini note that an investor who already holds a T-bill portfolio could use the futures market to improve the returns on the existing portfolio. This quasi-arbitrage opportunity exists since the investor holding a T-bill portfolio has lower marginal transaction costs than otherwise.

Also responding to the divergence of findings just noted, Anthony J. Vignola and Charles Dale approach the problem in a new way in The Efficiency of the Treasury Bill Futures Market: An Analysis of Alternative Specifications. The alternative specifications refer to the existence of pure and quasi-arbitrage opportunities as mentioned by Rendleman and Carabini. They find that markets are efficient with respect to pure arbitrage opportunities, but that quasi-arbitrage opportunities have existed. Therefore, they conclude that results concerning market efficiency depend largely on the cost of financing the arbitrage operation.

All of these papers deal with the efficiency of the T-bill futures market. To date no papers have appeared that appraise the efficiency of the other interest rate futures contracts. These tests are likely to be even more difficult. Commercial paper and T-note markets are insufficiently active to provide a good data source, leaving only T-bond and GNMA futures. The example of the T-bond futures market illustrates the special difficulties. In the T-bond futures market numerous delivery vehicles are possible. In order to determine which is likely to be cheapest to deliver, sophisticated term structure estimations are necessary. The GNMA futures market presents similar difficulties, as well as some unique ones. Consequently, in spite of all the attention to market efficiency, as witnessed by the papers in this part, the final resolution of the issue is not imminent.

5

Using T-Bill Futures to Gauge Interest-Rate Expectations*

William Poole[†]

Trading in three-month Treasury-bill futures began on January 6, 1976. Six contracts were traded originally: March, June, September, and December of 1976, and March and June of 1977. When each contract matured, trading began in a new contract dated three months beyond the most distant contract previously traded. More recently trading has been conducted in eight contracts.

The details of this market and its uses in various types of hedging, speculative, and tax-motivated transactions have been fully described elsewhere.[1] The purpose of this paper is to provide an analysis of the link between the futures market and the spot market in Treasury bills of varying maturities, and to examine the policy significance of the interest-rate expectations incorporated in the T-bill futures.

---

*Reprinted from the *Economic Review* of the Federal Reserve Bank of San Francisco, (Spring 1978). Reprinted by permission of the publisher.

[†]Professor of Economics, Brown University. The empirical work in this paper was conducted while the author was Visiting Scholar at the Federal Reserve Bank of San Francisco in Summer 1977. The views expressed are the responsibility of the author and do not necessarily reflect those of the Bank.

[1] See, for example: Albert E. Burger, Richard W. Lang, and Robert H. Rasche, "The Treasury Bill Futures Market and Market Expectations of Interest Rates," *Federal Reserve Bank of St. Louis Review*, June, 1977; Wallace H. Duncan, "Treasury Bill Futures–Opportunities and Pitfalls," *Federal Reserve Bank of Dallas Review*, July, 1977; Paul L. Kasriel, "Hedging Interest Rate Fluctuations," *Business Conditions* (Federal Reserve Bank of Chicago), April, 1976; and Linda Snyder, "How to Speculate on the World's Safest Investment," *Fortune*, July, 1977.

In the first section of the paper, it is shown that the spot and futures Treasury bill markets are closely linked in practice; profitable arbitrage opportunities between the two markets rarely exist, at least for the nearest futures maturity traded at any given point in time. (Only this maturity is examined in this paper.)

In the second section the issue of liquidity, or term premiums is examined. Studies of the term structure of interest rates have generally found that longer-term securities on average have higher yields than shorter-term securities. This finding is of importance in its own right, but it also implies that a term premium must be subtracted from a futures rate if that rate is to be interpreted as the market expectation of the future spot rate at the maturity of the futures contract. This rather technical issue is treated at some length, because it is of great importance in assessing the significance of yields in the futures market.

From evidence presented in previous studies of the term structure, and from new evidence on the futures market, it is argued that part of the observed term premiums may reflect transactions costs rather than risk aversion. The conclusion reached is that, since transaction costs in the futures market are almost non-existent, it is probably not necessary to make any allowance for term premiums when using futures rates to gauge market expectations of future spot rates.

In the last section, the policy implications of market interest-rate forecasts are explored. The major issue concerns the significance of differences between market forecasts and policymakers' forecasts of interest rates.

I. RELATIONSHIPS BETWEEN SPOT AND FUTURES T-BILL MARKETS

At the present time, eight contracts are traded in the Treasury-bill futures market. In August, 1977, for example, trading was conducted in futures for September and December, 1977; March, June, September and December of 1978; and March and June of 1979. Government security futures other than bills are also available. When yields on these securities get out of line with yields in the futures market, profitable risk-free arbitrage transactions are possible.

Only for short maturities, however, is it possible to find a perfect match of maturities in the spot and futures markets. For example, from March 24 through June 22, 1977, spot bills due June 23 and September 22 and June futures provided instruments with exactly matching maturities. Settlement on the June futures took place on June 23, and required delivery of the September 22 bill—a 91-day bill on June 23—on all June futures contracts still open. If held to maturity, an investment in the combination package of the June 23 spot bill and a long position in June futures had identical characteristics to an investment in the September 22 spot bill. The two investments should, therefore, have identical yields—except for possible differences in transactions costs should the investor desire to sell out before maturity. The yield differences are limited, however, by the possibility of arbitrage between the two markets.

Arbitrage opportunities for futures maturities other than the nearest one are not quite risk-free because the maturities do not quite match. For example, between December 23, 1976 and March 22, 1977, arbitrage involving June 1977 futures had to be based on bills dated September 20 and June 23; the September 22 bill was not issued until March 24.

In studying the completeness of arbitrage, we may limit the investigation to the nearest maturity futures contract, so as to avoid the need for extra assumptions concerning arbitrage when maturities do not quite match. In examining arbitrage, we may proceed as if the spot bill yields are fixed; the problem is the determination of the range of bill futures yields such that risk-free arbitrage profits are possible considering the explicit transaction costs involved. The range will be defined in terms of an upper critical point, F^U, above which substitution of the short spot bill and a long futures position for the long spot bill will be profitable; and a lower critical point, F^L, below which substitution of the long spot bill and a short futures position for the short spot bill will be profitable. Although we will be determining upper and lower critical points for the futures rate given the spot bill yields, we could just as well have determined upper and lower critical points for either spot bill given the yield on the other bill and the futures yield.

In the derivations below it is assumed that bills are infinitely divisible, and all calculations are per $100. In fact, the discreteness of bills and of futures contracts—each futures contract is for $1 million face value of bills—prevents arbitrage from being profitable precisely at these critical points. However, the critical points derived under the perfect divisibility assumption provide benchmarks against which the market may be judged with respect to the exhaustion of arbitrage opportunities.

Suppose that an n+91-day bill is owned, where n is the number of days to the maturity of the nearest futures contract. If the futures yield is high enough, the investor can raise his rate of return over the n+91-day horizon by selling the n+91-day bill and using the proceeds to buy an n-day bill and a long position in a futures maturing in n days. What futures yield will be high enough to make this substitution profitable?

Each n+91-day bill is worth $P^b_{n+91,t}$ at time t, where P^b is the dealer's bid price—the price at which investors other than dealers can sell the bill. By the definition of the banker's discount yield—the quotation

Interest Rate Futures: Concepts and Issues

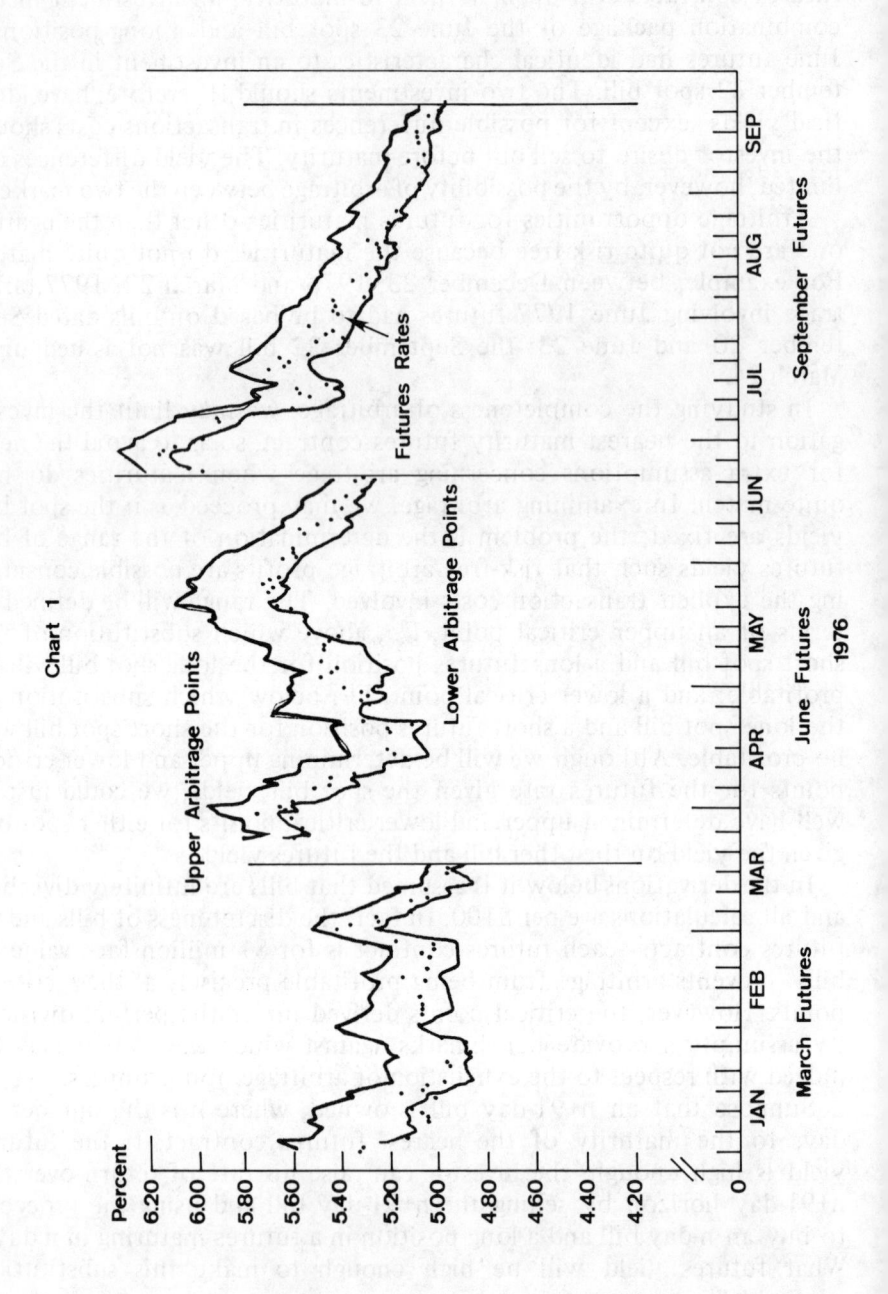

Chart 1

1976

Percent

Futures Rates

Upper Arbitrage Points

Lower Arbitrage Points

March Futures | June Futures | September Futures

JAN FEB MAR APR MAY JUN JUL AUG SEP

method used in the bill market—we have

$$P^b_{n+91,t} = 100 - \frac{n+91}{360} R^b_{n+91,t}$$

where R^b is the bid yield, in percent, on the banker's discount basis. In the arbitrage transaction being examined, enough n+91-day bills are sold to buy the n-day bills required to provide the cash needed in n days to settle the maturing long futures position. The cash requirement at time t also includes the futures market commission—$60 per contract—and the futures market margin requirement—$1500 per contract. Since each contract is for $1 million face value of bills, the commission and margin amount to only $0.006 and $0.15, respectively, per $100 of face value.[2]

Working backwards, in n days the amount needed to settle the long position in the futures market will be

$$q_{n,t} = 100 - \frac{91}{360} F_{n,t}$$

where $F_{n,t}$ is the yield at time t on the futures contract maturing in n days. However, when the futures contract matures, the $1500 per contract margin will be returned, and so the net cash requirement per $100 in n days is $q_{n,t} - 0.15$.

Each n-day bill will be worth 100 upon maturity in n days; thus a $(q_{n,t} - 0.15)/100$ fractional n-day bill must be purchased at time t to provide the cash needed at time t+n. For investors other than dealers, the purchase price of an n-day bill is the dealers' asked price, $p^a_{n,t}$, which is related to the asked yield by

$$P^a_{n,t} = 100 - \frac{n}{360} R^a_{n,t}.$$

Thus, the cash needed at time t is that required to buy the fractional bill at the price of $P^a_{n,t}$ per bill plus the amount needed for the futures contract margin requirement and commission, or $0.15 and $0.006 per $100. Thus, the total cash requirement at time t is

$$\left(\frac{q_{n,t} - 0.15}{100} \right) P^a_{n,t} + 0.15 + 0.006.$$

---

[2] The calculations discussed below are based on the assumptions that the $60 commission is paid when the futures position is taken and that the $1500 margin is put up in cash. In fact, the commission may in some cases be paid when the futures position is covered and the margin requirement may be satisfied by putting up interest-bearing securities. In addition, futures price fluctuations may lead to a requirement that additional cash or securities be added to the margin account or may permit some cash or securities to be withdrawn from the margin account. Because the amounts involved are so small, these considerations would have a negligible effect on the arbitrage calculations presented below and so are ignored.

Interest Rate Futures: Concepts and Issues

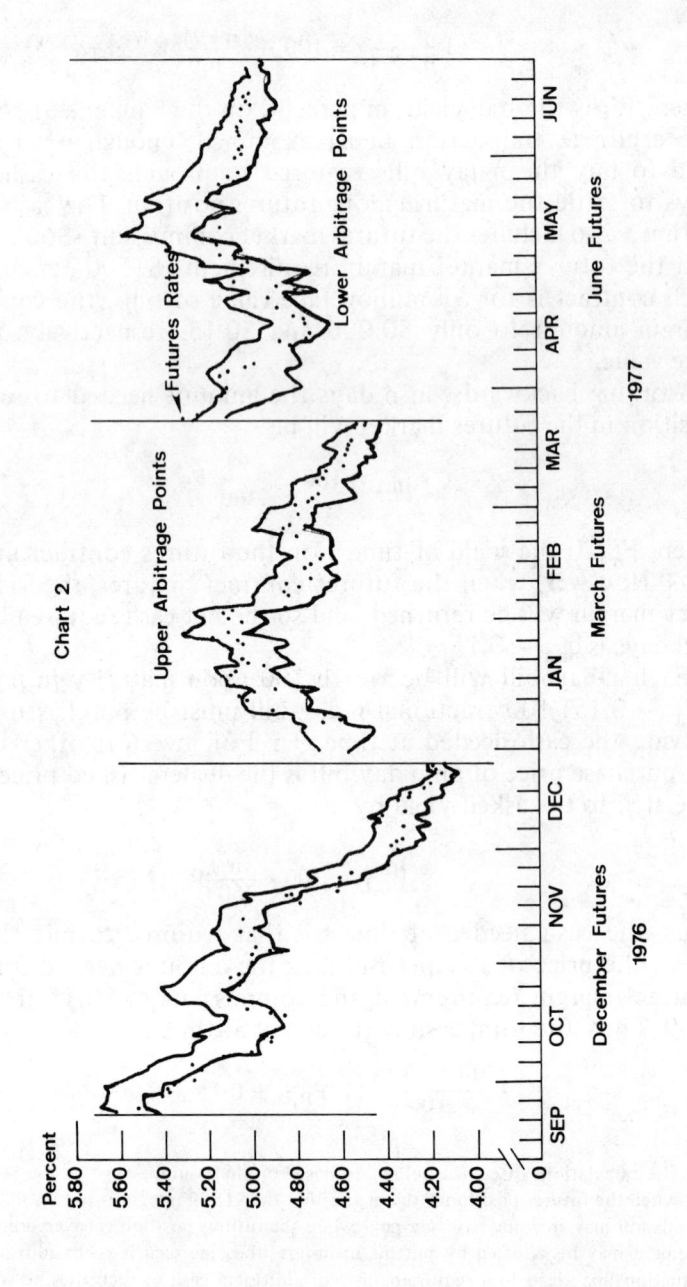

Chart 2

Using T-Bill Futures to Gauge Interest-Rate Expectations

The cash requirement at time t is to be raised by selling a fractional part, X, of the n+91-day bill already owned. If this fraction is less than one, then the arbitrage operation will be profitable. The purchase of the n-day bill and the futures contract package will produce $100 in n+91 days. Simply holding the n+91-day bill will also produce $100 in n+91 days. Thus, if the arbitrage transaction requires that a fraction less than one of the n+91-day bill be sold, then the fraction 1-X of an n+91-day bill will be a risk-free arbitrage profit.

From these considerations, the fraction, X, of n+91-day bills selling at price $P^b_{n+91,t}$ sold must be such that

$$X P^b_{n+91,t} = \left(\frac{q_{n,t} - 0.15}{100}\right) P^a_{n,t} + 0.15 + 0.006.$$

Dividing through by $P^b_{n+91,t}$ defines X; arbitrage is profitable if X < 1, or in yield terms,

$$(1) \quad F_{n,t} > \left(1 - \frac{n}{36000} R^a_{n,t}\right)^{-1} \left[\frac{n+91}{91} R^b_{n+91,t}\right.$$

$$\left. - \frac{n}{91} R^a_{n,t} + \frac{360}{91}(0.006) + \frac{n}{91}(0.0015 R^a_{n,t})\right].$$

The right-hand side of the inequality (1) defines the upper critical point for profitable arbitrage. The expression has been written so that the components due to explicit transactions costs in the futures market—the terms involving 0.006 and 0.0015—may be clearly identified.

It may also be noted that without the two futures market transaction-cost terms, the right-hand side of (1) defines the implicit forward rate of interest in the term structure calculated from the bid yield on the n+91-day bill and the asked yield on the n-day bill. In the example being discussed, the implicit forward rate is the rate of interest that would have to be earned on a 91-day bill to be issued at time t+n, so that the total yield over n+91 days would be the same on an n+91-day bill and on an n-day bill with the proceeds invested on maturity in a 91-day bill. The yield on a 91-day bill is, of course, unknown before the bill is issued, but the investor can (if desired) lock in a known yield by buying a bill futures contract. He can also lock in that yield implicitly by buying an n+91-day bill, provided he is willing to lock in the package combination of the equivalent of an n-day bill and the 91-day bill to be issued at time t+n.

From a similar line of reasoning, the lower critical point may be defined. A risk-free arbitrage opportunity exists if

$$(2) \quad F_{n,t} < \left(1 - \frac{n}{36000} R^b_{n,t}\right)^{-1} \left[\frac{n+91}{91} R^a_{n+91,t}\right.$$

$$\left. - \frac{n}{91} R^b_{n,t} - \frac{360}{91}(0.006) - \frac{n}{91}(0.0015 R^b_{n,t})\right].$$

The right-hand side of (2) defines the lower critical point for profitable arbitrage.

The critical points defined by (1) and (2) have been calculated from daily data for the period from January 6, 1976 to June 23, 1977, and plotted as solid lines in Charts 1 and 2.[3] The futures quotes are plotted as dots in the charts.

The charts suggest that profitable arbitrage opportunities rarely exist, and when they exist are small in magnitude. This finding is especially significant because only explicit costs were included in the calculation of the arbitrage points—no allowance was made, for example, for the labor time of the arbitrageur—and perfect divisibility was assumed.

Two other features stand out in the charts. First, there appears to be a tendency for the futures rate to fall closer to the lower than the upper arbitrage point, especially in the first month plotted for each contract. Second, there seems to be a tendency for the futures rate to fall in the last month of trading for each contract. These observations are directly related to the nature of term premiums in interest rates for securities of various maturities.

II. TERM PREMIUMS AND BID-ASKED SPREADS[4]

It is now generally agreed that longer-term securities have systematically higher yields than shorter-term securities, the differences being labled "term premiums," or "liquidity premiums." The existence of term premiums had been widely assumed, and so recent empirical findings have seemed to confirm the theoretical expectation that risk aversion would cause longer-term securities to sell at higher yields on the average than shorter-term securities.

To this author's knowledge, however, the relationship of transactions costs to term premiums has never been carefully investigated. The data used in previous studies of the term structure have consisted either of points drawn free-hand through yield observations—the Durand and Treasury *Bulletin* yield curves—or means of bid and asked yields. Given the significant size of bid-asked spreads—especially for short-term securities—it is clear that transactions costs need to be examined carefully.

The second and third columns of Table 1 suggest that transactions costs may be related to estimated term premiums. These two columns are reproduced from Tables 5-3 and 6-12 in Richard Roll's study of the

---

[3] The data base consists of closing bid and asked yields on bills, and closing futures quotes—all from the *Wall Street Journal*.

[4] This section is somewhat technical and may be skipped by the reader primarily interested in the policy implications of the bill futures market.

Using T-Bill Futures to Gauge Interest-Rate Expectations

Table 1 Bid-Asked Spreads and Term Premiums

Weeks to Maturity	Mean Spread[a]	Term Premium Marginal[b]	Term Premium Average[c]
1	.2336	0	0
2	.1762	.00704	.00352
3	.1486	.0555	.0208
4	.1288	.168	.058
5	.1121	.291	.104
6	.0993	.323	.141
7	.0893	.347	.170
8	.0813	.383	.197
9	.0753	.445	.224
10	.0695	.427	.245
11	.0649	.396	.258
12	.0580	.414	.271
13	.0424	.562	.294
14	.0843	.0403	.276
16	.0835	.0696	.262
16	.0831	.142	.254
17	.0822	.175	.250
18	.0810	.189	.246
19	.0788	.256	.247
20	.0762	.262	.248
21	.0734	.296	.250
22	.0710	.305	.252
23	.0681	.310	.255
24	.0620	.328	.258
25	.0555	.365	.262
26	.0415	NA	NA

NA: Not Available.

[a] Weighted (by number of observations) averages of mean spreads for March, 1959-December, 1961 and January, 1962-December, 1964 reported in Roll. R., *The Behavior of Interest Rates*, Table 5-3.

[b] For March, 1959-December, 1964, from Roll, Table 6-12.

[c] For maturity m, mean of marginal term premiums for maturities 1,2, . . . m.

Treasury bill market.[5] (The other column in Table 1 will be discussed later.) The sharp drop in Roll's estimated marginal term premium—the average difference between the one-week implicit forward rate m weeks in the future and the one-week spot rate realized in m weeks—between the 13- and 14-week maturities appears to be suspiciously related to the sharp increase in the mean spread between the same two maturities. Be-

[5] Richard Roll, The Behavior of Interest Rates (New York: Basic Books, 1970).

fore discussing this issue further, however, a review of some of the a priori arguments concerning term premiums will prove helpful.

As a matter of *arithmetic*, a given change in yield to maturity produces a larger change in the price of a longer-term security than in the price of a shorter-term security. As a matter of *fact*, long-term yields do not fluctuate as much as short-term yields, but the relative variability of long-term and short-term yields is such that the prices of long-term securities nevertheless fluctuate more than the prices of short-term securities; thus, the capital values of long-term securities are subject to more interest rate risk. If we assume that investors are risk averse, we would expect that the average yield on long-term securities will have to be higher to compensate investors for the greater risk.

Another argument suggesting the probable existence of term premiums depends on transactions costs. Consider the situation faced by a firm that temporarily has excess cash which it will need in m days. The firm could buy an m-day Treasury bill, which would mature just when the cash was needed.[6] Alternatively, the firm could buy a longer-term security and then sell it in m days. A firm that is not risk averse would compare the yield on the m-day bill with the expected yield over m days from buying a n-day bill, where n is larger than m, and selling it after m days. This yield would have to be calculated from the asked price of the n-day bill and the expected bid price of an n-m bill in m days.

Letting $P_{k,t}$ be the price at time t of a bill with k days to maturity, the continuously compounded yield to maturity is

$$R_{k,t} = \frac{365}{k}(\log 100 - \log P_{k,t}).$$

The expected continuously compounded holding-period yield $_nH^*_{m,t}$ from buying an n-day bill at the asked price $P^a_{n,t}$ and selling it m days later at the expected bid price $P^{b*}_{n-m,t+m}$ is

$$_nH^*_{m,t} = \frac{365}{m}(\log P^{b*}_{n-m,t+m} - \log P^a_{n,t})$$

$$= \frac{n}{m} R^a_{n,t} - \frac{n-m}{m} R^{b*}_{n-m,t+m}$$

The firm needing cash in m days will buy an m-day bill rather than an n-day bill if $R^a_{m,t} > {_nH^*_{m,t}}$. Using the definition of the bid-asked yield spread S_k on a bill with k days to maturity as the difference between

---
[6] Treasury bills, of course, do not mature every day. The firm wanting to invest in a maturing bill would have to select the existing bill with maturity best matching the firm's predicted cash needs. The following analysis ignores the fact that purchase of a bill with more than m days to maturity permits the firm to keep its funds invested right to the day its cash needs arise, since an existing bill can be sold on any business day.

the bid and asked yields, this inequality yields the expression

(3) $\quad R^a_{m,t} > \frac{n}{m} R^a_{n,t} - (\frac{n-m}{m}) (R^{a*}_{n-m,t+m} + S^*_{n-m,t+m})$.

A particularly convenient interpretation of inequality (3) arises for n = 2m. In this case, we have

(4) $\quad R^a_{m,t} > 2R^a_{2m,t} - (R^{a*}_{m,t+m} + S^*_{m,t+m})$.

Suppose interest rates on particular maturities are not expected to change so that $R^{a*}_{m,t+m} = R^a_{m,t}$, and suppose that bid-asked spreads for given maturities are constant over time so that $S^*_{m,t+m} = S_m$.[7] Then we can write (3) as

(5) $\quad R^a_{m,t} > R^a_{2m,t} - \frac{1}{2} S_m$.

Letting $R_{k,t} = \frac{1}{2} (R^b_{k,t} + R^a_{k,t}) = R^a_{k,t} + \frac{1}{2} S_{k,t}$,

(5) may be written in terms of yields defined as the means of bid and asked yields.

(6) $\quad R_{m,t} > R_{2m,t} - \frac{1}{2} S_{2m}$.

Since bid-asked mean yields have typically been employed in term structure studies (including Roll's), (6) is in a form that relates the present argument to previous work. The typical finding that short-term rates are on the average below long-term rates is consistent with (6) provided that the yield differential is not excessive compared to the spread. The average difference between the yield to maturity on an m-week bill and the yield on a one-week bill is the average of the marginal term premiums for maturities 2, 3, ..., m. This average term premium, calculated from Roll's estimates of marginal term premiums, is reported in Table 1. Using these estimates of average term premiums for various maturities and the estimated spreads in Table 1, inequality (6) is found to hold for maturities of 1, 2, 9, 10, 11, and 12 weeks but not for maturities of three through eight weeks.

It is interesting to note that Roll found the hypothesis of market efficiency well-supported except for maturities of 4 to 8 weeks.[8] For these maturities yields seem to be too low, on the average. We may conjecture, however, that the apparent anomaly would disappear with a fuller accounting of transactions costs.

---

[7] Rather than interpreting equation (4) as applying to a time when rates are not expected to change, the rates in (4) may be interpreted as the means of the rates over a long sample period in which there is no overall trend in the level of rates. The means of $R^a_{m,t+m}$ and $R^a_{m,t}$ differ only by virtue of one observation at each end of the sample.

[8] See Roll, p. 116.

A few numbers will provide a feel for the magnitudes involved. From inequality (6), the yield on a four-week bill is too low by about 10 basis points according to Roll's evidence. (A basis point is .01 percent.) Comparing the two sides of inequality (3) and using the fact that $R_m^a = R_m - 1/2\, S_m$, this 10 basis point discrepancy makes the right-hand side of (3) larger than the left-hand side by about 20 basis points. The firm with cash to invest for four weeks could, therefore, have a 20 basis points advantage on the average from investing in an eight-week bill (which would be sold after four weeks) rather than in a four-week bill.[9] These yields, however, are all expressed at annual rates. The yield advantage per four weeks is only 4/52 of 20 basis points, or about $154 per million of invested funds. It is easy to imagine that the extra transactions costs from buying an eight-week bill and selling it four weeks later as compared to simply buying a four-week bill and holding it to maturity would exceed $154 per million of funds invested.

The analysis of the transaction-cost effect in depressing yields on very short-term bills is, however, only indirectly relevant to the issue of the size of term premiums in bill futures-market quotes. We need to know whether the term premium should be subtracted in order to interpret the futures quotes as reflecting market expectations of future spot rates on three-month bills; the fact that a one-week bill has an average yield below that on a 13-week bill is not directly relevant to this issue.

The transaction-cost argument suggests that yields on very short-term bills could be depressed without there being any noticeable impact on longer-term bills. For example, in comparing the yield from holding a 13-week bill to maturity with the yield from holding a 26-week bill for 13 weeks, the bid-asked yield spreads are small enough, and the 13-week holding period long enough, so that there is little room for the average 13-week bill yield to fall below the average 26-week bill yield. From inequality (6) and the mean spread on 26-week bills (Table 1), the effect would be only two basis points.

Nevertheless, the transaction-cost effect on very short-term bills can affect term premiums (as estimated in previous studies) because of the way in which implicit forward rates are calculated. To understand the argument, consider first the expression defining the implicit forward rate of interest on a 13-week loan to begin m weeks in the future, calculated from the yields to maturity on spot bills with m and m+13 weeks to maturity. Using continuously compounded yields

$$(7) \quad 13\,r_{m,t} = \left(\frac{m+13}{13}\right) R_{m+13,t} - \frac{m}{13} R_{m,t},$$

---

[9] That the holding period yield advantage is greater than the discrepancy in yields to maturity can be seen readily from the fact that the yield to maturity, R_n, on an n-week bill is the weighted average of the yield over the first m weeks and the yield over the remaining n-m weeks. If the latter yield is below R_n, then the former yield must be above R_n.

where $_{13}r_{m,t}$ is the implicit forward rate as of time t on a 13-week loan to begin in m weeks and $R_{k,t}$ is the yield to maturity on a spot bill with k weeks to maturity. On the average, the yield on a k-week bill exceeds the yield on a one-week bill by the average term premium $\bar{L}_k$. Thus, on the average we have

$$(8) \quad _{13}r_{m,t} = (\frac{m+13}{13})(R_1 + \bar{L}_{m+13})$$
$$- \frac{m}{13}(R_1 + \bar{L}_m)$$
$$= R_1 + (\frac{m+13}{13})\bar{L}_{m+13} - \frac{m}{13}\bar{L}_m$$
$$= R_1 + \frac{1}{13}\sum_{j=m+1}^{m+13} L_j.$$

The third line in equation (8) is derived from the definition

$$\bar{L}_k = \frac{1}{k}\sum_{j=1}^{k} L_j.$$

Each L_j, it may be recalled, is the marginal term premium—the amount by which the implicit forward rate on a one-week loan to mature k weeks in the future exceeds the realized spot rate on a one-week loan maturing k weeks in the future.

The summation term in (8) contains 13 L_j's. If the L_j's were nondecreasing so that $L_{j+1} \geq L_j$, then

$$\frac{1}{13}\sum_{j=m+1}^{m+13} L_j \geq \frac{1}{13}\sum_{j=1}^{13} L_j = \bar{L}_{13}.$$

In this case the implicit forward rate $_{13}r_{m,t}$ would be an upward biased estimate of $R_{13} = R_1 + L_{13}$.

Roll's estimates of the L_j, however, are not nondecreasing for all j. When the summation term in (8) is calculated using Roll's estimates it is found that $_{13}r_m$ is an upward biased estimate of R_{13} for m from 1 to 7 weeks but a downward biased estimate for m from 8 to 12 weeks. The maximum size of the downward bias is about four basis points and the maximum size of the upward bias is about two basis points. While the size of the upward bias is very small based on Roll's estimates, the phenomenon may help to explain the appearance in the charts of a decline in the implicit forward rates underlying the arbitrage points in the last month of trading of a futures contract.

McCulloch provides another term-structure study of direct relevance to this issue.[10] Using somewhat different estimation methods than Roll

---

[10] J. Huston McCulloch, "An Estimate of the Liquidity Premium," *Journal of Political Economy*, 83 (February, 1975), 95-119.

and a sample period from March 1951 to March 1966, McCulloch reports estimates of the term premium attached to implicit forward 13-week rates at various periods in the future (Table 2). If these estimates are taken at face value, 10 to 20 basis points should be subtracted from implicit forward rates for 13-week bills one or more months in the future to obtain market expectations of future spot rates on 13-week bills.

These estimates of term premiums are above those relevant for the bill futures market if the argument on transaction costs is accepted, because transaction costs affect implicit forward rates calculated from spot bills of varying maturities but not the bill futures market. If this argument is correct, quotes in the futures market should generally be below the corresponding implicit forward rates.

This hypothesis was tested by calculating the mean futures rate and the mean implicit forward rate over the three-month period preceding the maturity date of the six futures contracts maturing between January, 1976 and June, 1977 (Table 3).[11] In every case the mean of the rate on a given futures contract is below the corresponding mean of the implicit forward rate calculated from bid-asked mean rates. The means of the upper and lower arbitrage points are also reported, although it is obvious from the charts that the futures rate almost always lies between the two arbitrage points.

A test of the statistical significance of the results in Table 3 is reported in Table 4. The test has been confined to the first 20 observations in each of the periods listed in Table 3, since there is much more interest in market forecasts of the bill rate a few months in the future than in forecasts a few weeks in the future. For the first 20 trading days in each period, the difference between the futures rate and the implicit

Table 2

McCulloch Estimates of Term Premiums in 13-week Implicit Forward Rates

Bill to be Issued in:	Term Premium Free Form Estimates	Exponential Form Estimates
1 month	0.10	0.09
2 months	0.15	0.14
3 months	0.16	0.17
6 months	0.12	0.21
9 months	0.11	0.22
1 year	0.13	0.22
2 years	0.12	0.22

[11] The yields in Table 3 are bankers' discount yields. The implicit forward rates were calculated with due regard for discounting considerations.

Table 3

Means of Futures Rates, Implicit Forward Rates, and Arbitrage Points for Selected Periods

Period	Futures Contract	Futures Rate	Implicit Forward Rate Bid-Asked Mean	Bid	Asked	Arbitrage Point Lower	Upper
1/6/76-3/17/76	March 1976	5.10	5.17	5.21	5.13	5.02	5.32
3/24/76-6/23/76	June 1976	5.48	5.54	5.57	5.50	5.38	5.69
6/24/76-9/22/76	Sept. 1976	5.42	5.45	5.49	5.42	5.34	5.57
9/23/76-12/22/76	Dec. 1976	4.84	4.95	4.98	4.92	4.84	5.05
12/23/76-3/23/77	March 1977	4.82	4.85	4.87	4.82	4.73	4.96
3/24/77-6/22/77	June 1977	5.05	5.11	5.12	5.10	4.99	5.23

forward rate was calculated; the means and standard deviations of these differences appear in Table 4 along with the statistic for testing the statistical significance of the mean difference. The mean difference is negative for all periods. Using a one-tailed t-test, the mean differences for the first, second, and fourth periods are significant at the .001 level, the third period at about the .02 level, the fifth period at almost the .05 level, and the last period at about the .15 level. From these results for the individual periods, it is obvious that, in the pooled sample for the six periods combined, the mean is statistically different from zero at a very high level of statistical significance.

The evidence suggests that yields on very short maturities are depressed by the existence of transaction costs. Investors depress the return on very short-term bills when they attempt to obtain a return on balances invested for only a few weeks' time. The return is apparently

Table 4

Futures and Implicit Forward Rates
(Differences, first 20 observations each period)

Differences	1/6/76-3/17/76	3/24/76-6/23/76	6/24/76-9/22/76	9/23/76-12/22/76	12/23/76-3/23/77	3/24/77-6/22/77
Mean, $\bar{X}$	−0.1345	−0.0505	−0.0285	−0.1590	−0.0405	−0.0205
Standard Deviation, S	0.0788	0.0511	0.0584	0.0397	0.1079	0.0894
Test Statistic, $\|\bar{X}/S\sqrt{20}\|$	7.63	4.42	2.18	17.91	1.68	1.03

slightly lower than can be explained by the bid-asked spreads on longer-term bills, but not by much. The term premiums involved, however, do not in any event extend very far into the yield structure. Beyond maturities of about 13 weeks, the average term structure is essentially flat.

Quotes on the nearest maturity in the bill futures market can, therefore, be interpreted for all practical purposes as the market's unbiased estimates of the future spot rates on 13-week bills. The policy significance of this finding will now be explored.

III. POLICY IMPLICATIONS OF T-BILL FUTURES

The evidence discussed above shows that for the nearest bill futures maturity there is a close correspondence between the futures rate and the implicit forward rate calculated from spot rates. If this finding also applies to the other bill futures maturities—and in this section it will be assumed that the finding does apply to all maturities—then it is clear that the opening of the bill futures market did not provide policymakers with much new information. Nevertheless, the futures rates, by displaying investors' expectations of future spot rates on 13-week bills explicitly, have focused attention on these expectations in a way implicit forward rates never did.

Since the start of trading in bill futures in January, 1976 the rates on more distant futures have always been higher than the rates on near futures; investors have been expecting spot bill rates to rise over time. As of this writing—early April, 1978—realized bill rates have been almost always below prior expectations as measured by rates on the more distant futures contracts. For example, on January 30, 1976 the futures rates for March, June, September, and December, 1976 were 4.89, 5.33, 5.64, and 5.86 percent, respectively.[12] The realized bill rates on the maturity of these futures were 4.97, 5.32, 5.01, and 4.25 percent, respectively. For a more recent example, on September 30, 1976 the futures rates for December, 1976, March, June, September, and December, 1977, and March, 1978 were 5.37, 5.71, 6.07, 6.44, 6.77, and 7.10 percent, respectively, whereas the realized spot rates were 4.25, 4.52, 5.00, 5.85, 5.96, and 6.22 percent, respectively.

If the findings in the previous section apply to all futures maturities, then the differences between the futures rates and the realized spot rates over the last two years reflect genuine expectational errors rather than term premiums attached to the futures rates. A variety of interpretations of these expectational errors is possible.

---

[12] The two longer futures contracts, March and June 1977, were not actively traded in the first several months after the futures market opened.

One starting point would be a hypothesis concerning the relationship between economic activity and inflation on the one hand and the spot bill rate on the other. It is generally argued that higher levels of economic activity add to the demand for funds to finance business inventories, purchases of consumers' durables, and so forth, and so tend to raise interest rates. Higher rates of inflation also tend to raise interest rates. Expectational errors, therefore, could have occurred if economic activity and the inflation rate had been below investors' anticipations. This explanation seems not very satisfactory, however, because the performance of the economy over the past two years has, if anything, been slightly stronger than earlier forecasts had suggested likely.

Another possible explanation of expectational errors emphasizes the influence of government policy on interest rates. In the short run, accelerated money growth probably tends to depress interest rates, and slower money growth to raise interest rates. If money growth is higher than anticipated, interest rates will tend to be lower than anticipated. Similarly, since government budget deficits require financing, smaller-than-anticipated budget deficits will tend to lead to lower-than-anticipated interest rates. Interpretation of the interest-rate effects of monetary policy is complicated, however, by the fact that higher money growth in the long-run raises the rate of inflation and, therefore, raises interest rates. It is not known exactly where the dividing line in time lies between the short-run effect of depressing interest rates and the long-run effect of raising interest rates.

The explanation for recent expectational errors that emphasizes errors in anticipating government policy fits the facts better than the explanation based on the performance of the economy. Money growth on the M_1 definition was higher in 1976 than in 1975, and higher in 1977 than in 1976; on the M_2 definition, money growth was higher in 1976 than in 1975, but lower in 1977 than in 1976.[13] And the total government-budget deficit—federal, state and local government combined—has been lower than anticipated by many observers because of below-budget federal spending and surprisingly large state-and-local budget surpluses.[14]

A third explanation—one consistent with much recent discussion—is that the demand for money may have declined over the past several years. Especially on the M_1 definition, money growth in 1975 and 1976 was much slower than would have been anticipated given the ob-

---

[13] Measuring money growth from December of one year to December of the next, M_1 growth was 4.1 percent in 1975, 6.1 percent in 1976, and 7.7 percent in 1977, while M_2 growth was 8.5, 11.4, and 9.2 percent, respectively.

[14] See Edward M. Gramlich, "State and Local Budgets the Day after it Rained: Why is the Surplus So High," in Arthur M. Okun and George L. Perry, eds., Brookings Papers on Economic Activity, 1978:1, 191-214.

served changes in income and interest rates. Or, viewed another way, interest rates were much lower than would have been anticipated given the observed growth in M_1 and income. From the point of view of a bill futures market participant in early 1976, the concensus forecast for income growth and the Federal Reserve's announced money growth targets implied, from the existing evidence on money demand relationships, higher interest rates than were in fact realized.

While this brief discussion may or may not be a correct analysis of the interest rate expectational errors of the past two years, it serves to introduce the nature of the problem faced by policymakers in interpreting the interest rate forecasts incorporated in T-bill futures rates. The key problem faced by policymakers is that of assessing the significance of market interest rate forecasts that differ from the policymaker's own forecasts.

Suppose, for example, that T-bill futures rates are higher than policymakers' forecasts of future interest rates. One possibility is that the market is anticipating a higher level of economic activity and/or a higher inflation rate than policymakers are anticipating. It is especially important to consider this possibility, because the market forecasts incorporated in bill futures rates reflect more than simply the interest-rate guesses of speculators. Firms may enter the bill futures market on the basis of their anticipated cash flows arising, for example, from the expected effects of current plans or commitments to accumulate inventories.

This type of activity in the bill futures market is similar to that in commodity futures markets; the wheat futures price, for example, reflects expected demands for wheat by bakeries and supplies of wheat by farmers. Trading in this market, therefore, reflects the impact of current decisions—bread supply commitments by bakeries and planting decisions by farmers—that will affect wheat supplies and demands and, therefore, wheat prices in the future.

If policymakers' forecasts of interest rates below those in the bill futures market do reflect mistaken forecasts by policymakers of the future strength of aggregate demand, then their decisions may provide for a more expansionary policy than is appropriate. The accuracy of the economic forecasts available to policymakers is not so high that the possibility that high futures rates are forecasting higher levels of economic activity and/or higher inflation can be ignored.

An even more troubling possibility, though, is that rates in the bill futures market may reflect anticipations concerning policy decisions that do not reflect actual policy plans. Failure of policy decisions to ratify private anticipations concerning policy then falsifies one of the assumptions under which business decisions are made and leads to less appropriate business decisions than would otherwise be the case.

To avoid private expectational errors, policy-makers must provide clear information, through formal announcements or otherwise, concerning-prospective policies. And if statements concerning policy intentions are to be believed, policymakers must in fact determine policy in accordance with those announced intentions. If policies typically do not reflect previously announced policy intentions, then statements of policy intent will simply not be believed. Business planning will be subject to unnecessary uncertainty, but so also will policy planning. To interpret current economic data in such a situation, policymakers will have to guess what businessmen are guessing the policymakers will do.

An apparently easy solution to this problem would be for policymakers to make clear announcements of their policy plans and then to ensure that these plans are realized. Under this approach, however, policy could not be adjusted in a flexible and timely manner when economic conditions change unexpectedly. The policy dilemma is clear. To encourage sound and sensible business planning, policymakers need to make their plans clear and must realize their plans to retain credibility. But policy plans should, presumably, be adjusted from time to time to reflect changing economic conditions.

Different policy analysts place differing degrees of emphasis on the relative importance of realizing policy plans and of retaining policy flexibility. Unfortunately, there is no simply way of determining how to strike a balance between those two goals. What can be done, though, is to broaden the concept of the announced policy plan by making clear the nature of the policy responses to the expected under specified conditions. It is well understood, for example, that the Federal Reserve will intervene heavily to stabilize money markets disrupted by a spectacular bankruptcy such as the Penn-Central failure in 1970, even if such intervention produces a temporary surge in money growth far above what had been planned.

But it is important to distinguish between specific intervention of this type and a more generalized intervention to cushion interest-rate increases. An excellent example of the benefits of *not* cushioning interest-rate increases occurred in April 1977, when M_1 increased at a 20-percent annual rate (since revised to 14 percent). That episode raised fears in the markets that the Federal Reserve was permitting money to expand at a rate far above its announced policy intentions. By permitting short-term interest rates to rise sharply at that time—the 13-week bill rates went from 4.57 percent in the week ending April 1 to 5.06 percent in the week ending May 27—the Federal Reserve convinced the markets that money growth would not be permitted to continue at clearly excessive rates.

While the rate on 13-week bills was rising in May 1977 rates on the more distant bill futures fell. Comparing weekly average rates for the week ending April 1 to weekly average rates for the week ending May 27, the September 1977 futures went from 5.88 to 5.65, the March

1978 futures from 7.03 to 6.62, and the September 1978 futures from 7.83 to 7.22. In this situation, expanding the rate of money growth even further to hold down the rate on 13-week bills might very well have led to heightened fears of future inflation which would have raised rates in the futures market.

IV. SUMMARY AND CONCLUSIONS

The evidence reviewed in this paper demonstrates that the Treasury-bill futures market is closely linked to the spot market in Treasury bills. Unexploited arbitrage opportunities between the two markets rarely exist.

A key question is whether term premiums must be subtracted from T-bill futures rates to convert those rates into market forecasts of future spot rates on Treasury bills. A review of evidence on term premiums from previous studies suggests that very short-term bills trade at lower yields than longer-term bills on the average but that much, and perhaps all, of the average yield differential probably reflects the extra transactions costs from selling longer-term bills before maturity compared to holding very short-term bills to maturity. Because transactions costs in trading bill futures are so very small, futures rates were hypothesized to be slightly lower than the forward rate implicit in the yields on spot bills of various maturities. This hypothesis is supported by the evidence presented in this paper.

What is the policy significance of the new market in Treasury bill futures? The existence of these explicit market interest-rate forecasts emphasizes the need for policymakers to understand the reasons for discrepancies between their own interest-rate forecasts and market interest-rate forecasts. If, at some point in time, rates in the bill futures market are based on forecasts of a stronger and/or more inflationary economy than projected by policymakers, and if the market is correct, then there is a danger than policymakers will determine a more expansionary policy than is appropriate for the needs of the economy.

Market interest-rate forecasts may also reflect forecasts of policies that differ from those that policymakers are actually planning. This possibility emphasizes the importance of policymakers making their plans known and maintaining credibility by ensuring that announced policy plans are realized. However, strict adherence to policy plans makes it difficult for policy to be adjusted flexibly in response to changing circumstances.

While there is no easy solution to this dilemma, the problems raised can be eased by including in the concept of a policy plan an understanding of the policy adjustments required by certain contingencies. For example, permitting temporarily high money growth to cushion market disruptions caused by a major bankruptcy, such as the Penn-Central failure, need not imply that long-run plans for money growth will not be realized.

Although the accuracy of the bill futures rates as predictors of future spot rates was not discussed in detail, it is clear that futures rates, even if unbiased, are not especially accurate forecasts. For this reason the policy significance of these interest rate forecasts ought not to be exaggerated. However, the policymakers' own forecasts of interest rates are not very accurate either. Unless policymakers have solid evidence that their own forecasts are more accurate than market forecasts, they cannot afford to ignore the T-bill futures market.

6

Is the Futures Market for Treasury Bills Effecient?*

Donald J. Puglisi[†]

On January 6, 1976, the International Monetary Market of the Chicago Mercantile Exchange began trading in ninety-day U.S. Treasury bill (T-bill) futures. This new product adds to a growing list of financial and/or interest rate sensitive commodity future contracts. Like other commodity futures, the T-bill futures are designed to provide either hedging or speculative attractions to interested traders. T-bill futures have an added attraction in that, should the market for these futures be inefficient, arbitrage opportunities involving futures and outstanding T-bills will be available to institutional portfolio managers who maintain positions in bills. The purpose of this paper is to (1) specify a model for the proper pricing of T-bill futures contracts in an efficient market; (2) test the efficiency of the market on a body of collected data; and (3) develop implications of the test findings for market efficiency and possible action by institutional portfolio managers.

---

*Reprinted from *The Journal of Portfolio Management*, Vol. 4, (Winter 1978). Reprinted by permission of Institutional Investor Systems, Inc., publisher.

[†]The author would like to acknowledge the assistance of James Widdoes and Janet Rzewnicki in collecting and analyzing the data examined in this study.

PRICING T-BILL FUTURES IN AN EFFICIENT MARKET

The T-bill futures contract represents the opportunity to buy (go long) or sell (short) $1 million of 90-day U.S. Treasury bills for future delivery. The price of the futures contract, F, is found by the following equation:

$$F = 1MM - \frac{(90.1MM \cdot d_F)}{360} \quad (1)$$

where d_F is the discount rate on the futures contract.

In the context of the expectations hypothesis of the term structure of interest rates, d_F is related to the expected short-term rate r_E in

$$(1 + r_L)^L = (1 + r_s)^S (1 + r_E)^{L-S} \quad (2)$$

where r_L is the yield on a long-term security for L units of time, r_s is the yield on current short-term securities for S units of time, and r_E is the expected short-term rate to cover (L-S) units of time. For example, assume that L equals 2 years, S equals 1 year, r_L equals 6%, and r_s equals 5%. Then

$$(1 + r_L)^L = (1 + r_s)^S (1 + r_E)^{(L-S)}$$

$$(1.06)^2 = (1.05)(1 + r_E)$$

$$r_E = .07$$

Equation (2) specifies, then, the manner in which future short-term rates can be determined. The discount rate on T-bill futures should follow from a variation on equation (2)—provided we can ignore costs of illiquidity, which can be assumed to be insignificant given the very short-term nature of the bill futures. If the rate does not conform to that developed from (2), arbitrage opportunities should exist between positions in outstanding bills and futures. Let us consider this point further.

THE SEARCH FOR ARBITRAGE OPPORTUNITIES

Let F represent a position in a given three-month T-bill futures contract, S represent an outstanding short-term T-bill maturing at the time of expiration of the futures contract, and L be defined as a long-term bill due to mature at the same time as the bill represented in the futures

Is the Futures Market for Treasury Bills Efficient?

contract. For example, the March, 1976 T-bill futures contract expired on March 17, 1976. It provided an investor the opportunity to buy or sell the T-bill due on June 22, 1976. F then is the futures contract, S is the March 18, 1976 bill, and L is the June 22, 1976 bill. An investor interested in investing funds to March 18 has two alternatives:

I. buy S
II. buy L and short F

In an efficient market, F should be priced so that the investor is indifferent between I and II. Alternatively, an investor interested in investing funds to June 22, 1976, has two choices:

I. buy L
II. buy S and long F

Again, F should be priced so that the investor is indifferent between I and II. For purposes of this paper, we will be concerned with the strategy where the investor has as his choices:

I. buy S
II. buy L and short F

The holding period return from alternative I is

$$R_1 = D_s/S \tag{3}$$

where R_1 = holding period return from buying short-term bill, D_s = discount on the short-term bill, and S = price of the short-term bill, and

$$D_s = (d_s . 1MM . N_s)/360 \tag{4}$$
$$S = 1MM - D_s \tag{5}$$

where d_s = discount rate on short-term bill and N_s = number of days to maturity on the short-term bill.

The annualized return on this alternative is

$$R_1^* = R_1 . (360/N_s) \tag{6}$$

The holding period return from alternative II is

$$R_2 = (F - L - T)/L \tag{7}$$

where R_2 = holding period return from strategy of buying long-term bill and shorting the futures contract, F = price of the futures contract, L = price of the long-term bill, and T = transactions costs ($60 per contract), and

$$F = 1MM - D_F \tag{8}$$
$$L = 1MM - D_L \tag{9}$$

where

$$D_F = (d_F \cdot 1MM \cdot 90)/360 \qquad (10)$$

$$D_L = (d_L \cdot 1MM \cdot N_L)/360 \qquad (11)$$

with D_F = dollar discount on futures contract, D_L = dollar discount on long-term bill, d_F = discount rate on futures contract, d_L = discount rate on long-term bill, and N_L = number of days to maturity on long-term bill.

The annualized return on strategy II, R_2^*, is

$$R_2^* = R_2 \cdot (360/N_S) \qquad (12)$$

The arbitrage profit opportunities are, on a holding period and annualized basis, respectively,

$$R_3 = R_2 - R_1 \qquad (13)$$

$$R_3^* = R_2^* - R_1^* \qquad (14)$$

Note that there is zero cost for margin since having a T-bill position eliminates the need for margin. If the T-bill futures market is efficient, both R_3 and R_3^* will approximate zero. A sufficient condition for this to occur is the existence of portfolios that are well-diversified with respect to T-bill maturities and can buy futures. Examples are major corporations, money-center banks, and dealers who make markets in T-bills and have seats on the IMM. It follows from this that if the market is efficient, the discount rate of T-bill futures is

$$d_F = (1MM - (D_s L/S) - L - T)/250M \qquad (15)$$

DATA SPECIFICATION AND FINDINGS

The efficiency of the T-bill futures market is tested by applying equation (14) to a body of assembled data. The data represent quotes on the March, 1976, June, 1976, September, 1976, December, 1976, March, 1977, June, 1977, and September, 1977 T-bill futures and the corresponding short-term and long-term T-bills necessary to compute returns for the bills-only and bills-futures strategies. For computing returns, the daily closing price on the futures contracts and the asked prices on the T-bills as reported in the *Wall Street Journal* were used. Transactions costs were assumed to be the minimum $60 commission charged per futures contract. The results of the tests are reported in Table I.

Rows (1) and (2), respectively, of Table I present the average annualized returns from bills-only and bills-futures strategies. Row (3) pre-

Is the Futures Market for Treasury Bills Efficient?

Table I. Returns from Bills-Only and Bills-Futures Strategies

	\multicolumn{7}{c}{Contract}
	March 76	June 76	Sept. 76	Dec. 76	March 77	June 77	Sept. 77
(1) $\bar{R}_1^*$	4.52%	4.92%	5.24%	5.20%	4.96%	4.77%	5.07%
(2) $\bar{R}_2^*$	4.81%	5.08%	3.97%	5.27%	4.95%	4.85%	5.03%
(3) $\bar{R}_3^*$	−0.29%	−0.16%	1.27%	−0.07%	0.01%	−0.08%	0.04%
(4) $SD(R_3^*)$	0.22%	0.37%	3.75%	0.37%	0.20%	0.34%	0.33%
(5) t	−1.32[1]	−0.43	0.34	−0.20	0.05	−0.23	0.12
(6) N	44	116	178	177	181	187	197
(7) $N(R_1^*) < N(R_2^*)$	42	92	5	103	74	90	72

[1] $\bar{R}_3^*$ significantly less than zero at .1 level.

Notes:
$\bar{R}_1^*$ is annualized return from bills-only strategy.
$\bar{R}_2^*$ is average annualized return from bills-futures strategy.
$\bar{R}_3^*$ is $\bar{R}_1^*$ less $\bar{R}_2^*$.
$SD(R_3^*)$ is standard deviation of differences in return between bills-only and bills-futures strategies.
t is t-statistic to determine if $\bar{R}_3^*$ is significantly different from zero.
N is the number of observations.
$N(R_1^*) < N(R_2^*)$ is the number of times the bills-only strategy returned less than the bills-futures strategies. A sign test on this figure indicates that $\bar{R}_3^*$ is significantly different from zero at the .01 level for the March, 76, June, 76, September, 76, and September, 77 contracts and at the .05 level for the December, 76 and March, 77 contracts.

sents the average annualized return from bills-only less bills-futures strategies.

For four of the seven cases—the March, 1976, June, 1976, December, 1976, and June, 1977 contracts—the use of futures in combination with bills would have resulted in higher returns than if a bills-only strategy were pursued. The annualized advantage from the bills-futures strategies averaged 29, 16, 7, and 8 basis points for the March, 1976, June, 1976, December, 1976, and June, 1977 contracts, respectively. The opposite was true in the case of the September, 1976, March, 1977, and September, 1977 contracts, where use of the futures in conjunction with bills would have given an average annualized return of 127, 1, and 4 basis points less than a bills-only strategy, respectively.

The t-statistics for testing whether the returns on the bills-only strategy are less than those on the bills-futures strategies—reported in row (5) of Table I—indicate that only in the case of the March, 1976 contract was the difference significantly less than zero. However, a sign test computed on the number of times the returns from the bills-only strategy were less than the returns on the bills-futures strategies—reported in row (7) of Table I—implies that the differences in return are significantly different from zero at the .01 level for four of the contract months tested and at the .05 level for two of the contract months tested. Given the sample sizes used and the proportion of cases in which one strategy dominated the other, the sign test is quite powerful.[1] An examination of the distribution of R_3^* revealed a number of outlier observations, many near the expiration date of the futures contracts. These outliers make the distributions non-normal and the t-test becomes invalid. This point is reinforced when the last ten observations for each of the first three contracts are dropped from the study, as shown in Table II. Now R_3^* for the March, 1976 contract becomes significantly less than zero while R_3^* for the September, 1976 contract is significantly greater than zero. Of course, it is questionable whether it is legitimate to drop these observations from study. In any event, the argument for use of the sign test is supported further.

IMPLICATIONS AND CONCLUSIONS

The results of the tests reported in this paper suggest that the T-bill futures market is inefficient. While the major inefficiencies occurred early in the life of the new commodity future and have ebbed as the market has continued to mature, the systematic mispricing of T-bill futures has not been completely corrected over time.[2] While this

Table II. Returns from Bills-Only and Bills-Futures Strategies on Reduced Sample (Omitting Last 10 Observations)

	Contract		
	March, 1976	June, 1976	September, 1976
(1) $\bar{R}_1^*$	4.54%	4.90%	5.30%
(2) $\bar{R}_2^*$	4.79%	5.03%	4.70%
(3) $\bar{R}_3^*$	−0.25%	−0.13%	0.60%
(4) $SD(R_3^*)$	0.13%	0.19%	0.38%
(5) t	−1.92[1]	−0.68	1.58[2]
(6) N	34	96	160

[1] $\bar{R}_3^*$ is significantly less than zero at .05 level.
[2] $\bar{R}_3^*$ is significantly greater than zero at .10 level.
Notes: Symbols on (1)-(6) are defined in Table I.

[1] An explanation of the use and power of the sign test can be found in W. J. Dixon and F. J. Massey, *Introduction to Statistical Analysis*, 3rd Edition (New York: McGraw-Hill Book Company, 1969).
[2] This, of course, assumes that the inefficiency lies in the futures market and not in the pricing of the short-term and long-term T-bills. Support for the notion that the market for T-bills is efficient can be found in Richard Roll, *The Behavior of Interest Rates: Application of the Efficient Market Model to the U.S. Treasury Bill Rates* (New York: Basic Books, Inc., 1970), and M. Hamburger and E. Platt, "The Expectations Hypothesis and the Efficiency of the Treasury Bill Market," *Review of Economics and Statistics*, May, 1975.

conclusion draws some support from the parametric-related tests, much more support is brought from the results of the non-parametric sign test. Given evidence of outlying observations and non-normality in the distribution of return-differentials between strategies, the sign test is especially valid in this study. Given the sample sizes and the proportions of cases in which one strategy dominated another, the sign test is quite powerful.

Many of the outlying observations occurred near the expiration of the futures contract. This can be expected to occur if the market is somewhat thin and speculators become nervous in trying to terminate their positions without taking or making delivery of T-bills at contract expiration. In any event, this should make for especially attractive investment opportunities for those who wish to take or make delivery of the bills, i.e., institutional portfolios.

Even if we ignore the violent price swings and gross mispricing at the contracts' ends, however, the market for T-bill futures is still inefficient. There are a number of possible explanations for this.

First, there might be inaccuracies in the data used in the study. The prices on the futures contracts are firm closing prices; on the other hand, the prices of the T-bills are nominal quotes. The spreads between bid and asked on T-bills as reported in the *Wall Street Journal* are much wider than those that exist in actual trading. The experience of the author, taken together with firm offers for a number of days of trading, however, suggests that the asked prices as reported in the *Journal* are good approximations of actual trades, although the bid sides can differ widely from actual experience. As the prices of the contracts and for the bills are reported at different times during the same day, this could also dirty the data. Nevertheless, one would expect that noise introduced into the data by this factor would tend to average out over the many days of observed transactions. Since the results are so supportive for the case of market inefficiency, as implied by the sign test that ignores the magnitude of the differences in returns, the findings and implications cannot be refuted by this factor.

A second possibility of market inefficiency would be bars to entry to institutions that could arbitrage the market for bills and for futures. Surely some banks and other institutional portfolios with large bill positions have not been able to receive permission from their boards of directors to invest in the T-bill futures market. Yet this author does know a number of institutional portfolios and T-bill dealers who also have seats on the IMM and are investing in T-bill futures. The growing involvement by institutions in this market is likely the reason why the arbitrage opportunities have tended to decline in frequency and profit opportunity as the market has matured.

The third possible reason why investors do not arbitrage the returns from the two markets to the extent possible is that the assumption of the insignificance of illiquidity is not valid. An investor with a more distant contract month bills-futures strategy might demand a premium for his investment position versus the bills-only strategy, since liquidation of the position involves selling bills and covering the futures contract. Should a contract go from overvalued (having too low a yield) to undervalued (having too high a yield), the benefit of the bills-futures strategy over the bills-only strategy could be lost in liquidation. Examination of daily trading results suggests that this was a very real possibility in the more recent contracts. As long as there are portfolios that have the capacity to maintain a position to expiration, however, such an argument lacks sufficient merit to support continued inefficiencies in the market.

Lastly, one might argue that the returns from arbitraging the market are too small to encourage institutional investors to try it. Although the return from this activity would be quite small to a well-diversified institutional portfolio and although the relatively huge profit opportunities that appeared when the market first started are unlikely to reappear, a profit opportunity does exist—and there should be investors willing to exploit it.

The conclusion of this study, then, is that the market for T-bill futures is inefficient. How long it will take investors to take advantage of these inefficiencies and force the correct pricing of T-bill futures remains to be seen. In the meantime, however, astute institutional investors can increase the returns on their portfolios by developing strategies that involve bills-futures as well as bills-only strategies. Such active portfolio management is consistent with the premise that most markets for securities are efficient: only by ferreting out opportunities that exist in some of the inefficient markets can a portfolio manager achieve above average returns.

Is the Futures Market for Treasury Bills Efficient?*

Anthony J. Vignola and Charles J. Dale[†]

In a recent article in this *Journal*,[1] Puglisi developed and tested a model for evaluating the efficiency of the Treasury bill futures market. His model was based on the expectations hypothesis of the term structure of interest rates whereby the futures market discount rate is related to the expected short-term, or forward, rate implied by the term structure. He found that the market for Treasury bill futures was not efficient because arbitrage opportunities existed involving transactions in futures and outstanding Treasury bills. He concluded, however, that such opportunities have "ebbed as the market has continued to mature."

These conclusions are based upon a comparison of the returns from investment strategies that involve only bills and a combination of bills and futures. The differences between the returns from these two strategies for equal holding periods were evaluated; it was shown that, although the mean difference was not significantly different from zero, except for the first futures contract (March, 1976), a sign test indicated that the number of times that the differences were significantly different from zero held for six of the seven futures contracts examined.

*Reprinted from *The Journal of Portfolio Management*, Vol. 5, (Winter 1979). Reprinted by permission of Institutional Investor Systems, Inc., publisher.

†The authors wish to acknowledge the assistance of Rosemarie Workman, without whose programming aid this work would not have been possible, and Jeanne Rickey of the Chicago Mercantile Exchange for providing data used on this paper. The views expressed here are those of the authors and do not necessarily reflect the views of the Treasury Department.

[1] D. Puglisi, "Is the Futures Market for Treasury Bills Efficient?", *Journal of Portfolio Management* (Winter, 1978), pp. 64-67.

The purpose of this comment is to show that the summary statistics reported by Puglisi are misleading and may be misinterpreted, that the Treasury bill futures market may be used to increase returns, and that the spot and futures markets must be evaluated for such purposes on a daily basis. The time series of the differences in returns from bills-only and bills-futures transactions clearly shows that, although the mean difference between these returns on average are small and their standard deviations large, there are distinct arbitrage returns from using the futures market. Moreover, these returns may be substantial on a given day, even though the mean return for all days of a particular contract is zero. These returns and the times series trends in these returns that may assist the portfolio manager in his use of the futures market become clearer when arbitrage returns are evaluated on a daily basis. Furthermore, our data show results substantially at odds with those reported by Puglisi, and we have found that, according to more recent data, the futures market has remained inefficient.[2]

Following the model developed by Puglisi, we have computed the annualized returns from a short-term bill that matures on the same date as the expiration of the futures contract, and the annualized return from a longer-term bill (one with three more months to maturity) that may be delivered against the short sale of the futures contract.[3] The annualized return from these two investments is given by equations 1 and 2, respectively.

$$R_S = \frac{D_s}{S} \times \frac{365}{N_s} \qquad (1)$$

$$R_L = \frac{F-L-T}{L} \times \frac{365}{N_s} \qquad (2)$$

where R_S = annualized return from a bills-only strategy, R_L = annualized return from a bills-futures strategy, D_s = discount on the short-term bill, S = price of the short-term bill, N_s = number of days to maturity, i.e., the number of days from the transaction date to the delivery date of the futures contract, F = price of the futures contract, as specified N_s days before delivery, L = price of the long-term bill, and T = minimum transaction costs on a futures contract ($60).[4]

[2] The market is assumed inefficient if there are arbitrage opportunities involving futures and outstanding Treasury bills.

[3] For the period three months prior to the contract delivery date, the outstanding spot market bills have the exact maturity date as the futures contract expiration and the maturity of the deliverable bill. For periods when the corresponding bills do not exist, the nearest one-year bill is used as an approximation.

[4] It is noteworthy to realize that, while we only consider the alternative for the short seller of the futures contract, symmetrical results hold for the buyer of a futures contract. That is, when the short-term investor increases his returns from buying a longer-term bill and selling a

Is the Futures Market for Treasury Bills Efficient?

The source of our spot market data is the Federal Reserve Bank of New York, which compiles composite quotes on all Treasury securities. The Chicago Mercantile Exchange provided futures market quotes. Daily settlement prices for futures contracts and closing bid and ask prices for spot market Treasury bills were used. We report results for bid and ask spot prices, because there are different conclusions depending on which prices are used and they confirm our findings that the market has remained inefficient. Furthermore, it has been conjectured that the Treasury bill market is a dealer dominated market, indicating that the bid side quotes for the spot market should determine the trading price. We offer no conclusion on this conjecture. However, the results using bid and ask prices are different enough to warrant reporting both results. On one half of the eight contracts evaluated, the spread is enough to change the sign of the arbitrage profits.

Tables 1 and 2 report our results for ask and bid spot prices, respectively. For each contract, the daily return from each investment strategy is computed for approximately nine months using the six-month bill for the last 91 days of the contract and the nearest one-year bill for all other days. Row 1 of each table gives the mean returns from an outright bill purchase (equation 1), and row 2 gives the mean returns from a bill purchase in combination with a futures market short sale (equation 2). Row 3 is the bills-only return minus the bills-future return. The table also gives the standard errors for each of these returns, along with the number of observations used for each contract and the results of a sign test.

Our results show that there were positive arbitrage profits from the covered short sale of a futures contract on only one contract out of the first eight, the December, 1977 contract, when using ask spot market prices. These results differ substantially from Puglisi's findings that there were positive returns from the March, June, December, 1976 and the June, 1977 contracts. Our findings indicate that positive arbitrage profits accrued to the long purchase of a futures contract on the first seven contracts. Using bid spot prices, there were positive arbitrage gains on the short of the futures market on five of the eight contracts. However, these conclusions are misleading, since the "t" statistics for all eight contracts indicate that none of the mean differences using bid or ask prices is significantly different from zero at any acceptable level of confidence.

We have also computed sign tests on the number of times that the returns from the bills-only strategy were less than the returns on the

---

futures contract, rather than purchasing the short-term bill outright, the long-term investor decreases his return by buying a short-term bill in combination with the purchase of a future market bill rather than buying the longer-term bill outright. The dollar amounts of gain or loss from these transactions are equal, but opposite in sign. The annualized returns, however, differ.

Table 1 Mean Returns from Bills-Only (R1) and Bills-Futures Strategies (R2) Ask Spot Market Prices Contracts

	Mar. 1976	June 1976	Sept. 1976	Dec. 1976	Mar. 1977	June 1977	Sept. 1977	Dec. 1977
R1	4.576%	4.994%	5.316%	5.335%	5.155%	4.863%	5.135%	5.608%
SD(R1)	(.142)	(.212)	(.283)	(.550)	(.676)	(.318)	(.229)	(.292)
R2	4.402%	4.940%	5.166%	5.274%	5.043%	4.813%	4.971%	5.714%
SD(R2)	(.540)	(.468)	(.270)	(.578)	(.666)	(.342)	(.408)	(.497)
R3	+.174%	+.054%	+.150%	+.061%	+.112%	+.048%	+.164%	−.106%
SD(R3)	(.489)	(.459)	(.213)	(.254)	(.191)	(.226)	(.437)	(.294)
t (R3)	0.356	0.118	0.704	0.240	0.586	0.212	0.375	0.361
N	48	113	175	198	200	191	197	184
N(R1) < N(R2)	20	67	73*	81*	45**	63**	47**	106*

R1 is annualized return from bills-only strategy, R2 is annualized return from bills-futures strategy, R3 is R1 less R2, SD is standard deviation, t is t-statistic, N is the number of observations, N(R1) < N(R2) is number of times bills-only strategy returned less than bills-futures strategy, MAE is mean absolute error, *significant at the $a = 0.01$, and **significant at the $a = 0.05$.

118

Table 2 Mean Returns from Bills-Only (R1) and Bills-Futures Strategies (R2) Bid Spot Market Prices Contracts

	Mar. 1976	June 1976	Sept. 1976	Dec. 1976	Mar. 1977	June 1977	Sept. 1977	Dec. 1977
R1	4.866%	5.197%	5.452%	5.452%	5.265%	5.005%	5.260%	5.730%
SD (R1)	(.157)	(.235)	(.265)	(.550)	(.664)	(.319)	(.310)	(.318)
R2	5.078%	5.410%	5.431%	5.490%	5.244%	5.015%	5.189%	5.907%
SD (R2)	(.262)	(.474)	(.231)	(.405)	(.535)	(.341)	(.376)	(.554)
R3	−.212%	−.217%	+.021%	−.037%	+.022	−.010	+.071	−.177
SD (R3)	(.184)	(.329)	(.161)	(.220)	(.179)	(.187)	(.186)	(.283)
t (R3)	1.512	0.660	0.160	0.1681	0.123	0.053	0.382	0.625
N	48	113	175	198	200	191	197	184
N(R1) < N(R2)	44**	102**	82	112	98	83	63**	123**

R1 is annualized return from bills-only strategy, R2 is annualized return from bills-futures strategy, R3 is R1 less R2, SD is standard deviation, t is t-statistic, N is the number of observations, N(R1) < N(R2) is number of times bills-only strategy returned less than bills-futures strategy, MAE is mean absolute error, *significant at the $a = 0.01$, and **significant at the $a = 0.05$.

bills-futures strategy. The sign tests indicate that the difference in returns was significantly different from zero at the .05 level of significance, or better, for six of the eight contracts on the ask side and for four contracts on the bid side. Our sign test results also differ from those reported by Puglisi. The sign tests indicate that the market has remained inefficient and that the arbitrage returns on Treasury bill futures has been increasing, not decreasing, This is further confirmed by the fact that the last two contracts analyzed, the September and December, 1977 contracts, are the only ones where the bid-ask spread does not change the sign of arbitrage returns and the sign tests are significant at the .01 level of confidence for both bid and ask spot market prices.

Our major concern is not that our results differ from those reported by Puglisi, since such differences may be because of our different data source, the use of different one-year bills, and the use of true bond yield equivalent rates. Instead, we are concerned that the distribution of the difference in returns from bills-only and bills-futures (R3) must be examined on a daily basis for the portfolio manager to assess adequately the profit possibilities or arbitrage. It is our conclusion that one can only obtain an adequate picture of the futures market by examining the distribution and time series properties of R3. For this reason, we have provided charts of the arbitrage returns for each contract.

The charts show the bills-futures returns minus the bills-only returns for each contract. The horizontal axis represents the number of days to the delivery of the futures contract, with time moving from the right to the left. Each chart begins roughly nine months prior to the contract delivery date. It should be recalled that, while positive numbers on these charts represent gains from arbitrage to the seller of a futures contract, the opposite is true for the purchaser of a futures contract. The charts clearly indicate that summary statistics are misleading and that there are time series trends in arbitrage returns. We have examined this trend and found that there is significant autocorrelation in arbitrage returns for each contract, confirming that the futures market is inefficient, not only in an arbitrage sense but also in the sense that the arbitrage returns are not distributed randomly over time.[5]

The time series of differences in returns for each contract present a more revealing overview of arbitrage and inefficiency in the Treasury bill futures market. Moreover, there is a great deal of similarity in the

---

[5] It is not our purpose to pass judgment on the appropriate test for market inefficiency, but to replicate and update the work of Puglisi. Others, however, have indicated that the sign test and the existence of autocorrelation are not strong enough tests to conclude that market inefficiency exists. See E. Fama, "Efficient Capital Markets: A Review of Theory and Empirical Work," *Journal of Finance* (May, 1970), pp. 383-420, and W. Cornell and J. Dietrick, "The Efficiency of the Market for Foreign Exchange Under Floating Exchange Rates," *Review of Economics and Statistics* (February, 1978), pp. 111-120.

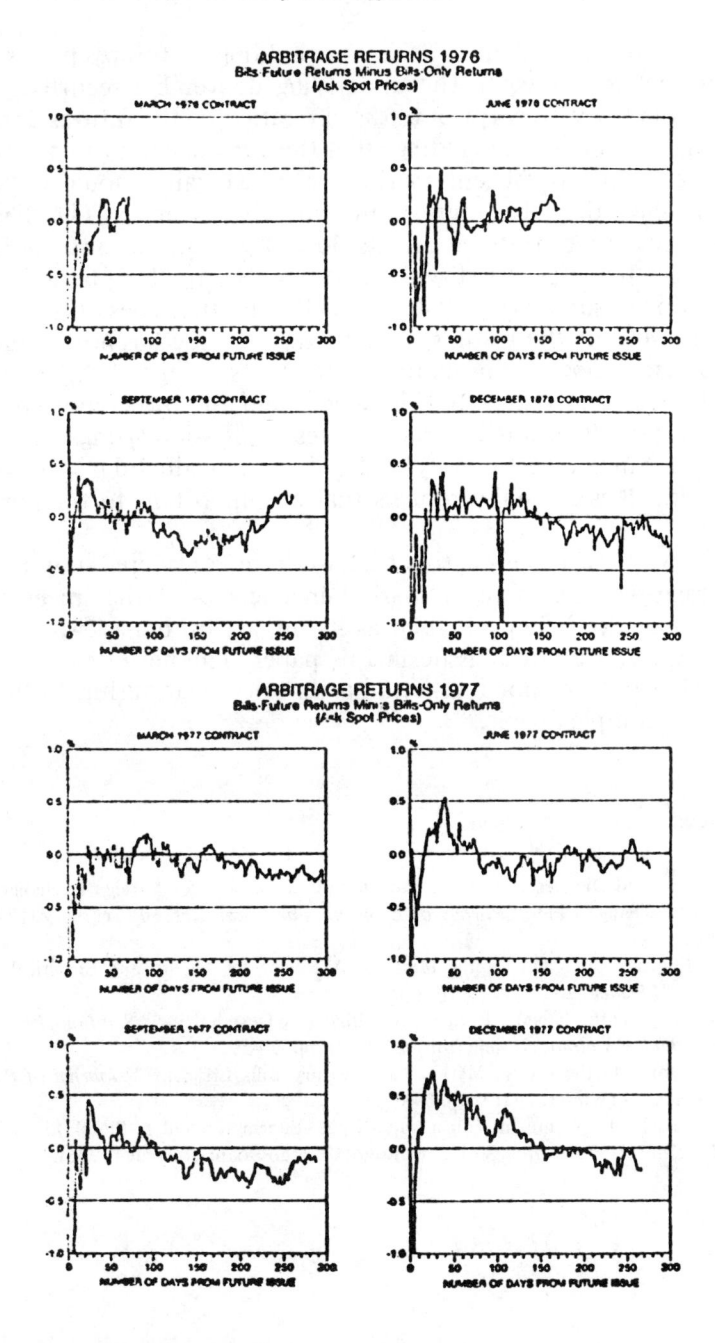

Is the Futures Market for Treasury Bills Efficient?

ARBITRAGE RETURNS 1976
Bills-Future Returns Minus Bills-Only Returns
(Ask Spot Prices)

ARBITRAGE RETURNS 1977
Bills-Future Returns Minus Bills-Only Returns
(Ask Spot Prices)

trend of these differences in all contracts since September, 1976. For the June, September, and December, 1977 contracts, in particular, there is an upward trend in arbitrage returns for the short seller. Such a situation implies that, for the more recent contracts, there has been an excess demand for futures contracts, bidding up futures prices, especially in the period when the underlying deliverable security is outstanding, roughly 91 days prior to the expiration of the futures contract.

The charts support the findings that the Treasury bill-futures market is inefficient. In an efficient market, arbitrage gains should rarely appear and when they do, they should quickly disappear. The diagrams not only show that arbitrage profits do not vanish, but also show that discrepancies tend to persist with the same sign for long periods. They refute, as do our summary statistics, that the inefficiencies only occurred early in the life of the futures market. Inefficiency has not diminished with the maturation of this market. The charts point out the reason for the small mean differences and the large standard errors reported in our results. The small means are the net result of wide swings above and below zero. Since investors buy and sell on individual days, not at the mean return, it is the daily returns that are important to the portfolio manager.

Finally we wish to emphasize that we have considered only the case of arbitrage as a measure of market inefficiency. Other measures of the futures market's impact, such as its impact on bid-ask spreads and price volatility, are not at issue in this paper. The net effect of the futures market on the spot market, and its price relationship to the spot market, is a complex topic.[6]

References

1. Cornell, W. and Dietrich, J., "The Efficiency of the Market for Foreign Exchange Under Floating Exchange Rates," *Review of Economics and Statistics*, 60 (February, 1978), pp. 111-120.
2. Fama, Eugene, "Efficient Capital Markets: A Review of Theory and Empirical Work," *Journal of Finance*, 25 (May, 1970), pp. 383-420.
3. Froewiss, Kenneth, "GNMA Futures: Stabilizing or Destabilizing," *San Francisco Federal Reserve Bank Economic Review* (Spring, 1978), pp. 20-29.
4. Puglisi, Don, "Is the Future Market for Treasury Bills Efficient?", *Journal of Portfolio Management*, 4 (Winter, 1978), pp. 64-67.
5. Sandor, Richard, "Comment (on a paper by L. Ederington and L. Plumly)," in *Futures Trading Seminar Proceeding*, Vol. 5, Chicago; Chicago Board of Trade (1976).

---

[6] See R. Sandor, "Comment (on a paper by L. Ederington and L. Plumly)," in *Futures Trading Seminar Proceedings* (1976), pp. 102-104, and K. Froewiss, "GNMA Futures: Stabilizing or Destabilizing," *San Francisco Federal Reserve Bank Economic Review* (Spring, 1978), pp. 20-29.

8

A Comparison of Yields on Futures Contracts and Implied Forward Rates*

Richard W. Lang and Robert H. Rasche

Since the introduction of futures trading in 3-month Treasury bills in 1976, yields on these futures contracts have been examined for clues as to market expectations of the future course of interest rates. Although there are difficulties in isolating these expectations, the yields on futures contracts do embody information about market expectations of future interest rates.[1] However, similar information is also embodied in the forward rates of interest that are implicit in the spot market yield curve.

Yields on Treasury bill futures contracts (futures rates) are essentially the market counterpart to the implied forward rates embodied in the Treasury yield curve. The correspondence between yields on financial futures contracts and forward rates derived from a yield curve is readily apparent in the work of Sir John Hicks. Hicks interpreted the term structure of interest rates as a futures market for loans in formulating his theory about the relationship of long- and short-term interest rates.[2] To the extent that futures rates and forward rates represent the yield on the same type of loan contract, market traders will arbitrage be-

---

*Reprinted from the Federal Reserve Bank of St. Louis *Review*, (December 1978). Reprinted by permission of the publisher.

[1] For a discussion of these difficulties, see Albert E. Burger, Richard W. Lang and Robert H. Rasche, "The Treasury Bill Futures Market and Market Expectations of Interest Rates," this *Review* (June 1977), pp. 2-9.

[2] J. R. Hicks, *Value and Capital: An Inquiry into Some Fundamental Principles of Economic Theory*. 2nd ed. (Oxford: Clarendon Press, 1946), pp. 144-47.

tween yields in the futures markets and yields in the spot market (from which implied forward rates are derived) if profitable trading opportunities exist. In this case, it would not be surprising to find yields on Treasury bill futures contracts to be closely related to implied forward rates embodied in the Treasury yield curve. This paper compares yields on 3-month Treasury bill futures contracts with forward rates derived from spot yields on Treasury securities, for comparable periods, to examine how closely these interest rates are related. Specifically, this paper tests the hypothesis that futures rates are equal to implied forward rates, and finds that this hypothesis must be rejected. Various explanations as to why the rates are not equal are then examined.

Recently, William Poole and others have argued that the yields on 3-month Treasury bill futures contracts can be expected to be less than the corresponding implied forward rates, that these futures rates are unbiased market estimates of future Treasury bill spot rates, and that it is not necessary to allow for risk premia when using yields on futures contracts to measure market expectations of future interest rates.[3] If these arguments are correct, a great deal of empirical work in economics that includes variables on interest rate expectations will be greatly simplified. In addition, such conclusions would allow policymakers to easily assess the differences between their own interest rate forecasts and the market's expectations of the future course of interest rates. As Poole notes, policymakers face difficult problems when market interest rate forecasts differ from the policymakers' forecasts, since they then must decide whether their own estimates of economic activity are incorrect or whether the market is misinterpreting the policymakers' plans.[4] Unfortunately, the results reported in this paper do not support these conclusions about the relationship between futures rates and forward rates for futures contracts, except for the ones closest to delivery, which were the ones investigated by Poole. Extrapolation of Poole's conclusions to other futures contracts is therefore unwarranted, and other explanations for the relationship between forward and futures rates must be explored. One factor considered here is the possibility of default risk affecting yields on futures contracts.

EXPECTATIONS OF INTEREST RATES AND FORWARD RATES

Expectations of future interest rates play an important role in many areas of economics; topics in both micro- and macroeconomics deal

---

[3] William Poole, "Using T-Bill Futures to Gauge Interest-Rate Expectations," Federal Reserve Bank of San Francisco *Economic Review* (Spring 1978), pp. 7, 14 and 15; and Kenneth Froewiss and Michael Gorham, "Everyman's Interest Rate Forecast," Federal Reserve Bank of San Francisco *Weekly Letter* (September 8, 1978), p. 1.

[4] Poole, "Using T-Bill Futures to Gauge Interest-Rate Expectations," pp. 16-17.

with interest rate expectations. Since such expectational variables generally are not observable, researchers have only been able to proxy them by using various substitutes, such as by constructing expectational variables on the basis of the past history of each variable. This approach is problematical in that when such expectational proxies are used in empirical research, a joint test is made: both the hypothesis and the assumed expectations-formation mechanism are tested.

One alternative to such joint tests is to survey a specific group (such as financial consultants) as to their expectations of interest rates for various future periods. Such a survey has been reported since 1969 in the Goldsmith and Nagan *Bond and Money Market Letter*.[5] However, such surveys are subject to problems that may limit their usefulness. One problem is basically statistical, but another deals with the *timing* of the survey. The Goldsmith-Nagan survey is quarterly, which makes its use for shorter periods very difficult.

An alternative approach that allows the use of daily data focuses upon *changes* in interest rate expectations rather than *levels*, and is based upon changes in the shape of the yield curve from one date to another. A yield curve relates the yields-to-maturity of a group of securities to their terms-to-maturity, for securities with similar characteristics other than maturity. In particular, all of the securities used in constructing a yield curve have similar default risk. For example, yield curves are usually drawn for Treasury securities, or for corporate Aaa bonds, as of a particular date. The yield curve indicates the structure of interest rates on a given date for securities with the same risk of default and different terms-to-maturity.

Changes in the shape of the yield curve from one date to another involve changes in implied forward rates. A forward rate is the yield on a loan or investment over some period beginning at a specified future time. Such a forward rate can be obtained by an appropriate combination of buying and selling bonds outstanding. For example, by selling a 1-year bond and buying a 2-year bond, a 1-year investment is effectively made that will begin 1 year hence at a rate of interest established by the difference in the spot market yields for the 1- and 2-year bonds. The forward rate on this loan is defined by:

$$(1+{}_1F_1) = \frac{(1+R_2)^2}{(1+R_1)^1}$$

where ${}_1F_1$ is the forward rate on a 1-year loan to begin in 1 year, R_2 is the spot rate on 2-year bonds, and R_1 is the spot rate on 1-year bonds. More generally, for a 1-period investment to begin n−1 periods in the

---

[5] Other interest rate surveys have been collected by various researchers, but are not regularly published. For example, see Edward J. Kane and Burton G. Malkiel, "The Term Structure of Interest Rates: An Analysis of a Survey of Interest-Rate Expectations," *The Review of Economics and Statistics* (August 1967), pp. 343-55.

future the forward rate is:

$$(1+_{n-1}F_1) = \frac{(1+R_n)^n}{(1+R_{n-1})^{n-1}}$$

where $_{n-1}F_1$ is the forward rate on a 1-period loan to begin in n−1 periods. R_n is the spot rate on n-period bonds, and R_{n-1} is the spot rate on (n−1)-period bonds. Thus, the yield curve at any given point in time implies a set of 1-period forward rates to prevail on forward (or future) transactions. Such forward rates have economic content, however, only if the implied transactions are possible in the market, and can be carried out by market traders.[6]

In theories of the term structure of interest rates, the forward rates ($_{n-1}F_1$) are often decomposed into a 1-period expected rate ($_{n-1}E_1$) plus a premium (a liquidity premium associated with interest-rate risk or a term premium associated with investors' preferences for bonds with specific ranges of maturities).[7]

$$_{n-1}F_1 = {_{n-1}E_1} + \text{Premium}$$

For a set of 1-period forward rates on a given date, there is then a set of 1-period expected rates stretching out into the future. Under the assumption that the premia are stable over time, changes in the structure of interest rates (measured by changes in the yield curve) reflect changes in interest rate expectations. Thus, by examining the changes in the implied forward rates contained in the term structure, researchers can obtain an estimate of the *changes* in interest rate expectations, even though the *level* of expected interest rates is not readily estimable.

However, such calculations are time consuming and costly—in terms of both data collection and computer time. One must obtain quotations on securities outstanding (e.g. Treasury issues), fill in missing data points by estimating a yield curve, then calculate forward rates. This is a difficult task if done monthly, and expensive to do weekly or daily. As a result, it is expensive to use yield curve data to assess the effect of new information about economic policies or of the state of the economy on expectations of future interest rates.

---

[6] For a thorough discussion of yield curves, forward rates of interest, and the term structure, see Burton Gordon Malkiel, *The Term Structure of Interest Rates: Expectations and Behavior Patterns* (Princeton: Princeton University Press, 1966), Chapters I and II.

[7] Malkiel, p. 26; Franco Modigliani and Richard Sutch, "Debt Management and the Term Structure of Interest Rates," *Journal of Political Economy* (Supplement: August 1967), pp. 571-73; Charles R. Nelson, *The Term Structure of Interest Rates* (New York: Basic Books, 1972) pp. 20 and 28-31.

FUTURES MARKETS IN FINANCIAL INSTRUMENTS

Starting in the fall of 1975, the difficulties of examining changes in market expectations of future interest rates on a weekly or daily basis have been alleviated. Trading in futures contracts in financial instruments began to develop in late 1975, and currently there are futures markets in seven financial instruments.[8] This paper focuses on the futures market in 3-month Treasury bills.

Futures markets in 3-month Treasury bills allow us to observe directly the yields or prices on 3-month bills to be delivered at certain dates in the future. Thus, they are the market counterpart of the implied forward loans or investments which can be constructed from Treasury yield curve data. But instead of requiring large efforts at data collection, estimation, and calculation, these yields are readily available from daily quotations in *The Wall Street Journal* and other newspapers.

As new information about the economy or economic policy becomes available to market traders, this information is incorporated into the market prices and yields of Treasury bill futures contracts. To the extent that such new information changes market expectations of interest rates, it is reflected in changes in the Treasury bill futures rates. Yields on futures contracts could also be broken down into expectational and premium components, just as in the case of forward rates implicit in the yield curve. Again, the *level* of expected future interest rates may not be readily estimable, but *changes* in market expectations of future interest rates can be observed from changes in yields on futures contracts, under the assumption that the premia are stable.[9]

YIELDS ON FUTURES CONTRACTS AND IMPLIED FORWARD RATES FROM YIELD CURVES

Since implied forward rates calculated from the yield curve are, in theory, rates on forward loans or investments such as those actually made in the Treasury bill futures market, the question arises as to whether yields on 3-month Treasury bill futures contracts are equal to

---

[8] Currently there are futures markets in 3-month and 1-year Treasury bills, 15-year Treasury bonds, 3-month commercial paper, and three GNMA instruments. A number of other futures markets in other financial instruments have also been proposed.

[9] Burger, Lang, and Rasche, "The Treasury Bill Futures Market and Market Expectations of Interest Rates," pp. 4-5.

3-month forward rates calculated from the Treasury yield curve. It would be convenient if the two sets of yields were equal, so that we would not have to be concerned with any separate informational content of either data set (especially since yields on Treasury bill futures are easier to obtain).

A test for the equality of the two yields, as of a quotation date, can be made by comparing yields on Treasury bill futures contracts with yields on implied forward contracts for the same periods. First, we choose a set of quotation dates. Then, we obtain the yields on Treasury bill futures contracts on those dates for each available delivery date. Next, we obtain quotations on U.S. Treasury securities outstanding on those same quotation dates. From these data we calculate implied 3-month forward rates that match the 3-month Treasury bill futures contracts. Finally, we calculate the difference (in absolute value) between the two sets of rates to determine whether they are significantly different from each other.

The Data

The selection of quotation dates for yields on Treasury bill futures contracts and yields on outstanding Treasury securities were obtained by random selections of thirty quotation dates from each of three periods of roughly equal length—eight to nine months.[10] The first thirty quotation dates were taken from the period March 1, 1976 to November 30, 1976 (Period I); the second thirty quotation dates were taken from the period December 1, 1976 to July 31, 1977 (Period II); and the last thirty quotation dates were taken from the period August 1, 1977 to March 31, 1978 (Period III). Yields on the available futures contracts for each quotation date were based on the settlement prices obtained from the "Daily Information Bulletin" of the International Monetary Market of the Chicago Mercantile Exchange. Yields on outstanding U.S. Treasury securities used to construct forward rates for each quotation date were obtained from the Federal Reserve Bank of New York's "Composite Closing Quotations for U.S. Government Securities." All yields were converted from a discount basis to a bond equivalent yield basis.

Forward rates were calculated for each quotation date to match up with each available Treasury bill futures contract. Thus, if a futures contract were to be delivered in 30 days, at which time the delivered Treasury bills would have 90 days to maturity, a forward rate was calculated using the yields on an outstanding Treasury bill maturing in

---

[10] The random numbers were obtained from The Rand Corporation, *A Million Random Digits with 100,000 Normal Deviates* (Glencoe, Illinois: The Free Press, 1955).

30 days and an outstanding Treasury bill maturing in 120 days. If no bills were outstanding with the exact number of days to maturity, say 120, then the yield was estimated by linearly interpolating from the yields on two securities with maturities surrounding 120 days—say one with 130 days and one with 115 days. The resulting forward rate is the implied yield on a loan or "security" that begins in 30 days and has 90 days to maturity—the same time frame as the futures contract.[11]

Once the forward rates matching the available futures contracts were calculated for each quotation date, they were compared to the yields on the futures contracts (futures rates) by taking the absolute difference between the two. For each quotation date, these differences were categorized as being associated with the futures contract nearest-to-delivery (Category 1), next nearest-to-delivery (Category 2), and so on. All the available contracts for each quotation date were categorized in this way. When the market was first formed in 1976, only four contracts were traded, extending out one year into the future. As trading in Treasury bill futures has increased, the number of contracts has been extended. By March 1978, the end of the third sample, there were eight contracts traded, extending out two years into the future. Consequently, the number of observations in Categories 4 through 8 are not always equal to 30 for each sample, and the first sample does not have as many categories as the last two samples.

Results

Summary statistics for the futures rates minus the associated forward rates are given in Table I for each category in each sample period. The mean of the absolute value of the differences between the rates are given for each category, as well as the standard deviation and the number of observations. For each category in each sample, the hypothesis that the futures rate is equal to the associated forward rate was tested by determining whether the mean absolute difference in each category is signi-

---

[11] Spot rates used to calculate forward rates were the average of the bid and asked yields in the spot market. For futures contracts to be delivered more than one year in the future, yields on Treasury coupon securities were used (since Treasury bills are not available) to calculate the forward rates. (This introduces a slight measurement error in the calculation of the forward rates since the formulae given below and in the text assume that the spot rates used are for non-coupon securities.) The formula used to calculate the forward rates is that given by Richard Roll, *The Behavior of Interest Rates: An Application of the Efficient Market Model to U.S. Treasury Bills* (New York: Basic Books, Inc., 1970), p. 16:

$$_{n-91}F_{91} = \frac{nR_n - (n-91)R_{n-91}}{91}$$

A comparison of the above formula's estimates of forward rates with estimates based on the traditional formula given in the text showed only minor differences. Consequently, the above formula was used for computational ease.

Table I

Summary Statistics for Absolute
Differences: Futures Rates Less Forward Rates

	Categories[1]							
	1	2	3	4	5	6	7	8
Period I (3/1/76 - 11/30/76)								
Mean, $\bar{X}$	0.13	0.16	0.35	0.58	0.58	0.51		
Standard Deviation, S	0.11	0.12	0.21	0.34	0.45	0.31		
Number of Observations, N	30	30	30	29	23	11		
t-statistic[2]	6.47	7.30	9.13	9.19	6.18	5.46		
Period II (12/1/76 - 7/31/77)								
Mean, $\bar{X}$	0.09	0.14	0.34	0.37	0.63	0.88	0.97	1.43
Standard Deviation, S	0.06	0.11	0.20	0.26	0.35	0.34	0.26	0.44
Number of Observations, N	30	30	30	30	30	29	12	12
t-statistic[2]	8.22	6.97	9.31	7.79	9.86	13.94	12.92	11.26
Period III (8/1/77 - 3/31/78)								
Mean, $\bar{X}$	0.19	0.26	0.16	0.34	0.48	0.56	0.55	1.01
Standard Deviation, S	0.13	0.15	0.11	0.22	0.29	0.27	0.31	0.36
Number of Observations, N	30	30	30	30	30	30	30	28
t-statistic[2]	8.01	9.49	7.97	8.46	9.07	11.36	9.72	14.85

[1]Category 1 includes futures rates for the futures contract closest-to-delivery; Category 2 includes futures rates for the futures contract next nearest-to-delivery; and so on.
[2]All t-statistics are significantly different from zero at the 1 percent level.

ficantly different from zero. The t-value for each test is also given in Table I.

The two futures contracts nearest to delivery (Categories 1 and 2) tended to have the smallest mean absolute differences between the futures and forward rates, while the contracts furthest from delivery tended to have the largest mean absolute differences. All of the mean absolute differences were significantly different from zero at the 1 percent level. Thus, although the mean absolute differences between the futures and forward rates for the two futures contracts closest to delivery (Categories 1 and 2) were generally less than 20 basis points, the hypothesis that the rates are equal is rejected in each sample.

Samples were taken from three different time periods in order to determine whether the differences between the futures and forward rates have narrowed over time. Such an observation would suggest that in its first year of trading the futures market might have been poorly developed, or "thin," in terms of the number of traders in the market and the availability of information about the market. We could then expect that as the volume of trading in this market increased and information about possible arbitrage opportunities between futures and spot markets was more effectively utilized, the differences between the futures and forward rates would decrease between the first and second samples, and would decrease further between the second and third samples.

Neither casual observation of the data in Table I nor statistical tests for significant differences across sample periods support the hypothesis that the differences between futures and forward rates have consistently narrowed over time. Table II presents the results of statistical tests to determine whether the mean absolute difference in each category of a sample was significantly different from the mean absolute difference in the same category in the other two samples.[12] The results shown in Table II do not present a consistent pattern over time.

For example, a comparison of the mean absolute differences between the first and second samples for Categories 1, 2, and 3 indicates that the means are not significantly different from each other at the 5 percent level. Thus, the slight declines in the mean absolute differences for the first three categories nearest to delivery between the first and second samples do not represent statistically significant differences in the rela-

---

[12] A t-test for the difference between two means generally requires the assumption that the variances of the two samples are equal. When this assumption cannot be made, one is faced with what has been called a "Behrens-Fisher problem." An approximation to the t-test due to Cochran that provides a solution is given in George W. Snedecor and William G. Cochran, *Statistical Methods*, 6th ed. (Ames, Iowa: Iowa State University Press, 1967), pp. 114-16. This method was used in calculating the t-values and their significance in Table II for the cases where an F-test of the equality of the variances of the samples being compared rejected the hypothesis of equality.

Table II

Test Values of Comparisons of Mean Absolute Differences Across Samples

Categories	I and II	II and III	I and III
1	−1.75[1]	3.83[1, 2]	1.93[3]
2	−0.67	3.53[1, 2]	2.85[2]
3	−0.19	−4.32[1, 2]	−4.39[1, 2]
4	−2.66[2]	−0.48	−3.21[1]
5	0.44	−1.81[3]	−0.93[1]
6	3.28[2]	−3.99[2]	0.47
7	—	−4.47[2]	—
8	—	−2.91[2]	—

[1] Indicates that critical value of the significance test was determined using Cochran's approximation to the Behrens-Fisher problem, see footnote 12 of text.
[2] Significantly different from zero at the 1 percent level.
[3] Significantly different from zero at the 5 percent level.

tionship of the futures and forward rates. On the other hand, the increases in the mean absolute differences between the second and third samples for the first two categories are statistically significant, as is the decrease for the third category.

On the basis of this evidence, we cannot conclude that the differences between the futures and forward rates have been narrowing consistently over time as the futures market for Treasury bills has become more developed. Other explanations for the statistically significant spreads between the futures and forward rates must be explored.

EXPLANATIONS OF THE DIFFERENTIAL

Given that there are significant differences between futures and forward rates that have not declined over time, the question arises as to whether or not these differences are systematic. If the differences are systematic, can we identify some factor or factors that would cause such systematic differences? A further issue is to re-examine the argument that market traders will arbitrage away differences between futures and forward rates. This argument was based on the assumption that a futures contract is essentially identical to an implied forward contract. If a futures contract is substantially different from an implied forward contract, then market traders will not necessarily drive futures rates to equality with forward rates. However, even if a futures contract is essentially identical to an implied forward contract, the existence of transactions costs in trading spot and future Treasury bills may provide few profitable arbitrage opportunities to traders. In this case, trading in spot and futures markets will not necessarily result in equalizing futures and forward rates.

To examine whether there are systematic differences between futures and forward rates, the mean arithmetic difference for each category in each sample period is given in Table III. The arithmetic differences are systematically negative in all periods for Category 1, zero or negative for Category 2, and systematically positive in all periods for Categories 3 through 8. With the exception of Category 2 in Periods I and II, all of the arithmetic differences are significantly different from zero. Thus, futures rates for contracts closest to delivery are generally lower than their associated forward rates, while futures rates for later-dated contracts are generally higher than their associated forward rates. Explanations of the spread between futures and forward rates must be able to account for both the spread itself and its change in sign as the delivery date is extended into the future.

Transactions Costs: Poole's Approach

In a recent article, William Poole hypothesizes that futures and forward rates should not be equal because of the effect of transactions costs on these yields.[13] He argues that transactions costs are basically zero for futures contracts but positive for trades in the spot market. Other factors affecting futures and forward rates (such as term or liquidity premia and interest rate expectations) are assumed to be about the same, while the effect of transactions costs would tend to increase forward rates. Consequently, Poole concludes that futures rates should be lower than forward rates.[14]

Poole obtains empirical support for his hypothesis by examining the futures contract closest to delivery (our Category I). He finds that the mean (arithmetic) difference between futures and forward rates is indeed negative, indicating that futures rates are lower than forward rates. The mean difference also tends to be significantly different from zero; a result consistent with that reported in our Table III.

In Poole's subsequent discussion of the policy implications of the Treasury bill futures market, he assumes that his findings apply to all futures maturities (i.e., all categories in Table III), not just to the contract closest to delivery.[15] This assumption is not supported by our

---
[13] Poole, "Using T-Bill Futures to Gauge Interest-Rate Expectations," pp. 7-19.
[14] Ibid., p. 14.
[15] Ibid., p. 15.

Table III

Summary Statistics for Arithmetic Differences: Futures Rates Less Forward Rates

	\multicolumn{8}{c}{Categories[1]}
	1	2	3	4	5	6	7	8
Period I (3/1/76 - 11/30/76)								
Mean, $\bar{X}$	−0.12	0.01	0.35	0.48	0.49	0.45		
Standard Deviation, S	0.12	0.21	0.22	0.48	0.55	0.40		
Number of Observations, N	30	30	30	29	23	11		
t-statistic[2]	−5.48	0.26[3]	8.71	5.39	4.27	3.73		
Period II (12/1/76 - 7/31/77)								
Mean, $\bar{X}$	−0.08	0.04	0.32	0.37	0.62	0.88	0.97	1.43
Standard Deviation, S	0.08	0.17	0.23	0.27	0.38	0.34	0.26	0.44
Number of Observations, N	30	30	30	30	30	29	12	12
t-statistic[2]	−5.48	1.29[3]	7.62	7.51	8.94	13.94	12.92	11.26
Period III (8/1/77 - 3/31/78)								
Mean, $\bar{X}$	−0.19	−0.23	0.08	0.33	0.47	0.56	0.52	1.01
Standard Deviation, S	0.13	0.19	0.18	0.24	0.31	0.27	0.37	0.36
Number of Observations, N	30	30	30	30	30	30	30	28
t-statistic[2]	−8.01	−6.63	2.43	7.53	8.30	11.36	7.70	14.85

[1] Category 1 includes futures rates for the futures contract closest-to-delivery; Category 2 includes futures rates for the futures contract next nearest-to-delivery, and so on.
[2] All t-statistics are significantly different from zero at the 1 percent level, except for those with footnote 3 references.
[3] Not significantly different from zero at the 5 percent level.

data. The results shown in Table III indicate that Poole's hypothesis holds only for Categories 1 and 2 (the two contracts closest to delivery). For the other contracts that are delivered further in the future, the futures rates are higher than the forward rates—contrary to Poole's hypothesis.

Poole seems to argue that futures rates are close to being equivalent to the market's expectations of future interest rates.

> Quotes on the nearest maturity in the bill futures market can, therefore, be interpreted for all practical purposes as the market's unbiased estimates of the future spot rates on 13-week bills.[16]
>
> If the findings in the previous section apply to all future maturities, then the differences between the futures rates and the realized spot rates over the last two years reflect genuine expectational errors rather than term premiums attached to the futures rates.[17]

The evidence presented here indicates that it is misleading to extrapolate from the evidence on the futures contract closest-to-delivery to the later-dated contracts. Futures rates on the later-dated contracts are generally 50 to 100 basis points higher than their associated forward rates, which suggests the existence of some substantial differences between the factors affecting the futures and forward rates.

A Digression—Arbitrage Opportunities

The relatively large and statistically significant differences in Table III between the futures and forward rates for the later-dated futures contracts raises the issue of whether substantial arbitrage opportunities exist for these contracts. Poole investigated this issue for the contract closest to delivery and found that few arbitrage opportunities exist.

Poole defined upper and lower critical points for profitable arbitrage for the futures rate given the spot yields, taking into account transactions costs. Values of the futures rates that lie between these upper and lower critical points indicate that profitable arbitrage opportunities do not exist. Poole calculated upper and lower arbitrage points using daily data between January 6, 1976 and June 23, 1977 for the contract closest to delivery. He found that profitable arbitrage opportunities rarely existed, and were small in magnitude when they did exist.

By converting Poole's formulae for the upper and lower arbitrage points to a bond equivalent yield basis (from his discount yield basis), we applied his approach to our three samples of data. In doing so, the

[16] Ibid.
[17] Ibid.

formulae are not exact since the transactions costs associated with arbitraging the futures contracts further from delivery are larger than for the contracts closest to delivery. This is because maturities for securities in the spot market do not exactly match up with the maturities associated with the futures contract. In addition, for futures contracts to be delivered more than one year out, yields on Treasury coupon securities were used to calculate forward rates (see footnote 11). Consequently, transactions costs associated with arbitraging the later-dated contracts would be higher than the ones used in Poole's formulae. This means that our adoption of Poole's formulae understates the upper arbitrage point, and overstates the lower arbitrage point. The spread between the upper and lower points is therefore understated, so that there may appear to be arbitrage opportunities which would not in fact be profitable if we took all the transactions costs into account.

Nevertheless, the application of Poole's formulae will at least indicate the extent of arbitrage opportunities using a conservative estimate of the transactions costs involved. For each category of contract in each sample period, Table IV shows the number of futures rates that are above the upper arbitrage point, below the lower arbitrage point, or within the upper and lower points. Table IV also shows the number of futures rates that are within or "close" to (defined as within .10 of) the upper or lower arbitrage points.

Aggregating over all three sample periods, the results for Categories 1 and 2 tend to support Poole's findings. Over 75 percent of the futures rates in Categories 1 and 2 are within, or "close" to, the upper and lower arbitrage points, taking all three periods as a whole. However, the percentage for Period III alone is considerably lower than for Periods I and II. Furthermore, the percentage tends to decline as the delivery date extends further into the future. For categories 6, 7, and 8 over all three sample periods, the number of futures rates within, or "close" to, the upper and lower arbitrage points are only 45, 36, and 5 percent, respectively. Of course, the calculation of the arbitrage points for these later-dated contracts are most likely to be subject to error since they are based on yields on Treasury coupon securities rather than Treasury bills, and since the spot maturities of the securities used do not match up exactly with the later-dated futures contracts. Nevertheless, there are still some puzzling features about the results.

First, when the futures rate falls outside the upper and lower arbitrage points for the two contracts closest to delivery (Categories 1 and 2), it is almost always *below* the lower arbitrage point. Futures rates for later-dated contracts, on the other hand, are almost always *above* the upper arbitrage point when they fall outside the upper and lower bounds. Second, when the futures rate is above the upper arbitrage point for the later-dated contracts, the difference between the futures rate and the upper bound ranges from less than 10 basis points to over 100 basis

Table IV
Futures Rates Relative to Arbitrage Points

	Category[1]							
	1	2	3	4	5	6	7	8
Period I (3/1/76 - 11/30/76)								
Number of Futures Rates:								
Below Lower Point	10	6	0	1	0	0		
Above Upper Point	0	1	19	18	12	5		
Within Points	20	23	11	10	11	6		
Within or "Close"[2]	28	27	18	11	13	8		
Number of Observations	30	30	30	29	23	11		
Period II (12/1/76 - 7/31/77)								
Number of Futures Rates:								
Below Lower Point	5	2	1	0	0	0	0	0
Above Upper Point	0	5	20	14	18	26	12	12
Within Points	25	23	9	16	12	3	0	0
Within or "Close"[2]	29	26	14	19	15	6	1	0
Number of Observations	30	30	30	30	30	29	12	12
Period III (8/1/77 - 3/31/78)								
Number of Futures Rates:								
Below Lower Point	21	17	4	0	0	0	0	0
Above Upper Point	0	0	5	8	12	15	17	27
Within Points	9	13	21	22	18	15	13	1
Within or "Close"[2]	17	17	28	23	22	18	14	2
Number of Observations	30	30	30	30	30	30	30	28

[1]Category 1 includes futures rates for the futures contract closest-to-delivery; Category 2 includes futures rates for the futures contract next nearest-to-delivery, and so on.

[2]Includes futures rates that are within the upper and lower arbitrage points as well as those that are "close" in that they are within .10 of the upper or lower points.

points (one full percentage point), and generally averages over 30 basis points in each category. Thus, unless the calculations of the upper arbitrage points for the later-dated contracts are substantially underestimated, it appears that systematic arbitrage opportunities frequently existed for the later-dated futures contracts during our sample periods.[18]

If profitable arbitrage opportunities exist but are not acted upon by market traders, then we should not expect futures and forward rates to

---

[18] That frequent arbitrage opportunities have existed in the futures market has also been argued in two other papers. See Donald J. Puglisi, "Is the Futures Market for Treasury Bills Efficient?" *The Journal of Portfolio Management* (Winter 1978), pp. 64-67; and Anthony J. Vignola and Charles J. Dale, "Is the Futures Market for Treasury Bills Efficient: A Comment," *The Journal of Portfolio Management* (Winter 1979), forthcoming.

be as closely related as we had earlier suggested, and we certainly should not expect them to be equalized. Such a situation could explain the results obtained earlier, that futures rates and forward rates are not equal. However, such a situation implies that there is a market inefficiency or failure present. Such inefficiency or failure could be due to lack of information about trading opportunities or to institutional constraints on trading. Since information about trading in futures markets is likely to improve over time, and since institutional constraints encourage innovations that reduce their effectiveness, such a situation of market inefficiency or failure will probably be reduced over time.

If transactions costs are substantially larger than those used here, it may be that profitable arbitrage opportunities rarely existed despite the large spreads between the futures and forward rates for the later-dated contracts. In this case, we again should not expect futures and forward rates to be as closely related as was earlier suggested. Given transactions costs, futures rates and forward rates may not be equalized.

However, Poole's argument based on transactions costs led him to conclude that futures rates should be lower than forward rates. Even though transactions costs might explain why futures rates and forward rates are not equalized, it is still puzzling that futures rates are substantially higher than their associated forward rates for the later-dated contracts, contrary to Poole's argument. This suggests that factors other than transactions costs may affect futures rates differently than forward rates, and we now turn to a consideration of these other factors.

Default Risk

Poole implicitly assumes that factors other than transactions costs have the same effects on both futures and forward rates. Thus, since transactions costs are expected to increase forward rates, and since transactions costs are close to zero for futures contracts, Poole concludes that futures rates will be less than their associated forward rates.[19] That this conclusion is not supported by evidence for the later-dated futures contracts suggests that there are other factors embodied in futures and forward rates that have effects *in the opposite direction* to the transaction-cost effect discussed by Poole. Furthermore, this effect is stronger for the later-dated futures contracts than for those close to delivery.

Both futures rates and forward rates can be broken down into expectational and premium components. Since one-period expectations of future interest rates should be the same in both rates, we must consider the premium components of these rates. The premium associated with a

---

[19] Poole, "Using T-Bill Futures to Gauge Interest-Rate Expectations," p. 14.

forward or futures rate is generally considered to be a liquidity premium associated with interest-rate risk, or a term premium associated with investors' maturity preferences.

For a liquidity premium embodied in a futures rate to be different from the liquidity premium embodied in a comparable forward rate implies that the interest-rate risk associated with the futures contract is different than that associated with the comparable implied forward contract. For futures rates to be higher than forward rates for the later-dated contracts as a result of differences in liquidity premia, a given rise in interest rates would have to generate a larger risk of capital loss in the futures contract than in the implied forward contract. It is not obvious why this would be the case.

For a term premium embodied in a futures rate to be different from the term premium embodied in a comparable forward rate implies that investors' maturity preferences vary both across maturities and across financial instruments. It is again not obvious why this would be the case.

One factor that has been ignored in the discussion of futures contracts is default risk. Treasury bills traded in the spot market are considered to be default free. Hence, implied forward rates would not embody premia related to default risk. However, a futures contract is not guaranteed by the U.S. Government, but is rather guaranteed by the exchange on which it is traded. Although the futures contract involves delivery of Treasury bills that are default free, the contract itself is not default free. Consequently, the futures rate may contain a risk premium associated with default risk.

This default risk factor would be more important for the futures contracts that are further from delivery, those for which Poole's hypothesis fails to be supported in our samples. The furthest-dated futures contracts involve delivery of Treasury bills which have not yet been issued; they do not exist. The possibility exists, although it may be small, that there would not be a sufficient amount of 3-month Treasury bills available to meet the deliveries required by the number of open futures contracts held for delivery. Although the Chicago Mercantile Exchange guarantees that a settlement would be made, at least a monetary settlement, the item promised for delivery (3-month Treasury bills) may not be delivered.[20]

This risk of default, or risk of non-delivery of the Treasury bills, would tend to make yields on the later-dated futures contracts higher than the yields on the two contracts closest to delivery (where Treasury bills that can be used for delivery have been issued), other things con-

---

[20] Defaults on futures contracts for commodities are rare, but result in quite an uproar when they do occur. A recent example was the May 1976 default on the delivery of Maine potato futures. Recently a bill was introduced in Congress that would ban all futures trading in potatoes.

stant. The results shown in Table III are consistent with this hypothesis. However, whether or not the size of the spreads between the futures and forward rates for the later-dated contracts can be accounted for solely by default risk is an open question.

SUMMARY AND CONCLUSIONS

Since yields on futures contracts are the market counterpart of implied forward rates of interest derived from the yield curve, the hypothesis that futures rates and forward rates are identical was tested using data from the Treasury bill futures market and the spot market for Treasury securities. The results indicate that futures rates are significantly different from the associated forward rates. Furthermore, the differences between the two rates have not narrowed consistently over time. Thus, it is difficult to attribute the significant differences between the two rates as being due to the initial "thinness" in the development of the Treasury bill futures market.

Poole's argument that the two rates should not be equal, but that the futures rate should be below the forward rate, was also examined. Poole's results were based on the effect of transactions costs on forward and futures rates, and were supported by evidence using the futures contract closest to delivery. Results from our samples for later-dated futures contracts do not support Poole's hypothesis. Instead, we find that the futures rates are consistently above the forward rates for the later-dated contracts. Thus, Poole's results on the contract closest-to-delivery should not be extrapolated to other futures contracts.[21]

An explanation which is consistent with the empirical results is that there is a default risk premium that affects and is embodied in the futures rates (since the futures contracts themselves are not obligations of the U.S. Government) but that does not affect the forward rates. The default risk would be greater for the later-dated contracts, which involve delivery of Treasury bills not yet issued, than for the contract closest to delivery, which Poole investigated. Although further testing and examination is required to fully explore the implications of the evidence given here, the consideration of the default risk of futures contracts should be a useful starting point.

The results of this study imply that we cannot interpret yields on later-dated 3-month Treasury bill futures contracts as the market's unbiased expectations of future spot rates on 3-month Treasury bills. Futures rates do not necessarily reflect the expected *level* of future

---

[21] Poole, "Using T-Bill Futures to Gauge Interest-Rate Expectations," p. 15.

interest rates. However, these results do not conflict with the proposition that *changes* in market expectations of future interest rates can be inferred from *changes* in futures rates.

The examination of interest rate expectations embodied in futures rates is therefore more complicated than Poole's results suggest. Furthermore, if default risk is a significant factor affecting futures rates, then estimates of term or liquidity premia in forward rates will not be comparable to the premia embodied in futures rates. This would make the estimation of the *levels* of expected future interest rates even more difficult. Consequently, policymakers who want to compare their own interest rate forecasts to the market's expectations should use caution in employing futures rates to measure market expectations.

9

Testing the Unbiased Expectations Theory of Interest Rates*

Ben Branch[†]

INTRODUCTION

Three different hypotheses have been advanced to explain the term structure of interest rates. The most intellectually appealing of the competing hypotheses is the unbiased expectations theory. According to the hypothesis the current term structure may be used to derive precisely the market's expectations of future short term rates. Thus any given long term rate is said to be equal to the market's expectation of a geometric average of the short term rates covering the same period.[1] That is, the yield on a one year security should be equal to the yield on a combination of a current six month security and the expected yield on

---

*Reprinted from *The Financial Review*, Vol. 13, pages 51-66, (Fall 1978). Reprinted by permission of the Eastern Finance Association, publisher. This paper is the 1978 EFA Competitive Paper Program winner.

[†]Associate Professor of Finance, University of Massachusetts. This research began as a project for the Instructional Seminar in Commodity Futures sponsored by the Chicago Board of Trade, July 11-22, 1977.

[1] More precisely stated, one plus the long rate is equal to the geometric average of one plus the average of the appropriate short rates:

$$(1 + R_n)^N = (1 + r_1)(1 + r_2)(1 + r_3)\ldots(1 + r_n)$$

where R_n = interest rate on long term security, n = number of periods to maturity of long term security, and r_i = expected short term interest rate for period i.

a six month security purchased six months hence. If the unbiased expectations model is correct, borrowers and lenders wishing to make a commitment of a particular length, should at the margin be indifferent between a single maturity transaction and a series of rolling maturities. Thus a borrower would for example expect equal financing costs from a single loan covering three years or borrowing the same amount for six months and then refinancing the loan each time it matures during the three year period.

The unbiased expectations hypothesis has two principal rivals: the liquidity premium and the segmented markets hypotheses. The unbiased expectations hypothesis depends on the existence of arbitrageurs who are indifferent between the terms of their lending or borrowing. If rates are out of line vis á vis expectations, the actions of these arbitrageurs are expected to drive them back into line. Under the liquidity premium model these arbitrageurs exist but have definite preferences which can only be overcome by offering a risk premium for non preferred maturities.[2] Lending long or borrowing short for long term needs are generally considered to be more risky to the prospective lenders and borrowers, than lending short or borrowing long for long term needs. Thus some sort of attractive ratio of long to short rates may be necessary to induce the marginal trader to shift to the non-preferred maturity commitment. This would lead to a divergence from unbiased expectations. More specifically the biased expectations or liquidity preference model predicts increasing risk premiums for longer term maturities. Thus the markets' actual expectations of future short term interest rates would be lower than those derived directly from the term structure.

The segmented markets hypothesis also rejects the notion of an indifferent arbitrageur assuming instead the borrowers and lenders have preferred habitats.[3] Thus most of the supply and demand for a particular maturity comes from potential borrowers and lenders who prefer that particular term. If the different maturity terms are largely separated with relatively little shifting between the various maturities, interest rates can diverge substantially from unbiased expectations. Thus the biased expectations and segmented markets hypotheses permit long rates to differ from the geometric average of the appropriate expected short rates. In the case of the biased expectations model, the term structure derived future short rate estimates are too high while the segmented markets hypothesis would permit divergence in either direction.

---

[2] P. Cagan, "A Study of Liquidity Premiums on Federal and Municipal Government Securities," *Essays on Interest Rates*, J. Guttentag and P. Cagan, editors, National Bureau of Economic Research, 1969, pp. 107-142.

[3] C. Campbell and R. Campbell, *An Introduction to Money and Banking*, Holt, Rinehart, and Winston, (New York 1972), pp. 49-50.

TESTING THE HYPOTHESES

Most of the empirical work to date has been unable to settle the controversy. The results are generally consistent with each of the three explanations for the term structure.[4] The basic problem with these earlier tests is that there was no accurate way to estimate the market's future interest expectations. Now, however, there may be. Since early 1976 there has been trading in interest rate futures. Both Treasury bill and mortgage futures have been traded since 1976.[5] Futures trading in long term U.S. bonds and commercial paper began in 1977. There are also plans to trade futures in other debt instruments.[6]

With these new interest rate futures contracts, it now appears to be possible to observe what a segment of the market anticipates for future interest rates. This paper reports on a study of the relations between the expected future short term rates derived from the term structure and that reflected in interest futures trading. The unbiased expectations hypothesis suggests that the two sets of rates should be equal. Because of imperfections in the data and methodology, we should not expect precise equality. If, however, the two sets of rates differ by more than the margin of error of the tests and particularly if there is a consistency to the direction of the difference, the results would conflict with the unbiased expectations hypothesis.

The liquidity premium hypothesis, would appear to imply that expected interest rate futures are lower than the corresponding term structure derived rates. This would be the case if we accept the assumption that the futures rates do accurately reflect market expectations while the term structure derived rates contain a risk premium. If on the other hand both rates are assumed to contain risk premiums, it may not be possible to determine which rate should be lower.

The segmented market hypothesis would allow either set of rates to be the higher one. In order to test these predictions, appropriate data need to be collected and analyzed.

Data

The future interest rate expectations for T bills may be derived directly from the futures quotes for such trading. To this end data were

---

[4] G. Kaufman, *Money the Financial System and the Economy*, Rand McNally, (Chicago 1973), pp. 167-170.
[5] A. Burger, R. Lang, and R. Rasche, "The Treasury Bill Futures Market and Market Expectations of Interest Rates," *Federal Reserve Bank of St. Louis Review*, (June 1977), pp. 2-9.
[6] The Chicago Board of Trade currently (July 1978) trades futures in GNMA mortgages, long term U.S. bonds and commercial paper while the Chicago Mercantile Exchange trades Treasury bill futures. There is talk of expanding the list to include municipals, long term corporates and intermediate term governments.

collected for the period from June 21, 1976 to July 3, 1978. During this period nine sets of three month futures contracts expired. The dates for data collection were chosen so as to obtain a quote just before and just after each of these contracts expired. This provided a total of eighteen observations.

There are three basic ways that the number of data points could have been expanded: collect earlier data, more frequent data for the time period covered or wait and gather more recent data as it is generated. The T bill futures market actually began on January 6, 1976, approximately six months prior to the first collected data point (June 21, 1976). No data were used from this initial period because at this time the market was still in its infancy. Most new markets require a period of testing before the more obvious inefficiencies are eliminated. It was felt that by not using the first half year of data, most of the shakedown-period anomalies would thereby be avoided.

Collecting data more often than twice every three months would have increased the amount of data but would not have increased the number of comparable data points. If data were collected at intervals more frequent than every three months, it would then be impossible to line the data up for relevant time series comparisons. That is since contracts expire only once every three months, a contract with exactly three months to run may be observed only once every three months. Clearly this is also true for six, nine, twelve month contracts and so on up to twenty-four month contracts. A month after such an observation is made all these securities are now two, five, eight, eleven and so on up to twenty-three month securities. Thus, they are no longer comparable to the original data. If, however, we wait an additional two months, a new set of data appears that is comparable to the original. Strictly speaking only nine data points are available over the June 21, 1976-July 3, 1978 period. By using data approximately ten days apart at each expiration point, the bulk of data points are essentially doubled. This permits us to observe the market as a contract is just about to expire and then again when a new contract has just begun trading and to observe all other contracts twice. With the collected data separated by ten days, enough time is allowed to elapse so that we may view the interest structure for the two separate time periods as essentially independent. On the other hand, the time that has elapsed is short enough so that we may view the two adjacent sets of data as having comparable maturities. Thus, for example, contracts with six months and contracts with six months and ten days are both treated as six months contracts for the purpose of this analysis.

Obtaining appropriate term structure interest quotes is a somewhat more complex task than the collection of interest futures quotes. T bills, the delivery vehicle, are not available for maturities longer than 12 months. And yet T bill futures are quoted for maturities as distant as

27 months (three month T bills delivered 24 months hence). Even within the relevant range for T bills, the appropriate delivery dates are not always quoted. That is a contract might call for delivery of T bills with a maturity of 6-29 while the nearest maturity that is currently traded may mature on 7-5. In such a case one may have to estimate what the appropriate rate would have been from the actual rate on nearby maturities.[7] Data were collected for T bill rates and tests run, but this provided at most, interest expectations for half of the traded futures contracts. To overcome this problem a longer maturity structure of debt instruments was needed.

The logical substitute for non traded longer term T bill rates are the rates on relatively short period Treasury notes. Such notes are similar to T bills in that they mature monthly, carry the same full faith and credit guarantee, are traded by the same government bond dealers and compete for the same general market. While they are not perfect substitutes, equivalent maturity U.S. notes and T bills do appear to bear very similar yields. The differences between them appear to be largely random.[8] Thus, even though U.S. notes are not substitutable for delivery in the contract specifications of T bill future contracts, they are considered close substitutes in the marketplace.

Methodology

With appropriately spaced interest rates on T bills or U.S. notes, one can derive the interest rate expectations implied by the unbiased expectations hypothesis. If, for example, one wishes the market's three month rate expectation for eighteen months hence, the first task is to

---

[7] There will of course ultimately be a 6-29 T bill but trading might not begin until 90 days prior to maturity. The futures contract on it, in contrast, may begin trading 27 months before maturity.

[8] There is a slight difference in the manner of how T bill and U.S. note yields are computed. The T bill yield is on a discount basis and a 360 day year while the notes are quoted on a semi-annual compound basis and a 365 day year. In this study, all discount rates are adjusted to the equivalent compound yield. First the actual issue price was determined from the quoted yield as follows:

$$\text{actual issue price} = \frac{100 - (\text{days to maturity} \times \text{T bill yield} \times 100)}{360}$$

Then the actual issue price and days to maturity was used to convert the T bill yield to the bond equivalent yield using the following formula.

$$\text{equivalent bond yield} = \frac{(\text{T bill face value} - \text{actual issued price}) \, 365}{\text{days to maturity}}$$
$$\overline{\text{actual issue price}}$$

These formulas were taken from: Chicago Mercantile Exchange, *T Bill Futures: Opportunities in Interest Rates* U.S.A., (February 1976), p. 31.

obtain the rates on the appropriate eighteen and twenty-one month debt securities. Next, the compound values of the two securities at maturity are computed. Then one determines that rate which, if earned for another three months on the eighteen month security's proceeds, would equal the compound value of the twenty-one month security.

Computations such as the one discussed above are relatively straightforward.[9] There are, however, some unavoidable errors in the process which should be borne in mind. In particular:

a. U.S. notes are a close but not perfect substitute for T bills.
b. Maturity dates on U.S. notes can be close but not precisely equal to that of the appropriate T bills.[10]
c. The reported yield on a debt security differs with respect to whether the price is considered the bid, asked, or an average.[11]
d. When the market price on a debt instrument differs from par, there are tax considerations. In particular below par issues offer a return which may be partially subject to tax preferred capital gains treatment. Above par issues, in contrast, have tax disadvantages relative to issues selling at or below par.
e. Quotations are not necessarily simultaneous. Futures rates may come from trades which take place either before or after those of the relevant debt securities.[12]
f. Rounding errors are possible at any stage of the computation.

Each of these imperfections can cause problems but none is likely to be of major proportions and most of the errors introduced should be random. For example the difference in maturity for the notes and ap-

---

[9] The basic procedure used was the following:

1) Find the compound values of the two relevant securities at their respective maturities.
2) Compute the ratio of these two compound values.
3) Determine the rate of return on that ratio which will make its present value equal one.

A computer program could easily have been written to make these same computations, but it was not necessary since the actual amount of time required for the hand computations was relatively modest.

[10] U.S. notes mature on the last day of the relevant month while T bills mature weekly on a Thursday (unless it is a holiday). Trading in a particular T bill future ends on the second business day following the T bill auction during the third week of the delivery month. Delivery is to be made on the day following the last day of trading. Acceptable delivery instruments are 90, 91 and 92 day T bills. In practice this means that the last maturing T bill of the appropriate month is usually the delivery instrument. Such a T bill can have a maturity differing by as much as three or four days from the nearest maturity U.S. note.

[11] Typically newspaper note quotations are based on the asked price while both the bid and asked prices are used to compute separate yields on T bills.

[12] The Chicago Mercantile Exchange permits trading during the hours of 8:35 and 1:35 Chicago time. The closing prices for a particular series, however, could conceivably be any time during the day. The *Wall Street Journal* bond quotes are taken at 3:30 New York time (2:30 Chicago time). Thus the two sets of quotes are usually at least an hour apart.

propriate bills are no more than a few days. Thus we might be substituting the rate on a 183 day security rather than a 181 day security. It is unlikely that the market could distinguish very much of difference between the appropriate interest rates on the two maturities. Similarly quoting the yield on the bid, asked or average are all acceptable as long as the same approach is used consistently. The future rate expectations are derived principally from the difference between the two rates rather than their level values *per se*. Whether one starts from a level which is a few basis points higher or lower matters little if the difference between the two levels are the same. To minimize the coupon effect notes were chosen selling closest to par when more than one maturity was listed in the same month. Because most notes in the relevant range (27 month or shorter maturity) generally trade close to par anyway (in almost every case the prices fall in the range of from 99 to 101), little or no coupon effect is likely to be present. It is true that the market is active and changing. The T bill and note quotes, however, are all derived from a very similar time frame. The timing of the futures quotes may vary somewhat but the differences are still unlikely to be more than a few hours (even for an inactively traded futures) and usually much less. Any such errors of timing should be essentially random. Computations were carried out to eight significant places to minimize rounding errors. The basic data (interest quotes), however, were only available to the nearest basis point. Thus rounding errors could lead to estimates which differed by a few basis points from what a precise estimate would have been.

All in all the methodology employed here should provide meaningful results. Random errors of perhaps five to ten basis points are certainly possible. Even these errors, however, should be reduced through the process of averaging several estimates. Random errors generally introduce a bias against finding statistically significant results. Thus if significant results are obtained, it would probably be in spite, not because of, the random errors.

RESULTS

One simple way of presenting the results from this analysis is to report the future interest rate estimates from both the futures market and the term structure. Table 1 reports the interest expectations both before and after delivery for the March 1977 cycle of expiration. Another eight such tables could have been presented. Only this one expiration cycle is included here as the others reveal a basically similar pattern. Unlike the traditional yield curve, this table does not report the yield to maturity but the interim expected three month yields for each of the relevant time periods. The futures yield is taken from the newspaper

Table 1 Interest Expectations Derived from Futures T Bills and Notes

Futures	T Bills	ΔT	Notes	ΔN
March 21, 1977				
M 4.69	4.62	.07	4.47	.22
J 5.33	5.44	−.11	5.29	.04
S 6.03	5.52	.51	5.99	.04
D 6.66			5.93	.72
M 7.17			6.57	.60
J 7.62			6.58	1.24
April 1, 1977				
J 5.26	5.13	.12	5.11	.15
S 6.01	5.54	.47	5.92	.09
D 6.68	5.64	1.04	5.88	.80
M 7.21			6.54	.67
J 7.69			6.60	1.09
S 8.05			6.52	1.54

quotations (adjusted from its quoted discount basis). The equivalent T bill and note yields were computed by the method described in footnote 9. The ΔT and ΔN columns report the difference between the futures expectations and the corresponding T bill and note expectations.

Looking at Table 1 one can easily make several observations. First, the future's, T bill's and U.S. note's term structures are related. At least for the period covered each market indicated that interest rates were expected to rise. Second, the delivery rates anchoring each structure are not very far from one another. That is the yield on three month T bills, notes and near delivery future contract's are always within a few basis points of one another. This reflects the well known tendency for futures contracts to move very close to the appropriate cash price as delivery approaches.[13] Emery and Scott obtained similar results using a somewhat difficult methodology and shorter time period.[14] Poole also found a close correspondence between the near maturity T bill and its equivalent contract.[15] Third, as the contract expiration period is length-

---

[13] R. Dahl and P. Henneberry, "Cash Futures Price Relationships," Station Bulletin 517-1977, Agricultural Experiment Station, University of Minnesota.

[14] Scott and Emery examined weekly data on a single interest futures contract (March 1977). Their data began in February 1976 and extended up to the expiration date. For this particular time series and contract they found a gap between the futures and term structure generated rates which narrowed over time. They did not, however, collect data on more than one contract or for prior periods longer than one year. S. Emery and R. Scott, "T Bill Futures and the Term Structure of Interest rates: A Means of Reconciling Market Forecasts and Values, Financial Assets," paper presented to April 1978 Eastern Finance Association meetings.

[15] W. Poole, "Using T Bill Futures to Gauge Interest-Rate Expectations," *Federal Reserve Bank of San Francisco Economic Review*, (Spring 1978), pp. 7-19.

ened, a substantial divergence is opened up between future rates and note derived futures rates. While the ΔN values for the June 1977 contract are less than twenty basis points, the June 1978 ΔN values exceed one hundred basis points. A similar pattern appears for most other dates.

While examples of divergent interest expectations such as those presented in Table 1 are interesting, a more systematic examination of these data is needed. Results of such an analysis are provided in Tables 2 and 3. Here the average gaps between the futures and term structure estimates are computed and tested to determine if they are significantly different from zero. That is the average of all ΔT's and ΔN's three months from expiration are averaged and these averages tested for significance. The same is done for each respective time period.

Looking at these tables and graphs one can easily observe the tendency of large gaps to narrow. With T bills for example the average gap narrows from 26.9 basis points nine months from the delivery month to -2.2 basis points a few days from contract expiration. Far more dramatic is the behavior of the gap for notes. The gaps for the three contracts nearest to delivery are all very close to zero indicating again the tendency for the spot and futures to move together when maturity is near. From nine months prior to delivery on the average gaps begin to widen from about 35 basis points all the way to over 100 basis points. All of these gaps are significantly different from zero at the 99% level. Clearly the futures market and the cash market produce rather different interest figures.

While these results are quite dramatic, one might well wonder if the phenomena of the positive gaps is something that is likely to persist over time. It might for example be that the positive gaps tended to be large in the earlier period (when the market was new) and much smaller later (as the market began to recognize its prior inefficiencies). Even though the data points are relatively limited, it is possible to make some

Table 2 Behavior of T Bill Gaps Over Time

	Average value of gap	Standard error of mean	t ratio	DF
Delivery in zero months	−.0222	.0183	1.21	8
3 months	−.1050**	.0571	1.84	17
6 months	.0517	.0761	.68	17
9 months	.2592**	.1155	2.24	11

*Significant at 90% level
**Significant at 95% level
***Significant at 99% level

Table 3 Behavior of Note Gaps Over Time

Delivery in	Mean value of gap	Standard error of the mean	t ratios	DF
zero months	.0211	.084	.25	8
3 months	−.1178**	.058	2.03	17
6 months	−.0183	.039	.47	17
9 months	.3589***	.067	5.38	17
12 months	.2850***	.074	3.90	17
15 months	.6906***	.121	5.72	16
18 months	.5507***	.138	4.01	13
21 months	.9833***	.151	6.52	8
24 months	1.1425***	.184	6.23	3

*Significant at 90% level
**Significant at 95% level
***Significant at 99% level

meaningful comparisons by splitting the sample into two time periods, at least for the three month to the fifteen month deliveries. In each of these cases we have eighteen (or in one case seventeen) observations so our data splitting still leaves us with nine (in one case eight) observations. With the data thus stratified the same basic tests run in Tables 2 and 3 were rerun and reported in Table 4.

Table 4 rather effectively dispels this notion that the gap has narrowed significantly over the period of study. As with the entire sample the two stratified three and six-month-from-delivery contract mean gaps are close to zero. For the nine, twelve and fifteen-months-from-delivery gaps, the means are all significantly positive. Moreover, the

Table 4 Behavior of Selected Note Gaps for Stratified Sample

Delivery in	Mean Gap Size for June 21, 1976-June 21, 1977	DF	July 1, 1977-July 3, 1978	DF
3 months	−.0667 (1.03)	8	−.1689* (1.71)	8
6 months	.0178 (.39)	8	−.0544 (.866)	8
9 months	.3767*** (2.93)	8	.3411*** (7.22)	8
12 months	.2944** (2.28)	8	.2756*** (3.33)	8
15 months	.8156*** (5.11)	8	.5500*** (3.05)	7

*Significant at 90% level
**Significant at 95% level
***Significant at 99% level

nine and twelve months gaps have essentially the same value (.3767 vs. .3411 and .2944 vs. .2756). Only the fifteen month gap shows a noticeable decline (from .8156 to .5500) and these two values are still within one standard error of the equivalent combined group mean (.6906).

Implications

It is true that these results apply to a specific time period. In particular they generally cover a period when interest rates were expected to increase but in most cases did not rise as much as anticipated. For that reason the behavior of the gap may be relevant to such a period but not to other periods with different expectations and market behaviors. Thus under different circumstances the typical gap might have the opposite sign. And yet the narrowing of the gap as delivery approaches is almost certainly likely to continue. It is a general characteristic of futures markets for the futures price to move toward the cash price as delivery approaches and T bill futures should not be an exception to this tendency.

It is however, surprising that a large gap should open up at all—particularly to those who subscribe to the unbiased expectations hypothesis. Unlike most futures-cash market relations, it is at least conceptually possible to construct a hedge which is equivalent to the futures contract. By going long on the more distant maturity combined with an equivalent short position in a three month shorter maturity, a hedge is created which should be very nearly equivalent to the appropriate futures. Indeed such a hedge should offer the yield derived from the unbiased expectations hypothesis. Thus by taking opposite positions on the futures contract and its equivalent hedge, one should be able to derive a gain proportional to the decline in the gap as it approaches the delivery month. The activity of arbitrageurs taking such positions and making such trades would then be expected to narrow the gap to the point where it is no longer profitable to arbitrage. A number of the gaps, however, appear to be large enough to attract arbitrageurs.

The failure of the market to arbitrage the gaps to a lower level is probably due to the relatively high cost of constructing the appropriate hedge. The standard fee between government bond deals for borrowing governments (so that they may be shorted) is 50 basis points. This means that in order to realize the profit potential in a given size gap one would have to overcome a total transaction cost equal to the sum of the following expenses: foregone interest on margin deposit for futures positions, commissions on each transaction, possible bid-asked spread on each transaction and a borrowing charge equal to an annualized 50 basis points for the period that any government is shorted. Since the 50 basis point charge applies to the entire length of the holding period and the profit potential gap is limited to a three month equivalent security, it is quite unlikely that even a government bond dealer could often effect a profitable type of hedge. In a few rare instances a governments dealer might be able to offset the 50 basis point charge on the short position by leading the long half of the position but it would be quite rare for one to be so lucky. Reverse repurchase agreements might also be used to effect a short position but these agreements rarely run for more than a week or so while the short position would generally need to be maintained for a much longer period. Thus it seems unlikely that even a governments dealer would be able to construct the needed hedges at profitable prices. Since any outsider would have to pay considerably more to construct such hedges, it seems highly unlikely that this type of arbitraging could take place at all frequently.

And yet even without any pure arbitraging, it still should be possible for an efficient market to reduce the gap to commissions and carrying costs. There are numerous financial intermediaries with relatively large portfolios of government bonds. Most intermediaries have a preferred maturity structure for their portfolios. Such a maturity structure can be constructed directly through long positions in the appropriate securities. It is also possible, however, to employ futures in the construction of the desired portfolio. For example, a bank might wish to lengthen the average maturity of its holdings. One approach would be to sell some of its short maturity governments and replace them with longer maturity securities. Alternatively the bank could replace the shorter maturity governments with long positions in relatively more distant T bill futures. Similar types of adjustments could be used to reduce the average maturity of the portfolio if that were desired. Indeed a wide variety of combinations of short and long positions on futures coupled with sales and/or purchases of governments can be used to produce almost any reasonable maturity structure. Clearly some of these approaches will offer a better portfolio yield than others. This will be true as long as gaps exist between the futures interest rates and the equivalent rates derived from the term structure. The following example should be sufficient to illustrate some of the possibilities. On July 19, 1977 (when an early draft of this paper was being written) U.S. notes due September 1979 were yielding 6.26%. It was also possible to construct a "security" with the same maturity date by purchasing March 78 U.S. notes and purchasing futures contracts which would carry the investment through September 79. The yield (ignoring commissions and the margin balances which would have been required) on this constructed T bill was 7.13%. Anyone wishing to own a government security expiring on September 1979 would have been able to obtain a far more attractive yield by trading in futures than by buying the note outright.[16]

---

[16] The gross advantage is 87 basis points on a 2.25 year term for $1,000,000. That is an extra interest income of about $21,200. This is offset in some degree by commissions and mar-

Were financial intermediaries to trade interest futures extensively and effectively, most of the gaps such as that illustrated above should be arbitraged away. Apparently the current participation in the futures market is either not extensive enough or not effective enough to accomplish this arbitraging. There are of course a number of barriers to some types of institutional participation in the futures market. An examination of the extent of the profit potential of institutional use of the futures market as well as a study of the reasons why there is not more such trading seems warranted.

Trading Possibilities

While the principal opportunities created by these gaps are afforded to the large financial intermediaries, one can not help but wonder whether the small investor could profit from such market imperfections. Several possibilities suggest themselves.

One might hypothesize that in general the narrowing of gaps is due at least in part to the movement of the futures price toward the term structure derived rate. If the later rate can be assumed to move randomly, the closing of the gap should yield a profit for the appropriate side of the futures contract. Thus one might on June 21, 1976 have observed a large gap associated with the September 1977 futures contract. The futures contract appears to be under priced relative to the derived rate (8.24 versus 7.04). By taking a long position in such contracts one could have hope to profit if the gap narrowed by more than the amount that the derived rate rises (if the derived rate falls, this would be even better). As it turned out this would have been a profitable trade as rates on September 1977's had fallen to 5.35 by July 1, 1976. Such a decline of 290 basis points would have been profitable indeed to the long side of the contract.[17] Unfortunately there is no assurance that such a strategy

gin balances. The standard commissions on four or fewer contracts is $60 per contract. Thus purchasing the required five separate contracts would cost $300. Assuming they were exercised, no further commissions would be incurred. The initial required margin is $1,500 while maintenance requirement is $1,000. Thus the initial margin deposits for the five separate contracts would be $7,500. The average margin balance that might have to be put up over the life of the contracts, is relatively difficult to predict as adverse fluctuations would require additional margin while needed margin would be reduced by favorable moves. Taking $10,000 as an average the foregone interest at 7.13% would equal $1,676. Thus the net advantage would be reduced by about $2,300 by commissions and foregone interest on margin. In other words margin and commissions would only offset a small fraction of the gross advantage. The net advantage is estimated at almost $19,000 per million.

[17] Opening a position in one contract would have cost the $1,500 margin plus $60 in commissions. The 290 basis point move in the 3 month T bill future would have produced a gross profit of $47,250. Subtracting commissions on both sides of the trade produces a net profit of $7,130, on an initial investment of $1,560. This amounts to a return of 457% on a holding period of one year. Indeed pyramiding the profits by using the increasing equity to purchase additional contracts could have yielded profits an order of magnitude higher still. Only the most risk oriented traders, however, would be likely to undertake such a pyramiding strategy.

would yield consistent profits. Indeed a strategy of identifying misvalued futures would need to be tested over a variety of market conditions before one could have any reasonable confidence in it. The problem is obvious: without an offsetting hedge, the risk of random market movements is quite substantial.

Next we wonder if some sort of partial hedge might be constructed. One could use either long positions in governments or short positions in other maturity futures to construct a spreadlike position.

On June 21, 1975 the September 1977 futures contract appeared to be overpriced relative to the derived rate. On the other hand the December 1976 futures contract appeared to be appropriately priced. A long December 1976 and short September 1977 position would be less subject to random market moves than the short position alone. The straddle would have been established with a difference of 131 basis points on December 21, 1976, near expiration of the December contract, this difference would have narrowed to 94 (5.18 − 4.24) or a narrowing of 37 basis points.[18] Again there is no assurance that such moves would repeat themselves with any consistency. On *a priori* grounds, however, it does appear that the spread would be much the safer strategy than the unhedged position.

A second type of hedge could be constructed through the use of different interest futures. For example, one might hedge T bill futures against GNMA futures. McCarthy studied such a strategy and found suggestive but not conclusive evidence of a profitable trading rule involving such hedging.[19]

This discussion of trading possibilities is necessarily *ad hoc*. A definitive test would require first that a reasonable sort of trading rule be formulated with reference to one set of data and then tested over a second and independent data set. While the data coverage is adequate for what has been done herein, there is insufficient data to make a reasonable test of a trading rule. One would need data covering several business cycles in order to have any confidence that the test results could have any long term predictive validity. Clearly we are a long way from having such a data set. Thus an effective trading rule analysis will have to wait for at least several more years.

CONCLUSION

We begin this analysis with the suggestion that futures trading of interest rates permits one to test the unbiased expectations hypothesis.

---

[18] The profit here is much more modest. A beginning investment of $3,060 would have yielded a gross profit of $925 and a net profit of $685. That amounts to a return of around 22% for six months: not bad but not exciting considering the risks.

[19] T. McCarthy, "Hedging Opportunities as Determined by the Relation of the Spread Between GNMA's and Treasury Bill Futures." Term paper for Finance 713, December 5, 1977, University of Massachusetts.

Having performed such a test, what now can we conclude? Such conclusions depend in large part on what interpretations we are to give to interest futures trading. Do such futures accurately reflect a portion of the overall market's expectations? Certainly they do reflect a portion of the market represented by those who are willing to put their money where their expectations are. If we are willing to go further and assume that interest futures trading reflects the market's unbiased expectations, we can make some rather definitive statements on the term structure hypothesis. While the question of bias in interest rate futures prices has not heretofore been raised, there is a very substantial literature on the subject as it relates to other commodities. Keynes hypothesized that hedgers were generally short and in order to induce sufficient speculative interest they had to pay a risk premium.[20] Thus according to the theory of normal backwardation futures prices were said to be downward biased vis-á-vis expected spot prices. Very extensive testing, however, has failed to substantiate the hypothesis. Indeed the evidence is quite consistent with the contrary view that futures prices are unbiased forecasts of the future spot price.[21] If what is true for commodity futures generally is also true of interest futures, we may proceed to use the futures prices as true expectations. Thus:

The gap between the term structure derived interest rates and the futures market's interest futures are just too large and differ in the same direction too often to be consistent with the unbiased expectations hypothesis. Confidence in this conclusion is strengthened by the consistency of the stratified sample results. Liquidity premiums would suggest higher term structure derived futures rates than the market expects and we generally found the opposite. Only the segmented markets hypothesis remains. It would permit expectations and term structure derived estimates to diverge as they do in this analysis. At a minimum we can conclude that there is a certain amount of segmentation between the interest futures market and the T bill and note markets. How much farther we go depends on how much confidence we place in the futures market as an index of expectations. If we accept the futures market rates as representative of the entire bond market's expectations of future interest rates, only the segmented markets hypothesis fits the data. If, however, we are unwilling to make the assumption, all that can be said for certain is that there is a substantial amount of segmentation between the government debt securities market and the futures market for such securities. The evidence presented here can be made consistent with the liquidity premium hypothesis only if we are willing to argue

---

[20] J. M. Keynes, "Some Aspects of Commodity Markets," *Manchester Guardian Commercial*, European Reconstruction Series, Section 13, March 29, 1923, pp. 784-86; and Keynes, *A Treatise on Money*, Vol. II, New York: Harcourt, 1930, pp. 143-44.

[21] R. Gray, "The Search for a Risk Premium, *Journal of Political Economy*, Vol. LXIX, No. 3, (June 1961); C. Rockwell, Normal Backwardation, Forecasting and the Returns to Commodity Futures Traders," *Feed Research Institute Studies*, Supplement to Vol. VII, (1967).

that there is a greater risk premium attached to futures interest rates than to the term structure derived rates.

Even if we do not interpret interest futures as expectations of future interest rates, they still should be consistent with the interest rates reflected in the term structure. An efficient market should drive the two sets of rates together. That this has not thus far happened and that there appears to be little or no progress in that direction is rather clear evidence of both a segmentation of the two markets (cash governments and futures governments) and an inefficiency in the linkage between the two markets.

While the present work only deals with the T bill futures market, it is certainly quite possible that similar segmentations and inefficiencies exist for some or all of the other interest futures markets. Perhaps greater efficiency among the various markets will have to wait until such studies are made and their results widely disseminated to the appropriate portfolio managers.

10

The U.S. Treasury Bill Futures Market and Hypotheses Regarding the Term Structure of Interest Rates[*]

Brian G. Chow[**] and
David J. Brophy[†]

INTRODUCTION

Theory of the term structure of interest rates dates at least from the work of Irving Fisher [1]. His proposition that expectations of future interest rates influence the term structure of rates became the foundation of the "expectations" hypothesis. In the 1930s, building on the Keynesian [2] notion of "normal backwardation" in the futures market, J. R. Hicks [3] suggested the "liquidity premium" term structure hypothesis. He argued that the forward rate would normally exceed the expected interest rate by a risk premium to compensate the investor for assuming the uncertainty of price fluctuations. In 1957, Culbertson [4] formalized the "market segmentation" hypothesis.

In time, studies of the term structure have developed and refined variants to interpret and analyze the term structure, but they have not produced a consensus. A factor contributing to the lack of consensus in term structure interpretation may be the lack of independent measures

---

[*]Reprinted from *The Financial Review*, Vol. 13, pages 36-50, (Fall 1978). Reprinted by permission of the Eastern Finance Association, publisher.
[**]Saginaw Valley State College.
[†]University of Michigan.
The authors wish to thank David Aker and Charles Curtiss for assistance and helpful discussion.

of interest rate expectations. Tests of the hypotheses cited above require the inclusion of such expectations, and the usual procedure has been to generate expectations with a model of some sort. Consequently, tests of term structure hypotheses turn out to be joint tests of the hypothesis in question and of the interest rate expectations model which the researcher is employing. Since the expectations model used is always open to challenge, the results of any test of term structure hypotheses done in this way are, at best, conditional.

In this paper we examine the proposition that observed interest rate expectations, generated by participants in an organized futures market, can be used in tests of term structure hypotheses to remove effectively the conditionality which is inherent in the model-generated expectations described above. We direct our tests specifically to the three major hypotheses: pure expectations, market segmentation and liquidity preference. The latter two are examined as special cases of the stationary variant of the market segmentation hypothesis.

The source of market-generated interest rate expectations is the U.S. Treasury Bill futures market, which has been in operation since 1976 and is maintained by the International Monetary Market of the Chicago Mercantile Exchange. Participants deal in contracts involving U.S. Treasury Bills with maturity of three months (13 weeks, 91 days) for delivery on specified dates in March, June, September, and December. The longest-term contract is for delivery in 21 months. The data are described in detail in the third section.

The body of this paper proceeds with sections and subsections devoted to each of the following: a specification and discussion of the pure expectations hypothesis and associated tests; description of data and the results of the tests of the pure expectations hypothesis; consideration of effects due to transactions costs; a test of the stationary variant of the market segmentation hypothesis; and conclusions.

FORMULATION OF A TEST OF THE PURE EXPECTATIONS HYPOTHESIS

Roll [5], states the fundamental dynamic equation for interest rates in an efficient market as

$$E_{t-1}(\tilde{r}_{j,t} - \tilde{L}_{j,t} \mid B_{t-1}) = r_{j+1,t-1} - L_{j+1,t-1} \qquad (1)$$

where $r_{j,t}$ is the one-period forward rate for j-periods hence, observed in period t, and $L_{j,t}$ is the j-period liquidity premium observed in period t. The E_{t-1} is the mathematical expectations operator as of period t-1.

Hypotheses Regarding the Term Structure of Interest Rates

B_{t-1} represents all available information about interest rates at time t-1. All random variables have a tilde superscribed above them. We follow Roll's [5] definition of an efficient market, namely, one which has: (1) zero transactions costs (an assumption we will relax below); (2) symmetric market rationality, which means that every trader acts rationally (i.e., desires more, rather than less, wealth, and uses all available information and believes all others do likewise); (3) information is free and becomes available to everyone at the same instant. These conditions are sufficient grounds for assuming that no trading rule which earns excess profits can be developed. Equation (1) states that the forward rate applicable to a fixed future date, less a liquidity premium, follows a martingale sequence, i.e.,

$$E_{t-1}(\tilde{X}_{j,t}) = X_{j+1,t-1}$$

$$E_{t-2}(\tilde{X}_{j+1,t-1}) = X_{j+2,t-2}; \text{etc.} \qquad (2)$$

In other words, $r_{j+1,t-1} - L_{j+1,t-1}$ is an unbiased estimator of the random variable $\tilde{r}_{j,t} - \tilde{L}_{j,t}$.

The pure expectations hypothesis can be stated mathematically as

$$L_{j,t} = 0 \text{ for all } j \text{ and } t. \qquad (3)$$

Thus, equation (1) can be written

$$E_{t-1}(\tilde{r}_{j,t} | B_{t-1}) = r_{j+1,t-1} \qquad (4)$$

The starting point of our test is the assumption that both the T-bill spot and futures markets are efficient in the sense attributed to Roll above. If both markets are efficient and open to the same body of investors, it follows that the same term structure theory should apply in both markets. Different theories in the two markets would permit the development of trading rules capable of producing excess profits. This, of course, is inconsistent with the efficient market assumption. On this basis, then, we expect the term structure derived from the T-bill spot market on any given date to be identical to the term structure derived from the T-bill futures market at the same time.

On the other hand, if it is found that none of the major term structure hypotheses is consistent with both the T-bill spot and futures markets under the assumption of market efficiency, there are strong grounds upon which to suspect that at least one of the two T-bill markets is inefficient. Such inefficiency, if it exists, is likely to be found in the T-bill futures market. We believe this for two reasons: first, the market is only two and one half years old at this writing and, second, Roll [5] shows the T-bill spot market to be efficient assuming that the term structure hypothesis used is valid.

For test purposes we compute the term structure implied by the T-bill futures market through the use of a pure expectations hypothesis formulation. We compare the observed discount yields from the T-bill spot market with the corresponding yields obtained from the derived term structure. The differences of the yields are then tested. We argue that the existence of any such differences indicates that investors must have used factors in addition to expectations in valuing the futures contracts. If investors are using different theories in the spot and futures markets, the pure expectations theory cannot hold; that is, expectations are not the *sole* factor determining the term structure.

The major difference between this approach and the "model-generated expectations" approach is, of course, that the futures interest rates are market-based and immediately observable. The question of whether the expectation coincides with actual spot rates observed later is, in a significant sense, not relevant to the question at hand. The T-bill futures market is important, therefore, in capital market analyses because it is both a source of expectations information and a vehicle for tests of consistency when compared to the T-bill spot market.

The prices in both the Treasury-bill spot and futures markets are quoted on a discount basis. The interest earned on a Treasury bill is the difference between the par price (face value) and the purchase price if it is held to maturity. Prices in the T-bill futures market are quoted in terms of the International Monetary Market Index, which is 100 minus the T-bill yield (discount) on an annual basis.

Let $D_{n_i,\Delta_i}(t)$ be the discount yield at time t for a bill to be delivered according to the terms of a futures contract n_i days from t and which will mature $n_i + \Delta_i$ days from t. The price of a $100 (at maturity) bill at time t, $P_{n_i,\Delta_i}(t)$, is

$$P_{n_i,\Delta_i}(t) = 100 - \frac{\Delta_i}{360} D_{n_i,\Delta_i}(t). \tag{5}$$

Furthermore, let us define the true rate of return $R_{n_i,\Delta_i}(t)$ as the internal rate of return at which the maturity value of the T-bill must be discounted to equal its price at time t. The subscripts of $P_{n_i,\Delta_i}(t)$ and $R_{n_i,\Delta_i}(t)$ have the same meaning as those of $D_{n_i,\Delta_i}(t)$. For mathematical simplification we will use continuous compounding. The true rate of return can be expressed in terms of the price of a T-bill as follows

$$P_{n_i,\Delta_i}(t) \, \text{Exp}\left[\frac{R_{n_i,\Delta_i}(t)\Delta_i}{36{,}500}\right] = 100$$

or,

$$R_{n_i,\Delta_i}(t) = -\frac{36{,}500}{\Delta_i} \ln \frac{P_{n_i,\Delta_i}(t)}{100}, \tag{6}$$

where $R_{n_j,\Delta_i}(t)$ is in percentage per annum and ln is the natural logarithm.

According to the pure expectations hypothesis, short- and long-term securities can be treated as perfect substitutes. Therefore

$$\text{Exp}\left[\frac{R_{0,\Delta_1+\Delta_2+\ldots\Delta_k}(t)}{36,500}(\Delta_1+\Delta_2\ldots\Delta_k)\right]$$

$$=\text{Exp}\left[\frac{R_{0,\Delta_1}(t)\Delta_1}{36,500}\right]\cdot\text{Exp}\left[\frac{R_{\Delta_1,\Delta_2}(t)\Delta_2}{36,500}\right]\cdot$$

$$\text{Exp}\left[\frac{R_{\Delta_1+\Delta_2,\Delta_3}(t)\Delta_3}{36,500}\right]$$

$$\ldots\text{Exp}\left[\frac{R_{\Delta_1+\Delta_2+\ldots\Delta_{k-1},\Delta_k}(t)\Delta_k}{36,500}\right]; \quad (7)$$

or,

$$R_{0,\Delta_1+\Delta_2\ldots\Delta_k}(t)=$$

$$[R_{0,\Delta_1}(t)\Delta_1 + R_{\Delta_1,\Delta_2}(t)\Delta_2 + R_{\Delta_1+\Delta_2,\Delta_3}(t)\Delta_3$$

$$\ldots + R_{\Delta_1+\Delta_2+\ldots\Delta_{k-1},\Delta_k}(t)\Delta_k] \div [\Delta_1+\Delta_2+\ldots+\Delta_k]. \quad (8)$$

In words, equation (8) states that the true rate of return of a bill which will mature in $\Delta_1 + \Delta_2 + \ldots \Delta_k$ days is the weighted average of the true rates of return of the T-bill future contracts. Since the T-bills are quoted in discount yields, $D_{n_j,\Delta_i}(t)$, instead of true rates of returns, $R_{n_j,\Delta_i}(t)$, we derive a relation among discount yields. Substituting equations (5) and (6) into (8), we obtain

$$D_{0,\Delta_1+\Delta_2+\ldots+\Delta_k}(t) = \frac{36,000}{\Delta_1+\Delta_2+\ldots\Delta_k}$$

$$\left[1-\left(1-\frac{\Delta_1 D_{0,\Delta_1}(t)}{36,000}\right)\left(1-\frac{\Delta_2 D_{\Delta_1,\Delta_2}(t)}{36,000}\right)\left(1-\frac{\Delta_3 D_{\Delta_1+\Delta_2,\Delta_3}(t)}{36,000}\right)\right.$$

$$\left.\ldots\left(1-\frac{\Delta_k D_{\Delta_1+\Delta_2+\ldots\Delta_{k-1},\Delta_k}(t)}{36,000}\right)\right] \quad (9)$$

where $D_{\Delta_1+\Delta_2+\ldots\Delta_{k-1},\Delta_k}(t)$ is the discount yield of a bill at time t to be delivered at $\Delta_1+\Delta_2+\ldots\Delta_{k-1}$ days from t and which will mature at $\Delta_1+\Delta_2+\ldots\Delta_k$ days from t.

Let us introduce a superscript s and f to the discount yield D to signify its origin. Thus, $D^s_{o,\Delta_i}(t)$ is the spot (observed) discount yield at time t while $D^f_{o,\Delta_i}(t)$ is the expected discount yield derived from Treasury-bill futures markets at time t by means of equation (9). If the pure expectations hypothesis is the sole determinant of interest rates and discount yields in the spot and futures markets, it requires:

$$D^s_{o,\Delta_i}(t) = D^f_{o,\Delta_i}(t) \text{ for all i and t.} \tag{10}$$

Since $D^s_{o,\Delta_i}(t)$'s are directly observable and $D^f_{o,\Delta_i}(t)$'s are completely determined by the observable discount yields in the T-bill futures market via equation (9) plus one spot yield, equation (10) is a testable hypothesis. The test of this hypothesis is referred to below as Test 1.

Test 1 employs *all* the observed discount yields of the currently outstanding T-bills in the spot market at any time t. Given a term structure hypothesis we incorporate all the data points by constructing the whole term structure via equation (9) implied by the Treasury-bill futures markets at time t with linear interpolation for intermediate yields. Then every discount yield observed in the spot T-bill market can be compared with the corresponding predicted yield. Other researchers such as Burger [6], Puglisi [7] and Branch [8] start with the yields in the T-bill futures market and then compute the corresponding yield from the spot market by utilizing a very small subset of the data. For example, using this approach, Branch obtains only three data points on each date from the spot T-bills market. In this analysis we are able to use roughly 40 data points. Under the former method, one can increase the data points by including yields from U.S. Notes, as in Branch's analysis. However, there are problems with such an approach. U.S. Notes are imperfect substitutes for T-bills because of tax and other considerations. The difference in discount yields between T-bills and U.S. Notes is frequently larger than those between the T-bills in the spot and futures market. At best, the inclusion of U.S. Notes introduces random errors of large magnitude. This, of course, reduces the efficiency and power of the test. In our approach, a sufficient number of data points is available from the spot and futures T-bill market alone.

Another important characteristic of Test 1 is that it permits the combination of data across time. As shown in equation (10), the spot discount yield of a given number of days to maturity observed at time t should be the same as the discount yield of the same maturity derived from the futures market. If a given term structure hypothesis is valid, and markets are efficient, the difference between the above two discount yields should be zero for every maturity and at any time, i.e., the differences are independent. Alternatively, the same conclusion may be reached by observing that the number of discount yields in the spot market is the same as the number of differences computed. Consequently, our method incorporates all these differences in one test.

Another way to test term structure hypotheses compares a "piggy back" combination of a short-term spot transaction and a futures contract, with a spot transaction in a T-bill of maturity equal to that of the combination. In essence, this tests

$$\bar{D}_{\Delta_i-91,\Delta_i}(t) \equiv D^f_{\Delta_i-91,\Delta_i}(t) - \frac{36{,}000}{91} \left[1 - \frac{1 - \dfrac{\Delta_i D^s_{0,\Delta_i}(t)}{36{,}000}}{1 - \dfrac{(\Delta_i-91) D^s_{0,\Delta_{i-91}}(t)}{36{,}000}} \right] = 0 \quad (11)$$

for all Δ_i and t, where $\bar{D}_{\Delta_i-91,\Delta_i}(t)$ is the difference between the observed discount yield of a 13-week T-bill futures contract which will mature Δ_i days from now and the discount yield deduced from the spot T-bill market yields. The test of the hypothesis represented by equation (11) is referred to below as Test 2.

Parenthetically we note that in contrast to Test 1 in which the researcher can use all the data available in the T-bill spot market, Test 2 uses only a small subset of the data. On the other hand, Test 2 is easier to correct for transactions costs and is a more convenient vehicle for testing whether the liquidity premium differs in the spot and futures markets. The following section describes the data and presents the results of hypothesis testing for both Test 1 and Test 2.

DESCRIPTION OF DATA AND RESULTS OF TESTS ON THE PURE EXPECTATIONS HYPOTHESIS

The data are the discount yields on U.S. Treasury bills available for direct transactions in the spot market and through contracts for future delivery in the T-bill futures market. For the spot market data, we employ the average of bid and ask yields. For the future contracts market data, the yields at market close are used. Transaction costs are ignored in these tests but are discussed below. It should be noted that the bid-ask spread for T-bills which will mature in less than 30 days is very large because of transaction costs. Consequently, these securities are not included in the test data. Our sample consists of biweekly discount yields from the spot market and the corresponding yields derived from the futures market covering the period from January 8, 1976, through January 26, 1978.

We proceed with Test 1 by using the following regression equation

$$D_{\Delta_i}(t) \equiv D^s_{0,\Delta_i}(t) - D^f_{0,\Delta_i}(t) = \alpha + \Delta_i \beta, \qquad (12)$$

where $D_{\Delta_i}(t)$ is the difference between the discount yield observed in the T-bill spot market and that derived from the futures market. The discount yields from the T-bill futures market are calculated by means of equation (9).

If the pure expectations hypothesis is valid according to equation (10), α and β in equation (12) will not be statistically different from zero. Our results are as follows

$$D_{\Delta_i}(t) = .1038 - .00027\, \Delta_i \qquad (13)$$

Std. Errors   (.0052) (.00003)
t-Statistics   (19.8)   (−9.2)
Number of observations   1,308

where $D_{\Delta_i}(t)$ is in percentage per annum and Δ_i in number of days to maturity. For both coefficients, the significance level is zero to four decimal places, which means that the chance for either α or β to be zero is practically nil. Thus, the pure expectations hypothesis predicting zero intercept and zero slope is not substantiated by this test.

One might argue that inefficiencies would be expected during the early months after the inception of T-bill futures trading. Thus, we have applied the same test to the biweekly data for a different period: July 1, 1976 to August 4, 1977. Similar results are obtained.

$$D_{\Delta_i}(t) = .0942 - .00042\, \Delta_i \qquad (14)$$

Std. Errors   (.0052) (.00003)
t-Statistics   (18.3)   (−14.5)
Number of observations   690

Thus, our conclusion that the pure expectations hypothesis is not substantiated remains unaltered even if the first six months of data are excluded.

We proceed with Test 2 by using the following regression equation

$$\bar{D}_{\Delta_i - 91, \Delta_i}(t) = \bar{\alpha} + \bar{\beta}\,(\Delta_i - 91). \qquad (15)$$

Our results are as follows and lead to the same conclusion as Test 1.

$$\bar{D}_{\Delta_i-91,\Delta_i}(t) = .199 - .00180\,(\Delta_i-91) \qquad (16)$$

     Std. Errors   (.025) (.00016)
     t-Statistics   (7.8) (−11.4)
  Number of observations   351

Effects Due to Transaction Costs

In the T-bill spot market, the dealer makes a profit through the bid-ask spread. Thus, it is reasonable to assume that the spot interest rates, in the absence of transaction costs, are the average of bid and ask rates if the spread is small. A typical spread for a T-bill with a week to maturity is around .4 percent while that with three months or more to maturity is around .1 percent or less. In Test 1, bills with maturity of less than one month are not included while in Test 2 bills with maturity of less than one week are not included.

In the T-bill futures market, although the size of a single contract is $1 million, one can buy or sell a contract on margin, and the round-turn commission per contract is $60. However, the commission rates vary from one brokerage house to another. Furthermore, marketable securities, treasury stock, or a letter of credit may be substituted for cash in fulfilling the margin requirement. Thus, the opportunity cost varies. For our purposes, however, it is not necessary to determine precisely the weighted-average opportunity cost for the T-bill futures transactions, because our conclusions are not sensitive to the opportunity cost. We thus assume that the average margin was $2,000 and commission was $60 per contract during the period of our investigation.

Let $\bar{D}_{\Delta_i+\Delta_2+\ldots+\Delta_{k-1},\Delta_k}(t)$ be the discount yield, after transaction cost adjustment, of a T-bill at time t to be delivered at $\Delta_i + \Delta_2 + \ldots + \Delta_{k-1}$ days from t and which will mature at $\Delta_i + \Delta_2 + \ldots + \Delta_k$ days from t. If the pure expectations hypothesis is valid, a piggyback combination of a spot transaction and a future contract will have the same yield as a spot contract of maturity equal to that of the combination. If the margin for a future contract is assumed to have been invested in the spot T-bill market to earn an interest rate of six percent per annum, the quoted discount yield for a T-bill futures contract with a maturity value of $1 million and a delivery date $\Delta_i - 91$ days from now, $D^f_{\Delta_i-91,\Delta_i}(t)$, should be adjusted downward by a percentage factor $A^f_{\Delta_i}$ according to the following formula to represent the discount yield net of transactions costs to the investor,

$$A^f_{\Delta_i} = \left[\frac{60 + (2{,}000)(.06)\frac{(\Delta_i-91)}{365}}{1{,}000{,}000}\right] \cdot \left[\frac{12}{3}\right] \cdot [100\%]$$

$$= 0.24 + .00013\,(\Delta_i-91) \tag{17}$$

For example, the adjustment for T-bill contracts to be delivered 13 weeks, 26 weeks, and 39 weeks from now are 0.036, 0.048, and 0.06 percent respectively. In the present study we will apply this modification to Test 2 to account for transactions costs in the T-bill futures market.

In equation (2), $D^f_{\Delta_i-91,\Delta_i}(t)$ should be adjusted downward by the value of $A^f_{\Delta_i}$. Alternatively, if we use the same $D^f_{\Delta_i-91,\Delta_i}$ values as data for testing, we are really testing that

$$\bar{\alpha} + \bar{\beta}(\Delta_i-91) = A^f_{\Delta_i} = .024 + .00013\,(\Delta_i-91). \tag{18}$$

But we have already found, in equation (16) that $\bar{\alpha} = .199$ and $\bar{\beta} = -.0018$. The t-statistics of the hypothesis test that $\bar{\alpha}$ and $\bar{\beta}$ are different from .024 and .00013 are 6.87 and -12.18 respectively. For both coefficients the significance level remains zero to four decimal places. Thus, even with an adjustment for transactions costs, the chance of the pure expectations hypothesis being valid is practically nil—provided, of course, that the spot and futures markets are otherwise efficient.

A special feature of the T-bill futures market is the requirement of daily "resettlement" on all contracts, also known as "marking to the market" or "daily marking." In essence, at the end of each day and based on the result of the day's price change, the profits are credited to and losses drawn from every futures market account. Recently, the argument has been made that the daily marking differentiates the futures market from the forward market (Morgan [9]).

For the testing of the pure expectations hypothesis, the effect of daily marking is zero. This is so because the chance of a gain or loss from daily marking occurs randomly and effectively cancels out to an expected value of zero. Thus it does not affect our tests or conclusions in any way. Furthermore, daily marking substantially reduces the default risk or the T-bill futures contract and strengthens our implicit assumption that the T-bill futures contract is default-free.

We will show later that the effect of daily marking is also negligible under the assumptions of market segmentation or liquidity preference for our data points. Consequently, we do not believe that daily marking distinguishes the futures market from the forward market.

Test of the Stationary Variant of the Market Segmentation Hypothesis

The basic premise of the market segmentation hypothesis is that securities which differ only with respect to maturity are imperfect substitutes. Stated in terms of equation (1),

$$E_{t-1}(\tilde{r}_{j,t} - \tilde{L}_{j,t} \mid B_{t-1}) = r_{j+1,t-1} - L_{j+1,t-1}, \qquad (19)$$

the segmentation hypothesis implies that at least some of the L's are non-zero. There are two major variants of the market-segmentation hypothesis. The time-dependent variant in Roll [5, p. 38] states that the maturities of the payment streams of many assets and liabilities depend on calendar time. If investors with calendar time-dependent maturity habitats dominate the market, the j-period liquidity premium observed in period t, $L_{j,t}$, should be about equal to the j + 1-period liquidity premium observed in period t-1, aside from random unexpected fluctuations.

In this paper we have chosen to test the stationary variant of the market segmentation hypothesis for three reasons. First, the market segmentation hypothesis to which reference is most commonly made is actually the stationary variant. Second, if we restrict the liquidity premium to be a monotonically increasing function of maturity, the stationary variant of the market segmentation hypothesis is reduced to the liquidity preference hypothesis [5, p. 44]. In other words, the latter is a refinement of the former. Thus, if we prove that the stationary variant is not substantiated, it follows that both the market segmentation and the liquidity preference hypotheses will not be substantiated. Third, Roll has shown that the stationary variant is well supported in the T-bill spot market.

Mathematically, in the stationary variant,

$$E_{t-1}(\tilde{L}_{j,t}) = L_{j,t-1}. \qquad (20)$$

Substituting equation (20) into (1) we obtain:

$$E_{t-1}(\tilde{r}_{j,t}) = r_{j+1,t-1} + L_{j,t-1} - L_{j+1,t-1}, \qquad (21)$$

or

$$E_t(\tilde{r}_{j,t+1} - r_{j+1,t}) = L_{j,t} - L_{j+1,t}.$$

Since

$$L_{1,t} = 0$$

then
$$-L_{2,t} = E_t(\tilde{r}_{1,t+1} - r_{2,t}).$$

Let the estimate of $L_{2,t}$ be $\hat{L}_{2,t}$:

then,
$$\hat{L}_{2,t} = \overline{r_{2,t} - r_{1,t+1}},$$

where the bar denotes a sample average.
Similarly,

$$\hat{L}_{2,t} - \hat{L}_{3,t} = \overline{r_{2,t+1} - r_{3,t}}$$

$$\hat{L}_{3,t} = \hat{L}_{2,t} + \overline{r_{3,t} - r_{2,t+1}}$$

$$= \overline{L_{2,t} - r_{1,t+1}} + \overline{r_{3,t} - r_{2,t+1}}$$

$$= \sum_{j=2}^{3} \left(\overline{r_{j,t} - r_{j-1,t+1}} \right).$$

In general,
$$\hat{L}_{j,t} = \sum_{i=2}^{j} \left(\overline{r_{i,t} - r_{i-1,t+1}} \right). \tag{22}$$

If the stationary variant of the market segmentation hypothesis is the determinant of the term structure, investors would use this same hypothesis to determine the term structure of interest rates in the spot and futures markets. That is to say, the expected interest rates after adjustment for liquidity premiums, derived from the spot and futures markets, should be the same. Mathematically,

$$E^s_{t-1}(\tilde{r}_{j,t}) = E^f_{t-1}(\tilde{r}_{j,t}) \text{ for all } j \text{ and } t,$$

or
$$r^s_{j+1,t-1} + L^s_{j,t-1} - L^s_{j+1,t-1} = r^f_{j+1,t-1} + L^f_{j,t-1} - L^f_{j+1,t-1} \tag{23}$$

where the superscripts s and f denote quantities in the spot and futures market respectively.

Given that the liquidity premiums in the spot and futures markets are identical, equation (23) becomes

$$r^s_{j+1,t-1} = r^f_{j+1,t-1},$$

or
$$r^s_{j,t} = r^f_{j,t}, \text{ for all } j \text{ and } t. \tag{24}$$

Thus such a test of the stationary variant of the market segmentation hypothesis is identical to that of the pure expectations hypothesis.

Since the latter is not substantiated above, the former is not substantiated in the present study.

One possible complication in this test is the daily marking discussed in the prior section. Morgan [9] claimed that its effect does not have to be zero under market segmentation or liquidity preference hypotheses, but he has not presented an estimate of its magnitude. We found that the magnitude of the daily marking effect under the market segmentation or liquidity preference hypothesis can be roughly estimated.[1] For all the data points used in our tests, the effect due to daily marking is only around .01%. Viewing the typical discrepancy of yields in T-bill spot and futures market of around .2% (see equation 16) we conclude that the daily marking effect is negligible in our analysis and explains very little of the observed differences. However, we note that daily marking can cause fluctuations in return under any term structure hypothesis. This fluctuation suggests the existence of a risk premium and, although our estimates indicate its size to be small, it deserves further investigative analysis.

Our results may suggest that inefficiency exists in one or both of the T-bill spot or futures markets. There are at least two approaches which can be used to test for inefficiency in the T-bill markets.

The first approach is to develop a trading rule by which excess profits may be generated. To date, despite efforts by researchers and practitioners, published proof of the existence of such a trading rule has not appeared. In one recent paper [7] Puglisi suggests the existence of such a trading rule based on market inefficiency which he believes to be temporary and a reflection of the immaturity of the market. The results of that paper, however, provide no evidence that the trading rule developed produced excess and consistent profits.

A second approach would show that price changes of futures contracts are serially correlated so that prices do not fully and quickly adjust to new information. However, the prerequisite for such an approach

---

[1] The daily marking effect, E, is estimated by the following formula:

$$E \approx \frac{\sigma}{2} \frac{T}{12} \frac{r}{100}$$

where E is stated as a percentage, T is the time period in months from now to delivery date of the futures contract, σ is the liquidity premium in % for the period T, and r is the average lending or borrowing rate in percentage during the period T.

For our data set, T is at most 9 months, σ is typically .5% and r is assumed to be 6%. Therefore, E is around .01%. To test this under extreme circumstances, we considered the longest possible T-bill futures contract, i.e., one with delivery in 21 months. With r still assumed to be 6%, σ is roughly 1½%. The value of E turns out to be about .08% and with the wrong sign if we assume that the liquidity preference hypothesis holds. Because of the small magnitude of this result, we conclude that the daily marking effect does not seem to be important.

is to have a term structure hypothesis which can be validly used to determine the expected discount yield $D^f_{o,\Delta_i}(t)$.

The assumption we propose is that the same term structure hypothesis must be used in both the spot and futures markets. In other words, after adjustments for features unique to spot or futures markets (such as transactions costs and daily marking) and assuming the markets are efficient, a single valid hypothesis must be capable of explaining yields in both markets. Our tests do not support the conventional term structure hypothesis if both T-bill spot and futures markets are assumed to be efficient. As a consequence, at least one of the following possibilities must hold.

The first possibility is that we have failed to include the key feature(s) unique to T-bill spot and/or futures markets. We can state that in our analysis and our survey of current research on T-bill spot and futures markets, none of the unique features so far identified is capable of explaining the differences in yields in the spot and futures markets. As a minimum, our methodology should be considered useful in analyzing the effect of any unique feature once that feature is identified.

The second possibility is that none of the three conventional term structure hypotheses is valid in their present form. If so, we contend that the T-bill spot and futures markets together provide an important medium for testing any modified or new term structure hypothesis.

Third, it may be that at least one of the T-bill spot and futures markets is inefficient. If this is true, the implications are far reaching since much of modern finance theory is based on the assumption of efficient markets. To practitioners, inefficiency in a new market is acceptable or even expected. But to the efficient-market advocates, any inefficiency lasting for two years or longer would be at least very disturbing.

CONCLUSIONS

We have sought to demonstrate that the comparison of the term structure of interest rates derived from the T-bill spot and futures markets offers a useful framework for empirical tests of term structure hypothesis. The value of this approach stems from the fact that observations of market-generated interest rate expectations are used rather than model-generated expectations. Thus, the results of hypotheses testing are not conditional upon the validity of the model underlying generation of interest rate expectations. This dependence has flawed previous tests of term structure hypotheses.

Our results show that none of the three conventional term structure hypotheses—pure expectations, market segmentation and liquidity preference—are valid, assuming that both the T-bill spot and futures market were efficient during the period of our investigation, namely from January 6, 1976 through January 26, 1978.

References

[1] Fisher, Irving. *The Theory of Interest*. New York: Macmillan Co., 1930, 210.
[2] Keynes, J. M. *A Treatise On Money*, II. New York: Harcourt, Brace, 1930, 142-44.
[3] Hicks, J. R. *Value and Capital*, 2d edition. London: Clarendon Press of the Oxford University Press, 1946, 138-39, 144-47.
[4] Culbertson, J. M. "The Term Structure of Interest Rates." *Quarterly Journal of Economics* 71 (Nov. 1957): 485-517.
[5] Roll, Richard. *Behavior of Interest Rates*. New York: Basic Books, 1970, 35-36.
[6] Burger, Albert E., *et al*. "The Treasury Bill Futures Market and Market Expectations of Interest Rates." *Monthly Review*, Federal Reserve Bank of St. Louis, 1977, 6.
[7] Puglisi, Donald J. "Is the Futures Market for Treasury Bills Efficient? *Journal of Portfolio Management*, Winter 1978, 64-67.
[8] Branch, Ben. "Testing the Unbiased Expectation Theory of Interest Rates." *Financial Review*, this issue.
[9] Morgan, George. "Pricing Treasury Bill Futures Contracts." Revised unpublished draft. Comptroller of the Currency, Washington, D. C., June 1978.

11

Treasury Bill Pricing in the Spot and Futures Markets*

Dennis R. Capozza and Bradford Cornell[†]

I. INTRODUCTION

Studies of the term structure of interest rates have a long tradition in the literature of finance and economics. Two prominent examples are Roll (1970) and Nelson (1971).[1] More recently, a parallel literature has evolved on the pricing of commodity contracts, spawned by the work of Dusak (1973) and Black (1976). With the advent of futures trading in Treasury bills on the Chicago Mercantile Exchange (CME) the direct relationship between the theory of the term structure of interest rates and the theory of commodity contract pricing has become apparent. Since arbitrage is possible between the spot and futures markets, appropriately defined returns in both markets should be identical.

In this paper we compare the returns in the spot and futures markets

---

*Reprinted from the *Review of Economics and Statistics*, Vol. 61, No. 4, (November 1979). Reprinted by permission of the North Holland Publishing Company, Amsterdam.

[†]University of Southern California and University of California, Los Angeles, respectively.

The authors thank Fischer Black, a referee for this *Review*, and Richard Roll for helpful comments on an earlier version of this paper. Don Keller of United California Bank's bond department provided information on the institutional operation of the Treasury bill market. Computational assistance was provided by Bernard Joei. The Chicago Mercantile Exchange provided partial funding.

[1] Studies of the efficiency of the spot market for Treasury bills include Fama (1975, 1976a,b), Hamburger (1975) and Roll (1970).

over the first 30 months of trading in the CME Treasury bill futures market. Surprisingly, we find that rather large deviations between returns in the two markets have persisted throughout the sample period, i.e., the one price law is violated. For this result to be obtained, arbitrage costs must be large, differential risk must exist, or traders in the two markets must be distinct non-overlapping groups.

In the next section an arbitrage condition connecting the two markets is derived. The condition specifies the relationship between returns in the spot and futures markets under the assumption of a perfect capital market. The third section presents the data and demonstrates that the arbitrage condition has not been satisfied. The fourth section offers a possible explanation for the failure of the arbitrage condition. The paper concludes with a summary of the results.

II. AN ARBITRAGE CONDITION

In developing the arbitrage condition the exposition is considerably simplified if continuously compounded daily rates of return are employed rather than the Treasury bill discounts quoted by dealers and the financial press. If 91-day bills are quoted at 98 (98 cents per dollar of maturity value) the corresponding Treasury bill discount will be quoted as 7.9% (=[100 − 98] × [360/91]). The continuously compounded annual return will be 8.1% (= [365/91] 1n[100/98]) or in daily terms 0.022%.

The futures contract as currently traded on the CME calls for delivery of 91-day bills on the maturity date.[2] For example, sale of the September contract obligates the seller to deliver $1 million of 91-day Treasury bills on the Wednesday following the third Treasury bill auction of September. The rates quoted on the futures contracts are annual Treasury bill rates. Thus, these rates can be converted to daily continuously compounded rates in the same way that spot bill returns are converted.

The arbitrage relation is derived by comparing the futures rates with the forward rates contained in the term structure. In general, the price of a bill per dollar of maturity value will be $P = \exp(-rT)$ where r is the daily continuously compounded rate and T is the number of days to maturity. The forward rate is defined as follows. Let r_n^s and r_{n+m}^s be the daily continuously compounded returns on spot bills with a matur-

---

[2] Those interested in further institutional details on futures trading in bills should consult *Treasury Bill Futures: Opportunities in Interest Rates*, which is available on request from the Chicago Mercantile Exchange. Similar material is contained in a review article by Burger, Lang and Rasche (1977).

ity of n and $n + m$ days, respectively. The prices of these bills will be $P_n = \exp(-r_n^s \cdot (n))$ and $P_{n+m} = \exp(-r_{n+m}^s \cdot (n+m))$. The forward rate on an m day bill, n days in the future is[3]

$$_n r_m^s = \ln(P_n/P_{n+m})$$
$$= (r_{n+m}^s \cdot (n+m) - r_n^s \cdot (n))/m. \quad (1)$$

All the notation is summarized in table 1.

Profitable arbitrage opportunities will exist if the forward rate is not equal to the futures rate at every point in time. Assume, for example, that the forward rate is less than the futures rate, that is, $_n r_m^s < {}_n r_m^f$. The arbitrager could take the following position:

1. Short a bill with maturity $n + m$ days.
2. Invest the proceeds in n-day bills.
3. Make a futures contract to purchase m-day bills, n-days hence.

The resulting cash flows per dollar invested are:

At time t:

Inflow from shorting $(n + m)$-day bill	$= P_{n+m} = \exp(-r_{n+m}^s \cdot (n+m))$
Outflow for investment in n-day bills	$=$ same
net	$= 0 \quad (2)$

At time $t + n$:

Inflow from maturation of n-day bills	$= \exp(-r_{n+m}^s \cdot (n+m)) \cdot \exp(r_n^s \cdot (n))$
	$= \exp(-{}_n r_m^s \cdot (m))$
Outflow from taking delivery of bills on the futures contracts	$= \exp(-{}_n r_m^f)$
net	$= \exp(-{}_n r_m^s \cdot (m)) - \exp(-{}_n r_m^f \cdot (m))$
	$> 0 \quad (3)$

[3] For a discussion of the concept of the forward rate see Fama (1976b) or Nelson (1971).

At time t + n + m:

Inflow from maturation of the m-day bill brought through the futures market	= 1
Outflow from maturation of the shorted $(n + m)$-day bill	= 1
net	= 0 (4)

TABLE 1.—EXPLANATION OF SYMBOLS

P_n = Spot price of an n-day bill per dollar of maturity value.
r_n^s = Daily continuously compounded return on an n-day bill in the spot market.
$_n r_m^f$ = The forward rate = the daily continuously compounded rate on an m-day bill, n days in the future implied by the spot market prices.
$_n r_m^f$ = The futures rate = the daily continuously compounded rate on an m-day bill, n days in the future in the futures market. In practice only m = 91 day bills are traded in the futures market.

The arbitrager receives a certain cash flow at time $t + n$ without the investment of any funds.

If the forward rate is greater than the futures rate the arbitrager would simply reverse his position and

1. Short a bill with n-day maturity.
2. Invest the proceeds in an $n + m$ day maturity bill.
3. Make a futures contract to deliver m day bills in n-days.

His certain cash flow at time $t + n$ would then be $\exp(-_n r_m^f \cdot (m)) - \exp(-_n r_m^s \cdot (m)) > 0$, again with no initial investment.

One could argue that the arbitrage condition may fail to hold because of the costs involved with taking short positions in bills.[4] Even if short-selling of bills were prohibited, however, divergence of the forward and futures rates implied that holders of Treasury bills could increase their return by using the futures market. Assume, for instance, that the forward rate is greater than the futures rate. Consider an investor who plans to hold bills for n-days. If he buys n-day bills, his return is r_n^s. If he buys $n + m$ day bills and enters into a futures contract to

---

[4] The costs incurred when shorting Treasury bills are discussed extensively in the fourth section.

sell them after m days, his return, denoted by r', is

$$r' = \frac{\ln[\exp {}_nr_m^f \cdot (m)/\exp(-r_{n+m}^s \cdot (n+m))]}{n}$$

$$r' = \frac{r_{n+m}^s(n+m) - {}_nr_m^f(m)}{n}.$$

Using equation (1) to decompose $r_{n+m}^s(n+m)$, we have

$$r' = \frac{r_n^s(n) + {}_nr_m^s(m) - {}_nr_m^f(m)}{n},$$

$$r' = r_n^s + \frac{{}_nr_m^s(m) - {}_nr_m^f(m)}{n} > r_n^s. \qquad (5)$$

The last inequality follows from the assumption that the forward rate is greater than the futures rate.

Should the forward rate be less than the futures rate, investors who plan to hold bills for $n + m$ days could increase their return by buying n-day bills and entering into futures contracts to buy m-day bills in n days, instead of buying $n + m$ day bills. The return, denoted by r'', would be

$$r'' = \frac{r_n^s(n) + {}_nr_m^f(m)}{n+m}.$$

Rewriting the above

$$r'' = \frac{r_n^s(n) + {}_nr_m^s(m)}{n+m} + \frac{{}_nr_m^f(m) - {}_nr_m^s(m)}{n+m}.$$

Again using equation (1)

$$r'' = r_{n+m}^s + \frac{{}_nr_m^f(m) - {}_nr_m^s(m)}{n+m} > r_{n+m}^s. \qquad (6)$$

Here, the inequality follows from the assumption that the futures rate is greater than the forward rate. Thus, whenever the forward rate differs from the futures rate, holders of Treasury bills could increase their return without altering the maturity of their investment. In a competitive capital market, therefore, the arbitrage conditions should hold even if short-selling is prohibited.

III. TEST RESULTS

To test whether the arbitrage conditions were satisfied, weekly data were collected on futures and spot Treasury bill rates. The futures returns were computed from Wednesday's closing prices for the first three futures contracts as reported in Thursday's *Wall Street Journal*. Correspondingly forward rates were computed from the returns on spot bills as reported in the Wall Street Journal. The average of the bid and the ask quotes was used in computing the forward rates.[5] The data were limited to the first three futures contracts, because beyond that horizon it is more difficult to compute a forward rate that closely corresponds to the futures rate. The sample period begins January 6, 1976, when the futures market opened, and runs through the maturity of the June 1978 futures contract.

The results are summarized in tables 2, 3a, 3b and 3c. Table 2 represents the average deviation and the average absolute deviation between the futures rate and the forward rate. The averages were computed by taking the first three futures contracts, subtracting the relevant forward rate from the futures rate, and averaging the difference over the thirteen weeks in the quarter. This means that the maturity of the futures contract is not held constant when the average is computed. For example, row one, column two was calculated by following the June 1976 contract over the quarter from January 6, 1976 to March 21, 1976. During this period the maturity of the contract dropped from 24 to 13 weeks.

Though the average deviation is generally small for the near contract, it tends to grow as maturity is increased. For the longest term contracts studied, those with a maturity of 26 to 39 weeks, column 3 of table 2 shows that the average deviation was typically of the order of 40 basis points. For these contracts the futures rate always exceeded the forward rate with the exception of two observations (this can be seen by noting that the average and average absolute differences are equal). In addition, there has been no tendency for the difference between the futures and forward rate to decline over time, despite the fact that the volume of trading has increased dramatically.[6]

To place these results in perspective, a discrepancy of one basis point implies a profit of about $25 when the arbitrage position described in the previous section is set up using bills with a maturity value of $1 million. A 40 basis point deviation will thus produce income of $1,000 per futures contract before transactions costs. Forty basis points or more of deviation is typical for the contract with 6 to 9 months to maturity.

The relationship between the deviation and the maturity of the futures contract is more clearly shown in tables 3a, 3b and 3c. The data

---

[5] All calculations were repeated using bid prices since some practitioners argue that bids more accurately reflect true market prices. No useful differences in the results appeared; therefore only the results from averaging bid and ask prices are reported.

[6] In the first quarter of 1976 trading was only of the order of 100 contracts a day, so the discrepancy could, perhaps, be attributed to a thin market in which investors could not take sizable positions at the previous transaction price. From early 1977 to the present, however, volume has averaged about 1,500 contracts a day and the discrepancy has not declined.

TABLE 2.—AVERAGE DEVIATION (1) AND AVERAGE ABSOLUTE DEVIATION (2) OF FUTURES RATE FROM THE IMPLIED FORWARD RATE (BASIS POINTS)

Quarter Ending	Near Contract	Near + 3 months	Near + 6 months
March 1976	(1) −4.8	−9.6	17.5
	(2) 7.4	11.5	32.4
June 1976	(1) −1.1	37.1	45.2
	(2) 5.4	37.5	45.2
Sept. 1976	(1) 1.2	2.2	57.1
	(2) 3.2	10.2	57.1
Dec. 1976	(1) −6.0	6.5	25.6
	(2) 7.3	10.2	25.6
March 1977	(1) −1.3	19.2	68.4
	(2) 5.0	19.9	68.4
June 1977	(1) −4.8	19.3	46.3
	(2) 8.4	21.7	46.3
Sept. 1977	(1) −1.0	−9.2	59.6
	(2) 5.7	20.7	59.6
Dec. 1977	(1) −10.8	−1.8	39.1
	(2) 11.3	18.3	39.1
March 1978	(1) −10.6	−2.88	39.7
	(2) 12.11	15.78	39.7
June 1978	(1) −12.4	−5.9	36.7
	(2) 13.4	25.11	38.0

in the tables are averages over contracts of a given maturity. Table 3a is for the entire period, while tables 3b and 3c present data for the subperiods from January 6, 1976 to June 22, 1977 and from June 23, 1977 to June 20, 1978. The sample was divided as a further test of the proposition that the discrepancy was the result of the newness of the bill futures market. Though there are some differences, the same general pattern appears in both periods. For the near term contracts, the deviations are close to zero, although negative deviations do appear in the later period. Beginning with the sixteen week maturity, however, the deviations turn positive and increase almost monotonically to a maximum of nearly 70 basis points at a maturity of 38 weeks.

In addition, it should be noted that we report *average* discrepancies. An investor could earn larger returns than these figures indicate by taking positions only when discrepancies were particularly large. In some cases the difference between the forward and futures rate was close to 100 basis points.

In summary, our results show that the arbitrage conditions set out in the previous section do not hold. With the exception of the first few weeks of trading, the average deviation between the two markets has been surprisingly stable. Further, the discrepancy between the arbitrage condition and the observed rates is a function of the maturity of the futures contract. Finally, the discrepancy has not disappeared despite the extensive publicity the market has received in recent years.

Table 3a.—Average Deviation and Average Absolute Deviation by Weeks to Maturity: January 6, 1976—June 20, 1978

Weeks to Maturity	Average Deviation	Average Absolute Deviation	Weeks to Maturity	Average Deviation	Average Absolute Deviation
0	0.1	2.1	20	12.5	15.9
1	0.9	2.5	21	13.2	16.1
2	3.1	7.3	22	14.2	20.6
3	−6.0	7.1	23	18.9	21.8
4	−8.3	8.4	24	24.3	24.3
5	−8.8	8.8	25	30.1	30.1
6	−12.0	13.9	26	27.4	27.6
7	−5.7	8.9	27	19.3	20.6
8	−10.3	11.5	28	36.8	36.8
9	−7.0	10.9	29	34.6	34.6
10	−2.6	8.6	30	37.9	39.1
11	−5.1	8.4	31	39.9	39.9
12	−8.8	15.9	32	47.7	47.7
13	−15.3	18.1	33	46.5	48.9
14	−13.2	15.5	34	44.4	48.6
15	−2.6	17.1	35	41.9	50.6
16	−0.5	13.6	36	41.8	43.7
17	3.5	16.9	37	58.6	58.6
18	7.1	10.2	38	65.5	65.5
19	15.1	20.1			

182

TABLE 3b.—AVERAGE DEVIATION AND AVERAGE ABSOLUTE DEVIATION BY WEEKS TO MATURITY: JANUARY 6, 1976—JUNE 22, 1977

Weeks to Maturity	Average Deviation	Average Absolute Deviation	Weeks to Maturity	Average Deviation	Average Absolute Deviation
0	−1.0	1.7	19	18.4	21.8
1	0.9	1.7	20	14.9	19.8
2	2.7	3.3	21	9.9	20.5
3	−2.2	4.0	22	17.4	22.2
4	−4.3	4.4	23	28.9	28.9
5	−7.7	7.8	24	36.6	36.6
6	−8.9	12.0	25	33.4	33.4
7	0.1	5.2	26	21.5	21.5
8	−6.0	8.0	27	44.2	44.2
9	−3.8	9.1	28	40.2	40.2
10	1.2	8.8	29	44.7	44.7
11	2.4	3.1	30	42.1	42.1
12	0.8	11.0	31	47.8	47.8
13	−2.3	7.0	32	47.5	51.4
14	−2.1	6.0	33	46.9	54.0
15	9.3	13.0	34	38.3	52.8
16	6.2	15.6	35	38.3	41.5
17	10.7	15.5	36	61.0	61.0
18	18.2	26.4			

183

TABLE 3c.—AVERAGE DEVIATION AND AVERAGE ABSOLUTE DEVIATION BY WEEKS TO MATURITY: JUNE 23, 1977—JUNE 20, 1978

Weeks to Maturity	Average Deviation	Average Absolute Deviation	Weeks to Maturity	Average Deviation	Average Absolute Deviation
0	1.2	2.6	20	3.7	6.9
1	1.0	3.8	21	10.6	10.6
2	3.6	13.4	22	20.7	20.7
3	−11.8	11.8	23	21.1	21.1
4	−14.3	14.3	24	17.4	17.4
5	−10.4	10.4	25	20.4	20.4
6	−16.7	16.7	26	18.4	19.0
7	−14.4	14.1	27	16.0	19.4
8	−16.7	17.0	28	25.7	25.7
9	−11.8	13.5	29	26.2	26.2
10	−8.4	8.4	30	27.7	31.5
11	−16.3	16.3	31	36.7	36.7
12	−23.2	23.2	32	47.6	47.6
13	−34.8	34.8	33	45.1	45.1
14	−29.8	29.8	34	40.6	40.6
15	−20.5	23.3	35	47.3	47.3
16	−10.5	10.5	36	47.0	47.0
17	−7.2	8.9	37	55.1	55.1
18	3.7	6.8	38	61.1	61.1
19	10.6	10.6			

184

IV. SHORT-SELLING AND THE ARBITRAGE CONDITION

The existence of a differential between the forward and futures rate does not imply that arbitrage will occur if arbitrage is costly. Potential arbitrage costs can be broken down into (1) the costs of opening and closing a futures position, (2) the costs of buying and selling spot bills, and (3) the cost of taking a short position in spot bills. The first two costs are minimal. Treasury bill futures contracts can be traded through discount commodity brokerage firms for $25 per round turn. The costs are even less for a large trader who can negotiate commissions or invest in a seat on the exchange. The cost of buying or selling one million of spot Treasury bills, represented by the bid-ask spread, is about $30 for actively traded bills, and can increase to about $100 on less active issues. In combination, these expenses can account for a differential of no more than 3 to 5 basis points between futures and forward rates.

The third cost is more significant. In order to borrow the bills from a government securities dealer for shorting, the investor must post collateral equal to the value of the bills borrowed. In terms of the arbitrage position, however, this is not a significant constraint because the dealer will accept other bills, on which the short seller receives the interest, as collateral.[7] More importantly, dealers require that borrowers pay a premium of 50 basis points per annum on the borrowed bills. The existence of this premium implies that short-selling costs are a function of time, because the borrower is forced to pay the premium as long as he maintains the short position. As a result, the differential between forward and futures rates can increase with maturity of the futures contract without arbitragers being attracted to the market.

The effects of the arbitrage costs on the differential are illustrated in figures 1a, 1b and 1c. Once again, the three figures correspond to the total period and the two subperiods. At a maturity of zero, trading costs would allow for a differential of about 4 basis points before arbitrage became profitable. The allowable differential grows at a rate of 3.85 basis points per week because of the premium arbitragers must pay on their short positions in Treasury bills.[8] All of the observations from the tables fall well within the bands set by these short-selling and transactions costs.

Closer inspection of the figures reveals that an arbitrager may not have to wait the full term to maturity to realize the profit from the

---

[7] Most dealers require that the bills posted as collateral have a shorter maturity than the bills borrowed. If such is not the case, some additional collateral must be posted. As long as the investor can post bills as collateral and receive the interest, the opportunity cost of posting collateral is zero.

[8] Fifty basis points is $5,000 per year on a million dollar bill. The 3.85 basis points per week is ($5,000 ÷ 52 weeks) ÷ $25 profit per basis point on the arbitrage position.

186   *Interest Rate Futures: Concepts and Issues*

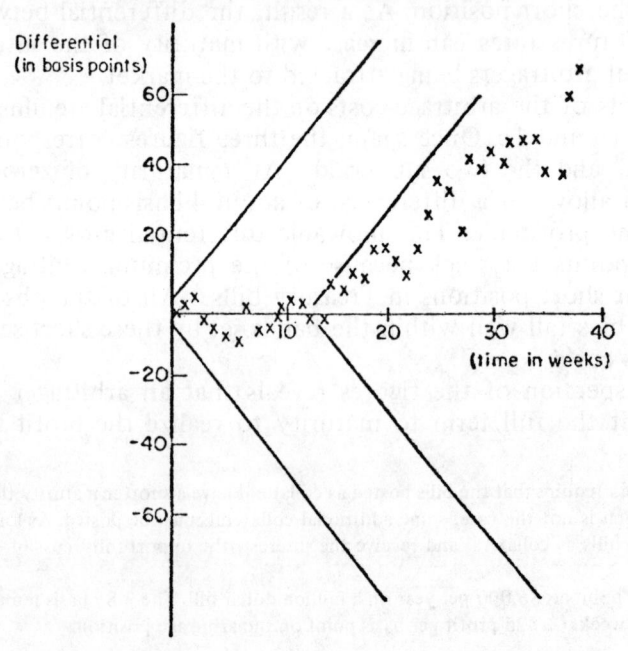

FIGURE 1a.—ARBITRAGE COSTS AND THE DIFFERENCE
BETWEEN FORWARD AND FUTURES RATES:
JANUARY 6, 1976—JUNE 20, 1978

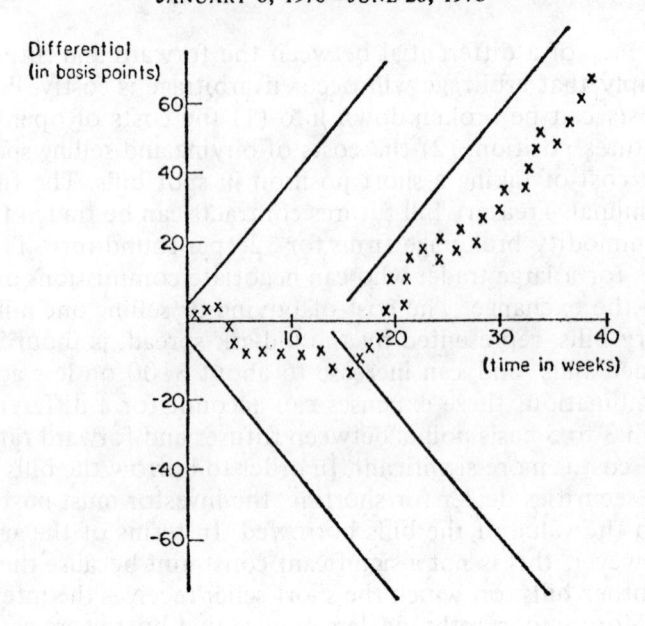

FIGURE 1b.—ARBITRAGE COSTS AND THE DIFFERENCE
BETWEEN FORWARD AND FUTURES RATES:
JANUARY 6, 1976—JUNE 23, 1977

FIGURE 1c.—ARBITRAGE COSTS AND THE DIFFERENCE
BETWEEN FORWARD AND FUTURES RATES:
JUNE 23, 1977—JUNE 20, 1978

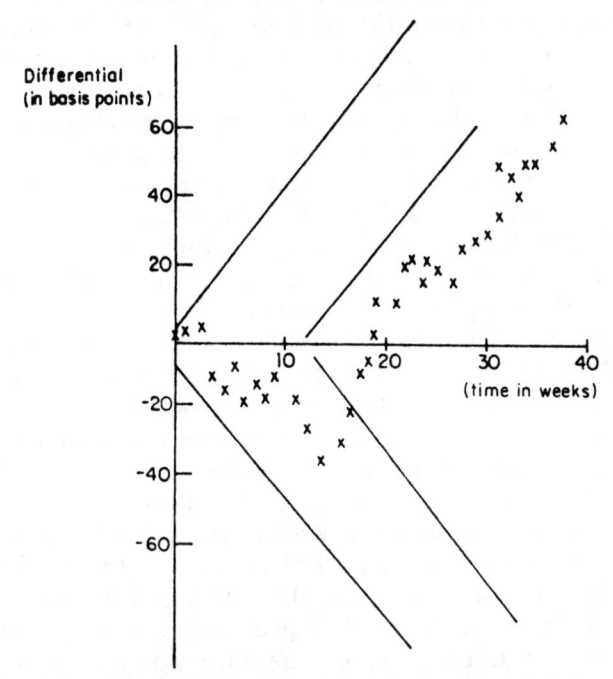

position. The positive discrepancies between forward and futures rates typically have disappeared by the time the maturity has fallen to 14 weeks. Thus an arbitrager with a position in 39 week (9 month) futures would obtain the entire profit from the position within 25 weeks.

If we redraw the arbitrage cost band to reflect the dogleg pattern (line B in figure 1), the differential tracks close to the upper boundary, but the points still lie inside the band. The average change in the differential from 14 to 38 weeks is 2.9 basis points per week, fairly close to the 3.85 basis point slope of the arbitrage cost band. One question that can be raised is why the dogleg pattern appears, i.e., why is there a small or negative differential on the near contract (0-13 weeks) but an increasing differential on more distant contracts? There does not appear to be a facile answer to the question. We hope future study will be able to resolve the problem.

The existence of short-selling costs is a necessary, but not a sufficient, condition for explaining the sustained differential between the forward and futures rates. As was observed in section II, the existence of a differential implies that holders of Treasury bills could increase their return by making judicious use of the futures market. The fact that the differential has failed to decline is evidence that corporations and commercial banks have not aggressively exploited the futures market. This is consistent with a study by Snyder (1977) which reported that institutions were not actively involved in the futures trading.[9,10] The same observation applies to short-selling. By lending bills to short sellers, firms could profit from the 50 basis point per year premium. Such activity would, in turn, reduce the lending premium and thereby make possible increased arbitrage between the spot and the futures markets.

Aside from concluding that management has been slack, there are a number of other explanations for why corporations and commercial banks have chosen not to enter the futures market. Entering a new market is not costless for a company. Traders and their superiors must be educated, the futures market must be monitored, new accounting methods must be developed for dealing with margin calls, and the firm must be prepared to explain any "speculative" losses to the stockholders (in the minds of many people all activity in the futures market is speculative). Whether the added return justifies bearing these costs depends on the number of contracts that could be traded at favorable prices, but a company has no way of knowing how long any discrepancy will persist. It is possible that by the time a trading operation could be established, the profit opportunities would have disappeared.

In addition, a futures contract in Treasury bills must always be riskier than the bills themselves. Both parties to the contract cannot give each other the same assurance that the U.S. Government can provide. For example, if the short seller gives large amounts of collateral to the purchaser as a security deposit, he must worry about whether his collateral will be returned. If both parties give collateral to a third party, such as the exchange, they must worry about the solvency of the exchange. The same comments apply to the shorting of bills in the cash market. A private party that issues the bills cannot match the government's guarantee. At least part of the 50 basis point premium, therefore, can be interpreted as compensation for bearing this added risk.

Whether these factors are sufficient to explain the reported discrepancies is a question that cannot be resolved by a priori argument. Detailed data would have to be collected on the internal organizational costs of entering the futures market, and an attempt would have to be made to measure the risk of purchasing shorted Treasury bills. Both of these tasks are beyond the scope of this paper.

---

[9] One possible explanation for institutional reluctance to enter the market is the fear of default on futures contracts. While both the brokerage firm and the exchange must guarantee the contract, default would be a possibility in the case of a very large position. Note, however, that if default occurs all the firm looses is the capital gain on the position. Because no actual purchase of securities occurs when a futures contract is made, the investor does not risk losing the face value of the Treasury bills. The contract is simply aborted and no delivery or payment takes place.

[10] In some cases legal restrictions have prevented institutions from entering the market. A plan by the State of California to use the futures market to increase the return on short-term cash balances was overruled by the State Attorney General.

V. SUMMARY AND CONCLUSIONS

This paper has studied the relationship between the rates on Treasury bill futures contracts and forward rates implied by the term structure of interest rates. An arbitrage condition was derived that predicted that the forward and futures rates would be equal. The empirical results, however, showed the existence of a differential between the forward and futures rates. This differential increased almost monotonically with the time to maturity of the futures contract, and exhibited no tendency to decline as the volume of futures trading increased.

The behavior of the differential can be rationalized by the existence of two institutional constraints: (1) short-selling costs in the form of a premium of 50 basis points per year on borrowed bills and (2) the reluctance of institutions to enter the futures market. These constraints, in turn, can be at least partially attributed to the existence of underlying costs and risk differentials. Internal reorganization and training is required before a firm can enter the futures market. Once a firm is in the market, personnel and data processing costs are involved in seeking profitable opportunities. A firm, or any purchaser of a shorted Treasury bill, also has the problem of determining the riskiness of that security. Since no private institution can match the government's guarantee, shorted bills must offer some risk premium. The same is true of futures contracts; because no collateral arrangement can be designed to give both parties to the contract the same assurance the U.S. Government can offer, positions involving futures contracts are not identical to positions in the cash market.

References

Black, Fischer, "The Pricing of Commodity Contracts," *Journal of Financial Economics* 3 (Mar. 1976), 167-179.
Burger, Albert E., Richard W. Lang, and Robert H. Rasche, "The Treasury Bill Futures Market and Market Expectations of Interest Rates," *Federal Reserve Bank of St. Louis Monthly Review* (June 1977), 1-9.
Dusak, K., "Futures Trading and Investor Returns: An Investigation of Commodity Market Risk Premiums," *Journal of Political Economy* 81 (Nov./Dec. 1973), 1387-1406.
Fama, Eugene F., "Short-term Interest Rates as Predictors of Inflation," *American Economic Review* 65 (June 1975), 269-282.
———, "Inflation Uncertainty and Expected Returns on Treasury Bills," *Journal of Political Economy* 84 (June 1976a), 427-448.
———, "Forward Rates as Predictors of Future Spot Rates," *Journal of Financial Economics* 3 (Oct. 1976b), 361-378.
Hamburger, Michael J., and E. N. Platt, "The Expectations Hypothesis and the Efficiency of the Treasury Bill Market," this *Review* 57 (May 1975), 190-199.
Nelson, Charles R., *The Term Structure of Interest Rates* (New York: Basic Books, 1971).
Roll, Richard, *The Behavior of Interest Rates* (New York: Basic Books, 1970).

———, "A Critique of the Asset Pricing Theory's Tests," *Journal of Financial Economics* 4 (Mar. 1977), 129-176.

Snyder, Linda, "How to Speculate in the World's Safest Investment," *Fortune Magazine* (July 1977).

The Efficiency of the Treasury Bill Futures Market[*]

Richard J. Rendleman, Jr. and Christopher E. Carabini[†]

On January 6, 1976, the International Monetary Market of the Chicago Mercantile Exchange began trading the Treasury bill futures contract. Compared with other financial instruments, the Treasury bill futures contract is relatively simple to price. As we will show, the equilibrium price of a contract can be determined or closely approximated from observable spot Treasury bill prices. Given the ease of pricing the contract, one would expect the market for Treasury bill futures to be highly efficient. The purpose of this paper is to test the efficiency of the Treasury bill futures market.

The specifications of the contract call for delivery of a $1,000,000 par value, 90-day U.S. Treasury bill, although 91 or 92 day bills are substitutable. The delivery months are March, June, September, and December, and eight contract maturities are currently traded. Contracts are deliverable on the second day following the Federal Reserve 3-month (13 week) Treasury bill auction of the third week of the delivery month. This generally falls on the third Thursday of the month.

---

[*]Reprinted from the *Journal of Finance*, Vol. 34, (September 1979). Reprinted by permission of the publisher and authors.

[†]Assistant Professor of Finance and Ph.D. student, Northwestern University, Graduate School of Management. The authors wish to thank the International Options Company for partial funding of this study, the Chicago Mercantile Exchange for providing futures price data, and Bruce Bagamery for providing computational assistance. We also wish to acknowledge Ronnie Anderson, Brit Bartter, Ben Branch, Uri Dothan, George Morgan, Joe Swanson, Robert Taggart, Joseph Williams, and especially, Richard McEnally for providing helpful comments.

Recently, several studies (Branch [2], Capozza and Cornell [3], Emery and Scott [5], Lang and Rasche [6], Oldfield [7], Poole [8], and Puglisi [9]) of the Treasury bill futures market have attempted either to test the efficiency of the market or to test the empirical validity of the Expectations Hypothesis of the term structure of interest rates. Both types of tests focused on the existence of arbitrage opportunities between the futures and spot markets. Although the nonexistence of arbitrage opportunities does not prove the Expectations Hypothesis, the studies that intended to test the Hypothesis can be viewed as indirect tests of market efficiency.[1]

These studies find conflicting evidence regarding the efficiency of the futures market. These conflicting results can be partially explained by differences in sample sizes and sample periods. However, it is possible that the same data may not have been employed in a consistent manner in all studies. For example, only in the Branch, Poole, and Lang and Rasche papers is there any recognition of the fact that the delivery vehicle for contracts, other than the nearby contract, has never existed. Therefore, it is not clear how this problem was resolved in the development of the data to be tested. In addition, several studies recognize the existence of transaction costs, either objectively or subjectively, but in some cases the treatment of transaction costs is inconsistent.

Emery and Scott, Poole, and Oldfield found that differences between futures prices and forward prices implied in spot bills were not of the magnitude to permit profitable arbitrage. Oldfield's tests showed a tendency for the market to become more efficient during the first year of trading. Poole focused only on the futures contract nearest to maturity.

Using weekly data for the first eighteen months of trading, Capozza and Cornell concluded that the nearest term contract was priced efficiently. The longer term contracts tended to be under-priced and the extent of under-pricing was directly related to the time remaining until the futures matured. However, none of these discrepancies could have been directly arbitraged due to the cost of shorting the spot bill necessary to establish the appropriate position.

Branch, Lang and Rasche, and Puglisi found the futures market to be inefficient. Branch's sample of only eighteen dates casts considerable doubt on any general conclusions about efficiency that can be inferred from his study. Much of the evidence in the Lang and Rasche study in support of inefficiency is provided by futures contracts with a year or more to maturity. The delivery vehicles for these contracts do not exist; therefore, Lang and Rasche used the yields of coupon securities to compute theoretical futures yields. Given the well-known problems associated with yield to maturity as a return measure which result from

---

[1] See Cox, Ingersoll and Ross [4] for an excellent description of the confusion surrounding the Expectations Hypothesis and other theories of the term structure of interest rates.

coupon and tax effects, it is unlikely that one can infer theoretical futures prices from the yields of such securities. As shown later, some of the empirical results obtained by Puglisi contrast sharply with the results of the present study. The conflicting findings of the above studies suggest that the question of market efficiency remains an unresolved issue.

I. PRICING THE FUTURES CONTRACT

The Equilibrium Futures Price

The equilibrium price of the futures contract can be determined on the basis of arbitrage relationships between the futures contract and spot bills. If the futures and spot markets are in equilibrium, there can be no pure arbitrage or quasi arbitrage opportunities available between the two markets.[2]

Consider the following graphical representation of the time dimensions of a typical Treasury bill futures contract.

```
Time 0 ──────────────── m ──────────────── n
                                            Maturity Date
                        Maturity            of Delivery
         Current        Date of             Vehicle for
         Date           Futures Contract    Futures Contract
```

The futures contract allows the investor to contract to either buy or sell a Treasury bill that will mature at time n for a fixed commitment price at time m.

Let P_m and P_n represent the spot prices per $100 of par value for T-bills maturing at time m and n, respectively. In addition, let FP represent the futures price per $100 of par. Consider a situation in which the bill maturing at time n is purchased for P_n at the present time and its time m selling price is locked in at FP through a futures contract. If this transaction offers a different return than could be obtained by simply purchasing a bill for P_m (FP/100) with a time m maturity value of FP, market pressures should eventually bring the returns into parity. Similarly, it might be possible to purchase a bill for P_m (FP/100) with a time m maturity value of FP and use the maturity proceeds of the bill to fund a position in the futures contract that would provide a higher return than could be obtained by paying P_n for the bill maturing at time n. Again, one would expect market pressures to close this gap until the prices of the two equivalent portfolios were the same. In the absence of

---

[2] Pure arbitrage refers to shorting a security or portfolio to fund a position in an economically equivalent security or portfolio at a lower price. Quasi arbitrage refers to selling securities from an existing portfolio to fund an economically equivalent position at a lower price.

transaction costs, both of these situations imply that equilibrium will be attained in the futures market when

$$P_m (FP/100) = P_n \qquad (1A)$$

or

$$FP = 100\, P_n/P_m, \qquad (2A)$$

where FP is the theoretical no-arbitrage futures price.[3]

Even if the actual and theoretical futures prices are not the same, the transaction costs involved with using futures to improve a portfolio's yield may eliminate much of the potential gain. Prior to negotiated rates,[4] round-trip commissions on the futures contract were $60.00 or $.006 per $100 of par. Unlike commissions on stocks, these brokerage fees are paid when the position in the futures contract is reversed.

---

[3] This derivation treats the futures contract as if it is a forward contract. Futures contracts differ from forward contracts, however, in that day-to-day changes in the futures prices are either debited or credited to the customer's account with any deficits having to be replenished with cash. Thus, to be technically correct, any futures pricing model should take these day-to-day changes into account.

Cox, Ingersoll and Ross (4) have shown that (2A) will not hold if interest rates are uncertain. They develop a closed form solution for pricing unit discount bonds (Treasury bills) and futures contracts under the assumption that the instantaneous interest rate (which might be viewed as the Federal Funds rate in practice) follows a mean reverting square root diffusion process. The inputs to the unit discount bond model are the current instantaneous interest rate, the natural rate, the variance of percentage changes in the interest rate, the mean reverting diffusion process speed of adjustment coefficient, the covariance of changes in interest rates with percentage changes in optimally invested wealth, and the time to maturity of the bond. The inputs to the futures pricing model are the same except that one must specify the time to maturity for both the futures contract and the bond that serves as the contract's delivery vehicle.

Using a variety of inputs, we have computed futures prices using the Cox, Ingersoll and Ross model. For input parameters that give rise to "reasonable" unit discount bond prices, the difference between theoretical forward and futures IMM Index values (which we define later) is generally less than 3-4 basis points for contracts with 270 days to maturity. The difference is generally less for shorter maturities. An example of a "reasonable" unit discount bond price would be $.92 per $1.00 of par for a one year bond if the instantaneous (Federal Funds) rate were 6%. We would not consider a $.75 price per $1.00 of par to be reasonable, however, given a 6% instantaneous rate. At the "unreasonable" prices, we do find wide discrepancies.

Using numerical methods, we have also computed futures and forward prices using an alternative model that assumes that the Expectations Hypothesis of the term structure of interest rates holds and that the instantaneous interest rate follows a lognormal distribution. The inputs to this model are the current instantaneous rate, the expected drift and variance of the rate, and the time parameters associated with the maturity of the various securities. Using a wide range of input parameters, we were unable to find any differences between futures and forward prices that we could view as significant (all differences were generally less than one basis point). Based on these calculations, we feel that it is unlikely that our tests, which price the futures contract as if it was a forward contract, are significantly biased.

[4] Fixed rates were phased out completely in March, 1978, the final month of our sample period.

The Efficiency of the Treasury Bill Futures Market

In addition to this cost, the buying and selling prices of Treasury bills are not the same due to the dealer's bid-asked spread. These transaction costs imply that a range of futures prices will exist over which arbitrage between the futures and spot markets will not be possible.

To determine the lower bound of this range, consider the situation in which the time m bill and the futures contract are purchased as a substitute for the bill maturing at time n. With transaction costs, the bill that matures at time m must be purchased to fund both the futures contract and the commission on the contract. In addition, the bill must be purchased at the dealer's asking price.

Let P_m^A represent the asking price of the bill maturing at time m per $100 of par. The amount paid to fund the long position in the bill maturing at time m for FP + $.006 would be $P_m^A [(FP + .006)/100]$. This long position in the time m bill in conjunction with the long position in the futures contract will ensure a return of $100 at time n. If the dealer's bid price, P_n^B, for the bill maturing at time n for $100 is greater than $P_m^A [(FP + .006)/100]$, arbitrage would be possible. Thus, in an efficient market, one would expect the futures price to be set so that this type of arbitrage opportunity would not be present,

or
$$P_m^A \left(\frac{FP + .006}{100} \right) \geq P_n^B. \tag{1B}$$

This implies that the equilibrium futures price will meet the following condition:

$$FP \geq 100\, P_n^B/P_m^A - .006. \tag{2B}$$

In a similar manner, it can be shown that the upper bound of the equilibrium futures price is given by:

$$FP \leq 100\, P_n^A/P_m^B + .006. \tag{2C}$$

Determining the Equilibrium Value of the IMM Index

The International Monetary Market of the Chicago Mercantile Exchange has adopted the IMM Index for pricing the Treasury bill futures contract. This index is quite similar to the bankers' discount method of pricing Treasury bills. The index value is simply the difference between the par value of the bill (on a $100 basis) and its annualized discount from par, assuming 360 days to the year. For example, an IMM Index value of $92 corresponds to an actual contract price of $100 − $(100−92) (90/360) = $98 for a futures contract on a 90-day bill. The futures contract is actually written in terms of $1,000,000 or par rather than $100. Therefore, a one basis point move in the index represents a

$.01 [$1,000,000/$100] × 90/360 = $25 gain or loss in the actual price of the contract.[5]

Subtracting the futures prices in (2B) and (2C) from $100 and multiplying by 360/91, the annualized discounts from par of the futures prices can be determined. These discounts can then be subtracted from $100 to obtain the following range of equilibrium IMM Index values:

$$100 - 395.6\,[1 - P_n^B/P_m^A] - .0237 \leq \text{IMM}$$
$$\leq 100 - 395.6\,[1 - P_n^A/P_m^B] + .0237. \quad (3)$$

If P_m and P_n are expanded in terms of the bankers' discount pricing convention, and one basis point is subtracted from the lower bound of the IMM Index and added to the upper bound to allow for the market maker's spread in the futures contract, the equilibrium range for the index can be restated in terms of the percentage discount yields (Y_m and Y_n) and days to maturity (D_m and D_n) of the two bills.[6]

$$100 - 395.6\left[\frac{Y_n^B D_n/360 - Y_m^A D_m/360}{100 - Y_m^A D_m/360}\right] - .0337 \leq \text{IMM}$$
$$\leq 100 - 395.6\left[\frac{Y_n^A D_n/360 - Y_m^B D_m/360}{100 - Y_m^B D_m/360}\right] + .0337 \quad (4)$$

In the absence of all transaction costs, the equilibrium IMM Index value reduces to:

$$\text{IMM} = 100 - 395.6\left[\frac{Y_n D_n/360 - Y_m D_m/360}{100 - Y_m D_m/360}\right], \quad (5)$$

which is the IMM Index value corresponding to the futures price given in (2A).

II. ANALYSIS

If the spot and futures markets are in equilibrium, observed IMM Index values should fall within the bounds of (4). Otherwise, it would be possible to improve the yield of an existing portfolio by trading fu-

---

[5] If a position in a futures contract is reversed prior to maturity, the investor's gain or loss is $25 per basis point difference in the IMM Index values at which the contract is bought and sold. Therefore, prior to maturity, settlement in the contract is based on a 90-day maturity, even if 90 days will not be the maturity of the delivery vehicle. During the period of this study, a 91-day bill has always served as the delivery vehicle for the futures contract. If one either makes or takes delivery in a 91-day bill, the settlement price is adjusted to reflect the extra day. Thus, each basis point move in the IMM Index represents a $25 × 91/90 or $25.28 gain or loss in a contract in which delivery takes place. In the remaining analysis, we compute all IMM Index values on a 91 day basis.

[6] According to the research department of the Chicago Mercantile Exchange, the market maker's bid-asked spread is typically two basis points.

tures. As we explain later, one might also expect to observe a tendency for prices to converge to the no-transaction cost price of (5), even in the presence of transaction costs. Thus, to test the efficiency of these markets, we examine the relationship between actual IMM Index values and theoretical values given by (4) and (5).

Description of the Data

Price data for the futures contracts were provided by the Chicago Mercantile Exchange. These data contained the price and time of trade of every transaction from the commencement of trading on January 6, 1976, through March 31, 1978. From this data source, the prices of the last trades and trading times for each contract included in our analysis were collected on a daily basis for this study. Since the maximum maturity of a Treasury bill is one year, a more complicated pricing model would have to be developed to price futures beyond the first three maturities. Therefore, we limited our analysis to the first three contract months trading at any given date. For those days in which a trade did not take place in a given contract, the contract in question was omitted from the analysis for that day.

Bid and asked bankers' discount yields of Treasury bills maturing on the maturity date of each contract as well as the bill maturing 91 days thereafter were collected on a daily basis from the Federal Reserve Bank of New York's "Composite Closing Quotations for U.S. Government Securities." In many cases, the actual bill that would serve as the delivery vehicle for a given contract or the bill that would mature on the contract's maturity date did not exist.[7] For these contracts, we recorded the bid and asked quotes of the Treasury bills whose maturity dates most closely surrounded the date in question. In a limited number of cases, the longest term bill matured prior to the maturity date of the delivery vehicle for the third contract month. In these cases, we omitted the contract from the analysis for the day. Finally, only those days in which both the futures and Treasury bill markets were open were included in the analysis. The resulting data contained 1606 observations.

Measurement Problems

To compute the range of no-arbitrage IMM Index values, one must know the bid and asked bankers' discount yields of Treasury bills ma-

___
[7] As a general rule, the actual delivery vehicle for each contract is auctioned 93 days prior to the contract's maturity date. Except for the period 1/06/76 through 3/18/76, the maturity date of the delivery vehicle for any contract month corresponded to the maturity date of the futures contract for the next contract month.

turing on the futures' maturity dates and 91 days thereafter. In many cases, these Treasury bills had not been auctioned, making it necessary to estimate what the yields would have been had these maturities been available.

Our method of estimating such yields is based on the assumption that the yield curve can be well approximated by a linear function between any two dates that are "reasonably" close.[8] Let Y^- and Y^+ denote the bankers' discount yields of bills maturing just before and just after the maturity date of the bill for which the yield estimate is being made. Similarly, let D^*, D^- and D^+ represent the days to maturity of the bill in question and the days to maturity of the bills maturing just prior and just after this bill, respectively. A linear yield curve between days D^* and D^+ implies the following yield estimate:

$$Y^* = \frac{Y^-(D^+ - D^*) + Y^+(D^* - D^-)}{D^+ - D^-} \qquad (6)$$

When estimating either bid or asked yields to determine the range of equilibrium IMM Index values, the appropriate bid or asked yields are input into (6). When estimating yields to determine the equilibrium IMM Index without transaction costs, we use the means of the bid and asked yields as inputs into (6).

Comparison of Actual and Theoretical IMM Index Values (Transaction Costs not Considered)

The existence of transaction costs gives rise to a range of values for the IMM Index over which arbitrage opportunities are not available. Assuming that buyers and sellers of futures contracts face transaction costs of the same order of magnitude, neither group would be expected to dominate the market. Therefore, one should not expect a preponderance of trades to take place at either the high or low end of the no-arbitrage price range. Instead, the typical or average trade is likely to take place near the no-transaction cost value of the index, which will also approximate the mid-point of the no-arbitrage range. If the actual prices deviate from the no-arbitrage values, market inefficiency would not be implied due to the existence of trading costs. However, an average deviation of zero between the actual and theoretical IMM Index val-

---

[8] Technically, the "yield curve" describes the relationship between annual rates of return and maturity. We actually assume a linear relationship between bankers' discount yields and maturity. Although the bankers' discount yield approximates the true rate of return, these two measures are not the same. It is easy to show, however, that the yield estimates that we obtain would not be significantly different had we assumed a linear relationship between rates of return, rather than discounts.

ues of equation (5) would at least suggest a long-run tendency toward equilibrium.

In Table I, we present summary statistics for the difference between actual and theoretical index values. A positive difference indicates that the futures is overpriced. Summary statistics are cross-tabulated for each of the three contract months over each of the three nine-month periods of the sample. In addition, summary statistics are shown for the entire sample.

In Table I, the term "first contract month" refers to the futures contract with the least time to maturity at any given date. These contracts will always have 1-91 days until maturity. The second and third contract months refer to those contracts which mature on the two subsequent maturity dates.

These statistics suggest that futures for the nearest contract month have tended to be over-priced, while the longer-term futures have been under-priced. However, average deviations of actual IMM values from their no-transaction cost theoretical values do not appear to be consistent over time. For example, during the first eighteen months of the same period, the average deviation for the first contract month was approximately 6 basis points. The average difference increased to 15 basis points, however, during the last nine month period of the sample. During the second nine months, the second contract was under-priced by an average of 4 basis points, but during the next nine months, the relationship reversed; the contract was over-priced on average by approximately 14 basis points. Although the average deviation for the longest term contract was consistently negative, the average deviation varied by approximately 21 basis points from the second nine months to the third. Four of nine trading period-contract month cells of Table I show an average deviation that is not significantly different from zero.[9] The

---

[9] t statistics were adjusted to reflect autocorrelated basis point differentials. Let $\Delta \tau$ represent the differential observed at time τ. The following autoregressive model was fit to the data presented in both Tables 1 and 2:

$$\Delta_\tau = \delta + \phi_1 \Delta_{\tau-1} + \phi_2 \Delta_{\tau-2} + \epsilon_\tau.$$

The coefficients ϕ_1 and ϕ_2, and the standard error of estimate, σ_ϵ, are reported in the tables. In addition, the Box-Pierce (1970) Q statistic is presented. This statistic, which follows a chi-square distribution, can be used to test the residuals for significant departures from white noise. Except for a few cases which are noted in the tables, one cannot reject the hypothesis of zero autocorrelation in the residuals at the 5% level.

Letting μ and N represent the sample mean and sample size, respectively, the t statistic for testing the hypothesis of a zero mean basis point differential is:

$$t = \frac{\mu(1 - \phi_1 - \phi_2)}{(\sigma_\epsilon/\sqrt{N})}$$

With zero first and second order autocorrelation (i.e., $\phi_1 = \phi_2 = 0$), the standard error of estimate equals the estimate of the population standard deviation, and we obtain the usual t statistic.

Table I
Summary Statistics for Basis Points Differential Between Actual and No-Transaction Cost Values of IMM Index

		Contract			
Trading Period		1st Contract Month	2nd Contract Month	3rd Contract Month	All Contracts
1st 9 Months	μ	5.599	.322	−26.788	−6.260
1/06/76–9/30/76	$\|\mu\|$	6.670	17.468	35.219	19.245
	σ	7.113	21.393	28.811	25.008
	σ_ϵ	4.940	8.004	8.945	N/A
	ϕ_1, ϕ_2	.633, .124	.752, .179	.855, .083	N/A
	N	187	187	168	542
	t	3.766[a]	.038	−2.407[a]	N/A
	$Q(21, N)$	19.746	23.911	40.328[b]	N/A
2nd 9 Months	μ	6.472	−4.349	−30.884	−8.700
10/1/76–6/30/77	$\|\mu\|$	8.089	11.344	32.545	16.688
	σ	7.880	14.055	24.857	22.689
	σ_ϵ	4.693	8.119	10.627	N/A
	ϕ_1, ϕ_2	.709, .108	.743, .087	.883, .017	N/A
	N	185	186	163	534
	t	3.433[a]	−1.236	−.242	N/A
	$Q(21, N)$	16.494	30.216	21.266	N/A
3rd 9 Months	μ	15.421	13.811	−10.140	7.236
7/1/77–3/31/78	$\|\mu\|$	15.681	17.691	15.471	16.324
	σ	11.182	15.943	17.200	18.694
	σ_ϵ	5.745	7.443	5.940	N/A
	ϕ_1, ϕ_2	.716, .163	.665, .236	.939, −.002	N/A
	N	186	186	158	530
	t	4.430[a]	2.505[a]	−1.430	N/A
	$Q(21, N)$	28.999	17.132	21.467	N/A
Entire sample period	μ	9.162	3.256	−22.774	−2.670
	$\|\mu\|$	10.144	15.504	27.947	17.431
	σ	9.934	19.016	25.759	23.362
	σ_ϵ	5.159	7.887	8.794	N/A
	ϕ_1, ϕ_2	.715, .160	.743, .176	.879, .059	N/A
	N	558	559	489	1606
	t	5.244[a]	.701	3.528[a]	N/A
	$Q(21, N)$	17.957	26.060	35.312[b]	N/A

Legend:
μ = sample mean
$|\mu|$ = sample mean of absolute value
σ = sample standard deviation
σ_ϵ = standard error of estimate of second order autoregressive process
ϕ_1, ϕ_2 = first and second order autocorrelation coefficients
N = sample size
$t = \mu(1 - \phi_1 - \phi_2)/(\sigma_\epsilon/\sqrt{N})$
$Q(21, N)$ = Box-Pierce Q statistic using 21 residual autocorrelations with sample size N.
[a] Significantly different from zero at 5% level.
[b] Null hypothesis that residuals follow a white noise process is rejected at the 5% level.

relatively low t values in the remaining cells together with an average basis point differential of only -2.6 for the entire sample suggests that one could not expect to have made large excess profits in the Treasury bill futures market, even in the absence of transaction costs.

An average basis point differential of zero does not necessarily imply market efficiency, since deviations of opposite sign will tend to offset when a simple average is taken. Therefore, in Table I, the mean of the absolute value of the basis point differential is also presented.

The average absolute differential over all contracts in the entire sample is 17.431 basis points. The mean of the differentials in the first and third contract are roughly equivalent to the means of the absolute values of the differentials. This implies that the first contract was generally over-priced and the third contract was generally under-priced over the sample period. Except for the third nine month period, the average absolute differential increased with contract maturity.

Although the average absolute basis point differential has declined by approximately three basis points from the first nine months to the third, there does not appear to be significant evidence to suggest that the Treasury bill futures market has become more efficient. A reduction in the mean of the absolute basis point differential in the third contract from 35.219 to 15.471 from the first to the third nine months suggests that the contract has become more efficiently priced over time. In contrast, the mean of the absolute basis point differential in the first contract month increased from 6.670 to 15.681, indicating a tendency to become less efficiently priced.

The standard deviations of the basis point differential increased monotonically across contract maturities, indicating less predictability for the prices of the longer term contracts. It is interesting to note that the standard deviation across all maturities has decreased over time. This suggests that prices have become more predictable, but not necessarily more efficient.

In Figure 1, we present the basis point differential plotted against the number of days remaining on the contract. In this figure, as well as Figures 2 and 3, ten percent of the data points are plotted on a random basis.[10]

The same types of relationships discussed above can be seen in Figure 1. In addition, we can see that very few contracts have been under-priced during the last 120 days to maturity. Only during the last two weeks of the contract does there appear to be a convergence to the equilibrium price. The fact that the longer term contracts have been generally under-priced while the shorter-term contracts have been over-priced for all subperiods, suggests that one could expect to earn

---

[10] Separate graphs of each subperiod showing all data points will be furnished by the authors upon request.

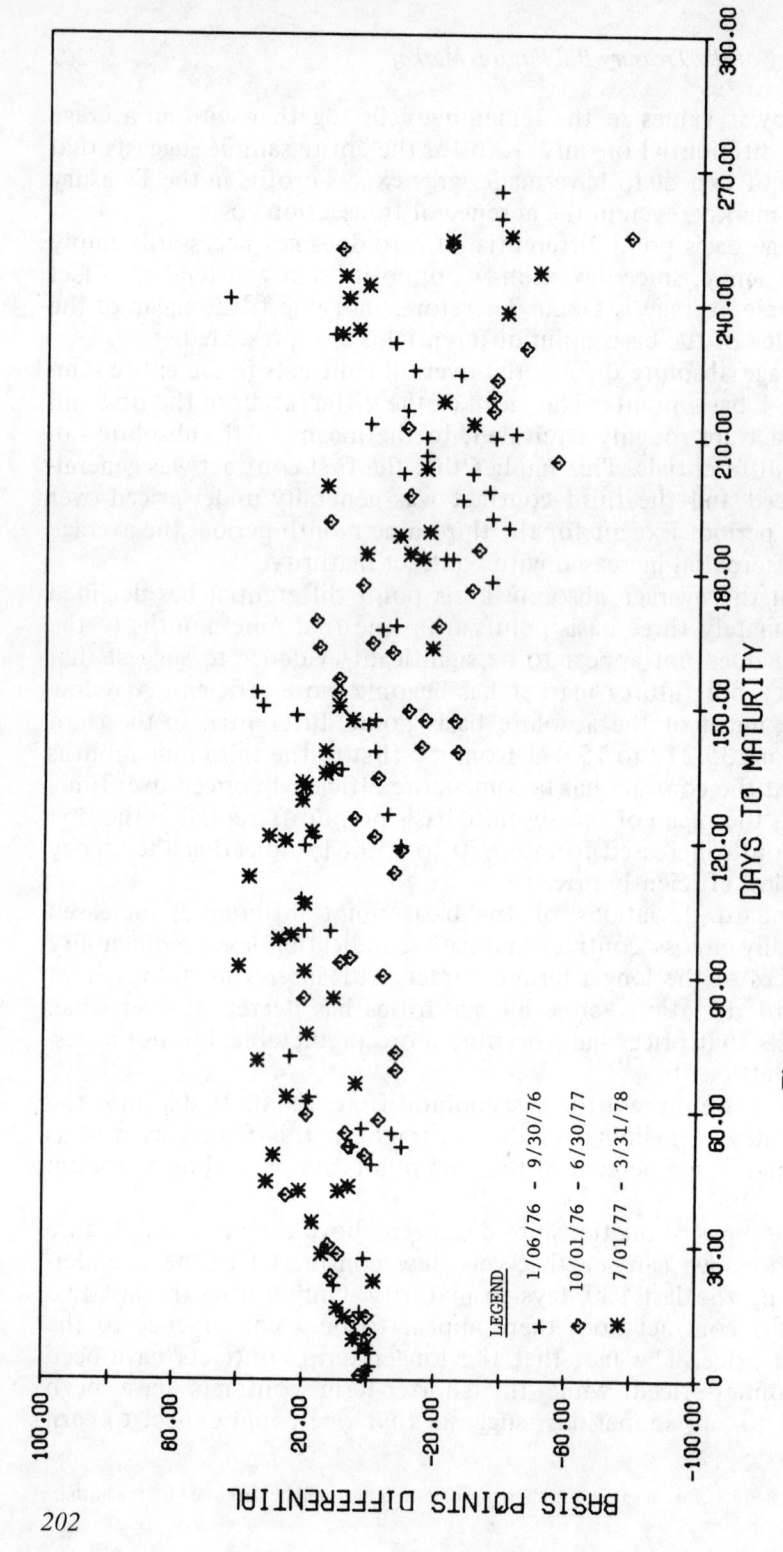

Figure 1. Non-annualized basis points differential vs. days to maturity

Figure 2. Annualized basis points differential vs. days to maturity

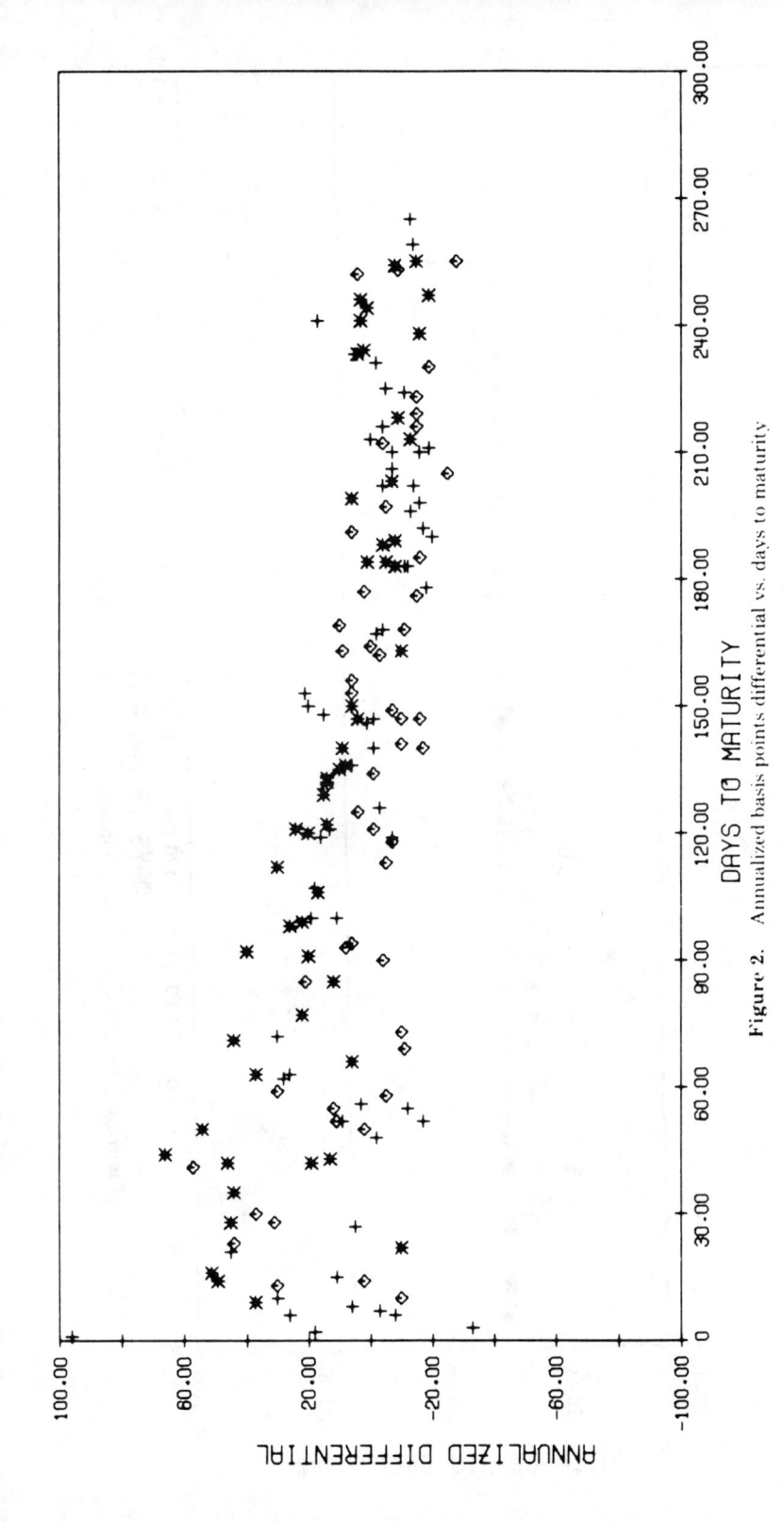

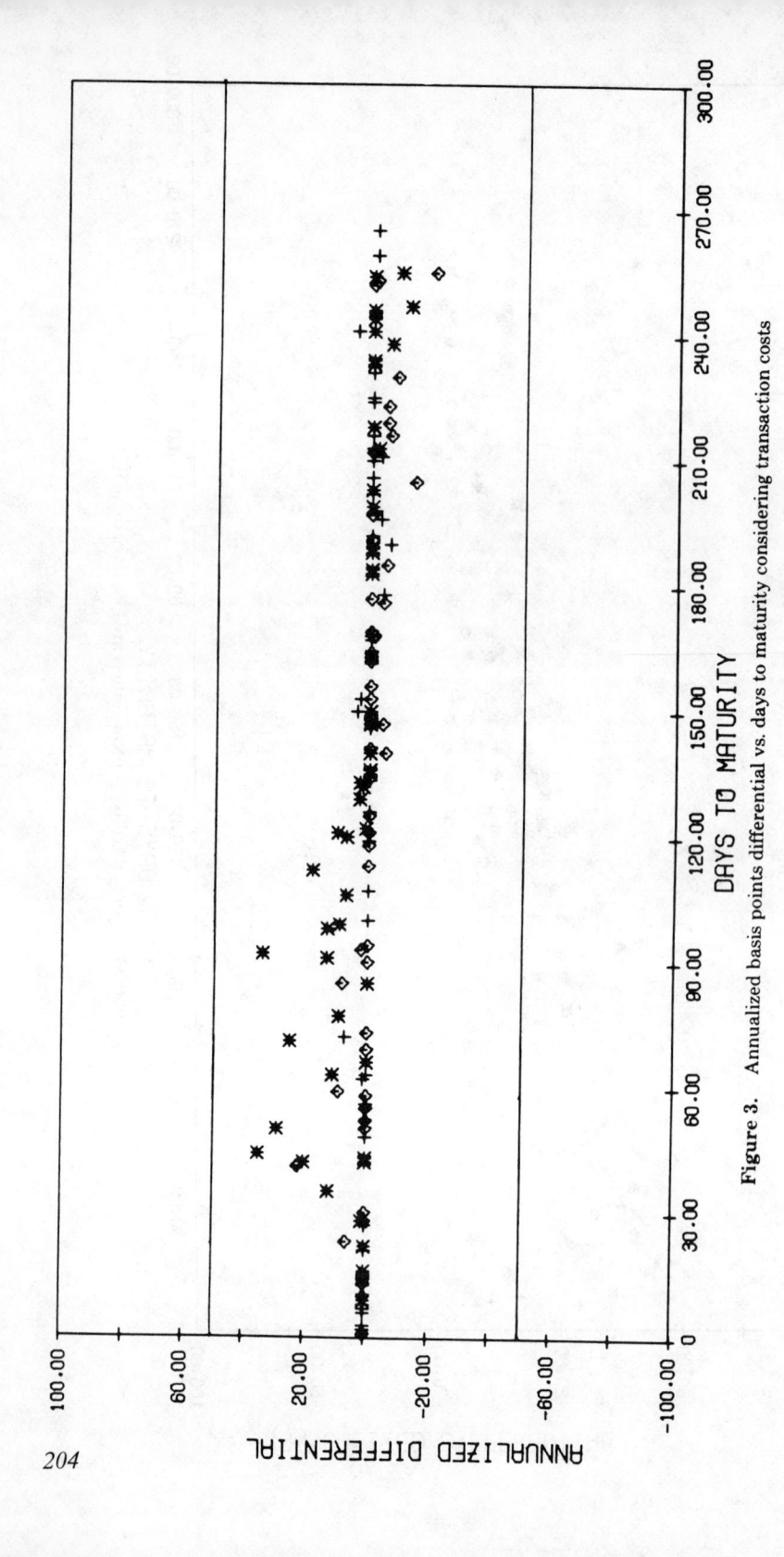

Figure 3. Annualized basis points differential vs. days to maturity considering transaction costs

excess returns beyond the original basis point differential by purchasing a long-term contract in an arbitrage arrangement and reversing the position 30 to 120 days prior to the contract's maturity.

The data presented thus far, as well as results obtained by Branch and Capozza and Cornell, suggest that futures contracts with shorter maturities appear to be more efficiently priced. These results can be misleading, however, if one does not recognize the fact that the arbitrage profits in the shorter term contracts can be earned in a shorter time period than those in the longer term contracts. With frequent trading in near term contracts, it might be possible to earn a higher return in the long run than could be earned in a long-term contract, even though the basis point differential in the longer term contract is higher. To adjust the basis point differential to reflect the time period over which the arbitrage profit is earned, the differential can be multiplied by $(91/360) \times (365/D_m)$. The first term converts the differential from IMM Index units to dollar units. The second term annualizes the return by multiplying the dollar return by the number of times per year it can be earned. In this adjustment it is assumed that the futures and spot markets will converge to equilibrium on the maturity date of the contract and that similar investment opportunities will be available in the future.

Table II presents summary statistics for the basis point differential on an annualized basis. Figure 2 presents a graphical representation of the annualized basis point differential and days to maturity.

It should be noted that these data contrast sharply with those of Puglisi. Puglisi found an average of 127 basis points difference between annualized yields in the spot market and those of equivalent positions in the September 1976 futures contract. In contrast, we find that no single data point in our sample provides a basis point differential of this magnitude. Moreover, in three of nine contract month-subperiod cells, the mean annualized basis point differential is not significantly different from zero.

In contrast to the non-annualized data, these exhibits illustrate that the arbitrage return potential has been the highest in the shortest term contracts. The dispersion in annualized arbitrage profit as measured by σ and σ_ϵ has been highest in the nearest term contracts and has tended to increase over time. The average absolute basis point differential has also increased in the shortest term contracts through time. On the other hand, the absolute deviation has decreased for the longest term contracts. This evidence supports the earlier conclusion that the efficiency in the pricing of the longest term contract has improved, while the pricing in the shortest term contract has become less efficient. Therefore, none of the evidence presented thus far suggests that the market as a whole has become more efficient since trading began. However, before reaching any firm conclusions about the degree of efficiency in the

Table II
Summary Statistics for Annualized Basis Points Differential Between Actual and No-Transaction Cost Values of IMM Index

		Contract			
Trading Period		1st Contract Month	2nd Contract Month	3rd Contract Month	All Contract
1st 9 Months	μ	14.406	1.195	−10.991	1.97
1/06/76–9/30/76	$\|\mu\|$	17.971	11.497	14.135	14.54
	σ	23.370	13.651	11.023	19.87
	σ_ϵ	21.661	5.350	3.665	N/A
	ϕ_1, ϕ_2	.292, .184	.739, .189	.836, .095	N/A
	N	187	187	168	542
	t	4.766[a]	.220	−2.682[a]	N/A
	$Q(21, N)$	15.560	21.365	40.655[b]	N/A
2nd 9 Months	μ	17.694	−2.314	−12.429	1.53
10/1/76–6/30/77	$\|\mu\|$	21.080	7.563	13.182	13.96
	σ	26.144	9.218	9.827	21.21
	σ_ϵ	23.132	5.507	4.084	N/A
	ϕ_1, ϕ_2	.400, .143	.670, .125	.878, .028	N/A
	N	185	186	163	534
	t	4.755[a]	−1.152	−3.652[a]	N/A
	$Q(21, N)$	14.587	28.208	23.673	N/A
3rd 9 Months	μ	31.651	11.409	−3.940	13.9
7/1/77–3/31/78	$\|\mu\|$	35.671	13.537	6.273	19.1
	σ	28.096	12.635	6.854	23.5
	σ_ϵ	24.871	5.615	2.504	N/A
	ϕ_1, ϕ_2	.197, .378	.766, .140	.924, .008	N/A
	N	186	186	158	530
	t	7.376[a]	2.605[a]	−1.345	N/A
	$Q(21, N)$	25.577	21.427	21.346	N/A
Entire sample period	μ	21.244	3.426	−9.192	5.7
	$\|\mu\|$	24.902	10.867	11.277	15.8
	σ	26.952	13.308	10.114	22.3
	σ_ϵ	23.460	5.498	3.516	N/A
	ϕ_1, ϕ_2	.308, .280	.755, .167	.863, .074	N/A
	N	558	559	489	1606
	t	8.813	1.149	−3.642[a]	N/A
	$Q(21, N)$	25.031	24.072	35.341[b]	N/A

Legend:

μ = sample mean
$|\mu|$ = sample mean of absolute value
σ = sample standard deviation
σ_ϵ = standard error of estimate of second order autoregressive process
ϕ_1, ϕ_2 = first and second order autocorrelation coefficients
N = sample size
$t = \mu(1 - \phi_1 - \phi_2)/(\sigma_\epsilon/\sqrt{N})$
$Q(21, N)$ = Box-Pierce Q statistic using 21 residual autocorrelations with sample size N.
[a] Significantly different from zero at 5% level.
[b] Null hypothesis that residuals follow a white noise process is rejected at the 5% level.

Treasury bill futures market, the impact of trading costs must be considered.

Comparison of Actual and Theoretical IMM Index Values in the Presence of Transaction Costs

Table III presents the means of the non-annualized and annualized basis point differential net of transaction costs in cross tabular form. For those contracts for which the actual IMM Index falls below the theoretical lower bound of equation (4), the basis point differential is the difference between the actual index value and the lower bound. Similarly, for those contracts for which the index falls above the upper bound, the basis point differential is the difference between the actual value and the upper bound. For those contracts for which the index falls within the two bounds, the basis point differential is the difference between the actual index value and the no-transaction cost value of equation (5).

Figure 3 presents a plot of the annualized basis point differential and days to maturity after considering transaction costs. The values plotted are the annualized differences between the actual index values and the appropriate bounds. For those contracts for which the actual prices fall within the bounds, a value for zero is plotted.

Table III shows that 66% of the observations could not have been arbitraged, given the existence of transaction costs. As observed earlier, the average annualized arbitrage returns decreased with the length of time to maturity. Of course, the returns that actually could have been earned on an annualized basis would have been less than those indicated in the table, because many contracts did not provide recurring profitable arbitrage opportunities.

In contrast to Oldfield's observation that the market became more efficient during the first year of trading, this analysis suggests that the market became less efficient during the first twenty-seven months of trading. The percentage of observations that fell between the two no-arbitrage price bounds decreased from 72% to 58% from the first to the third nine month subperiod. Most of this decline was in the first and second contract months in which the percentage of nonarbitrageable observations fell from 89% to 45% and from 78% to 55%, respectively. However, during this same period, the pricing of the third contract became more efficient as evidenced by an increase from 43% to 77% in the number of contracts that could not be arbitraged profitably.[11]

These relationships can be seen visually in Figure 3 in which very

---

[11] Given the autocorrelation in the data reported earlier, caution should be used in interpreting these results.

Table III
Summary Statistics for Basis Points Differential when Transaction Costs are Considered

Trading Period		1st Contract Month			2nd Contract Month				3rd Contract Month				All Contracts			
		N	%	μ	μ_a	N	%	μ	μ_a	N	%	μ	μ_a	N	%	μ	μ_a
1/06/76–9/30/76	B	0	0	0.000	0.000	18	10	−8.076	−4.994	77	46	−17.433	−6.674	95	18	−15.660	−6.335
	W	167	89	4.241	13.458	146	78	−0.020	1.045	80	48	−15.511	−7.034	393	72	−1.348	4.675
	A	20	11	3.445	4.113	23	12	7.535	5.053	11	6	10.031	3.724	54	10	6.529	4.430
		187	100			187	100			168	100			542	100		
10/1/76–6/30/77	B	1	1	−0.574	−0.582	30	16	−8.645	−4.890	98	60	−23.006	−9.103	129	24	−19.492	−8.057
	W	140	76	3.261	14.295	148	80	−0.730	0.410	65	40	−6.625	−2.762	353	66	−0.233	4.989
	A	44	23	4.417	7.166	8	4	6.486	6.309	0	0	0.000	0.000	52	10	4.735	7.034
		185	100			186	100			163	100			534	100		
7/1/77–3/31/78	B	0	0	0.000	0.000	3	1	−7.957	−4.074	37	23	−13.657	−5.159	40	7	−13.230	−5.113
	W	84	45	5.258	17.332	102	55	3.461	2.508	121	77	−2.544	−1.025	307	58	1.586	5.172
	A	102	55	10.771	17.950	81	44	13.566	11.537	0	0	0.000	0.000	183	35	12.009	15.112
		186	100			186	100			158	100			530	100		
Entire sample period	B	1	0	−0.574	−0.582	51	9	−8.404	−4.879	212	43	−19.350	−7.539	264	16	−17.164	−6.999
	W	391	70	4.108	14.590	396	71	0.626	0.878	266	54	−7.441	3.257	1053	66	−0.119	4.925
	A	166	30	8.204	13.425	112	22	11.822	9.830	11	3	10.031	3.724	289	18	9.676	11.662
		558	100			559	100			489	100			1606	100		

Legend:
N = Number of observations
% = % of total observations within cell
μ = Sample mean, not annualized
μ_a = Sample mean, annualized
B = Below lower index bound (Means are differences between actual IMM Index values and lower Index bound)
W = Within index bounds (Means are differences between actual and no-transaction cost Index values)
A = Above upper index bound (Means are differences between actual IMM Index values and upper Index bound)

few contracts with less than 130 days until maturity provided arbitrage opportunities in the first nine months of trading, while a large number of near term contracts would have provided arbitrage profits in the last nine months. It is also apparent from these graphs that the pricing of the longest term contracts became more efficient. One can observe that contracts with 130 to 210 days to maturity were the most efficiently priced during the sample period.

It is possible that timing differences in the reporting of prices in the futures and spot markets could create the appearance of arbitrage opportunities when, in fact, such opportunities do not exist.[12] Trading in futures halts at 2:35 p.m. EST, whereas trading in the underlying Treasury bills continues until 3:30 p.m. EST. Of course, it is possible that the last trade in each market may occur prior to the close.

If apparent arbitrage opportunities can be explained by timing differences, one would expect to observe the greatest difference in the timing of trades in those contracts that appear to sell for disequilibrium prices. Our futures data provide the time of last trade for each futures contract. According to the Federal Reserve Bank of New York's trading room, the spot quotations reflect "representative" closing bids and offers of the various dealers in the U.S. Government Securities Market. Therefore, the greatest timing differences should occur in futures contracts with the earliest time of last trade.

In Table IV, the average time of last trade is presented for the futures contract classifications in Table 3. Surprisingly, the average trading time for non-arbitrageable contracts for the entire sample is earlier than that of contracts which fall outside the no arbitrage bounds. Only in one trading period-contract month classification (3rd contract month for the period 1/06/76-9/30/76) does there appear to be any support of the hypothesis that arbitrage opportunities can be explained by timing differences in the trading of futures and spot T-bills.[13]

The potential arbitrage profits observed thus far can be viewed as quasi-arbitrage profits that could have been earned by using futures contracts to improve the return of an existing portfolio. To form a pure arbitrage position, however, one must short a spot Treasury bill. Capozza and Cornell have pointed out that the cost of borrowing a spot bill is approximately 50 basis points per year. This cost is shown in Figure 3 by the parallel lines at the +50 and −50 annualized basis point differen-

---

[12] It may also be possible for the opposite to occur, disequilibrium prices may appear to be equilibrium prices due to timing differences in the reporting of prices.

[13] The upper bound on the time of trade casts doubt on the appropriateness of conventional statistical tests of significance based on normally distributed trading times. Moreover, in many cases the average trading time was later for the arbitrageable contracts. Thus, we believe that tests to determine whether average trading times in the arbitrageable contracts are significantly lower than the trading times in the non-arbitrageable contracts would provide little additional insight.

Table IV
Average Time of Last Futures Trade

Trading Period		1st Contract Month			2nd Contract Month			3rd Contract Month			All Contracts		
		N	$\%$	$\bar{T}$	N	$\%$	$\bar{T}$	N	$\%$	$\bar{T}$	N	$\%$	$\bar{T}$
1/06/76–9/30/76	B	0	0	N/A	18	10	14.536	77	46	14.124	95	18	14.202
	W	167	89	14.125	146	78	14.437	80	48	14.142	393	72	14.244
	A	20	11	14.539	23	12	14.196	11	6	11.851	54	10	13.845
		187	100		187	100		168	100		542	100	
10/1/76–6/30/77	B	1	1	14.594	30	16	14.578	98	60	14.554	129	24	14.559
	W	140	76	14.098	148	80	14.554	65	40	14.569	353	66	14.376
	A	44	23	14.441	8	4	14.542	0	0	N/A	52	10	14.456
		185	100		186	100		163	100		534	100	
7/1/77–3/31/78	B	0	0	N/A	3	1	14.536	37	23	14.510	40	7	14.512
	W	84	45	14.234	102	55	14.562	121	77	14.448	307	58	14.427
	A	102	55	14.413	81	44	14.550	0	0	N/A	183	35	14.473
		186	100		186	100		158	100		530	100	
Entire sample period	B	1	0	14.594	51	9	14.561	212	43	14.390	264	16	14.424
	W	391	70	14.139	396	71	14.513	266	54	14.386	1053	66	14.342
	A	166	30	14.436	112	20	14.476	11	3	11.851	289	18	14.353
		558	100		509	100		489	100		1606	100	

Legend:
N = number of observations
$\%$ = % of total observations within cell
$\bar{T}$ = average time of last trade expressed in hours and fractions thereof after midnight EST
B = mean of basis point differential falls below lower index bound
W = mean of basis point differential falls within index bounds
A = mean of basis point differential falls above upper index bound

tials. This 50 annualized basis point cost can be offset if the absolute value of the annualized return potential of the arbitrage position exceeds 50 basis points. Consistent with Capozza and Cornell's results, no observations in Figure 3 fall outside the bounds. A plot of all data points would show the same result. This implies that no pure arbitrage opportunities were available in the market during the sample period, assuming that all positions would have been maintained to maturity. Therefore, the Treasury bill futures market appears to have been highly efficient with respect to pure arbitrage opportunities. However, it appears that the futures could have been used to improve the return of a Treasury bill portfolio.

III. CONCLUDING REMARKS

The evidence in this study suggests that many quasi-arbitrage opportunities have existed in the Treasury bill futures market. To determine the extent of inefficiency in the market, it is necessary to assess the significance of the quasi-arbitrage returns that could have been earned.

From the cell of Table 3 that describes the potential arbitrage returns for all contracts during the entire sample period, a potential annualized return of 7-12 basis points can be observed. Considering that profitable arbitrage opportunities were not continuously available, the true annualized return would have been lower.

It is doubtful that these potential arbitrage returns would have been worth exploiting, given the indirect costs of educating traders and policymakers within financial institutions, the costs of monitoring the futures market, the inability (in some cases) to cover a futures obligation with the exact Treasury bill required, and the reluctance by many financial institutions to alter the present maturity structure of their short term portfolios. Moreover, if a portfolio manager were to trade futures more frequently than is implied by the hold-to-maturity strategy underlying our analysis, trading costs would be significantly higher than those considered here. Finally, if a portfolio manager desired to improve the yield of an existing short term portfolio, financial instruments such as high grade commercial paper and negotiable certificates of deposit are likely to provide higher returns and greater acceptance within financial institutions than futures contracts.[14] Thus, the inefficiencies in the Treasury bill futures market do not appear to be significant enough to

---

[14] Some financial institutions may view the futures contract as containing an element of default risk. Although the clearing members of the Chicago Mercantile Exchange guarantee the contract, the recent default on the Maine potato contract of the New York Mercantile Exchange may cast doubt on the Exchange members' guarantee. Thus, a portion of the apparent quasi-arbitrage opportunities that we observe may actually reflect a premium for default risk.

offer attractive investment alternatives to the short-term portfolio manager.

To the extent that quasi-arbitrage opportunities have existed in the market, there appears to have been a tendency for the market to become less efficient over time. The pricing of the near term contract has become less efficient while the pricing of the third contract has become more efficient. However, it is doubtful that these inefficiencies have been large enough to induce portfolio managers to alter their investment policies.

References

1. Box, G. E. P. and Pierce, D. A. Distribution of residual autocorrelations in auto-regressive-integrated moving average time series models. *Journal of the American Statistical Association* (December 1970).
2. Branch, Ben. Testing the unbiased expectations theory of interest rates. *Proceedings of the Eastern Finance Association* (Summer 1978).
3. Capozza, D. R. and Cornell, B. Treasury bill pricing in the spot and futures markets, forthcoming, *Review of Economics and Statistics* (1978).
4. Cox, J. C., Ingersoll, J., and Ross, S. A theory of the term structure of interest rates and the valuation of interest dependent claims. Working paper (1977).
5. Emery, J. T. and Scott, R. H. T-bill futures and the term structure of interest rates: A means of reconciling market forecasts and valuing financial assets. Working paper (1978).
6. Lang, R. W. and Rasche, R. H. A comparison of yields on futures contracts and implied forward rates, *Federal Reserve Bank of St. Louis Review* (December 1978).
7. Oldfield, G. S. Jr. The relationship between U.S. Treasury bill spot and futures prices. Working paper (1977).
8. Poole, W. Using T-bill futures to gauge interest rate expectations. *Federal Reserve Bank of San Francisco Economic Review* (Spring 1978).
9. Puglisi, D. J. 1978. Is the futures market for Treasury bills efficient? *The Journal of Portfolio Management* (Winter 1978).

13

The Efficiency of the Treasury Bill Futures Market: An Analysis of Alternative Specifications*

Anthony J. Vignola and Charles Dale[†]

Treasury-bill futures began trading on January 6, 1976, on the International Monetary Market (*IMM*) of the Chicago Mercantile Exchange. The *IMM* trades Treasury Bill futures contracts for delivery in March, June, September, and December. Trading in each contract ends on the second business day following the Treasury Bill auction of the third week of the delivery month. Contracts call for the delivery of $1 million of Treasury Bills to mature in 90 days. Until the existence of financial futures, testing the determinants and the informational content of futures market prices has been difficult because of the vagaries associated with commodity markets. In the case of financial futures, and in particular, Treasury Bill futures, the existence of an active secondary market and the resulting term structure of interest rates enables one to test alternative hypotheses about the prices of future contracts. The merits of futures markets as a mechanism for price discovery have been debated for a considerable length of time.

In the present study, the pricing of Treasury Bill futures contracts is examined. Actual futures prices are compared with two alternative specifications of equilibrium futures prices, *i.e.*, those implied by carrying charges and those derived from the unbiased expectations hypothesis of the theory of the term structure of interest rates. Specifically, we

---

*Reprinted from the *Journal of Financial Research*, Vol. 3, No. 2, (Fall 1980). Reprinted by permission of the publisher.
[†]Economists, Office of Government Financing, U.S. Treasury Dept., Washington, D.C.

present and empirically test two alternative specifications of Treasury Bill futures market efficiency.[1] These are: (1) the determination of pure-arbitrage opportunities between the futures and the cash market and (2) the determination of quasi-arbitrage opportunities between the futures and the cash market.[2] The pure-arbitrage model is based upon Working's theory of storage costs.[3] The quasi-arbitrage model is based on the expectations hypothesis of forward rates.

I. RECENT EMPIRICAL ANALYSES

The secondary market for Treasury securities gives rise to a well defined term structure of interest rates, or yield curve.[4] Since theories and tests of the term structure abound in the economic and financial literature, it is natural for economists to turn to term structure theories for the analysis of Treasury Bill futures, since implied forward rates embodied in the term structure are the spot market's assessment of future rates of interest.[5] Several recent papers have been written that empirically evaluate the futures market using the expectations hypothesis of the term structure as a basis for establishing the equilibrium price of a futures contract. These papers have been concerned with verifying various term structure hypotheses and testing the efficiency of the Trea-

---

[1] In recent studies of the futures market, inefficiency has been assumed to exist when there are profitable arbitrage opportunities. In this paper, the writers adopt the terminology of market inefficiency in the current context to mean that arbitrage possibilities exist between the cash and futures market.

[2] Pure arbitrage refers to arbitrage where the position must be financed from borrowed funds, as in the case of a fully leveraged firm. Quasi-arbitrage refers to situations involving existing portfolios. For example, in the case of quasi-arbitrage a holder of Treasury Bills can alter his his portfolio mix and obtain arbitrage profits by selling a three-month bill, buying a six-month bill and shorting a futures contract for delivery in three months. The terms of the portfolio will be unchanged, but the composition will be altered.

[3] According to Working, any divergence between spot prices and futures prices can be explained by carrying charges, that is, the cost of storing the commodity until future delivery. For futures in tangible commodities, these costs have traditionally included insurance, warehousing, interest and transportation. See Working [22, 23]. Of course, a necessary condition is that a commodity be storable. Technically, deliverable Treasury bills are only storable for approximately 91 days prior to delivery. Prior to that period, only proxies for storable bills exist.

[4] For a thorough discussion of yield curves, forward rates and the term structure, see Malkiel [11], especially Chapters I and II, Nelson [13] and Roll [18]. See Cox, Ingersoll and Ross [5] for explicit specification of the differences among alternative theories of the term structure.

[5] Since Working postulated that spot and futures prices are intimately connected, his theories are more general but consistent with term structure theories since they also embody an implied cost of storage. In fact, the Hicksian development of the theory of the term structure is based on concepts derived from commodity futures markets. Hicks viewed all markets, spot, futures and forward as mutually interdependent. See Hicks [8], especially Chapter 11.

sury Bill futures markets.[6] Using the traditional approach to the term structure for evaluating the efficiency of the futures market poses difficulties, for it assumes that the same term structure theories that apply to the spot market hold for the futures market.

Poole [15] examined the case of arbitrage between the cash market returns to a bill holder and the returns to a combination of bills and futures transactions. He found that profitable arbitrage opportunities rarely exist, and are small when they do exist, implying that the markets are efficiently priced. Lang and Rasche [9] rejected the hypothesis that Poole's findings can be extrapolated to more distant contracts, and also rejected his findings for the case of arbitrage for more recent periods. Branch [2], Chow and Brophy [4] and Morgan [12] obtained similar results. However, Morgan showed that the characteristics of futures contracts may result in differences between futures prices and implied forward prices, even in an efficient market.

Puglisi [16] and Vignola and Dale [21] also found market inefficiencies that present opportunities for portfolio investors in Treasury Bills. Capozza and Cornell [3] concluded that for approximately 18 weeks prior to contract delivery, futures prices (rates) were too high (low) and that they were too low (high) for more distant periods when forward rates were compared to futures rates. They attributed these differences to transactions costs, but they were unable to explain the differences for the contract nearest delivery. On the other hand, Oldfield [14] concluded that profitable arbitrage opportunities do not exist.

Rendleman and Carabini [17] compared actual futures prices with estimated equilibrium prices treating futures contracts as forward contracts. They found significant price differences between actual and hypothetical equilibrium prices, when no transaction costs were included. Nearby futures contracts were generally overpriced and longer term contracts were generally underpriced. When transaction costs were introduced, the number of arbitrage possibilities declined. However, they found that a significant number of arbitrage opportunities remained and that the tendency for such opportunities to exist was increasing, particularly for the nearby contract.

Despite the conflicting evidence, in general, futures prices (rates) are found to differ from prices implied by the term structure, with nearby contracts showing futures prices too high and more distant contracts having prices too low. Some of the confusion seems to be due to differences in annualization periods, compounding assumptions, and rate approximation formulas. Some price differences are annualized over the number of days to the delivery of the futures contract, some to the ma-

---

[6] Studies that use the expectations hypothesis to evaluate the efficiency of the futures are performing joint tests of the forward rate and the efficiency of the futures market.

turity of the deliverable security, others over a constant 91-day period.[7]

The findings that actual futures prices do not equal equilibrium futures price have resulted in a myriad of explanations for this apparent market inefficiency. Nearly all authors revert to some form of transactions cost for an explanation, ranging from the cost of borrowing a security (50 basis points) to the implied transactions costs in the spot market as represented by bid and ask spreads.[8] Other explanations include the riskiness of futures as compared to spot bills, the effects of marking to the market, the newness of the markets, the lack of use by institutional investors, and where these reasons are unable to explain the differences, the conclusion is reached that the futures market is inefficient.[9]

The conflicting evidence regarding the pricing and efficiency of the Treasury Bill futures markets makes it clear that a number of unresolved issues remain. The extant literature has centered on quasi-arbitrage tests of the efficiency of the Treasury Bill futures market. Only Rendleman and Carabini raise the issue of pure arbitrage versus quasi-arbitrage. By examining both pure and quasi-arbitrage, the present paper offers a reconciliation of the conflicting findings with regard to pricing and efficiency of the Treasury Bill futures market and offers a valuable approach for analyzing other markets of financial futures.

II. DEVELOPMENT OF MODEL

This section describes two specifications of equilibrium Treasury Bill futures prices. A later section evaluates them using a consistent set of data. Hypothetical equilibrium futures prices are derived from (1) the theory of storage costs and (2) the expectations hypothesis of forward rates implied by the term structure. These hypothetical equilibrium prices are then compared to actual futures prices.

[7] Only Rendleman and Carabini [17] and Vignola and Dale [21] specifically note this effect. Vignola and Dale [21] show that when only bid or ask prices are used, the dollar difference for the long and the short of a futures contract are the same, but the annualized basis point differential is dramatically affected depending on whether the time period of arbitrage profit is to the delivery of a futures contract or to the maturity of the deliverable bill.

[8] Explanations of differences between prices that are caused by bid-ask spreads in the spot market are not without shortcomings. Bid-ask spreads in the spot market are a function of many factors, particularly the time since issue and the dollar amount of a basis point. (See Baker and Vignola [1] for a discussion of this issue). A further complication in the present context arises from the discontinuous nature of the spread as one moves from one-year bills as proxies for deliverable bills to six- and three-month bills.

[9] The conclusion that the futures market is inefficient may merely be the result of the use of inappropriate carrying charges. Dusak [6] shows that the appropriate discount for cash or, equivalently, the financing charge is the only issue in the pricing of futures contracts.

An Analysis of Alternative Specifications

For simplification, the following notations are adapted: time is assumed to flow from right to left, t represents the present time, m is the delivery date of the futures contract, and n is the maturity date of the deliverable instrument.

```
n                          m                       t
<_____ 91 days _____>  | <_____ SD days _____>
```

The time from t to m is referred to as SD days, and the time from m to n is always 91 days. Therefore, from time t to time n, the maturity of the deliverable bill is $SD + 91$ days. The price of a futures contract, PF, is that price which is established at time t and is to be paid at m, SD days later. The prices of spot market bills are subscripted with the time period to which they apply.

The relation between the quoted price of a futures contract and the actual price of a futures contract is easily established:

$$PF = 100 - (100 \times Df \times 90) / 360 \qquad (1)$$

where PF = actual price of futures contract, and Df = discount rate at time t on the futures contract (100-futures price index).

Since the Treasury issues 91- and 182-day bills, which are perfectly interchangeable, there is a period of 91 days when the futures contract trades for the delivery of an existing commodity which may be stored for future delivery. As a result, during the three-month period before the expiration of a futures contract, perfect arbitrage possibilities may exist. For periods greater than 91 days prior to the expiration of the futures contract, arbitrage conditions may be explored by using the one-year bill, as a proxy for the deliverable security.

A. Cost of Carry Equilibrium

According to Working's theory of carrying charges, arbitrage possibilities arise when the price of the commodity in the spot market plus the cost of storage differ from the price of the futures contract.[10] In the case of Treasury Bills, the relevant cost of the spot commodity is the price of the deliverable bill. The spot price of a bill is given by:

$$PBn = 100 - (100 \times Rn \times (SD + 91)) / 360 \qquad (2)$$

---

[10] Working [23] defines the price of storage as the difference between the price of a futures contract and the current cash price which may be positive or negative. Therefore, one could solve for the equilibrium financing charge and evaluate the futures market on the basis of whether that financing charge were available. In order to establish the equilibrium price of a futures contract and compute prices for forward rates, take the cost of storage as given and compute equilibrium prices.

where PBn = actual price of a bill with n days to maturity, Rn = discount rate on a bill with n days to maturity, and SD = number of days to the futures contract expiration.

The cost of storage is the financing cost necessary to store the commodity (which can be purchased for a price of PB) until the delivery of the futures contract, SD days from the present. The cost of storage is therefore given by:

$$C = PBn \times Rs \times SD / 365 \qquad (3)$$

where C = cost of storage, PBn = amount borrowed—the cost of the deliverable bill, and Rs = the annualized storage rate of interest.

Therefore, according to the cost of carry theory of futures prices, the price of a futures contract, $ARBc$, in dollar terms should be:

$$ARBc = PBn + C. \qquad (4)$$

Several problems arise when attempting to determine the relevant cost of storage for Treasury Bills. Initially, one may conclude that the financing rate, rm, given by a Treasury Bill with SD days to maturity, represents the proper financing cost. Such an assumption, however, does not necessarily reflect either profit-maximizing behavior or the institutional characteristics of the Treasury Bill spot market or the futures market. The rate, rm, does not take into account the opportunity cost of money to the holder of a bill or to the seller of a bill. Such a rate is appropriate for "quasi-arbitrage," in which an investor already holds Treasury Bills and uses futures to increase his net return. However, for the case of "pure arbitrage," which may more appropriately typify firms engaging in futures markets arbitrage, the additional cost of shorting a Treasury Bill would have to be included.[11]

However, even the rate for establishing a short position in an inappropriate financing cost, due to the fact that institutional developments in repurchase agreements ($RP's$) have resulted in the near elimination of short selling. For example, an effective short position can be established by simultaneously purchasing a security under a reverse-RP, and selling the security. The current popularity of this technique means that the RP rate is the most representative rate for financing Treasury Bills.[12]

[11] In a short-sale, an investor borrows a security and immediately sells it, anticipating that the security can be purchased at a lower price and returned to the original owner. The borrower must pay interest accruing on the security plus the borrowing fee. A 1979 survey of futures market participants by the Commodity Future Trading Commission showed commercial traders which include security dealers, held 34% of the outstanding bill contracts. These firms are marginal net borrowers of funds for which pure arbitrage would apply.

[12] A repurchase agreement involves the sale of a security with the simultaneous agreement for the repurchase at some later date. A reverse RP refers to the purchase of a security or the opposite side of a repurchase agreement. For a review of developments in the RP market, see

In order to have riskless arbitrage, a holding period, or term RP rate is warranted. This presents a two-fold dilemma; the term RP market is thin and not uniformly priced and the holding period RP rate involving a particular bill, the "special" RP rate, entails significant premiums. Therefore, one must resort to proxies of the appropriate financing rate. The most representative rate characterizing the marginal financing costs of firms engaged in government securities arbitrage is the overnight rate. Since these firms are also major arbitrage participants in the futures market, the overnight RP rate may also reflect their marginal borrowing needs to finance arbitrage as it is often referred to and carried out in the futures market. If an overnight rate is used, the necessary economic assumption is that the expected value of that rate over the holding period will be equal to the current rate.[13] This specification is consistent with a random walk model of short term rates. In a practical sense, such an assumption is not unrealistic given the uncertainties of market forecasts of short-term rates. However, arbitrage using an overnight borrowing rate is not riskless and requires equation (3) to be specified in the form:

$$C = PBn \left[(1 + Rs)^{SD/365} - 1 \right]. \quad (5)$$

Unfortunately, no representative overnight RP rate is either published or readily available. The closest proxy for the rate is the federal funds rate. The use of the federal funds rate as a proxy for the overnight RP rate introduces a negative bias in the calculation of the cost of carry since the federal funds rate is generally higher than the RP rate.[14] The writers, therefore, test the pure arbitrage model with the federal funds rate, recognizing as Dusak [6] does that the empirical question in pric-

---

Lucas, Jones and Thurston [10], Simpson [19] and Smith [20]. The reverse RP for acquiring a specific bill is called a "special." The market for such transactions is very thin and can entail premiums ranging from 50 to 100 basis points.

[13] Other studies of short-term rates, for example Hamburger and Platt [7], show that short-term rates are consistent with the efficient market model and that "investors appear to behave as if they expect rates of interest . . . to be the same as the current rates." Morgan [12], shows that the price of a futures contract not only depends upon the interest rate expected to prevail on the delivery date but also depends on the expected course of interest rates between the date of agreement and the delivery date.

[14] The RP rate is a secured loan rate and is generally lower than federal funds rate by 1/8 to 1/4 percent. The federal funds rate is the rate on unsecured overnight loans. See Simpson [19]. For the more aggressive banks and government securities dealers who participate in the futures market, the federal funds rate may properly reflect marginal borrowing costs for Treasury Bill futures. Daily observations on the federal funds rate are sometimes greatly influenced by bank reserve excesses and shortages and are frequently not representative on Wednesday as a result of the end of the statement week for reserve requirement purposes. This results in many outlier observations for Wednesday. Therefore, when this rate is used the model is estimated without Wednesday observations.

ing futures contracts reduces to the determination of the appropriate financing costs.[15]

B. Implied Forward Rate Equilibrium Prices

According to the expectations theory of the term structure of interest rates, the relationship between the futures market and the cash market is determined by the fact that the purchase and sale of securities in the spot market can result in the same position as can be established in the futures market. The costs of undergoing such transactions, however, generally preclude carrying them out. Nonetheless, such transactions should be expected to yield a return equivalent to the forward rate implied by the expectations hypothesis of the term structure of interest rates. For example, the expectations hypothesis holds that an investor should be indifferent between an investment in a six-month Treasury Bill and two consecutive purchases of three-month bills. The expected forward rate to prevail three months from today, therefore, is a function of the relationship between the yields on three-month bills and six-month bills. The expected three-month rate Re, is frequently given by the expression:

$$Re = 1 - [(1-Rn)^{((SD + 91)/360)} \times (1-Rm)^{-(SD/360)}] (360/91) \quad (6)$$

where Rn = discount bill rate for n days, Rm = discount bill rate for m days, Re = expected three-month discount rate, and SD = number of days to maturity of Rm, the delivery date of a futures contract.

Equation (6) gives the futures market equilibrium rate according to the expectations hypothesis. In dollar terms, the price of a bill ($ARBe$) with the expected discount rate, Re, to prevail in m days follows from the formula for the price of a bill:

$$ARBe = 100 - 100 \times Re \times 91/360. \quad (7)$$

Equations (6) and (7) are approximations to the arbitrage price of a futures contract since they assume interest rates are determinate. Since Treasury Bills are discount instruments and are traded in terms of price, the arbitrage price, $ARBe$, can be solved for directly. Letting Pm represent the price of a discount instrument that is worth 100 at maturity, $100/Pm$ defines the closed form pure rate of interest over the period m, that is, $Pm \times (1 - Rm)^{-m} = 100$. $100/Pm$ defines the rate of interest without assumptions about compounding or linear approximations.

---

[15] Since the October 6, 1979, policy changes by the Federal Reserve in conducting monetary policy, the historical relationship between the federal funds rate and the RP rate has broken down, making updated analysis based on this relationship impossible.

By substitution, equations (6) and (7) reduce to:

$$ARBe = (100/Pm) \times Pn. \qquad (7')$$

In this form, it becomes clear that the relationship between the expectations hypothesis and the cost of carry formulation reduces to a difference in the appropriate discounting rate since $100/Pm = (1 - Rm)^{-m}$. The only difference is the implied financing charge.

Equations (5) and (7') are arbitrage conditions: equation (5) appropriate for pure arbitrage; equation (7') for quasi-arbitrage. Arbitrage will take place if the arbitrage price does not equal the futures price, that is, if $ARB \neq FP$.[16] If $FP > ARB$, indicating that the price (rate) of a futures contract is too high (low) relative to the spot market, the arbitrager would purchase the long bill (the deliverable bill) and short the futures contract. His profit would be:

$$DIFF = FP - ARB. \qquad (8)$$

On the other hand, if $ARB > FP$, indicating that the futures price (rate) is too low (high) relative to the spot market, the arbitrager should buy a shorter bill, one with SD days to maturity, and go long the futures contract rather than hold a longer term bill.

To calculate the arbitrage price, ARB, the writers use the bid-ask mean for all trades, rather than the separate bid or ask prices for selling or buying. The reasons for using bid/ask means follow from theoretical and institutional considerations. Neither buyers no sellers of Treasury Bills or futures contracts should inordinately influence either of these markets, implying equilibrium should approach the mean. Furthermore, bills have different spreads depending on their characteristics. Since three- and six-month bills are used, as well as one-year bills as a proxy until the six-month bills are issued, this eliminates discontinuities.[17] Using bid-ask means further simplifies the analysis. When bid-ask means are used the dollar gain (loss) from the combination of a long bill purchase and a short sale of a futures equals the dollar loss (gain) to the buyer of a short bill and the purchaser of a futures contract.

---

[16] Futures market transactions costs are ignored. Such costs are minimal. Initially round-trip commissions were $60. Since March 1978, they have been negotiable. Margin requirements are also small ($800), and their effective cost is the earnings on such funds. Furthermore, they may be satisfied with no initial cash outlay by letters of credit or marketable securities.

[17] Spot market transactions for Treasury Bills rarely take place at the bid or ask price. The quoted bid price is a lower bound for selling a security and the ask price an upper bound for buying a security. Both are paid by only the less frequent participants in this market. In addition, spreads are a function of many factors. Amont these are the time since issue and the dollar value of a basis point for a given term to maturity. Bid-ask spreads in the spot market are frequently as much as 50 basis points for bills with less than 13 weeks to delivery. If an arbitrage band is calculated using such spreads, as many authors have done, it is unlikely that any profitable arbitrage situations will be found.

Two daily series of differences between the arbitrage or equilibrium price of a futures contract and the actual price of the contract were computed. One series used the theory of carrying charges ($ARBc$) while the other series used the expectations hypothesis ($ARBe$). The data sample included all contracts since the beginning of trading in Treasury Bill futures, January 6, 1976, through the December 1978 contract. For both cases, a positive difference represents a price which benefits the short seller of a futures contract, and a negative difference represents a loss to the short seller but a gain to the purchaser of a short bill in conjunction with a futures contract.

III. RESULTS

Tables 1 and 2 contain summary statistics for the dollar amounts of the differences between actual futures prices and computed equilibrium prices for the cost-of-carry model and the forward-rate model, respectively. Tables 3 and 4 give the annualized rates of return for these differences. Each table separates the results into three quarterly subperiods. The nearby period for each contract refers to the 91-day period immediately preceding the futures contract maturity, the period when the exact deliverable security exists. The second and third quarters refer to the subsequent 91-day periods. Thus, summary statistics for a cross section of contracts at the same time relative to their maturity are arrayed horizontally and a time series over the last nine months of any one contract is listed vertically.

As noted above, summary statistics about contracts must be viewed cautiously and may be misleading because of the distribution and time series properties evident in the data. Therefore, charts of the daily results are given in Figures I-IV. The figures show the dollar difference and annualized percent differences for all contracts, grouping the data according to the year in which the contract matured. The horizontal axis of the figures represents the number of days until the delivery of the futures contract, with time flowing from the right to the left. The vertical axis in Figures I and II give the dollar difference between actual futures prices and calculated equilibrium prices. Figures III and IV give the annualized percentage rates of return represented by these dollar differences.

A positive difference between the actual futures price and the equilibrium price means that returns can be increased over the period SD, the time to maturity of the futures contract, by purchasing a security with ($SD + 91$) days to maturity and selling a futures contract instead of buying a security with SD days to maturity. A negative difference indicates that returns can be increased over the period $SD + 91$, the peri-

TABLE 1. Cost of Carry Model Summary Statistics for Dollar Differences: Futures Price Less Equilibrium Price**

		1976				1977				1978			All (contracts)
		Mar.	Jun.	Sep.	Dec.	Mar.	Jun.	Sep.	Dec.	Mar.	Jun.	Sep.	Dec.	
Nearby Contract	μ	134	110	−32	66	−86	−120	−171	61	24	−320	−519	−212	−85
		(27)*	(32)	(17)	(14)	(23)	(37)	(26)	(16)	(36)	(38)	(38)	(57)	(433)
	$|\mu|$	194	242	124	124	144	210	187	128	198	330	532	429	268
		(39)	(50)	(44)	(28)	(55)	(76)	(75)	(30)	(58)	(120)	(176)	(137)	(351)
	+	27	26	17	32	14	17	8	25	19	9	3	18	215
	−	12	22	33	16	34	33	41	26	29	40	46	30	462
Second Quarter	μ		1839	691	893	315	382	−118	306	466	637	281	519	550
			(93)	(91)	(68)	(48)	(67)	(75)	(32)	(050)	(080)	(042)	(057)	(753)
	$|\mu|$		1839	734	921	469	536	549	383	538	765	362	729	704
			(93)	(94)	(68)	(66)	(87)	(149)	(47)	(59)	(098)	(052)	(079)	(600)
	+		43	40	49	36	40	16	41	39	43	35	41	423
	−		0	7	0	14	9	34	8	8	4	13	21	118
Third Quarter	μ			4049	4001	2561	984	1146	865	952	1609	1627	1973	2031
				(156)	(235)	(151)	(95)	(108)	(166)	(183)	(140)	(120)	(100)	(1647)
	$|\mu|$			4049	4101	2561	1039	1295	1071	952	1611	1763	1973	2086
				(156)	(235)	(151)	(99)	(124)	(181)	(183)	(140)	(157)	(100)	(1572)
	+			43	61	62	45	50	36	40	49	45	48	479
	−			0	0	0	7	7	10	1	1	2	0	28

μ = mean
$|\mu|$ = mean absolute value
+ = number of + observations
− = number of − observations
* = numbers in parentheses are standard errors
** = Differences are in dollars for $1,000,000 contract.

TABLE 2. Forward Rate Model Summary Statistics for Dollar Differences: Futures Price Less Equilibrium Price**

		1976				1977				1978				All (contracts)
		Mar.	June	Sep.	Dec.	Mar.	Jun.	Sep.	Dec.	Mar.	Jun.	Sep.	Dec.	
Nearby Contract	μ	175	119	81	265	76	165	166	552	401	345	371	612	282
		(18)*	(14)	(9)	(17)	(15)	(17)	(12)	(30)	(29)	(28)	(41)	(65)	(379)
	$\|\mu\|$	178	151	93	273	121	208	176	549	413	413	517	802	342
		(22)	(22)	(16)	(19)	(24)	(25)	(16)	(30)	(30)	(38)	(57)	(83)	(317)
	+	39	44	46	54	41	54	50	64	56	45	44	47	584
	−	9	15	15	5	19	9	12	0	5	15	18	13	135
Second Quarter	μ		540	655	247	114	−255	−316	385	351	367	755	1417	269
			(39)	(48)	(27)	(19)	(30)	(42)	(35)	(32)	(32)	(55)	(54)	(664)
	$\|\mu\|$		547	664	344	259	308	373	440	498	399	801	1417	555
			(40)	(198)	(43)	(43)	(96)	(117)	(42)	(55)	(36)	(59)	(54)	(444)
	+		51	4	50	39	14	16	49	45	54	53	62	437
	−		3	55	11	23	48	47	13	15	6	8	0	229
Third Quarter	μ			−162	−898	−1086	−233	−1227	−583	−738	88	−333	303	−500
				(47)	(62)	(70)	(36)	(50)	(65)	(55)	(25)	(41)	(36)	(727)
	$\|\mu\|$			846	898	1086	416	1227	606	738	233	361	530	713
				(193)	(229)	(270)	(112)	(310)	(189)	(230)	(48)	(715)	(62)	(539)
	+			22	0	1	23	0	7	0	49	8	51	161
	−			33	77	77	43	72	51	52	15	53	26	499

μ = mean
$\|\mu\|$ = mean absolute value
+ = number of + observations
− = number of − observations
* = numbers in parentheses are standard errors
** = Differences are in dollars for $1,000,000 contract.

TABLE 3. Cost of Carry Model Summary Statistics for Annualized Dollar Differences: Futures Price Less Equilibrium Price (Percent)

		1976			1977				1978				All (contracts)
		Mar.	Jun.	Sep.	Dec.	Mar.	Jun.	Sep.	Dec.	Mar.	Jun.	Sep.	Dec.	
Nearby Contract	μ	.136 (.019)	.125 (.026)	.006 (.006)	.068 (.011)	.015 (.012)	.032 (.030)	−.031 (.009)	.051 (.009)	.035 (.017)	−.067 (.015)	−.148 (.011)	−.029 (.017)	.020 (.159)
	$\|\mu\|$	.160 (.021)	.162 (.027)	.050 (.010)	.089 (.013)	.069 (.015)	.118 (.034)	.063 (.017)	.072 (.010)	.085 (.020)	.112 (.032)	.154 (.046)	.157 (.038)	.105 (.121)
	+	27	26	17	32	14	17	8	25	19	9	3	18	215
	−	12	22	33	16	34	33	41	26	29	40	46	30	462
Second Quarter	μ		.515 (.016)	.172 (.020)	.240 (.014)	.076 (.011)	.108 (.015)	−.005 (.017)	.094 (.008)	.130 (.012)	.173 (.017)	.072 (.009)	.121 (.011)	.149 (.177)
	$\|\mu\|$		.515 (.016)	.179 (.020)	.240 (.014)	.106 (.014)	.133 (.018)	.107 (.026)	.105 (.009)	.141 (.013)	.193 (.020)	.087 (.010)	.158 (.014)	.174 (.152)
	+		43	40	49	36	40	16	41	39	43	35	41	423
	−		0	7	0	14	9	34	8	8	4	13	21	118
Third Quarter	μ			.671 (.018)	.611 (.026)	.381 (.017)	.148 (.014)	.192 (.016)	.139 (.025)	.155 (.027)	.260 (.024)	.267 (.017)	.292 (.013)	.317 (.236)
	$\|\mu\|$			.671 (.018)	.611 (.026)	.381 (.017)	.156 (.014)	.208 (.017)	.163 (.026)	.155 (.027)	.261 (.024)	.281 (.020)	.292 (.013)	.323 (.228)
	+			43	61	62	45	50	36	40	49	45	48	479
	−			0	0	0	7	7	10	1	1	2	0	28

μ = mean
$|\mu|$ = mean absolute value
+ = number of + observations
− = number of − observations
* = numbers in parentheses are standard errors

TABLE 4. Forward Rate Model Summary Statistics for Annualized Dollar Differences: Futures Price Less Equilibrium Price (Percent)

		1976			1977				1978				All (contracts)
		Mar.	Jun.	Sep.	Dec.	Mar.	Jun.	Sep.	Dec.	Mar.	Jun.	Sep.	Dec.	
Nearby Contract	μ	.163 (.018)	.164 (.026)	.097 (.012)	.223 (.016)	.089 (.012)	.220 (.029)	.146 (.016)	.529 (.045)	.349 (.043)	.256 (.020)	.247 (.023)	.458 (.043)	.248 (.291)
	$|\mu|$	.170 (.018)	.176 (.026)	.104 (.012)	.227 (.016)	.103 (.012)	.221 (.030)	.152 (.016)	.529 (.045)	.353 (.043)	.279 (.021)	.300 (.026)	.513 (.045)	.264 (.276)
	+	39	44	46	54	41	54	50	64	56	45	44	47	584
	–	9	15	15	5	19	9	12	0	5	15	18	13	135
Second Quarter	μ		.150 (.009)	–.099 (.007)	.087 (.009)	.043 (.006)	–.038 (.004)	–.041 (.006)	.126 (.013)	.126 (.012)	.122 (.013)	.241 (.021)	.389 (.014)	.100 (.169)
	$|\mu|$		.152 (.009)	.107 (.029)	.101 (.010)	.067 (.008)	.052 (.014)	.063 (.016)	.134 (.013)	.147 (.013)	.127 (.013)	.248 (.021)	.389 (.014)	.144 (.135)
	+		51	4	50	39	14	16	49	45	54	53	62	437
	–		3	55	11	23	48	47	13	15	6	8	0	229
Third Quarter	μ			.013 (.007)	–.098 (.006)	–.117 (.007)	–.021 (.004)	–.141 (.006)	–.065 (.007)	–.085 (.006)	.020 (.003)	–.036 (.004)	.064 (.007)	–.056 (.073)
	$|\mu|$			.115 (.023)	.098 (.023)	.117 (.028)	.052 (.012)	.141 (.034)	.070 (.020)	.085 (.024)	.035 (.005)	.042 (.012)	.087 (.009)	.074 (.054)
	+			22	0	1	23	0	7	0	49	8	51	161
	–			33	77	77	43	72	51	52	15	53	26	499

μ = mean
$|\mu|$ = mean absolute value
+ = number of + observations
– = number of – observations
* = numbers in parentheses are standard errors

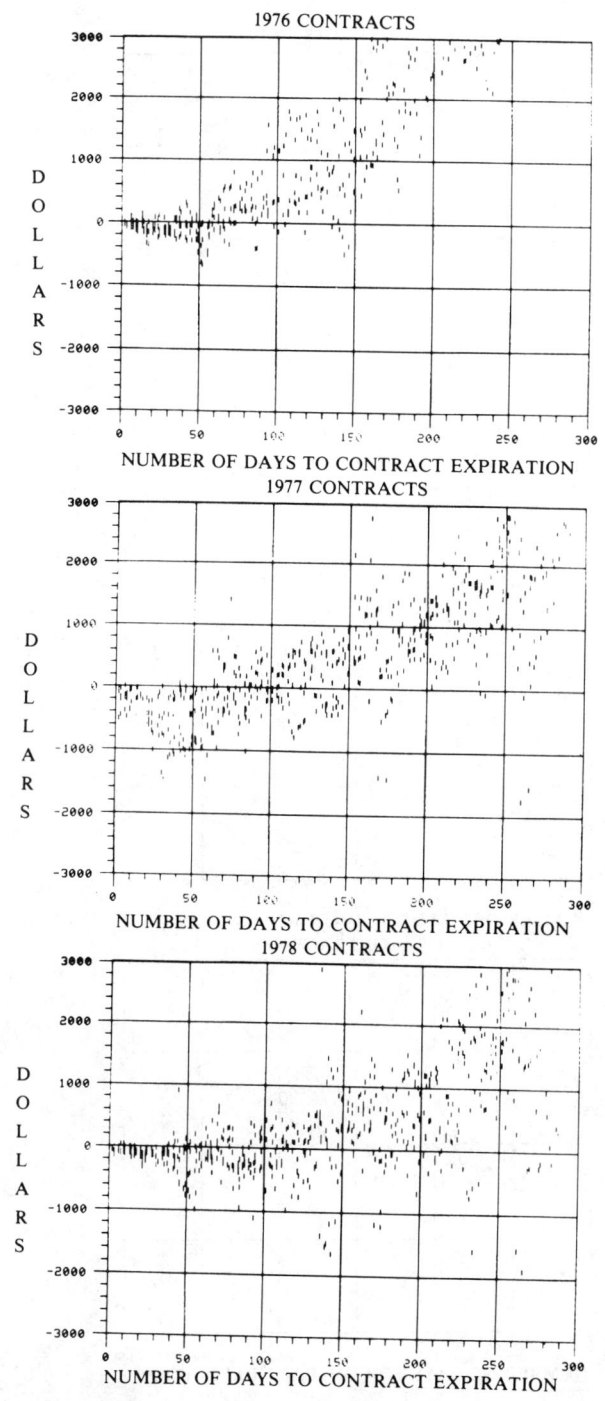

FIGURE I. Cost-of-Carry Model Dollar Differences: Futures Price Less Equilibrium Price

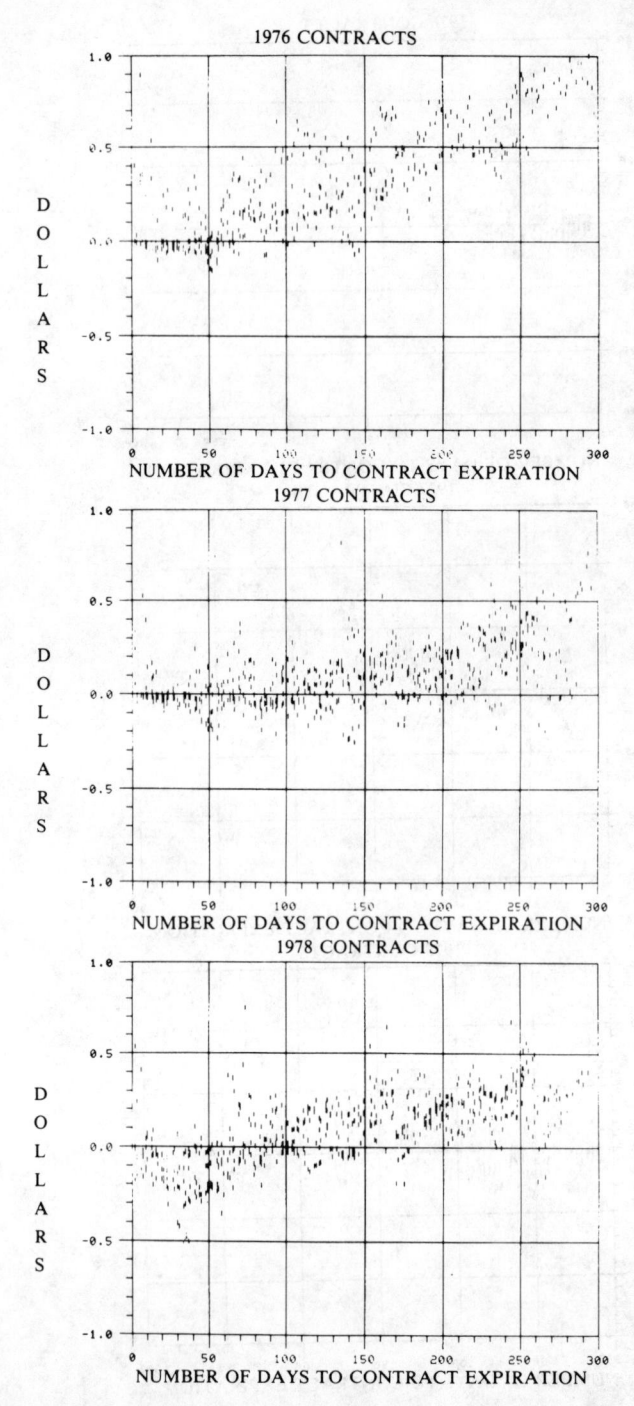

FIGURE II. Forward Rate Model Dollar Differences: Futures Price Less Equilibrium Price

Interest Rate Futures: Concepts and Issues 229

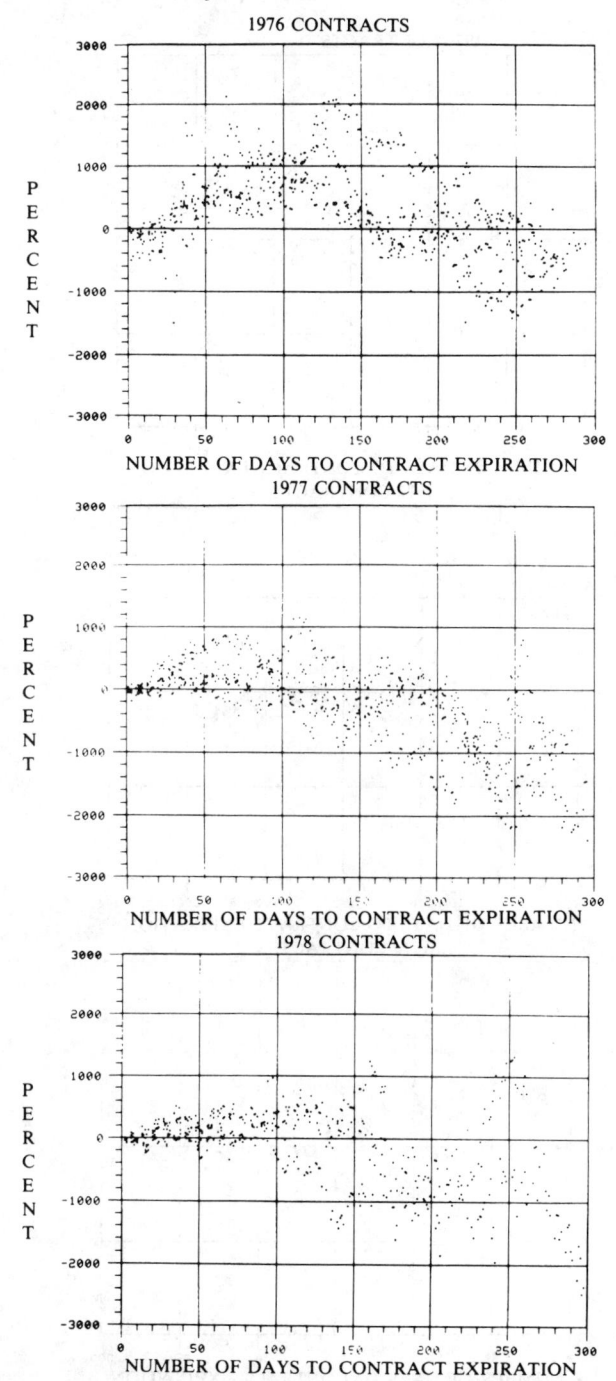

FIGURE III. Cost of Carry Model Annualized Dollar Differences: Futures Price Less Equilibrium Price

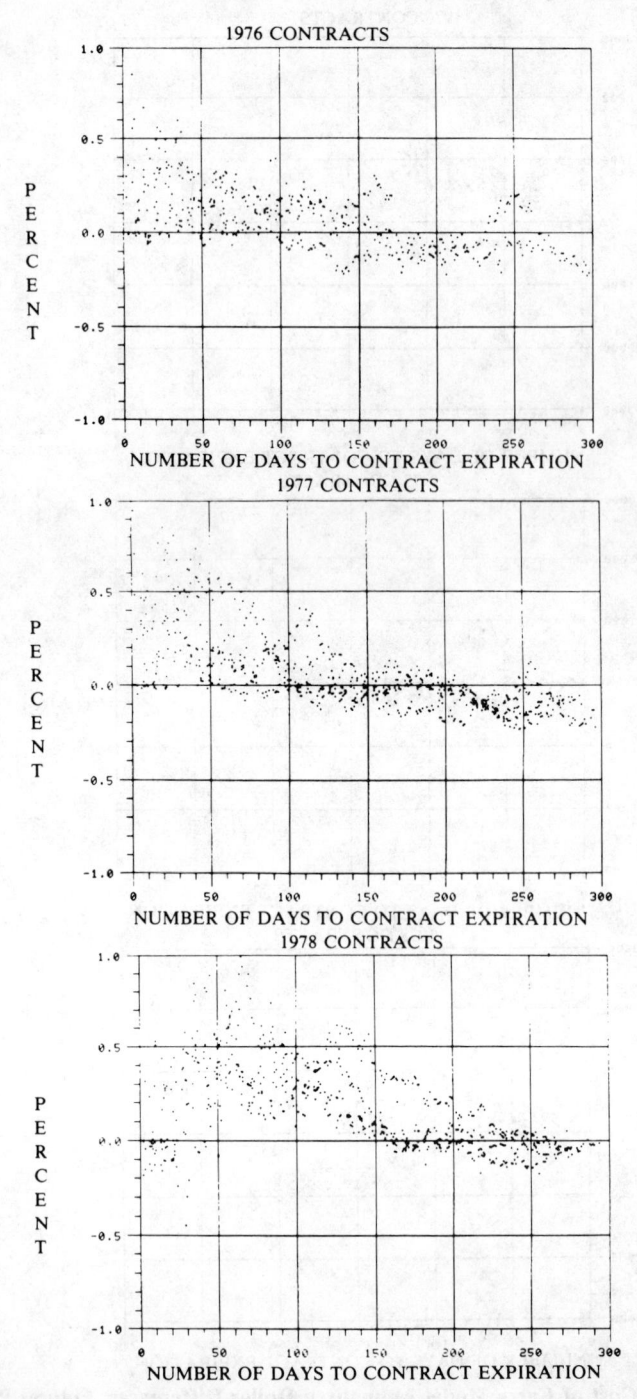

FIGURE IV. Forward Rate Model Annualized Dollar Differences: Futures Price Less Equilibrium Price

od to the maturity of the security deliverable on the futures contract, by purchasing a security with SD day to maturity and buying a futures contract instead of buying a security with $(SD + 91)$ days to maturity. Because these arbitrage conditions derive from positive and negative differences between the actual and theoretical price, they are referred to as overpriced and underpriced situations. For the forward rate model, overpriced and underpriced situations are applicable to the cash investor in Treasury Bill, the case of quasi-arbitrage. The cost-of-carry results more appropriately apply to the opportunity cost of funds, the case of pure arbitrage.

The data show that there are different conclusions to be drawn as to the pricing of futures contracts and its implications for market efficiency depending upon the implied financing charge or, equivalently, on whether equilibrium prices are derived from the cost-of-carry specification or the forward-rate specification of the model.

In terms of the summary statistics, the dollar differences (per $1,000,000 contract, Tables 1 and 2) show that the mean price difference for all contracts is $282 for the nearby contract for forward rates and only $85 for the cost-of-carry model. For both theories the sign of the price difference tends to reverse as the time from contract maturity increases. The cost-of-carry differences tend to increase as the time from maturity increases, and the forward-rate differences decrease. These trends are highlighted in Figures I and II.

Since the inception of futures trading, the price differences derived from forward rates for the nearby contracts have been increasing,[18] and those for the cost of carry have fluctuated around zero. For the more distant contracts, the cost-of-carry price differences have declined over time from large positive values, while those derived from forward rates have been persistently negative. The forward rate data in Table 2 and Figure II show that roughly 150 days from contract maturity there is a switching from overpricing to underpricing of the futures contract. The mean absolute differences confirm these tendencies. For both the nearby and the third-quarter contracts, the mean absolute difference is nearly equal to the mean difference, but in the second quarter it is nearly double the mean difference. These findings for forward rates are consistent with those of other researchers who have examined futures prices, and have led some to conclude that theories of backwardation hold for longer-term contracts, or that futures contract risk exists which requires excess returns. The dollar differences for the cost-of-carry model (Table 1 and Figure I) are positive for distant contracts and move toward zero for nearby contracts.

The annualized data present a much more striking indication of the differences between the two models and the trends within these models.

---

[18] Rendleman and Carabini [17] found a similar trend in differences that were based on forward rates.

differences between the two models and the trends within these models. Since the overpricing in the cost-of-carry model occurs in the third quarter, it is much less significant in increasing annual rates of return than the overpricing in the forward rate model, where the overpricing occurs in the nearby contracts and the implicit annualization assumption is that it can be replicated many times throughout the year.[19] Tables 3 and 4 give the summary statistics for the annualized basis point difference for the two models, and Figures III and IV plot the daily data segmented by yearly periods.

Unlike the dollar data, the annualized basis point data show that the two theories differ considerably with respect to the nearby contract and the more distant, third-quarter contract. The mean annualized basis point differential for the nearby contract using forward rates is 25 basis points. In the contract month of December 1977, it reached a high of 53 basis points (Table 4).[20] Confirmation of the consistency of this overpricing is given by the mean absolute difference which is nearly equal to the mean in every contract. On the other hand, the annualized cost-of-carry differences for the nearby contract were only 2 basis points. Furthermore, unlike the forward-price differences, the mean absolute of the cost-of-carry differences is far greater than the mean, indicating fluctuations around zero are common.

The second quarter shows only slight overpricing for both theories. The third quarter, however, supports the earlier conclusions that the forward-rate model results in underpricing and the cost-of-carry model in overpricing. Figures III and IV show the different conclusions concerning futures market pricing and market efficiency that result from alternative assumptions about financing charges. For the nearby contract, it is evident that the financing cost plays an important role in influencing arbitrage decisions. For quasi-arbitrage, returns can be en-

---

[19] For example, a difference of $1,000 on an investment of $1,000,000, if obtained over a period of 91 days, is at an annual rate of 0.40 percent (40 basis points); if obtained over 30 days or 182 days, the annual rate would be approximately 1.20 or 0.20 percent, respectively. In recent work on this subject the annualization period seems to have been a major reason for conflicting findings. For example, Puglisi [16] and Vignola and Dale [21] annualized all dollar differences over SD days, consistent with their narrow approach aimed at portfolio holders. Others [17] appear to use an annualization period of 91 days for all their differences. Using forward rates generally implicitly assumes a 91-day period for annualization. Because of these difficulties, it is preferable first to calculate the price differences of arbitrage, then explicitly to take annualization into account.

[20] This study uses closing prices for futures and spot markets. Since the futures market closes earlier than the cash markets, our results are affected by spot market price changes that occur late in the day. The spot market closes roughly one hour later than the futures market. Thus, the existence or nonexistence of arbitrage possibilities may be due to data reporting. For example, for the December 1978 contract, when the money market was highly volatile due to Federal Reserve policy changes and the November 1, 1978, actions to support the dollar in foreign exchange markets, the closing price data resulted in a number of outlier observations. Examination of these observations, however, did not indicate any unidirectional bias.

hanced by using the futures markets, since overpricing is generally present (Figure IV). For pure arbitrage, however, there is a slight underpricing of nearby contracts (Figure III).

The pure arbitrage findings must be viewed cautiously since the results are sensitive to the storage-cost rate. The writers have used the overnight federal funds rate throughout the paper. Had an *RP* rate been used, the financing costs would have been lowered by 1/8 to 1/4 percent, resulting in a lower equilibrium price.[21] Even though the overnight *RP* rate is lower than the federal funds rate, the federal funds rate may give more realistic results since the term structure of *RP* rates generally reflects the upward sloping term structure found in Treasury Bills. Unfortunately, the necessary *RP* series or proxies for such series do not exist. Factoring in these considerations, the futures market appears to have been priced efficiently with respect to pure arbitrage opportunities.

IV. CONCLUSIONS

The effects of alternative financing costs on the pricing of Treasury Bill futures are clearly demonstrated in this paper. In general, the writers' results show that the overnight cost-of-carry model is better for explaining futures prices than are forward rates derived from the yield curve. The conclusion is that the cost-of-carry and pure arbitrage dominate futures prices, although there are cases of pure arbitrage. However, there are more significant opportunities for quasi-arbitrage. If one uses the existence or nonexistence of arbitrage profits to draw conclusions about market efficiency, as many authors have, one will reach a different conclusion depending on which price model is adopted and what financing costs are implicity assumed. The fact that forward rates are inappropriate for determining the equilibrium price of futures contracts has been responsible for the often-cited underpricing and overpricing of the futures market and the implication that the market is inefficient. However, these findings are appropriate for portfolio holders of Treasury Bills who may increase their returns by using Treasury Bill futures.

The use of the cost-of-carry model removes the need to resort to the explanations that have been forthcoming to rationalize the findings when forward rates are used as the basis for judging futures markets pricing and efficiency. It is reasonable for economists to have turned to traditional theories of the term structure in exploring futures markets. However, in doing so they have explicitly considered only a narrow

---

[21] For the average term of 45 days for the nearby contract, 1/8 of a percent results in a financing cost difference of approximately $150.

framework for drawing their conclusions and have had to explain their findings by referring to transactions costs, institutional practices, risk premiums and other market imperfections. A more flexible model based on the cost-of-carry does not need to revert to such *ad hoc* explanations. The conclusion is, therefore, the question of futures market efficiency and pricing reduces to the question of the use of the appropriate financing charges.

References

1. C. C. Baker and A. J. Vignola, "Market Liquidity, Security Trading, and the Estimation of Empirical Yield Curves," *The Review of Economics and Statistics*, Volume LXI, Number 1, (February, 1979), 131-135.
2. B. Branch, "Testing the Unbiased Expectations Theory of Interest Rates," *The Financial Review*, (Fall, 1978), 51-66.
3. D. R. Capozza and B. Cornell, "Treasury Bill Pricing in the Spot and Futures Markets," *Review of Economics and Statistics*, Volume LXI, Number 4, (November, 1979), 513-520.
4. B. G. Chow and D. J. Brophy, "The U.S. Treasury Bill Market and Hypotheses Regarding the Term Structure of Interest Rates," *The Financial Review*, (Fall, 1978), 36-50.
5. J. C. Cox, J. E. Ingersoll, and S. A. Ross, "A Theory of the Term Structure of Interest Rates," Research Paper No. 468, Graduate School of Business, Stanford University, (August, 1978).
6. K. Dusak, "Futures Trading and Investor Returns: An Investigation of Commodity Market Risk Premiums," *Journal of Political Economy*, Volume LXXXI, Number 6, (November, 1973), 1387-1406.
7. M. Hamburger and E. Platt, "The Expectations Hypothesis and the Efficiency of theTreasury Bill Market," *The Review of Economics and Statistics*, Volume LVII, Number 1, (May, 1975), 190-199.
8. J. R. Hicks, *Value and Capital*, Oxford: The Clarendon Press, (1939).
9. R. W. Lang, and R. H. Rasche, "A Comparison of Yields on Futures Contracts and Implied Forward Rates," *Federal Reserve Bank of St. Louis Monthly Review*, Volume 60, Number 12, (December, 1978), 21-30.
10. C. Lucas, M. Jones, and T. Thurston, "Federal Funds and Repurchase Agreements," *Federal Reserve Bank of New York Quarterly Review*, Volume 2, Number 2, (Summer, 1977), 33-48.
11. B. G. Malkiel, *The Term Structure of Interest Rates: Expectations and Behavior Patterns*, Princeton: Princeton University Press, (1966).
12. G. E. Morgan, "Forward and Futures Pricing of Treasury Bills," College of Business Administration, University of Texas, Manuscript (1979).
13. C. R. Nelson, *The Term Structure of Interest Rates*, New York: Basic Books, Inc., (1972).
14. G. S. Oldfield, "The Relationship Between U.S. Treasury Bill Spot and Futures Prices," School of Business Administration, Dartmouth College, Manuscript (1977).
15. W. Poole, "Using T-Bill Futures to Gauge Interest Rate Expectations," *Federal Reserve Bank of San Francisco Economic Review*, (Spring, 1978), 7-19.
16. D. J. Puglisi, "Is the Futures Market for Treasury Bills Efficient," *The Journal of Portfolio Management*, Volume 5, Number 1, (Winter, 1978), 64-67.
17. R. J. Rendleman and C. E. Carabini, "The Efficiency of the Treasury Bill Futures Market," *The Journal of Finance*, Volume XXXIX, Number 4, (September, 1979), 895-914.
18. E. Roll, *The Behavior of Interest Rates*, New York: Basic Books, Inc. (1970).
19. T. D. Simpson, "The Market for Federal Funds and Repurchase Agreements," *Federal Reserve Board Staff Study*, Number 2106, (July, 1979).

20. W. J. Smith, "Repurchase Agreements and Federal Funds," *Federal Reserve Bulletin*, (May, 1978), 353-360.
21. A. J. Vignola and C. J. Dale, "Is the Futures Market for Treasury Bills Efficient?," *The Journal of Portfolio Management*, Volume 5, Number 2, (Winter, 1978), 78-81.
22. Holbrook Working, "The Theory of the Inverse Carrying Charge in Futures Markets," *Journal of Farm Economics*, Volume 30, (1948), 1-28.
23. Holbrook Working, "The Theory of Price of Storage," *American Economic Review*, Volume XXXIX, Number 6, (December, 1949), 1254-1262.

PART III

HEDGING WITH INTEREST RATE FUTURES

One of the most important social functions that futures markets provide is a means of transferring risk. While it is difficult to give exact definitions of hedgers and speculators, the following seem usable. A speculator increases risk by entering the future market in the hopes of realizing a profit. By contrast, a hedger enters the futures market in order to reduce risk exposure. To a large extent the success or failure of a new futures market will depend on its success in attracting a large volume of hedging activity. The amount of hedging activity a market attracts depends in turn on the hedging effectiveness of the market. Consequently, the papers in this section all deal with assessments of the hedging effectiveness of the interest rate futures market or proposed strategies for increasing hedging effectiveness.

The first paper, Interest Rate Futures: New Tool for the Financial Manager, *by Peter W. Bacon and Richard E. Williams,* explains the nature of the GNMA futures contract and indicates several ways in which hedges can be initiated. In Hedging for Better Spread Management, *Robert W. McLeod and George M. McCabe* focus on the role of interest rate futures in bank spread management—the spread being the rate difference between borrowed and loaned funds for the bank. McLeod and McCabe find T-bill futures to be the most appropriate vehicle for a variety of different hedging applications.

Richard W. McEnally and Michael L. Rice distinguish three alternative hedging strategies in their paper, Hedging Possibilities in the Flotation of Debt Securities. *When the instruments* to be hedged and the deliverable instruments on the futures contract are matched with respect to maturity, coupon, and risk level, one may hedge one dollar of the hedged instrument with one dollar of the futures contract. However, when the instruments are not so well matched, the 1:1 hedge ratio is not appropriate. McEnally and Rice go on to discuss two more sophisticated techniques for selecting the proper hedge ratio, which they call a "duration hedge" and a "historically optimal hedge." Additionally, they provide the first empirical data on the relative effectiveness of these alternative hedging approaches.

The historically optimal hedge of McEnally and Rice is quite similar to the hedging strategy developed by Stein. (See Part I.) Louis H. Ederington recognized the usefulness of Stein's approach and applied it to hedging with T-bill and GNMA futures. After deriving the variance-minimizing hedge ratio, Ederington tested the hedging effectiveness of the interest rate futures market in comparison to that for agricultural commodities. He found considerable hedging effectiveness for interest rate futures, but less than that of the agricultural commodities.

Charles T. Franckle responded to Ederington's paper in The Hedging Performance of the New Futures Markets: Comment. He points out several problems with Ederington's technique. Notably, Ederington did not fully allow for the expected price change that would normally occur for a T-bill simply due to the fact that the T-bill would be approaching its maturity. Also, Franckle notes, as time progresses the interest sensitivity of a T-bill will naturally change, and Ederington's method does not fully account for this phenomenon either. However, Franckle is able to show the necessary modifications to Ederington's method to correct the hedge ratio for T-bills. As a result, the hedging performance of the T-bill futures is improved substantially. Although his method works for T-bills, Franckle does not apply it to the GNMA futures.

Working in the tradition of Stein and Ederington, Joanne Hill and Thomas Schneeweis apply the minimum-variance technique to hedging corporate bonds in Risk Reduction Potential of Financial Futures for Corporate Bond Positions. Since no futures contract is traded on corporate bonds, any hedge of corporate bonds must be a "cross hedge." A cross hedge is a hedge involving instruments differing in coupon, maturity, risk level or other institutional features—such as callability or tax status. Since the kinds of instruments covered in the interest rate futures market are necessarily few, most hedges will involve cross hedging. Therefore, Hill and Schneeweis want to appraise the usefulness of the interest rate futures market for cross-hedging, and they find considerable hedging effectiveness for corporate bonds using GNMA and T-bond futures.

All consideration of hedging necessarily depends on the relationship between the cash and futures market. Likewise, market efficiency tests (see Part II) also depend upon this relationship. In their paper, The Error Learning Model and the Financial Futures Market, George E. Morgan and Charles T. Franckle argue that tests of market efficiency and hedging effectiveness both depend upon a theory linking the cash and futures markets. Morgan and Franckle believe that the error-learning model of Meiselman provides such a theory. Basically, the error-learning model states that observed forecast errors of interest rates constitute new information that market observers incorporate into new interest rate forecasts. Morgan and Franckle find that the error-learning model helps to promote a better understanding of the interest rate futures market. They also go on to draw important implications for tests of market efficiency and hedging effectiveness.

In addition to the historically optimal hedge, McEnally and Rice also explored the duration hedge. As has been seen, the historically optimal hedge has been developed by Ederington, Franckle, Hill and Schneeweis, and others. The duration hedge is developed by Robert W. Kolb and Raymond Chiang in Improving Hedging Performance Using Interest Rate Futures. Kolb and Chiang derive a hedge ratio that gives a perfect hedge, assuming flat yield curves. A perfect hedge is a hedge that leaves the hedger's wealth unchanged. This price sensitivity (PS) strategy, as Kolb and Chiang call it, is designed to handle mismatches in the maturity, coupon, and risk level between the hedged and hedging instruments. As such, it is particularly applicable to cross-hedging situations. Since the PS strategy explicitly considers the price sensitivity of both the hedged and hedging instruments, it escapes the adjustment problems that Franckle encountered with Ederington's methodology. Consequently, the PS strategy is equally applicable to all interest rate futures instruments, not just the T-bill futures. To demonstrate this applicability, Kolb and Chiang conclude with two examples of the implementation of the PS strategy.

In a second paper, Duration, Immunization, and Hedging

with Interest Rate Futures, *Kolb and Chiang* extend the work of their first paper. In that earlier paper, Kolb and Chiang assumed that yield curves were flat, which is not usually the case. Consequently, they extend the analysis to situations where term structures have various shapes, and yields move differently on the hedged and hedging instruments.

As is often true in other fields of finance, different models of hedging are advocated by various authors. To a large extent, for the practical hedger, these methods are complementary, not competitive. The ultimate goal of the hedger is to avoid wealth changes due to shifts in yields. Each of the methods proposed is valuable to the extent it aids that goal. Much remains to be learned about hedging, but the articles in this part point the way to more effective hedging strategies.

14

Interest Rate Futures: New Tool for the Financial Manager[*]

Peter W. Bacon and Richard E. Williams[†]

One of the many problems facing the financial manager today is how to deal with the possibility of wide fluctuations in interest rates. For years, buyers and sellers of a wide variety of commodities have used the futures markets to offset much of the risk of future price fluctuations. Until recently, however, there was no effective, inexpensive way for the financial manager to hedge against the possibility of rising or falling future interest rates. Fortunately, in October 1975, the Chicago Board of Trade opened a futures market in Government National Mortgage Association pass-through certificates (GNMA's), and in January 1976, the International Monetary Market of the Chicago Mercantile Exchange provided a market for futures trading in 3-month Treasury Bills (T-bills). The purpose of this article is to review the operations of these two futures markets and to demonstrate how futures trading in either GNMA or T-bill securities might be used to reduce the risk of future interest rate fluctuations.

---

[*]Reprinted from *Financial Management*, Vol. 5, No. 1, (Spring 1976). Reprinted by permission of the publisher and authors.

[†]Dr. Bacon is Associate Professor of Finance at Wright State University and an Associate Editor of Financial Management. He received his DBA from Indiana University. A previous article by Professor Bacon appeared in the Summer 1972 issue of *Financial Management*. Dr. Williams is Assistant Professor of Finance at Wright State University and received his PhD from Michigan State University.

GNMA FUTURES MARKET

Development of a futures market in mortgage-backed securities came at the behest of financial institutions dealing in the mortgage market. These institutions (e.g. mortgage bankers, insurance companies, savings and loan associations) found themselves faced with the problem of having to make commitments of funds at current interest rate levels in an era of increasingly volatile rate structures. At least a partial solution was achieved by the development of an interest rate futures market by the Chicago Board of Trade (CBT). This market uses mortgage-backed certificates guaranteed by the Government National Mortgage Association as the unit of trading. The GNMA certificates represent marketable shares in pools of Federal Housing Administration and Veterans Administration mortgage loans. The trading unit has a principal amount of $100,000, a stated interest of 8%, and an assumed maturity of 12 years. Exhibit 1 indicates the prices at which GNMA futures contracts will trade for a variety of interest rate assumptions. A detailed explanation of yield and price relationships is contained in Appendix A.

All trading in GNMA futures is conducted on the floor of the CBT. However, each trader's contract is with the CBT Clearing Corporation rather than with his counterpart in trade. The Clearing Corporation guarantees payment and delivery, and permits buyers and sellers to operate independently. Moreover, as in the case of futures trading in other commodities, few actual deliveries are expected. Rather, most

Exhibit 1 Yield and Price Table for GNMA Futures Contracts[3]

Yield[1]	Price[2]	Yield[1]	Price[2]
6.75%	109-13	9.25%	91-02
7.00%	107-12	9.50%	89-15
7.25%	105-12	9.75%	87-29
7.50%	103-13	10.00%	86-12
	to 103-14		—
7.75%	101-17	10.25%	84-28
8.00%	99-21	10.50%	83-14
	to 99-22		
8.25%	97-27	10.75%	82-00
	to 97-28		
8.50%	96-03	11.25%	79-09
8.75%	94-12	11.50%	77-30
			to 77-31
9.00%	92-22	11.75%	76-21

[1] Yields represent simple, uncompounded monthly payments of principal and interest on 30-year certificates bearing stated interest rate of 8.00%, under the assumption that the certificate is prepaid in the 12th year.

[2] Digits to right of dash are 32nds. (109-13 means 109 13/32).

[3] See Appendix A for further explanation.

Source: Merrill Lynch Pierce Fenner and Smith, Inc.

sellers will "close" by buying another contract and most buyers will "close" by selling a contract prior to the termination of trading.

Of particular interest to the potential participants in the GNMA futures market is the fact that yields and prices on GNMA certificates are highly correlated with those of other long-term securities. For example, the correlation coefficient between the yields on GNMA 8% certificates and AAA Corporate bonds is in excess of 90% [11]. Consequently, GNMA futures trading should prove useful not only to those directly involved with residential mortgages, but to financial managers of non-financial corporations as well. Moreover, commission charges and margin requirements are modest, which should increase the attractiveness of the market to speculators as well as hedgers.

HEDGING OPPORTUNITIES WITH GNMA FUTURES CONTRACTS

The existence of a futures market in GNMA certificates presents an opportunity for the financial manager to hedge against rising or falling rates. Two types of hedging positions are possible—a short and a long hedge.

Short Hedging with GNMA Futures

A short hedge involves the sale of a futures contract and is used to protect the firm, individual, or institution against the possibility of an increase in the future level of interest rates. Institutions most likely to be adversely affected by an increase in interest rates are (1) those expecting to borrow in the futures and (2) those investing today in interest sensitive assets. Either group could offset the risk by selling a futures contract. If rates rose above the level implicit in the futures contract, the market value of the contract would decline and the position could be closed by purchasing another contract at the lower price. The gain would help offset increased borrowing costs for the first group and the reduced market value of the original investment for the second.

For example, consider the situation where the financial manager knows that he must issue $10 million of intermediate-term (12-year) bonds six months from now to pay for a plant currently under construction, but fears that interest rates may rise in the interim. Sale of $10 million in futures contracts now would allow him to offset at least some of the effects of the possible increase in interest rates prior to the time the bonds are actually issued. Assume that the current price on GNMA future contracts with a delivery date in six months is 99-22/32 (equivalent to an 8% yield to maturity on a 30-year certificate assumed to be prepaid in the 12th year), and that the corporate borrowing rate is currently 8%. The financial manager could sell 100 GNMA contracts for delivery in six months. If interest rates for both GNMA certificates and corporate bonds rise by 1% over the next six months, then the price of the contracts sold will decline to 92-22/32 (see Exhibit 1). The financial manager can then cover his short position by buying 100 contracts, earning a $700,000 profit before commissions. This profit can be used to reduce the amount of bonds that will have to be issued from $10 million to $9,300,000.

The effective cost of financing produced by this futures market operation can be calculated by finding the interest rate which makes the present value of the future interest and principal on a 9%, 12-year bond issue with a principal amount of $9,300,000 equal to the $10 million that would have been issued in the absence of the futures market dealing. If interest is paid semi-annually, then

$$\$10,000,000 = \sum_{t=1}^{24} \frac{(\$9,300,000)(.045)}{(1+k/2)^t} + \frac{\$9,300,000}{(1+k/2)^{24}}$$

Solving for k results in an effective annual interest rate of 8%, and the financial manager has completed a perfect hedge if the nominal commissions are ignored. The perfect hedge in this example is the result of assuming (1) equal coupon rates for both securities, (2) equal maturities and, (3) equal absolute increases in interest rates. If each of the assumptions is relaxed, then it can be shown that the hedges are no longer perfect but do still allow the financial manager to offset at least a portion of the interest rate increase.

Unequal Coupon Rates. Relax first the assumption of equal coupon rates on both the corporate bond and the GNMA certificate by as assuming that while the GNMA rate is rising from 8% to 9% over the six-month period, the corporate bond rate is rising from 9% to 10%. If maturities for both issues are still assumed to be twelve years, then

$$\$10,000,000 = \sum_{t=1}^{24} \frac{(\$9,300,000)(.05)}{(1+k/2)^t} + \frac{\$9,300,000}{(1+k/2)^{24}}$$

and the effective or hedged rate is about 8.96% compared with an unhedged rate of 10% and a 9% rate that prevailed when the hedge was undertaken. The slightly more than perfect nature of the hedge is due to the fact that the present value of future amounts decreases at a decreasing rate as interest rates rise. Thus, discounting at 9% instead of the 8% rate used in the previous example more than offsets the higher interest payments accompanying the 10% rate assumption for the bond issue.

Unequal Maturities. Now assume that both the GNMA and the corporate bond rates increase from 8% to 9%, but that the maturity of the corporate issue is 20 years rather than 12. Here the hedge is less than perfect. In this case,

$$\$10,000,000 = \sum_{t=1}^{40} \frac{(\$9,300,000)(.045)}{(1+k/2)^{40}} + \frac{\$9,300,000}{(1+k/2)^{40}}$$

and the hedged rate is about 8.24% compared to a perfectly hedged rate of 8%. Thus, when the financial manager issues bonds with a maturity different from the assumed 12-year maturity of the GNMA certificates, the hedging operation is unlikely to completely lock in the current rate of interest.

Partial Correlation. Next, assume that the GNMA and corporate bond rates do not increase by the same absolute percentage amounts, but rather that the GNMA issue goes from 8% to 8½%, while the corporate rate is rising from 8% to 9%. The profit earned on the short sale of GNMA futures contracts will decrease to $359,400 from the $700,000 of previous examples and the dollar amount of the bond issue will increase to $9,640,600. If a 12-year maturity for both securities is assumed, then

$$\$10,000,000 = \sum_{t=1}^{24} \frac{(\$9,640,600)(.045)}{(1+k/2)^t} + \frac{\$9,640,600}{(1+k/2)^{24}}$$

and the effective rate is approximately 8.51%. The financial manager has managed to offset about one-half of the increase in interest rates by using the futures market.

Finally, relax all the assumptions and assume that GNMA rates are going from 8% to 8½% while rates on a 20-year corporate bond are rising from 9% to 10%. In this case,

$$\$10,000,000 = \sum_{t=1}^{40} \frac{(\$9,640,600)(.05)}{(1+k/2)^t} + \frac{\$9,640,600}{(1+k/2)^{40}}$$

and the hedged rate is about 9.59%. Therefore, even when the bonds to be issued have considerably different features than the GNMA certificates, the financial manager is still able to offset some of the increase in interest rates.

Inaccurate Forecasts. The effects of an inaccurate forecast of future rates by the financial manager should also be considered. Assume that both the GNMA futures rate and the current corporate bond rate are 8% and that a short hedge is executed by the financial manager in anticipation of a rise in rates. If, instead of rising, interest rates fall to 7%, there will be a loss on the futures market contract amounting to $768,700. Consequently, the financial manager will effectively have to issue $10,768,700 worth of 7%, 12-year bonds. Since

$$\$10{,}000{,}000 = \sum_{t=1}^{24} \frac{(10{,}768{,}700)(.035)}{(1+k/2)^t} + \frac{\$10{,}768{,}700}{(1+k/2)^{24}}$$

the hedged rate will be approximately 7.94%. Consequently, by executing a short hedge, the financial manager locks the firm into the rate structure implied in the futures contract; no benefits will accrue if a lower rate prevails when the bonds are actually issued. To gain the risk-reducing advantages of hedging, the opportunity to profit from favorable interest rate movements is forfeited.

Investor Expectations. In all the previous examples it was assumed that the cash market interest rate and the futures market rate were identical. In practice, the futures rate should reflect a consensus of investors' expectations regarding future interest rate levels. For example, on May 14, 1976 the yield on 8% GNMA certificates in the cash market was 8.42%. Exhibit 2 shows the relationship between expiration date and yield to maturity for GNMA futures contracts. At that time investors generally were anticipating higher interest rates, and this expectation was reflected in futures contract yields higher than the cash market yield.

The sale of GNMA futures contracts locks in the rate contained in the futures market rather than the rate prevailing in the cash market. Therefore, a short hedging operation will not protect the financial manager against interest rate changes that have already been anticipated by the futures market. In fact, if actual future interest rates were always perfectly anticipated, then the hedging operation would serve no monetary purpose. Of course, if such were the case there would be no futures market whose very existence depends upon the inability to accurately predict future prices. This is not meant to suggest that the GNMA futures market will be "inefficient." An efficient market implies that new information is immediately reflected in the price of the asset, not that the future price will be perfectly forecast.

Since it is unlikely that the futures market will precisely predict future interest rates, it is imperative that the financial manager formulate his own interest rate forecast. If he is confident that the futures market

Exhibit 2 Yield Curve for GNMA Futures Contracts

Futures contract expiration date	Yield to maturity
June '76	8.604%
Sept. '76	8.736
Dec. '76	8.819
March '77	8.898
June '77	8.968
Sept. '77	9.025

Source: *Wall Street Journal*, May 17, 1976.

has over-estimated future rate levels, then a short hedge will not be undertaken.

Even if a risk-averse financial manager agrees with the consensus forecast, a hedging transaction might be appropriate. If one views the consensus forecast as representing the mean of a probability distribution of expected future rates, utility theory suggests that unfavorable deviations will be given greater weight than favorable deviations.

Finally, it should be emphasized that the primary objective of hedging (as contrasted with speculation) is to substitute a known acceptable future rate for an unknown, possibly *unacceptable* interest rate. By protecting against the unacceptable rate, financial planning should be facilitated.

Other GNMA Short-Term Hedging Opportunities

The sale of a GNMA futures contract can also be used to effectively reduce the interest rate risk associated with investing in longer term securities. Given the upward-sloping yield curve that has prevailed in recent decades, it can be expected that long-term securities will normally provide higher yields to maturity than short-term securities. Unfortunately, long-term securities are also subject to significantly greater loss in value for a given increase in interest rates. Such principal losses could result in low or possibly negative holding period returns if the securities were sold prior to maturity. Because of this higher level of interest-rate risk, financial managers are often reluctant to invest temporary excess funds in long-term securities. However, the purchase of a GNMA pass-through certificate in the cash market coupled with the sale of a GNMA futures contract can effectively eliminate interest rate risk by fixing the future sales price of the long-term security. By locking in the future sales price, the financial manager is able to compare the now essentially risk-free yield on the long-term certificate with current short-term rates. Given an upward-sloping yield curve, the financial manager may find that he can substantially increase return with little, if any, increase in risk.

For example, a large bank recently reported purchasing GNMA certificates in the cash market and simultaneously selling futures contracts at a price that guaranteed a 7.5% yield on a 2-month investment. At the time commercial paper was yielding 4.75% to 4.875% [7]. Although the existence of an efficient market would imply that such opportunities should be rare, alert financial managers should be aware of these opportunities and capitalize on them when possible.

Long Hedge with GNMA Futures

A long hedge always involves the purchase of a futures contract and is used to offset the risk that future interest rates will fall. Those most likely to be adversely affected by a fall in the future interest rate levels include 1) institutions with future investable funds and 2) institutions that are borrowing at today's high rate. If interest rates do fall over the contract period, the long hedger can sell his contract at an increased price. This gain would increase the amount of future investable funds and help to preserve the level of interest income despite the fall in interest rates. Likewise, firms that borrowed at an earlier higher rate could view the gain as offsetting their high borrowing costs. Since the mechanics are similar to those covered in the short hedge example, they are left for the reader's investigation.

TREASURY BILL FUTURES TRADING

Futures trading in GNMA pass-through certificates provides a useful technique for hedging against changes in long-term interest rates. The Treasury bill futures market, by contrast, provides a vehicle for short-term borrowers and lenders to hedge against changes in money market rates.

T-Bill Futures Market

Trading in T-bill futures is conducted on the floor of the International Monetary Market (I.M.M.) of the Chicago Mercantile Exchange. The trading vehicle is the 90-day Treasury bill with a face value of $1,000,000. This instrument was selected because 1) its yield is highly correlated with other money market instruments, 2) there is no variation in quality, 3) terms are standard and, 4) a rapid, efficient transfer system was in place for delivery and settlement.

Contracts are currently being traded with delivery dates in March, June, September and December with payment and delivery made on the business day after the last trading day. Each trader's contract is with the I.M.M. Clearing House, which guarantees both payment and delivery.

Prices are quoted in terms of the I.M.M. index, which is simply the difference between the actual T-bill yield and 100.00. For example, a T-bill yield of 6% would be quoted as 94. Note, however, that the I.M.M. index is not the actual price of the contract. Rather, that price is computed by means of the following formula: Price = $1,000,000 − (days to maturity × T-bill yield × $1,000,000)/360. Thus, an I.M.M. index of 94 would translate to an actual price of $985,000 for 90-day bills yielding 6% with a face value of $1 million.

Hedging Against Falling Short-Term Rates

A long hedge involving the purchase of a T-bill contract is identical in concept to the long hedge with GNMA's. The purpose is to reduce the risk of a fall in interest rates.

Assume that in March a financial manager anticipates investing $10 million in September. Further assume that the futures price in March for a September T-bill contract is 94, which implies a yield of 6% and a delivery value of $985,000 per contract. The financial manager, fearing that the September interest rate may fall below 6%, buys 10 September T-Bill contracts.

The effectiveness of this hedge will, of course, depend upon the actual level of interest rates in September. If the T-bill rate prevailing in September has fallen to say 5.5%, 90-day T-bills with a maturity value of $10 million would be selling at $9,862,500. The financial manager might, therefore, elect to accept delivery on his contract paying only $9,850,000 (rather than the unhedged amount of $9,862,500) and earn a 6% annual return during the next 3 months. As an alternative, he could also sell his futures contracts at their September value of $9,862,500 and realize a $12,500 gain. Investing this gain in other money market instruments would tend to offset the decline in interest income due to the fall in rates.

Unfortunately, if interest rates rise rather than fall, the long hedger will suffer a loss. For example if the T-bill rate prevailing in September was 6.5%, the financial manager could sell his contracts for only $9,837,500 resulting in a $12,500 loss. The loss in turn would offset the higher income to be earned because of the prevailing higher interest rates.

The results of a variety of outcomes of a long hedge in T-bills are summarized in Exhibit 3. Analysis of this exhibit results in the following conclusions. First, the long hedge insures that the investor can at least earn the return implicit in the futures contract by accepting delivery on the contract. Second, if the investor chooses to invest in a money-market instrument other than T-bills, the effectiveness of the hedge depends upon both the correlation between the yield on T-bills and other money-market instruments, and on the maturity of the instrument selected. If other money market rates fall by a greater amount than the T-bill rate, only a portion of this fall will be offset. If other money market rates rise by more than the T-bill rate, the investor will benefit to some extent from this increase. As the maturity of the futures investment exceeds 90 days, the hedge becomes less effective.

Hedging Against Rising Short-Term Rates

Potential borrowers in the money markets can use T-bill futures to protect themselves against increases in short term interest rates with

Exhibit 3   Selected outcomes of a Long Hedge with a 6% T-Bill Futures Contract

Security	Rate prevailing at purchase date	Rate prevailing at delivery date	Effective yield on future investment
90 day bills	6.0	5.5	6.0
90 day paper	7.0	6.5	7.0
180 day paper	7.0	6.5	6.75
90 day bills	6.0	5.5	6.0
90 day paper	7.0	6.0	6.5
180 day paper	7.0	6.0	6.25
90 day bills	6.0	6.5	6.0
90 day paper	7.0	7.5	7.0
180 day paper	7.0	7.5	7.25
90 day bills	6.0	6.0	6.0
90 day paper	7.0	8.0	7.5
180 day paper	7.0	8.0	7.75

a short hedge. If interest rates rise between the sale date and delivery date, the delivery value of the futures contract will fall and the hedger can profit by repurchasing his contract at the lower price. The gain can then be viewed as reducing his future cash borrowing costs.

For example, assume that the financial manager anticipates borrowing $10 million in September through the commercial paper market. The current commercial paper rate is 7% and a September T-bill contract can be sold at a yield of 6%. Anticipating a rise in rates, the financial manager sells 10 September T-bill futures contracts at an equivalent delivery price of $9,850,000. If the bill rate in September has risen to 6.5% and the commercial paper rate to 7.5%, the financial manager could repurchase his contracts for $9,837,500 and use his gain of $12,500 to offset his increased borrowing cost.

The effectiveness of a short hedge in anticipation of rising rates depends on the same factors that influenced the effectiveness of the long hedge. If, in the preceeding example, the commercial paper rate increases more than the T-bill rate, only a portion of the increase will be offset. Likewise, if the maturity of the firm's future debt instrument exceeds 3 months, the firm is still partially exposed to the risk of rising rates.

The sale of T-bill futures contracts can also be used to eliminate the interest rate risk, while preserving the higher yields associated with longer term money market investments. For example, purchase of a six-month T-bill in today's cash market coupled with the sale of a T-bill futures contract for delivery in 3 months effectively converts todays 6-month into a 3-month instrument. Depending upon the slope of the yield curve and the relationship between the cash market and the futures market rates, higher returns with no increase in risk may often be achieved.

THE FUTURE FOR INTEREST RATE FUTURES

Hedging against rising or falling interest rates is not yet a widely used strategy of financial managers. Given the newness of the concept, this is certainly understandable. There are, however, several factors in addition to increased familiarity that will determine the potential usefulness of the technique.

One consideration is that the Securities and Exchange Commission and the recently formed Commodities Futures Trading Commission both claim jurisdiction over Treasury Bill and GNMA futures. The outcome of this dispute will affect financial disclosure, jurisdiction over brokers and dealers, rules to prevent market manipulation and potential registration of the contracts as securities.

Perhaps the most important factor influencing the use of the futures markets by financial managers is the extent to which speculators will participate in these markets. The hedger is attempting to reduce the risk of interest rate fluctuations by passing this risk to a speculator who is willing to assume the risk in the hope of making a profit. The profit potential and risk from speculating in interest futures is considerable. For example, the value of a T-bill futures contract will change by $25 for each basis point change in yield. Thus, a 25 basis-point change in T-bill rates could lead to a $625 profit (or loss) on a $1,500 initial margined investment.

Early reports on trading activity were not particularly encouraging in this regard. During the first month of T-bill futures trading, about 100 to 150 contracts were being traded each day. By April, however, 300 to 400 T-bill contracts were being traded daily and analysts were predicting between 2,000 and 3,000 contracts a day within a year [7]. GNMA futures trading is currently running at about 400 contracts per day, up from approximately 250 per day in February. As the futures volume continues to expand, large transactions will be accommodated with increasing ease.

A final factor influencing the use of interest rate futures markets concerns the problem of having only two maturities available. That is, the financial manager is only able to perfectly hedge against changes in very short term (3-month) or intermediate term (12-year) maturities. A broader spectrum of maturities would appear to be appropriate.

To the extent that these problems are resolved, the interest rate futures market should become an important vehicle for reducing the uncertainty regarding future interest rate levels.

APPENDIX A. YIELD AND PRICE CALCULATIONS FOR GNMA CERTIFICATES

The following factors enter into the calculation of the trading price or yield to maturity of the GNMA certificates:

1. Unlike a bond, GNMA certificates pay interest and principal monthly rather than paying only interest semi-annually.
2. The compounding effects of the monthly payment are ignored. In effect, six monthly payments are treated as one semi-annual payment.
3. It is assumed that prepayment of principal occurs in the twelfth year.
4. The first payment on a GNMA pass-through certificate actually occurs 45 days after the certificate is issued rather than one-month. Subsequent payments are made at monthly intervals thereafter. This delay lowers the true yield on the investment. Thus to yield 8%, the certificate will sell at slightly less than par (see Exhibit 1).

In equation form, the yield and price relationship can be expressed as follows:

$$V = \frac{\sum_{t=1}^{24} \frac{M_t}{(1+i/2)^t} + \frac{P}{(1+i/2)^{24}}}{(1+i/24)}$$

where V = Price of GNMA certificate, M_t = the sum of the six monthly payments of interest and principal in period t, P = outstanding principal at the end of 12 years, i.e., 24 semiannual periods, and i = yield to maturity.

The reader should note that the denominator adjusts for the 15 day delay as discussed in item 4 above.

References

1. Richard A. Donnelly, *Barrons* (Jan. 12, 1976), pp. 68-69.
2. Les Gapay, "Two U.S. Agencies Dispute Jurisdiction Over Treasury Bill, Ginnie Mae Futures," *Wall Street Journal* (June 12, 1976), p. 16.
3. International Monetary Market, "IMM Treasury Bill Futures Contract Specifications," Chicago.
4. International Monetary Market, "T-Bill Futures: Opportunities in Interest Rates," Chicago.
5. Steven Jacobs and James R. Kozach, "Is There a Future For a Mortgage Futures Market?" *Real Estate Review* (Spring 1975).
6. Byron Klapper, "New T-bill Futures Market Has Light Volume–," *Wall Street Journal* (Jan. 23, 1976), p. 24.

7. Valerie Mackie, "Interest Rate Futures offer A New Hedging Alternative," *Pensions and Investments* (April 12, 1976), p. 17.
8. Trevvett Matthews, "Possible GNMA Futures Market Should Alert Mortgage Bankers to Workings of Commodity Exchanges," *Mortgage Banker* (July 1975).
9. Merrill Lynch Pierce Fenner and Smith, Inc., "Hedge Guide for Mortgage Bankers and Institutional Investors."
10. Merrill Lynch Pierce Fenner and Smith, Inc., "GNMA Mortgage Futures: Trading Facts."
11. Shearson Hayden Stone Inc., "Guide to Speculating and Hedging in Mortgage Futures" (Oct. 10, 1975).
12. Joseph Winsk: "Interest-Rate Futures Trades Set Today; Mechanism May Help Mortgage Lenders," *Wall Street Journal* (Oct. 20, 1975), p. 16.

15

Hedging for Better Spread Management*

Robert W. McLeod and George M. McCabe†

In recent years, large commercial banks have increasingly relied on purchased funds, such as CDs, to finance an expanded loan portfolio. This procedure, widely termed "spread management banking," enables the bank to make a profit as long as it maintains a positive spread between the rate earned on the loan and the rate paid on the purchased funds. To the extent that the maturities of the loans and CDs can be matched, this procedure carries little more risk than the traditional banking approach, where loans are funded from the demand and savings accounts of regular bank customers. If the maturities are not matched, then the bank is faced with the possibility of a narrowing of the spread (which would reduce expected earnings) or even a negative spread (which would result in a loss).

---

*Reprinted by permission from *The Bankers Magazine*, Vol. 163, No. 4, July-August 1980. Copyright © 1981, Warren, Gorham and Lamont Inc., 210 South Street, Boston, Mass. All rights reserved.

†Robert W. McLeod is an assistant professor of finance at the University of Alabama. He has a B.S. in business administration and an M.B.A. from the University of Southern Mississippi and a Ph.D. from the University of Texas at Austin.

George M. McCabe is an associate professor of finance at the University of Alabama. He has an A.B. and an M.B.A. from the University of Michigan and a Ph.D. from the Wharton School of the University of Pennsylvania.

APPROACHES TO INTEREST-RATE RISK

Money center banks that practice spread management widely use two basic techniques to control this risk. The first involves floating-rate loans. With floating rates, the interest on the loan is tied to the prime and thus varies over the life of the loan. As the cost of funds increases, the prime rate should also increase, preserving the spread.

In actuality, however, there are several problems with floating-rate loans. Since the prime rate and the floating rate on the loan must be based on existing monetary conditions and cannot be adjusted instantaneously, there is always a lag between changes in money market conditions and changes in the rate on loans. This means that in periods of rising interest rates, the spread narrows. The major problem with floating-rate loans, though, is that they do not eliminate the risk of variation in the cost of funds; instead, they merely transfer it to the borrower.[1] Those bank customers who are hesitant to incur the risk of a floating-rate loan because of the uncertain cash flows have other options available. They can take out fixed-rate loans with specific maturities or even cap-rate loans. The problem with these is that the bank usually charges a fairly large premium for them. The size of these premiums has many times forced borrowers who want these loans to seek other sources of funds, such as smaller banks that have not expanded beyond their deposit base and still make mostly fixed-rate loans, insurance companies or the commercial paper market.

Layering

The other technique used to control the risk of variations in the spread is called "layering." The basic idea is essentially to match the maturities of the asset with those of the CD funding it. Since banks do not associate a loan with a specific source of funds (nor is this recommended), matching of maturities of individual loans and individual CDs is not practicable. Layering is, in essence, an approximation to individual matching. The bank divides its balance sheet into maturity categories. The more categories, the more involved the technique becomes, but the more closely the variation in the spread can be controlled. The easiest way to explain the technique is through an example. Consider the bank whose balance sheet is shown in Table 1.

---

[1] There is ample evidence that many borrowers are not in favor of floating-rate loans. For example, Harry Kane, Financial Vice President of Georgia Pacific, states: "The problem is you're still looking mainly at variable interest rates when you're looking at bank debt. And when you invest in bricks and mortar, like we do, that's like playing Russian roulette." Jansson, "Why Have Corporations Been Giving the Cold Shoulder to Their Banks," *Institutional Investor*, Dec. 1976, at 31-38.

Hedging for Better Spread Management

Table 1 Commercial Bank Balance Sheet

Assets		Liabilities	
T-bills	$ 800	DD	$ 800
Loans	2,500	Savings accts.	800
Bldg., etc.	200	CDs	1,500
		Shareholders' Equity	400
	$3,500		$3,500

The first-step in the layering process is to separate the non-sensitive assets and liabilities from the interest-sensitive assets and liabilities.[2] The second step involves the ordering of the interest-sensitive assets and liabilities by maturity layer. It is assumed in this example that the bank does not have any asset or liability with a maturity of greater than one year. The results of this process are shown in Table 2.

Once the bank has analyzed its position in regard to interest-sensitive assets and liabilities, it should try to match them at each maturity layer. The bank represented in Table 2 clearly has not done so. It should lengthen the maturity of its CDs or shorten the maturity of its loans or investments. With its current balance sheet, it faces considerable risk if interest rates rise. Within ninety days, it would have to refinance $1,500 of CDs at the new higher rate, yet it only has $500 of assets maturing in that time on which it could adjust rates. Its overall spread will narrow.

One might argue that layering is not essential to risk-reduction, and all that is necessary is to match the durations of the bank's interest-sensitive liabilities with those of its interest-sensitive assets. This is not sufficient. First, banks generally wish to avoid undue fluctuations in earnings; matching durations would mean that losses in one quarter or

Table 2 Interest-Sensitive Assets and Liabilities by Maturity Class

Maturity	Assets	Liabilities
0-90 days	$ 500	$1,500
21-180 days	600	
181-270 days	1,000	
271-365	1,200	
No maturity of non-interest-sensitive	200	2,000
	$3,500	$3,500

[2] Basically we mean by interest-sensitive assets (or liabilities) those for which we can compute a present value and whose present value will vary directly (as opposed to indirectly) with interest rates. This means that the asset (or liability) must have a *fixed-payment* scheme and a *definite maturity*. Thus, the balance sheet T-bills, loans, and CDs in Table 1 are interest-sensitive. The problem of spread management and variations in the spread is relevant only for interest-sensitive assets and liabilities.

year would be offset by profits in another. Second, there is no assurance that interest rates would not fall again, so there would be no offset. If, in our example, interest rates rose in the first quarter, the bank would roll over the $1,500 of CDs at the new higher rate with the rollover of the $500 of short-term assets only partly offsetting the increased costs. If interest rates now fall, the $600 of 91-180-day assets would be rolled over at a lower rate and there would be no gain to offset the loss in the first quarter. Indeed, there may be an additional loss. So, if the bank wishes to stabilize earnings and protect itself against variations in the spread, it needs to match interest-sensitive assets and liabilities at each maturity layer. Therefore, the bank needs to shorten the maturity of its loan portfolio and/or lengthen the maturity of its CD portfolio.

In theory, this is simple to do; in practice, there are considerable difficulties. A bank must orient its loan portfolio and loan policies to customer needs. If it wishes to compete, it will find that the terms and maturity distribution of its loan portfolio are dictated by its customers' needs for funds and not by its own liquidity needs. This means that any adjustments of maturities, in order to achieve matchings of interest-sensitive assets and liabilities, must be made on the liabilities side and largely in the CD portfolio. Although it is fairly easy to adjust the maturity distribution of the bank's shorter-term CDs, the longer-term CD market is quite thin, so adjustments of the maturity distribution become quite difficult or impossible to make. Beyond one-year maturity, there are very few funds available, so the bank would have almost no flexibility in choosing the maturities of CDs. As a practical matter, layering becomes infeasible for longer-term maturities.

HEDGING AND SPREAD MANAGEMENT

With the advent of interest rate futures markets at the Chicago Board of Trade and the Chicago Mercantile Exchange, it is now possible to modify the layering strategy and make it more useful. These interest rate futures markets can be used to make fixed-rate loans and avoid the risk of variations in the spread. Integrating a hedging strategy with spread management makes it possible to reduce the variations in the spread without matching individual assets and liabilities.

The first step in integrating hedging into the general spread management procedure is to determine the extent of the unmatched balances at each maturity layer. This is done simply by finding the net asset or liability balance at each maturity layer. For our example, this is done in Table 3.

For hedging purposes, we need to deal only with the net balances. The

Hedging for Better Spread Management

Table 3 Net Asset or Liability Balances at Each Maturity Layer

Maturity	Assets	Liabilities	Net Exposed Balance	Asset or Liability
0-90 days	$ 500	$1,500	$1,000	Liability
91-180 days	600		600	Asset
181-270 days	1,000		1,000	Asset
271-365 days	1,200		1,200	Asset
Non-interest-sensitive	$ 200	2,000		
	$3,500	$3,500		

portion of assets and liabilities that are matched and netted out can be viewed as a sort of natural hedge. The $500 of 0-90-day interest-sensitive assets will not affect the spread because they are matched with $500 of the $1,500 of 0-90-day liabilities. When interest rates rise and $500 of the 0-90 day CDs must be rolled over at a higher rate, the $500 of a 0-90-day assets have also matured and can be reinvested at the new rate, which would maintain the spread.[3] Likewise, when interest rates fall, the $500 of 0-90-day assets mature and must be reinvested at a lower rate, but $500 of the CDs mature also and can be refinanced at a lower rate; therefore, the spread can be maintained. When we have a matching, we have a natural hedge that maintains itself over time.

This risk can be removed or reduced by hedging in the interest rate futures market. As can be seen in Table 3, the bank has a net exposed liability balance of $1,000 of CDs in the 0-90-day maturity layer which it must refinance. If the bank issues new 90-day CDs, $600 of these must be rolled over once before $600 of assets (the 91-180-day assets) mature and can be reinvested at a rate that will maintain the desired spread. In other words, the bank is exposed to an interest-rate squeeze on $600 for 90 days. The other $400 of the $1,000 must be rolled over twice before a matching exposed asset balance can be reinvested, so the bank is exposed for 180 days to an interest-rate squeeze on the $400. As noted above, if the CD market were such that the appropriate maturities of funds were available, the bank could have avoided the problem by floating $600 of 91-180-day CDs and $400 of 181-270-day CDs in place of the $1,000 of 0-90-day CDs. But this is not necessary. The bank can achieve the same result by hedging the rollovers.

By appropriately structuring a hedge, the bank can effectively lock in or insure the interest rate it will have to pay on each rollover. In the above example, the bank would need to sell an appropriate amount of futures contracts to hedge each anticipated rollover. Thus, since the en-

---

[3] Of course, there will always be some mismatching within each maturity layer. Thirty-day liabilities must be rolled over before 60-day assets mature. But the extent of the problem is much less than, say, 30-day liabilities and 360-day assets.

tire $1,000 must be rolled over in the next quarter, it should sell $1,000 of 90-day T-bill futures contracts with a delivery date in the next quarter. Since $400 must be rolled over again into the third quarter, the bank needs to sell a $400, 90-day futures contract with a delivery date in the third quarter in order to be hedged.

The effect on the spread of this approach can be seen by another example. Assume that the current interest rate on 90-day CDs is 10 percent and that this rate is expected to remain constant for the next year so that the futures contracts are purchased at a 10 percent discount. Also, suppose that the bank's assets are all invested at 12 percent for a 2 percent spread. If CD rates rise to 11 percent in the next quarter, the bank will want to raise its rate of return on loans and investments to 13 percent to maintain the spread. It can reinvest the $500 of 0-90-day assets at 13 percent, since they mature at about the same time as the CDs. The rate on the loans of 91-180 and 181-270 cannot be raised, but the sales of the futures has prevented variations in the spread.

The easiest way to analyze this is to treat the futures contracts as hedging the cost of funds. The bank has priced its loans on the assumption that the CDs can be rolled over at 10 percent; to maintain the spread, it needs to be able to do that. If CD rates have risen to 11 percent, it will have to pay 11 percent to roll over the $1,000 of CDs, but the extra one percent will be offset by a profit on the futures contracts (Table 4).

The change in value of the futures contract was due to the increase in the rate of interest from 10 percent to 11 percent. Therefore, the gain in the futures market exactly offsets the loss in the cash market so that the spread is maintained for that period. Likewise, by the end of the second quarter, the bank will have to roll over another $400 of CDs at 11 percent for $0.01 \times \$400 = \$4$ more than it expected while pricing loans. But the $400 T-bills futures contract it sold will have risen in value by $4, so its net or hedged cost of funds will still be 10 percent.

Table 4 Gain or Loss from Hedged Position*

Time	Cash-Market Transactions	Offsetting Futures Market Transactions
Loan origination and flotation of first CD	Anticipated CD cost 10% (10%) ($1,000) = $100	Sell $1,000 T-bill contract (1-.10) ($1,000) = $900
Rollover of CD	Actual CD cost 100% (11%) ($1,000) = $110	Buy $1,000 T-bill contract (1-.11) ($1,000) = $890
	Loss = $110 − 100 = $10	Gain = $900 − 890 = $10
	Net Result = 0	

*For a more complete discussion of this type of hedge, see McCabe & Blackwell, "The Hedging Strategy: A New Approach to Spread Management Banking and Commercial Lending," *Journal of Bank Research* (in press).

Table 5   Net Exposed Balances After Hedging

Maturity	Net Exposed Balance	Asset or Liability
0-90 days	0	
91-180 days	0	
181-270 days	$ 600	Asset
271-365 days	1,200	Asset
Non-interest sensitive	$1,800	Liability

Another and perhaps simpler way to view this hedging process is to note that the hedges described above have converted the $1,000 of net exposed 90-day liability balances into the equivalent of $600 of 91-180-day liabilities and $400 of 181-270-day balances. From the point of view of spread management, $600 of 90-day CDs plus the ability to refinance them for another 90 days at an essentially guaranteed rate is the equivalent of $600 of 180-day CDs. Hedging, then, has converted our net exposed balances from those shown in Table 3 to those shown in Table 5.

The object of spread management, to match interest-sensitive assets and liabilities at each maturity layer so as to eliminate variations in the spread, has been achieved by hedging. There are no longer any net exposed positions that can be matched against one another so as to reduce risk. The $600 and $1,200 of net exposed assets are funded by non-interest-sensitive sources, such as shareholders' equity and demand deposits. In fact, for these funds, the spread, as the term is normally used in the banking literature, does not exist. The $1,800 of non-interest-sensitive liabilities does not have an explicit cost that must be recouped; the cost of these funds is an implicit or opportunity cost. In a sense, they have infinite maturity. There is no possibility of an interest-rate squeeze.

FUNDING SHORT-TERM ASSETS WITH LONG-TERM LIABILITIES

Although this discussion has focused on a money center bank that funds longer-term loans out of shorter-term CDs, there are other cases where the hedging approach can be used. Consider the bank whose balance sheet is given in Table 6 broken down by maturity classes.

This bank has $600 of subordinated debentures due in the fourth quarter that must be refinanced. In this case, the spread (which may be negative) is caused by investing long-term fixed rate funds in short-term assets. And, as before, the size of this spread could vary, causing

Table 6 Balance Sheet Broken Down by Maturity Classes

Days to Maturity	Quarter of Maturity	Assets	Liabilities	Net Exposed Position	Asset or Liability
0-90	1	$ 500	$ 100	$400	Asset
91-180	2	500		500	Asset
181-270	3	400		400	Asset
271-365	4	300	600	300	
Non-interest-sensitive		200	1,200		Liability
		$1,900	$1,900		

variations in profits. These variations could be reduced by the same techniques. The bank could lengthen the maturity of its investments or assets so as to match the $300 of net exposed liabilities in the fourth quarter. This would be traditional layering. Alternatively, it could hedge the reinvestment of $400 of funds it will have to invest in the third quarter by buying $400 of a TB futures contract. It can essentially convert $400 of 181-270-day funds into the equivalent of 271-365-day funds. Using either approach, the bank's net exposed positions would be as shown in Table 7.

As with the previous bank whose post-hedging position was shown in Table 5, the objectives of spread management have been achieved. All remaining interest-sensitive asset balances are funded with non-interest-sensitive funds.

In both of the above examples, the two banks could still use the interest rate futures markets to hedge their net exposed balances, but their purposes would change. Previously, the idea was to effectively convert a net exposed asset or liability to another maturity so as to match an opposite net exposed position. This would result in a situation where their interest rates would vary together with market interest rates and the spread would remain constant. Now the object must be to lock in a rate of return that is thought to be acceptable.

Essentially, the bank is hedging its rate of return on assets. It must reinvest its 0-90-day assets in ninety days at some rate. It can wait until they mature and then accept the prevailing rate, or it can immediately lock in the reinvestment rate implied by the futures markets by pur-

Table 7 Net Exposed Positions

Days to Maturity	Quarter	Net Exposed Position	Asset or Liability
0-90	1	$ 400	Asset
91-180	2	500	Asset
181-270	3	100	Asset
271-365	4	0	
Non-interest-sensitive		$1,000	

chasing $400 of second-quarter T-bill futures contracts. Since the rate of return on its other assets for the second quarter are already known, this will mean that it knows its profits in the second quarter. This would be true because if interest rates decreased, the lost profit on the investment of second-quarter funds would be offset by the gain on the T-bill contracts so as to lock in a predetermined rate of return.

The same process can be repeated for the third quarter by purchasing $900 of T-bill futures contracts. This procedure reduces uncertainty, but it does not reduce the risk of variations in the spread because that risk does not exist here.[4] That risk occurs only when the bank has fixed-rate assets funded from fixed-rate liabilities and has to refinance or reinvest one or the other at a certain rate to maintain the spread.

CONCLUSION

As has been shown, commercial banks can reduce the risk of loss due to unfavorable changes in interest rates by hedging net interest-sensitive balances at each maturity layer. The use of the financial futures markets and the layering approach enables the bank to maintain a predetermined spread and to, therefore, lock in an anticipated rate of return.

In this article, the authors have assumed perfect matching at each maturity layer. Of course, in practice, this would not be the case. The approach to risk reduction outlined in this article is obviously more effective the shorter or finer the maturity layers chosen.

---

[4] This is not strictly true in the case of savings accounts. If interest rates on savings accounts are fixed at 5 percent, the bank may wish to hedge its loan portfolio to insure that the rate of return stays above 5 percent. But since savings accounts have no maturity, there is no natural stopping point, so complete elimination of the risk is not possible. In any case, with rates on savings accounts constrained so far below market rates, the problem is of little relevance today.

16

Hedging Possibilities in the Flotation of Debt Securities*

Richard W. McEnally and Michael L. Rice[†]

When a firm decides to issue debt securities, typically there is a time lapse of 12 weeks or more between the decision to issue and the date the securities come to market. This causes the borrower considerable uncertainty about just what the final cost of debt will be. Until recently, about the only recourse available to a borrower was to rush the flotation procedure along and to maintain adequate financial flexibility so it would be possible to postpone the debt issue should rates become too high.

Recent developments in the commodities markets have opened up an alternative strategy. Since October of 1975, futures contracts on Government National Mortgage Association pass-through certificates (GNMAs) have been traded on the Chicago Board of Trade. More recently, futures contracts have become available in other debt instruments, specifically Treasury bills, Treasury bonds, and commercial paper. In principle, a firm can cross-hedge (hedge a position in one commodity with an offsetting position in a different but presumably related commodity) its constructive long position in its own soon-to-be issued

---

*Reprinted from *Financial Management*, Vol. 8, No. 4, (Winter 1979). Reprinted by permission of the publisher and authors.

[†]Richard W. McEnally is Professor of Finance at the University of North Carolina at Chapel Hill, where Michael L. Rice is Assistant Professor of Business Administration. They are grateful to Tom McClish for programming and data analysis and to George Morgan for insights into interest rate hedging.

bonds by going short in a related interest rate futures contract. Such cross-hedging against corporate debt securities has been seriously advanced as a potential use of GNMA futures contracts [1].

A HEDGING EXAMPLE

As an aid to understanding the mechanics of this operation, it may be helpful to review a typical hedging example using actual market yields and prices in the latter part of 1976 and the opening months of 1977. Your AAA-rated firm decides late in November to issue $100 million dollars in bonds. The prevailing yield on comparable bonds is 7.85%; yields have been declining most of the year, and you anticipate an interest rate within a few basis points of today's figure when the bonds are taken to market in late February. As you proceed through pre-sale activities with your investment banker, you watch prevailing yields climb 40 basis points by the last week in February. Your options are limited. If your firm is counting on the issue, and alternative sources of funds are unattractive, you may be forced to proceed with the sale. The loss: $400,000 per year in interest costs; in present value terms (on a 35-year bond), about $4.6 million.

Consider the alternative of hedging your constructive long position with GNMA futures contracts. When the decision to issue was made in late November, the contract for GNMAs to be delivered the following September was market-priced at 98.437. In a move to hedge the risk of long-term interest rates moving during pre-sale activities, you ask your broker to sell short 1,000 September GNMA futures contracts ($100 million face amount). As the market date for your bond issue nears, where do you stand? The 40 basis point rise in AAA bond rates has coincided with a decrease in the price of your futures contract (increase in the value of your short position). On market day, with the futures contract priced at 95.437, your short position yields a cash gain of $3 million (ignoring commissions and margin costs), resulting in a substantially smaller net loss.

The example raises a number of questions that are vital to the evaluation of the usefulness of cross-hedging techniques in the issuing of corporate debt:

1. What are the appropriate goals and evaluation criteria for a hedging strategy? How large a hedged position is optimal? (In the above example, a short position in 1,500 contracts rather than 1,000 would have nearly eliminated the firm's implicit losses in securities.)

2. How effective are various hedging strategies? How consistently do prices of the hedged issue and the futures contract move together? (Parallel price movement is clearly critical to the success of such cross-hedges.)
3. What is the effect of institutional constraints, such as brokerage and margin costs, accounting treatment and tax effects, thin futures markets?

This paper is intended to be suggestive in nature, addressing these specific issues without attempting an exhaustive treatment of cross-hedging possibilities. Although the paper deals specifically with the efficacy of hedging interest rate risk during the flotation of debt securities, the principles may be applied to the broader issue of using interest rate futures contracts to hedge against changes in interest rates for any purpose.

CHARACTERISTICS OF THE GNMA FUTURES MARKET

A brief description of the GNMA futures market may be in order. A more extensive exploration of hedging instruments and markets is provided in Bacon and Williams [1].

The contract traded on the Chicago Board of Trade is for delivery of $100,000 principal amount of marketable pass-through certificates representing shares in pools of mortgages guaranteed as to repayment by the Government National Mortgage Association (that is, VA and FHA mortgage loans).

Conversations with Board of Trade officials indicate clearly that the GNMA futures contract was not devised-exclusively or even primarily to appeal to hedgers of positions in GNMA pass-through certificates. Indeed, an informal but active forward commitment market in GNMA pass-throughs already existed to serve the hedging needs of this group. Rather, GNMA were chosen because the underlying instrument is 1) protected against default risk and hence likely to respond to fundamental changes in supply and demand in credit markets rather than to changes in risk premiums; 2) long-term, and hence more likely to reflect changes in long-term credit markets than, say, Teasury bills; and 3) a familiar, standardized item available in large quantity with an active spot market.

The upshot is that, at least in the hopes of the Chicago Board of Trade, GNMA futures should be useful for hedging positions in a much broader range of the intermediate- to long-term securities than simply GNMA pass-throughs.

HEDGING STRATEGIES

The goal of any hedging operation is risk transformation. In hedging new issues of corporate bonds, the objective is the reduction of uncertainty caused by movement of interest rates over the period of pre-sale activities. In our example, the rise in interest rates between the decision to issue bonds and market day represented significant losses to the firm. Had interest rates moved lower during the pre-sale time lapse, the firm would have benefited. As with any other risky venture, uncertainty due to interest rate movements is a two-edged sword. The goal of a hedging strategy is to reduce the gains or losses in dollar terms due to unexpected variations of interest rates in either direction. Any attempt on the part of the financial manager to hedge only when adverse rate activity is anticipated is speculative in nature.

As Bacon and Williams [1] correctly emphasize, hedging can at best only eliminate gains or losses due to *unexpected* changes in interest rates. Generally anticipated changes in interest rates will tend to be built into the structure of futures prices and thus cannot be neutralized by hedging operations.

If hedging is to be used to reduce the effect of uncertainty of interest rate movements during pre-sale activities, a key decision is determining the size of the position that should be taken in the hedging instrument relative to the size of the bond issue. A convenient way to express the size of the hedging position is the *hedge ratio*, that is, the ratio of the investment in the short hedging position to the implicit long position in the bond markets:

$$\text{Hedge ratio} = \frac{\$ \text{ position in GNMA futures}}{\$ \text{ size of bond issue}}$$

A hedge ratio of -1.5 for a \$100 million offering would mean a \$150 million short position in GNMA futures contracts.

Although there are any number of different hedge ratio strategies available to the financial manager, we propose three:

1. A "naive" hedge: simply going short a number of initial dollars of GNMA futures equal to the initial dollar value of the proposed offering. This represents a hedge ratio of -1.0.
2. A "duration" hedge: based on the theoretical responsiveness of the proposed bond issue price to changes in market yields.
3. An "historically optimal" hedge: based on the minimum-variance hedge ratio during a period immediately preceding the hedging decision.

The first strategy, using a hedge ratio of -1.0, has the advantage of simplicity. In subsequent testing of the three hedge ratio strategies, we will use the naive hedge as a benchmark of comparison.

The duration hedge strategy has its basis in bond yield price theory. There is no *a priori* reason to expect the prices of GNMA futures contracts and corporate bonds to move together in a one-to-one manner even if their yields are highly correlated. It is well known that the duration of a bond measures the responsiveness of its price to changes in its yield (for example, see Hopewell and Kaufman [5] or McEnally[6]). There is also evidence that the volatility of yields decreases with term to maturity (Yawitz, Hempel, and Marshall [7]). Combining these elements, and assuming the GNMA futures contract has the same yield volatility as the 8% pass-through certificates, we can compute the duration hedge ratio which will equate the price volatilities

$$(D_B' \cdot YV_B) = HR \, (D_F' \cdot YV_V)$$

$$HR = \frac{D_B' \cdot YV_B}{D_F' \cdot YV_F}$$

where D_B' and D_F' are "adjusted" durations of the bond and futures instruments. (This adjustment, which simply consists of dividing the conventionally computed duration by its yield to maturity, is needed to maintain consistency with discrete compounding: see [6, p. 55].) YV_B and YV_F are the estimated yield volatilities of securities with maturities equal to the bond and futures instruments, respectively.[1] In effect, the hedge ratio is equal to the forecasted price volatility of the bond relative to the forecasted price volatility of the GNMA.

The third strategy, employing historically optimal hedge ratios, simply involves using the hedge ratio that provides the minimum variance of the hedged outcome over a period immediately preceding the hedging decision. The length of the period used to calculate the historically optimal hedge ratio should be equal to the time required to float the proposed issue. This optimal hedge ratio is calculated in the following way:

Let HR be the hedge ratio, S be the realized gain or loss in a bond price series over the hedging period, and F be the gain or loss in the basic futures contract price series. For this purpose, gains or losses can

---

[1] Yawitz, Hempel, and Marshall [7] give values for the mean monthly absolute change in yields for U.S. government securities of 1-, 2-, 3-, 4-, 5-, 10-, 20-, and 30-year maturities. The volatility values we employ were estimated from fitting the equation:

$$YV_t = a + b_1 \, (1/t) + b_2 \, (1/t^2)$$

to these values, were YV_t is the mean monthly absolute change in yields for a security with term to maturity t. There are, of course, dangers in assuming that yield volatilities for other time periods and securities will be appropriate in the future.

be expressed in either dollar or percentage terms. The net gain or loss from the hedged position is then:

$$HR \cdot F + S$$

The variation of the gain or loss in the hedged position, which we are trying to minimize, can be measured by its variance and written:

$$\text{Var}(HR \cdot F + S) = HR^2 \, \text{Var}(F) + \text{Var}(S) + 2HR \cdot \text{Cov}(F,S).$$

Differentiating with respect to the hedge ratio gives:

$$\frac{d}{dHR} \text{Var}(HR \cdot F + S) = 2HR \cdot \text{Var}(F) + 2\text{Cov}(F,S).$$

Setting this expression equal to zero and solving for the minimum-variance hedge ratio, HR*, yields:

$$HR^* = \frac{-\text{Cov}(F,S)}{\text{Var}(F)}.$$

That is, the minimum-variance hedge ratio is the ratio of the covariance between the bond series and the futures contract price series to the variance of the futures contract price series. The negative sign simply implies a short position in the futures contract against the implicit long position in corporate bonds.

TEST OF HEDGING STRATEGIES

In order to test the usefulness of hedging to the financial manager, we have empirically tested the three hedge ratio strategies suggested above as well as a "perfect foresight" strategy using the minimum-variance hedge ratio over the test period. This last strategy is, of course, not possible to use in practice, but it serves the purpose of demonstrating the maximum benefit attainable from hedging.

The hedging strategy tests are based on weekly observations of GNMA futures contract prices and prices of several bond price series between December 26, 1975, and March 8, 1977. The bond series used include the two Salomon Brothers new issue series for Aaa- and Baa-rated bonds, and the Standard & Poor's series based on seasoned AAA- and BBB-rated bonds. Also included for comparison are government bonds represented by the Treasury 8½s of 1994-99 issue and the Standard & Poor's Municipal Bond Index. Bond series yields were converted into prices using the conventions explained in Exhibit 1.

Unfortunately, the Salomon Brothers series only relates to utility

Exhibit 1. Key to Series used in Testing Hedging Activity

GNMA Futures Contracts—Closing trading prices on the CBT on Friday of each week, with conversion into yields using the standard formulation.

S & P AAA—Yields on Standard & Poor's AAA Composite Bond Yield Index, converted into prices by assuming a 6.65% coupon and 25 years to maturity, in accordance with values given in Garard [4]. These figures are based on the Wednesday of the week and thus lead the GNMA futures by two days.

S & P BBB—Yields on Standard & Poor's BBB Composite Bond Yield Index, converted into prices by assuming a 6.5% coupon and 20 years to maturity in accordance with the values given in [4]. These figures are based on Wednesday of the week and thus lead the GNMA futures by two days.

Salomon New Aaa—Estimates of the market yield on newly issued Aaa utility bonds by Salomon Brothers & Hutzler, for Friday of the week, as reported in *Business Week*. Conversion into prices was made by assuming an 8% coupon and 35 years to maturity.

Salomon New Baa—Estimates of the market yield on newly issued Baa utility bonds by Salomon Brothers & Hutzler, for Friday of the week, as reported in *Business Week*. Conversion into prices was made by assuming a 9% coupon and 30 years to maturity.

Treasury Bond—Closing weekly "bid" prices on the U.S. Treasury 8½s of 1994-99, from the *Wall Street Journal*.

S & P Municipals—Yields on Standard & Poor's Municipal Bond Index, converted into prices by assuming a 4% coupon and 20 years to maturity—the same assumption S&P use to obtain their municipal bond price series from this yield series. These figures are based on the Wednesday of the week and thus lead the GNMA futures by two days.

---

bonds. Moreover, these series are based on traders' judgments regarding the yield on newly-issued bonds of standard characteristics. There are many weeks when few or no bonds with these characteristics are brought to market. Thus, these series probably contain measurement errors. The Standard & Poor's series is based on seasoned bonds. Therefore it is susceptible to all the well-known problems of measurement error, tax biases, infrequent trading, and sluggish response to changing market conditions [4].

To get some idea of the usefulness of hedging in the flotation or corporate debt securities, we have utilized the price series in some simple tests. We have uniformly assumed that positions are open 12 weeks, since this corresponds approximately to the time that would be required to float a bond issue once the decision is made to do so. We have ignored commissions, margin requirements, income taxes, and other frictions. Most importantly, we have assumed that GNMA futures contract prices over the study period were representative of those in a more mature market, even though this may not be a valid proposition. Therefore, our results must be regarded as preliminary.

In order to gain maximum information from our limited data, we have considered all possible overlapping periods of 12 consecutive weeks. There are 65 price observations in the basic series; one is lost in the formation of ratios, and 11 more are lost at the end of the run of data. Therefore, the tabulated values are based on 53 observations of the form:

$$PR_t = \frac{P_{t+12}}{P_t}$$

(t = 1, ..., 53) where PR_t is the price relative (1.0 plus the rate of return) return over the period (t, t + 12), and P_t is the closing value of the price series for week t. In effect, these price relatives represent gains or losses in the basic bond price series standardized by the value of the series at the beginning of the period.

The major results are summarized in Exhibit 2, which relates only to hedging via the March 1977 GNMA futures contract. (Results for the contracts maturing in June and September 1977 were also determined, but since they were similar we have not reproduced them here.) An alternative strategy would utilize futures contracts maturing near the

Exhibit 2. Results of Various Hedging Strategies Over the Period 12/26/75-3/18/77 in the March 1977 GNMA Contract

Basic Instrument	Standard Deviation of Gain or Loss in Dollars per $100 of invested position*				Hedge Ratios	
	Unhedged	Minimum-Variance Hedge	Naive Hedge	Duration Hedge	Minimum-Variance	Duration
S&P AAA	2.46	1.41	1.41	1.48	1.008	1.240
S&P BBB	1.72	1.43	1.76	1.86	0.482	1.080
Salomon New Aaa	4.04	2.62	2.83	2.70	1.535	1.216
Salomon New Baa	6.12	5.23	5.36	5.34	1.584	1.065
Treasury Bond	2.43	.88	.92	.88	1.134	1.136
S&P Municipals	2.46	1.39	1.39	1.88	1.014	1.645

*Guide to Interpretation: The standard deviation figures are × 10^2, so they may be read as dollars lost or gained per $100 of invested position. A one standard deviation of the unhedged S&P AAA Index, for example, could be interpreted as a gain or loss of $2.46 per $100 of invested position ($2,460,000 on a $100 million offering).

date of the anticipated bond issue. Practical problems may arise from such a strategy because of the three-month "gaps" between maturity dates, which make exact matching impossible. Our results are biased against the efficiency of the hedging strategy if the degree of parallelism of price movements decreases as the contract maturity date is further from the dates on which spot rates are observed.

The first column of Exhibit 2, labeled "unhedged," is intended to convey the risk of price change associated with an unhedged long position held open for a 12-week interval. The values that are presented are the conventional measure of price risk and the standard deviations of price relative returns around the mean price relative (σPR_t). (Standard deviations are computed around the mean, since there is no reason to expect the price series to be trendless. Limited experimentation suggests that the results would be similar if the standard deviations were computed around the price relatives of 1.0—that is, zero gain or loss.)

As is evident from the exhibit, far and away the greatest risk is found in the new issue debt series, especially the new issue medium grade bonds, while the lowest risk is found in the seasoned medium grade bonds. The noncorporate bonds occupy intermediate risk positions.

The second column, labeled "Minimum-Variance Hedge," shows the standard deviation of returns for the same 53 12-week periods when each long position is matched by a short position in the March 1977 GNMA futures contract according to the minimum-variance hedge ratio. That is, each of the 53 price relatives reflects the change in value of a "portfolio" of the two positions and is equal to:

$$PR_t = 1 + HR \cdot \frac{Q_t + 12}{Q_t} + \frac{P_t + 12}{P_t},$$

where Q_t is the closing value of the futures contract and other terms are as before. These optimal hedge ratios are contained in columns 5 of Exhibit 2.

In all six cases, hedging reduces the variation of the price relative series, and in several instances the reduction is large. For example, the standard deviation for the hedged Treasury bond series is only 36% as large as for the unhedged series. Hedging is prospectively less successful with the corporate debt series, especially of the seasoned medium grade bond series is reduced by 17%, while the standard deviation of the new issue medium grade series is only reduced by 15%. In contrast, 43% and 35% of the standard deviation of the high grade seasoned and new issue series, respectively, is eliminated by hedging. As one might expect, cross-hedging appears most effective when the hedged series is most like the security underlying the hedging instrument. Prices of medium grade bonds are likely to be affected more by factors extraneous to the movements of basic interest rates—such as changes in default premiums—than are government and high grade corporate bond prices.[2]

The naive hedging strategy based on a simple hedge ratio of −1.0 provides risk reduction in five cases out of six. Only for the medium grade seasoned series is a naive hedge not productive. The naive strategy does nearly as well as the optimal hedge in several cases.

The results of the strategy based on duration, in column 3 of Exhibit 2, are mixed. In one case involving the seasoned corporate bond series, this strategy produces results that are inferior to those of the naive strategy in two out of the six cases. Once again, the strategy appears to work best in those situations where the securities in question are most like the GNMA series.

A test of the historically optimal hedge ratio strategy (the minimum-variance hedge ratio over a period preceding the hedging decision) required that we split our data into two roughly equal time periods and estimate minimum-variance hedge ratios over the first period. The results of applying these hedge ratios, as well as hedge ratios obtained in previously described ways, to the second period are contained in Exhibit 3. Compared to unhedged positions, hedging with historically optimal hedge ratios is rewarding in four of the six cases. On the other hand, the historical strategy is inferior to the naive and duration strategies in three of the six cases. It is interesting that the historical strategy outperforms the naive and duration strategies with the seasoned bond series—

Exhibit 3. Results of Historically Optimal Hedge and Other Hedging Strategies*
8/13/76-3/18/77 in March 1977 Contract

Basic Instrument	Unhedged	Minimum-Variance Hedge	Historically Optimal Hedge	Naive Hedge	Duration Hedge
S&P AAA	3.02	1.64	1.64	1.65	1.67
S&P BBB	1.16	.83	1.18	1.72	1.89
Salomon New Aaa	4.16	2.46	3.28	2.67	2.52
Salomon New Baa	4.49	3.15	4.14	3.28	3.24
Treasury Bond	2.94	9.54	.61	0.79	0.60
S&P Municipal	2.09	1.19	2.95	1.34	2.41

Standard Deviation of Gain of Loss

*See guide to interpretation, Exhibit 2.

[2] When the correlation between the GNMA futures contract and the bond price series is low, as happens for the medium grade bond series, the hedged position may be nearly as risky as or more risky than the unhedged position. That is:

$$\sigma(HR \cdot F + S) = (HR^2 \, Var(F) + Var(S) + 2HR \cdot r_{FS} \, \sigma_F \, \sigma_s)^{1/2}$$

where r_{FS} is the correlation coefficient (always negative) between the short position in futures and long position in the bond price series.

just the instances in which one might expect that explicit recognition of the historical (and presumably dampened) behavior of the price series would be most useful.

SOME PRACTICAL CONSIDERATIONS IN THE HEDGING DECISION

Although our empirical tests of various hedging strategies are encouraging, a number of institutional considerations will be important to financial managers considering hedging:

1. *Brokerage fees:* The minimum Chicago Board of Trade round-trip brokerage fee is $60 per $100,000 GNMA contract. However, conversations with several brokerage houses indicate that considerable discounts are the rule on larger transactions with good clients. On a large issue, the investment banker handling the transaction might well include brokerage fees for hedging as part of the package.

2. *Opportunity costs of margin positions:* The minimum margin requirement is $1,500 per GNMA contract. Moreover, an adverse move on the futures side of a hedge could, in theory, lead to further margin calls up to the entire face value of the contract. If the margin requirement is made in cash, it would be appropriate to consider the forgone return as a cost of the hedge. However, it is possible to meet initial margin requirements by putting up Treasury bills or other negotiable securities. Since the contract owner would continue to accrue the interest on such securities, there would be no opportunity cost for at least the initial margin position.

3. *Size of the market:* Volume in the GNMA futures market has grown substantially since the inception of trading in late 1975. It is now running upward from around 6,000 contracts per day. Even so, it is not at all evident what the impact might be of trading in the magnitude that would be required to hedge a corporate debt issue. For example, a bond issue of $60 million would today be regarded as only of moderate size when issues of $500 million and above are not uncommon. Yet the CBT imposes a "position limit" of 600 contracts on each trader who does not qualify as a hedger, in order to reduce the possibility of domination or manipulation of the market. These 600 contracts would repre-

sent approximately 10% of one day's trading and somewhat less than 1% of the total open interest, based on the dimensions of the market in mid-1978. Therefore, there are grounds for concern that the trading activity necessary to effect a hedge might generate price moves that would affect the prospective gains from the hedge.

4. *Taxes:* All our analysis has ignored income taxes, yet gains or losses on the short side of a hedging transaction will produce an increment or decrement in corporate income taxes that will have no direct offset. That is, a gain or loss resulting from hedging activity is taxable during the year in which the gain or loss occurred. Offsetting gains or losses due to changes in market yields over the financing period will be realized over the maturity of the debt instrument. Since income taxes reduce the size of both gains and losses on the short side of the hedge, hedge ratios should be adjusted upward in a taxed environment.

5. *Corporate financial accounting:* In the major areas where corporations typically employ hedging techniques—to reduce exposure to exchange rate fluctuations and changes in raw materials prices—the prospective loss being realized within an accounting period. Similarly, the gain or loss on the short side of a hedging transaction will nearly always be realized within an accounting period. Therefore, in these cases, matching the offsetting gains and losses in corporate financial reports is not a problem. However, in the corporate debt securities area, the loss or cost that is being hedged against is only realized over the life of the debt issue in the form of increased interest costs. This characteristic may make it difficult to report the results of the hedging transaction in a manner that corporate executives will find appealing.

The ideal accounting treatment, both on theoretical grounds and from the corporate viewpoint, would be to treat a gain on the short side of the hedge as a deferred income item (credit) or a loss as a deferred cost item (debit), and to amortize whichever occurs over the life of the debt issue as an adjustment to interest expense. This is the treatment currently given to similar items associated with a debt issue, such as initial premiums or discounts.

However, accountants with whom we have consulted inform us that there would be strong pressure under current accounting practices to pass the entire gain or loss in the short position through the income statement in the period in which it is closed out. Such a treatment would increase the volatility of net income in the period of debt issuance and have no visible effect on interest expense in subsequent years. For this reason, we feel that hedging in the flotation of corporate debt securities will be somewhat less attractive to corporate management than would otherwise be the case, in view of managers' strong preference for stable earnings from period to period. Presumably, active hedging of the type we have examined will lead at some point to appropriate accounting treatment.

SUMMARY AND DIRECTIONS FOR FURTHER RESEARCH

A first look at hedging in floating of corporate debt suggests that it may be promising, in the sense that prospectively it can reduce the risk of interest rate changes while the new securities are constructively in the firm's inventory. We believe, however, that there are many practical barriers to its widespread use.

The most pressing research needs lie in two directions. First, we need a much better conceptual understanding of interest rate futures hedging and the price generating process in the interest rate futures market. Second, we need much better readings on price behavior in the interest rate futures markets in order to make better judgments about matters such as appropriate hedge ratios. A major barrier in this respect is the brevity of the historical record on interest rate futures contracts.

References

1. P. W. Bacon and K. E. Williams, "Interest Rate Futures: New Tool for the Financial Manager," *Financial Management* (Spring 1976), pp. 32-38.
2. Chicago Board of Trade, *Hedging in GNMA Mortgage Interest Rate Futures*. Chicago, 1975.
3. Chicago Board of Trade, *Origination and Delivery of Due Bills: GNMA Mortgage Interest Rate Futures*, Chicago, 1975.
4. F. F. Garard, "Fixed Income Portfolio Performance: A Discussion of the Issues," *Journal of Banking Research* (Winter 1974), pp. 280-287.
5. M. Hopewell and G. Kaufman, "Bond Price Volatility and Term to Maturity: A Generalized Respecification," *American Economic Review* (September 1973), pp. 749-753.
6. R. W. McEnally, "Duration As a Practical Tool for Bond Management," *Journal of Portfolio Management* (Summer 1977), pp. 53-57.
7. J. B. Yawitz, G. H. Hempel, and W. J. Marshall, "The Use of Average Maturity As a Risk Proxy in Investment Portfolios," *Journal of Finance* (May 1975), pp. 325-333.

17

The Hedging Performance of the New Futures Market[*]

Louis H. Ederington[†]

Organized futures markets in financial securities were first established in the U.S. on October 20, 1975 when the Chicago Board of Trade opened a futures market in Government National Mortgage Association 8% Pass-Through Certificates. This was followed in January, 1976 by a 90 day Treasury Bill futures market on the International Monetary Market of the Chicago Mercantile Exchange. In terms of trading volume both have been clear commercial successes and this has led to the establishment, in 1977, of futures markets in Long Term Government Bonds and 90-day Commercial Paper and, in 1978, of a market in One-Year Treasury notes and new GNMA markets.

The classic economic rationale for futures markets is, of course, that they facilitate hedging—that they allow those who deal in a commodity to transfer the risk of price changes in that commodity to speculators more willing to bear such risks. The primary purpose of the present paper is to evaluate the GNMA and T-Bill futures markets as instruments for such hedging. Obviously it is possible to hedge by entering into forward contracts outside a futures market, but, as Telser and Higinbotham [19] point out, an organized futures market facilitates

---

*Reprinted from the *Journal of Finance*, Vol. 34, No. 1, (March 1979). Reprinted by permission of the publisher and author.

†Associate Professor, Georgia State University. The author would like to acknowledge the helpful comments of Bruce Fielitz, Ed Ulveling, and Jerome Stein. This research was supported in part by the Bureau of Business and Economic Research of Georgia State University.

such transactions by providing a standardized contract and by substituting the trustworthiness of the exchange for that of the individual trader.

In the futures market, price change risk can be eliminated entirely by making or taking delivery on futures sold or bought, but few hedges are concluded in this manner.[1] The major problem with making or taking delivery is that there are only four delivery periods per year for financial security futures so it is often impossible to hedge in this manner over the desired time period. Moreover, the desired time period may change or may be uncertain. The most common hedge, therefore, is one in which the seller (buyer) of the futures contract cancels his delivery commitment by buying (selling) a contract of the same future prior to delivery. It is this type of hedge, in which futures positions are liquidated by offsetting trades, which has received the most attention in the hedging literature and is examined in this paper.

In order to illustrate such a hedge and the potential of the new markets for risk avoidance, let us suppose that on September 16, 1977 a mortgage lending institution committed itself to a future loan at a set interest rate. Suppose, further, it was the lender's intention to finance this loan by issuing or selling $100,000 of 30 year GNMA Pass-Through Certificates with an 8% coupon rate which were selling at that time (September 16, 1977) at $99,531 or an effective yield of 8.02%.[2] Fearing that interest rates would rise and GNMA prices would fall by the time it actually sold its certificates, the mortgagor decided to hedge

---

[1] It should perhaps be noted that in the GNMA market there would, however, be some uncertainty regarding the amount one would need to hold to make delivery. The futures contract is for $100,000 of GNMA 8% Pass-Through Certificates. Since prepayment on these certificates might occur prior to delivery, there is some uncertainty regarding the quantity one would need to hold at present in order to deliver $100,000 of certificates. This is mitigated by the fact that one can deliver certificates of between $97,500 and $102,500 face value with the deficiency or excess to be settled in cash but some uncertainty remains. In addition, the person who accepts delivery of GNMA futures faces uncertainty regarding the type and relative market value of the certificates to be received. While trading is in 8% certificates, certificates of any mortgage rate can be delivered as long as the quantity delivered is equivalent to $100,000 of 8% certificates assuming a thirty year certificate with total prepayment at the end of twelve years. Since the market doesn't always accept such arbitrary prepayment assumptions, it may be cheaper to deliver 6½% or 9% or some other certificates. Indeed, it has generally been cheaper to deliver 9% certificates [6]. Consequently, those accepting delivery may not receive $100,000 of 8% certificates or their market equivalent. This also means that at delivery the futures price for GNMA's will generally remain somewhat below the cash price.

It should also be noted that over the observed period, January 1976 through July 1977, futures prices were below cash prices except for a few occasions within a few weeks of delivery. Purchasers of GNMA or T-Bill futures could therefore lock-in a lower price as well as a certain price but sellers of futures would have to be willing to lock-in a loss. On GNMA's, for example, the futures price averaged 1.9 below the cash price two months before delivery over the observed period and ranged from 1.1% below the cash price to 2.5% below.

[2] GNMA yields are calculated on the assumption of a prepayment after 12 years. The published market yields also take into account, as the face yields do not, that there is an interest free delay of 15 days in payments of principal and interest.

Table 1 A Possible Short Hedge Based on Actual Prices

Cash Market	Futures Market
September 16, 1977	
Makes mortgage commitment and makes plan to sell $100,000 face value of GNMA 8% Certificates	Sells one December futures contract at $98,219
Current price $99,531	
October 14, 1977	
Sells GNMA 8% certificates ($100,000 face value)	Buys one December futures contract at $97,156
Current price $98,281	
Results: Loss from delay on cash market	$1250
Gain on futures market	1063
Net Loss	$ 187

against this risk by selling December 1977 GNMA futures which were trading at $98,219 or an effective yield of 8.20% on September 16.[3] This transaction is summarized in the top half of Table 1.

In this particular case, our firm's fears of an interest rate rise were realized and the hedge was successful. By October 14, 1977, when the firm closed its loan and sold the GNMA certificates, cash market yields had risen 17 basis points to 8.19%. However, futures market yields had also risen 15 basis points to 8.30% so, as shown in Table 1, the futures market gain largely offset the cash market loss. This is a short hedge. If an individual or firm plans to purchase GNMA's, T-Bills, or some other security in the future, it could attempt to protect against the contingency of a decline in interest rates by buying GNMA or T-Bill futures, i.e., entering a long hedge. In this particular example, the hedge was successful because cash and futures prices both fell, but this may not always be the case.

There is not perfect agreement in the futures market literature as to what hedging is or why it is undertaken. The paper begins in Part I, therefore, with a survey of three major theories of hedging: the traditional theory, the theories of Holbrook Working, and the portfolio theory. The portfolio theory, which the author finds superior to the other two, suggests a method for measuring the hedging effectiveness of

---

[3] Note that if the firm were to wait until December and make delivery, it would lock in exactly this price and yield but if it closes the hedge prior to delivery the price and yield are still somewhat uncertain.

At the present time there is no good data on what sort of firms are hedging in the market so this example is hypothetical. In addition, there are regulatory constraints on the participation of banks and S & L's (See Ederington and Plumly, 1976).

a futures market and this measure is used in Part II to evaluate the GNMA and T-Bill futures markets. These financial security futures are compared with each other and with two more established and heavily traded futures markets: corn and wheat. The portfolio theory also provides a method for measuring the costs of hedging and these costs are examined for the two financial security futures. The article closes with a summary of the conclusions and some observations on possible future research in futures in Part III.

I. THEORIES OF HEDGING

A. Traditional Hedging Theory

While traditional hedging theory predates the work of Working and the application of portfolio theory to hedging, it continues to be important. Indeed, it is the traditional theory which underlies almost all the early "How To" articles on hedging which accompanied the establishment of the GNMA and T-Bill Futures markets.[4]

Traditional hedging theory emphasizes the risk-avoidance potential of futures markets. Hedgers are envisioned as taking futures market positions equal in magnitude but of opposite sign to their position in the cash market as in the example in Table 1. For instance, holders of an inventory of X units would protect themselves against the loss from a decline in the cash price by selling X futures of the same commodity or security. When the inventory is sold, futures contracts would be purchased canceling both positions.

If the cash or spot prices at times t_1 and t_2 are P_s^1 and P_s^2 respectively, the gain or loss on an unhedged position, U, of X units is $X[P_s^2 - P_s^1]$, but the gain or loss on a hedged position, H, is $X([P_s^2 - P_s^1] - [P_f^2 - P_f^1])$ where the f subscript denotes the futures price. Traditional theory argues that spot and futures prices generally move together so that the absolute value of H is less than U or that $\text{Var}(H) < \text{Var}(U)$. This question is often discussed in terms of the change in the cash price versus the change in the "Basis," where the basis is defined as the difference between the futures and spot prices so that the change in the basis is $([P_f^2 - P_s^2] - [P_f^1 - P_s^1])$ or $-([P_s^2 - P_s^1] - [P_f^2 - P_f^1])$. A hedge is viewed as perfect if the change in the basis is zero. It is commonly argued that the basis and changes in the basis are small because of the possibility of making or taking delivery, hence $\text{Var}(H) < \text{Var}(U)$. The question of smallness is, of course, relative. While it is true that delivery

---

[4] Examples are the Chicago Board of Trade's "Hedging in GNMA Interest Rate Futures" (1975) and articles by Smith [6], Jacobs and Kozuch [10], Sandor [5], Stevens [8], and Duncan [5].

possibilities limit changes in the basis, a range for variation obviously remains.

Certainly, the familiar theory of adaptive expectations implies that if futures prices reflect market expectations they should not normally match changes in cash prices. According to the theory of adaptive expectations

$$E_n^2 - E_n^1 = a[P_s^2 - E_2^1] + u$$

where E_n^2 and E_n^1 represent the cash prices expected to prevail in period n as of periods 2 and 1 respectively and E_2^1 represents the price which had in period 1, been expected to prevail in period 2. If one assumes that $P_f^2 = E_n^2$ and $P_f^1 = E_n^1$, one obtains

$$P_f^2 - P_f^1 = a[P_s^2 - P_s^1] - a[E_2^1 - P_s^1]$$

If, therefore, no change in spot prices is expected between periods 1 and 2 ($E_2^1 = P_s^1$) and $a \neq 1$, this theory implies that any change in the spot price will be accompanied by a proportional but unequal movement of the futures price. If, on the other hand, cash prices change in exactly the manner which had been expected ($P_s^2 = E_2^1$), then certainly there will be no change in futures prices.

While it is clear that the basis changes so that most traditional hedges are not perfect, Working [20] complained that many writers of the time were conveniently ignoring this fact:

> A major source of mistaken notions of hedging is the conventional practice of illustrating hedging with a hypothetical example in which the price of the future bought or sold as a hedge is supposed to rise or fall by the same amount that the spot price rises or falls. [20, pp. 320-321.]

In perusing articles and pamphlets on hedging in GNMA's and T-Bills, I have been surprised to note that many continue to follow the same practice almost 25 years later. This includes not only publications of the exchanges and brokerage houses and articles in trade publications, such as *Savings and Loan News* [16] and *The Mortgage Banker* [10], but also articles in the *Review of the Federal Reserve Bank of St. Louis* [18] and the *Federal Home Loan Bank Board Journal* [15]. In these articles, any caveat that cash and futures price changes may not be equal is relegated to a footnote or a discussion of cross-hedging.

B. Working's Hypothesis

Working [20 and 21] challenged the view of hedgers as pure risk minimizers and emphasized expected profit maximization. In his view hedgers functioned much like speculators, but, since they held positions in the cash market as well, they were concerned with relative not absolute price changes. Instead of expecting cash and futures prices to move together, he argued that "most hedging is done in expectation of a change in spot-futures price relations [20]." Holders of a long position in the cash market would, according to Working, hedge if the basis was expected to fall and would not hedge if the basis was expected to rise.

C. Portfolio and Hedging Theory

By viewing hedging as a simple application of basic portfolio theory Johnson [11] and Stein [17] were able to integrate the risk avoidance of traditional theory with Working's expected profits maximization. Johnson and Stein argued that one buys or sells futures for the same risk-return reasons that one buys any other security. While traditional theory argued that hedgers should always be completely hedged and Working's hypothesis indicated (though he realized such was not always the case) that hedgers would be completely hedged or unhedged, the application of portfolio theory allowed Johnson and Stein to explain why hedgers would hold both hedged and unhedged commodity stocks.

While the portfolio model of hedging may contain nothing which is new to those in the finance field, it is less familiar to analysts of commodity futures markets and has experienced a somewhat slower acceptance in this field. Since we will use this model to evaluate the GNMA and T-Bill futures as hedging instruments in the next section, let us briefly summarize its important characteristics.

One difference between this and the more familiar portfolio model is that cash and futures market holdings are not viewed as substitutes. Instead, spot market holdings, X_s, are viewed as fixed and the decision is how much of this stock to hedge. Following Johnson and Stein, let us restrict our attention to the case in which the potential hedger holds only one spot market commodity or security. Since spot market holdings are exogenous, any interest payments may also be viewed as predetermined and therefore irrelevant to the hedging decision. Letting U represent once again the return on an unhedged position,

$$E(U) = X_s E[P_s^2 - P_s^1] \tag{1}$$

$$\text{Var}(U) = X_s^2 \sigma_s^2 \tag{2}$$

Let R represent the return on a portfolio which includes both spot market holdings, X_s, and futures market holding[5], X_f.

$$E(R) = X_s E[P_s^2 - P_s^1] + X_f E[P_f^2 - P_f^1] - K(X_f) \quad (3)$$

$$\text{Var}(R) = X_s^2 \sigma_s^2 + X_f^2 \sigma_f^2 + 2 X_s X_f \sigma_{sf} \quad (4)$$

where X_s and X_f represent spot and futures market holdings. $K(X_f)$ are brokerage and other costs of engaging in futures transactions including the cost of providing margin. σ_s^2, σ_f^2, σ_{sf} represent the subjective variances and the covariance of the possible price changes from time 1 to time 2.

Note that the portfolio, whose returns are represented by R, may be a portfolio which is either completely or partially hedged. There is no presumption, as in traditional theory, that $X_f = -X_s$ (in which case $R = H$). Indeed cash and futures market holdings may even have the same sign.

Let $b = -X_f/X_s$ represent the proportion of the spot position which is hedged. Since in a hedge X_s and X_f have opposite signs, b is usually positive.

$$\text{Var}(R) = X_s^2 \{\sigma_s^2 + b^2 \sigma_f^2 - 2 b \sigma_{sf}\} \quad \text{and} \quad (5)$$

$$E(R) = X_s \{E(P_s^2 - P_s^1) - b E(P_f^2 - P_f^1)\} - K(X_s, b)$$
$$= X_s \{(1 - b) E(P_s^2 - P_s^1) + b E(P_s^2 - P_s^1) - b E(P_f^2 - P_f^1)\}$$
$$- K(X_s, b) \quad (6)$$

or letting $E(\Delta b) = E([P_f^2 - P_s^2] - [P_f^1 - P_s^1])$ represent the expected change in the basis,

$$E(R) = X_s[(1 - b) E(S) - b E(\Delta B)] - K(X_s, b) \quad (7)$$

where $E(S) = E(P_s^2 - P_s^1)$ is the expected price change on one unit of the spot commodity.

If the expected change in the basis is zero, then clearly the expected gain or loss is reduced as $b \to 1$. It is also obvious that expected changes in the basis may add to or subtract from the gain or loss which would have been expected on an unhedged portfolio ($E(U) = X_s E[S]$).

Holding X_s constant, let us consider the effect of a change in b, the proportion hedged, on the expected return and variance of the portfolio R.

$$\frac{\partial \text{Var}(R)}{\partial b} = X_s^2 \{2 b \sigma_f^2 - 2 \sigma_{sf}\} \quad (8)$$

so the risk minimizing b, b^*, is

$$b^* = \frac{\sigma_{sf}}{\sigma_f^2} \qquad (9)$$

$$\frac{\partial E(R)}{\partial b} = -X_s[E(\Delta B) + E(S)] - \frac{\partial K(X_s, b)}{\partial b} \qquad (10)$$

Since $E(\Delta B)$ and $E(S)$ may be either positive or negative, the opportunity locus of the possible combinations of $E(R)$ and $Var(R)$, which are shown in figure 1, may lie in either the first or second quadrant or both. Moreover, as b increases one moves either clockwise or counterclockwise around the locus depending on the sign of equation 10.

In this model there is no riskless asset. Treasury bills, which are a usual candidate for a riskless asset, are themselves being hedged. One may wish to liquidate a position in bills prior to maturity in which case there is a price risk however small. Consequently, the optimal b, $\hat{b}$, will be that associated with the point on the indifference curve which is just tangent to the highest indifference curve, II'. Not only need $\hat{b}$ not equal one as traditional hedging theory presumed, but $\hat{b}$ may be greater than one, in which case one takes a greater position in the futures than in the cash market, or $\hat{b}$ may be less than zero, in which case one takes the same position (either short or long) in both the spot and futures markets.[5]

II. EVALUATING THE GNMA AND T-BILL FUTURES MARKETS

The purpose of this section is to estimate the effectiveness of the new futures markets in reducing the risk associated with a cash position in GNMA's or T-Bills based on the market experience to date and to estimate the costs of hedging (the impact on expected returns).

While traditional theory indicates that the risk reduction to be achieved by hedging can be measured by comparing the variance of the change in the basis to the variance of the change in the cash price, this presumes that $b = 1$ which as shown above may not be the case. Fortunately, portfolio theory also provides a measure of hedging effectiveness. While the risk reduction achieved by any one hedger depends on the chosen b, the futures markets' potential for risk reduction can be measured by comparing the risk on an unhedged portfolio with the minimum risk that can be obtained on a portfolio containing both spot and forward securities. This minimum risk is represented by the left most point of the opportunity locus in figure 1, and corresponds to the variance of

---

[5] Since one would normally assume that $\sigma_{sf} > 0$, $b^* > 0$ but since b may be either increasing or decreasing as one moves counterclockwise around the opportunity locus, the portion of the locus above b^* may represent either $b < b^*$ or $b > b^*$.

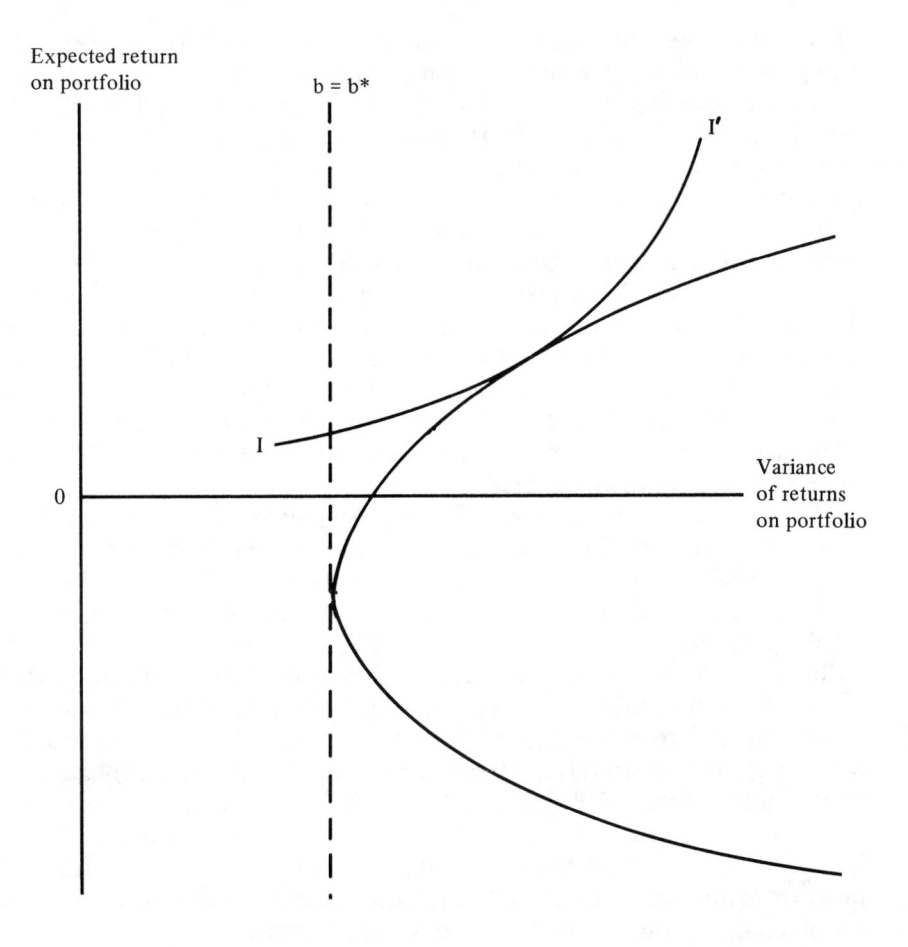

The Hedging Performance of the New Futures Markets

Figure 1

the return on a portfolio where b equals the b^* defined in equation 9. The measure of hedging effectiveness used in this paper is, therefore, the percent reduction in the variance or

$$e = 1 - \frac{\text{Var}(R^*)}{\text{Var}(U)}$$

where var(R^*) denotes the minimum variance on a portfolio containing security futures.

Substituting equation 9 into equation 5 yields

$$\text{Var}(R^*) = X_s^2 \left\{ \sigma_s^2 + \frac{\sigma_{sf}^2}{\sigma_f^2} - 2\frac{\sigma_{sf}^2}{\sigma_f^2} \right\} = X_s^2 \left(\sigma_s^2 - \frac{\sigma_{sf}^2}{\sigma_f^2} \right)$$

Consequently

$$e = \frac{\sigma_{sf}^2}{\sigma_s^2 \sigma_f^2} = \rho^2$$

where ρ^2 is the population coefficient of determination between the change in the cash price and the change in the future's price.

In order to judge the market's effectiveness at reducing risk, we estimated e using the sample coefficient of determination, r^2, for hedges of two arbitrary lengths (two and four weeks) and using the sample variances and sample covariance of the two and four week price changes over the observed period to estimate b^* as well as σ_s^2, σ_f^2 and σ_{sf}. As noted above, the GNMA and T-Bill markets were established in October 1975 and January 1976 respectively. Since it seemed prudent to allow the markets to gain some depth before analyzing them, weekly data collection for the GNMA market began in January 1976 and for the T-Bill market in March 1976. Both data sets were continued through December 1977. For comparison purposes we also collected data (January 1976–December 1977) and calculated e for two established and heavily traded futures: corn and wheat.[6]

For T-Bill cash prices, 90-day T-Bill prices were consistently used because they were readily available. This ignores the fact that over the hedge period the term to maturity of any T-Bills held will decline. Actual hedgers would need to adjust their b according to the term of the T-Bills held and the length of the hedge [5].

Since a hedger can buy futures with near or distant delivery dates, hedges in futures with a delivery date in 3 months or less (the nearby contract), in 3 to 6 months, in 6 to 9 months, and in 9 to 12 months were evaluated separately.[7] It could be argued that one's expectations of the near future will be affected more by unexpected changes in the cash price than one's expectation of the more distant futures, and this is supported by some work on adaptive expectations using forward rates from the term structure [12]. Consequently, we hypothesize that e will decline as one considers more distant contracts.

In addition, it is hypothesized that e will be greater for four week than for two week hedges because absolute changes in cash prices should generally be greater and futures prices would have more time to respond (if there is a lag) over the longer period.

The results for two week hedges are shown in Table 2 and the results for four week hedges are shown in Table 3. The most striking result is the marked superiority of the GNMA market to the T-Bill market particularly for the shorter hedges. While it appears less effective than the

---

[6] The futures prices were weekly closing prices as reported in the *Wall Street Journal*. For the spot price of wheat, we used the price of #2 Kansas City hard and for corn we used the price of #2 Chicago yellow as reported in the *Journal*.

[7] Two or four week periods in which the nearby contract expired were dropped from the sample. During the harvest season, futures contracts are available for every other month for corn and wheat, so the time periods for these differ somewhat from those for GNMA's and T-Bills.

Table 2 Two Week Hedges

The Futures Contract	Estimated e	Estimated b*
8% GNMA's (46 observations)		
The Nearby Contract	.664	.801*
3 to 6 Month Contract	.675	.832
6 to 9 Month Contract	.677	.854
9 to 12 Month Contract	.661	.852
90 Day Treasury Bills (41 observations)		
The Nearby Contract	.272	.307*
3 to 6 Month Contract	.256	.237*
6 to 9 Month Contract	.178	.143*
9 to 12 Month Contract	.140	.116
Wheat (45 observations)		
The Nearby Contract	.898	.864*
2 to 6 Month Contract	.889	.815*
4 to 8 Month Contract	.868	.784*
6 to 10 Month Contract	.841	.778*
Corn (45 observations)		
The Nearby Contract	.649	.915
2 to 6 Month Contract	.605	.905
4 to 8 Month Contract	.541	.868
6 to 10 Month Contract	.450	.764

*Significantly different from 1 at .05 level.

wheat market, the GNMA market compares quite favorably with the corn market as a hedging instrument. With the puzzling exception of hedges in the nearby contract for a four week period, the T-Bill market appears rather ineffective in reducing exposure to price change risk particularly over the shorter period. Indeed, if one followed the prescription of traditional theory and set $b = 1$, the hedged T-Bill portfolio would have been more risky than the unhedged portfolio in all cases except for four week hedges in the nearby contract. The author feels that this may be due to the fact that the T-Bill rate is closely related to the federal funds rate which, given current Federal Reserve operating procedures, is basically controlled by the Fed over short periods. If short-run changes in T-Bill rates are viewed as induced by monetary authorities, market participants may see no need to adjust their expectations of future rates.

While the author is unaware of any way to statistically test this hypothesis, the results in Tables 1 and 2 are certainly consistent with the hypothesis that e will be larger for the longer hedges. This difference in

Table 3 Four Week Hedges

The Futures Contract	Estimated e	Estimated b*
8% GNMA's (23 observations)		
The Nearby Contract	.785	.848
3 to 6 Month Contract	.817	.993
6 to 9 Month Contract	.799	1.019
9 to 12 Month Contract	.780	1.035
90 Day Treasury Bills (21 observations)		
The Nearby Contract	.741	.651*
3 to 6 Month Contract	.571	.427*
6 to 9 Month Contract	.406	.242*
9 to 12 Month Contract	.369	.228*
Wheat (21 observations)		
The Nearby Contract	.918	.917
2 to 6 Month Contract	.921	.862*
4 to 8 Month Contract	.909	.840*
6 to 10 Month Contract	.887	.843*
Corn (21 observations)		
The Nearby Contract	.725	1.021
2 to 6 Month Contract	.666	1.011
4 to 8 Month Contract	.608	.969
6 to 10 Month Contract	.560	.887

*Significantly different from 1 at .05 level.

hedging effectiveness appears particularly pronounced for the financial security futures.

The hypothesis that short-term hedges in nearby contracts are more effective than hedges in more distant contracts appears to hold for all except the GNMA market.

In estimating e we also estimated $b*$.[8] These estimates, which are also reported in the Tables, are themselves of interest since traditional theory implies that $b* = 1$. In most cases $b*$ was significantly different from 1 and in general was less than 1. The hypothesis that $b* = 1$ is therefore rejected.

Since these are ex-post estimates of $b*$ and since hedgers may be unable because of the individuality of the futures contract to achieve the desired b, the question of the sensitivity of e to the chosen b is one of some importance. To address this question, we calculated e or r^2 for b's ten percent greater and lower than those shown in Tables 1 and 2.

---

[8] Let us note again that hedgers in T-Bills must adjust these estimates of $b*$ to reflect the term to maturity and the hedging period of their own portfolio.

For hedges in either GNMA's or T-Bills, in either the nearby or the next closest contract, and over either a two or four week period, raising or lowering b ten percent from the estimated b^* resulted in a reduction in e of approximately 1%. We conclude, therefore, that these results are not very sensitive to small deviations in b.

While real cross-hedging was not considered, the effectiveness of the GNMA futures market in hedging positions in 6½% and 9% certificates was examined. As mentioned earlier, one can deliver these certificates to satisfy a futures contract and an earlier study (Ederington and Plumly, 1976) indicated that, at least in 1976, it would have been cheaper to deliver 9% certificates than 8% certificates and more expensive to deliver 6½% certificates. For this reason we expected e to be higher for 9% than for either 8 or 6½% certificates. This proved to be the case for all two-week hedges. Indeed, for all futures contracts e was highest for a hedge against 9% certificates, lower for 8% certificates, and lowest for 6½% certificates. For hedges in the nearby contract over a two week period, for instance, the measures of e were .820, .664, and .662 respectively.

Having found that, at least for GNMA's, one can lower the risk (as measured by the variance) associated with holding securities by holding futures, attention is now turned to the impact of hedging on expected returns. Two points are clear from equation 7. One, expected returns are lowered by the amount of the brokerage and other costs associated with the futures. Two, if the expected change in the basis is zero and $0 < b < 1$, partial hedging reduces the gain or loss associated with an unhedged position ($X_s E[S]$). Attention is therefore centered on the term, $E(\Delta B)$. The important question is whether over the long run $E(\Delta B)$ will tend to be consistently negative or positive i.e., whether the expected value of the expected change in the basis is positive or negative. Since the basis must be approximately zero at the delivery date,[9] $E(\Delta B)$ will generally be positive if the current cash price exceeds the current futures price and will generally be negative if the futures price exceeds the cash price.

The longer the hedge and the closer the delivery date, the closer this relationship between $E(\Delta B)$ and the initial basis should be. The question basically reduces, therefore, to whether there is any reason to anticipate that in the long-run futures prices will generally be above or below cash prices.

Over the observed period, cash prices on GNMA's and T-Bills consistently exceeded futures prices (except occasionally at delivery). To provide an idea of what changes in the basis might have been expected dur-

---

[9] If it is cheaper to deliver GNMA certificates with a mortgage rate other than 8%, the basis for GNMA's will not be eliminated completely. A negative basis remains depending on the difference in costs.

ing this period, the average change in the basis as a percent of the cash price (for comparison) was calculated for four week hedge periods.[10] The results are shown in Table 4.[11] As expected, the average change in the basis was positive so that over this period the change in the basis tended to add to (subtract from) the expected returns of those taking a long (short) position in the futures market.[12] In addition, it is interesting to note that for GNMA's the average change in the basis tended to vary inversely with the length of the futures contract. Since the risk reduction was approximately the same for all four contracts, this suggests that long (short) hedgers would have been well advised to hedge in the nearby (distant) contract.

While over the observed period cash prices on GNMA's and T-Bills consistently exceeded futures prices so that positive changes in the basis could generally be expected, this was not always the case in 1978 and may not be the case in the future. The author is much more reluctant to accept Table 4 as a guide to the future than Tables 2 and 3. The crucial question is whether futures prices are unbiased measures of market expectations of future spot rates or whether they are biased downward by "normal-backwardation." There isn't enough data to answer this question since the lower futures prices to date could simply reflect consistent expectations of rising interest rates.

There continues to be a theoretical and empirical debate over "normal backwardation," the Keynes-Hicks argument from which the liquid-

Table 4 Average Change in the Basis Over 4 Week Periods
January 1976 (March for T-Bills)-December 1977

Futures Contract	GNMA Certificates	Treasury Bills
The Nearby Contract	.271%	.184%
3 to 6 Month Contract	.162%	.220%
6 to 9 Month Contract	.133%	.161%
9 to 12 Month Contract	.098%	.164%

Average Change in the Basis as a % of the Cash Price

[10] The average change for four weeks is not exactly double the change for two weeks because the periods do not completely overlap since periods in which the nearby contract matured were eliminated.

[11] The author does not feel that corn and wheat provide a meaningful comparison in this case because the basis on these varies with the time till harvest and storage costs.

[12] Note that when the basis is negative, those who take a long position in the futures market and take delivery lock in the lower buying price and higher interest rate. Those who are short and make delivery lock-in a selling price which is below the current selling price.

ity premium theory of the term structure was developed.[13] However, it is questionable whether evidence from other futures markets is applicable to GNMA and T-Bill markets. Hicks' argument [8, pp. 136-139] was that most hedgers of agricultural commodities maintain a long position in the cash and a short position in the futures market so that there is a weakness on the demand side of the futures market which speculators will not step in and absorb until the futures price is sufficiently low so that the expected favorable price change will compensate for the risk. Since it is an open question whether hedgers in GNMA's and T-Bills are generally long or short, the existence and sign of any liquidity premium in these markets is less certain.

For the T-Bill market there is an additional consideration. Since one can satisfy the delivery commitment by delivering longer T-Bills on which all but three months have elapsed, the possibility of riskless arbitrage should theoretically keep the futures rate close to the forward rates implicit in the term structure.[14] If, therefore, there are liquidity premiums in the term structure they should be reflected in the futures market. While there is still debate on this point, the bulk of recent evidence indicates that the term structure does contain liquidity premiums [7 and 9]. For T-Bills, therefore, it may be that futures prices normally tend to be below cash prices so that $E(\Delta B)$ is generally positive.

III. CONCLUSIONS AND OBSERVATIONS

The conclusions of this study may be summarized as follows:

1. The decision to hedge a cash or forward market position in the futures market is no different from any other investment decision—investors hedge to obtain the best combination of risk and return. Basic portfolio theory, which best explains when and how much holders of financial portfolios will wish to hedge, encompasses both the traditional hedging theory and Working's theory as special cases.
2. The implication of many "How-To" articles in the popular financial press that hedges in GNMA's and T-Bills are perfect because cash and futures prices change by equal amounts is completely indefensible.
3. Contrary to traditional hedging theory (but consistent with the theory of adaptive expectations), our empirical results indicate

---

[13] See Peck, Section I [4], Burger, Lang and Rasche [3], Fama [7], and Cornell [4].

[14] While this should theoretically be the case, surprisingly large differences between future and forward rates have been observed [2].

that even pure risk-minimizers may wish to hedge only a portion of their portfolios. In most cases the estimated b^* was less than one.
4. Based on the experience to date, the GNMA futures market appears to be a more effective instrument for risk avoidance than the T-Bill market particularly for short-term (i.e., two-week) hedges.
5. Both the GNMA and the T-Bill market appear to be more effective in reducing the price change risk over long (four-week) than over short (two-week) periods.
6. While changes in the basis were generally positive over the observed period (adding to the return on long hedges and subtracting from that on short hedges), the financial futures markets have not been in existence long enough to tell whether this is the usual case because of "normal backwardation" or whether it merely reflects expectations during the observed period.

A number of unanswered questions and topics for future research regarding futures markets in financial securities obviously remain. One which the author regards as particularly important is the effectiveness of the new futures markets for cross-hedging, i.e., for reducing the risk of portfolios containing securities other than GNMA's or T-Bills. Since mortgage lenders must often commit themselves months before the funds are lent, the effectiveness of the GNMA future in hedging against changes in conventional mortgage rates (or in the cost of funds) seems to be an important unanswered question. [However, our results are appropriate if the lender plans to finance the mortgages by issuing GNMA Pass-Through Certificates as in Table 1.] Unfortunately, the only data series for local mortgage rates of which the author is aware—the Federal Home Loan Bank Board series—measures the rate on loans made and these loans may reflect commitments made months ago. What are needed are localized data on new commitments.

References

1. P. W. Bacon, and R. E. Williams, 1976. "Interest Rate Futures: New Tool for the Financial Manager," *Financial Management* (Spring, 1976), pp. 32-38.
2. B. Branch, 1978. "Testing the Unbiased Expectations Theory of Interest Rates." Paper presented at 1978 annual meeting of the Eastern Finance Association.
3. A. E. Burger, R. W. Lang, and R. H. Rasche, 1977. "The Treasury Bill Futures Market and Market Expectations of Interest Rates," *Review* of the Federal Reserve Bank of St. Louis, Vol 59, No. 6, pp 2-11.
4. Bradford Cornell, 1977. "Spot Rates, Forward Rates and Exchange Market Efficiency," *Journal of Financial Economics* (August, 1977), pp. 55-60.
5. W. H. Duncan, 1977. "Treasury Bill Futures—Opportunities and Pitfalls," *Review* of the Federal Reserve Bank of Dallas (July, 1977).

6. L. E. Ederington, and W. E. Plumly, 1976. "The New Futures Market in Financial Securities," Futures Trading Seminar Proceedings, Vol IV, Chicago Board of Trade.
7. E. F. Fama, 1976. "Forward Rates as Predictors of Future Spot Rates," *Journal of Financial Economics* (Oct., 1976), pp 361-378.
8. J. R. Hicks, 1946. *Value and Capital* (London: Oxford University Press) second edition.
9. T. E. Holland, 1965. "A Note on the Traditional Theory of the Term Structure of Interest Rates on Three-and-Six-Month Treasury Bills," *International Economic Review* (September, 1965), pp 330-36.
10. S. F. Jacobs, and J. R. Kozuch, 1975. "Is There a Future for a Mortgage Futures Market," *The Mortgage Banker*.
11. L. L. Johnson, 1960. "The Theory of Hedging and Speculation in Commodity Futures," *Review of Economic Studies*, Vol 27, No. 3, pp 139-51.
12. J. B. Michaelsen, 1973. *The Term Structure of Interest Rates* (New York: Interest Educational Publishers).
13. J. H. McCulloch, 1975. "An Estimate of the Liquidity Premium," *Journal of Political Economy* (February, 1975), pp 95-119.
14. A. E. Peck, 1977. *Selected Writings on Futures Markets*, Vol II (Chicago: Board of Trade of the City of Chicago).
15. R. L. Sandor, 1975. "Trading Mortgage Interest Rate Futures," *Federal Home Loan Bank Board Journal* (September, 1975), pp 2-9.
16. B. Smith, 1976. "Trading Complexities, FHLBB Rules Impede Association Activity," *Savings and Loan News* (January, 1976).
17. J. L. Stein, 1961. "The Simultaneous Determination of Spot and Futures Prices," *American Economic Review*, Vol LI, No. 5.
18. N. A. Stevens, 1976. "A Mortgage Futures Market: Its Development, Uses, Benefits and Cost," *Review* of the Federal Reserve Bank of St. Louis (April, 1976).
19. L. G. Telser, and H. N. Higinbotham, 1977. "Organized Futures Markets: Costs and Benefits," *Journal of Political Economy* (October, 1977), Vol 85, pp 969-1000.
20. H. Working, 1953. "Futures Trading and Hedging." *American Economic Review* (June, 1953), pp 314-343.
21. ———. 1962. "New Concepts Concerning Futures Markets and Prices," *American Economic Review* (June, 1962), pp 431-459.

18

The Hedging Performance of the New Futures Market: Comment[*]

Charles T. Franckle[†]

I. INTRODUCTION

In a recent article appearing in this Journal, Louis Ederington [2] examines the hedging performance of the futures markets in financial securities by using a basic portfolio model that was previously applied to the analysis of commodities futures markets by Johnson [3] and Stein [4]. A conclusion he reaches is that two week hedges using 90 day Treasury Bill futures are rather ineffective in reducing exposure to price change risk. One purpose of this comment is to show that within the context of Ederington's analysis two week hedges using T-Bill futures are more effective than he found and in fact compare favorably with similar hedges in other markets. One aspect of this type of hedge which is unique to the financial markets is that the maturity of the cash position decreases during the hedge. This comment extends Ederington's work by estimating for the T-Bill market the effects of changing maturity on the variance minimizing hedge ratio. Furthermore, it is shown that the decreasing maturity tends to limit the flexibility of the timing of hedges in financial markets relative to those in commodity markets.

[*]Reprinted from the *Journal of Finance*, Vol. 35, No. 5, (December 1980). Reprinted by permission of the publisher and author.
[†]The University of Texas at Austin. I wish to thank Louis Ederington for providing his data and for his encouragement. The comments of Steve Magee and George Morgan are gratefully acknowledged.

II. EFFECTIVENESS OF HEDGES USING T-BILLS

If a portfolio has both par value spot holdings of X_s and futures market holdings of X_f, then $b = -X_f/X_s$ is the proportion of the spot position which is hedged. Ederington shows that the risk minimizing b, b*, is

$$b^* = \frac{\sigma_{sf}}{\sigma_f^2} \qquad (1)$$

where σ_f^2 is the subjective variance of the price change of the futures during the period hedged and σ_{sf} is the covariance of the spot and futures price changes. Furthermore, when $b = b^*$, the percent reduction in variance from the unhedged portfolio is 100e, where

$$e = \frac{\sigma_{sf}^2}{\sigma_s^2 \sigma_f^2} = \rho^2 \qquad (2)$$

σ_s^2 is the subjective variance of the spot price change and p^2 is the population coefficient of determination between the change in the cash price and the change in the price of the futures contract.

In order to judge the market's effectiveness at reducing risk, Ederington estimated e using the sample coefficient of determination, r^2, for hedges of two and four weeks. The sample variances and sample covariances of these price changes over the observed period were used to estimate b*. One puzzling result is the relative ineffectiveness of the T-Bill market, particularly for two week hedges. The primary reason for this result is his choice of the cash T-Bill rate. Although the Friday settlement prices are used for the futures, the 90-day T-Bill prices are weekly averages. Thus, much of the relevant change in cash price may be masked by the use of weekly averages.

The first line of Table I shows Ederington's original results for the two week hedge using T-Bills. An error in the data for the nearby contract is partially responsible for the low estimated value of e and b*; however, even after correcting for this error (line 2), the estimated reduction in variance is still much less than for hedges in the corn, wheat, and GNMA markets, where estimated e is .649, .898 and .664 respectively. Line 3 in Table I matches Friday to Friday changes in the futures price with Friday to Friday changes in the bid price of 90 day T-Bills as reported in the *Wall Street Journal*.[1] The T-Bill market now compares favorably with the corn and GNMA markets.

---

[1] The bid yields were used for both the purchase and sales prices of the T-Bills. Otherwise, there would be a change in price of the T-Bill without any real change in market rates. The difference between bid and ask could be included by assuming it is constant and subtracting it from the expected return.

Table I Hedges Using the Nearby Contract for 90 Day Treasury Bills

Day of Hedge	T-Bill Rate	Maturity of T-Bill when Hedge is Lifted	Estimated e	Estimated b*	Observations
		Two Week Hedges			
1. Friday (Ederington's original data)	weekly average	90 Days	.272	.307[a]	41
2. Friday (Ederington's corrected data)	weekly average	90 Days	.428	.442[a]	41
3. Friday	same day	90 Days	.679	.610[a]	41
4. Thursday	same day	90 Days	.645	.765[a]	43
5. Thursday	same day	90 Days	.693	.850[a]	78
6. Thursday	same day	76 Days	.640	.589[a]	43
7. Thursday	same day	76 Days	.686	.698[a]	78
		Four Week Hedges			
8. Friday	weekly average	90 Days	.741	.651[a]	21
9. Thursday	same day	90 Days	.756	.801	21
10. Thursday	same day	90 Days	.678	.918	39
11. Thursday	same day	62 Days	.649	.557[a]	21
12. Thursday	same day	62 Days	.661	.669[a]	39

[a] Significantly different from 1 at .05 level.

This substantial reduction in variance is due to the increased covariance of the daily price changes with the futures prices, which is reflected in the increase in estimated b*. This large reduction is also partially due to the fact that there is more variance to reduce in the first place because the variance of the daily cash price is greater than the variance of the weekly price; however, the increase in covariance is so great that there is an actual reduction (by about one-third) in the variance of the hedged portfolio using daily prices as compared to the variance of the hedged portfolio using weekly prices.

In order to see how sensitive the results are to the particular day of the hedge, a Thursday to Thursday comparison was made for the same period, March, 1976 to December, 1977.[2] The results of this are shown on line 4, and they appear to be similar to the Friday results. When the sample period is extended through May, 1979 (line 5) the estimated maximum reduction in variance increases to 69.3 percent.

Using weekly averages for the four week hedges (line 8) does not seem to give as biased an estimate of e. When Thursday to Thursday data is used (line 9) the estimated e increased only slightly. The estimated value of b*, however, increases to the extent that it is no longer statistically different from one at the .05 level. It seems that even though the covariance is increased by using the proper price, the expected gain in effectiveness is offset by the greater variance of the daily cash price relative to the variance of the weekly average cash price. Whereas the two week hedges seemed to improve with the extended sample period, the four week hedges appear to be slightly less effective. The estimated b*, however, is still closer to one than Ederington believed.

III. ADJUSTING b* FOR MATURITY

Ederington recognizes that the value of b* needs to be adjusted because of the decreasing maturity of the T-Bill during the period of the hedge,[3] but he makes no estimates of the necessary adjustments. In his empirical tests he assumes that we have a 90 day T-Bill at both the beginning and at the end of the hedge when actually if we purchase a 90 day T-Bill at the start of the hedge we would sell a 76 day T-Bill at the end of a two week hedge or a 62 day T-Bill at the end of a four

---

[2] Since the futures contracts are delivered on Thursdays, some periods in which the contracts expired and were dropped from the Friday sample coincided with the end of the Thursday hedges and were included in the Thursday sample. Thus, neither the timing nor the number of observations in the Thursday and Friday hedges are the same.

[3] See Ederington [p. 164]. The problems arising from using a constant maturity futures contract to hedge a cash position with decreasing maturity were also identified by Duncan [1].

week hedge. Alternatively, if we end with a 90 day T-Bill for each hedge, then the original purchase must have been of a 104 day or 118 day T-Bill.

When a constant maturity T-Bill is used in the estimations, it is possible to distinguish two factors which would cause estimates of the variances of the cash price changes and the covariances of these changes with the changes in the futures prices to be biased. The first is the imperfect correlation between 90 day rates and 76 or 62 day rates, which would be expected to affect both b^* and e, and the second is that as the maturity of the T-Bill decreases the price sensitivity to changes in the discount rate decreases, which would affect only b^*. To understand these factors, it must be realized that the price changes that are considered in the model are due solely to changes in the discount rate and not to the normal price appreciation of the T-Bill as it approaches maturity. Thus, Ederington was measuring the variance of changes in the 90 day discount rate over two and four week periods and the covariance of this rate with the changes in the discount rate on a futures contract. Assuming we start with a 90 day T-Bill, to correct for the first factor the proper variance would have been that for the difference between a 90 day discount rate at the beginning of the hedge and a 76 or 62 day discount rate at the end of the hedge period, and the proper covariance would have been between these changes in rates and the change in rate on a futures contract.

The other problem is due to the fact that even if the changes in discount rates on T-Bills of different maturities were identical, they would have different impacts on the prices of the T-Bills. If all discount rates were 8 percent at the beginning of the hedge and all discount rates were 9 percent at the end of the hedge the final maturity of the cash T-Bill is very important for the proper hedge ratio. For example, if the discount rate was not expected to change, then the relevant price change for a $1MM face value 90 day T-Bill would be from $980,000 to $977,500, a $2,500 decrease in value, while the relevant price change for a $1MM face value 62 day T-Bill would be from $986,222 to $984,500, a decrease in value of only $1,722. Since an equal change in discount rates caused a smaller price change for the shorter maturity T-Bill, it follows that the quantity of future contracts needed would be less for the shorter term T-Bill.

The effect of the imperfect correlation between the 90 day rate and other T-Bill rates was estimated by assuming that the 90 day T-Bill that was purchased was the same T-Bill that was sold at the termination of the hedge. Since the only price change to be measured is that due to changes in interest rates, the selling price was calculated assuming the T-Bill still had 90 days to maturity but using the 76 and 62 day bid yields for two and four week hedges respectively.

The effects of this adjustment are shown in Table I. Lines 6 and 7 show the effect for the original and extended periods of the two week hedge and lines 11 and 12 for the four week hedge. Although there is a decrease in estimated e and the decrease is greater for the longer hedge, it is not very great, which suggests that this has a very small effect on the potential effectiveness of such a hedge. There is a much greater decrease, however, in the estimated b*. In the case of the four week hedge, estimated b* is significantly different from 1 at the .05 level, whereas previously it had not been.

The decrease in estimated b* is due to the decrease in sample covariance, which was expected. The lower estimated value of e is somewhat misleading. It should be remembered that e is the potential percent reduction in variance of the hedged portfolio relative to an unhedged cash position. In each case the sample variance of the unhedged cash position is greater (from 30 to over 80 percent greater) for the constant maturity T-Bills than for the decreasing maturity T-Bills. Consequently, even though the percent reduction in variance is not quite as great for the maturity adjusted hedges, their sample variances were 15 to 42 percent less than the sample variances of the constant maturity hedges.

The second effect of changing maturity, that of decreasing price elasticity, can be measured by assuming that the changes in discount rates of all T-Bills are identical. Since the change in price per one dollar face value of a T-Bill with n days to maturity is related to a change in the discount rate, d, by

$$\Delta_n P_s = -\frac{n}{360} \Delta d, \qquad (3)$$

the relationship between the expected return and variance of a T-Bill with n days to maturity and those of a 90 day T-Bill would be

$$E(\Delta_n P_s) = \frac{n}{90} E(\Delta_{90} P_s) \qquad (4)$$

and

$$\text{Var}(\Delta_n P_s) = \left(\frac{n}{90}\right)^2 \text{Var}(\Delta_{90} P_s). \qquad (5)$$

Thus, for a T-Bill with n days to maturity, the variance minimizing ratio, $_n b^*$, relative to that ratio for a 90 day T-Bill would be

$$_n b^* = \frac{n}{90} (_{90} b^*) \qquad (6)$$

To see how this might be applied, assume that a hedger uses the estimates from line 12 of Table I to construct a minimum variance four week hedge. Since the estimate of b* has already corrected for the effect of different maturity on the correlation between futures and cash interest rates, it is now necessary to correct only for the fact that changes in the futures rate affect the price of a 90 day T-Bill while changes in the cash rate affect the price of a 62 day T-Bill. Thus, the fully corrected estimate of the minimum variance hedge ratio would be

$$_{62}\hat{b}^* = \frac{62}{90}(.669)$$

$$= .461.$$

If this is compared to the estimated b* of .918 (from line 10), we can see that the estimated quantity of futures that should be sold in order to minimize the variance is only about half the quantity we estimated when neither of the effects of decreasing maturity were considered.

IV. EFFECTS OF DECREASING MATURITY ON THE TIMING OF THE HEDGE

This knowledge of the proper adjustment for a hedge of any given length cannot be used to construct a continuous hedge over any arbitrary period.[4] Suppose we tried to create a continuous hedge for a $90MM par value cash position in 90 day T-Bills. Assuming that all T-Bill discount rates are identical and $_{90}b^* = 1$, this requires that we be short (90 − i) futures contracts of the ith day of the hedge in order to offset any price change due to changes in the discount rate. In order to be short (90 − i) contracts we would have sold 90 contracts at the beginning of the hedge and purchased one contract each day of the hedge. The gains and/or losses on the i contracts would depend upon the daily changes in the discount rate during that period, while any change in price of the cash position after i days is determined by the discount rate at that time and is completely offset by the remaining (90 − i) futures contracts. Thus, the actual return on the hedged position would be affected by the unforeseeable gains and/or losses resulting from the daily rebalancing.

Thus, b* must be interpreted with care. It is valid only if the length of the hedge is known at the beginning, since changing the hedge ratio would result in unknown and possibly large gains or losses. A T-Bill futures contract can be duplicated in the cash market by the proper choice of maturities and combination of short and long positions. Therefore, it should not be surprising that these futures markets cannot provide a continuous hedge that is unobtainable with the cash markets.

---

[4] Duncan [p. 4] suggested that continual adjustment is a solution to the changing maturity problem.

Whether the futures market is used or not, a risk free nominal rate can be obtained only for a predetermined investment period.

This model when applied to the commodities markets also assumes that the subjective variances and covariances are for a specific time period; however, in many cases it seems reasonable to assume that the optimal hedge ratio would be fairly stable over time. Thus, a hedge that was originally intended to last two weeks may be almost as effective if it were lifted after four weeks. Also, decreasing maturity would not be a serious problem for short hedges with GNMA futures since the maturity of GNMA securities is so much longer than that of T-Bills.

Ederington neither claims that this model is applicable to nor that these markets are appropriate for such a continuous hedge. On the other hand, many hedging examples suggest that the date of termination is not crucial to the hedge; thus, it is important to demonstrate just how important this aspect is. Furthermore, it highlights the fact that there is a risk free rate to compare to the hedged rate, which is the rate on the T-Bill that matures on the day the hedge is lifted. Further investigations into the effectiveness of such hedging should use this shorter term T-Bill rate as one standard.

IV. SUMMARY

Within the framework of the model that Ederington has applied to hedging with financial futures, it was found that by matching the futures prices with the correct cash T-Bill price the effectiveness of this market is much better than originally claimed for two week hedges using T-Bills.[5] Estimates of the effect of the changing maturity of the cash position on e and b* show that potential reduction in variance is almost as great, but it requires a substantially smaller quantity of futures contracts to achieve. Furthermore, it was demonstrated that the condition of having a predetermined length of hedge is a crucial assumption for the proper application of this model.

References

1. W. H. Duncan. "Treasury Bill Futures—Opportunities and Pitfalls." *Review* of the Federal Reserve Bank of Dallas (July 1977).
2. L. H. Ederington. "The Hedging Performance of the New Futures Markets." *Journal of Finance*, 34 (March 1979).

[5] In correspondence with the Editor, Professor Ederington acknowledges that he did use weekly averages for Treasury Bill returns rather than Friday closing prices and that this error has undoubtedly affected his results. For the other series, GNMA, wheat & corn, he did use, as he wrote in his article, Friday closing prices. (Footnote added by Editor).

3. L. L. Johnson. "The Theory of Hedging and Speculation in Commodity Futures." *Review of Economic Studies*, 27 (October 1960).
4. J. L. Stein. "The Simultaneous Determination of Spot and Futures Prices." *American Economic Review*, 51 (December 1961).

19

Risk Reduction Potential of Financial Futures for Corporate Bond Positions*

Joanne Hill and
Thomas Schneeweis

ABSTRACT

This study is an empirical analysis of the usefulness of GNMA and T-bond futures for hedging the risk of holding and/or issuing corporate bonds. Hedging effectiveness is examined using monthly price changes for a sample consisting of corporate bond indices. Sensitivity of hedging effectiveness to bond coupon rate, rating, industry class of issues, and the time to delivery of the futures contract is analyzed. In addition, the return and risk levels of minimum risk hedged positions are compared to the risk and return performance of unhedged positions. Results indicate substantial reduction in interest rate risk through hedging especially for high quality corporate and public utility bonds.

I. INTRODUCTION

Investment in and financing with fixed income securities is affected by uncertainty as to the cost of financing or return on investment. Sales or purchases of financial instrument futures permits security issuers or

*Reprinted by permission of the authors who are Assistant and Associate Professors of Finance at the University of Massachusetts (Amherst).

investors to hedge long or short positions in the fixed-income spot market. Corporate bond issuers or the investment bankers who represent them may reduce their interest rate risk exposure between the time of the flotation decision and issue date by selling financial futures. Institutional and individual holders of corporate bonds are also interested in selling futures to reduce the short-term volatility of their corporate bond portfolio values. Risk is reduced to the extent that the gain (loss) in the futures position offsets the loss (gain) on the spot position.

This study consists of an empirical analysis of the value of a particular type of hedge: a minimum risk cross-hedge involving a spot position (long = investment, short = financing) in corporate bonds and a futures position in the GNMA mortgage-backed certificate futures or U.S. Treasury bond futures.[1] GNMA futures call for delivery of shares in pools of Federal Housing Administration and Veterans Administration mortgage loans. The trading unit has a principal amount of $100,000, a stated interest of 8% and an average maturity of 12 years. U.S. Treasury bond (T-bond) futures contracts call for delivery of $100,000 of U.S. T-Bonds with a stated interest rate of 8%. For both of these contracts, certificates or bonds of rates other than 8% are also deliverable at discounts or premiums set according to a CBT formula.[2]

The scope of this analysis is limited to hedging behavior directed at minimizing the price volatility of a predetermined position in corporate bonds. The case examined here is one in which the size or timing (horizon) of the corporate bond position is independent of risk reduction and return opportunities in the financial futures markets. This dimension of the hedging problem is similar to that explored by Johnson [3] and Stein [8] for commodities and by Ederington [1] for Treasury bills and GNMA certificates. This application of hedging is particularly relevant for institutional bond holders who have long-term horizons for corporate bond investment and who select bonds based on their long-term properties, but who at the same time have short-run performance goals to meet. For example a pension or mutual fund may for various reasons be unable to liquidate bond positions despite a pessimistic short-term outlook for the bond market.

The alternative approach to deriving optimal positions involving financial futures is to adopt the Markowitz single horizon framework; the level of investment (financing) of corporate bond and financial instrument futures is simultaneously determined and based on the expected return, variance/covariance structure and desired risk/return tradeoff. This theoretically defensible formulation of the problem is easily

---

[1] Although corporate bonds are subject to substantial interest rate risk there are presently no futures available calling for corporate bond delivery. One reason for this is the heterogeneity of corporate bonds which arises from the perceived default risk associated with each issue.

[2] At any point in time, the expected price at delivery of the cheapest deliverable coupon (based on these formulae) will be the major factor in futures price determination.

solvable; however, it is less interesting because its treatment of spot and futures positions as simultaneous decisions does not reflect the realities of actual bond portfolio management and debt financing practices.

Earlier studies [2,4] have examined aspects of the risk reduction effectiveness of cross-hedgers using the GNMA contracts. This present study serves to update these previous results using 1979 data and to expand the analysis to examine the T-bond futures contract as well. This larger data set permits analysis of changes in hedging effectiveness as the futures market matures as well as a comparison between GNMA and T-bond futures as cross-hedging vehicles for corporate bonds of different ratings and coupons. The average change in portfolio value and risk during 1979 for unhedged and hedged positions is also determined using the minimum risk hedge ratio based on the 1976-1978 data.

In the following section existing empirical evidence on financial instrument hedging effectiveness and theoretical basis of hedging measures used in this analysis are discussed. In Section III, the analysis to be performed and the financial instrument data set to be used are described. Empirical results of monthly cross-hedging are presented and discussed in Section IV along with the results of the simulated hedged and unhedged positions. The major findings and their implications for corporate managers and bond investors are summarized in the final section.

II. HEDGING EFFECTIVENESS MEASURES AND EVIDENCE

Ederington [1] was among the first to analyze the hedging effectiveness of financial instrument futures in his study of the U.S. Treasury bill and GNMA futures market as hedges for their deliverable instruments. Based on a small data set, he concluded that it was possible to eliminate approximately 75% of the price change risk of a spot position in the deliverable instruments with the nearby GNMA or T-bill contract. In addition he presented the formulation of the minimum risk hedge ratios for financial instruments hedges drawing on the work on commodity hedging by Johnson [3] and Stein [8].

The optimal hedge ratio, (HR*) and hedging effectiveness of a market or contract(s) is related to the covariance between spot and futures price changes and the variances of futures price changes. This hedge ratio can be interpreted as the weight of the futures position in the portfolio or proportion of the given spot positions (long or short) that is hedged. A positive (negative) HR* indicates a purchase (sale) of futures and is the solution to the problem below:

$$\min \text{Var}(C_{Ht}) = \text{Var}(C_{st}) + X_f^2 \text{Var}(C_{ft}) + 2X_f \text{cov}(C_{st},C_{ft}) \tag{1}$$

$$\text{subject to } C_{Ht}^o = E(C_{st}) + X_f E(C_{ft}) \tag{2}$$

where C_{st}, C_{ft} = the value change during period t of the spot position and futures contracts, C_{Ht}^o = the target change in value during period t of the hedged position, and X_f = the proportion of the portfolio held in future contracts; X_f^* would equal the optimal hedge ratio (HR*) with $X_f < 0$ representing a short position and $X_f > 0$ a long position in futures.

Since the object of hedging as analyzed here is to minimize the value of a predetermined corporate bond position, the minimum risk hedge ratio HR_m^* is simply the value of X_f at which the unconstrained objective function (1) reaches a minimum. One can then measure the hedging effectiveness for these risk minimizing hedges represented by a futures position in the proportion of HR_m^*. This minimum risk hedge ratio can be found by setting the partial derivative of the portfolio variance with respect to X_f equal to 0 and solving for X_f^*.

$$\frac{\delta \text{Var}(C_{Ht})}{\delta X_f} = 2X_f \text{Var}(C_f) + 2\text{cov}(C_s,C_f) = 0 \tag{3}$$

$$X_f^* = -\frac{\text{cov}(C_s,C_f)}{\text{Var}(C_f)} = HR_m^*$$

The result is equivalent to the negative of the slope coefficient of a regression of spot price changes on futures price changes.

The measure of hedging effectiveness E_f^* for the minimum risk hedge is defined as the proportional reduction in variance that comes from maintaining a hedged ($X_f \neq 0$) rather than unhedged position ($X_f = 0$). E_f^* reduces to the coefficient of determination for the regression of spot on futures' price changes.

$$E_f^* = \frac{\text{Var}(C_s) - \text{Var}(C_H)}{\text{Var}(C_s)} = 1 - \frac{\text{Var}(C_H)}{\text{Var}(C_s)} \tag{4}$$

$$E_f^* = \left[\frac{\text{cov}(C_s,C_f)}{SD(C_s)SD(C_f)}\right]^2 = R^2$$

The higher the correlation between spot and futures price changes the more effective is the futures contract for reducing the risk of a particular spot position. A perfect hedge (total risk reduction) is possible if E_f^* or $R^2 = 1.0$.

Studies of cross-hedging between corporate bond indices and GNMA futures contracts using this methodology have been conducted by

McEnally and Rice [4] and by Hill and Schneeweis [2]. The former study used weekly price change data and a corporate index sample of Salomon Brothers and Standard and Poor's bond indices from December 1976 to March 1977 and indicated the presence of significant risk reduction using GNMA futures. The latter work utilized both monthly (Moody's and Merrill Lynch indices) and weekly (S&P indices) price changes over the 1976-1978 period and compared effectiveness of hedges for bond indices of different rating and coupon level and for futures contracts with different numbers of months to delivery. Hill and Schneeweis found evidence of significant risk reduction with GNMA hedges that was highest for high-rated corporate or public utility bonds and for bonds with coupon rates in the 6-8% range.

III. DESCRIPTION OF DATA AND FRAMEWORK FOR ANALYSIS

The data set of futures price changes includes month-end to month-end contract value differences beginning with the end of January 1976 for the GNMA futures and with the end of August 1977 for the T-bond futures and ending with the December 1979 closing price. A total of 19 contracts are included in the GNMA sample which covers the June 1976 to December 1980 contract.[3] The first of 13 T-bond contracts is the December 1977 future. Price changes for each contract are differentiated by the number of months remaining to delivery; e.g., the May 1976 price change on the June 1976 future would be identified as one month before delivery.[4] The source of the futures price data is the daily futures price tapes made available by the Chicago Board of Trade.

The sample of corporate bond index value changes includes long-term Moody's and Merrill Lynch Taxable Bond (ML) indices. The ML indices measure the performance of groups of bonds having similar issuers (corporate vs. utility), ratings, coupon level and remaining maturities of at least 15 years; they are monitored over time to replace bonds that no longer fit the maturity and/or rating criteria. These indices are therefore comparable to actual segments of bond portfolios

---

[3] Observations on the 1981 and some 1982 futures contracts were also available but were not included because of the long period of time to delivery.

[4] The last observation in each contract is the closing price in the month prior to the delivery month. Since cross-hedges are involved here no delivery could occur; therefore, the price observation just prior to delivery was not used. The minimum and maximum number of observations per contract were 3 and 32.

having the index characteristics that would be typically held by institutional investors.[5]

Moody's indices are reported in the form of a yield that would be available on 20 year corporate bonds selling at par value. The AAA and A corporate and utility Moody's indices that are included in the sample to represent bond portfolios of relatively high and low risk. Monthly index value changes for Moody's bond yield indices are computed by assuming the purchase of a par value bond at the beginning of each month yielding that month's index and the sale of the bond at the beginning of the following month priced to yield that month's index yield. The index values assuming semiannual interest payments, are calculated using the following expression:

$$V = [(P^*r/2)(1-(1+i/2)^{-2n})/i/2] + P^*(1+i/2)^{-2n} \qquad (5)$$

where V = the selling price of the bond at the end of the month (week), P = par value of bond ($1,000) − Price of bond at beginning of month (week), i = yield at sale, r = coupon rate, and n = years to maturity.

It should be noted that these corporate bond portfolios or indices would through diversification have eliminated most individual bond default risk and would have most of their price variability resulting from movements in general interest rate levels. Since financial instrument futures are directed toward interest rate risk reduction, cross-hedging or bond portfolios would lead to a much greater relative reduction in risk than cross-hedging individual bonds.

The first part of the analysis consists of regressions of each set of ML and Moody's monthly index changes on contemporaneous GNMA and T-bond futures price changes to estimate hedging effectiveness (R^2) and minimum risk hedge ratios (HR* = B from regression). To determine if contracts defined in terms of distance to delivery exhibited different hedging effectiveness, separate regressions are run for price changes on contracts with 1-4, 5-8, 9-12, and more than 12 months remaining to delivery. The hedging effectiveness of the near-term contract, for example, would be a measure of the average reduction in spot position variance that could be realized over the sample period by continuing to maintain a futures position in the contract with 4 months or less remaining to delivery. The near term contract is hypothesized to be the most useful in hedging because it is the most liquid (has the highest open interest up to the end of the month prior to delivery).

The data set is then divided into pre-1979 and 1979 price change ob-

---

[5] The ML index values reflect the market value of the included bonds, net accrued interest paid or received, coupon income paid, and compounded reinvested coupon payments. The authors wish to thank Merrill Lynch for providing this data for research.

servations.[6] Sub-period hedging effectiveness measures and hedge ratios are analyzed to see if they are stable across periods or if the futures markets exhibit greater effectiveness in the more recent period. In addition, using hedge ratios estimated from the pre-1979 data, minimum risk hedges in near delivery futures are constructed and implemented using the 1979 data. The mean and standard deviation of price changes of these hedges during 1979 are then compared to that of unhedged positions to indicate the ex post value of hedging using minimum risk hedge ratios estimated from historical data.

IV. PRESENTATION AND ANALYSIS OF RESULTS

Tables 1, 2, and 3 contain the hedging effectiveness measures (E_f^*) and minimum risk hedge ratios (X_f^*) for the entire sample period and sub-periods for both GNMA and T-bond futures hedges of corporate bond positions. The level of E_f^* can be interpreted as the average proportion of monthly price change variance that could have been eliminated by implementing the minimum risk hedge during the sample period over *all* sample contracts with particular time to delivery characteristics. The 1976-79 results as well as subperiod results presented in Table 1, 2, 3 indicate that in all delivery periods and for all indices examined a statistically significant and sizable amount of risk can be eliminated by utilizing cross-hedges.[7] Several observations on relationships that occur consistently in the sample can be made regarding comparable hedging effectiveness.

GNMA vs T-Bond Hedges

Across all ratings, issuers, and coupon levels, T-bond future cross-hedges appear slightly more effective than those with GNMA futures.

---

[6] The 1976-78 sub-period only contains contracts through the December 1979 contract (15 contracts for GNMA and 11 for T-bonds futures).

[7] It is important to note that in this study only month-end to month-end price changes are reflected in hedging effectiveness measures. In fact hedgers must maintain margin during the month based on daily price changes and therefore face uncertainty regarding the amount of funds committed to hedging within their horizon. As shown by Ederington [1] the shorter the horizon the smaller tends to be the risk reduction. Large economic units must consider futures market liquidity for large-volume hedge initiation and termination. Although this becomes less a problem as futures markets grow in size, diversification across different delivery month contracts may be used to reduce some of the liquidity risk and exposure to technical market conditions in specific contracts.

Table 1 GNMA and T-Bond Futures Hedging Effectiveness

Index	Months to Delivery	E_f^* GNMA	E_f^* T-Bond	HR* GNMA	HR* T-Bond
Moody's					
Corporate AAA	⩽ 4	.728	.848	.930	.951
	5 to 8	.744	.871	1.002	1.103
	9 to 12	.662	.828	.870	1.037
	⩾ 13	.593	.228	.807	.216
Corporate A	⩽ 4	.431	.519	.650	.706
	5 to 8	.515	.635	.816	.922
	9 to 12	.429	.506	.670	.768
	⩾ 13	.297	.107	.502	.139
Utility AAA	⩽ 4	.705	.798	.903	.887
	5 to 8	.732	.831	.985	1.037
	9 to 12	.662	.730	.870	.980
	⩾ 13	.610	.208	.802	.200
Utility A	⩽ 4	.637	.712	1.064	1.131
	5 to 8	.644	.777	1.157	1.297
	9 to 12	.586	.708	.983	1.166
	⩾ 13	.439	.152	.778	.203
Merrill Lynch					
High Quality Corporate 6-7.99%	⩽ 4	.825	.891	1.448	1.375
	5 to 8	.841	.904	1.536	1.529
	9 to 12	.789	.873	1.436	1.470
	⩾ 13	.715	.209	1.354	.287
High Quality Corporate 8-9.99%	⩽ 4	.862	.929	1.411	1.419
	5 to 8	.884	.936	1.477	1.515
	9 to 12	.816	.892	1.338	1.468
	⩾ 13	.775	.160	1.200	.257
Medium Quality Corporate 6-7.99%	⩽ 4	.707	.741	1.185	1.067
	5 to 8	.762	.804	1.331	1.314
	9 to 12	.677	.774	1.189	1.174
	⩾ 13	.626	.260	1.076	.259

*Merrill Lynch High Quality includes ratings AAA and AA; Medium Quality includes ratings A and Baa.
All HR* are significant at confidence level of 5%.

The difference in effectiveness is usually less than a .10 proportional reduction in variance. An analysis of the sub-period results does show an increased advantage of T-bond to GNMA hedging in the more recent period. Since GNMA futures are sensitive to specific mortgage market conditions and are influenced by governmental intermediation and regulation, the T-bond futures would be expected to provide a better hedge for corporate bond positions. Before 1979, however, the T-bond market was still relatively new and had less volume than GNMA futures. Hence, T-bond futures were very likely not superior to GNMA's for hedging during this period because of their greater liquidity risk.

Time to Delivery

Contracts having less than nine months remaining to delivery were consistently the most useful in monthly cross-hedging. In the pre-1979

Table 1 (continued)

Index	Months to Delivery	E_f^* GNMA	E_f^* T-Bond	HR^* GNMA	HR^* T-Bond
Merrill Lynch					
Medium Quality	⩽ 4	.846	.895	1.403	1.421
Corporate	5 to 8	.857	.913	1.510	1.590
8-9.99%	9 to 12	.797	.865	1.333	1.482
	⩾ 13	.754	.151	1.231	.243
High Quality	⩽ 4	.745	.802	1.488	1.464
Utility	5 to 8	.801	.840	1.527	1.537
4-5.99%	9 to 12	.735	.755	1.466	1.499
	⩾ 13	.642	.327	1.427	.440
High Quality	⩽ 4	.760	.851	1.395	1.293
Utility	5 to 8	.823	.874	1.440	1.382
6-7.99%	9 to 12	.754	.826	1.395	1.383
	⩾ 13	.736	.197	1.450	.307
High Quality	⩽ 4	.739	.825	1.216	1.197
Utility	5 to 8	.806	.861	1.312	1.329
8-9.99%	9 to 12	.737	.798	1.217	1.267
	⩾ 13	.702	.175	1.118	.259
Medium Quality	⩽ 4	.727	.768	1.462	1.370
Utility	5 to 8	.798	.816	1.562	1.527
6-7.99%	9 to 12	.743	.732	1.555	1.557
	⩾ 13	.702	.197	1.483	.331
Medium Quality	⩽ 4	.639	.702	1.320	1.299
Utility	5 to 8	.735	.776	1.439	1.454
8-9.99%	9 to 12	.673	.675	1.432	1.469
	⩾ 13	.630	.160	1.315	.296
Medium Quality	⩽ 4	.560	.684	1.176	1.270
Utility	5 to 8	.659	.767	1.329	1.445
10-11.99%	9 to 12	.599	.664	1.260	1.390
	⩾ 13	.527	.167	1.111	.294

Number of observations:	GNMA	T-Bond
⩽ 4	61	36
5 to 8	61	36
8 to 12	61	61
⩾ 13	170	92

subperiod the near term contract in most cases dominates the 5-8 month contract in terms of effectiveness.[8] This relationship is reversed in the 1979 data set. One reason for the instability between these delivery periods is that capital gains on those 5-8 month contracts that are held for 6 months are treated as long-term capital gains for tax purposes. Tax considerations may have affected the pricing of these contracts and the consistency of their performance. Contracts with a year or more

---

[8] For the full time period analysis of hedge ratios across industry, coupon, and quality for the most liquid of contracts (less than 4 months) shows for both GNMA and T-bond futures significant differences between (1) 6-8% and 8-10% medium quality corporates as well as high quality public utility, (2) medium and high quality 6-8% coupon corporate, and (3) corporate and public utility 8-10% high quality and 6-8% medium quality. Results are available from the authors.

Table 2 GNMA Futures Hedging Effectiveness by Sup-period

Index	Months to Delivery	E_f^* 1976-78	1979	HR* 1976-78	1979
Moody's					
Corporate AAA	≤ 4	.719	.718	.865	.978
	5 to 8	.605	.812	.717	1.167
	9 to 12	.597	.681	.755	.950
	≥ 13	.499	.717	.696	1.009
Corporate A	≤ 4	.376	.430	.484	.722
	5 to 8	.283	.600	.432	.989
	9 to 12	.326	.427	.493	.707
	≥ 13	.253	.323	.373	.610
Utility AAA	≤ 4	.709	.681	.849	.931
	5 to 8	.633	.769	.760	1.103
	9 to 12	.627	.657	.776	.921
	≥ 13	.572	.649	.725	.930
Utility A	≤ 4	.500	.722	.750	1.289
	5 to 8	.391	.765	.667	1.417
	9 to 12	.421	.653	.700	1.137
	≥ 13	.346	.555	.578	1.027
Merrill Lynch					
High Quality	≤ 4	.845	.810	1.461	1.475
Corporate	5 to 8	.826	.850	1.458	1.636
6-7.99%	9 to 12	.760	.794	1.505	1.402
	≥ 13	.711	.784	1.436	1.474
High Quality	≤ 4	.888	.861	1.268	1.557
Corporate	5 to 8	.886	.894	1.271	1.625
8-9.99%	9 to 12	.797	.827	1.229	1.445
	≥ 13	.783	.821	1.220	1.585
Medium Quality	≤ 4	.807	.618	1.265	1.125
Corporate	5 to 8	.785	.742	1.218	1.417
6-7.99%	9 to 12	.703	.630	1.290	1.111
	≥ 13	.686	.603	1.247	1.098

*Merrill Lynch High Quality includes rating AAA and AA; Medium Quality includes ratings A and BAA.
All HR* are significant at confidence level of 5%.

remaining to delivery have the lowest hedging effectiveness in both periods and overall.[9]

Rating and Coupon Level

Hedging effectiveness is lower for corporate and utility bonds with higher levels of default risk (lower ratings). This result, apparent for

[9] The reason the effectiveness for this delivery period is so low in the entire period relative to the subperiods is because several observations of price changes quite far from delivery (more than 2 years) are included in the Table 1 results that are omitted in Table 2 and Table 3 because of the method in which sub-periods were constructed. Since the first subperiod only has through the December 1979 contract, observations on 1980 contracts in 1977 and 1978 are not included but are present in the entire data set.

Risk Reduction Potential of Financial Futures 317

Table 2 (continued)

Index	Months to Delivery	E_f^* 1976-78	1979	HR* 1976-78	1979
Merrill Lynch					
Medium Quality	≤ 4	.865	.865	1.152	1.624
Corporate	5 to 8	.872	.883	1.146	1.744
8-9.99%	9 to 12	.793	.804	1.125	1.482
	≥ 13	.761	.828	1.090	1.609
High Quality	≤ 4	.610	.860	1.402	1.570
Utility	5 to 8	.652	.889	1.357	1.662
4-5.99%	9 to 12	.549	.854	1.388	1.484
	≥ 13	.520	.828	1.269	1.582
High Quality	≤ 4	.835	.684	1.603	1.211
Utility	5 to 8	.842	.803	1.542	1.398
6-7.99%	9 to 12	.769	.729	1.568	1.232
	≥ 13	.752	.719	1.529	1.367
High Quality	≤ 4	.839	.648	1.232	1.169
Utility	5 to 8	.806	.783	1.312	1.375
8-9.99%	9 to 12	.757	.687	1.209	1.171
	≥ 13	.736	.691	1.132	1.310
Medium Quality	≤ 4	.738	.691	1.466	1.386
Utility	5 to 8	.737	.813	1.448	1.612
6-7.99%	9 to 12	.675	.755	1.425	1.536
	≥ 13	.676	.749	1.419	1.567
Medium Quality	≤ 4	.680	.578	1.276	1.245
Utility	5 to 8	.652	.752	1.227	1.510
8-9.99%	9 to 12	.598	.680	1.234	1.443
	≥ 13	.581	.670	1.137	1.447
Medium Quality	≤ 4	.522	.550	.998	1.204
Utility	5 to 8	.471	.731	.937	1.504
10-11.99%	9 to 12	.438	.650	.943	1.353
	≥ 13	.377	.640	.779	1.386

Number of observations:	1976-78	1979
≤ 4	45	15
5 to 8	45	15
9 to 12	45	15
≥ 13	99	26

both GNMA and T-bond hedges, can be explained by the fact that a greater proportion of the price volatility of higher quality bonds arises from movements in the general level of interest rates rather than changes in risk premia. As noted earlier interest rate futures are primarily used to reduce interest rate risk as opposed to default risk.

Differences in hedging potential across coupon levels can be studied using the ML indices. The 8-10% coupon level tended to have the greatest hedging effectiveness in 1979, especially for the corporate portion of the sample. In the entire sample and earlier subperiods, however, cross-hedging effectiveness was roughly equivalent in the 6-8% as well as 8-10% coupons. The greater hedging effectiveness in the 1979 period for the 8-10% coupons can be explained by the fact that T-bond and GNMA futures price changes are influenced by expectations of price

Table 3 T-Bond Futures Hedging Effectiveness by Sub-period

Index	Months to Delivery	8/1977-78	1979	8/1977-78	1979
Moody's					
Corporate AAA	≤ 4	.775	.880	.753	1.030
	5 to 8	.720	.914	.772	1.187
	9 to 12	.684	.878	.747	1.160
	≥ 13	.697	.840	.721	1.100
Corporate A	≤ 4	.310	.582	.423	.798
	5 to 8	.252	.722	.403	1.040
	9 to 12	.136	.632	.291	.925
	≥ 13	.348	.408	.447	.690
Utility AAA	≤ 4	.646	.858	.607	.994
	5 to 8	.610	.889	.644	1.136
	9 to 12	.537	.864	.555	1.137
	≥ 13	.643	.807	.616	1.044
Utility A	≤ 4	.654	.744	.850	1.244
	5 to 8	.593	.830	.839	1.415
	9 to 12	.539	.791	.775	1.345
	≥ 13	.621	.585	.847	1.062
Merrill Lynch					
High Quality	≤ 4	.849	.919	1.058	1.494
Corporate	5 to 8	.829	.933	1.094	1.642
6-7.99%	9 to 12	.734	.919	1.050	1.238
	≥ 13	.781	.873	1.009	1.566
High Quality	≤ 4	.829	.982	1.019	1.581
Corporate	5 to 8	.810	.980	1.058	1.630
8-9.99%	9 to 12	.737	.967	.962	1.679
	≥ 13	.745	.960	.978	1.725
Medium Quality	≤ 4	.760	.765	.739	1.191
Corporate	5 to 8	.742	.844	.774	1.448
6-7.99%	9 to 12	.588	.798	.746	1.344
	≥ 13	.722	.685	.726	1.179

*Merrill Lynch High Quality includes ratings AAA and AA; Medium Quality includes ratings A and BAA.

All HR* are significant at confidence level of 5%.

changes of the cheapest deliverable T-bond or GNMA. In this period the cheapest delivery bonds had coupon rates in the 8-10% range.

Type of Issuer

Consistent with earlier results [2] for GNMA futures hedges, holders of corporate and utility bond portfolios realized on average equivalent risk reduction from T-bond futures hedges in the 1976-78 period. In 1979 a change occurs in that hedging effectiveness and hedge ratios for corporate bond indices become markedly higher than for utilities of comparable rating and coupon range. Utility interest rates in 1979 were affected by the Three Mile Island nuclear accident. This and subsequent information influenced the default risk of many utility bonds and the

Table 3 (continued)

Index	Months to Delivery	8/1977-78	1979	8/1977-78	1979
Merrill Lynch					
Medium Quality	≤ 4	.736	.975	.853	1.640
Corporate	5 to 8	.739	.972	.927	1.754
8-9.99%	9 to 12	.652	.960	.795	1.741
	≥ 13	.691	.946	.856	1.730
High Quality	≤ 4	.563	.904	1.245	1.531
Utility	5 to 8	.540	.916	1.183	1.617
4-5.99%	9 to 12	.422	.868	1.074	1.608
	≤ 13	.539	.850	1.183	1.615
High Quality	≤ 4	.875	.841	1.276	1.277
Utility	5 to 8	.825	.885	1.251	1.406
6-7.99%	9 to 12	.782	.834	1.180	1.417
	≥ 13	.810	.827	1.171	1.477
High Quality	≤ 4	.846	.824	1.005	1.254
Utility	5 to 8	.793	.878	1.032	1.395
8-9.99%	9 to 12	.744	.828	.914	1.381
	≥ 13	.779	.822	.941	1.438
Medium Quality	≤ 4	.761	.767	1.228	1.389
Utility	5 to 8	.735	.831	1.325	1.561
6-7.99%	9 to 12	.687	.755	1.195	1.651
	≥ 13	.768	.781	1.230	1.611
Medium Quality	≤ 4	.786	.675	1.265	1.280
Corporate	5 to 8	.757	.776	1.298	1.471
8-9.99%	9 to 12	.693	.692	1.158	1.565
	≥ 13	.717	.719	1.214	1.509
Medium Quality	≤ 4	.741	.775	1.200	1.268
Utility	5 to 8	.690	.785	1.148	1.494
10-11.99%	9 to 12	.596	.708	1.037	1.518
	≥ 13	.638	.711	1.111	1.471

Number of observations:	1977-78	1979
≤ 4	20	15
5 to 8	20	15
9 to 12	20	15
≥ 13	27	26

effectiveness of T-bonds or GNMA futures to hedge utility interest rate movements.

Hedge Implementation Results

In Table 4 and 5 the mean change in the value of hedged (GNMA and T-bond futures) and unhedged positions in these indices during 1979 is shown. Hedge performance results are presented for strategies of maintaining both the minimum risk hedge ratio estimated from the 1976-1978 historical data for near term (≤4) contracts and for the naive hedge ratio of equal size positions in both futures and spots (HR = 1.0). In 1979 the hedged portfolios consisting of a long corporate and short

Table 4 Mean and σ of Monthly Price Changes for Hedged and Unhedged Positions During 1979 (GNMA Futures with ≤ 4 Months to Delivery)

Index	Mean Unhedged	Mean RH=1.0	Mean HR*	Standard Deviation σ Unhedged	Standard Deviation σ HR=1.0	Standard Deviation σ HR*	Proportion of σ^2 Eliminated
Moody's							
Corporate AAA	−.767	−.230	−.307	2.840	1.508	1.532	.709
Corporate A	−.949	−.411	−.688	2.708	2.156	2.125	.384
Utility AAA	−.886	−.349	−.430	2.777	1.577	1.581	.659
Utility A	−.880	−.342	−.477	3.732	2.091	2.371	.597
Merrill Lynch							
High Quality Corp							
6-7.99%	.146	.683	.931	4.034	2.112	1.759	.810
8-9.99%	.088	.625	.769	4.130	2.061	1.696	.831
Medium Quality Corp							
6-7.99%	−.068	.469	.618	3.524	2.201	2.206	.608
8-9.99%	.170	.707	.789	4.300	2.203	1.964	.791
High Quality Util							
4-5.99%	.172	.709	.925	4.169	2.098	1.613	.850
6-7.99%	−.094	.444	.768	3.605	2.092	2.243	.612
8-9.99%	−.236	.301	.425	3.574	2.160	2.126	.646
Medium Quality Util							
6-7.99%	−.401	.136	.387	4.105	2.472	2.291	.688
8-9.99%	−.643	−.105	.043	5.315	2.689	2.622	.756
10-11.99%	−.447	.091	.089	3.996	2.726	2.727	.534

Table 5 Mean and σ of Monthly Price Changes for Hedged and Unhedged Positions During 1979 (T-Bond Futures with ≤ 4 Months to Delivery)

	Mean			Standard Deviation σ			Proportion of σ^2 Eliminated
Index	Unhedged	HR=1.0	HR*	Unhedged	HR=1.0	HR*	
Moody's							
Corporate AAA	−.767	−.216	−.352	2.840	.985	1.216	.817
Corporate A	−.949	−.397	−.716	2.708	1.826	2.002	.453
Utility AAA	−.886	−.335	−.551	2.777	1.048	1.448	.728
Utility A	−.880	−.328	−.411	2.732	1.991	2.146	.382
Merrill Lynch							
High Quality Corp							
6-7.99%	.146	.698	.730	4.034	1.719	1.611	.840
8-9.99%	.088	.639	.650	4.130	1.604	1.558	.858
Medium Quality Corp							
6-7.99%	−.068	.484	.370	3.524	1.778	1.995	.679
8-9.99%	.170	.722	.641	4.300	1.788	2.146	.751
High Quality Util							
4-5.99%	.172	.724	.859	4.169	1.888	1.491	.872
6-7.99%	−.094	.458	.611	3.605	1.607	1.438	.841
8-9.99%	−.236	.316	.318	3.574	1.636	1.630	.792
Medium Quality Util							
6-7.99%	−.401	.151	.276	4.105	2.222	2.024	.757
8-9.99%	−.643	−.091	.056	5.314	2.412	2.301	.812
10-11.99%	−.447	.105	.216	3.996	2.382	2.286	.672

future position had a higher (lower) increase (decrease) in value than the unhedged. This is due to the fact that this was a period of sharp interest rate increases. The opposite effect would occur to those hedging corporate bond financing (short in corporate bonds).

Hedging performance results for 1979 imply that historical data is useful in forecasting hedging effectiveness and in estimating hedge ratios to be implemented in subsequent periods. In Tables 4 and 5 the comparisons are made between standard deviation of hedged and unhedged corporate and utility bond portfolios. The magnitude of the risk reduction follows the patterns discussed in previous sections. Risk reduction is greatest for hedges with T-bond futures and for hedging high quality, 8-10% corporate bonds. The last column indicates the realized E_f^* or average proportional reduction in variance achieved through minimum risk hedges. These values are very close to the expected reduction (E_f^*) contained in pre-1979 results (Tables 2 and 3). For example, with GNMA futures hedges on Moody's indices, estimated E_f^* levels are .719, .376, .709, and .500 and the comparable realized levels are .709, .384, .659, and .597. The ML corporates have estimated E_f^* of .849, .829, .760, and .736 with T-bond futures hedges and realized proportional variance reductions equal to .840, .858, .679, and .736. Naive hedge ratios also reduced variance but with a smaller reduction than when hedging with ratios equal to HR*.[10]

V. SUMMARY AND CONCLUDING REMARKS

Existing portfolio theory and evidence presented here demonstrates that the risk of a long or short position in corporate bonds can be significantly reduced by an offsetting position in a GNMA or T-bond future. The size of the futures position for those seeking risk-minimizing hedges is a function of the variance of and covariance between corporate bond and T-bond or GNMA futures value changes over a particular time period.

Moody's and Merrill Lynch corporate and utility bond indices are used here to measure hedging effectiveness of these markets and to estimate minimum risk hedge ratios. Results show that usually more than half and in certain cases 80-90% of the variance of value changes on corporate bond positions can be eliminated with T-bond or GNMA hedges of a month's duration at the appropriate hedge ratio. These futures markets are most effective for those seeking hedges for high-quality

---

[10] The only exception was the medium quality corporate hedge ratios. T-statistics are available from the authors upon request.

corporate bond portfolios in the 8-10% coupon range. Slightly lower levels of risk reduction are possible for hedges of sets of high-quality utility bonds or of both corporate and utility bonds in the 6-8% coupon range. Futures contracts with less than 9 months to delivery have historically provided the best hedge. An analysis of realized risk reduction in 1979 based on implementation of hedge ratios estimated from historical data reveals a close correspondence between actual and expected results and reaffirmed the comparable effectiveness analysis summarized above.

Although these empirical results establishing the value of cross-hedging for corporate bonds are very encouraging, research should be directed to the analysis of technical factors involved in implementing cross-hedging strategies. For example, the cost associated with maintaining margin balances and the uncertainty associated with the level of these balances during the hedging horizon needs to be explored. Liquidity aspects of moving in and out of the futures markets is a problem to users of these markets but has not been adequately addressed in the literature. Also of interest are the determinants of price differences among contracts delivering at different times and the advantages of diversification across delivery months. The growth of research interest, opportunities, and results in this area should keep pace with growth in trading volume and available contracts in the markets.

References

1. Ederington, Louis, "The Hedging Performance of the New Futures Market," *Journal of Finance*, (March 1979), pp. 157-170.
2. Hill, Joanne and Schneeweis, Thomas, "Risk Reduction Potential of GNMA Futures for Issuers and Holders of Corporate Bonds," presented at International Research Seminar, Chicago Board of Trade, May 1980.
3. Johnson, L. L., "The Theory of Hedging and Speculation in Commodity Futures," *Review of Economic Studies*, (1959-1960), pp. 559-66.
4. McEnally, Richard W. and Michael L. Rice, "Hedging Possibilities in the Flotation of Debt Securities," *Financial Management* (Winter 1979), 12-18.
5. Miller, Edward, "Tax-Induced Bias in Markets for Futures Contracts," *Financial Review*, (Spring 1980), pp. 35-38.
6. Markowitz, H. M., "Portfolio Selection," *Journal of Finance*, (March 1952), pp. 77-91.
7. Norgard, Richard, "Bond Indices and Optimal Portfolios," *The Financial Review*, (Fall 1978), 12-21.
8. J. L. Stein, "The Simultaneous Determination of Spot and Futures Prices," *American Economic Review*, Vol. LI, No. 5, 1961.
9. *Taxable Bond Indices*, Merrill Lynch, Pierce, Fenner and Smith, Inc., (August 1979).
10. Working, H., "Futures Trading and Hedging," *American Economic Review*, (June 1953), pp. 314-343.

20

The Error Learning Model and the Financial Futures Market*

George Emir Morgan and Charles T. Franckle

The emergence of interest rate futures contracts as viable financial instruments has spurred research in the areas of pricing and use of these contracts. A number of authors have aimed at directly testing the efficiency of the interest rate futures markets, Puglisi (1978), Vignola and Dale (1979), Capozza and Cornell (1978), and Rendleman and Carabini (1980). Some authors have explored the empirical relationship between the cash and spot markets without the motive of testing market efficiency. Ederington (1979) has reported work in which he examined the hedging performance of some financial futures against constant maturity spot instruments. He suggests that T-bill futures contracts are surprisingly ineffective in some cases, but Franckle (1980) has provided evidence that Ederington's technique has understated the effectiveness.

In this paper we will address the relationship between the spot and cash markets, but we will not focus on testing efficiency or hedging effectiveness (though, the results will have implications for hedgers which we will explore later in the paper). We suggest that before one can embark on an empirical investigation one needs a theory which links the two markets. Meiselman (1962) first expressed many of the important concepts in his formulation of the "error-learning" hypothesis. Because an explicit financial futures market did not exist in 1962, Meiselman's empirical efforts involved testing the error-learning model in the spot

*Reprinted by permission of the authors who are Assistant Professors of Finance at the University of Texas at Austin.

market with annual observations of U.S. corporate bonds using the futures prices implied therein. The newly formed futures markets provide an opportunity to directly test the error-learning hypothesis regarding the way in which forecasts of future interest rates are adjusted given the revelation of new information. Moreover, since the hypothesis is not restricted to particular maturities, the various futures contracts can be used to provide observations on a much more frequent basis than annually.

In this paper we will use the error-learning model to test the way in which forecasts are adjusted in the 91 day Treasury bill futures market. In the next section we describe the attractiveness of Meiselman's error-learning model for examining the financial futures markets and contrast Meiselman's and Ederington's model. Section II describes our methodology, and Section III reports the empirical results. Section IV summarizes our conclusions and suggests some implications of the results for hedging.

I. THE ERROR LEARNING MODEL

Meiselman's error-learning model is a behavioral formulation of how interest rate forecasts are adjusted. The formulation is based on the effects of new information that is revealed in spot markets. Given a forecast of tomorrow's short-term rate, one observes a deviation of the actual rate revealed tomorrow from the expected rate. This forecasting error is "new information," and Meiselman's hypothesis is that the forecasting error will be linearly related to the adjustment of forecasts of next week's and next month's interest rates with a declining impact as the period to which forecasts apply becomes farther in the future. Thus Meiselman's model is based on causation from the spot market to the futures markets. Although futures prices may change for many reasons, Meiselman's model suggests a systematic (error learning) component of changes in forecasts in addition to the random component.

Meiselman's linear specification of the error learning relationship is

$$_{t+d+n}FR_t - {}_{t+d+n}FR_{t-1} = b_{d+n}[{}_tR_t - {}_tFR_{t-1}] + {}_{d+n}\epsilon_t \qquad (1)$$

where FR represents futures rates with left subscript signifying the delivery date of the contract and right subscript signifying the date on which the futures rate is observed and $_tR_t$ is the 91 day spot rate observed at time t. In this paper, all futures rates (forecasts) pertain to 91 day T-bills as does the spot rate, and one period is taken to be one month. Meiselman allows for the relationship to be different the farther one is from the delivery date of the contract, and thus b is subscripted by d+n. We have designated the length of time between the initial forecast and delivery as d+n where d is the length of time until delivery on the *nearest* contract and n is the length of time between d and the delivery date for the futures contract under consideration. The reasons for introducing this complication will become apparent later in the paper.

Ederington (1979) has suggested a model that is similar in some respects to Meiselman's model but some important distinctions should be noted. First, Ederington considers the relationship between changes in spot rates and changes in futures rates, that is $_tR_t - _{t-1}R_{t-1}$ versus $_{t+d+n}FR_t - _{t+d+n}FR_{t-1}$. (Grant and Hempel (1980) take a similar approach.) Thus Ederington uses the fiction of a constant maturity T-bill for examining the relationship. Meiselman's formulation clearly indicates that a constant maturity instrument is inappropriate and that following the same instrument from t−1 to t (even though the maturity of the instrument is one period shorter at t than at t−1) is the pertinent focus. Put slightly differently, Meiselman argues that it is unexpected movements in the spot rate $_tR_t$ which is important to changes in forecasts. If $_tR_t$ is exactly equal to the expected rate, then no change will be required in other forecasts even though the spot rate at time t may be higher or lower than the spot rate at t−1. Meiselman's point is relevant in the hedging framework adopted by Ederington. One cannot hedge away *expected* changes in rates. Hedging can reduce the risk that the realized rate will be different from what had been expected (i.e., risk is variation about the mean not the fact that the mean is higher or lower in one period relative to another), but hedging cannot be used to reduce the costs resulting from expected movements. Of course, one can bet against the market expectation by taking unhedged positions, but that is not the focus of Ederington's tests.

Another difference between Ederington and Meiselman is the choice of independent and dependent variables. Meiselman specifies futures changes as the dependent variable as a result of the behavioral causation behind his error-learning model. Ederington's specification is based on consideration of a given dollar spot position which an investor wants to hedge. Thus Ederington uses spot changes as the dependent variable and futures changes as the independent variable. That is, the analog to equation (1) using Ederington's specification would be

$$_tR_t - _tFR_{t-1} = C_{d+n}(_{t+d+n}FR_t - _{t+d+n}FR_{t-1}) + _{t+d+n}\eta_t. \qquad (2)$$

We prefer Meiselman's formulation because its grounding in behavioral assumptions seems a more reliable representation of the underlying process generating price movements.

Although we adopt Meiselman's formulation, we do not adopt it without alteration. Meiselman used changes on forecasts of *yields* and realized *yields* in his tests, but we will use changes of forecasts of (futures) *prices* and realized *prices*. This seems more appropriate for two reasons: 1) as Carleton and Cooper (1977) have noted, traders are more directly concerned with the price of the security being traded because profits arise from the difference between buying and selling prices not yields and more importantly, 2) the Meiselman hypothesis is stated in terms of linear adjustment which is more likely to be a representation of adjustments to forecasted prices rather than yields. The use of yields may create specification errors in linear regressions because the relationship between prices and yields is non-linear. (The bankers discount on T-bills is linearly related to price.) Meiselman did not use bond price data because of its unavailability. For the T-bill futures market and the T-bill spot market, prices are readily available, and we employ them.

II. METHODOLOGY

Our tests of the error-learning model in the 91 day T-bill futures market will use one month ahead forecasts of spot rates to calculate the forecast errors. Ideally, we would use futures prices to generate those forecasts, but there are only four dates each year on which futures are deliverable. Thus to obtain observations on monthly forecast errors, we calculated the implied forecast of 91 day T-bills from the one month T-bill price and the four month T-bill price.[1] We observe these prices every two weeks. The actual forecast error is used as the independent variable in a regression against one month changes in futures prices.

The altered Meiselman regressions we estimate are

$$_{t+d+n}F_t - {}_{t+d+n}F_t = a_{d+n} + b_{d+n} ({}_tP_t - {}_tf_{t-1}) + {}_{d+n}\eta_t \qquad (3)$$

where F is a futures price, ${}_tP_t$ is the realized price of a 91 day T-bill on date t, and ${}_tf_{t-1}$ is the implied forward price forecast made at time t−1 for 91 day bills on date t. In Meiselman's empirical work, the distance to delivery, d+n was important, i.e., $b_{d+n} \neq b_{d+k}$ for n≠k. Therefore the regressions must be estimated separately for each value of d+n. The estimation process is somewhat simplified by the institutional setting. Futures contracts traded on 91 day T-bills have delivery dates set by the International Monetary Market at March, June, September, and

---

[1] The expectations hypothesis is employed as a good description of one month ahead forward pricing. Evidence of liquidity premium has been found (eg. Van Horne [1965]) in longer term forward rates. Our empirical tests allow for tests of the suitability of the expectations hypothesis in the short term.

December. Therefore the largest value d, distance to nearest delivery date, can take is 2 months. For example, the change in a futures price and the forecast error $(_tP_t - {_tf_{t-1}})$ for the third week in December to the third week in January is approximately 2 months from the next delivery date in the third week of March. Also this change is 5½ months from the June delivery date, 9 months from the September delivery date, etc. In this case, d + n = 2, 5½, 9, 12½, ... or d = 2 and n = 3½, 7, 10½, ... months. Also it can be noted that the price change from the third week in March to the third week in April is 2 months from the delivery of the nearest contract (the June contract) and is 5½, 9, 12½, ... months from delivery of each of the other delivery dates. Thus data observations for the third weeks of December-January, March-April, June-July, September-November are used in regressions where d + n = 2, 5½ months, and so on. We call this set of regressions the d = 2 regressions. There are a total of 5 possible sets of regressions where d = 0, ½, 1, 1½, and 2 months.[2] For example, the first weeks of February-March, May-June, August-September, and November-December are the d = ½ set of regressions. Within each of the sets of regressions approximately 8 regression coefficients are estimated corresponding to the eight contracts outstanding at any time. Within each set, the same independent variable is used for all eight regressions. It should be noted that this data segmentation is entirely due to the institutional structure and the ease of data file manipulation.

Based on Meiselman's findings, we expect to find that the regression coefficients, b_{d+n}, will decline as the delivery date gets farther away, i.e., as d+n gets larger, both within the sets of regressions and across the six sets. In other words, we expect that the impact of current events on forecasts (as reflected in the forecast error) will be smaller the more distant is the forecast period. Similarly, we expect to find (as Meiselman did) that the proportion of the variance of futures price changes explained by current events will also decline with increasing distance to delivery. The R^2 of the regression equation (3) will measure the explanatory power.

We have included the constant term, a_{d+n}, in equation (3) even though it does not appear in equation (1). Meiselman pointed out the possibility that the constant term could be non-zero if a liquidity premium existed in forward rates.[3] Also if our use of an implied forward rate in the independent variable and explicit futures prices in the dependent variable introduces some biases (e.g. due to differential forecasting

---

[2] More precisely, the values of d are 0, 2, 4, 7, and 9 weeks. We use the term "month" to refer to a 4 week period, approximately. There is the opportunity to obtain data for d = 11 weeks. See footnote 8.

[3] Wood (1963) has noted that a constant term of zero is not evidence against the liquidity premium hypothesis.

power), then the constant term would be non-zero. That is directly testable, and we expect to find a constant term of zero as did Meiselman.[4] Ederington's theory presumes a zero constant term since a non-zero constant term would imply an excess return (cost) to using the futures market to hedge. Ederington does not report estimates of constant terms so it is difficult to compare studies; however, if Ederington's model (2) with η independent of futures changes) represented the true underlying generating mechanism, then estimation using Meiselman's model would result in a non-zero constant term.

We obtained settlement prices for T-bill futures contracts from the *Wall Street Journal* for the period of January 1976 to September 1980. Prices were observed for Wednesdays on a bi-weekly basis.

Similarly, the spot prices (bids) for four week, thirteen week, and seventeen week Treasury bills were collected for every other Wednesday from the *Wall Street Journal*. Franckle (1981) has demonstrated the importance of using actual spot quotations for the same dates as the futures prices instead of using daily averages over the week as are available in the *Federal Reserve Bulletin*. Over the time period chosen, there are approximately 18 data points for each of the 37 regressions, and the period spans episodes of rapidly rising as well as rapidly falling interest rates, an expansionary period as well as a recession.

III. EMPIRICAL RESULTS

Table 1 presents the coefficient estimates, standard errors, R^2, and Durbin-Watson statistic for each of the regression equations (3) ordered by d+n. In four cases out of 37, the constant term is significantly different from zero and in 3 of these cases the regressions use the near futures contract as dependent variable, i.e., d+n = d or n = 0. This suggests the existence of a liquidity premium or cost of hedging risk of between three and six basis points per month on the near contracts.[5] Otherwise,

---

[4] Holland (1965) purports to examine the error learning model in the T-bill market and to find very low R^2 and b but does not actually test Meiselman's model. Instead, Holland has used

$$\frac{(1 + {}_tR_t^M \times 100)}{(1 + {}_tR_t^N \times 100)} = X_t$$

(where ${}_tR_t^M$ is the spot rate on an M period bill, M>N) in place of the forward rate, f_t, and runs regressions of the form

$$X_{t+3} - X_{t+2} = a + \beta (X_{t+3} - {}_tR_t) + E_t.$$

Of course, Meiselman's model is unrelated to the difference between current spot rates, ${}_tR_t$, and "forecasts" to be made three periods in the future, X_{t+3}.

[5] It is more likely that the significant constant term results because the forecast power of implied prices is weak in the near term where bid-ask spreads are widest. For all spot data, we have used bid prices only and this may introduce some spurious bias.

the constant terms are insignificant for all other regressions supporting the unbiased expectations hypothesis and our use of implied forward prices to forecast.

On the other hand, the b_{d+n} and R^2_{d+n} present a confusing picture. It does not appear that they decline monotonely as d+n increases although the values of b_{d+n} and R^2_{d+n} for large values of d+n are generally lower than for small values of d+n. In only two cases are the slope coefficients (the "error learning coefficients") not significantly different from zero. Even the coefficients for futures contracts 22 months from delivery are significantly affected by Meiselman's forecast error. There are many cases where the error learning coefficient is not significantly less than one. The insignificant difference from one usually occurs for low values of d+n, though there are some b_{d+n} which are indistinguishable from one for large d+n.

In Figure 1 we have graphed the error learning coefficients[6] as a function of d+n and connected the points which share the same value of d, the distance to the nearest delivery date. Figure 1 brings order to the chaos of Table 1. We observe for fixed d that (with only two exceptions) the Meiselman error learning coefficients decline monotonely as n gets large. The regularity of the decline of b_{d+n} and the striking order such that the lines almost never cross are readily apparent even to the casual observer. Moreover, there appears to be a pattern in the location of the various functions. With the exception of the d = ½ month coefficients, as d gets larger the error learning coefficient also gets larger! That is, the farther away the date of delivery on the *nearest* contract (regardless of whether that nearest contract is the futures contract employed in the regression), the greater the impact of spot "fundamentals" on futures prices. We also observe that coefficients which are not significantly different from one generally occur for values for d+n which are less than 7 months. In the case of d = 2, the coefficient is significantly higher than one for periods which are 2 months and 5½ months from the nearest delivery date.

The implication of these observations for hedging are important. As the hedger gets closer to the delivery date on the nearest contract, the number of spot instruments which a single futures contract will hedge gets larger. At a distance of 2 months, a single futures contract will perform in a manner to hedge fewer than one spot T-bill. Whichever futures contract is employed in the hedge, as time passes a larger number of spot instruments can be hedged with the single futures contract.

The greater sensitivity of futures prices to unexpected spot movements as the nearest delivery date is farther away necessitates that any investigation of hedging effectiveness or market efficiency disaggregate

---

[6] In Figure 1 the coefficients have been estimated with regressions forced through the origin since the constant was insignificantly different from zero.

Table 1 Error Learning Regression Results

d+n	Constant	b_{d+n}	R^2_{d+n}	Durbin-Watson
½	−.29* (.011)	1.101*+ (.047)	.969	1.27
1	−.054* (.023)	.923* (.080)	.886	1.58
1½	−.032 (.041)	.794* (.133)	.689	.68
2	−.043* (.020)	1.327* (.139)	.851	2.72
3	−.021 (.014)	.701*+ (.098)	.762	1.29
3½	−.018 (.011)	1.023* (.104)	.851	1.79
4	−.072 (.038)	.851* (.133)	.707	1.58
5	−.060 (.041)	.790* (.134)	.684	.78
5½	−.043 (.022)	1.387*+ (.154)	.835	2.62
6½	−.002 (.014)	.574*+ (.096)	.692	1.83
7	−.025 (.033)	.954* (.144)	.719	1.96
7½	−.083 (.044)	.739* (.155)	.573	1.52
8½	−.046 (.035)	.740* (.112)	.730	.89
9	−.026 (.023)	1.253* (.161)	.791	2.45
10	.009 (.017)	.410*+ (.119)	.424	1.83
10½	−.028 (.038)	.847* (.169)	.598	1.95
11	−.082 (.045)	.661*+ (.158)	.507	1.34
11½	−.042 (.029)	.692*+ (.095)	.769	1.43
12	−.009 (.026)	1.102* (.179)	.703	2.47

the data into groups based on distance to nearest delivery date. While the coefficients in the d = 0, d = 1, and d = 1½ groups may not be significantly different from each other,[7] the d = 2 coefficients appear to be different from the three lower groups. That is, the sample with the highest error learning coefficient is always the sample based on changes in futures prices from the third weeks of December to January, March to April, June to July, and September to November.

[7] It seems unlikely that the differences between the coefficients in these groups is due to purely random influence when the orderliness of the patterns is so strong.

Table 1 (continued)

d+n	Constant	b_{d+n}	R^2_{d+n}	Durbin-Watson
13	.009	.294*+	.304	2.51
	(.017)	(.115)		
13½	−.004	.714*	.564	1.97
	(.037)	(.157)		
14	−.071	.604+	.485	1.28
	(.045)	(.156)		
15	−.045*	.644*+	.879	2.37
	(.021)	(.064)		
15½	−.008	.951*	.609	2.73
	(.029)	(.197)		
16½	.008	.254+	.207	2.51
	(.019)	(.133)		
17	−.002	.598*	.504	1.88
	(.039)	(.159)		
17½	−.054	.523*+	.398	1.17
	(.050)	(.166)		
18½	−.034	.589*+	.926	2.28
	(.018)	(.050)		
19	.010	.718*	.511	2.10
	(.034)	(.212)		
20	.008	.246+	.188	2.46
	(.024)	(.154)		
20½	.004	.602*+	.636	1.76
	(.037)	(.137)		
21	−.099	.486*+	.430	1.05
	(.057)	(.169)		
22	−.026	.554*+	.914	2.64
	(.018)	(.051)		
22½	.016	.625*	.453	2.14
	(.033)	(.207)		
23	.011	.207+	.132	2.46
	(.025)	(.159)		
23½	−.003	.562*+	.614	1.58
	(.036)	(.134)		
24	−.100	.430*+	.365	1.01
	(.058)	(.171)		

*Significantly different from zero at the 5% level.
+Significantly different from one at the 5% level.

We cannot state unequivocally that the value of d is significant since the d = ½ regressions do not fit the pattern and because we have no statistical test to check our hypothesis. On the other hand, the pattern is apparent for 4 of the 5 sets of regressions and thus we believe that, at the very least, future investigators need to exercise care with respect to the value of d.

To further examine the influence of d we have plotted the R^2_{d+n} in a similar fashion in Figure 2. As a general rule, R^2 decreases as d+n increases for a fixed value of d. The major exception to the rule is the behavior of R^2_{d+n} for d = 1½; however, we attribute the odd behavior to

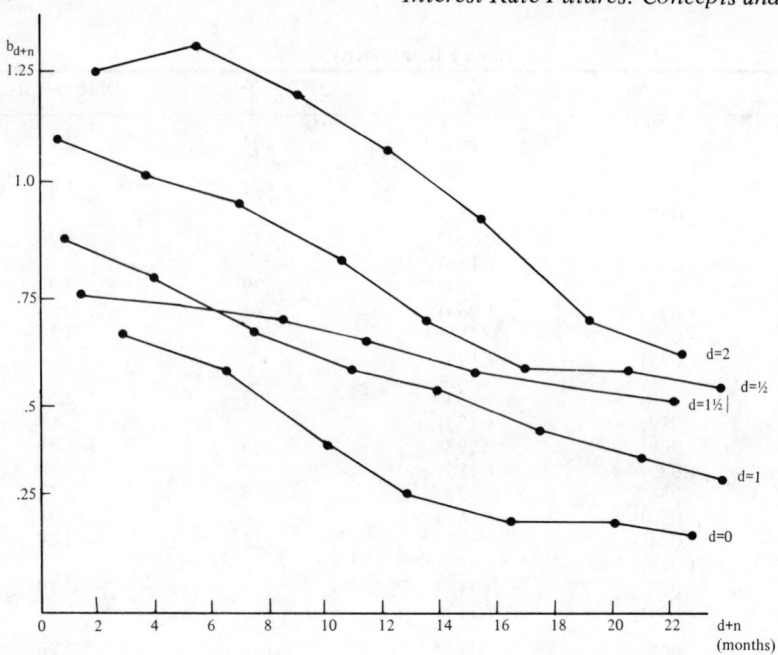

Figure 1 b_{d+n} for regressions of unexpected changes in spot prices against futures price changes for various futures contracts grouped by distance to delivery on nearest contract.

the positive autocorrelation as exhibited by the low Durbin-Watson statistics. Over all the regressions, the Durbin-Watson were frequently above the upper cut-off point and in the first three regressions for d = 1½ the D-W were below the lower critical value. In those three cases, therefore, the R^2_{d+n} values are unreliable even though the regression coefficient estimates are unbiased.

The pattern with respect to d does not appear as strong for R^2_{d+n} as for b_{d+n}; however, there is still some pattern visible, for example, by comparing d = 0 to d = 1 to d = 2, comparing d = ½, to d = 1½, and over the intermediate range comparing d = ½ to d = 2. In those cases it again appears that as d gets larger, the R^2 gets larger. That is, as the delivery date on the nearest contract gets closer, the explanatory power of the spot forecast error becomes smaller and other factors become more important in affecting futures prices. The results do not show conclusively that lower d means lower explanatory power since some of the data is not consistent with this theory (e.g., compare d = 0 with d = ½), but the results lend strong support to the hypothesis that not only is the maturity date of the futures contract important, but also the number of months to delivery on the *nearest* contract is important. The results do suggest that the farther away one is from the delivery date on

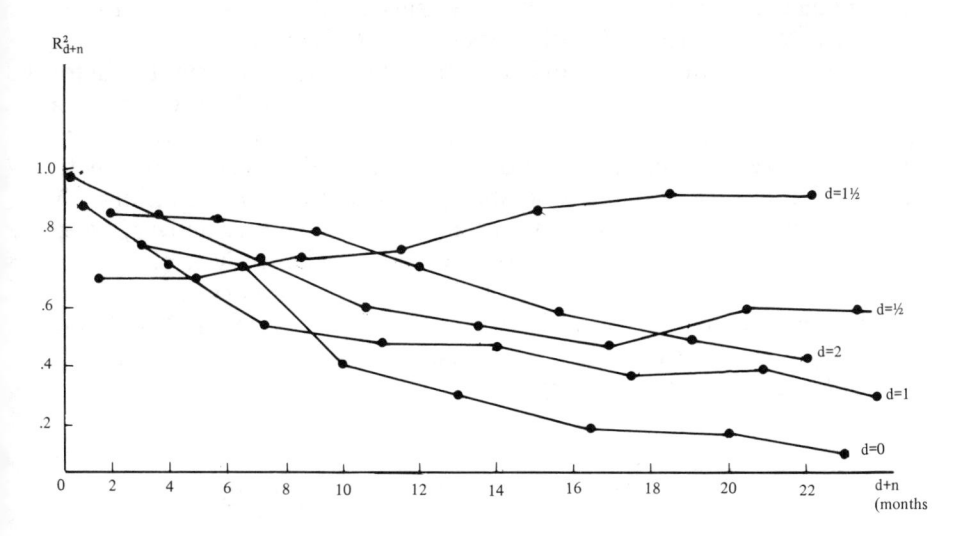

Figure 2 R^2 of regressions of unexpected changes in spot prices against futures price changes for various futures contracts grouped by distance to delivery on nearest contract.

the *nearest* contract, the larger the impact of unexpected spot changes is on futures prices *regardless* of the delivery date of the futures contract in question. Put another way, in the month immediately prior to delivery of a contract, *all* contracts are less sensitive to and have a lower correlation with the Meiselman forecast error.[8,9]

These results are surprising and seem inconsistent with Meiselman's work, but it must be noted that Meiselman could not explore this phenomenon. In some ways, our results are consistent with Rendleman and Carabini's (1979) conclusions that the closer one moves to delivery the greater the annualized excess profit opportunities. We cannot find

---

[8] We also ran regressions for "d = 2½" months but since the observations of price changes included a price for ½ month before delivery of the last contract and a price for ½ month after last delivery, the R^2 were extremely low and coefficients were erratic as well as insignificant. This further substantiates the importance of d since the "d = 2½" regressions were a mixture of the closest and farthest away observations resulting in what appeared to be statistical garbage.

[9] We also ran the regressions on spot and futures prices generated on Fridays in addition to the Wednesday results in order to determine if there was any effect on the day of the week as a result of factors such as the end of the Federal Reserve settlement week. Friday's coefficients closely paralleled Wednesday's coefficients and were always lower than Wednesday's coefficients with only 4 exceptions out of the 37 regressions! This reaffirms that the closer one is to delivery on the nearest contract, the lower the coefficient. The R^2 results for Friday's were similar to the Wednesday results but Friday R^2 were not always below Wednesday's.

a convincing explanation of the surprising results, except that the R^2 do seem to be consistent with market lore. It is frequently asserted by market participants that as delivery months arrive fundamental factors become less important and less informative in pricing futures contracts because of pressure from participants with open positions who do not want to take or make delivery on the contract. Thus, the unexpected spot price change explains a smaller proportion of the variation in futures prices on the nearest contract, i.e., R^2 is smaller as delivery weeks approach. Although this explanation directly applies only to the nearest contract, evidence of strong correlation across futures contracts found by Franckle and McCabe (1979) and Grant and Hempel (1980) indicates that such pressure in the nearest month is generally transmitted to contracts with later delivery.

IV. SUMMARY AND CONCLUSIONS

We have tested Meiselman's error learning model in the explicit futures market for financial instruments. Meiselman used the futures market implicit in the spot market for his original tests because he did not have the opportunity to perform tests in an explicit market. We have verified that the expectations adjustment process delineated by Meiselman does have empirical content in the explicit futures market similar to that which Meiselman found in the spot (implicit) market in 1962.

An important difference between our results and Meiselman's results is the significance for all contracts of the distance (0, ½, 1, 1½, or 2 months) from the delivery date of the *nearest* contract. The farther the current date is from the next delivery date, the larger is the impact of forecast errors and the higher the explanatory power of the forecast errors. Those results suggest that previous research on the efficiency and hedging effectiveness of the T-bill futures market has not correctly specified all of the relevant variables. They have mixed together heterogeneous observations making their results difficult to interpret. The significant difference between the month after a delivery month and other months of the year suggests that any studies of the efficiency or hedging effectiveness of the T-bill futures markets must account for the distance to delivery on the nearest contract. (For a recent example, Grant and Hempel (1980) pool together the samples after noting the potential biases this might induce.) Otherwise, the data are drawn from different regimes and are not from the same generating mechanism. No previous study of financial futures has separated the observations by the distance from delivery on the nearest contract.

Although our tests are not intended to thoroughly explore the question of the efficiency of the T-bill futures markets, the market appears to be efficient in the sense that the results are consistent with Meiselman's work but appears to have some inefficiency in the sense that the proximity to delivery of the nearest contract increases the influence of factors other than the underlying fundamentals in the spot market.

We have not designed or intended our tests of the error learning model, by themselves, to measure hedging effectiveness of T-bill futures. Nonetheless, there are two implications for hedgers that can be drawn from both the expected and unexpected empirical results. First, the use of "strips" or other nonconsecutive combinations of futures contracts to hedge a spot instrument appears to have some potential because the reduction of R^2 over the first few contracts is not very large. Benefits from diversifying across contracts could be obtained with little loss in correlation between the two sides of the hedge. Since the error learning coefficients give the relative proportions of futures to spot, the coefficients can be used to guide in setting up combinations of contracts to hedge spot instruments of different maturities. An investigation of the properties of such combinations is a subject for future research.

Second and more important, the hedge ratio is a function of the month. Contracts behave differently relative to the spot market in January, April, July, and October than in March, June, September and December. As time passes the optimal hedge ratio changes necessitating restructuring of the hedge perhaps as frequently as bi-weekly. For a hedge period of long duration, say two years, the changing optimal hedge ratio has two components. As time passes, both d and n change. Decreasing n implies fewer spot instruments relative to futures, but a decrease in d implies an increase in the number of spot instruments relative to futures. Examination of the empirical content of these implications has the potential for interesting future research efforts.

References

Capozza, D. R. and B. Cornell (1979), "Treasury Bill Pricing in Spot and Futures Markets," *Review of Economics and Statistics*, November, 1979.

Ederington, Louis (1979), "The Hedging Performance of the New Futures Markets," *Journal of Finance*, March 1979.

Franckle, Charles (1980), "The Hedging Performance of the New Futures Markets: Comment," *Journal of Finance*, December.

Franckle, Charles and George McCabe (1979), "The Effectiveness of Rolling the Hedge Forward in the Interest Rate Futures Market," University of Texas at Austin, Graduate School of Business Working Paper Series, No. 80-10.

Grant, Dwight and George Hempel (1980), "Bank Portfolio Management: The Role of Financial Futures," Southern Methodist University, Working Paper 90-900.

Holland, Thomas (1965), "A Note on the Traditional Theory of the Term Structure of Interest Rates on Three- and Six-Month Treasury Bills," *International Economic Review*, September.

Puglisi, Donald (1978), "Is the Futures Market for Treasury Bills Efficient?" *Journal of Portfolio Management*, Winter, 1978.

Rendleman, Richard and Chris Carabini (1979), "The Efficiency of the Treasury Bill Futures Market," *Journal of Finance*, September 1979.

Van Horne, James (1965), "Interest Rate Risk and the Term Structure of Interest Rates," *Journal of Political Economy*, October.

Vignola, Anthony and Charles Dale (1979), "Is the Futures Market for Treasury Bills Efficient?" *Journal of Portfolio Management*, Winter, 1979.

Wood, John (1963), "Expectations, Errors, and the Term Structure of Interest Rates," *Journal of Political Economy*, April.

21

Improving Hedging Performance Using Interest Rate Futures*

Robert W. Kolb and
Raymond Chiang[†]

ABSTRACT

The recent advent of interest rate futures markets greatly enriches the hedging opportunities of market participants faced with high interest rate risk. Today, with extremely volatile yields affecting bankers, investors, corporations, and underwriters to a much greater extent than before, efficient hedging techniques are crucial.

We develop a hedging strategy that matches the price sensitivity of the bond to be hedged with the correspondingly sensitive position in the future market. Only in the most coincidental circumstances will the two techniques suggest the same commitment size in the futures market as in the spot market. We illustrate the hedging effectiveness of the price sensitivity strategy by calculating gains and losses for several possible strategies drawn from the hedging literature.

Effective hedging of interest rate risk depends on four key factors:
1. The maturity of the hedged and hedging instrument;
2. The coupon structure of the hedged and hedging instruments;
3. The varying risk structure of interest rates; and
4. The changes in the term structure of interest rates.

*Reprinted from *Financial Management*, Autumn, 1981, pp. 72-79. Reprinted by permission of the publisher and authors.

[†]The authors would like to thank the Center for Econometrics and Decision Science at the University of Florida for its financial support.

Many practical guides to hedging interest rate risk utilize examples in which equal face value amounts of the hedged and hedging instrument are employed [1, 5, 6, 10, 13]. For a hedger seeking to minimize interest rate risk, this is almost always incorrect. The only time it is correct is when all four of the factors mentioned above are perfectly matched.[1] Under any other circumstances a better hedge can be devised.[2]

In the past, when interest rates have fluctuated relatively little, naive approaches to hedging interest rate risk have served relatively well. Today, with extremely volatile interest rates affecting bankers, investors, corporations, and underwriters to a much greater extent than ever before, the development of more efficient hedging techniques has become crucial. Furthermore, the recent development of interest rate futures markets with standardized contracts has enriched the hedging opportunities of all market participants and lowered the cost of hedging. This paper formulates more efficient hedging rules in and illustrates their application and usefulness.

MORE EFFICIENT HEDGING TECHNIQUES

Upon entering the futures market to hedge some interest rate risk, the hedger knows the maturity and coupon structure of the hedged and hedging instruments. He does not know the changes in the risk and term structure of interest rates that will occur while the hedge is in effect. (If he could know the future course of interest rates, the prospective hedger would not hedge anyway. He would simply alter his portfolio to profit from the rate changes that were about to occur.)

Because these two elements are unknown when the hedge is initiated, it is impossible to guarantee in advance that the hedge will be perfect. (A perfect hedge is one that leaves the hedger's wealth unchanged.) If changes in the term and risk structure are assumed known, it is possible to derive a hedge ratio that protects against interest rate risk caused by a mismatch of maturity and coupon between the hedged and hedging instrument.

All hedging strategies make some implicit assumption about the kinds of interest rate changes that will occur, and any hedging rule implies beliefs about the future course of interest rates. In the derivation of our hedge ratio, we explicitly assume that the yield curve remains

---

[1] When these four factors match perfectly, the hedged and hedging instruments will respond in the same way to interest rate changes (factors 1 and 2), and they will experience the same changes in their risk and term structures (factors 3 and 4). The conceptual background is common to the bond immunization literature. See [2].

[2] See [5] and [14] for another approach to developing more efficient hedging strategies. The "portfolio approach" attempts to minimize the variance of the value of the entire hedge over its life; [14] also develops an approach similar in spirit to ours.

that for the life of the hedge. (Throughout the paper we ignore the difference between the yield to maturity and the expected return, which is tantamount to assume that both instruments have zero default risk.) We make this assumption for several reasons. First, it helps to make the mathematics tractable. Second, a flat yield curve is a convenient approximation to the more realistic case of a yield curve that has "shape," but that maintains the same shape, changing only its level.

The basic strategy revolves around choosing some number of units (N) of futures contract j to hedge one unit of asset i with the goal that, over the life of the hedge:

$$\Delta P_i + \Delta P_j (N) = 0. \qquad (1)$$

where P_i and P_j are, respectively, the values of the bond to be hedged and the futures contract. Clearly, for any given interest rate shock the size of ΔP_i and ΔP_j depends on the sensitivity of i and j to a change in interest rates. Our problem, then, is to choose the number of futures contracts to trade (N) to balance out the different interest rate sensitivities of i and j, and thereby to preserve the truth of Equation (1). (Note that the technique hedges against a single interest rate shock.) As the equation implies, the perfect hedge we wish to find is the hedge that makes wealth invariant to a change in interest rates.

One important and useful measure of a financial asset sensitivity to interest rates is its duration (D), which we may define as:

$$D_k = \frac{\sum_{t=1}^{K} \frac{tC_{kt}}{(R_k)^t}}{\sum_{t=1}^{K} \frac{C_{tk}}{(R_k)^t}}. \qquad (2)$$

where C_{kt} = the tth period cash flow from asset k; $R_k = 1 + r_k$; r_k = yield to maturity on k; and k = term to maturity.

This is the duration measure as developed by Macaulay. For an exposition of the concept, see [14]; [9] gives an account of duration's development.

In Equation (2) the denominator is simply the price of asset k. The numerator is the present value of a single cash flow (C_{kt}) multiplied by (t), the number of periods until the payment is received. The result, duration, is the negative of the asset's price elasticity with respect to a change in the discount factor (R_k).

We show in Appendix A that, to hedge one unit of asset i with financial futures contract j, one should trade N units of j, where N is given by:

$$N = \frac{-\bar{R}_j P_i D_i}{\bar{R}_i F P_j D_j}. \qquad (3)$$

where $R_F = 1 +$ the risk-free rate; $\bar{R}_j = 1 +$ the rate expected to obtain on the asset *underlying* future contract j; $\bar{R}_i = 1 +$ the expected yield to maturity on asset i; $FP_j =$ the price agreed upon in the futures contract j to be paid upon maturity of the futures contract for title to the asset *underlying* j; $P_i =$ the price of asset i expected to prevail on the planned termination date of the hedge; $D_i =$ the duration of asset i expected to prevail on the planned termination date of the hedge; and $D_j =$ the duration of the asset *underlying* futures contract j expected to prevail on the planned termination date of the hedge.

THE TREASURY BILL FUTURES CONTRACT

Treasury bill futures contracts call for the delivery of \$1,000,000 face value of 90-day Treasury bills upon maturity of the futures contract. Consequently, for every Treasury bill hedge $D_j = \frac{1}{4}$ year. Prices of Treasury bill futures are quoted according to the IMM Index, which is simply 100–bank discount rate. (See [10] for an exposition of the IMM Index.) This is not a true yield and requires conversion to $\bar{R}_j$. For example, if the IMM Index is 87.47, the bank discount rate is 12.53% which is equivalent to a true yield of 13.576%, or an $\bar{R}_j = 1.13576$. This means that:

$$FP_j = \frac{\$1{,}000{,}000}{(\bar{R}_j)^{0.25}}. \tag{4}$$

For a hedge with a Treasury bill futures contract N is given by the simpler expression:[3]

$$N = \frac{-4(\bar{R}_j)^{1.25} P_i D_i}{\bar{R}_i (\$1{,}000{,}000)} \tag{5}$$

The values needed to calculate N in Equation (5) are easily determined with the *Wall Street Journal*.

THE TREASURY BOND FUTURES CONTRACT

The Treasury bond futures hedge is slightly more complicated because of the fact that Treasury bonds have coupons. Treasury bond futures contracts call for the delivery of \$100,000 face value of 8% coupon

---

[3] Note that N is calculated to hedge the position as of some one moment in time—the planned termination date of the hedge. $\bar{R}_i$ and $\bar{R}_j$ are the rates expected at that time, and the P_i and D_i are the price and duration expected to prevail at that time, given $\bar{R}_i$.

Treasury bonds having a maturity of at least 15 years, or at least 15 years to their first call date. Bonds with a coupon other than 8% may be delivered in fulfillment of the futures contract subject to an adjustment. Long maturity bonds having an 8% coupon may be delivered against the futures contract with no adjustment. Generally, it is cheapest to deliver the longest maturity lowest coupon Treasury bond against the future contract.

From discussions with representatives of the Chicago Board of Trade, it appears that the market is well aware of this fact. For the most recent month on record the bonds delivered were all of maturity in excess of 21 years. The *Wall Street Journal* reports implicit yields assuming a 20-year 8% coupon bond. However, the futures market must be pricing the actual bond that is to be delivered if it is efficient. Currently, the longest-maturity lowest-coupon bonds mature between 2005-2010 and have a coupon of 10%. However, to be consistent with the values reported in the *Wall Street Journal*, we assume an 8% 20-year bond for delivery against the futures contract.

In the *Wall Street Journal*, Treasury bond futures prices are quoted in "points and 32^{nd}s of par." A futures price of 71-24 means that the price is 71 24/32% of par. Since for the whole contract par = $100,000, a futures price quoted as 71 24/32 would correspond to an FP_j = $71,750 (71 24/32% × $100,000 = $71,750). Because Treasury bonds have coupons, D_j varies with $\bar{R}_j$. Exhibit A provides a table of D_j and $\bar{R}_j$ for selected bonds with prices between 60-00 and 100-00 assuming a 20-year maturity and an 8% coupon. The values in Exhibit A make it easy to calculate N for the Treasury bond futures hedge with Equation (3).

HOW TO APPLY THE HEDGING RULES

To illustrate the hedging rules developed, consider a portfolio manager who learns on March 1 that he will receive $5 million dollars to invest on June 1 in AAA corporate bonds with a coupon rate of 5% and a maturity of 10 years. The manager finds current AAA yields attractive, and he wishes to lock in that rate for his June 1 investment by trading in the futures market now. There are two possibilities. In the first case, rates on the hedged and hedging instruments change by the same amount, while in the second, they change by different amounts. For the two alternatives we can examine the hedging actions and outcomes for the naive strategy (face value dollar for face value dollar) and the method developed earlier, which we call the price-sensitivity (PS) strategy.

CASE 1

Assume the following rates obtain:[4]

	Treasury Bill Futures	Treasury Bond Futures	AAA
March 1	8.00%	8.50%	9.50%
June 1	7.58	8.08	9.08

As of March 1, when the hedge is initiated, the price expected to hold June 1 for the AAA bond must be $717.45 ($P_i$), given the current rate of 9.5%. Its duration (D_i) on June 1 will be 7.709 years. We can now calculate the hedge-ratio (N) for hedging with Treasury bill futures from Equation (5) above:

$$N = \frac{-4(1.08)^{1.25}(-\$717.45)(7.709)}{(1.095)(\$1,000,000)} = 0.022244. \qquad (6)$$

This means that 0.022244 Treasury bill futures contracts should be traded for each bond. As the manager knows he will have $5 million to invest, expecting the price of the bond to be $717.45 on June 1, he is planning to buy 6,969.1268 bonds ($5,000,000/$717.45). Consequently, he should buy 155.0213 Treasury bill futures contracts[5] (6,969.1268 × 0.022244).

Given the interest rate changes shown above, the price of the bond on June 1, is $739.08, not the expected $717.45. For the manager buying the bonds on June 1, this represents an opportunity loss of $21.63 on each bond, and $150,742.21 on the entire position. Let us now compare the hedging effectiveness of the two strategies: the naive vs. the PS.

According to the naive strategy, one will trade one dollar of face value in the futures market per dollar of bonds. The naive hedge is to buy five Treasury bill futures contracts, whereas the PS strategy recommends 155.0213 contracts. When the rates dropped from 8.00 to 7.58%, this generates a gain on a futures contract of $956.02.

$$\frac{\$1,000,000}{(1.0758)^{0.25}} - \frac{\$1,000,000}{(1.08)^{0.25}} = \$956.02.$$

---

[4] Numerically these Treasury bond yields are the same as those used in an example of a perfect hedge in [7], page 8. However, we assume that the rates are the true rates, corresponding to the $\bar{R}_j$ and the $\bar{R}_i$. Compare our results with that of the CBT example.

[5] The cost of a Treasury bill futures contract is negligible. It takes $60 in transaction costs and a margin of $1,000 for daily resettlement for one contract ($1 million in denomination). In our example, we assume interest rates change at the end of the hedge period. With interest rates changing frequently in the real world, the manager will need a small amount of cash for daily resettlement and rebalancing will be necessary.

For the naive strategy the total gain in the futures market is $4,780.10, while for the PS strategy it is $148,203.46. The following table depicts the results:

Bond Market	Treasury Bill Futures Market	
	Naive Strategy	PS Strategy
Opportunity Loss	+$4,780.10	+$148,203.46
−$150,742.21		
ERROR	−$145,962.11	−$2,538.75

The PS strategy is not perfect, losing $2,539, because of the fact that the change in rates was discrete. The error from the naive strategy is 57.5 times the error from the PS strategy.

Part of the explanation for this difference in the performance of the two strategies stems from the short maturity and absence of coupons of Treasury bills. The naive strategy should be closer in dollar amount to the performance of the PS strategy using Treasury bond futures, for Treasury bonds more closely match the maturity and coupon structure of the bond being hedged. To hedge with Treasury bond futures, the correct hedge ratio is given by Equation (3):

$$N = \frac{-(1.085)(-\$717.45)(7.709)}{(1.095)(\$96,875)(10.143)} = 0.005577.$$

To implement the hedge with Treasury bond futures, we will trade 38.8667 (0.005577 × 6,969.1268) contracts according to the PS strategy, and 50 contracts according to the naive strategy (the Treasury bond future contract is for $100,000 face value of bonds).

From Exhibit A one observes that a drop in rates from 8.5 to 8.08% causes the futures price to rise from $96,875 to $100,750, for a gain of $3,875 per contract. For the two strategies this gives the following hedging results:

	Treasury Bond Futures Market	
	Naive Strategy	PS Strategy
Opportunity Loss	$193,750.00	+$150,608.46
−$150,742.21		
ERROR	$43,007.79	−$133.75

In this case, the error of the naive strategy is 411.5 times that of the PS strategy, but the dollar difference between the two is smaller, as the price sensitivity of Treasury bonds is closer to that of the bond being hedged than is the case with Treasury bills. The PS strategy is almost perfect, hedging 99.91% of the $150,742.21 opportunity loss in the bond market.

CASE 2

This case allows the rates to change by different amounts from the same original starting point. Assume now that the following rates obtain:

	Treasury Bill Futures	Treasury Bond Futures	AAA
March 1	8.00%	8.50%	9.50%
June 1	7.58	8.08	9.25

As long as the starting rates are all the same, the hedge ratios will all be the same as above. For the futures, the rates conform to the previous example, but the yield change for the bonds has been decreased. With a rate of 9.25% the price of the bond will be $730.24 on June 1. For the bond position the total opportunity losses is $89,135.13 (6,969.9268 × $12.79). For the Treasury bill hedge the new results are:

Bond Market	Treasury Bill Futures Market	
Opportunity Loss	Naive Strategy	PS Strategy
−$89,135.13	+4,780.10	+$148,203.46
ERROR	−$84,335.03	+$59,068.33

For the Treasury bond hedge the result would be:

Bond Market	Treasury Bond Futures Market	
Opportunity Loss	Naive Strategy	PS Strategy
−$89,135.13	+$205,779.50	+$150,608.46
ERROR	+$116,664.37	+$61,473.33

In both cases, the PS strategy gives a smaller error. If rates change by different amounts on the hedged and hedging instruments, it is possible for the naive strategy to outperform the PS strategy, but that would occur only by infrequent coincidence. This possibility notwithstanding, the naive hedger subjects himself to considerable risk that the hedger following the PS strategy can avoid.

SOME FINAL HINTS

The PS strategy presented here provides a rational procedure for hedging interest rate risk by trading in the Treasury bill and Treasury bond futures market. The method takes account of differences between the maturity and coupon structures of the hedged and hedging instruments. With a flat yield curve and an infinitesimal change in interest rates, the PS strategy results in a perfect hedge. In the real world one cannot expect the PS strategy to provide a perfect hedge, for rates change constantly by discrete amounts, and the term structure is not flat. Yet the method we develop can be expected to improve hedging performance in actual trading.

To apply the PS strategy, it is better to use a futures instrument with a maturity and coupon structure matching that of the bond to be hedged. (That is why the error was smaller with the Treasury bond hedge.) The method can also be applied to bond portfolios by simply using portfolio values, durations, and interest rates. Finally, as rates vary over time, the hedging performance can be improved by periodic rebalancing of the hedge. The PS strategy is designed to hedge against a single interest rate shock. Hedging performance can be improved by periodic recalculation of N and by adjusting the hedge accordingly. The frequency of rebalancing depends upon the size of the position, transactions costs of changing the hedge, and the anticipated volatility of interest rates.

References

1. P. Bacon and R. Williams, "Interest Rate Futures: New Tool for the Financial Manager," *Financial Management* (Spring 1976), pp. 32-38.
2. G. Bierwag, G. Kaufman, and C. Khang, "Duration and Bond Portfolio Analysis: An Overview," *Journal of Financial and Quantitative Analysis* (November 1978), pp. 671-682.
3. J. Cox, J. Ingersoll, and S. Ross, "A Re-Examination of Traditional Hypotheses about the Term Structure of Interest Rates," University of Chicago Working Paper (November 1980).
4. J. Cox, J. Ingersoll, and S. Ross, "A Theory of the Term Structure of Interest Rates," University of Chicago Working Paper (August 1978).
5. L. Ederington, "The Hedging Performance of the New Futures Market," *Journal of Finance* (March 1979), pp. 157-170.
6. W. Feller, *An Introduction to Probability Theory and Its Applications*, Volume II, New York, John Wiley & Sons, 1971.
7. Chicago Board of Trade, "Hedging Interest Rate Risks," Chicago, 1977.
8. J. Ingersoll, J. Skelton, and R. Weil, "Duration Forty Years Later," *Journal of Financial and Quantitative Analysis* (November 1978), pp. 627-650.
9. Chicago Board of Trade, "An Introduction to the Interest Rate Futures Market," Chicago, 1978.
10. E. Kane, "Market Incompleteness and Divergences between Forward and Futures Interest Rates," *Journal of Finance* (May 1980), pp. 221-234.
11. R. Kolb and R. Chiang, "Duration, Immunization, and Hedging with Interest Rate Futures," *Journal of Financial Research* (forthcoming).
12. A. Loosigian, *Interest Rate Futures*, Princeton, N.J., Dow Jones Books, 1980.
13. R. McEnally, "Duration as a Practical Tool for Bond Management," *Journal of Portfolio Management* (Summer 1977), pp. 53-57.
14. R. McEnally and M. Rice, "Hedging Possibilities in the Flotation of Debt Securities," *Financial Management* (Winter 1979), pp. 12-18.
15. International Monetary Market, "Treasury Bill Futures," Chicago, 1977.

APPENDIX A

This appendix shows the derivation of the hedge ratios used. Assume:

1. That the yield curves are flat for each instrument, so that all future payments associated with an instrument are appropriately discounted at a single rate—the instruments' yield to maturity; and
2. That cash flows occur on a futures contract immediately upon a change in its value, which corresponds to the current institutional arrangement of daily resettlement.

Notation:

Instrument i is to be hedged by financial futures contract j, where: P_i, P_j = the value of instruments i and j, respectively; C_{it}, C_{jt} = the tth period cash flows for instrument i and for the financial asset underlying financial futures contract j, respectively; FP_j = the price specified for the delivery of the instrument in futures contract j; D_i, D_j = Macaulay's duration measure for instrument i and the asset underlying financial futures contract j, respectively; R_F = 1 + the risk-free rate; $\tilde{R}_i$, $\bar{R}_i$ = 1 + the yield to maturity on i and the expected value of $\tilde{R}_i$, respectively; $\tilde{R}_j$, $\bar{R}_j$ = 1 + the yield to maturity on the asset underlying financial futures contract j expected to obtain at the planned termination date of the hedge, and the expected value of $\tilde{R}_j$, respectively; R_j^* = the yield to maturity implied by FP_j for the instrument underlying financial futures contract j; N = the hedge ratio to be derived—the number of futures contracts j to trade to hedge a one-unit position in asset i; and I, J = the term to maturity of asset i and the term to maturity of the financial asset underlying futures contract j.

The goal of the hedge is to insure, insofar as possible, that as of the planned termination date of the hedge:

$$\Delta P_i + (\Delta P_j) N = 0. \tag{A.1}$$

To find N we must solve the equation:

$$\frac{dP_i}{dR_F} + \frac{dP_j}{dR_F} N = 0. \tag{A.2}$$

As i is a bond, its price is given at any time by:

$$P_i = \sum_{t=1}^{I} \frac{C_{it}}{(R_i^*)^t} \tag{A.3}$$

Improving Hedging Performance Using Interest Rate Futures 349

At any time the value of the futures contract is given by (ignoring the problem of Jensen's Inequality):

$$P_j = \sum_{t=1}^{J} \frac{C_{jt}}{(\bar{R}_j)^t} - \sum_{t=1}^{J} \frac{C_{jt}}{(R_j^*)^t}. \qquad (A.4)$$

Equation (A.4) has an important economic interpretation. When one purchases a futures contract, he agrees to pay the futures price, FP_j, at the maturity of the futures contract, in exchange for the series of flows C_{jt}. Consequently, it must be the case that:

$$FP_j = \sum_{t=1}^{J} \frac{C_{jt}}{(R_j^*)^t}. \qquad (A.5)$$

It is reasonable to agree to pay FP_j only if one believes, at the time of entering the futures contract, that $\bar{R}_j = R_j^*$. Otherwise one of the parties to the futures contract expects a loss. Consequently, at the time of entering the futures contract, $P_j = 0$ for Equation (A.4). Later, during the life of the futures contract, it may be that $\bar{R}_j \neq R_j^*$, and then $P_j \neq 0$.

Substituting (A.3) and (A.4) into (A.2) gives:

$$\frac{d \sum_{t=1}^{I} \frac{C_{it}}{(\bar{R}_i)^t}}{d \bar{R}_i} \frac{d \bar{R}_i}{d R_F} + \frac{d \left[\sum_{t=1}^{J} \frac{C_{jt}}{(\bar{R}_j)^t} - \sum_{t=1}^{J} \frac{C_{jt}}{(R_j^*)^t} \right]}{d \bar{R}_j} \frac{d \bar{R}_j}{d R_F} N = 0, \qquad (A.6)$$

from which we derive:

$$\frac{1}{\bar{R}_i} \sum_{t=1}^{I} \frac{-tC_{it}}{(\bar{R}_i)^t} \frac{d\bar{R}_i}{dR_F} + \frac{N}{\bar{R}_j} \sum_{t=1}^{J} \frac{-tC_{jt}}{(\bar{R}_j)^t} \frac{d\bar{R}_j}{dR_F} = 0 \qquad (A.7)$$

Solving for N, we find

$$N = - \frac{\bar{R}_j}{\bar{R}_i} \frac{\sum_{t=1}^{I} \frac{tC_{it}}{(\bar{R}_i)^t} \frac{d\bar{R}_i}{dR_F}}{\sum_{t=1}^{J} \frac{tC_{jt}}{(\bar{R}_j)^t} \frac{d\bar{R}_j}{dR_F}} \qquad (A.8)$$

Equation (A.8) is a general expression for N applying to any bond i and any futures contract j. Recall Macaulay's duration measure, D, is:

$$D_i = \frac{\sum_{t=1}^{I} \frac{tC_{it}}{(\bar{R}_i)^t}}{\sum_{t=1}^{I} \frac{C_{it}}{(\bar{R}_i)^t}}.\qquad (A.9)$$

Substituting (A.3) and (A.9) into (A.8) gives:

$$N = \frac{-R_j P_i D_i \dfrac{d\bar{R}_i}{dR_F}}{\bar{R}_i FP_j D_j \dfrac{d\bar{R}_j}{dR_F}} \qquad (A.10)$$

Note that, in Equation (A.10), P_i, D_i, FP_j, and D_j are all evaluated as of the planned termination date of the hedge. Because we have assumed that the yield curve is flat, they are the prices and durations that will obtain at current rates.

Assuming $d\bar{R}_i/dR_F$ and $d\bar{R}_j/dR_F$ can be estimated, those estimates should be included in the computation of N for improved hedging performance. For illustrative purposes, we assume $d\bar{R}_i/dR_F = d\bar{R}_j/dR_F$, so Equation (A.10) becomes:

$$N = \frac{-\bar{R}_j P_i D_i}{\bar{R}_i FP_j D_j}, \qquad (A.11)$$

and Equation (A.11) is used for the computation of N throughout the paper.

Exhibit A presents prices, discount rates, and durations for a wide variety of Treasury bonds assuming 20 years to maturity and an 8% coupon paid semiannually. These values of R_j and D_j may be used in Equation (3) from the text for the calculation of the proper hedge-ratio N. Prices are presented in "points and 32nds of par" to correspond to the *Wall Street Journal* listings. To calculate N, the prices of this exhibit must be converted to FP_j. For bonds with prices not in the exhibit, one may simply interpolate.

Exhibit A: Prices, Yields, and Durations for a 20-year 8% Treasury Bond

60- 0	1.1449	7.746
60- 8	1.1443	7.768
60-16	1.1437	7.789
60-24	1.1431	7.810
61- 0	1.1425	7.831
61- 8	1.1419	7.853
61-16	1.1413	7.874
61-24	1.1407	7.894
62- 0	1.1401	7.916
62- 8	1.1395	7.937
62-16	1.1390	7.957
62-24	1.1384	7.977
63- 0	1.1378	7.998
63- 8	1.1373	8.018
63-16	1.1367	8.039
63-24	1.1361	8.060
64- 0	1.1356	8.079
64- 8	1.1351	8.099
64-16	1.1345	8.120
64-24	1.1340	8.139
65- 0	1.1334	8.159
65- 8	1.1329	8.179
65-16	1.1324	8.199
65-24	1.1318	8.219
66- 0	1.1313	8.238
66- 8	1.1306	8.256
66-16	1.1303	8.277
66-24	1.1298	8.296
67- 0	1.1293	8.315
67- 8	1.1288	8.334
67-16	1.1283	8.353
67-24	1.1278	8.372
68- 0	1.1273	8.391
68- 8	1.1268	8.410
68-16	1.1263	8.428
68-24	1.1258	8.447
69- 0	1.1253	8.466
69- 8	1.1248	8.484
69-16	1.1244	8.502
69-24	1.1239	8.521
70- 0	1.1234	8.539
70- 8	1.1229	8.558
70-16	1.1225	8.576
70-24	1.1220	8.594
71- 0	1.1216	8.611
71- 8	1.1211	8.629
71-16	1.1207	8.647
71-24	1.1202	8.665
72- 0	1.1197	8.683
72- 8	1.1193	8.700
72-16	1.1189	8.718
72-24	1.1184	8.735
73- 0	1.1180	8.753
73- 8	1.1175	8.770
73-16	1.1171	8.787
73-24	1.1167	8.804

Exhibit A: (continued)

74- 0	1.1163	8.821
74- 8	1.1158	8.839
74-16	1.1154	8.856
74-24	1.1150	8.873
75- 0	1.1145	8.890
75- 8	1.1141	8.906
75-16	1.1137	8.923
75-24	1.1133	8.939
76- 0	1.1129	8.956
76- 8	1.1125	8.972
76-16	1.1121	8.989
76-24	1.1117	9.006
77- 0	1.1113	9.022
77- 8	1.1109	9.038
77-16	1.1105	9.054
77-24	1.1101	9.070
78- 0	1.1097	9.087
78- 8	1.1093	9.102
78-16	1.1089	9.119
78-24	1.1085	9.134
79- 0	1.1082	9.150
79- 8	1.1078	9.166
79-16	1.1074	9.181
79-24	1.1070	9.187
80- 0	1.1066	9.213
80- 8	1.1063	9.228
80-16	1.1059	9.244
80-24	1.1055	9.259
81- 0	1.1051	9.275
81- 8	1.1048	9.290
81-16	1.1044	9.305
81-24	1.1041	9.320
82- 0	1.1037	9.335
82- 8	1.1033	9.350
82-16	1.1030	9.365
82-24	1.1026	9.380
83- 0	1.1023	9.395
83- 8	1.1019	9.410
83-16	1.1016	9.425
83-24	1.1012	9.439
84- 0	1.1009	9.454
84- 8	1.1005	9.469
84-16	1.1002	9.484
84-24	1.0998	9.498
85- 0	1.0995	9.512
85- 8	1.0991	9.527
85-16	1.0988	9.542
85-24	1.0985	9.556
86- 0	1.0981	9.570
86- 8	1.0978	9.584
86-16	1.0975	9.598
86-24	1.0972	9.612
87- 0	1.0963	9.627
87- 8	1.0965	9.640
87-16	1.0962	9.655

Exhibit A: (continued)

87-24	1.0959	9.668
88- 0	1.0955	9.682
88- 8	1.0952	9.696
88-16	1.0949	9.709
88-24	1.0946	9.723
89- 0	1.0942	9.737
89- 8	1.0939	9.751
89-16	1.0936	9.764
89-24	1.0933	9.778
90- 0	1.0930	9.791
90- 8	1.0927	9.804
90-16	1.0924	9.818
90-24	1.0921	9.832
91- 0	1.0918	9.844
91- 8	1.0915	9.858
91-16	1.0912	9.871
91-24	1.0909	9.884
92- 0	1.0906	9.897
92- 8	1.0903	9.910
92-16	1.0900	9.923
92-24	1.0897	9.936
93- 0	1.0984	9.949
93- 8	1.0891	9.962
93-16	1.0888	9.975
93-24	1.0885	9.987
94- 0	1.0882	10.000
94- 8	1.0879	10.013
94-16	1.0876	10.026
94-24	1.0873	10.038
95- 0	1.0871	10.051
95- 8	1.0868	10.063
95-16	1.0865	10.075
95-24	1.0862	10.088
96- 0	1.0859	10.100
96- 8	1.0856	10.113
96-16	1.0854	10.125
96-24	1.0851	10.137
97- 0	1.0848	10.149
97- 8	1.0845	10.162
97-16	1.0843	10.174
97-24	1.0840	10.186
98- 0	1.0837	10.198
98- 8	1.0835	10.210
98-16	1.0832	10.222
98-24	1.0829	10.234
99- 0	1.0826	10.246
99- 8	1.0824	10.257
99-16	1.0821	10.269
100- 0	1.0816	10.292
100- 8	1.0813	10.304
100-16	1.0811	10.316
100-24	1.0808	10.327

22

Duration, Immunization, and Hedging with Interest Rate Futures

Robert W. Kolb
Raymond Chiang*

INTRODUCTION

The recent advent of interest rate futures markets has greatly enriched the hedging opportunities of market participants faced with undesired interest rate risk. The variety of futures contracts presently spans a number of instruments with different risk, maturity, and coupon characteristics. One may find futures contracts on treasury bills, notes, and bonds, GNMA pass-through certificates, and commercial paper, and even more variety in the contracts may be anticipated for the future.[1]

Yet in spite of the diversity of instruments, it is clear that not every hedger wishes to hedge an instrument with exactly the same characteristics as one of the instruments for which a futures contract exists. This lack of correspondence between the risk, maturity, and coupon of the hedged and hedging instruments is often dismissed or avoided in discussions of practical hedging techniques.[2] On other occasions, when the problem is treated, the difficulty is handled on an *ad hoc* basis, with no

---

*The authors would like to thank the Center for Econometrics and Decision Science at the University of Florida for its financial support.
[1] Currently both the International Monetary Market of the Chicago Mercantile Exchange and the Chicago Board of Trade are seeking permission to trade futures contracts on bank CDs.
[2] Illustrations of this can be found in Bacon and Williams (1976) and CBT (1977).

obvious rationale.[3] For example, a hedger may wish to hedge a risky long-term coupon bond, but no futures contracts exist on instruments of that type. Consequently, the optimal hedge cannot be simply dollar for dollar of face value, since the price response of each instrument to interest rate changes depends on risk, maturity, and coupon. This paper develops an analytical solution to problems of this type that exploits the concept of duration as applied to financial futures contracts.

Many properties of duration as an immunization technique have been summarized by Bierwag, Kaufman, and Khang (1978) and Ingersoll, Skelton, and Weil (1978). However, their analyses can apply only to nonzero price assets, but futures contracts have zero prices.[4] Consequently, their durations are undefined, and the previously developed hedging techniques cannot be applied to these instruments. We develop strategies (which correspond to the traditional duration immunization methods) to hedge interest rate and flotation risk using futures contracts. In Section II, we present a survey of the literature, together with a definition of our problem. The principle of immunization and the concept of duration are used to derive the strategies for hedging business operations risk under three specific interest rate patterns in Section III. Section IV provides a summary of our results and the implications for practical hedging.

SURVEY OF LITERATURE AND DEFINITION OF PROBLEMS

Since the late 1930s when Macaulay and Hicks first developed the concept of duration, a rich and growing literature has emerged. Subsequently, duration has become an important tool in controlling the maturity structure of bond portfolios. Further, it has found extensions to such uses as capital budgeting and profitability analysis (Durand 1974), portfolio management evaluation (Tito and Wagner 1977), and has even been embedded within a CAPM framework (Lanstein and Sharpe 1978). Perhaps the greatest interest has focused on the use of duration in various "immunization" strategies—the attempt to eliminate interest rate risk by matching the duration of two sides of a position.[5] The elimina-

---

[3] See, for example, CBT (1981), pp. 46-7.

[4] Futures contracts have zero price in the following sense. The "futures price" that is quoted in the financial press is the price to be paid at the time of delivery for title to the deliverable asset underlying the futures contract. But the futures contract does not have a price itself since it costs nothing (except for a small commission fee and margin requirements) to enter it.

[5] There are two fundamentally different approaches to immunization. For a portfolio to be held over time to the end of some planning period, the duration of the portfolio can be manipulated so that the duration equals the time remaining in the planning period. Then, the realized

tion of interest rate risk is attainable under highly restrictive assumptions regarding the permissible pattern of the yield curve or the stochastic process underlying the interest rate movements. Often, each kind of permissible rate shift requires its own specialized measurement of duration. Ingersoll, Skelton, and Weil (1978), and Bierwag, Kaufman, and Khang (1978) have provided outstanding surveys of the properties, usefulness, and limitations of duration. A significant breakthrough in this area has been made by Cox, Ingersoll, and Ross (1979). They established an alternative measure of duration with its own immunization procedure that allows consideration of multiple shocks that can change the shape as well as the location of the yield curve. Though all these immunization techniques cover a wide range of stochastic processes underlying interest rate movements, they apply to positive price assets only. Bacon and Williams (1976) illustrated several hedging strategies with GNMA futures when the interest rate is known to rise or fall. Of course, if the direction of interest rate movement is known, immunization will be suboptimal.

Immunization strategies can be applied only when one controls two sides of a position. When one controls the asset and liability portfolios of a bank or other corporation, one may attempt to immunize the firm from interest rate risk by equating the duration of the asset and liability portfolios (Grove 1974). Likewise, when one has a planning period in view, one may attempt to immunize the portfolio held over this period against interest rate risk (the chance of realized yield falling below the promised yield) by equating the duration of the portfolio with the planning period (Kaufman 1978). In both cases the immunization attempt depends critically on the measure of duration, since the choice of the measure of duration must correspond to the form of the anticipated interest rate shock.

We extend the concepts of duration and immunization to a new use—to form hedges using interest rate futures to offset the price risk of interest sensitive assets.[6] As mentioned before, duration cannot be applied directly to instruments having zero price. Consequently, Section III develops a modified concept of duration applicable to futures contracts, and uses this to develop more sophisticated hedging strategies.

---

return will be no less than the promised return (Kaufman, 1978). Alternatively, one can immunize by a balance sheet approach. When the duration of the assets equals that of the liabilities, both will change in value by equal amounts, leaving the value of the equity unchanged (Grove, 1974). Both approaches make certain assumptions about the kinds of interest rate changes that will occur.

[6] Getting rid of price risk is similar to the avoidance of interest rate risk. Both are minimization of risk arising from interest rate fluctuations. The only difference lies in the objective functions. It just so happens that duration is useful in both cases.

DURATION AND HEDGING WITH FUTURES CONTRACTS

When Macaulay first developed the concept,[7] he defined duration as:

$$D = \sum_{t=1}^{n} t \left[\frac{\frac{C_t}{R^t}}{\sum_{t=1}^{n} \frac{C_t}{R^t}} \right] \quad (1)$$

where C_t = payment received at t, r = yield to maturity, R = 1 + r, and n = time to maturity.

The denominator for the bracketed expression is simply the price of the security, while the entire bracketed expression gives the proportion of the net present value of the security that is returned to the owner at time t. Duration, then is a weighted average, where the weights are the times at which the cash flows are received, and the average is across proportions of net present value. Duration is basically an elasticity measure, with the negative of duration equaling the price elasticity of the instrument with respect to a change in the discount rate, i.e.,

$$-D = \frac{\frac{dP}{P}}{\frac{dR}{R}} \quad (2)$$

where P represents the price of bond. As apparent from both (1) and (2)[8] the ability to calculate the duration of an asset requires that its price be non-zero. However, futures contracts have no price. As a result, the duration concept of hedging cannot be applied directly to hedging with futures.

Let us form a portfolio q with one unit of asset i and N units of j. Then $P^q = P^i + P^j N$, where P^k denotes the price of the kth asset. For the portfolio to be free of interest rate risk, it requires:

$$\frac{dP^q}{dR} = \frac{dP^i}{dR} + N \frac{dP^j}{dR} = 0 \quad (3)$$

or

$$N = - \frac{\frac{dP^i}{dR}}{\frac{dP^j}{dR}}$$

---

[7] Notice that Macaulay's duration measure implicity assumes a flat term structure. This is reflected in (1) by the discounting of all cash flows at the common rate R.

Duration, Immunization, and Hedging with Interest Rate Futures

In other words, the ratio of price sensitivities of both assets with respect to interest rates determines the hedge factor N. The price sensitivity of an asset is just

$$\frac{dP^k}{dR} = \frac{-1}{R} \sum_{t=1}^{n} \frac{tC_t^k}{R^t} \tag{4}$$

where k denotes the particular asset involved. Note that the expression in equation (4) does not include price. Consequently, it can be used in immunization techniques even if the hedging asset has a zero price (such as a futures instrument).

In the particular case of i and j both being bonds[9] (and therefore having positive prices):

$$N = -\frac{P^i D^i}{P^j D^j} \tag{5}$$

Equation (3) gives the general solution for N, but (5) does not, since duration is not defined for every instrument. For hedging this is particularly crucial. Since financial futures contracts have zero price, (except between resettlements) their duration is undefined.

Let us apply the modified concept of immunization just developed to hedge interest rate risk[10] with futures contracts[11] under three specific regimes: (1) the hedged instrument is risk-free and the term structure is flat; (2) the hedged instrument is risk-free, but the long spot rate is linear in the short spot rate; and (3) the asset is risky, with a flat term structure.

---

[8] $\dfrac{dP}{dR} = -\dfrac{1}{R} \sum_{t=1}^{n} \dfrac{tC_t}{R^t}$

$\therefore \dfrac{dP}{dR} \cdot \dfrac{R}{P} = -D$

[9] $N = -\dfrac{dP^i}{dR} \Big/ \dfrac{dP^j}{dR}$

For $P^i, P^j > 0$, then

$N = -\left(\dfrac{dP^i}{dR} \dfrac{R}{P^i}\right) P^i \Big/ \left(\dfrac{dP^j}{dR} \dfrac{R}{P^j}\right) P^j$

$= -\dfrac{D^i P^i}{D^j P^j}$

[10] For a general equilibrium model in bond pricing see Cox, Ingersoll and Ross (1980).

[11] We have ignored the potential bias from the tax treatment of the implicit interest receipts on the T-bill. For the importance of taxes in the interest rate futures market see Kane (1980), and Cornell (1981).

Regime (1) Riskless Hedged Asset, Flat Yield Curve

Let V be the value of a futures contract, hence

$$V = E\left[\Sigma \frac{C_t}{\tilde{R}^t} - \Sigma \frac{C_t}{R^{*t}}\right] \quad (6)$$

where $\tilde{R}$ is the random interest rate to prevail in the future, and R^* is the contractual yield implied by the futures contract. Since the range of $\tilde{R}$ is small, we will ignore the problem of Jensen's Inequality.[12] Because we have stipulated that the term structure is flat (i.e., the expected rate, $\bar{R}$, is the same as the spot rate),

$$V \approx \Sigma \frac{C_t}{\bar{R}^t} - \Sigma \frac{C_t}{R^{*t}} \quad (7)$$

To see how to lay down the hedge, consider i as a bond maturing in m periods and j as a T-bill futures contact, with denomination F^j. The value of the portfolio will be

$$P^q = P^i + \left[\frac{F^j}{\bar{R}} - \frac{F^j}{R^*}\right] N \quad (8)$$

Our immunization conditions, as in (3), becomes:

$$\frac{dP^q}{dR} = \frac{dP^i}{dR} + \frac{d\left(\frac{F^j}{\bar{R}} - \frac{F^j}{R^*}\right)}{dR} N = 0 \quad (9)$$

and[13]

$$N = -P^i D^i \frac{\bar{R}}{F^j} \quad (10)$$

Equations (5) and (10) are similar in spirit, but for a T-bill futures hedge the correct value of N is given by (10), since the T-bill futures contract has no duration. The last term on the right-hand side of equation (10) ($\bar{R}/F^j$) represents the reciprocal of the sensitivity of the T-bill futures contract to the interest rate. As in equation (3), the hedge ratio is just a ratio of price sensitivities to interest rates.

Now consider hedging the flotation risk of bond i with a T-bill fu-

---

[12] I.e., $E(1/\tilde{R}) \neq 1/\bar{R}$. See W. Feller (1971), pp. 153-154.

[13] Note

$$\frac{dP^i}{dR} = -\frac{P^i D^i}{R}$$

and

$$\frac{d\left[\frac{F^j}{\bar{R}} - \frac{F^j}{R^*}\right]}{dR} = -\frac{F^j}{\bar{R}^2}$$

Duration, Immunization, and Hedging with Interest Rate Futures

tures contract j, where i is to be issued in one period, with maturity n (maturing at n + 1). In essence this is equivalent to hedging bond i' with futures contract j, where i' has the following cash flows:

$$C_1^{i'} = 0, C_{t+1}^{i'} = C_t^i, \text{ for all } t \geq 1.$$

Then

$$P^{i'} = \sum_{t=1}^{n+1} \frac{C_t^{i'}}{R^t} = \frac{P^i}{R} \qquad (11)$$

Consequently,

$$N = -P^{i'} D^{i'} \frac{\bar{R}}{F^j} \qquad (12)$$

Next we offer an analysis of hedging bond i with a T-bond futures contract j. For portfolio q composed of bond i and T-bond futures contract j:

$$P^q = P^i + \left[\sum \frac{C_t^j}{\bar{R}^t} - \sum \frac{C_t^j}{R^{*t}} \right] N$$

and

$$\frac{dP^q}{dR} = -\sum \frac{tC_t^i}{R^{t+1}} - \sum \frac{tC_t^j}{R^{t+1}} N \qquad (13)$$

since $R = R^* = \bar{R}$ in this regime.

$$\therefore N = -\frac{\sum \frac{tC_t^i}{R^t}}{\sum \frac{tC_t^j}{R^t}} = -\frac{D^i P^i}{\sum \frac{tC_t^j}{R^t}}$$

where C_t^j is the tth period cash flow of the instrument deliverable on the futures contract.

Since, at the time the futures contract is undertaken to initiate the hedge, $R = R^*$, the futures price FP_j is given by:

$$FP_j = \sum \frac{C_t^j}{R^t}$$

and letting D_{F_j} = the duration of the deliverable instrument underlying the futures contract, then

$$N = -\frac{D^i P^i}{D_{F_j} FP_j} \qquad (14)$$

Again, the denominator of equation (13) or (14) is simply the measure of the sensitivity of T-bond futures' value to the interest rate. In the particular case where $C_t^j = 0$ for all $t > 1$, then j is just a T-bill futures contract and equation (13) or (14) becomes equation (10). If we are issuing bond i a period later and intend to immunize the flotation risk, the hedge ratio can be obtained by just replacing D^i and P^i with $D^{i'}$ and $P^{i'}$ as defined by equation (11).

Regime (2) Riskless Assets, and the Long Spot Rate is Linear in the Short Spot Rate

Having delineated the solution to the hedging problem with a flat term structure, we relax that restrictive assumption and now allow a term structure in which the long spot rates are linear functions of the one period spot rate, i.e.,

$$R_{k,t} = a_k + b_k R_{1,t} \qquad a_1 = 0, b_1 = 1, b_k \geq 1, \text{ for all } k \geq 2 \qquad (15)$$

where $R_{k,t}$ equals one plus the k period spot rate in effect at t. In the particular case where b_k is equal to one for all k, (15) becomes

$$R_{k,t} = a_k + R_{1,t}$$

Then any change in the short rate will lead to an equal change in the long rates, i.e., we have parallel shifts in the yield curves. If in addition to b_k equal to 1 for all k, the "a_k" terms are proportional to time,[14] the yield curve would be linear. Without placing any restrictions on the a_k and b_k terms, we allow the shape of the yield curve to be more general than linear.

Given the yield structure follows relationship (15) the hedge ratio for hedging a bond i (with n periods to maturity) with a T-bill futures contract j is[15]

$$N = - \sum_{\tau=1}^{n} \frac{\tau C_\tau^i b_\tau}{R_{\tau,t}^{\tau+1}} \cdot \frac{R_{2,t}^3}{F^j} \cdot \frac{1}{(bR_1 - a_2)} \qquad (16)$$

---

[14] When the yield curve is linear (15) can be expressed $R_{k,t} = R_{1,t} + (k-1)a$ where a is a constant. Thus $b_k = 1$ for all k and $a_k = a(k-1)$, i.e., a_k is proportional to k minus 1 (the number of periods from t).

[15] When the yield curve is not flat, the value of the T-bill futures contract is

$$V = \frac{F^j}{f_{1,t}} - \frac{F^j}{f^*_{1,t}}$$

where f_{1t} is the one-period forward rate (at t), and $f^*_{1,t}$ is the implicit one-period forward rate from the T-bill futures contract. Re-arranging terms

$$V = \frac{R_{1,t} \cdot F^j}{R_{1,t} \cdot f_{1,t}} - \frac{F^j}{f^*_{1,t}} = R_{1,t} \frac{F^j}{R_{2,t}^2} - \frac{F^j}{f^*_{1,t}}$$

$$\therefore \frac{dV}{dR_{1,t}} = \frac{F^j}{R_{2,t}^2} (1 - \frac{2 R_1 b_2}{R_2})$$

Duration as defined in equation (2) cannot be used here since the yield curve may not be flat. An alternative definition of duration will be necessary if it is to be used in equation (16). In the particular case where $a_k = 0$ and $b_k = 1$ for all $k \geq 1$ (i.e., a flat yield curve) equation (16) reduces to equation (10). When $b_k = 1$ for all k, the hedge ratio from equation (16) will be similar to the hedge ratio derived by Fisher and Weil (1971) for assets with non-zero prices. On the other hand, if bond i is to be issued a period later, the hedge ratio for the flotation risk can be derived by the hedge ratio of bond i' with futures contract j where i' has cash flow $c^{i'} = 0$, and $C_{\tau+1}^i = C_\tau^i$. Notice the form of (16) is quite robust. As long as $R_{k,t}$ is a well-defined differentiable function of $R_{1,t}$, the hedge ratio will bear the form of (16). If the T-bill futures contract is replaced by a T-bond futures, one can obtain the hedge ratio by replacing the second term on the right-hand side of equation (16) by the sensitivity of the T-bond futures to the current one-period spot rate.

Regime (3) Risky Hedged Asset and Flat Yield Curve

Let us consider the regime of a corporate bond being hedged with a T-bill futures contract under the assumption that the yield curve of the risk-free rate is flat. A change in the risk-free rate can affect risky and riskless bonds differently, due to the effect on the risk premium. To deal with this let us assume δ, which is one plus the discount rate[16] on the corporate bond i, is a well-defined function[17] of the risk-free rate. With a risky corporate bond i, $\delta > R$ and

$$P^i = \Sigma \frac{C_t^i}{\delta^t}$$

Assuming that portfolio q is formed in the usual way:

$$\frac{dP^q}{dR} = -\frac{1}{\delta}\frac{d\delta}{dR} \Sigma \frac{tC_t^i}{\delta^t} - \frac{F^j}{R^2} N$$

For bond i, the price

$$P^i = \sum_{t=1}^{n} \frac{C_t^i}{R_{t,t}^t}$$

$$\therefore \frac{dP^i}{dR_{1,t}} = \sum_{t=1}^{n} \frac{tb_t C_t^i}{R_{t,t}^{t+1}}$$

Matching the two price sensitivities we have (16).

[16] Since the yield curve is flat, the yield-to-maturity and the discount rate are identical.
[17] In this context a well-defined function is continuous and differentiable.

Then:

$$N = -\frac{1}{\delta}\frac{d\delta}{dR} \Sigma \frac{tC_t^i}{\delta^t} \cdot \frac{R^2}{F^j}$$

or

$$N = -\frac{1}{\delta}\frac{d\delta}{dR} \frac{P^i D^i R^2}{F^j} \quad (17)$$

and D^i, the duration of (corporate) bond i, is re-defined to reflect the risk adjusted discount rate, δ, as:

$$D^i \equiv \sum_{t=1}^{n} \frac{tC_t^i}{\frac{\delta^t}{P^i}}$$

If δ is a linear function of the risk-free rate, $d\delta/dR$ would be replaced by a constant in equation (17). Further, if $\delta = R$, bond i is riskless. In that case equation (17) would have the same value as equation (10).

Alternatively, one can use a T-bond futures contract as the hedging instrument. Then for the standard portfolio q

$$\frac{dP^q}{dR} = -\frac{1}{\delta}\frac{d\delta}{dR} P^i D^i - \frac{1}{R} \Sigma \frac{tC_t}{R^t} N \quad (18)$$

$$\therefore N = -\frac{R}{\delta}\frac{d\delta}{dR} \frac{P^i D^i}{\Sigma \frac{tC_t^j}{R^t}}$$

In (17) the hedge ratio is the same as in (16) except that the price sensitivity of the T-bond futures replaces that of the T-bill futures.

In hedging the flotation risk of bond i, N becomes

$$N = -\frac{1}{\delta} P^{i'} D^{i'} \frac{R^2}{F^j} \frac{d\delta}{dR} \quad (19)$$

where $P^{i'}$ and $D^{i'}$ are, respectively, the price and duration of bond i' which is defined in Regime (1).

CONCLUSION

When the maturity, coupon, and risk of a hedged and hedging instrument are not matched, the optimal hedge will not be dollar for dollar of face value. The duration literature has developed techniques for dealing with this problem for positive price assets. However, these techniques cannot be applied to hedging with futures contracts, since these latter instruments have no price, and consequently no duration.

This paper modifies the concept of duration, and extends the duration hedging approach, suitably modified, to cases where one uses futures contracts as the hedging instrument. Here we have derived hedge ratios that take into account differences in coupon, maturity, and risk for three different regimes. Additionally, the hedge ratios were derived for both the case of hedging a portfolio and the flotation of new securities. Use of these hedge ratios should lead to more efficient hedging of interest rate risk.[18] Finally, the results of the paper may be extended to even more realistic situations by allowing interest rates to follow more complex stochastic processes.

References

1. Bacon, P. and R. Williams. "Interest Rate Futures: New Tool for the Financial Manager," *Financial Management* 5 (Spring 1976), 32-38.
2. Bierwag, G., G. Kaufman and C. Khang. "Duration and Bond Portfolio Analysis: An Overview," *Journal of Finance and Quantitative Analysis* 13 (November 1978), 671-682.
3. Bierwag, G. and C. Khang. "An Immunization Strategy Is a Minimax Strategy," *Journal of Finance* 34 (May 1979), 389-399.
4. Black, F. "The Pricing of Commodity Contracts," *Journal of Financial Economics* 3 (January/March 1976), 167-179.
5. Chicago Board of Trade. *Hedging Interest Rate Risks*, Chicago, 1977.
6. Chicago Board of Trade. *An Introduction to Financial Futures*, Chicago, 1981.
7. Cornell, B. "Taxes and the Pricing of Treasury Bill Futures Contracts," forthcoming, *Journal of Finance* (1981).
8. Cox, J., J. Ingersoll and S. Ross. "Duration and the Measurement of Basis Risk," *Journal of Business* 52 (January 1979), 51-61.
9. Cox, J., J. Ingersoll and S. Ross. "An Intertemporal Asset Pricing Model with Rational Expectations," unpublished working paper, Stanford University, (1980).
10. Durand, D. "Payout Period, Time Spread, and Duration: Aids to Judgement in Capital Budgeting," *Journal of Bank Research* 5 (Spring 1974), 20-34.
11. Feller, W. *An Introduction to Probability Theory and Its Applications*, Volume II, Wiley (1971).
12. Fisher, L. and R. Weil. "Coping with the Risk of Interest-Rate Fluctuations: Returns to Bondholders from Naive and Optimal Strategies," *Journal of Business* 44 (October 1971), 408-431.
13. Gay, G., R. Kolb, and R. Chiang. "Interest Rate Hedging: An Empirical Test of Alternative Strategies," working paper, 1981.
14. Grove, M. "On Duration and the Optimal Maturity Structure of the Balance Sheet," *Bell Journal of Economics* 5 (Autumn 1974), 696-709.
15. Hicks, J. *Value and Capital*, Oxford: Clarendon Press (1939).
16. Ingersoll, J., J. Skelton and R. Weil. "Duration Forty Years Later," *Journal of Financial and Quantitative Analysis* 13 (November 1978), 627-650.

---

[18] For practical applications of this technique see Kolb and Chiang (1981). Gay, Kolb and Chiang (1981) provides an empirical test of the technique.

17. Kane, E. J. "Market Incompleteness and Divergence between Forward and Futures Interest Rates," *Journal of Finance* (May 1980), 221-34.
18. Kaufman, G. "Duration, Planning Period, and Tests of Capital Asset Pricing Model," paper prepared for the annual meeting of the Eastern Finance Association, Atlanta (April 1978).
19. Kaufman, G. "Measuring Risk and Return for Bonds: A New Approach," *Journal of Bank Research* (Summer 1978), 82-90.
20. Kolb, R. and R. Chiang. "Improving Hedging Performance Using Interest Rate Futures," *Financial Management* (Autumn 1981).
21. Lanstein, R. and W. Sharpe. "Duration and Security Risk," *Journal of Financial and Quantitative Analysis* (November 1978), 653-668.
22. McEnally, R. and M. Rice. "Hedging Possibilities in the Flotation of Debt Securities," *Financial Management* 8 (Winter 1979), 12-18.
23. Tito, D. and W. Wagner. "Definite New Measures of Bond Performance and Risk," Wilshire Associates (1977).

PART IV

THE INSTITUTIONAL ENVIRONMENT

The explosive growth of the interest rate futures market has outpaced the understanding of its institutional environment. For any other financial market of comparable size, one will find much more widespread agreement about the institutional principles that govern the market. The financial futures market, in particular, poses special difficulties regarding the meaning of futures rates, the consequences and treatment of taxes, the appropriate accounting techniques for futures, and the optimal regulatory structure. The readings in this part address each of these issues.

From the literature on the efficiency of the interest rate futures market, it is clear that one of the most vexing problems was the discrepancy between yields on futures contracts and the corresponding yields from the spot market. (See Part II.) This was often regarded as evidence of market inefficiency. In his paper, Market Incompleteness and Divergence Between Forward and Futures Interest Rates, *Edward J. Kane argues that the two rates should not necessarily be equal. Because the institutional environments of financial futures and spot bond markets differ, there is little reason to expect exact equality between forward and futures rates. Kane points out important tax differences that would cause the forward and futures rates to diverge. Also the futures market exhibits less certainty of performance than the spot market for government bonds. Additionally, one would expect perfect equality of rates, in the absence of these factors, only if the pure expectations theory of the term structure holds.*

Consequently, Kane concludes that forward and futures rates constrain each other, but not to the point of equality.

The noted difference between forward and futures rates is approached from another perspective by George E. Morgan in Forward and Futures Pricing of Treasury Bills. *In the futures markets additions to, or withdrawals from, a margin account can occur daily during the life of the futures contract. If one creates a comparable forward contract by trading in the spot market, then no cash flow would occur until the forward contract is terminated. Thus, even if the futures and forward contracts mature with exactly the same yield, that does not mean they are equally profitable. The relative profitability, Morgan argues, will depend on the time pattern of interest rates over the contracts' lives. This is the case, since fluctuations in interest rates will generate profits or losses on the futures and forward contracts, but the profits or losses will be realized on the futures contracts due to the institutional requirement that futures contracts be "marked to market" daily. Therefore, forward and futures rates need not be equal even in a perfect market.*

Regarding the persistent issue of taxation, Edward Miller argues that there exists a Tax-Induced Bias in Markets for Futures Contracts. *The futures price need not be the estimate of a future price at some point in time, due to the tax structure, Miller argues. Because of tax rules concerning ordinary income as capital gains and the rules for speculation, tax benefits can be reaped by following certain simple rules. Potentially, one of the biggest users of interest rate futures is the banking industry. In* Tax Topics: Interest Rate Futures—Commercial Banks, *James G. O'Brien discusses the legal aspects of taxation of interest rate futures. He distinguishes long and short positions and treats hedging as well. O'Brien also points the reader to the most important legal precedents in the field.*

One of the principal impediments to bank activity in the interest rate futures market is the accounting procedure imposed upon banks. In particular, straightforward hedging activity can have deleterious effects on accounting income since different rules apply to the recognition of gains and losses on futures contracts and bonds themselves. Kurt Dew explores these issues in Bank Regulations for Futures Accounting. *One accounting proposal, "mark to market accounting" would require that futures traders recognize gains or losses in the quarter* in which they occur. Dew argues that this technique makes the bank's accounting income appear more volatile than it really is. Consequently, he advocates "deferral" or hedge accounting as being more representative of the bank's actual position.

Bank regulatory agencies play an important role in determining the accounting rules that banks must follow, so a consideration of accounting principles naturally leads into broader issues of regulation. In Futures Trading by National Banks, Robert C. Lower and Scott W. Ryan examine both the accounting issues and other regulatory factors as well. In addition to stipulating accounting procedures for banks, the Office of the Comptroller of the Currency also controls the kinds of activity that banks can undertake in the futures market. Regulators are concerned that banks may increase their risk exposure too much by unwise future trading, so they attempt to restrict the kinds of futures positions that bonds may take. Other financial institutions fall under different regulatory purview.

In spite of a regulatory framework that is sometimes bewilderingly complex, Phillip Cagan broaches the question: Financial Futures Markets: Is More Regulation Needed? Largely concerned with the Treasury-Federal Reserve Study *of interest rate futures,* Cagan details the principles behind the existing regulatory structure. He emphasizes the fact that the existence of interest rate futures is due to the volatility of interest rates brought about by recent inflationary trends. It is important, Cagan argues, that the regulatory framework be left sufficiently flexible to accommodate continued innovation in the face of new economic circumstances.

That there will be significant regulatory, tax, and accounting changes cannot be denied. As noted at the outset the institutional environment will be evolving continually. The problem will not concern whether change will occur, but how rapid it will be, and what economic dislocations will result.

Consistent with its history of rapid growth and innovative contract design, the financial futures market continues to move toward new and expanded offerings. Currently, several exchanges have proposals before the Commodity Futures Trading Commission seeking permission to trade interest rate futures contracts on certificates of deposit (CDs). Additionally, it appears that options contracts on GNMA certificates will soon be trading, and that these may well be options on GNMA futures *contracts. Additionally, a strong movement is underway to initiate futures contracts in Euro-CDs.*

The innovations discussed by the articles in this section go even farther, by aiming at the risk associated with purchasing power and the fluctuation in the value of real assets. Both risks are ultimately related to interest rate risk.

In his article, Living with Inflation: A Proposal for New Futures and Options Markets, *Louis H. Ederington proposes strategies for hedging inflation by the establishment of new futures and options contracts. There is widespread agreement that high rates of inflation cause high interest rates. Consequently, being able to hedge against inflation is a very important way of controlling interest rate risk. Ederington proposes that the new contracts could be tied to the Consumer Price Index (CPI).*

Victor Niederhoffer and Richard Zeckhauser, in Market Index Futures Contracts, *discuss the potential for futures contracts written on stock market indices. Several exchanges are already working on this idea. With a futures market for market indices one can hedge against unexpected future movements in equity. From capital market theory it is clear that equity values depend largely upon overall market movements and changes in the risk-free rate. Consequently, a market index futures contract allows hedging simultaneously against the "tidal movement" of the equities market and movement in the risk-free rate of interest.*

These last two articles indicate the way in which interest rate risk touches all areas of the economy. Since interest rate risk is so pervasive, it is not surprising to find innovation in interest rate futures taking two distinct courses. First, one can expect continued innovation in futures on fixed income securities such as CDs and Euro-CDs. But also, innovation can be expected on securities that have multi-faceted risk characteristics, interest rate risk being one of several dimensions. The strong interest in stock index futures contracts is the best current example of this second kind of innovation.

23

Market Incompleteness and Divergences Between Forward and Futures Interest Rates[*]

Edward J. Kane[†]

INTRODUCTION

A presidential address is a solemn ceremonial event. The words should perhaps be sung rather than recited. Not being in very good voice, I intend to give the shortest presidential address in AFA history. The presidential address is 1600 Pennsylvania Avenue, N.W. In the rest of the time allotted to me, I profess only to deliver a paper.

My paper offers some new perspectives on the logical basis for expecting divergences between yields quoted for futures contracts and parallel forward yields implicit in the term structure of interest rates. The presentation proceeds by focusing on the equilibrium *prices* of alternative ways of making two-period investments and on assumptions that *differentially* affect the ways that spot, futures, and options markets can be completed. Implications are drawn regarding observable divergences between expected, forward, and futures prices of post-dated bonds. Since we are free to interpret the first or the second period in our two-period equilibrium conditions to be as long or as short as we

---

[*]Reprinted from the *Journal of Finance*, Vol. 35, No. 2, (May 1980). Reprinted by permission of the publisher and author.

[†]Everett D. Reese Professor of Banking and Monetary Economics at The Ohio State University. For valuable comments on earlier drafts of this paper, the author wishes to thank Stephen Buser, Andrew Chen, Charles Cox, Kurt Dew, Patrick Hess, Gailen Hite, E. Han Kim, Richard Lang, J. Huston McCulloch, Gordon Roberts, and Akio Yasuhara.

please, our results readily generalize to investments of any maturity.

My specific objective is to develop an efficient-market explanation of the allegedly "confusing" time-series behavior of the differential between the forward and futures interest rates on U.S. Treasury securities. Forward rates implicit in the term structure have been close to parallel yields on futures contracts traded on the Chicago Mercantile Exchange only for the Treasury bill contract closest to execution (Poole; Lang and Rasche). Differentials on more distant contracts have been consistently large and in 1977 reversed sign (Struble). Even allowing for transactions and carrying costs, most scholars find these events puzzling (Capozza and Cornell; Vignola and Dale). A few even interpret the persistent failure of futures and forward rates to converge as evidence of segmentation (Branch) or "inefficiency" (Rendleman and Carabini). I argue instead that, once we recognize the implicit and explicit costs of guaranteeing futures-market performance and the capital-gains tax treatment of futures-market profit and loss, divergence becomes the typical equilibrium state.

I. PRICES VERSUS YIELDS

Traditional term-structure theory focuses on single-payment securities, uncomplicated by default risk or special features of any kind. The unit price, $P_{n,t}$, of a security that matures in n periods is the discounted present value of a dollar at the maturity date. We find this value by discounting the future dollar n times at $R_{n,t}$, the yield to maturity on an n-period bond:

$$P_{n,t} \equiv 1/(1 + R_{n,t})^n, \quad \text{for} \quad n = 1, 2, 3, \ldots \quad (1)$$

In this discrete-time conception, the term to maturity of any bond spans n unit maturities. As against the continuous-time conception, we can defend the notion of a "unit maturity" as a minimum period for economical investment in open-market securities. Much empirical work arbitrarily treats this interval as the calendar quarter.

Discounting may proceed in terms of either nominal or real yields. Term-structure theory seeks only to explain differential or relative yields, so that one yield (or one bond price) may be given exogenously. It is convenient to conceive of this exogenous yield as the shortest rate in the system, which we can term the "bill rate."

Traditional economic analyses root their explanations in the yield side of the pricing identity (1), asymmetrically viewing hypothetical changes in equilibrium yields as driving observable changes in bond prices. On the other hand, modern finance theory roots itself in state-preference theory, treating the equation's price side as a dog that wags an interest-rate tail. In this approach, bond prices arise as the sums of values of state-dependent claims, with yields viewed as artificial by-products (e.g., see Banz and Miller).

As the identity sign implies, apparent differences between a price and yield approach can only be matters of emphasis, not of substance (Malkiel). Nevertheless, I hope to convince you that reformulating expectational theories of the term structure of interest rates as arbitrage theories of bond *prices*, provides new insights into the ways in which futures markets function.

II. THE PURE-EXPECTATIONS THEORY REVISITED

A. Alternative Strategies for Term Lending. In modern contingent-claims theory (e.g., Black and Scholes), the trick is to define a hedge portfolio. Since the long and short sides of a hedge portfolio must be perfect substitutes, their value is governed by the Law of One Price. Investments maturing in exactly n periods can be made in at least seven distinct ways. In turn, these seven basic investment strategies can be broken down into two strategies for holding strips of maturities *shorter* than the planned holding period (i.e., the planned maturity of the overall investment), two strategies for *matching* the maturities to be held with the planned holding period, and three strategies for holding maturities *longer* than the planned holding period:

Strip or Unit-Maturity Strategies

1. The "naked rollover" or "uncovered rollover strategy" of buying a one-period bond (i.e., a "bill") in the current spot market and planning to let the matured funds ride in the one-period spot market for each of the next $n - 1$ periods.
2. The "covered rollover" or "futures-market strategy" of buying a bill in the current spot market and simultaneously contracting in the futures market for a sequence of bill purchases over the next $n - 1$ periods.

Matching Strategies

3. The "repurchase-agreement strategy" of buying an n-period security today and arranging to borrow against it *via* a series of one-period "buy-back" agreements.

4. The "buy-and-hold strategy" of buying an n-period bond in the current spot market and planning to hold it until it matures. This strategy is also called the "implicit forward-market strategy," to emphasize that the investor may be viewed as executing a series of implicit "forward" transactions in future one-periods bonds.

Yield-Curve Rides

5. The "uncovered roll-out strategy" of buying a bond whose maturity is longer than n periods and planning to sell it in the spot market n periods later for whatever it will bring at the time.
6. The "covered roll-out strategy" of buying a bond whose maturity is longer than n periods and simultaneously contracting in the futures market to sell it in exactly n periods.
7. The "options strategy" of buying a bond whose maturity is longer than n periods and simultaneously selling a call option and buying a put option on the bond, both exercisable n periods in the future at an identical striking price.

Metaphorically, each investment strategy maps out a set of roads along which current funds can travel to a destination n periods in the future. For any planned period of investment, each strategy constructs a point-input, point-output transaction in bond, options, and futures markets that converts an outflow of present dollars into a larger return flow of future dollars. Assuming that bond denominations are perfectly divisible, all strategies can be scaled to offer the same *expected* payoff of one dollar n periods hence.

B. Prices in Perfect Markets With Risk Neutrality and Perfect Performance Guarantees. We begin by assuming risk neutrality, identical expectations, perfect divisibility, costless transacting, identical tax treatment of interest and capital-gains income, *and* costless guarantees of futures-market performance. Under these assumptions, all n-period investment strategies have the same present value, since certain and expected future dollars are equally desirable. This is the situation contemplated in the pure-expectations theory of the term structure (PET), in which so-called term premia do not exist. By definition, term premia are differences between the market yield on n-period securities and the expected average yield on an n-period naked rollover in bills.

Under the PET assumptions, futures, spot, repurchase, and options markets are complete. For each holding period, all seven strategies must have the same price. To see what theorems equilibrium pricing entails, it is convenient to focus on two-period investments. Although we have not yet explained our notation, Table 1 gives the equilibrium price

Table 1
Value of an Expected Dollar Receivable Two Periods Later From Each of the Seven Basic Investment Strategies, Given PET Assumptions

1. Naked Rollover:

$$P_{2,t}^{NS} = P_{1,t}E_t(P_{1,t+1}).$$

2. Covered Rollover:

$$P_{2,t}^{CS} = P_{1,t}P_1^*(t, t+1).$$

3. Implicit Forward Contract:

$$P_{2,t} = P_{1,t}P_1^F(t, t+1).$$

4. Repurchase Agreement:

$$P_{2,t}^{RP} = [P_{2,t} - P_{2,t}] + P_{1,t}P_1^{BB}(t, t+1) = P_{1,t}P_1^{BB}(t, t+1).$$

5. Naked Rollout:

$$P_{2,t}^{NL} = P_{n,t}[E_t(P_{n-2,t+2})]^{-1}, \quad n > 2.$$

6. Covered Rollout:

$$P_{2,t}^{CL} = P_{n,t}[P_{n-2}^*(t, t+2)]^{-1}, \quad n > 2.$$

7. Options Strategy:

$$P_{2,t}^O = \{P_{n,t} - P^{\text{call}}[t, t+2; E_t(P_{n-2,t+2})]$$

$$+ P^{\text{put}}[t, t+2; E_t(P_{n-2,t+2})]\}$$

$$\cdot [E_t(P_{n-2,t+2})]^{-1}, \quad n > 2.$$

under PET of an expected dollar generated by each of the seven basic investment strategies.

On the left-hand side of the equals sign, $P_{2,t}$ represents the current price of a dollar receivable for sure in two periods. Superscripts designate each of the other strategies being valued. N signifies naked or uncovered positions, C covered ones. S indicates that the maturity bought in the spot market is shorter than the planned holding period, while L indicates that the maturity purchased in the spot market is longer than the planned holding period. RP and O stand for repurchase agreement and options, respectively.

On the righthand side, $E_t(P_{n,t+k})$ represents the expected value as of time t of the price of n-period bonds k periods in the future. Superscripts are used to designate explicit and implicit per-dollar prices of futures, forward, repurchase, and options contracts. In these contracts, each price has two timing dimensions. The first index represents the date at which the contract is entered. The second gives the future date at which the contract is scheduled for execution. Asterisks indicate futures prices, while BB denotes a "buy-back" price. The notation used for prices of call and put options includes as a third argument the "striking price" at which the option may be executed at $t + 2$. The reader may recognize that we have priced the options strategy by drawing on Hans Stoll's "put-call parity."

Finally, the forward price of $t + 1$ bills implicit in the term structure of interest rates at time t is defined as:

$$P_1^F(t, t + 1) \equiv P_{2,t}/P_{1,t}. \tag{2}$$

We can clarify the mechanics of the first six strategies by interpreting the righthand side of each equation as the product of the price and quantity of the security purchased at t. The second term of each product tells us *how many* securities we must buy today to produce an expected inflow of one dollar at $t + 2$. As an example, suppose that $P_{1,t}$ and $E_t(P_{1,t+1})$ were each 0.87. Then, a naked rollover would require us to buy 0.87 of current bills, thereby putting ourselves in the position to be able to put $E_t(P_{1,t+1})$ into bills at $t + 1$. The price of two-period bonds—indeed the price of all two-period strategies—would of course be $(0.87) \cdot (0.87) = 0.76$. In passing, we may note that unless interest-rate expectations are single-valued:

$$E_t(P_{1,t+k}) = E_t[1/(1 + R_{1,t+k})] \neq 1/[1 + E_t(R_{1,t+k})], k \geq 1. \tag{3}$$

To illustrate a naked roll-out, let us suppose that $P_{3,t}$ is 0.701 and $E_t(P_{1,t+2})$ is 0.926. Purchasing $(0.926)^{-1}$ or 1.08 three-period bonds at time t would produce an expected dollar's worth of bills to sell at $t + 2$. To carry out the options strategy, we must buy the same amount of three-period bonds at t and sell put and call options on an expected dollar's worth of the bills that these bonds evolve into at $t + 2$.

Since all strategies with the same expected future payoff must have the same current price, we can establish three theorems. First, the expected, futures, forward, and repurchase prices of next period's bills must all be equal:

$$E_t(P_{1,t+1}) = P_1^*(t, t + 1) = P_1^F(t, t + 1) = P_1^{BB}(t, t + 1). \tag{4}$$

Substituting (4) into expressions for successively longer investment strategies would let us establish that futures, forward, and repurchase prices for every future bill must each also equal the contemporary forecast of the relevant bill price.

Second, the expected and futures prices of all longer bonds must also be equal:

$$E_t(P_{n-2,t+2}) = P_{n-2}^*(t, t + 2), \quad n > 2. \tag{5}$$

By increasing the length of investment period to $k > 1$, we can easily establish that:

$$E_t(P_{n-k,t+k}) = P^*_{n-k}(t, t+k), \quad n > k > 1. \tag{5'}$$

Implicit forward and repurchase prices for bonds would also equal these same values.

Third, the options strategy constructs a *riskless* combination of bond-market and options transactions. Whatever happens to the price of $(n-2)$-period bonds at $t+2$, the investor is assured of receiving exactly one dollar. If $P_{n-2,t+2}$ turns out to exceed its expected value, the put option becomes valueless and the call would be exercised. If $P_{n-2,t+2}$ falls short of its expected value, the call becomes valueless and the investor would exercise the put. Either way, the bonds are exchanged for their expected value.

Setting $P^O_{2,t}$ equal to $P^{NL}_{2,t}$, we can easily establish that the PET assumptions imply that a put and call whose common striking price equals the bond's expected price have the same value. Cancelling the expected-value term, we get:

$$P_{n,t} - P_{n,t} = 0 = -P^{\text{call}}[t, t+2; E_t(P_{n-2,t+2})] + P^{\text{put}}[t, t+2; E_t(P_{n-2,t+2})]. \tag{6}$$

Replacing $t+2$ by $t+k$ (where $n > k \geq 1$) extends the result to cover holding periods of any length.

III. RELAXING PET ASSUMPTIONS

Term-structure theory is concerned with costs and benefits generated by moving funds through time. In the pure-expectations theory, risks are irrelevant and temporal "transportation" costs are zero. Hence, every conceivable n-period path of investment offers the same equilibrium expected return. All n-period strategies are equally efficient.

If we introduce differential tax rates or transactions costs, different individuals may find some n-period paths more efficient than others. Since efficient paths dominate inefficient paths, n-period securities must always be priced according to the risks and transportation costs encountered along what are the most efficient paths for the marginal investor.

A. Introducing Risk Aversion: The Risk-Averse Pricing Theory of the Term Structure.[1]
Leaving the other PET assumptions untouched, we now remove the assumption of risk neutrality. Instead we assume

---

[1] Observable implications developed in this section parallel those in section V of Cox, Ingersoll, and Ross. However, our approach makes it possible to finesse the specific stochastic assumptions required to implement their "general-equilibrium" continuous-time model.

that a positive price is paid for risk-bearing and that some nonarbitrageable risk exists in every future bill and every current bond. Perhaps the easiest way to justify this assumption is to postulate the absence of perfect hedges against unanticipated inflation.

These new assumptions break the equivalence between cash flows that are certain and those that are merely expected. While covered strategies remain priced as before, the risk-bearing inherent in *uncovered* strategies must now be priced. Parallel futures and implicit forward bond prices remain equal to each other, but they can no longer also equal the *expected* price. We can see this clearly in the two-period case. If the futures price *did* equal the expected price, the risk-adjusted value of the naked rollover strategy would be too high. No lender would go unhedged. The forward and futures-market strategies would *dominate* the uncovered rollover. To complete markets again, the risk-bearing inherent in the uncovered strategy must be compensated. The price paid for *not* covering is the market exchange rate between a dollar certain and a dollar expected to be generated at $t + 1$ *by the particular rollover or rollout opportunity*. In the multiperiod CAPM (Merton), this difference would be the compensation paid for bearing undiversifiable or "systematic" risk. We denote the t-period price of $t + 1$ certainty equivalence in bills as $a_{t,t+1}$. Risk-averse pricing implies that this price be *less* than unity.[2] It is, however, an instrument-specific measure.

As compared to the risk-neutral situation, the certainty-equivalence factor scales down the equilibrium price of the naked-rollover strategy to:

$$P_{2,t}^{NS'} = P_{2,t}^{NS} a_{t,t+1} = P_{1,t}[E_t(P_{1,t+1})a_{t,t+1}]. \tag{7}$$

Referring again to our price-quantity interpretation of these pricing equations, we need to buy *fewer* bills today to acquire an uncertain opportunity whose two-period expectation is one dollar than to purchase a certain opportunity with the same expectation.

Drawing again on the Law of One Price and the concept of market completeness, riskless futures, forward, rollout, and options strategies must sell at this same risk-adjusted price. As long as performance can be costlessly guaranteed in markets for options on future bills or bonds, riskless options strategies can also be constructed. This means that put and call options on securities that are exercisable at expected prices would still have equal values.

[2] Risk-averse pricing is, of course, merely an hypothesis. If all interest-rate risk could be costlessly arbitraged away, $a_{t,t+k}$ would equal unity for all k. Alternatively, in the preferred-habitat theory of Modigliani and Sutch, where $a_{t,t+k}$ is interpreted as manifesting the balance of borrower and lender maturity preferences, the certainty-equivalence factors can equal or even exceed unity. Other researchers (e.g., Green; Hirshleifer; Roberts) suggest still-different interpretations and restrictions. However, empirical research on the term structure (e.g., Kessel; Nelson; Kane and Malkiel; McCulloch; Pesando) supports the hypothesis of risk-averse pricing.

Equation (7) has an important observable implication. Risk-averse pricing implies that forward, futures, and repurchase-agreement prices for bills and bonds should *lie below* expected prices:

$$P_1^F(t, t+k) = P_1^*(t, t+k)$$
$$= P_1^{BB}(t, t+1) = E_t(P_{1,t+k})a_{t,t+k}, \quad k = 1, 2, 3, \ldots \quad (8)$$

$$E_t \left[\prod_{k=1}^{n-1} P_{1,t+k} \right] a_{t,t+n}^n = \prod_{k=1}^{n-1} P_1^*(t, t+k). \quad (9)$$

In equation (9), all forecasts are conditional on the t-period information set and $a_{t,t+n}^n$ represents the certainty-equivalence conversion factor for $t+n$ cash flows in n-period bonds evaluated at time t. Substituting (8) into (9) recursively, we can show that

$$a_{t,t+n}^n = \prod_{k=1}^{n-1} a_{t,t+k}. \quad (10)$$

With each $a_{t,t+k}$ assumed to be less than unity, bond-market certainty-equivalence factors decline with maturity. Translated to yield space, this cumulative "term price" implies conventionally positive term premia. By definition

$$T_{n,t} \equiv [P_{1,t}E_t \prod_{k=1}^{n-1}(P_{1,t+k})a_{t,t+k}]^{-1/n} - [P_{1,t}E_t \prod_{k=1}^{n-1}(P_{1,t+k})]^{-1/n}. \quad (11)[3]$$

Moreover, term-price theory can be turned into an explicit theory of term-price *incrementation*. In particular, if the price of bill-market certainty-equivalence is anticipated to be the same for all future periods, the term price would increase (at a decreasing rate) with maturity. In yield space, this would produce term premia that increase to an asymptote at a decreasing rate. This theory is observationally equivalent to the Hicksian Liquidity-Premium Theory of the term structure. In our theory, the $a_{t,t+k}$ are marginal elements parallel to Hicksian liquidity premia, while the term price is a cumulative average on the order of a term premium.

We can illustrate by extending the numerical example we used to illustrate Table 1. If for all k ($k = 1, 2, \ldots$), $a_{t,t+k} = 0.98$ and $E(P_{1,t+k}) = P_{1,t} = 0.87$, we obtain $P_{2,t} = 0.74$ and $P_{4,t} = 0.539$, with $T_2 = 0.012$, $T_4 = 0.018$, and $\text{Lim}_{n \to \infty} T_n = 0.0235$.

Implications can also be drawn from this theory concerning the effect of interest-rate levels on term premia. For a given term price, the term premium on any maturity *increases* with the average expected yield on interim bills. (See footnote 3.) Existing writings on this issue (Kessel; Cagan; Van Horne; Nelson; Pesando) do not distinguish the possible indirect effect of interest rates through the term price from the direct effect shown here.

---

[3] Defining the expected yield on an n-period naked rollover as $h_{n,t}$, (11) simplifies to:

$$T_{n,t} = (1 + h_{n,t})[(a_{t+n}^n)^{-1/n} - 1]. \quad (11')$$

B. Introducing Differential Capital-Gains Taxes.[4] With risk-averse pricing, interest-rate futures contracts carry an *anticipated* capital gain. U.S. tax law designates futures contracts—unlike Treasury bills themselves, but like options on bonds—as capital assets (*The Bank Tax Report*). Net capital gains are taxed differently from ordinary interest income.

In principle, the deferral of capital-gains taxes until realization and scheduled revisions in the capital-gains tax structure, along with changes in the tax situation of marginal investors in interest-rate futures, go a long way toward explaining observed variations in the average differences between forward and futures prices. The major tax law revisions are:

1. For assets other than the long side of a futures contract traded in an organized market, the holding period necessary for trading profits to qualify as long-term capital gains increased from 6 months to 9 months in 1977 and to one year from 1978 forward. Profits-earned on the *short side* of futures contracts are always classified as *short-term* capital gains, regardless of the holding period.
2. In 1979, taxpayers' long-term capital-gains tax rate was lowered from 50 percent of the statutory marginal tax rate on ordinary income to 40 percent of the statutory rate, producing a maximum capital-gains tax of 28 percent.
3. The optional "alternative tax," which had placed a cap of 25 percent on the rate for a household's first $50,000 in net long-term gains, was eliminated in 1979. For corporate taxpayers, the alternative ceiling on the long-term capital-gains tax rate was at the same time lowered from 30 to 28 percent.
4. Except for market-makers (for whom these assets are deemed stock-in-trade), net futures losses are not fully deductible from ordinary income. In any year, household taxpayers may deduct the sum of short-term losses and 50 percent of long-term losses only up to a maximum of $3,000 (up from $2,000 in 1978 and $1,000 before). However, by taking delivery rather than closing out a loss position, capital losses on T-bill futures can be converted into ordinary income.

Three important points emerge. First, except for market-makers, net *losses* on futures contracts are potentially tax-disadvantaged. Second, only net *long-term* capital gains are taxed advantageously. Third, favorable tax treatment applies only to *net* realized long-term gains on the aggregate of calendar-year transactions. Capital losses developed else-

---

[4] I am grateful to Stephen Buser for suggesting a role for capital-gains tax rates.

where in the portfolio lessen the effective tax preference afforded gains on long futures.

Recognizing these complications breaks the completeness of the hypothetical cover provided by futures-market transactions. Gains on long futures more than offset equal losses in bill markets, while losses on long futures may not offset equal gains in bill markets. Contract values must price both the tax advantage and the incompleteness. Equilibrium requires an equality of *after-tax* risk-adjusted returns on all strategies.

We can pull the risks and net potential tax advantages into a "futures factor," $f_{t,t+k}$. We hypothesize that:

$$P_1^*(t, t+1) = P_1^F(t, t+1) f_{t,t+k}, \tag{12}$$

where $f_{t,t+k} > 1$ for contracts with six months or more to run. In holding that long bill-rate futures are bid to a premium relative to implicit forward prices, we are assuming that, for the *marginal investor* in long futures, the lure of tax-favored expected capital gains outweighs the risks of unanticipated adverse price declines here and elsewhere in the investor's portfolio.[5]

C. *Prices in Perfect Markets with Risk Neutrality But with Costly Performance Guarantees.* We now restore the assumptions of equal tax rates and risk neutrality and relax the assumption that the ability to execute futures contracts and to exercise options can be guaranteed costlessly. This introduces a new probability into the pricing equations: the *probability of nonperformance.*

1. Implicit Prices Serve to Complete Markets

Unless the performance of futures and option contracts is costlessly guaranteed, spot, futures, and options markets are no longer complete. We need an implicit market for insurance against nonperformance to complete them again. When real rather than nominal discount rates are employed, the probability distributions of one-period prices are unbounded on both sides. Even using nominal rates, the upper tail is unbounded. In either case, it is unprofitable for producers of costly guarantees to carry them to perfection. This means that some unlikely events cannot be hedged against in futures markets. If investors can acquire only *partial* performance guarantees, it is impossible for them to construct a perfectly hedged portfolio by going long in current bonds

---

[5] To pursue the tax-effect issue, readers may consult Scholes. His paper analyzes tax effects on options pricing for investors in different tax brackets.

and short in an intervening series of interest-rate futures on one-period bonds or by trading in puts and calls on two-period bonds. The "fatter" the uninsured tail (or tails) of the bond-price distributions, the more severe the moral hazard.

To complete the spot and future markets, we must include the implicit prices of perfect-performance guarantees. Assuming that bonds are default-free does not imply that future commitments by individuals to buy and sell these bonds are also default-free. A would-be hedger has to recognize that futures-market or options transactors who take positions opposite to the hedger's act to maximize their own wealth position. As maximizers, they must be expected to default on their contracts whenever the benefit from reneging exceeds the penalties imposed on them for doing so. Similarly, a hedger retains the implicit option to engage in advantageous default himself. Even with universal risk neutrality, transactors in default-free long-term bonds offer the other side of the market a commitment that is valuable because it is irrevocable. Because they are executed immediately, implicit forward transactions are free from the moral hazard that besets a futures contract.

Investment strategies that take long positions in real-world futures markets are equivalent to the simultaneous issuance of *three* contracts:

1. Spot purchase of a one-period bill and a futures-market long position in a rollover portfolio of the same maturity;
2. An implicit put option allowing holders of short positions in futures markets ("shorters") to default whenever the one-period spot rate of interest becomes sufficiently *low*;
3. An implicit call option allowing long positions in futures markets (the "longers") to default on futures-market commitments whenever the spot rate becomes sufficiently *high*.

Although exercising either option constitutes nonperformance of the explicit futures contract, the true price of a long position in the futures market must have three components, one for each of the explicit contracts issued.

Introducing the possibility of nonperformance does not disturb the PET equilibrium conditions. The expected and forward prices of postdated bills continue to equal futures prices, but each futures price now has implicit as well as explicit elements. Hence, the unobservable *true* price of futures transactions will seldom be the contract execution price quoted in the marketplace, $P^{ex}_1(t, t+1)$.

2. Technology of Contemporary Performance Guarantees

Without external constraints, only in the razor's edge case where $P^{ex}_1(t, t+k)$ happens to equal $P_{1,t+k}$ would maximizing individuals on *both* sides of the futures market be willing to live up to their contractual commitments.

In the contemporary United States, Chicago Mercantile Exchange (CME) rules provide futures-market transactors with *partial* performance guarantees, whose value is hidden in escrow deposits, net-worth screening, negotiated brokerage fees (usually $60 per roundtrip million-dollar contract), and costs of margin maintenance. These guarantees narrow the effective range of potential defaults, improving the deliverability of the product but increasing explicit transactions and maintenance costs.[6]

First, brokers require most transactors to deposit $10,000 in escrow and to put up an "initial margin" of at least $1500 per million-dollar transaction. Since these deposits may take the form of a letter of credit or pledges of interest-bearing securities, they impose only minor costs on *wealthy* individuals. However, subsequent gains and losses in the value of the contract cumulate as cash in the margin account. Accounts are marked to market daily. Positions that fall below a "maintenance margin" of $1200 are subject to a margin call for cash, on which the broker keeps the subsequent interest. Customers who fail to meet a margin call are promptly sold out.[7] However, because of exchange limits on daily price changes, sell-outs cannot always take place immediately. Occasionally, brokers must wait for futures markets to "catch up" with spot markets. Balances in excess of escrow and initial margin requirements generate interim cash inflows that need to be invested at interest. When the futures price is *expected* to change in a specific direction (as, for example, it is expected to *rise* under risk-averse pricing), margin accounts introduce an *asymmetry* in expected cash flows for long and short positions that the contract execution price must adjust away.

Additionally, each brokerage firm is pledged to make good all defaults by its own customers and to bring suit in civil court against the defaulting party. Finally, the Exchange operates an emergency fund, which backstops transactors against individual-broker bankruptcy, even to the extent of authorizing the Exchange to levy make-good charges on surviving members of the Exchange.

In perfect markets, the quality of Exchange guarantees would increase with their cost. Hence, they would have a conflicting dual effect on the true futures price, $P_1^*(t, t+1)$. The more costly the guarantee, the higher the probability of performance, but also the greater the implicit charge for the guarantee. In practice, performance guarantees are produced from various combinations of high-rated cosigners, letters of

---

[6] I am grateful to Kurt Dew for clarifying the mechanics of CME margin requirements and guarantees.

[7] The probability of nonperformance may be particularly high for repurchase agreements, because interim changes in contract value and collateral are not systematically monitored.

credit, escrow accounts, and Exchange commitments. If we assume that guarantee quality is produced at nondecreasing costs, the *optimal quality* of guarantee would *never* be perfect.

Especially if the distribution of bond-price changes should be stable Paretian (Roll, McCulloch), one-day interest-rate movements could in principle have a sharp-enough spike to exhaust the finite sum of reserves implicit in Exchange arrangements. For a given set of penalties, the "fatter" the uninsured tails of the distribution of future one-period bond prices, the greater the probability of nonperformance.

CME arrangements only approximate guarantees of perfect futures performance. Persons who take long and short positions in interest-rate futures are *forced* by Exchange rules implicitly to sell their brokers almost all of their unconstrained default option. They retain only a residual option exercisable at a highly unlikely striking price. Still, with risk neutrality and perfect markets, the value of the options sold and retained must enter the true price of the overall futures contract.

3. Guarantee Costs and True Futures Prices

For futures-market commitments maturing in any period, three possibilities exist:

1. S_s = default by short positions;
2. S_l = default by long positions;
3. S_{ex} = execution of all maturing commitments.

The true price of a two-period futures strategy is its expected value. This is the product of $P_{1,t}$ and the net expected value of three second-period components. We let G_{t+1} equal the cost of Exchange guarantees and $\Pr(S_{ex})$ represent the conditional probability of execution, given the set of guarantees in force. If substantial inflows are expected to accrue to long-position margin accounts, G_{t+1} could well be negative. $Y_{t+1,l}$ and $Y_{t+1,s}$ denote the conditional expected values of Exchange penalties and make-good payments in the event of the indicated type of default. The alternative expected second-period cash flows become:

1. $\Pr(S_{ex})P_1^{ex}(t, t+1) - G_{t+1}$
2. $-Y_{t+1,l}$
3. $Y_{t+1,s}.$ (13)

The first of these expected cash flows may be interpreted as the price of a hypothetical perfect futures contract, with the indicated expected value, $P_1^{**}(t,t+1)$. The other two elements may be interpreted as the values of the *residual* long-position and short-position options to violate the contract, $N_1^L(t,t+1)$ and $N_1^S(t,t+1)$. Defining the "net option value,"

$$N_1(t, t+1) = N^L(t, t+1) - N^S(t, t+1), \quad (14)$$

the true price of the futures contract becomes:

$$P_1^*(t, t+1) = P_1^{**}(t, t+1) - N_1(t, t+1). \quad (15)$$

4. Relation Between Futures Contract Prices and Forward Prices

Risk neutrality requires that forward prices and true future prices be the same. But equation (15) implies that futures-contract execution prices may differ in either direction from both of these.

If the net option value just happens to equal zero, contract execution prices would probably *exceed* forward prices. But when price appreciation is expected on the futures contract (as it would be under risk-averse pricing), the reverse could be true. The differential depends on both the quality and the net cost of performance guarantees. Assuming that guarantees of given quality are cheap to produce for near-term contracts but progressively more costly to produce as the delivery date becomes more distant in time would let us explain the pattern of differentials on *T*-bill futures observed since mid-1977. The gap between forward and futures prices has been negligible for contracts close to delivery and increased with the futurity of the contract.

To explain the pre-1977 pattern without either appealing to tax effects or relaxing the assumption of risk neutrality, we must argue either that in 1976 and early 1977 the mechanics of CME guarantees promised large interim net cash *in*flows to long positions or that the net option value was positive and increased with maturity.

D. Prices in Perfect Markets with Risk-Averse Pricing and Costly Guarantees.

Retaining costly guarantees *and* introducing a positive price for risk-bearing breaks the equality between expected and forward rates. For futures and options markets, the major implication is that nonperformance *risk* must be priced, too. In the two-period model, equilibrium requires:

$$E_t(P_{1,t+1})a_{t,t+1} = P_1^F(t, t+1)$$
$$= P_1^{**}(t, t+1)a_{t,t+1}^{**} - Y_{t+1,t}a_{t,t+1}^L + Y_{t+1,s}a_{t,t+1}^S. \quad (16)$$

In this more realistic model, variations in the systematic risk of postdated bills and each of the three elements of the futures contracts combine with changes in their expected values to explain divergences between forward prices, expected prices, and contract prices for interest-rate futures. The equilibrium condition makes it clear that expected and forward bill prices can depart substantially, not only from each other, but especially from the execution prices of futures-market contracts. Reintroducing capital-gains tax differentials would further increase opportunities for divergence.

IV. CONCLUSIONS AND AGENDA FOR FUTURE RESEARCH

Recognizing that it is costly to guarantee futures-market performance is sufficient to destroy any presumed identity between futures and forward interest rates. Introducing a positive price for risk-bearing services, applicable to whatever nonarbitrageable risk inheres in every risky opportunity, suffices both to make forward interest rates differ from expected rates and, especially when capital gains are taxed preferentially, to make the representation of futures rates very complicated indeed. When PET assumptions are relaxed, expected, forward, and futures yields are free to travel different roads. Movements in comparable expected, forward, and futures yields *constrain* each other, but not to the point of equality.

Although the various parameters identified in this paper may be estimated in principle, data on the true prices of different contracts and options and on the cost functions for performance guarantees will be difficult to align.

References

Banz, Rolf W., and Miller, Merton H., "Prices for State-Contingent Claims: Some Estimates and Applications," *Journal of Business*, 51 (October 1978), pp. 653-672.

Black, Fisher, and Scholes, Myron, "The Pricing of Options and Corporate Liabilities," *Journal of Political Economy*, 81 (May/June 1973), pp. 637-654.

Branch, Ben, "Testing the Unbiased Expectations Theory of Interest Rates," *Financial Review*, (Fall 1978), pp. 51-66.

Cagan, Phillip, "A Study of Liquidity Premiums on Federal and Municipal Government Securities," in J. Guttentag and P. Cagan (ed.), *Essays on Interest Rates*, Vol. I, New York: National Bureau of Economic Research, 1969, pp. 107-142.

Capozza, Dennis R. and Cornell, Bradford, "Treasury Bill Pricing in the Spot and Futures Market," *Review of Economics and Statistics*, 61 (November 1979), pp. 513-520.

Cox, John C., Ingersoll, Jonathan E., Jr., and Ross, Stephen A., "A Theory of the Term Structure of Interest Rates," Stanford University Graduate School of Business (mimeographed, August 1978).

Green, H. A. J., "Uncertainty and the 'Expectations Hypothesis,'" *Review of Economic Studies*, 34 (October 1967), pp. 387-398.

Hicks, John R., *Value and Capital: An Inquiry into Some Fundamental Principles of Economic Theory*, 2nd edition, Oxford: Clarendon Press, 1946.

Hirshleifer, Jack, "Liquidity, Uncertainty, and the Accumulation of Information" in C. F. Carter (Ed.), *Uncertainty and Expectation in Economics: Essays in Honor of G. L. S. Shackle*, Cliffton, N.J.: A. M. Kelly, 1972.

Kane, Edward J., and Malkiel, Burton G., "The Term Structure of Interest Rates: An Analysis of a Survey of Expectations," *Review of Economics and Statistics*, 49 (August 1967), pp. 343-355.

Kessel, Reuben A., *The Cyclical Behavior of the Term Structure of Interest Rates*, New York: National Bureau of Economic Research, 1965.

Lang, Richard W., and Rasche, Robert H., "A Comparison of Yields on Futures Contracts and Implied Forward Rates," *Federal Reserve Bank of St. Louis Monthly Review*, 60 (December 1978), pp. 21-30.

Malkiel, Burton G., "Expectations, Bond Prices, and the Term Structure of Interest Rates," *Quarterly Journal of Economics*, 76 (May 1962), pp. 197-218.

McCulloch, J. Huston, "An Estimate of the Liquidity Premium," *Journal of Political Economy*, 83 (February 1975), pp. 95-119.

Merton, Robert, "An Intertemporal Capital Asset Pricing Model," *Econometrica*, 41 (September 1973), pp. 867-887.

Modigliani, Franco, and Sutch, Richard, "Innovations in Interest Policy," *American Economic Review (Papers and Proceedings)*, 56 (May 1966), pp. 178-197.

Nelson, Charles, "Estimation of Term Premiums from Average Yield Differentials in the Term Structure of Interest Rates," *Econometrica*, 40 (March 1972), pp. 277-287.

Pesando, James E., "Determinants of Term Premiums in the Market for Treasury Bills," *Journal of Finance*, 30 (June 1975), pp. 761-771.

Poole, William, "Using *T*-Bill Futures to Gauge Interest-Rate Expectations," *Federal Reserve Bank of San Francisco Economic Review*, (Spring 1978), pp. 7-19.

Rendleman, Richard J., and Carabini, Christopher E., "The Efficiency of the Treasury Bill Futures Market," *Journal of Finance*, 34 (September 1979), pp. 895-914.

Roberts, Gordon, "Term Premiums in the Term Structure of Interest Rates," *Journal of Money, Credit and Banking* (forthcoming).

Roll, Richard, *The Behavior of Interest Rates*, New York: Basic Books, 1970.

Scholes, Myron, "Taxes and the Pricing of Options," *Journal of Finance*, 31 (May 1976), pp. 319-332.

Stoll, Hans, "The Relationship Between Put and Call Option Prices," *Journal of Finance*, 24 (December 1969), pp. 802-824.

Struble, Frederick M., "Issues on Financial Futures Requiring Research," Board of Governors of the Federal Reserve System (mimeographed, November 1979).

The Bank Tax Report, 16 (November 7, 1975).

Van Horne, James, "Interest-Rate Risk and the Term Structure of Interest Rates," *Journal of Political Economy*, 73 (August 1965), pp. 344-351.

Vignola, Anthony J., and Dale, Charles, "Price Determination and the Treasury Bill Futures Market," Washington: U.S. Treasury Department (mimeographed, April 1979).

24

Forward and Futures Pricing of Treasury Bills[*]

George Emir Morgan[†]

Interest rate futures have been touted as futures contracts in the ultimate commodity, money, and indeed the rapid rise in volume and open interest have made interest rate futures contracts one of the success stories of the 70's (along with the success of options contracts). Paralleling the explosion of volume of trading in T-bill futures contracts,[1] there has been a substantial increase in the number of papers and articles devoted to empirical investigation of interest rate futures prices. See Poole (1978); Lang and Rasche (1978); Puglisi (1978); Vignola and Dale (1979); Chow and Brophy (1978); Ederington (1979); and Rendleman and Carabini (1979).

Poole (1978) provides convincing evidence that no arbitrage opportunities exist in the near futures contract once transaction costs are in-

---

[*]Reprinted from the *Journal of Banking and Finance* (forthcoming). Reprinted by permission of the North Holland Publishing Company, Amsterdam.

[†]Assistant Professor of Finance, University of Texas at Austin. My appreciation is due Bob Kolb, Dick Rendleman, and Richard McEnally for their valuable comments on earlier drafts of this paper and to an anonymous referee who significantly enhanced the clarity of the presentation in the third section.

[1] In this paper only 91 day T-bill futures will be discussed explicitly, but many of the points made apply to any interest rate futures contracts. Arthur (1971) is an excellent description of futures markets in general and Bacon and Williams (1976), Hamburger and Platt (1975), or Puglisi (1978) can be consulted for background material on T-bill futures.

cluded. Lang and Rasche (1978) have examined behavior of distant contracts as well as the near contract and found substantive differences between prices implied by the cash market and futures prices. Puglisi (1978) asserts that such differences present opportunities for profits by hedgers. Rendleman and Carabini (1979) have found that there is no consistent divergence between T-bills and futures prices, but they do find an unusual number of circumstances where divergences occur. There is even confusion over what instrument should be used to hedge an interest rate futures contract, for example, Ederington (1979).

Fischer Black (1976) has come closest to a careful analysis of the underlying qualities of futures and forward contracts. Black carefully points out that futures contracts have no "value" at the end of the trading day whereas forward contracts may have "value." The difference results from the daily resettlement process that the exchanges require of both sides to a futures contract. Unfortunately after Black recognizes this difference between forward and futures, he reverts back to the standard formulation when he assumes that the forward "price is always equal to the current futures price" when the forward contract is initiated. This assumption is not consistent with daily resettlement.

It will be shown in what follows that Black (1976) and others have not adequately incorporated the effects of the daily resettlement process where profits are denominated in terms of changes in price, and therefore, futures prices cannot equal forward prices even when the forward contract is initiated and *even in an efficient market*.

It is the purpose of this paper to show that observed discrepancies between forward and futures prices are not necessarily the result of inefficiencies but rather should be expected to occur in an efficient futures market. The paper presents a means of describing the way in which differences will arise and cannot be arbitraged away. The differences in prices result from the effects of the anticipated course of interest rates over the time to expiration. The course of interest rates is irrelevant to forward contract pricing but is important to buyers and sellers who must agree on a futures contract price.

The paper continues with a section that describes forward contracts, futures contracts, and daily marking to the market. The third section demonstrates that the expected course of interest rates is as important to the pricing of futures contracts as the expected future price of T-bills on the delivery date. The fourth section is a short digression on the need for futures contracts followed by sections analyzing the theoretical price discrepancy and the effects of relaxing some assumptions. The last section is a summary. Throughout the paper, an attempt is made to synthesize the traditional futures literature and the literature on the term structure of interest rates.

THE NATURE OF FUTURES CONTRACTS

Some background discussion in futures and forward contracts is necessary for a full understanding of futures contracts because the two are very similar. In fact, some writers have considered futures contracts as a type of forward contract.[2] It will be shown in the next section that futures contracts can be constructed from forward contracts.[3] Prior to discussing pricing, this section will provide a definition of forward and futures contracts and describe the nature of futures contracts as they are currently traded on the Chicago exchanges.[4]

A forward contract is a contract whereby the seller agrees to deliver a commodity to the buyer at a specified date and price. There is no initial cash flow between the two parties at the time of agreement, and the price cannot change between date of agreement and delivery date.[5] Forward contracts, thus, can be used to "lock-in" the price for a transaction in the future and avoid the risk of price fluctuations. With a futures contract, the price at which delivery will actually occur is not fixed. Instead, the price changes from day to day with recontracting occurring. The purpose of this institutional structure is the next topic considered.

In general, the possibility of default by either party to a forward contract is a major deterrent to forward contracting. Therefore, futures trading (which only occurs on organized exchanges) has been backed by clearinghouses of each of the exchanges that guarantee performance on contracts and match buyers and sellers at the delivery date. Futures contracts are only traded on standardized commodities, and the specific characteristics of a deliverable commodity are established by the exchanges. Telser and Higinbotham (1977) have noted that the commodities exchanges perform an insurance function and thus broaden participation in contracts relating to future delivery of a commodity. They suggest that their viewpoint is consistent with the fact that nearly all forward contracts are held to delivery date while only a small percentage of futures contracts result in delivery of the commodity. Telser and Higinbotham recognize that an integral part of the insurance function is the imposition of limits on daily price movements and a daily "marking

---

[2] For example, Sharpe (1978).

[3] Sharpe (1978) makes a similar argument. The question of the need for both kinds of contracts is deferred to a later section.

[4] The Chicago Board of Trade and The Chicago Mercantile Exchange. See Arthur (1971) or Hoel (1976) for a more detailed discussion.

[5] The definition is consistent with Black (1976) and Telser and Higinbotham (1977). Often "futures contract" is defined in this manner.

to the market" of all open contracts. Essentially, the mechanics of marking to the market are that the profit or loss reflected in the change in price during the day's trading must be settled at the end of the day. Profits are credited to the investor's account or losses are withdrawn.

The combination of required resettlement and price limits accomplishes the goal of eliminating a large part of the exposure of the clearinghouse and the brokers.[6] Those two features of futures contracts are the major differences between forward contracts and futures contracts and may be the source of any differences in prices.[7]

Lang and Rasche (1978) recently provided evidence that a pattern of discrepancies between forward and futures prices has persisted since the initial trading of T-bill futures contracts. The discrepancies get larger as the distance of the delivery date gets farther away. Early explanations of such differences concentrated on market inefficiencies and the inexperience of market participants in the new interest rate futures market. Lang and Rasche (1978) have argued that a differential default risk is a possible source of differential pricing. While it is agreed that futures and forward contracts are different though related instruments, it is argued here that a major aspect of futures contracts—the daily resettlement based on price changes—has not been properly accounted for in any empirical research to date. More will be said in a later section regarding the default risk hypothesis.

T-BILL FUTURES PRICES RELATIVE TO FORWARD PRICES

The traditional arbitrage[8] of one 91 day T-bill futures contract versus a spot T-bill[9] can be used to determine the equilibrium price of a futures contract. The traditional assumptions of no market frictions or

---

[6] It is clear that risk is not entirely eliminated since there may be no trading at all due to price limits. Brokers may not be able to liquidate the positions of customers in default, and the broker may take a loss on the position that is not covered by the maintenance margin.

[7] Currency forward and futures markets have existed side by side, but unfortunately, the maturities have been so seldomly synchronized that observations on price differentials are difficult to obtain. Denis (1976) did find some significant differences in prices; however, he concluded that the parameters of the model are "close" to being equal.

[8] Most often the arbitrage is described in terms of shorting one maturity T-bill while buying a longer maturity to create an implicit forward contract. It can be shown that the forward contract implicit in the term structure is priced the same as if it were a default free explicit forward contract. See Burger, Lang, and Rasche (1977) or Bacon and Williams (1978) for a more detailed discussion of the arbitrage.

[9] Ederington (1979) uses the 91 day T-bill as the hedging vehicle against the futures contract when the correct vehicle must have a maturity greater than 91 days (or alternatively, should be the forward contract implicit in the term structure).

transaction costs,[10] perfectly divisible securities, symmetric distributions, homogeneous beliefs, and risk neutrality[11] are adopted here. The effects of relaxing some of these assumptions is addressed in a later section.

Consider the choices facing an arbitrageur on the day before the futures contract's delivery date:

(a) buy a 92 day T-bill or
(b) "buy" the futures contract to a 91 day T-bill

The present values are determined by the 1 day spot T-bill rate. The cost of (a) is already in present dollars and must equal the present value of (b) if no arbitrage opportunities are to prevail. Thus in equilibrium:

$$P^1_{92} = \frac{1}{1+r_1{}^1} P^1_{fut}, \qquad (1)$$

where superscripts denote the date (in terms of number of days before delivery) at which the price prevails, subscripts are number of days to maturity, and "fut" denotes a futures contract for delivery of a 91 day T-bill to be delivered on day 0. Equation (1) implies that on the day prior to delivery

$$P^1_{for} = P^1_{fut} \qquad (2)$$

This is the commonly recognized relationship between futures and forward prices, but as will be shown below, it can be generally true only when the number of days to delivery is 1 or 0.

If there is more than one day to the delivery date, say D days, then the choices an arbitrageur has are basically the same but with the added obligation in a futures contract to "mark to the market." The choices are

(a) buy a D + 91 day T-bill or
(b) 1. "buy" the futures contract to a 91 day T-bill thus
    2. obligating oneself to abide by the exchange's clearinghouse process of daily resettlement of futures contracts.

[10] Transactions costs on futures contracts are very small relative to the face value. For example, round trip commissions on a $1 million T-bill Futures contract is $60. Initial margin is usually required as a performance bond, but a hedger can use the hedged T-bill as initial margin. To make the arbitrage opportunities equivalent, the cash used to purchase a spot contract must be used to purchase a T-bill when buying a futures contract. Thus initial margin is irrelevant to equilibrium pricing.
[11] It is well known that in valuing a riskless arbitrage in complete markets that any utility function can be employed. Risk neutrality is the most convenient. Implications of risk aversion are included in the section on relaxation of assumptions.

The no-arbitrage condition now requires that the present value (as determined by the D day T-bill rate) of (a) equal the present value of (b) 1. plus (b) 2. Because the daily settlement process creates realized daily "profits" or "losses," the present value of the benefits of those cash flows over the life of the contract may be positive or negative. In equilibrium in an (otherwise) perfect market

$$P_{D+91}^D = \frac{1}{1+r_D^D} P_{fut}^D + \frac{1}{1+r_D^D} \sum_{t=1}^{D-1} (\Delta P_{fut}^{D-t}) r_{D-t}^{D-t}, \qquad (3)$$

where Δ is the backward difference operator and r_D^D is the D day interest rate defined by the spot price P_D^D which is observed D days prior to delivery as defined earlier. The second term on the right hand side of (3) is the interest expense or revenue that results from the daily resettlement of the futures contract. The interest expense or revenue is realized at the delivery date and therefore the D day rate is employed as the discount rate in (3) similar to (1). (Note that the prices P_{fut}^{D-t} are *not* prices on futures contracts with delivery at D−t. The futures prices in the second term of (3) all refer to the same futures contract observed at the various times D−t). If marking to the market results in the necessity to send cash to the clearinghouse, there is an interest expense of borrowing the cash until the delivery date when the loss is recouped. On the other hand, a cash inflow generates the reinvestment income of interest revenues. These additional flows may be called the "cost of carrying" the arbitrage. Equation (3) can be rewritten as

$$P_{for}^D = P_{fut}^D + \sum_{t=1}^{D-1} (\Delta P_{fut}^{D-t}) r_{D-t}^{D-t} \qquad (4)$$

from which it can be seen that as long as futures prices are expected to change, futures and forward prices will not be equal. (The relationship between r_{D-t}^{D-t} and ΔP_{fut}^{D-t} is derived below in (6), but substitution of (6) in (3) and (4) only results in making the second terms in (3) and (4) appear as functions of changes in forward prices rather than futures prices.)

If equation (4) did not hold true, riskless arbitrage could be undertaken. The cash flows from rebalancing would go to finance the daily resettlement on the futures contract with any excess or deficiency loaned or borrowed until delivery date with a net profit accumulated at that time. Thus the presumption by most researchers that futures and forward prices should be equal in an efficient market is incorrect. Futures prices *must* be different from forward prices as long as it is believed that there is some chance that futures prices will change through time. Equation (4) shows that the difference between the futures price and the forward price is related to the expected changes in forward rates between agreement and delivery and related to the expected discounting rates over the time period. That is, the course of rates over time is important to the pricing of futures contracts. Equation (4) also implies that autocorrelation will be observed in the time series of differences. Thus it is not surprising and is supportive of the analysis here that Vignola and Dale (1979) have found autocorrelation (putting aside their annualizing factor which itself induces autocorrelation) as Rendleman and Carabini (1979) also have found.

Equation (3) may be more enlightening in its dynamic form. Consider the change in the value of alternatives (a) and (b) from D+1 to D where only the forward price changes. The change in value of the two alternatives must be equal if the no-arbitrage condition holds. Therefore the present value of the change in the futures price plus the change in the present value of the interest expense or revenue must equal the change in the price of a T-bill that will be deliverable on the futures contract, i.e.,

$$\frac{1}{1+r_D^D} \Delta P_{for}^D = \frac{1}{1+r_D^D} \Delta P_{fut}^D + \frac{1}{1+r_D^D} r_D^D \Delta P_{fut}^D \tag{5}$$

or

$$\frac{\Delta P_{for}^D}{1+r_D^D} = \Delta P_{fut}^D \tag{6}$$

Notice that the change in value of alternative (a) is exactly the amount required for marking to the market, but *because* that is true, futures and forward prices *cannot* be equal. Otherwise the two alternatives would not have equivalent changes in value. The forward price and changes in the forward price relate to a future event (the delivery) and thus must be discounted while the daily resettlement and the change in the futures price occurs in the present.

When the alternatives are viewed as an implicit forward contract versus a futures contract it can be seen with equation (6) that a futures contract can be created with continual rebalancing of an implicit forward contract to create cash flows exactly equal to the flows from daily resettlement on a futures contract. For a hedger, then, the daily resettlement poses no hardship and in fact is a crucial part of the daily rebalancing of the hedge.[12] Nonetheless, futures and forward prices must differ by virtue of the daily resettlement.

The insurance function of the clearinghouse has dictated the process of resettlement which is based on the denomination of profits in terms of the change in price. So the futures-forward differential is related to resettlement under the current institutional arrangement; however, resettlement based on denomination of profit and loss in terms of

---

[12] The hedging and arbitrage discussed here is the discrete time analog of the continuously rebalanced Black-Scholes (1973) riskless hedge. In discrete time models recursive or enumerative methods are commonly used. See Rendleman and Bartter (1979) for an example from the options literature.

discounted forward prices would remove any futures-forward price differential.

ARE FUTURES CONTRACT NEEDED?

Given the analysis developed in the previous section and the traditional analysis, the need for the existence of futures contracts can be questioned. If futures contracts can be constructed by rebalancing forward contracts, then what does a futures market offer to an economy? First it must be realized that the arbitrage strategy outlined above may not be available to all investors. Large investors (banks, corporations, mutual funds, government securities dealers) can perform quasi-arbitrage and are more likely to incur low transaction costs in shorting T-bills. Part of the lower transaction costs relate to the lower perceived (perhaps because of better information that is more easily obtainable) risk of default in dealing with such institutions. Thus there will be enough market participants to assure that equilibrium prices will prevail; however, not all investors can transact with low costs and good information.

The existence of futures contracts offers more economic units the opportunity to hedge cash positions than would be the case with either explicit or implicit forward contracts. The clearinghouse, as discussed above, provides insurance to investors so that there is no need to acquire information about the other side of the contract. This is particularly important for taking a short forward or futures position since there are restrictions (related to default potential in some senses) on shorting in the cash market where forward contracts are "bundled" with spot contracts. This is a substantial problem in the commodity cash markets and is a problem of only slightly lesser magnitude in the T-bill market.

These restrictions and frictions in T-bill cash markets and the explicit forward market are important from the viewpoint provided by Stein (1961). Stein argues that given a utility function and beliefs about return distributions there is an optimal proportion of a portfolio that should be hedged. Factors which prevent investors from achieving the optimal hedged position (which will only be 100 percent or zero percent in unusual circumstances) result in investors holding a portfolio that is suboptimal in terms of risk of investment. The existence of forwardlike contracts for which there are fewer restrictions (either economic or institutional) facilitates the attainment of the optimal portfolio allocation among risky investment opportunities in a world where there are short restrictions and forward contracts are bundled with spot contracts.

The next section examines and analyzes the character of the price differential implied by the theoretical relationship shown in equation (6).

ANALYSIS OF THE PRICE DIFFERENTIAL

Under the unbiased expectations theory of the term structure of interest rates,[13] forward prices are expectations of future prices of T-bills. The theory implies that the expected change in the forward price is zero. Because there is no expected change in future forward rates, all the terms in the summation on the right hand side of (4) are zero, and the difference between the forward price and the futures price is zero. Under the unbiased expectations hypothesis, then, forward and futures prices will be the same. That implies that tests of the equality of the implicit forward rate and the futures rate are tests of the expectations hypothesis. The evidence provided by Lang and Rasche (1978) indicates rejection of the null hypothesis of unbiased expectations since significant, consistent differences are observable.

The Lang and Rasche (1978) and Puglisi (1978) analyses indicate that futures prices have been consistently lower than forward prices in most contracts. The theory developed here provides some explanations for this observed phenomenon that appear more plausible than other explanations advanced. From equation (4), their observations are consistent with an expectation that forward prices would fall over the time period or that rates would rise over the relevant time periods. As an approximation, the Lang and Rasche difference of 60 basis points would correspond to expectations that rates would rise at a rate of 100 basis points a month. Rates did not rise *that* quickly, but, in fact, did rise over the periods considered. Assuming investors are rational though not infallible, the evidence is consistent with the theory developed here. Lang and Rasche (1978) found some cases where futures prices have been significantly higher than forward prices particularly in contracts nearer to delivery. The default risk explanation cannot fit comfortably with both positive and negative differentials in different contracts at the same point in time whereas the analysis presented here suggests that different portions of the timepaths of interest rates were relevant.[14] That is, over a short period, rates could be expected to fall while over longer periods rates could be expected to rise.

---

[13] There is a parallel theory of "futures" (forward) pricing that asserts that prices are unbiased forecasts of future spot prices. See Fama (1976), Teweles, Harlow, and Stone (1969), and Stevenson and Bear (1970). On term structure theories, see Hamburger and Platt (1974), Wood (1964), Malkiel (1966).

[14] More is said on the issue of risk premia at the end of this section.

On the other hand, there is a theory of forward interest rates that suggests that forward rates incorporate not only expectations but also a liquidity premium to compensate investors for potential losses incurred in the event that the securities are liquidated prior to maturity.[15] In other words, the expected change in the forward price is positive.[16] From equation (4), the liquidity premium theory produces futures prices that are higher than forward prices and the more distant the delivery date, the greater the difference between forwards and futures. The Lang and Rasche empirical analysis does not appear to verify the liquidity premium theory in any but the nearest-to-delivery contracts since futures prices have been observed consistently below forward prices, and because using Roll's (1970) estimates of liquidity premia, the magnitude of the effects would be on the order of 5 basis points which is much smaller than the observed effects; however, segmentation or preferred habitat theories may be consistent with the data since no smooth or monotone pattern of premia are presumed in those theories. In addition, the effect of expected shifts in the liquidity premium structure itself could create larger differential prices. If it were believed that the liquidity premium would increase to a peak and then drop during the period between agreement and delivery date,[17] the forward price might be, on net, lower than the future price. Unfortunately, there is no method known to measure expectations regarding the time path of the liquidity premium.

THE EFFECT OF RELAXING SOME ASSUMPTIONS

The qualitative effects of relaxing four assumptions can be examined to provide insight into more realistic futures pricing. The existence of a differential between rates at which gains can be reinvested and losses can be borrowed should magnify the size of the effects discussed here.

---

[15] See Malkiel (1966), Nelson (1972), Roll (1970) or Modigliani and Schiller (1973).

[16] In the "futures" (forward) pricing literature this is called normal backwardation. The contango theory asserts that forward prices should be higher than expected prices and thus prices are expected to fall over time. The two theories differ in the assumption of who the hedgers in the market are. A theory of bond pricing analagous to the contango theory would be a theory that concentrates on "income risk" instead of "liquidity risk." I am indebted to Professor Henry Latane for bringing this latter point to my attention and for suggesting that a more general theory of the term structure would include both risk factors working against one another in determining forward interest rates.

[17] This may occur in consonance with a cyclical rise in risk premia as examined in Fisher (1959), or as the result of increased uncertainty regarding the direction of monetary policy in a rapidly changing economic environment. Friedman (1979) also provides evidence that the size of the liquidity premia may be related to the level of interest rates.

An asymmetric distribution of price changes is more appealing than symmetric distributions because of the lower bound on price changes (i.e., −100 percent) and because empirically a lognormal distribution appears to fit the data better than a normal distribution. The skewness of the distribution of price changes becomes important when there is also a borrowing-lending rate differential and will increase the magnification of other effects such as the movement of liquidity premia over time.

Upon relaxing the assumption of risk neutrality, the issue of risk premia[18] in the futures market that are not already contained in the forward market is important for pricing. The existence of a premium cannot be justified based on traditional arguments. In the traditional literature the controversy over the existence of premia centers on different assumptions regarding who the hedgers are. Are the hedgers short hedgers or long hedgers? In the first case, speculators must be paid a risk premium to take long futures positions. In the second case, speculators must be compensated for short positions that allow the hedger to get the desired insurance. In some markets, these distinctions are not meaningful. For example, Burns (1976) points out that whether a premium or discount exists in foreign exchange futures depends on "which side of the coin" is considered. Furthermore, as is the case in the T-bill markets, there are few restrictions on active market participants[19] creating short hedges or long hedges.[20] That is, any observed price discrepancies can be captured by entering into a riskless arbitrage. The activity of market participants to capture premia while taking a riskless position will result in the premia being bid away.

The differences between the traditional literature and the arguments made here are the result of the different instruments given consideration. Traditionally, two different agreements are considered: one to buy a commodity at a future date and one to buy a commodity immediately. The price in each case is different and there is reason to believe that hedgers of the *spot* commodity would pay an insurance premium that would systematically bias *forward* prices. In contrast, there appears to be little support for the contention that T-bill *futures* contracts are systematically biased by an insurance premium paid by hedgers of *forward* contracts.

Although Lang and Rasche (1978) note the implausibility of a risk premium in futures markets when riskless arbitrage possibilities exist, they suggest that default risk may account for some of the differential.

---

[18] Dusak (1973) recently pointed out that conceptually only systematic risk is relevant to the existence of a risk premium.

[19] In both these markets, banks and large corporations can easily arbitrage the futures markets either way.

[20] In some cases, riskless arbitrage (or what Rendleman and Carabini (1978) call quasi-arbitrage) is a more accurate description of the process.

The default to which they refer is the default of an investor, his broker, the exchange clearinghouse, *and* the exchange membership on either resettlement or delivery. Although this risk could be considered entirely non-diversifiable, the event is so remote that the resulting premium could not be large enough to explain observable differences. For example, interest rate risk/horizon risk is many orders of magnitude larger than this default risk, yet it is generally believed that 50 to 100 basis points is the magnitude of the liquidity premium. Furthermore, it is not entirely clear how the default premium explanation used by Lang and Rasche (1978) necessarily implies a premium for the long side of the contract for distant contracts since the long side may also default, and as discussed earlier, the clearinghouse guarantees both sides of the contract. Similarly, it is unclear why the short side of the contract should receive a premium on near contracts.

A risk premium of another sort may be justified if the assumption of homogeneous beliefs is relaxed. If an investor is unaware what other investors believe about the course of interest rates, then it may be possible for the investor to exact risk compensation because the current equilibrium price from (4) is unknown. But even that risk premium has some implausibility since there are two parties subject to that same risk on every contract. Furthermore, if in developing equation (3) a risk adjusted discount rate were used to discount to the present net cash flows received at delivery date, no change in the ensuing equations would be required and the futures-forward differential would still be given by (4) in terms of expected changes in forward rates.

SUMMARY AND CONCLUSIONS

A discussion of the nature and usefulness of futures contracts revealed that there are a number of differences between futures and forward contracts. A major difference, that results from the insurance role of the clearinghouse of a futures exchange, is the requirement of daily marking to the market.

It was demonstrated that this difference would result in different prices for forward and futures contracts. Even in an efficient market, there will be a difference between forward and futures prices because futures prices incorporate expectations regarding the course of interest rates between agreement and delivery dates whereas forward prices do not. Empirical studies have all presumed that in efficient markets forward and futures were the same. Thus their analysis of the empirical evidence must be suspect. For example, Puglisi (1978) advises that the observed discrepancies are profit opportunities waiting to be exploited by simple riskless hedges or arbitrage strategies. Similarly, many brokerage houses tout the profit opportunities by referring to the standard formula that presumes forward and futures are the same. This is particularly troublesome given that the analysis here indicates that the "discrepancies" *can* result from efficient pricing based on expectations that rates will rise over the relevant time period.

Unfortunately, the analysis presented here dashes any hopes of testing term structure hypotheses a la Chow and Brophy (1978) or more generally of using futures prices as easily accessible, direct, market forecasts of future interest rates at a single future time *point*, Poole (1978).[21] By their construction, futures prices also include data regarding market expectations of the future course of interest rates over a time *period*. The analysis suggests that empirical tests can provide evidence regarding the validity of *some* of the theories of the term structure because some of those theories imply hypotheses regarding the course of interest rates. The evidence, so far, seems to favor rejection of the expectations hypothesis.[22] On the other hand, it appears that it will be difficult to test the appropriateness of other term structure theories versus the liquidity premium theory since so little has been done on the movement of liquidity premia over time. That is, it appears that term structure efforts are back at the starting point. In order to test the theories, an "independent" source of interest rate expectations is needed (and in the case of T-bill futures, expectations about movements in *forward* rates). T-bill futures prices are not such a source in either case, even in an efficient market, contrary to the presumptions made by Lang and Rasche (1978), Poole (1978), Chow and Brophy (1978), and Puglisi (1978).

References

Arthur, H. B. (1971), *Commodity Futures as a Business Management Tool*, Graduate School of Business Administration, Harvard University, Boston, Massachusetts.

Bacon, Peter W. and Richard E. Williams (1976), "Interest Rate Futures: New Tool for the Financial Manager," *Financial Management*, Spring, p. 32-8.

Black, Fischer (1976), "The Pricing of Commodity Contracts," *Journal of Financial Economics*, January-March, p. 167-79.

Black, Fischer and Myron Scholes (1974), "The Pricing of Options and Corporate Liabilities," *Journal of Political Economy*, May/June, p. 637-54.

Burger, Albert E., Richard W. Lang, and Robert H. Rasche (1977), "The Treasury Bill Futures Market and Market Expectations of Interest Rates," *Review*, Federal Reserve Bank of St. Louis, June, p. 2-9.

---

[21] This has no implication for Poole's empirical work since he only considered the contract nearest to delivery where the effects analyzed here have little impact.

[22] Rendleman and Carabini (1978) could be used as evidence to support the acceptance of the expectations hypothesis.

Burns, Joseph (1976), *Accounting Standards and International Finance*, American Enterprise Institute, Washington, D.C.

Chow, Brian and David Brophy (1978), "The U.S. Treasury Bill Futures Market and Hypotheses Regarding the Term Structure of Interest Rates," *Financial Review*, Fall, p. 36-50.

Denis, Jack Jr. (1976), "How Well Does the IMM Track the Interbank Forward Market?" *Financial Analysts Journal*, January, p. 50-54.

Dusak, Katherine (1973), "Futures Trading and Investor Returns: An Investigation of Commodity Market Risk Premiums," *Journal of Political Economy*, November, p. 1387-1406.

Ederington, Louis H. (1979), "The Hedging Performance of the New Futures Markets," *Journal of Finance*, March, p. 157-170.

Fama, Eugene (1976), "Forward Rates as Predictors of Future Spot Rates," *Journal of Financial Economics*, October, p. 361-77.

Fisher, Lawrence (1959), "Determinants of Risk Premiums on Corporate Bonds," *Journal of Political Economy*, June, p. 217-37.

Friedman, Benjamin (1979), "Interest Rate Expectations Versus Forward Rates: Evidence from an Expectations Survey," *Journal of Finance*, September, p. 965-973.

Hamburger and Platt (1975), "The Expectations Hypothesis and the Efficiency of the Treasury Bill Market," *Review of Economics and Statistics*, May, p. 190-99.

Hoel, Arline (1976), "A Primer on the Futures Markets for Treasury Bills," Research paper, Federal Reserve Bank of New York.

Kaldor, Nicholas (1939), "Speculation and Economic Stability," *Review of Economic Studies*, October, p. 1-27.

Keynes, J. M. (1930), *A Treatise on Money*, Harcourt, New York.

Lang, Richard W. and Robert Rasche (1978), "A Comparison of Yields on Futures Contracts and Implied Forward Rates," *Review*, Federal Reserve Bank of St. Louis, December, p. 21-30.

Malkiel, Burton (1966), *The Term Structure of Interes Rates*, Princeton University Press, Princeton, N. J.

Modigliani, F. and R. J. Schiller (1973), "Inflation, Rational Expectations, and the Term Structure of Interest Rates," *Economica*, February, p. 12-43.

Nelson, C. R. (1972), *The Term Structure of Interest Rates*, Basic Books, Inc. New York.

Poole, William (1978), "Using T-Bill Futures to Gauge Interest Rate Expectations," *Review*, San Francisco Federal Reserve, Spring, p. 7-19.

Puglisi, Donald (1978), "Is the Futures Market for Treasury Bills Efficient?" *Journal of Portfolio Management*, Winter, p. 64-7.

Roll, Richard (1970), *The Behavior of Interest Rates*, Basic Books, New York.

Rendleman, Richard and Brit Bartter (1979), "Two State Option Pricing," *Journal of Finance*, December, p. 1093-1111.

Rendleman, Richard and Christopher Carabini (1979), "The Efficiency of the Treasury Bill Futures Market," *Journal of Finance*, September, p. 895-914.

Sharpe, William (1978), "Investments," Prentice-Hall, New York.

Stein, Jerome (1961), "The Simultaneous Determination of Spot and Futures Prices," *American Economic Review*, December, p. 1012-25.

Stevenson, Richard and Robert Bear (1970), "Commodity Futures—Trends or Random Walks," *Journal of Finance*, March, p. 65-81.

Telser, L. G. and H. N. Higinbotham (1977), "Organized Futures Markets: Costs and Benefits," *Journal of Political Economy*, October, p. 969-1000.

Teweles, R. J., C. V. Harlow and H. L. Stone (1969), *The Commodity Futures Guide*, McGraw-Hill.

Vignola, Anthony and Charles Dale (1979), "Is the Futures Market for Treasury Bills Efficient?", *Journal of Portfolio Management*, Winter, p. 78-81.

Wood, John (1964), "The Expectations Hypothesis, the Yield Curve, and Monetary Policy," *Quarterly Journal of Economics*, August p. 457-74.

25

Tax-Induced Bias in Markets for Futures Contracts*

Edward Miller[†]

Conventional wisdom holds that prices for futures contracts should equal the expected value for the same contracts in future months, including the delivery month. It will be shown that this conclusion does not hold under the United States tax system (both before and after the 1978 changes). The argument will be developed using commodity futures contracts where markets are relatively simple, and there are no complications arising from lack of symmetry for long and short selling [2, 3]. However, similar effects may occur in the security markets since the applicable tax laws are the same (except that the holding period required for long-term gains is six months for commodities and one year for other capital assets, including securities).

Prices on futures markets are a result of the interaction of both hedgers and speculators. Hedgers are those who anticipate buying or selling the commodity in the future and are setting up positions in futures intended to hedge against adverse changes in the price of the commodity. They are subject to the same economic motives as the pure speculators, and the argument given here easily extends to include them. This discussion will focus on the role of the speculators rather than the hedgers. This is partially because the contribution of this article relates

*Reprinted from *The Financial Review*, Vol. 15, pages 35-38, (Spring 1980). Reprinted by permission of the Eastern Finance Association, publisher.

[†]SANOFF Professor of Public Affairs, Jones School of Administration, Rice University, Houston, Texas.

to their behavior and there is little to add to the previous discussion of hedgers by other authors [1, 6, 7]. However, the primary reason is that the number of speculators is potentially far larger (in theory at least) than the number of hedgers and prices cannot long remain at levels where the typical speculator would desire to take a position. Virtually any investor is a potential speculator, and if he believes that a commodity position offers risk adjusted returns in excess of other investments he will include in his portfolio a commodity position (for reasons of risk this will probably be small in relation to his total portfolio).

The conventional argument[1] is that if speculators thought that the current price of a futures contract exceeded the expected value for any future date they would sell it short forcing the price back to equality with the expected future price. Likewise, if speculators believe the current price to be less than the expected price at any future date, they would purchase the contract and hold it until that date. This would force the price upwards until it equaled the expected future price. If delivery conditions for the contract are the same as for the spot commodity, this implies that the price of a futures contract will be equal to the spot price expected in the delivery month. Thus, in the traditional two-person, zero sum context, the future price should equal the expected spot price.

However, commodity trading is not a simple two-person game. It is a three-person game, with the third person, Uncle Sam, following a passive strategy. This makes it possible for both of the other players to be winners, and to have an incentive to keep on playing.

THE TAX TREATMENT OF COMMODITY FUTURES

For those who buy and sell futures contracts as part of their business, profits and losses from futures contracts are treated as ordinary income.[2] However, for professional speculators, contracts are capital assets and are treated as such assets in most respects. The major exception is that the holding period for long-term gains is still only six months rather than the one year applicable to other capital assets. If long positions are held for more than six months, the resulting capital gains and losses are taxed at preferential rates. If held for less than six months, gains and

---

[1] Probably the most elegant discussion is by Black [1]. He explicitly excludes the tax effects which are the subject of this paper. Working [7] is often given credit for first developing the anticipatory model. Other good treatments are by Sharpe [5] and by Teweles, Harlow, and Stone [6].

[2] The discussion of taxes in this paper is based on *Prentice Hall's Federal Tax Course*, Student Edition [4], except for the 1978 changes.

losses are considered short-term and are taxed at the ordinary income rate (except that no more than $3,000 of capital losses can be deducted from ordinary income). Short positions in futures are treated the same as short positions in other capital assets: All gains and losses are short-term regardless of the holding period. This difference in treatment between short and long positions is the key to the argument to be presented.

Given the tax law, there is an optimal strategy for the speculator on the long side. He holds his position until just before the end of the short-term holding period. If at that time he has a loss, he sells the position, recording a short-term loss. If he has a gain he holds the position a bit longer, and records a long-term gain. By this strategy, all gains are taxed as long-term gains, and all losses are short-term. If prices of futures contracts were unbiased predictors of future prices, the expected after-tax profits from a long position would be positive. Since there are no similar expected profits from a short position (losses are expected after commissions), all speculators would desire to take the long side. Such an unbalanced situation is not consistent with equilibrium.

The same argument can be made in symbolic form. Let: p = the probability of gain on the futures contract; $(1 - p)$ = probability of a loss on the futures contract; G = expected value of gain, if there is one; L = expected value of a loss, if there is one; t = income tax rate on short-term gains and losses and on ordinary income; and c = tax rate on long-term gains and losses.

A market in which the current price of a futures contract is equal to the expected price in any future year and to the spot price in the delivery month (adjusted for any difference in delivery conditions) will be referred to as an unbiased market. Thus by definition, an unbiased market is one whose price is such that expected gains and loss are equal. Thus, in an unbiased market:

$$pG = (1 - p)L$$

Using the strategy described above, gains are taxed at the long-term rate and losses are deducted at the short-term rate (assuming they are less than $3,000 or are not offset by short-term gains). The expected after-tax net gains are

$$pG(1 - c) - (1 - p)L(1 - t)$$

Substituting pG for $(1 - p)L$, this simplifies to:

$$pG(1 - c) - pG(1 - t) \text{ and}$$
$$pG(t - c)$$

Thus if the tax rate on long-term gains is below the rate on short-term gains, the expected after-tax profit is positive in an unbiased market. Under current law, only 40% of the long-term gains are taxed, while all of the short-term gains are taxed. In addition, the individual with substantial long-term gains may be subject to a minimum tax on the excluded portions of the gains, but this does not eliminate the preferential treatment of long-term gains. To summarize, there is a tax subsidy available for trading commodity futures from the long side but not from the short side, and this prevents the market from being unbiased.

Since an unbiased market offers an expectation of after-tax profits on the long side and losses on the short side (due to commissions), an absence of sellers (other than hedgers) on the short side would prevent prices from remaining at the levels required for an unbiased market. Instead, prices would rise to offer before-tax profits to those taking the short side. This would attract individuals in low tax brackets to the short side of the market.[3] Those in high tax brackets would take the long side, where small before-tax losses can be converted to after-tax gains by a proper timing of transactions. Thus, the only player with expected losses in an efficient market is Uncle Sam.[4]

References

[1] Black, Fischer, "Pricing of Commodity Contracts," *Journal of Financial Economics*, Vol. 3, Nos. 1 and 2, (January/March 1976), 167-179.
[2] Miller, Edward, "Risk, Uncertainty, and Divergence of Opinion," *Journal of Finance* (September 1977).
[3] Miller, Edward, "How to Win at the Loser's Game," *Journal of Portfolio Management*, Vol. 5, No. 1, (Fall 1978), 17-24.
[4] *Prentice Hall, 1978 Federal Tax Course*, Student Edition (Englewood Cliffs, N.J., 1977), 1608-1610.
[5] Sharpe, William F., *Investments* (Englewood Cliffs, N.J.: Prentice Hall, 1978), 418-419.
[6] Teweles, Richard J., Charles V. Harlow, and Herbert L. Stone. *The Commodity Futures Game* (New York: McGraw-Hill, 1974), Chapter 4.
[7] Workings, Holbrook, "A Theory of Anticipatory Prices," *American Economic Review*, Vol. 48, No. 2, (May 1958), 188-199.

---

[3] High tax bracket investors would not also take the short side because that could lead to short-term losses offsetting the tax favored long-term gains, since any net short-term losses are subtracted from net long-term gains to determine total capital gains and losses.

[4] Uncle Sam has expected tax loss only if all speculators are rational (which implies that prices fluctuate randomly). If speculators took large positions, they would run the risk of incurring losses in excess of the amount that can be offset against other income (no more than $3,000 can be offset against ordinary income in any one year) and the risk of having their gains taxed in substantially higher brackets than those in which their losses are deducted. Since strategies that involve taking large positions in an efficient market have expected after-tax losses, rational speculators will limit themselves to positions sufficiently small to avoid such problems. In the real world, speculators appear to take large enough positions that Uncle Sam benefits from taxing gains at higher rates than those at which losses are deducted.

26

Tax Topics: Interest Rates Futures–Commercial Banks*

James G. O'Brien[†]

INTEREST RATES FUTURES–COMMERCIAL BANKS

A Hypothetical Situation

A bank is a dealer in securities. It inventories securities on hand at the close of the taxable year.[1] In addition, the bank is an investor in securities. It identifies securities at the purchase date as investment securities or dealer securities.[2] Investment securities held by the bank are capital assets.[3] However, upon the sale of investment securities the bank realizes ordinary gain or loss.[4] It enters into certain interest rate futures contracts that when made are identified as attributable to either its investment account or its trading account activities. The contracts

---

*Reprinted by permission from The Banking Law Journal, Volume 98, Number 3, March 1981. Copyright © 1981, Warren, Gorham and Lamont Inc., 210 South Street, Boston, Mass. All rights reserved.

†Senior Vice-President and General Tax Counsel for Bankers Trust Company. Former chairman, Tax and Accounting Committee, New York Clearing House; former chairman, Tax Section, American Bankers Association; President of the USA Branch, International Fiscal Association. This column is based on the author's presentation at the 16th Annual Bank Tax Institute, December 4-5, 1980.

[1] I.R.C. § 471; Reg. § 1.471-5(c).
[2] I.R.C. § 1236.
[3] I.R.C. § 1221; Reg. § 1.582-1(d).
[4] I.R.C. § 582(c).

involve both long (a contract to accept delivery of securities at a future date) and short (a contract to make delivery of securities at a future date) positions. The contracts are subject to the rules of an organized board of trade or commodity exchange and are closed by either offset or delivery more than six months from the contract date.

Long Futures Contract

The bank enters into a long futures contract involving Treasury bonds. Its expressed intent in entering into the contract is an investment motive; the bank believes interest rates will fall and outstanding bond prices will rise. The bank intends, should its expectations concerning future interest rates prove correct (bond prices rise), to close the contract by an offsetting short contract. Should its expectations prove incorrect (bond prices fall), the bank will take delivery and sell the Treasury bonds so acquired.

The Issues

The contract described immediately above would be a capital asset.[5] The contract is a separate asset which represents *rights* to Treasury bonds, not the underlying Treasury bonds.[6] No federal income tax consequence arises as a result of the bank entering into the contract.[7] Such a contract, which is held for more than six months, would satisfy the *holding period rules* for qualification for long-term capital gain or loss.[8]

Subject to the various caveats discussed below, "closing" of the contract by entering into an offsetting contract would produce long-term capital gain.[9] That "closing" would constitute a sale or exchange[10] of

---

[5] I.R.C. § 1221.

[6] Rev. Rul. 78-414, 1978-1 C.B. 213; Faroll v. Jacecki, 231 F.2d 281 (1956), and the concurring opinion (Holmes) in Covington v. Comm'r. 120 F.2d 768 (1941), *cert. denied* 315 U.S. 822 (1942). See also Kane, "Tax Treatment of Treasury Bond Futures," 52 So. Calif. L. Rev. 1555 (1979). The issues presented in Revenue Ruling 78-414 are similar to the present discussion. T-bills, the underlying property in that ruling, always produce ordinary income or ordinary loss. It should be stated that in the view of the IRS, Revenue Ruling 78-414 is intended to, in part, close an unwarranted tax-shelter practice (i.e., straddling).

[7] Rev. Rul. 78-182, 1971-1 C.B. 265 (a "put" and "call" ruling); Rev. Rul. 74-223, 1974-1 C.B. 23.

[8] I.R.C. § 1222. The last sentence of Section 1222 provides that in the case of futures transactions in any commodity subject to the rules of a board of trade or commodity exchange the length of the holding period for long-term capital gain shall continue to be six months.

It is not clear that such gain or loss is long-term capital gain or loss. See discussion under the short sale rules in the cases discussed below. In the absence of a sale or exchange, taxpayer would have been allowed ordinary losses.

[9] Rev. Rul. 78-414, note 7 *supra*.

[10] Covington v. Comm'r, note 6 *supra*: Faroll v. Jacecki, note 6 *supra*.

rights to Treasury bonds.[11]

In summary, the historical issue has been whether the sale or exchange requirement has been satisfied; once it is established that "closing" or "offsetting" constitutes a sale or exchange most investors realize capital gain or capital loss regardless of whether that exchange is deemed to involve a sale of the underlying property (Treasury bonds) or a sale of separate contractual rights. The latter issue is of course critical for commercial banks.[12] Revenue Ruling 78-414 holds that the closing transac-

---

[11] The "separate property" issue poses difficulties. The questions is whether securities, the Treasury bonds, have been sold. "The set-off or ringing-off transactions under the rules of the exchanges are considered to be legal deliveries (of the underlying property, i.e., the Treasury bonds)." Board of Trade v. Christie Grain & Stock Co., 198 U.S. 236 (1905). Cf. Rev. Rul. 78-414, note 7 *supra*. See also Note, "Trading in Commodity Futures Under Federal Income Tax Statutes," 51 Yale L.J. 505, 508-509 (1942).

In Covington v. Comm'r, note 6 *supra*, Judge Holmes noted:

> Conceding, arguendo, that the taxpayer merely entered into executory contracts, on margins, for the delivery of commodities at a future date which were terminated before the time therein named for delivery, such contracts were intangible property which are deemed to have a value the instant they are made; their subsequent value or lack of value depends upon the market price of the commodity at the time of valuation. *These contracts are capable of ownership and of being transferred by act of the parties or by operation of law.* They are capital assets within the meaning of Sec. 117(b) and (d) of the Revenue Act of 1936....

In Lyons Milling Co. v. Goffe & Carkener, 46 F.2d 241, 247, the court said: "A set-off is a method by which a contract to purchase is set off against a contract to sell without the formality of an exchange of warehouse receipts or other actual delivery and, in legal effect, is a delivery."

In Board of Trade v. Christie Grain & Stock Co., *supra*, the court said:

> We must suppose that from the beginning, as now, if a member had a contract with another member to buy a certain amount of wheat at a certain time, and another to sell the same amount at the same time, it would be deemed unnecessary to exchange warehouse receipts. *We must suppose that then as now, a settlement would be made by the payment of differences, after the analogy of a clearing house. This naturally would take place no less than the contracts were made in good faith, for actual delivery, since the result of actual delivery would be to leave the parties just where they were before. Set-off has all the effects of delivery.*

In United States v. Coffee Exch., 263 U.S. 611, 619, the Court said:

> *For purposes of taxation it is immaterial whether this taxpayer was a trader in the actual commodities or in rights to the commodities.* In either event his losses which resulted from trading in commodity futures contracts were properly classified as capital losses subject to the limitations of Sec. 177(d) of the Revenue Act of 1936. The substance of the transaction is the same whether the taxpayer acquired tangible or intangible property. It was the primary purpose of Congress in imposing the capital loss limitation to prevent such trading losses from wiping out all ordinary income for tax purposes. [Emphasis added.]

H. R. Rep. No. 704, 73d Cong. 2d Sess. 30-31.

[12] I.R.C. § 582(c).

tion involves separate property rights, not the underlying Treasury bills which were the subject of that ruling. The holding in that ruling will be litigated.

There would be no federal income tax incident on performance of the contract by taking delivery of the securities and their placement in the investment account.[13] Ordinary income or ordinary loss would be realized upon later sale of the securities.[14]

Does the *Corn Products*[15] doctrine change the result described above? Revenue Ruling 78-94[16] provides in part:

> The Internal Revenue Service has reconsidered Rev. Rul. 75-13, 1975-1 C.B. 67, because of the decisions by the United States Tax Court in *W. W. Windle Co. v. Commissioner*, 65 T.C. 692 (1976), appeal dismissed, 550 F.2d 43 (1st Cir. 1977), and *Bell Fibre Products Corporation*, T. C. Memo. 1977-42 (1977). Rev. Rul. 75-13 holds that the sale or exchange of shares of stock gives rise to capital gain or loss if investment is the *predominant motive* for purchasing and holding the stock. In the *Windle* and *Bell Fibre* cases the court concluded that stock purchased with a *substantial investment purpose* is a capital asset even though there was a more substantial business motive for the purchase. [Emphasis added.][17]

Is It a Hedge?

All of the above assumes that the long futures contract is not a hedge. A futures contract which is, for tax purposes, a "hedge" will always result in ordinary income or loss. To date, a hedge has been viewed as a form of "price insurance" for businesses which intend to profit from a

---

[13] See note 7 *supra*.
[14] I.R.C. § 582(c).
[15] 350 U.S. 46, *rehearing denied* 350 U.S. 943 (1955).
[16] 1978-1 C.B. 58.
[17] The extent to which the *Corn Products* doctrine encompasses "everyday business income" realized with an investment motive is unclear.

Nonetheless, Congress has in effect deemed a bank's purchases and sales of investment account securities to be an everyday business activity which generates ordinary income and ordinary loss. This occurred in 1969 when Congress amended Section 582(c) of the Code to provide that investment securities of banks and certain other financial institutions will yield ordinary income and ordinary losses instead of the capital gain (gain year) and ordinary loss (loss year) that had previously been allowed.

Congress though that "[t]ransactions of financial institutions in corporate and government bonds and other evidences of indebtedness do not appear to be true capital transactions; they are more akin to transactions in inventory or stock in view of the size of the bank's holdings of these items and the extent of their transactions in them." H.R. Rep. No. 91-413 (Part 1), 91st Cong., 1st Sess. 129-130 (Aug. 2, 1969); S. Rep. No. 91-552, 91st Cong., 1st Sess. 167 (Nov. 21, 1969).

"markup" on their inventory and not from market price fluctuations. Thus, hedging treatment has been allowed for manufacturers, merchants, etc., who use futures contracts to protect themselves from the risk of declines in inventory values[18] or from increased manufacturing costs.[19] The balanced market position which the futures contracts provide allows the taxpayer to realize approximately the same amount of income he would have if there were no price fluctuations.[20] Since the contracts are so closely related to the taxpayer's business operations, they are not viewed as capital assets.

It is very unlikely that the long contract described in our assumed facts constitutes a hedge for tax purposes.

Note: All of the above discussion suggests an uncertain possibility to realizing capital gain on closing investment account long interest-rate futures contract entered into by a commercial bank which is subject to Section 582(c). The reverse of that rule is capital loss on closing such contracts.

We shall now turn to "short" sales.

Short Futures Contract

Assume the same facts as above except that the contract is a short futures contract.

The contract would be a capital asset. No federal income tax consequence arises when the bank enters into the contract. And, by reason of Section 1233(a), there is no sale or exchange issue in the short sale. The "separate property" issue remains.[21] The short sale provisions of Section 1233, involve a complex set of rules generally designed to prevent conversion of certain items of ordinary income into capital gain and to prevent, through a set of special holding period provisions, the conversion of economic long-term loss into short-term loss or economic short-term gain into long-term gain. There is considerable confusion concerning the scope of (what constitutes a short sale) and the application of Section 1233.

Section 1233(a) provides:

> For purposes of this subtitle, gain or loss of property shall be considered as gain or loss from the sale or exchange of a capital asset to the

---

[18] See, e.g., Rev. Rul. 72-179, 1972-1 C.B. 57; Wool Distributing Corp. v. Comm'r, 34 T.C. 323 (1960); Silk v. Comm'r, 9 T.C. 174 (1947).

[19] See, e.g., Rev. Rul. 72-179, note 18 *supra*.

[20] *Id*. See Letter Ruling 7838099, which allows ordinary loss deductions for fat cattle futures that do not involve a "balanced market position" on the ground that the futures allowed the taxpayer to maintain his prior level of (business) income rule. This ruling seems incorrect unless it is assumed that the taxpayer intends to take delivery of the fat cattle.

[21] See discussion in note 11 *supra*.

extent that the property, including a commodity future, used to close the short sale constitutes a capital asset in the hands of the taxpayer.

"The term 'short sale' means any sale of [property] which the seller does not own or any sale which is consummated by the delivery of [property] borrowed by, or for account of, the seller."[22] A short sale remains "open" (no gain or loss) until the borrowed property is delivered (the short sale is closed). A short sale may be "naked" (the seller does not own identical property) or "against the box" (the seller owns identical property).

A *naked* short *always* produces short-term gain or loss; regardless of how long the short sale remains "open," during which time the seller is at risk.[23]

Why has this incorrect result been retained by the tax law for more than fifty years when:

(1) The "investment" is the same in a long and a short; and
(2) The "separate property" right rules are the same?

Now assume the short futures contract is entered into by the bank when identical property—Treasury bonds (cost equals market at date of contract)—has been held for more than one year in the investment account. This is a short sale against the box. Assume that the contract (the short sale) is profitable and that it is closed seven months later by (1) delivery of the identical Treasury bonds, or (2) an offsetting contract. Delivery would produce ordinary income under Section 582(c). An offsetting contract would produce short-term capital gain (the holding period of the offsetting contract is deemed to be less than six months under Section 1233).

---

[22] Richardson v. Comm'r, 121 F.2d 1, 4 (2d Cir. 1940) (dictum), *cert. denied* 314 U.S. 684 (1941).

[23] It has been suggested that a distinction should be made between ordinary short sales where the seller does not own the stock which he is selling and sales against the box. For an ordinary short sale, it is argued that the time between the sale of the borrowed stock and the covering transaction should be determinative, whereas for a sale against the box, the length of time the covering stock was held should control. Hendricks, *Federal Income Tax: Capital Gains and Losses* (1935) Harv. L. Rev. 262, 268-70. The theory advanced for such a treatment of an ordinary short sale is that the seller is under a commitment for the length of the time that he is short on the market. *Id.* at 269. Apparently this rests on an analogy between such a commitment and an investment in a capital asset for an equal length of time. *It is to be noted, however, that in such a situation the seller in fact has none of his original capital tied up, for the amount deposited with the lender generally will not exceed that realized from the sale of the borrowed stock.* [Emphasis added.]

Note, "Federal Taxation of Short Sales of Securities," 56 Harv. L. Rev. 274, 276. n. 17 (1942). Note that the amount of loss possible in a naked short sale is infinite where the amount of loss possible in a short sale against the box is limited to the cost of the long identical security. The rule that a naked short always produces short-term gain or loss is incorrect, but the courts—with good reason—have repeatedly refused to tamper with the short sale rules.

Now assume that the short futures contract proves profitable. Assuming such contracts can be "sold" other than closed by entering into an offsetting contract through the exchange, does such sale produce long-term capital gain?[24]

Performance of the contract (e.g., purchase of the securities and their delivery) would be considered a sale of the underlying securities. Ordinary income or ordinary loss would be realized upon such sale.[25]

When the Bank's Intent Is to Protect a Trading Account Position

Assume the same as above, except that the bank's motive is to protect its trading account position.

The sole issue is whether futures contracts (long or short) constitute a "hedge."[26] If so, all gains and losses are ordinary (and the contracts may be valued as inventory although not held for sale); if not, see the discussion of long and short futures contracts above. Presumably futures in the trading account are hedges when they *offset* existing cash positions (or securities purchased on a when-issued basis).

Is the intent, the motive, of the trader controlling?

Query. Can a commercial bank hedge, in the tax sense, a mismatched position in its loan portfolio (fixed rate) and its deposits (floating rates)?

If so, gains and losses from all futures contracts entered into by commercial banks will generally constitute ordinary income and ordinary

---

[24] See American Home Prods. Corp. v. United States, 601 F.2d 240 (1979); Hoover Co. v. Comm'r, 72 T.C. 206 (1979); The Carborundum Co. v. Comm'r, 74 T.C. (1979) No. 57 (July 21, 1980); Ltr. Rul. 8016004.

These cases are critical to the ultimate resolution of the bank case under discussion—both the long and the short contract—and these cases are today's variations of the discussion set forth in the notes 8 and 9 *supra*. For an excellent summary of the government's position (assignment of the forward sale of foreign currency contract constitutes a closing of the short sale—purchase and delivery of identical property—the British pounds—the holding period of which would make the gain short term in almost all instances), see the Reply Brief for the United States, Dec. 11, 1978, American Home Prods., Corp. v. United States, *supra*. Thus the government is arguing that the assignment of the contract is equivalent to the delivery of the underlying subject of the contract (i.e., the foreign currency—the Treasury bonds).

Further, in that brief the government notes at page 15:

> The objective sought to be achieved by this limitation was to remove the possibility of obtaining long-term capital gain treatment for the profit from a short-sale of stocks, securities, or commodities without actually holding the asset for the length of time necessary to support this treatment.

The quoted statement is exactly the same argument as set forth some forty years earlier in Note, note 23 *supra*. It seems peculiar that this argument is not raised to deny long-term gain on long futures.

[25] I.R.C. § 582(c).
[26] I.R.C. § 1233(e).

loss; if not, such gains and losses—determined contract by contract—will generally constitute capital gain and capital loss. To the writer's knowledge, there is simply no published authority concerning the tax character of future contracts entered into by commercial banks, at least outside the parameters of "hedging" inventory (i.e., securities in the dealer account).

It would be speculative to predict the ultimate framework of the tax law in this area. Nonetheless, the trend is toward a more restrictive definition of the term "hedging" for tax purposes, which is to say that the trend is toward a more restrictive application of the *Corn Products* doctrine.

In conclusion, it is noted that Congress did not contemplate the present activities of commercial banks in the futures market when it, in 1969, amended Section 582 of the Internal Revenue Code to provide that gains and losses on evidences of indebtedness shall be ordinary income or ordinary loss.

27

Bank Regulations for Futures Accounting*

James Kurt Dew[†]

The Federal Reserve System, the Comptroller of the Currency and the Federal Deposit Insurance Corporation issued a joint policy statement, effective January 1, 1980, setting forth how banks should account for their futures positions. This policy states that *"all futures contracts (will) be marked to the market at least monthly"* by commercial banks. More recently, the accounting regulations promulgated by the regulatory agencies have been revised to replace mark-to-market for futures to lower of cost or market. Since this change has no substantive impact on the conclusions or analysis here, it is not taken into account.

This policy could eliminate a liability and asset management strategy that might allow banks to compete more effectively for corporate loan business, and at the same time reduce the riskiness of banking. In this article, the aspects of the current banking environment that are relevant to considering the impact of this regulation are discussed. Second, the accounting procedures for bank loans and investments are discussed, and the difference between mark-to-market and deferral accounting is described. Finally, an example of a hedge that banks have not yet begun to use, but one that could potentially do much to enhance the competitive position of banks while simultaneously reducing bank risk will be described.

*Reprinted with permission from the Spring 1981 issue of *Issues in Bank Regulation*, published by Bank Administration Institute.
[†]Senior Financial Economist, Chicago Mercantile Exchange. Research assistance for this paper was provided by Susan Sjo. Opinions expressed are those of the author and do not necessarily reflect the opinions of the Chicago Mercantile Exchange.

BANK RISKS

There is a great deal of evidence that banking risks have significantly increased during the last decade. This riskiness was forced upon banks by the unstable economic environment of the late 1960s and the 1970s. Although they have assiduously attempted to reduce their risk exposure, this has not been possible, due to the two-pronged nature of the risks banks face.

Commercial banks are always subject to two kinds of risk—interest rate risk and credit risk. Interest rate risk is the risk that the cost of liabilities purchased by banks to fund loans and to purchase other assets will rise above bank earnings from these assets, causing the bank to take a net loss. Credit risk, on the other hand, is the risk that borrowers from banks will fail to meet their scheduled repayment obligations.

Prior to the 1970s banks chose to absorb considerable interest rate risk. That is, banks would make loans for maturities longer than the average maturities of their liabilities, at interest rates fixed over the duration of the loan. A corporate customer taking advantage of such a loan was assured that, although short-term rates might rise subsequent to his use of the borrowed funds for capital expenditure purposes, his interest costs would not rise. This banking service was of social worth, as well as being profitable to banks, since it encouraged corporate investment and thus tended to increase productivity.

Beginning in the last half of the 1960s, however, interest rates became extremely volatile and banks were forced to reduce their exposure to interest rate risk. Banks were forced to "hedge" their exposure to interest rate risk by issuing floating rate loans—loans whose earnings would change in tandem with the cost of bank liabilities. In other words, they reduced their interest rate risk by passing this risk along to their corporate customers. The biggest and most creditworthy of these customers rebelled. Since they could not reduce their interest rate risk through fixed rate bank loans, and since they could place their own short-term borrowing directly in the commercial paper market at a lower cost, they no longer borrowed from banks.

This had an adverse impact upon banks in two ways. First, they lost some of their share of the market for corporate funds. Second, and most relevant to our argument, they lost their most creditworthy customers and took on new, less creditworthy customers.[1] In short, the banks did not effectively reduce their total risk through the move from fixed rate loans to floating rate loans; they reduced their interest rate risk but increased their credit risk.

---

[1] For a discussion of the defection of corporations to the commercial paper market, and the impact of this defection on bank risk exposure, see Judd (3).

MARK-TO-MARKET ACCOUNTING AND DEFERRAL ACCOUNTING FOR CASH POSITIONS

Mark-to-market accounting, simply stated, means accounting for an asset or liability on the balance sheet at current market value, and determining current income by measuring changes in market value along with accrued earnings as income in the case of assets, or cost in the case of liabilities. In areas of a banking operation where mark-to-market accounting is used for cash positions—for example, a bank's dealer operation—it makes abundant sense to mark futures positions to market also, since in this case marking futures positions to market reflects the current earnings of banks using futures with reasonable accuracy. But in most areas of the bank, assets and liabilities are not marked to market.

Consider, for example, the case of a corporate loan. In the current bank accounting procedure, the quarterly earnings from a loan are recorded at equal quarterly increments of the yield in dollars, and any capital gains or losses due to changes in loan rates during the year are ignored. For example, suppose the loan in question was in a principal amount of $20 million at 9.25% for a one-year term to maturity. Then assuming the terms of the loan were met by the borrower, income statements in the four subsequent quarters would indicate quarterly revenues from the loan of $462,500 and total earnings over the year of $1,850,000. This is different from mark-to-market treatment in that effects of changes in interest rates on the market value of the loan itself, capital gains and losses, are ignored. Thus, this accounting treatment for loans does not "mark the loan to market" but "defers" the recognition of capital gains and losses on the loan until the maturity of the loan (or the date when the loan is sold in the unlikely event that the bank does not hold the loan to maturity). This practice of deferring capital gains and losses gives rise to the name "deferral" accounting, the accounting technique used by banks for their loans and for bank assets.

MARK-TO-MARKET AND HEDGE ACCOUNTING FOR FUTURES POSITIONS

The proposed accounting requirement that banks mark their futures positions to the market on a monthly basis is reasonable in divisions of a bank or subsidiaries of a bank holding company where cash positions are also marked to the market. As long as cash and futures positions are accounted for symmetrically so that cash gains and losses appear on the bank income statement along with futures gains and losses, mark-to-market accounting is consistent with the hedging uses of futures and somewhat representative of the true risk exposure of the bank. However, in areas of a bank where cash positions are not marked to market, the risk reduction implicit in a futures hedge is most accurately reflected if the hedge is accounted for in the same way as the cash position. If futures losses are recorded on the income statement of the bank, but the offsetting gains on the cash items being hedged are ignored, the hedge will make the bank's position appear more risky, when risk has actually been reduced. (An example of how mark-to-market accounting adversely effects income statements is provided in the next section.)

The longer the duration of the hedge, the more serious the impact of this accounting regulation on hedging operations. A hedge taken for only one week, for example, would be accounted for in the same way with deferral accounting as with mark-to-market accounting, since the proposal requires mark-to-market on a monthly basis. Thus, the one-week hedge would be closed out and accounted for at the close-out price under either set of accounting regulations. But if a hedge is maintained for longer than one month, the two accounting procedures would be different—and mark-to-market for futures only accounting would state the futures hedge gains and losses but not gains and losses on the cash item being hedged. Hence, this accounting procedure has a more severe impact the longer the duration of the hedge and will thus tend to reduce the duration of hedges used by banks. This is exactly the opposite direction that regulators interested in reducing the risk factor of banks should be sending the industry.

In the case of hedges in particular, the duration of the hedge is an important factor in reducing the riskiness of the hedged asset or liability. The longer a hedge is maintained, the greater the risk reduction provided by the futures portion of the portfolio. This is due to the increased correlation between futures price changes and cash price changes as the length of time over which this comparison is made rises. Accounting practice is intended to reflect the philosophy of the firm as well as its earnings. With banks, the philosophy is one of avoiding risk. Since this philosophy is consistent with hedges of a longer duration, it is clear that deferral accounting is consistent with good bank management.

FUTURE USE OF FUTURES BY BANKS

The Chicago Mercantile Exchange is aware of the current exposure of banks to risk and of the need to provide banks with risk reduction vehicles. For this reason, the CME, the American Commodities Exchange (ACE) and the Chicago Board of Trade (CBT) have developed a futures contract in Domestic Certificates of Deposit (CDs). A futures contract in domestic CDs will offer banks a vehicle through which they can effectively hedge their interest rate exposure on loans. In doing this, banks should be able to grant these loans in greater volume than they have in the past. This is the most important function provided by a futures market—risk protection at low transactions costs.

The Federal Reserve presently encourages banks to issue long term fixed rate loans at low risk by encouraging the issuance of longer term CDs, an alternative to futures in hedging risk of long term lending. The Federal Reserve has done this through lower reserve requirements for longer term CDs than for short term CDs. Despite this incentive, banks have tended to issue few long term CDs, perhaps due to a lack of demand on the part of traditional CD customers.

With futures contracts, a long term lower risk loan can be funded with short term CDs and futures hedges. Figure 1 describes how such a hedge would work. This table illustrates the making of a one-year fixed term $20 million loan, funded through the issue of a series of 90-day CDs and hedged by a strip of short sales of CD futures, all entered simultaneously. The profitability of such a fixed term loan, funded by a series of futures contracts, is compared to the profitability of the same loan funded in the same way without futures hedged, during a period where short term rates moved in such a way that long term loans funded through short term liabilities became unprofitable (September 1978 to September 1979). The table suggests that this sort of hedge would reduce the interest rate risk of such loans.

How would the proposed mark-to-market accounting and hedge accounting have affected the income statement in this instance? In order to answer this, the various relevant futures and cash yields at the date the hedge was entered and the following quarterly statement dates are provided in Figure 2. In constructing these, we used the actual futures yields on the appropriate 90-day Treasury bill contracts at mid-month in each case, and added 60 basis points, to reflect the fact that CD yields are somewhat higher than Treasury bill yields. With the CD cash and futures prices indicated, Figure 3 shows futures gains and losses by quarter and by futures contract.

With mark-to-market accounting on a quarterly basis, futures gains and losses on all futures contracts must be realized in the quarter they occur. Thus, with mark-to-market accounting for futures only, the appropriate accounting entries are computed by summing the entries in Figure 3 horizontally. For example, the futures gain during the first quarterly accounting period (Q1) is the accumulated gain in the December 1978, March 1979 and June 1979 futures contracts (the first entry

Figure 1.

Assumption: In the second half of September a bank grants a loan of $20 million to a customer at 9¼% fixed rate for 1 year.

Loan principle + interest	$21,850,000
Loan principle	- 20,000,000
= Revenue	$ 1,850,000

Cash Market

Bank simultaneously issue $20 million, 90-day CD and rolls it over quarterly for 1 year

		Yields
September 90-day CD		
Principle	$20,000,000	7.95%
× interest	× .0795	
= annual rate	$ 1,590,000	
÷ quarterly rate	÷ 4	
= Sept. CD interest cost	$ 397,500	
Dec. 90-day CD	$ 508,000	10.16%
March 90-day CD	$ 498,000	9.96%
June 90-day CD	$ 498,500	9.97%
Effective interest cost and yield rolling over cash CDs	$ 1,902,000	9.51%

Futures Market

Bank simultaneously sells $20 million, 90-day cash CD and $20 million of $1 million 90-day Dec., Mar., Jun. CD futures contracts

		Yields
Sept. Cash CD interest cost	$ 397,500	7.95%
Dec. CD futures		
20 contracts at $1 million	$20,000,000	
× discount rate	× .0854	
= interest pd. annual	$ 1,708,000	
÷ quarterly rate	÷ 4	
= Dec. CD interest cost	$ 427,000	8.54%
March CD futures	$ 432,500	8.65%
June CD futures	$ 437,000	8.74%
Effective interest cost and yield using cash CDs + CD futures contracts	$ 1,694,000	8.47%

	Revenue and Costs	Yields
Revenue from Loan	$1,850,000	9.25%
Cost of Funding Loan Without CD Hedge	$1,902,000	9.50%
Cost of Funding Loan With CD Hedge	$1,694,000	8.47%
Net Gain from Using Futures Hedges	$ 156,000	

Figure 2. CD Cash and Futures Prices at the Quarterly Statement Dates

	Accounting Period		September	Futures Contract Months December	March	June
Issue loan	(Sep. '78)		7.95 (cash)	8.54	8.65	8.74
Q1	(Dec. '78)		—	10.16 (cash)	9.99	10.10
Q2	(Mar. '79)		—	—	9.96 (cash)	10.10
Q3	(Jun '79)		—	—	—	9.97 (cash)

Futures yields are T-bill futures yields plus the average cash spread between T-bills and CDs—60 points. Cash yields are actual CD yields on the 15th of the month in question. In each case, the yield used was from the appropriate date in the year between September 1978 and June 1979.

Bank Regulations for Futures Accounting

Figure 3. Futures Gains and Losses by Quarter for Each Futures Contract*

	Quarter End	Contract Months Dec '78	Mar '79	June '79	Total Quarterly Gains (Losses)
Q1	(ends Dec. 15 '78)	$81,000	$67,000	$68,000	$216,000
Q2	(ends Mar. 15 '79)	—	−1,500	-0-	−1,500
Q3	(ends Jun. 15 '79)	—	—	−6,500	−6,500
Q4	(ends Sep. 14 '79)	—	—	—	—
Total gains for each futures contract		$81,000	$65,500	$61,500	—
Total gains due to futures		—	—	—	$208,000

*Gains and losses were computed using cash and futures prices from Figure 5.

in the column on the far right). Using the column on the far right, the appropriate accounting entries may be seen in Figure 4, "Balance Sheet for Mark-to-Market Futures Accounting."

With deferral or hedge accounting, on the other hand, the futures position is entered on the balance sheet at the time the hedge is closed. That is, the sum of the columns in Figure 3, which represent accumulated gains and losses for a given futures contract, are entered on the balance sheet at the time the cash CD is issued in fulfillment of delivery on the futures contract in question. For example, the accumulated gains on the June 1979 futures contract are entered in June, when a three-month cash CD is issued. The futures gains and losses due to the cash item being hedged are entered simultaneously. The result is displayed in Figure 5.

Futures Accounting

Figure 4. Balance Sheet for Mark-to-Market Futures Accounting

Loan Issued Sep '78		Loan Revenue	(−)	Cash CD int. Cost	(+)	CD Futures Margin Gains/ Losses	(=)	Net Income
Q1	(Dec. '78)	$ 462,500		$ 397,500		$216,000		$281,000
Q2	(Mar. '79)	$ 462,500		$ 508,000		− 1,500		− 47,000
Q3	(Jun. '79)	$ 462,500		$ 498,000		− 6,500		− 42,000
Q4	(Sep. '79)	$ 462,500		$ 498,500				− 36,000
Total		$1,850,000 (−)		$1,902,000 (+)		$208,000 (=)		$156,000

Figure 5. Balance Sheet with Hedge Accounting

Quarter	Interest Income	(−)	Interest Cost	(+)	Futures Gains and Losses	(=)	Net Income
Q1	$ 462,500		$ 397,500		-0-		$ 65,000
Q2	$ 462,500		$ 508,000		$ 81,000		$ 35,500
Q3	$ 462,500		$ 498,000		$ 65,500		$ 30,000
Q4	$ 462,500		$ 498,500		$ 61,500		$ 25,500
Total	$1,850,000 (−)		$1,902,000 (+)		$208,000 (=)		$156,000

By comparing Figure 4 net income with Figure 5 net income, one can see that mark-to-market for futures only makes the balance sheet far more volatile and not representative of the bank's actual risk. Since hedging reduces the risk to which a bank is exposed if used appropriately, and hedge accounting reflects the extent of the bank's risk exposure more accurately than mark-to-market for futures only, hedge accounting is clearly the more appropriate accounting procedure in this case.

Bibliography

Beebe, Jack. "A Perspective on Liability Management and Bank Risk," *Federal Reserve Bank of San Francisco Economic Review*, Winter 1979.

Boltz, Paul and Campbell, Tim. "Innovations in Bank Loan Contracting, Recent Evidence," Staff Studies, Board of Governors of the Federal Reserve System, May 1979.

Judd, John. "Competition Between the Commercial Paper Market and Commercial Banks," *Federal Reserve Bank of San Francisco Economic Review*, Winter 1979.

Rosenberg, Barr and Perry, Phillip. "The Fundamental Determinants of Risk in Banking," Proceedings of the 1978 Bank Structure Conference, Federal Reserve Bank of Chicago, pp. 402-471.

28

Futures Trading by National Banks*

Robert C. Lower** and Scott W. Ryan†

> The interest rate futures markets, according to the authors, have tremendous potential for national banks. The authors explain the increased efficiencies in financial instrument futures trading on the exchanges in comparison with the risks involved in traditional forward contract systems. The recent guidelines issued by the Comptroller are examined and their controversial accounting requirements are explained and evaluated.

COMMODITY FUTURES MARKETS

In a brief banking circular issued on November 2, 1976,[1] the Comptroller of the Currency authorized national banks to trade in financial instrument futures contracts to reduce the risk of loss resulting from interest rate fluctuations.[2] With this pronouncement, the chief regula-

---

*Reprinted by permission from *The Banking Law Journal*, Volume 98, Number 3, March 1981, copyright © 1981, Warren, Gorham and Lamont Inc., 210 South Street, Boston, Mass. All rights reserved.

**Partner, Alston, Miller & Gaines, Atlanta, Georgia and Washington, D.C.

†Mr. Ryan was appointed by the Presidential Commission on Executive Exchange in September of 1979 to serve as Executive Advisor for Banking and Securities to the Comptroller of the Currency.

[1] Comptroller of the Currency Banking Circular No. 79 (Nov. 2, 1976), [1978-1978 Transfer Binder] CCH Fed. Banking L. Rep. ¶ 96.977 (hereinafter cited as Circular 79).

[2] The original Circular 79 authorized banks to trade in Treasury bills and certificates guaranteed by the Government National Mortgage Association (GNMA). *Id.*

421

tor of national banks introduced a regulatory framework for a vast new area of financial activity for the national banking system.

The commodity futures markets are certainly not a new feature of economic activity in this country. As early as 1848, the grain merchants in the City of Chicago began trading in "to arrive" contracts for cash grain, which served the purpose of locking in prices for future delivery of grain. The activities of those merchants led to the creation of the Board of Trade of the City of Chicago—the oldest and still the largest commodity futures exchange in the United States.[3] For well over a century, the Chicago Board of Trade conducted trading in an ever-expanding realm of futures contracts—all relating to various agricultural products. Through this device, both producers, on the selling side, and processors and consumers, on the buying side, have been able to protect themselves against the volatile price fluctuations for agricultural products.

The economic uncertainties of the early 1970s led the two largest exchanges, the Chicago Board of Trade and the Chicago Mercantile Exchange, to begin futures trading in financial instruments.[4] In October 1975, the Chicago Board of Trade obtained approval for a futures contract covering mortgage-backed securities guaranteed by the Government National Mortgage Association (GNMA Futures). Shortly thereafter, in January of 1976, the Chicago Mercantile Exchange through its division known as the International Monetary Market initiated trading in futures contracts based on ninety-day Treasury bills. Thus, for the first time, futures contracts were offered on interest rate-sensitive securities—allowing parties vulnerable to interest rate fluctuations to protect themselves in the same manner used by the producers and processors of agricultural products for many decades.[5]

---

[3] Chicago Board of Trade, *Commodity Trading Manual* 4 (1977).

[4] Financial instrument futures contracts would not have been permitted prior to 1974, since before that time the definition of "commodity" under the commodity Exchange Act, which delineates the permissible activities in futures trading, referred only to specific agricultural commodities. In the course of the major overhaul of the Commodity Exchange Act and the creation of the Commodity Futures Trading Commission in 1974, the definition of commodity was greatly expanded to cover not only the previously enumerated commodities, but also "all other goods and articles, ... and all services, rights and interests in which contracts for future delivery are presently or in the future dealt in." Commodity Futures Trading Commission Act of 1974, Pub. L. 93-463, § 201(b), 88 Stat. 1389, 1395, 7 U.S.C. § 2 (1976).

[5] One of the principal reasons for the existence of the futures markets is price protection or "hedging." In the case of agricultural products, a farmer or producer can insure a certain price for his anticipated harvest by selling "short" in the futures market; on the other hand, a processor or consumer of the same commodity can lock in the cost of raw materials by purchasing a "long" position in the same contract. See discussion of the definition of hedging at note 10 *infra*.

In the case of financial instrument contracts, the strategies appear to be reversed. A party expecting to have funds to invest at a specific date in the future can obtain protection against a decline in interest rates by purchasing a *long* position in the financial instrument futures market; while a party needing to borrow at some future time can protect against an increase in interest

A futures contract is an agreement to buy or sell a specified quantity of a particular item—traditionally, an agricultural commodity like soybeans or wheat—to be delivered at some specified future time, but at a price determined by current competitive bidding on the floor of an exchange. By agreeing on a present price for the future transaction, a party needing a particular item at a future time can lock in the future cost of that item. Conversely, a party knowing that it will have the item to sell at a future time can lock in the sales price for that item.

In the case of financial instrument futures, the commodity to be delivered consists of a security such as a Treasury Bill or GNMA certificate, rather than soybeans, wheat, or some other agricultural commodity. Each such futures contract has a standard set of specifications so that the same quality, quantity, and delivery requirements apply to each transaction. Only the price is negotiated in the "pit" of the exchange.[6]

Even though delivery is required under the terms of a futures contract,[7] the futures markets normally are not used as delivery markets. Rather, contract positions generally are offset prior to the final delivery

---

rates by selling *short*. The reason for this turnabout in strategies is that an *increase* in interest rates results in a *decrease* in the price of money market instruments; whereas a *decrease* in rates produces an *increase* in price.

[6] For example, the GNMA contract traded at the Chicago Board of Trade (CBOT) provides for delivery of $100,000 principal balance of GNMA pass-through certificates with a stated interest rate of 8 percent; the Treasury bill contract offered at the Chicago Mercantile Exchange (CME) calls for delivery of $1 million par value of three-month Treasury bills. In the case of the GNMA contract, the contract holder with a "long" position who decides to take delivery receives a Collateralized Depository Receipt (CDR)—which is a claim on GNMA certificates being held in safekeeping by a specified depository—rather than the actual instruments. The "short" position holder is allowed to satisfy his obligations by delivering to the "long" position holder depository certificates bearing an 8 percent coupon, or he can substitute issues with other coupon rates in amounts sufficient to provide the same yield as the specified GNMA 8s under certain assumptions about the payments that will be made over the lives of the mortgages. Under the Treasury bill contract, the "short" delivers either a newly auctioned three-month bill or the outstanding bill which was originally issued as a 182-day Treasury bill that has three months left to maturity.

The other financial instrument futures contracts presently available cover several different instruments: Treasury bonds (CBOT), three-month commercial paper (CBOT), one-year Treasury bills (CME), and GNMA pass-through certificates calling for direct delivery of GNMA certificates, instead of the CDRs (American Commodity Exchange). 2 *Treasury/Federal Reserve Study of Treasury Futures Markets* 2-7 (1979) (hereinafter cited as *Treasury/Fed Study*).

An indication of the popularity of financial instrument futures generally is the fact that twelve additional applications are pending before the CFTC for contract approval. Many of these would provide duplicate contracts on the New York exchanges for those traded in Chicago. Others would introduce trading on new items such as Eurodollar certificates of deposit, five-to-seven-year Treasury notes, and one covering a designated index of stock prices. *Id.* at 10.

[7] See e.g., Rules and Regulations of the Chicago Board of Trade, Rules 1035 et seq.

date and the actual purchase of the item takes place in some other forum.[8]

Unlike the situation with "forward placement contracts"—which are essentially over-the-counter transactions between buyer and seller, with delivery to occur at some future time—the futures markets interpose a party between the buyer and seller. This intermediary, the clearinghouse, demands from each side that a security deposit be posted (referred to as "original margin") and thereafter makes adjustments in the amount of deposit posted by each side to reflect the gain or loss due to each day's price movement for that futures contract (known as the "variation margin"). This process is called "marking to market." Probably the most important feature of this system is that the clearinghouse of each exchange *guarantees* performance to both sides of each transaction. This guaranty is backed up first by the guaranty fund put up by clearing members of the exchange and, secondly, by the margin deposit posted by each side in every transaction.[9]

TRADITIONAL HEDGING ACTIVITIES OF BANKS

In the banking industry, the process of obtaining protection against adverse interest rate fluctuations—i.e., the hedging process—has traditionally occurred through the use of a variety of forward placement and standby contract transactions.[10] Under a forward placement contract,

---

[8] Deliveries with respect to agricultural commodities traditionally have been 2-3 percent of the maximum open interest. *Commodity Trading Manual*, note 3 *supra*, at 31. In the case of GNMA futures, deliveries have been running in the neighborhood of 15 percent, with Treasury bonds much higher. *Treasury/Fed Study*, not 6 *supra*, at 9.

[9] See generally, Hieronymous, *Economics of Futures Trading* 43-46 (1971). All transactions occurring on an exchange must be "cleared" through the accounts of a clearing member of the exchange, which involves a matching of information submitted by the two sides of each transaction. Once cleared, the clearinghouse guaranty runs in favor of those clearing members.

[10] The CFTC has adopted a very broad general definition of the term "hedging" which reads as follows:

> Bona fide hedging transactions and positions shall mean transactions or positions in a contract for future delivery on any contract market, where such transactions or positions normally represent a substitute for transactions to be made or positions to be taken at a later time in a physical marketing channel and where they are economically appropriate to the reduction of risks in the conduct and management of a commercial enterprise, and where they arise from:
>
> (i) The potential change in the value of assets which a person owns, produces, manufactures, processes, or merchandises or anticipates owning, producing, manufacturing, processing, or merchandising.
>
> (ii) The potential change in the value of liabilities which a person owes or anticipates incurring, or

the two parties enter into an agreement which is binding upon both of them to deliver a specified security at a future date for an agreed upon price. In the case of a standby contract, the party issuing the standby commitment is bound to accept delivery of the specified security if the purchaser of the standby elects to make delivery. The contract is essentially a "put" option on a security. In the case of both forward placement contracts and standbys, the two parties involved generally deal directly with each other. No clearinghouse intermediary is involved and traditionally the contracts have not been margined or marked to market. Through such agreements, however, banks have been able to obtain protection against adverse interest rate movements, with the various interested parties being brought together through a highly developed dealer network.[11]

The introduction of financial instrument futures trading on the exchanges, however, has created an opportunity for certain advantages and efficiencies over the traditional forward contract system. For example, the existence of a central marketplace (the exchange) reduces the costs involved in searching out a party with whom to transact business. The auction system of trading introduces a highly competitive pricing mechanism and the existence of the exchange clearing corporation adds a very significant financial safeguard against default by the opposite party. Because of the high degree of efficiency achieved in the futures markets, price dissemination is extremely rapid and widespread—providing important information to all interested parties. Finally, one of the most beneficial features of futures contracts is that they can be disposed of easily in the generally liquid futures markets, whereas under a forward contract, each party is always at the mercy of the other side with respect to making or taking delivery. In effect, the futures exchanges provide a "secondary" market in which any party with an open contract can close out its position without seeking the cooperation of the other side.

(iii) The potential change in the value of services which a person provides, purchases or anticipates providing or purchasing.

Notwithstanding the foregoing, no transactions or positions shall be classified as bona fide hedging . . . unless their purpose is to offset price risks incidental to commercial cash or spot operations and such positions are established and liquidated in an orderly manner in accordance with sound commercial practices. . . ."

17 C.F.R. § 1.3(z)(1)(1980).
    The term "hedging" will be used throughout this article in the more generic sense of activities undertaken for the purpose of protecting against loss due to fluctuations in the price of a commodity. The specific view of the Comptroller of the Currency with respect to the meaning of "hedging" for purposes of national bank regulation is discussed below.

    [11] *Treasury/Fed Study*, note 6 *supra*, at 23-29.

THE AUTHORITY TO TRADE FUTURES

The potential value to banks of futures market activity was recognized in the original issuance of Circular 79 by the Comptroller of the Currency in November of 1976. In that Circular, the Comptroller issued the following authorization:

> "National Banks may participate in (1) the GNMA mortgage futures market through the Chicago Board of Trade and (2) the T-bill futures market through the International Money [sic] Market of the Chicago Mercantile Exchange in order to reduce the risk of interest rate fluctuation in the corresponding cash markets...."[12]

In order to control this activity strictly, the original version of Circular 79 required that any bank planning to engage in futures market activity had to present a proposal to the Comptroller of the Currency for prior approval. Such a proposal was required to set forth certain information, including the background and experience of the traders, trading limits to be imposed upon those traders, procedures designed to prevent unauthorized trading and details regarding the timing and scope of internal audit and control procedures. Once a plan was approved, the bank was required to match each GNMA or T-bill futures contract to an appropriate cash transaction and to enter into a futures contract only for the purpose of substantially reducing the bank's risk of loss due to interest rate fluctuations.[13]

Pursuant to the authority granted in Circular 79, fifty national banks eventually obtained approval from the Comptroller to engage in futures trading.[14] However, not all of those authorized ever engaged in a significant amount of hedging activity. While the reasons for this low degree of actual participation no doubt vary from bank to bank, a major factor has been the lack of a thorough understanding of futures trading by national banks and, in particular, the lack of experienced personnel who could conduct such trading for those banks.

Perhaps another important explanation for the reluctance of banks to undertake futures market activity has been the factor of market liquidity. The informal network of financial institutions involved in trading forward placement and standby contracts was already quite highly developed and has continued to absorb much of the potential futures trading activity. Also, the conduct of business with other financial in-

---

[12] Circular 79, note 1 *supra*.
[13] *Id.*
[14] Cf. "Broker a 'Catalyst' to Lure Banks Into Interest Futures," *Chicago Tribune*, Feb. 6, 1980, Sec. 4, p. 3, col. 1.

stitutions may seem more secure than dealing with the somewhat mysterious and alien futures exchanges.

PROBLEMS IN FORWARD CONTRACTING

Whatever the reasons, the reluctance of financial institutions to use the financial futures markets has led to some serious regulatory problems.[15] For example, a number of savings and loans have encountered serious difficulties in the GNMA forward placement market by engaging in transactions that were primarily speculative.[16] Rather than trading in forward commitments to protect against rate fluctuations, some institutions have sought to profit from correctly anticipating those fluctuations.

These much publicized examples may be only the tip of the iceberg. There is no way to assess the degree of speculative forward contract activity which exists throughout the banking industry. However, recent scandals point out certain basic deficiencies of the forward contract market.

One of the first problems with forward contracts was discovered in early 1977 when Winters Government Securities of Ft. Lauderdale went out of business owing $3 million to Wall Street GNMA dealers.[17] This occurred because twenty-five banks and credit unions had refused to pay $8 million in losses on forward contracts.[18] Another scandal occurred in the celebrated case involving the University of Houston. The manager of short-term investments used repurchase agreements in what amounted to a pyramid scheme. He purchased a portfolio of $250 million in government securities, most of them via GNMA forward contracts. When the pyramid collapsed, the university had lost $17 million.[19] According to a recent estimate by the Comptroller of the Currency, approximately forty cases of trading abuses and speculative investment practices have been discovered since 1976 by bank examiners.[20]

---

[15] As the joint *Treasury/Federal Reserve Study* has pointed out, no commercial bank appears to have failed or required supervisory attention as a result of its involvement in futures trading: whereas solvency has been threatened in some banks as a result of their trading in forward and standby contracts for GNMA securities. *Treasury/Fed Study*, note 6 *supra*, at 59.

[16] It has also been alleged that certain securities dealers have engaged in illegal sales practices including misrepresentation, unauthorized trading, recommendations of unsuitable speculative transactions, and "churning." See SEC v. Winters Gov't Sec. Corp., [1977-78 Transfer Binder] CCH Fed. Sec. L. Rep. ¶ 96.128 (S. D. Fla., Civ. Act. No. 77-6345).

[17] Ruskin, "Securities Firm's Flop Reveals Big Risks Run by Some Small Banks," *Wall Street Journal*, Oct. 28, 1977, p. 1, col. 8.

[18] *Id.*

[19] "Ginnie Mae Futures Scrutinized." *The Washington Post*, March 9, 1980, Sec. G, p. 6.

[20] See 126 Cong. Rec., S. 3346 (April 1, 1980) (Remarks of Sen. Williams). In introducing S. 2515, a bill to provide for comprehensive regulation of the cash markets in government-

Since there currently exists no standardized mechanism to require the posting of margins in connection with such transactions, the risk of default in forward contracting has involved two significant levels of risk: First, the parties have borne the risk of interest rate fluctuations, and, second, they have incurred a "credit risk" in relying upon the ability of the other side to perform under the contract. Thus, the risk of default under such contracts is greater than the risk of default on a corresponding futures contract.

RECENT REGULATORY DEVELOPMENTS

Such scandals and abuses have led to a great amount of activity among the federal regulators of financial institutions.[21] In the case of

guaranteed securities, Senator Williams referred also the the takeover of a savings and loan association in Cleveland by the Federal Savings and Loan Insurance Corporation (FSLIC) because of an overcommitment in GNMA securities. Reportedly, Washington Federal Savings and Loan had about $176.6 million in deposits and almost three times that amount—or some $500 million—in outstanding commitments to purchase GNMA securities. The FSLIC was forced to intervene in order to protect the insured deposits of the institution. Senator Williams also cited the failure of Reliance Mortgage Corporation in Denver to take delivery of some $350 million in GNMA securities and the substantial losses this caused to some of the large Wall Street broker/dealers. *Id.* at S. 3349.

[21] The general issue of the regulation of financial instrument futures was raised in connection with the reauthorization of the CFTC during 1978. As a result of the concerns expressed by the Treasury Department, the Board of Governors of the Federal Reserve System, and the Securities and Exchange Commission, Congress amended the Commodity Exchange Act to require that the CFTC maintain communications with those agencies. Specifically, the amendment reads as follows:

> The Commission shall maintain communications with the Department of the Treasury, the Board of Governors of the Federal Reserve System, and the Securities and Exchange Commission for the purpose of keeping such agencies fully informed of Commission activities that relate to the responsibilities of those agencies, for the purpose of seeking the views of those agencies on such activities, and for considering the relationships between the volume and nature of investment and trading in contracts of sale of a commodity for future delivery and in securities and financial instruments under the jurisdiction of such agencies.

Futures Trading Act of 1978, Pub. L. 95-405, § 2, 92 Stat. 866 (to be codified at 5 U.S.C. § 5332). The 1978 Act also requires that any time a board of trade applies for permission to trade a futures contract on any security issued or guaranteed by the United States or any agency thereof, the CFTC must deliver a copy of such application to the Department of the Treasury and the Board of Governors of the Federal Reserve System. Those agencies are then given a period of forty-five days in which to comment on the application. Finally, the CFTC is required to take into consideration the effect that approval of such a futures contract or any other regulatory action which might be taken with respect to such contract would have on the national banks, this regulator concern resulted in the issuance of a revision of Banking Circular 79 by the Comptroller of the Currency.[22] This new version of the circular on futures trading was originally issued on November 15, 1979 and was subsequently modified by Banking Circular 79 (2d Revision) which was issued on March 19, 1980.[23]

In this new set of guidelines, the Comptroller combined the previous policy statements concerning futures contracts and forward placement and standby contracts.[24] Thus the Comptroller placed under a single set of guidelines most of the activities relating to the hedging of interest rate risk. In issuing the new circular, the Comptroller made the following statement:

> We view these contracts [futures, forward placements, and standbys] as neither inherently prudent nor imprudent. Evidence has shown that they can be used effectively to reduce interest rate risk. The use of these contracts by national banks should be in accordance with safe and sound banking practices and with levels of activity reasonably related to the bank's business needs and capacity to fulfill its obligations under the contracts.[25]

Probably the greatest significance of this pronouncement is the recognition that hedging interest rate risks is a legally appropriate activity for national banks. However, this pronouncement is subject to certain important qualifications.

Essentially, the Comptroller has taken the position that futures mar-

---

debt financing requirements of the United States Government and the continued efficiency and integrity of the underlying market for government securities. *Id.* (to be codified at 7 U.S.C. § 12a).

[22] Comptroller of the Currency Banking Circular 79 (Revised), 44 Fed. Reg. 66711 (Nov. 20, 1979), CCH Fed. Banking L. Rep. ¶ 98.038.

[23] Comptroller of the Currency Banking Circular 79 (2d Revision) (issued on March 19, 1980) (hereinafter cited as Circular 79 [2d Revision]).

[24] The Comptroller had previously issued a banking circular to cover national bank participation in forward placement or deferred delivery contracts for GNMA or other securities. Comptroller of the Currency Banking Circular No. 79, Supplement No. 1, August 1, 1977, CCH Fed. Banking L. Rep. ¶ 97.210.

[25] Circular 79 (2d Revision), note 23 *supra*, at 1. It is important to note that the final version of these guidelines imposes the responsibility for establishing a proper futures trading program on the board of directors of the bank. Specifically, the board is required to establish specific written policies and procedures which set forth the following: (1) policy objectives specific enough to outline permissible futures contract strategies and their relationship to other banking activities, (2) record keeping systems which provide sufficient detail to permit internal auditors and examiners to determine whether operating personnel have adhered to authorized objectives, (3) limitations applicable to futures, forwards, and standby contract positions for each category of authorized activity, and (4) the designation of a duly authorized committee of the board or the bank's internal auditors to review all outstanding contract positions on at least a monthly basis to insure that the established limits are not exceeded. *Id.* at 2-3.

ket activities do not involve the purchase of "investment securities" under the specific authority set forth in the National Bank Act.[26] Thus, futures trading in general is not a specifically authorized activity. Rather, certain activities involving the use of futures contracts are authorized as being "incidental to banking."[27] In order to give some guidance with respect to the activities which would fall in this category, the Comptroller has set forth certain distinctions:

1. For *investment portfolio* or *non-dealer operations* in fixed rate assets, banks should evaluate the interest rate risk exposure resulting from their overall investment activities to insure that the positions they take in futures, forwards and standby contract markets will *reduce* their risk exposure. Short positions in futures and forward contracts should reasonably relate to existing or anticipated cash positions, and should be used to enhance liquidity of the portfolio. Rather than using short hedges against portfolio holdings for purposes of income generation, we would expect,

---

[26] U.S.C. § 24 ¶ Seventh (1976). The Act defines "investment securities" as "marketable obligations, evidencing indebtedness of any person, copartnership, association or corporation in the form of bonds, notes and/or debentures commonly known as investment securities under such further definitions of the term "investment securities" as may by regulation be prescribed by the Comptroller of the Currency." *Id.* In his regulations, the Comptroller has added that the definition "does not include investments which are predominantly speculative in nature." 12 C.F.R. § 1.3(b) (1980).

[27] Circular 79 (2d Revision), note 23 *supra*. Under the National Bank Act, a national bank may exercise only those powers which are expressly conferred under federal law together with "all such incidental powers as shall be necessary to carry on the business of banking." 12 U.S.C. § 24 ¶ Seventh (1976). The scope of activities encompassed by the "incidental powers" provision has been the subject of considerable judicial scrutiny over the past few years. Recent decisions have rejected the extremely narrow interpretation that the only permissible incidental activities are those which are *indispensible* to the business of banking. Arnold Tours, Inc. v. Camp. 472 F.2d 427 (1972), but nonetheless have taken a limited view of the scope of permitted activities. In *Arnold Tours*, the First Circuit Court of Appeals determined that a particular activity undertaken by a national bank is authorized as an incidental power "if it is convenient or useful in connection with the performance of one of the bank's established activities pursuant to its express powers under the National Bank Act." *Id.* at 432. Under that standard, the court determined that the operation of a full service travel agency was not authorized as an incidental power. *Id.* Accord, American Soc'y of Travel Agents, Inc. v. Bank of American Nat'l Trust & Savings Ass'n, 385 F. Supp. 1084 (1974). One of the reasons expressed for disallowing activities which are not directly related to an express banking power is that such nonbanking ventures might put pressure on the bank to use its resources to bail out an unsuccessful business affiliate. See Investment Co. Inst. v. Camp, 401 U.S. 617(1971). Independent commercial activities have been struck down in a number of cases: Georgia Ass'n of Independent Ins. Agents, Inc. v. Saxon, 268 F. Supp. 236 (N.D. Ga. 1967), *aff'd* 399 F.2d 1010 (5th Cir. 1968) (general insurance business); First Nat'l Bank v. Dickinson, 396 U.S. 122 (1969) (armored car service); Investment Co. Inst. v. Camp, *supra*. (mutual investment fund); M & M Leasing Corp. v. Seattle First Nat'l Bank, 563 F.2d 1377 (9th Cir. 1977), *cert. denied* 436 U.S. 956 (1978) (repair and maintenance service in connection with vehicle leasing); National Retailers Corp. of Ariz. v. Valley Nat'l Bank of Ariz., 684 F.2d 34(1979) (general electronic data processing service).

where practicable, that contract gains would be used to offset losses resulting from the sale of portfolio securities as asset yields are upgraded. Long positions in futures and forwards should reasonably reflect the bank's investment strategy and ability to fulfill its commitments.

2. *Asset-liability management* involves the matching of fixed rate and interest-sensitive assets and liabilities in order to maintain liquidity and profitability. Futures and forward contracts may be used as a general hedge against the interest rate exposure associated with undesired mismatches in interest-sensitive assets and liabilities. Long positions in contracts could be used as a hedge against funding interest-sensitive assets with fixed-rate sources of funds; short positions in contracts could be used as a hedge against funding fixed-rate assets with interest-sensitive liabilities.

3. *Dealer-bank trading activities* that employ futures, forwards and standby contracts should be in accordance with safe and sound banking practices reasonably related to the bank's legally permitted trading activities.[28]

On the other hand, the Comptroller has taken the firm position that "spreading" futures contracts is not a banking activity authorized under the National Bank Act.[29] The Comptroller regards futures contract spreads as an offensive trading strategy which will be profitable only if a bank's speculation on the future price relationship between the spread contracts proves to be correct. Also, presumably futures market arbitrage activities would be similarly viewed as an activity which is not "incidental to banking."[30]

The regulatory approach is thus very specific. Banks are not authorized to engage in futures trading per se; rather, they are authorized to undertake certain activities which may involve futures trading. The philosophy of Circular 79 seems to be that *hedging* activities are permitted, but even the parameters of this function are not completely spelled out. In the original version of Circular 79, the Comptroller appeared to intend that only specific assets or liabilities could be hedged in the futures markets. Each bank was, in fact, required to match each futures

---

[28] Circular 79 (2d Revision), note 23 *supra*.

[29] A "spread" position in futures trading consists of a long position in a nearby delivery month which is coupled with a short position in the same commodity taken out in a later delivery month. Such a strategy locks in a particular difference or spread in prices between the two delivery months. Hieronymous, *Economics of Futures Trading* 63 (1971).

[30] The Comptroller does allow the type of "arbitrage" transactions where the bank has a cash security in its trading account. For example, a bank would be allowed to enter into a short futures position on a Treasury bond if the futures price were higher than the cost of the bond in the bank's trading account. See Circular 79 (2d Revision), note 23 *supra*.

position with a specific asset or liability.[31] Under the latest revision of the circular, however, a bank may hedge its interest rate exposure, but only as to its "overall investment activities."[32] In the case of asset-liability management, futures contracts are authorized as a "general hedge" against mismatches in interest-sensitive assets and liabilities.[33]

This concept of hedging with respect to the overall portfolio or balance sheet of a bank represents a major change from 1976, but one which reflects a greater sophistication in understanding the potential for futures market activities by financial institutions. The danger in following the earlier requirement of matching futures positions with particular assets or liabilities was that such a limited "hedge" could, in fact, *increase* the overall interest rate vulnerability of a bank. It can be argued that "hedging" a specific transaction within a bank has no real banking justification. The basic business of banking is to "hedge" or match assets and liabilities and to profit on the interest rate differential which results. To isolate a hedge on an individual portfolio security without regard to the corresponding source-fund liability may, in fact, be exposing the bank to increased risk in connection with the overall balance sheet of the bank. This then is the keystone of the Comptroller's philosophy: If futures market activities are entered into to protect the differential between the cost of its liabilities and the return on its assets, then they are "incidental to banking."

ACCOUNTING ISSUES

Probably the most controversial aspect of the revised version of Circular 79 is its accounting requirements. Specifically, the circular requires that all futures positions be "marked to market" on a monthly basis or marked to the lower of cost or market.[34] All losses resulting from such a monthly contract value determination are to be recognized as a current expense item, with any gains resulting from the marking to market recognized as a current income item.[35]

One difficulty this creates is that it may result in different accounting treatment for the two sides of a hedging transaction. For example, if a bank is hedging an investment portfolio item with a futures con-

---

[31] Circular 79, note 1 *supra*.
[32] Circular 79 (2d Revision), note 23 *supra*, at 2.
[33] *Id*. For a thorough discussion of the problems associated with establishing a general balance sheet hedge, see McCabe & McLeod, "Regulation and Bank Trading in the Futures Market," 3 Issues in Bank Regulation 6 (1979).
[34] Circular 79 (2d Revision), note 23 *supra*, at 3.
[35] *Id*.

Futures Trading by National Banks

tract, current practice would probably treat the two sides of the hedge differently. Many accountants would require the bank to carry the portfolio item at cost, but to mark the futures position to market. Thus, a loss on the futures side would be reflected in the bank's income statement, while the offsetting paper gain in the investment portfolio would not be so reflected. Thus, the present accounting treatment might prove to be a disincentive for banks to hedge in the futures market.

The rationale for the Comptroller's position on this issue is the need for regulatory uniformity. Since there is no generally accepted accounting principle with respect to the treatment of futures and forward contracts, accounting firms have different methods for treating such contracts.[36] Pending development of an acceptable accounting industry standard, the Comptroller has felt compelled to establish uniform reporting standards for national banks. There is no general disagreement among accountants with marking to market futures and forward contracts in a trading account or in asset/liability management. The objections which have been raised to the Comptroller's requirement all deal with the use of futures and forward contracts in hedging an investment account, either with a short hedge or a so-called long anticipatory hedge.

The Long Anticipatory Hedge

The so-called long anticipatory hedge involves the purchase of a futures or forward contract position for purposes of acquiring the underlying security at a future date. The problem with using deferred accounting in this activity is that it appears to encourage the taking of gains and deferring of losses. For example, if a futures position has a gain, it could be sold and the gain realized; however, a loss could be deferred by taking delivery of the security into the investment portfolio at contract cost. The use of SFAS No. 8 as a precedent for the use of deferred accounting would probably require that each futures contract or forward contract be a firm, noncancellable contract. In the case of a futures position, which can be cancelled by offset, this treatment might not be justified. On the other hand, if a more liberal position were taken with regard to the noncancellation feature, it would probably have the undesired result of encouraging the taking of gains and the deferring of losses as described above. Indeed, a prominent accounting firm has admitted that

---

[36] Some accountants have advocated treatment for futures positions on the basis of Financial Accounting Standards Board Statement of Financial Accounting Standard No. 8 (SFAS No. 8) which appears to permit the deferred recognition of loss or gain on futures contracts if the purpose is to hedge an identifiable bank asset. The Comptroller has specifically disagreed with this approach, however.

a strict interpretation of the criteria set forth under SFAS #8 would not seem to provide for the deferral of gains and losses of interest rate futures contracts entered into as a hedge against anticipated security purchases, primarily because the matching process would be artificial since the intended purchases are not necessarily going to be fulfilled.[37]

The concept of a long hedge makes some sense for banks, especially when there is an inverted yield curve. Rather than buying long-term bonds in the cash/spot market, a bank could buy Treasury Bond or GNMA futures or forward placement contracts to lock in long-term yield, and invest the cash in short-term money market instruments, thereby earning higher interim interest income until delivery. As an alternative, knowing a bond or other asset will be maturing at a specific date in the future, a futures or forward placement contract can be purchased to lock in an acceptable yield for reinvestment of the proceeds. However, this strategy is speculative since the motivation behind it is an anticipation of declining rates. Additionally, in most cases this would ignore the cost of funding the supporting liability—i.e., a long hedge locks in asset yields but not the liability costs that will fund the asset. Under the Comptroller's view, losses on futures and forward contracts should be recognized as a cost involved in generating the higher interim interest or of avoiding the negative cost of carry.

Short Hedges

Legitimate portfolio short hedges, viewed in isolation, could result in monthly swings in the income statement using a mark-to-market approach. Again, however, the Comptroller's Office feels that this ignores the liability funding cost. In a bank, unlike a pension fund or insurance company, investment securities are already a hedge against bank liabilities. By using futures or forward contracts to hedge an investment security, the bank may actually be increasing its interest rate exposure. The problem with deferred short-hedge accounting as proposed by several accounting firms, however, is not intent but correlation. In order to qualify for deferred accounting, a "high correlation" must exist during the hedge period.[38] This obviously is a hindsight determination. Given the periods of negative correlations that have existed between cash and futures markets in recent months, especially in cross hedges, a deferred accounting method would result in some short hedges having to be marked to market and thereby causing revisions of income statements. This is clearly an inconsistent practice and is unacceptable to the Comp-

---

[37] See Arthur Andersen & Co., "Interest Rate Futures Contracts: Accounting and Control Techniques for Banks," at 16.

[38] See *Treasury/Fed Study*, note 6 *supra*. at 54.

troller. Those methods of deferred accounting which would recognize just the gain or loss on a futures or forward contract when the hedge is terminated, rather than contemporaneously adjusting the carrying value of the security, are not acceptable to the Comptroller because such methods would encourage the taking of gains and deferring of losses.

While the Comptroller's Office has indicated its disfavor of isolating a short hedge against a portfolio security and demanding uniform treatment of both sides, it has indicated its willingness to accept a reasonable alternative. An accounting method which would require marking to market both the futures or forward contract *and* the portfolio security being hedged during the life of the hedge may be more acceptable. Accumulated depreciation on the security should not have to be recognized, only the basis gain or loss during the hedge would be shown on the income statement. Any net realized gain or loss upon repurchasing the contract would then be used to adjust the carrying value of the portfolio security. Such treatment might represent a reasonable compromise in the event the demand for such a pairing is strong in the banking industry. This compromise would, of course, require a modification of the existing generally accepted accounting principle for investment portfolio treatment.[39]

A task force of the American Institute of Certified Public Accountants was created to examine the accounting standards for futures and forward contracts; they submitted a report of their study to the Financial Accounting Standards Board (FASB) in late 1980, in which deferred accounting was recommended for short hedges and for anticipatory hedges. In the case of short hedges, when the hedge is terminated gain or loss in the future or forward would be used to adjust the carrying value of the hedged security within certain limits. Long anticipatory hedges would set the cost basis of the acquired security; any gain or loss from short anticipatory hedges (hedging future debt issuance) would be amortized over the life of the issue. The FASB is currently studying this report and will issue a position paper for comment later this year. Hopefully, the various regulatory agencies, industry officials, and the FASB can resolve their differences and develop a uniform accounting and reporting standard.

CONCLUSIONS

The Comptroller's Office has indicated its belief that forward contracts, and especially interest rate futures contracts, can be used effec-

---

[39] See *Treasury/Fed Study*, note 6 *supra*. at 61.

tively to reduce the interest rate exposure of national banks. The Comptroller encourages this use, especially in correcting mismatches in total bank interest-sensitive assets and liabilities by hedging an interest rate differential. The recent guidelines contained in Banking Circular 79 (2d Revision) indicate, however, that the isolation of individual "price hedges" on investment securities is not necessary, since it can result in a further mismatch in total asset and liability interest rate spreads.

Used properly, the interest rate futures markets have tremendous potential for the banking industry—particularly in this age of uncertainty and volatility with respect to interest rates. Futures trading may, in fact, become a necessary part of banking activities. However, the recent guidelines issued by the Comptroller make it clear that a program for futures trading must be carefully designed and must contain safeguards to assure that this activity is undertaken in a way which is closely related to the business of safe and sound banking. The Comptroller has made an excellent start toward defining the basic parameters. It is now up to the banks themselves to take advantage of the beneficial aspects of futures trading.

29

Financial Futures Markets: Is More Regulation Needed?*

Phillip Cagan[†]

INTRODUCTION

With the recent growth in volume of trading in futures contracts for Treasury securities and the likely further expansion in the range of contracts available, the Treasury and the Congress have become concerned over possible harmful consequences for debt management and monetary policy. The *Treasury-Federal Reserve Study*[1] of May 1979 (cited hereafter as the *Study*) described these concerns. My discussion of the regulatory issues will in part be a review of this *Study* and the Senate *Hearings*[2] in May 1980 on the proposed Proxmire bill for margin requirements.

*Reprinted from *The Journal of Futures Markets*, Issue No. 2, (Summer 1981). Reprinted by permission of John Wiley & Sons, Inc., Copyright © 1981.

†Phillip Cagan is Professor of Economics at Columbia University. He also is a research associate of the National Bureau of Economic Research and an adjunct scholar of the American Enterprise Institute. He earned his Ph.D. from the University of Chicago.

The author has benefited from comments of Franklin Edwards of Columbia University and Paula Tosini of the CFTC.

[1] *Treasury-Federal Reserve Study of Treasury Futures Markets*, Vol. 1: *Summary and Recommendations*, Vol. II: *A Study by the Staffs of the U.S. Treasury and Federal Reserve System*, May 1979 (cited as *Study*).

[2] U.S. Senate, Committee on Banking, Housing, and Urban Affairs (96th Cong., 2nd Sess.), *Margin Requirements for Transactions in Financial Instruments*, May 29 and 30, 1980 (cited as Senate *Hearings*).

The *Study* was largely devoted to the effects of futures trading on the cash markets for Treasury securities. There was concern that attempted corners or squeezes of the delivery of futures contracts, particularly for proposed new contracts on Treasury notes, would affect prices in the cash markets, rendering Treasury securities less attractive to regular investors, and could create pressures on the Treasury to increase the supply of certain new issues whenever threatened by a corner or squeeze. This was viewed as an undesirable intrusion on debt management policy. The *Hearings*, held in early 1980 just after the bubble in silver prices, were concerned that such gyrations in basic commodity prices traded on exchanges could produce inflationary pressures when the prices rose and lead to serious bankruptcies affecting lending institutions when the prices collapsed. The *Hearings* advanced the view that speculative trading needs tighter controls, particularly higher margin requirements, and assumed that such controls are needed for financial as well as commodity futures markets.

I shall assess the validity of the various arguments for regulation of financial futures markets advanced in the *Study* and the *Hearings* and elsewhere. Public opinion has recently begun to turn away from the view that had prevailed since the 1930s that government regulation is the way to improve the inefficiencies of the private economy and to promote various public benefits that cannot otherwise be achieved. The theoretical justification for government regulation, now viewed more critically than it used to be, pertains to private markets that lack competition or that produce harmful externalities. Externalities are those costs of products and services that the buyers and sellers do not bear. As in pollution from automobiles or from the production of electricity, producers and users have no incentive to reduce the pollution detrimental to the public except through regulation in the public interest.

The projected benefits of regulation need to be weighed carefully against its constraints on the use and development of futures markets. I shall begin with a brief look at the advantages usually given in support of futures markets and my own view of the disadvantages of regulation. Then I shall take up the externality arguments in favor of regulation. These pertain to corners and squeezes, price volatility due to speculation in futures markets, the absorption of credit by speculation, and the protection of inexperienced traders. The emphasis will be on financial futures markets, though some of the arguments made pertain mainly to commodity markets and have been applied inappropriately to financial futures markets.

THE ADVANTAGES OF FINANCIAL FUTURES MARKETS

The literature on futures markets (which includes the *Study*) is rich in fulsome praise of the public service of futures prices in providing information. The idea is sound enough: Futures prices reflect the collective wisdom of those willing to put their money on the line, and this information is available to the entire economy for making consistent and rational decisions about resource allocation. However, the emphasis on the price information of futures markets is more an outgrowth of the recent attention to the role of information in economic literature than of the reality of these markets. While futures prices for agricultural products are largely determined by crop and animal herd projections, interest rates have no well defined set of influences that have been demonstrated to produce adequate predictions. As a result, the price information provided by financial futures markets is of limited value. The information is in principle the same as has been provided all along by forward rates embedded in yield curves; and, as with forward rates, prices in futures markets have not displayed any consistent ability to predict future spot rates.[3] The prices are essentially projections of current spot rates, and the deviations of futures from concurrent spot rates have generally not had predictive value. Unanticipated movements in interest rates dominate any movements that traders may be capable of predicting. It may be that futures markets help to bring spot yields on bonds in line with future developments, so that futures markets in bond yields cannot be expected to contain more information about future yields than the spot market does. But this would not explain why future and spot short term interest rates, which need not correspond as do spot and future bond yields, fail to show differences that predict future movements. Apparently the relevant information on the economy is readily available from published sources of data, and the expertise of futures traders, such as it is, has not added perceptibly to the accuracy of this information or the analysis of it. To the vaunted "price discovery" service of financial futures markets, the assessment must be that they do not discover much.

A better claim for the contribution of financial futures markets is that they indicate the average expectation prevailing in the market of future prices, and this is provided more effectively by futures markets than by forward rates embedded in yield curves. Such information may help to narrow the range of expectations that prevail in the market and

---

[3] William Poole (1978): "Using T-Bill Futures to Gauge Interest-Rate Expectations," *Federal Reserve Bank of San Francisco, Economic Review*, Spring: 7-19; Albert E. Burger, Richard W. Lang, and Robert H. Rasche (1977): "The Treasury Bill Futures Market and Market Expectations of Interest Rates," *Federal Reserve Bank of St. Louis, Review*, 59, June: 2-9; Michael J. Hamburger and E. N. Platt (1975): "The Expectations Hypothesis and the Efficiency of the Treasury Bill Market," *Review of Economics and Statistics*, 57, May: 190-199; Eugene F. Fama (1976): "Forward Rates as Predictors of Future Spot Rates," *Journal of Financial Economics*, 3, October: 361-378; Michael Mussa (1979): "Empirical Regularities in the Behavior of Exchange Rates and Theories of the Foreign Exchange Market," in *Policies for Employment, Prices and Exchange Rates*, K. Brunner and A. Meltzer, Eds., supplement to the *Journal of Monetary Economics*, 1979.

to bring financial decisions made throughout the economy into more consistent alignment with each other.

It is not clear, however, that economic activity benefits from narrowing the range of expectations around a single value that is no more accurate than a simple projection of spot rates. The narrowing may possibly reduce the number of large expectation errors, which is a help to poor forecasters, but there could be disadvantages to a uniformity of expectations in the market. If expectations are uniform rather than diverse, shifts in expectations may produce sharper short run price movements, creating the bandwagon effect characteristic of overshooting price adjustments. Although such an effect of the uniformity of expectations on price dynamics lacks solid evidence, it does raise the possibility that financial futures markets may have negative externalities on the stability of prices, if the range of expectations is narrowed without becoming more accurate. Of course, this disadvantage of futures trading is hardly a justification for regulating it. Not even the champions of regulation in Washington would want to suppress a market for disseminating information! Indeed, enhancement of the public's access to information, even of a confidential nature, is the high-minded purpose of much recent legislation.

The main rationale and advantage of financial futures markets must surely be the traditional one of providing an inexpensive method of hedging against interest rate movements and thus of reducing the risks taken by financial institutions and others who are not in the best position to bear risk. This rationale is considerably weakened, however, by evidence that few hedgers have so far made use of Treasury futures, particularly for bills, which are mainly traded by speculators on both sides of contracts.[4] Except for the use of GNMA futures by mortgage brokers, financial institutions have so far not taken much advantage of the hedging opportunities opened up by futures markets. A case could be made, therefore, that the economy would not lose important benefits if, to serve regulatory purposes, futures trading, except in GNMAs and possibly U.S. bonds, were curtailed.

That would be a mistaken conclusion, however, and not only for the obvious counterargument that the freedom to speculate on interest rates is a benefit for those who want to. The more fundamental reason for avoiding regulatory curtailments is the potential of markets to evolve. Economic practices should be allowed to evolve by a trial-and-error process to changing conditions. A government regulatory agency cannot judge what benefits are being provided by particular markets to all participants and especially cannot know what benefits may be provided in the future by new developments over the horizon. Hedging with finan-

---

[4] Marcelle Arak and Christopher J. McCurdy (1979-1980): "Interest Rate Futures," Federal Reserve Bank of New York, *Quarterly Review*, 4, Winter: Table 1.

cial bill futures, which is still at a low level, seems to be expanding as more financial institutions and businesses discover ways to benefit from it, and others may find it more useful under future conditions than at present. Perhaps some new form of financial activity will evolve out of present futures trading. A free economy reveals its benefits in the adaptability to new developments. We see this again and again in the historical record. A wise government hesitates to interfere with this evolution.

The opportunity for markets to evolve in new directions and to develop new functions is in my view the strongest argument against regulation, since regulatory constraints almost always stifle evolution. Unfortunately, such an argument does not carry much weight against regulatory proposals designed to meet present problems widely viewed as serious. It is important, therefore, to ask whether such "problems" really exist and whether the proposed regulations will solve them.

CORNERS AND SQUEEZES IN TREASURY SECURITIES

The externality of financial futures trading that is the main concern of the *Study* is the effect on the cash markets for Treasury securities, particularly an increase in price variability that reflects delivery problems of futures contracts. Increased price variability might reduce the attractiveness of Treasury securities to investors and thus raise average yields.

It is understandable why the Treasury is concerned about futures trading in its securities. In most futures markets the delivery price cannot be influenced by individual demanders or suppliers. The Treasury, on the other hand, is a monopoly supplier of its securities. To be sure, its control over the new-issue price is limited by substitute financial instruments in the private sector and competition on the demand side, and the amount supplied is largely determined by budgetary considerations. Nonetheless, within its budgetary constraints the Treasury wants to take advantage of the monopoly benefits of being a sole supplier and resents the intrusion of futures trading on its control of the cash market.

The *Study* discusses at length the possibility of attempted corners or squeezes that would affect the price of new issues that are deliverable on futures contracts. Such effects are within the power of the Treasury as sole supplier to eliminate, and it objects to the likely pressures that would arise for it to increase supplies under such circumstances. Failure to supplement supplies under these circumstances would allow price variability to increase, while an adjustment of supplies would interfere with the objective of managing the federal debt in the public interest. The *Study* alludes reverently to the maturity distribution of the federal debt as though this followed some grand design that would be spoiled by any tinkering necessitated by futures trading. In fact, the design of the federal debt is largely *ad hoc*; although variations in the maturity distribution may affect the yield curve, it is doubtful that the national interest benefits from any particular yield curve over another.[5]

One wonders why a well functioning futures market is not also in the public interest to which the Treasury might contribute its services. To be sure, traders might well recoil at the prospect of the Treasury using its control over the supply to influence delivery prices. But, given the Treasury's objective of maintaining a stable market for its securities, this influence could be accepted as benign.

In an evaluation of these concerns, the bugaboo of corners should be laid to rest. Although their possibility always seems to cast an ominous shadow over futures markets, corners are almost never achieved. The analogy that best describes them is not some financial Waterloo but rather *The Charge of the Light Brigade,* in which the attackers, in an adventurous display of high-stakes bravado, are decimated with few casualties inflicted on the defenders.

I should think that the Treasury's position would be that it stands ready to break any corner in its securities. Such a stand would decisively end the threat. I do not see that such a stand would in fact create serious problems, even in the unlikely event that such threats occasionally required the Treasury to act. One is reminded of the attempt by Gould and Fisk to corner the gold market in 1869, when the Civil War suspension of dollar convertibility into gold was still in effect. They had the resources to corner the 20 million gold dollars in circulation before foreign shipments could be brought in, but faced a danger from the Treasury's reserve of 100 million gold dollars. They thought they had the danger contained by the Administration's announced intention not to interfere in the gold market—a policy of noninterference strengthened by bringing President Grant's brother-in-law in on the corner. Unfortunately for the corner, imagined assurances from Grant of Treasury noninterference turned out to be misinterpreted. When gold hit $164 an ounce on Friday, September 24, the Treasury announced its intention to sell, and the price plummeted to $133 to produce the first "Black Friday" in Wall Street history.[6] Gould, incidentally, had no CFTC to

---

[5] A well known study by Franco Modigliani and Richard Sutch ("Debt Management and the Term Structure of Interest Rates: An Empirical Analysis of Recent Experience," *Journal of Political Economy*, 75, No. 4, Part II, August 1967: 569-589) found no effect of relative supplies on the yield curve. A recent study claims to find such an effect (V. Vance Roley, "The Effect of Federal Debt Management Policy on Corporate Bond and Equity Yields," National Bureau of Economic Research Working Paper 586, December 1980). For a criticism of the traditional theory of debt management based on aggregate demand effects, see Phillip Cagan (1966): "A Partial Reconciliation Between Two Views of Debt Management," *Journal of Political Economy* 74, No. 6, December: 624-628.

[6] See Larry T. Wimmer (1975): "The Gold Crisis of 1869: Stabilizing or Destabilizing Speculation Under Floating Exchange Rates?" *Exploration in Economic History*, 12, April: 105-122.

contend with and reportedly came out well ahead by getting out in time, thanks to inside information conveyed from Mrs. Grant to her brother.

The Treasury might, of course, wish to put limits on a stand to break all corners. It might want the option of discontinuing the issue of notes of certain maturities, which could be awkward until futures contracts in those issues were terminated. This is primarily a problem for traders in note futures, however, rather than for the Treasury. The Treasury could at any time announce that it is not committed to continuing the issue of certain notes, in which case the anemic futures market in notes might expire altogether. The traders in note futures, in view of the risks of no forthcoming supply, could then decide for themselves whether such a market should survive. If trading were continued, the governing bodies of the exchanges have provisions for dealing with the settlement of contracts caught in the wake of a sudden discontinuance of a note issue.

In general, however, imposed settlements offer no solution to ordinary difficulties in the delivery of a contract, which is what troubles the Treasury because of the effects on cash market prices. Nevertheless, aside from corners, it would be best for the Treasury to disregard any effects of the futures market on the cash market in order to avoid any question that it might try to influence prices. This would mean disregarding squeezes, which the *Study* viewed as a serious problem and as possible justification for restricting futures trading.

A squeeze on futures contracts occurs when potential deliveries are large relative to the available supply, which can raise prices on the cash market. A squeeze could reflect an attempted corner or more likely a large number of contracts that are held for delivery, in most cases apparently for tax reasons. Most squeezes probably reflect fortuitous developments rather than intended manipulation. The *Study* fears that squeezes could occur more frequently if the already large volume of futures trading continues to increase. Contrary to the *Study*, however, this argues for the introduction of more bill contracts on different delivery dates, which would spread the demand among various issues and diminish the possibility of squeezes.

Since a squeeze does not by definition reflect an increase in total demand to *hold* the delivered security as an investment, the higher price to meet deliveries disappears in the cash market after delivery. Holders of a squeezed futures contract, therefore, cannot gain from the higher price by taking delivery. A squeeze can provide gains to the longs only to the extent that they sell out before delivery. But the sale of contracts before delivery takes pressure off the delivery price. In making delivery

---

Gould may not have had a gold corner as his objective. He reportedly desired to raise the price of gold (and thus depreciate the value of the dollar in relation to sterling) in order to stimulate grain exports, and thus increase profits on his railroad stocks by expanding grain shipments to Eastern ports.

of a squeezed contract, the shorts pay a higher price in the cash market for the security, which benefits sellers of the security in the cash market but not the holders of long futures contracts taking delivery.

Whether a pool could gain from a planned squeeze is therefore difficult to predict. It depends on the relationship between the higher prices the pool would pay to acquire a large position and the higher prices it would receive in selling before delivery. Barring a corner, the pool would have to take a sizable delivery to avoid driving futures prices down to the point that profits from the squeeze disappeared. The subsequent sale of the delivered securities themselves would generate no profit and perhaps produce a loss. Whether a planned squeeze could therefore produce an overall profit from the sales that were made prior to delivery is unclear. Yet, since the risk of loss for a pool is small, manipulation of the market, however unlikely on a regular basis, cannot be ruled out as an occasional possibility.

At first sight there appears to be evidence of squeezes in recent data. Deliveries on Treasury Bill contracts on the IMM have increased substantially with the June 1979 contract (see Table A), and market observers report that the deliverable six-month Treasury Bill has sometimes traded at prices that are high (yields low) in relation to adjacent maturities. A New York Federal Reserve study reports that the June 1979 contract pushed the deliverable six-month T-Bill yield 4 basis points below the adjacent shorter maturity, and the December 1979 contract pushed the deliverable bill 8 basis points below.[7]

Whatever the effect of futures trading on predelivery yields, I can find no systematic effect around the time of delivery, which would affect yields on new issues and which is the Treasury's primary concern. A squeeze can be expected to raise the price of the deliverable security until the last day of trading, after which it should fall in price relative to adjacent maturities. I have examined the bill futures contracts on the IMM for these effects. The evidence is discussed in Appendix A. The yields on deliverable six-month T-Bills after futures trading ended have not risen systematically relative to yields on adjacent maturities, which is the movement indicative of a squeeze. If squeezes have occurred, the effect on the yields has been too small to distinguish from normal daily variations. The data can be easily misinterpreted as indicating squeezes in particular cases, because daily changes in yields have generally become much larger since mid-1979, which has led to an associated sharp increase in futures trading. Such a development is ready-made to show isolated signs of squeezes that do not exist.

Although any effect on new issue prices has so far been minimal, conceivably deliveries could become large enough in future years to affect new issue prices significantly. There appears to be no practical way

---

[7] Arak and McCurdy, *op. cit.*, 33-46.

to prevent squeezes or to control them. Since the effects of a squeeze would always be in the Treasury's favor, however, namely to raise the price and reduce the auction rate on new issues, an objective of minimizing interest costs would call for the encouragement of squeezes! But the *Study* quite rightly avoids this implication, and everyone would agree that squeezes are detrimental to the integrity of a market. They subject sellers of contracts to greater risk. To be sure, this risk is likely to be small relative to the ordinary risks of rate movements, because cash market investors arbitrage differences between adjacent weekly bill yields. To some extent the risk is limited further, because the exchanges have the authority and the means to impose settlements on contract deliveries subject to special influences such as squeezes. Despite this authority, however, the risk is not eliminated. An imposed settlement, aside from its disadvantages, cannot be relied on to deal with all squeezes. This authority is difficult to invoke except in extreme cases, since squeezes are not well defined phenomenon like corners. To overcome this arbitrariness one might propose some *non*discretionary rule for imposing cash settlements. Such a rule would trigger a settlement if the price went outside a band based on some average of prices on adjacent maturities. I doubt that traders would find such a constraint attractive, and therefore imposed settlements offer no solution to the problem of squeezes.

The *Study* takes the position that squeezes are unacceptable and manages to leave the impression that they are due to manipulation. Although it should not make any difference in practice to the shorts or others in the futures market whether a squeeze is due to manipulation or not, the recommendations of the *Study* pertain only to manipulation. The *Study* wants the positions of traders closely monitored, and complains that the CFTC lacks the manpower to do this properly, particularly if the large number of proposed new futures contracts are approved. Coordinated monitoring of different exchanges is difficult, however, and alternative regulatory methods might be more effective. Manipulation of a market price is essentially a monopoly problem which is traditionally handled by limiting concentration. This could be accomplished by lawful position limits on the total of specified contracts held by an associated group of traders on U.S. exchanges. The limits would be set to be some appropriate fraction of the expected deliverable supply or, conceivably, of the number of contracts outstanding at time of purchase. Collusion among traders may be hard to prevent, but, if the penalty were a stiff fine on all contracts in excess of the limit, I should think the risks would far exceed any possible profit to undetected pools.

Position limits should be imposed when a contract is first traded, however, and not subsequently changed for that contract in midstream. It is an unfair use of regulatory authority to impose a liquidation of positions that were initially undertaken lawfully and in good faith. To avoid the forced liquidation that appeared necessary in silver in 1980, preannounced position limits seem preferable.

Most squeezes, however, are unlikely to reflect intentional manipulation. Even without collusion many contract holders may desire delivery for ordinary investment or for tax purposes, owing to the fact that futures contracts give rise to capital gains or losses while the discount on Treasury Bills is treated as income with the opportunity to take losses against income. Also, short futures positions give rise to short-term capital gains or losses, regardless of the time period held. Because of the importance of taxes, IRS rulings could be changed to eliminate the incentives to take delivery on contracts. The Treasury should drop its distrust of futures trading in its short term securities and help to devise tax laws and regulations that contribute to the stability and usefulness of these markets.

Squeezes in financial and commodity markets, though undesirable, should be kept in perspective. The *Study* treats them as an intolerable intrusion of supply deficiencies into smoothly functioning financial markets. But squeezes occur all the time in the economy when a buoyant business expansion carries demand to peak levels or supply disruptions cause temporary scarcities. No one likes a sqeeeze on available supplies, generally speaking not even the sellers, because of the disruption to normal business practices. Yet such conditions of economic life are not ordinarily viewed as intolerable. Since squeezes (unlike corners) are a widely experienced even though infrequent part of economic life, they should be of no greater concern in the market for Treasury securities than elsewhere, Treasury debt managers have no special reason for invoking the public interest in hopes of banishing the problem from their own market.

Except to lament unbridled speculation, the *Study* expresses no parallel concern for squeezes in the markets for other instruments, such as commercial paper, where delivery pressures could also affect new issue prices and affect the quantity supplied. The recommendations of the *Study* have the mark of a government agency careful to be on record with warnings of all imaginable troubles, lest it ever be criticized for not anticipating whatever difficulties might arise. It searches earnestly for all possible problems, but in my view comes up largely with trivia. The *Study* is honest, however, in recognizing the paucity of the evidence to support its concerns.

PRICE VARIABILITY DUE TO SPECULATION IN FUTURES MARKETS

Effects on Dealers and Investors

Squeezes are a rare special case of a more general concern that futures markets impart an undesirable volatility to cash markets. While no one except speculators would want market prices to be volatile solely to provide speculative opportunities, if the prices faithfully reflect a volatility in underlying economic conditions, as is generally the case, the reflection of this volatility in futures prices is natural and good for the economy. But the *Study* expresses the fear that futures trading increases volatility and that the bond dealers who make a market in Treasury securities, as well as many long term investors in these securities, are vulnerable to fluctuations in prices and would require a higher yield on the average to compensate for the greater risk. I doubt that most buyers of Treasury securities have anywhere else to go to find dollar investments that are safer, but some dealers could of course go out of this business if they could not handle the volatility, which thus might widen bid-ask spreads. Yet it is unclear whether futures trading, even if responsible for increased volatility, would have such consequences, because futures markets also offer low cost means of hedging against volatility.

Whatever the effect of futures trading on the volatility of prices has been, it is surely responsible for only a small fraction if any at all of the considerable volatility these markets have displayed in recent years. It is the rampant inflation and the swings in monetary and federal budget policies that have disrupted financial markets and fostered the growth of futures trading, not *vice versa*. Despite these developments, the bond dealers are still in business, and the new issue market has not been impaired. Any effect of futures trading on volatility has not been a serious detriment to the new issue market.

Possible Effects on Monetary Policy

If futures markets were to add to the variability of interest rates, however, they would have an adverse effect on the conduct of monetary policy that deserves attention, though the *Study* barely mentioned it. Monetary policy is guided to a considerable extent by the behavior of interest rates. It operates through financial markets as the channel for controlling general economic activity, and it relies on signals from financial markets to judge the desirable scale of its actions for achieving its economic targets. Despite the recent shift in operating technique to focus on monetary growth,[8] monetary policy still monitors the federal funds rate closely and operates to hold it within particular bands (now wider than before). Misdirected movements in interest rates can lead policy to take actions that are not justified by underlying economic

---

[8] "The New Federal Reserve Technical Procedures for Controlling Money," January 30, 1980, press release. For the background to the new policy see Phillip Cagan (1980): "The New Monetary Policy and Inflation," in *Contemporary Economic Problems 1980*, W. Fellner, Ed., Washington, D.C.: American Enterprise Institute, pp. 9-38.

conditions and that produce undesirable fluctuations in financial credit flows and aggregate economic activity.

A view held by Federal Reserve officials is that financial markets have in recent years overreacted to current developments, exacerbating market instability and obstructing the performance of monetary policy. An extreme example was the large gyrations in interest rates in February and March 1980, when three-month T-Bill yields rose 350 basis points in several weeks and then fell 900 points by early June. These gyrations can hardly be blamed on the existence of futures trading, of course. Market expectations have been volatile because of the instability of monetary policy. The present inflationary environment, which reflects past expansionist monetary policies, has fostered a jittery and highly sensitive financial behavior that adds to market instability and the difficulty of conducting monetary policy. Whatever the basic reason for interest rate gyrations, however, the high priority of an effective antiinflationary monetary policy calls for strengthening monetary controls over the economy in any feasible way. If futures markets contribute significantly to interest rate instability, that would be a possible justification for further regulation. This case for regulation depends crucially on whether such effects exist and is discussed next.

Price Variability and Speculation

The strongest condemnation of futures trading in the *Hearings* concerned the alleged increase in price variability produced by speculation. This view reflects a public opinion that is practically unanimous in believing that speculative activity increases price variability—not in the desirable sense of transmitting to prices all the underlying volatility in economic conditions, but in the critical sense that if speculation were constrained the variability of spot prices would be less without adversely affecting the allocation of resources. Public opinion unfortunately reveals little understanding of speculative activities and parallels an age-old religious condemnation of "money changers" and "unproductive" economic activities including practically everything except agriculture and manufactures. Modern economics teaches the opposite view that speculation is beneficial and tends to stabilize prices. In the view of economists, speculators pay attention to present and future economic conditions and bear the risks of future price movements. They make gains by moving prices into line with demand and supply developments as rapidly as those developments can be ascertained. If the result is to produce more variation in prices, the reason would be that market prices have become more sensitive and responsive to actual market developments. Without this responsiveness market prices would be less efficient, in the sense of not reflecting immediately all available information on market developments. The finding that changes in prices on commodity and financial exchanges are unpredictable by any statistical or econometric methods provides important empirical support for this view of speculation. The finding implies that speculators are not missing any obvious or even sophisticated opportunities for further profits and tend to make prices at any time as consistent with future levels as the available information allows. Such efficiency is clearly a good thing.

If speculation were to move prices away from levels consistent with future developments and to produce movements that increased the variability of prices, the traders responsible for these misdirected movements would incur losses on the average. The losses would gradually thin the ranks of speculators down to those who knew how to gain; as the thinning out proceeded, the unstable speculation would disappear.

There is one qualification to this "survival" argument, however. The demonstration that market price movements are not predictable or that destabilizing movements produce losses does not prove conclusively that speculation stabilizes prices. Destabilizing price movements might also be unpredictable and might be produced by amateur speculators who lose money on the average and are forced to retire from the market but are continually replaced by others equally inept. To Lincoln's truth, paraphrased, that "Market traders can't continue to be fooled indefinitely," the retort is that speculative markets do it with turnover. If speculation tended to increase price variability, futures markets, which make speculative trading very inexpensive through low margin costs, would help to increase the variability of spot prices.

Yet, when we turn from popular opinion to the statistical evidence, studies generally find that speculation is neutral or actually stabilizes prices, both for futures markets and corresponding cash markets. To be sure, commodity prices and interest rates have displayed greater variability in recent years as financial futures markets have started up and expanded, but the escalation of inflation in this period has been the primary source of variability. It is admittedly not a simple matter to disentangle the separate effect of futures trading. Nevertheless, when price variability in cash markets is examined before and after futures trading began, and when comparison is made with prices in related markets to allow for differences in price behavior over time for other reasons, prices are found to be less variable with futures trading.[9]

---

[9] See Kenneth C. Froewiss (1978): "GNMA Futures: Stabilizing or Destabilizing?" *Federal Reserve Bank of San Francisco, Economic Review*, Spring: 20-29. For a discussion of other empirical studies, see Senate *Hearings*, pp. 395-403. The vast empirical literature on the "efficiency of capital markets" also supports the view that they accurately reflect all the information available on relevant economic conditions. For a review of this literature see Eugene F. Fama (1970): "Efficient Capital Markets: A Review of Theory and Empirical Work," *Journal of Finance*, May: 383-417, and Richard Roll (1970): *The Behavior of Interest Rates: An Application of the Efficient Market Model to U.S. Treasury Bills*, New York: Basic Books.

The evidence of these statistical studies seem to be valid. I would qualify them in only one respect. Their evidence that price movements are stabilizing pertains to average behavior over a period of time. These studies do not demonstrate that speculation may not occasionally drive prices out of line, typically with buying on upswings. Many rapid price increases that end in a sudden collapse appear to exhibit the phenomenon of overshooting. The price increases may be initiated by changes in economic conditions, but the magnitude and speed of the upswing and the subsequent collapse do not make sense in terms of subsequent economic developments.[10] Examples are stock prices in 1929, grain prices in 1950, and recently gold and silver prices in 1979 and 1980. In these and other episodes an initial price movement, based on some new development, appears to gather momentum and to be carried further by speculative buying attracted by prospects of quick profits. The price overshoots a sustainable level and subsequently collapses before settling at a new temporary equilibrium. Such episodes appear detached from underlying economic conditions. The view that speculation occasionally produces overshooting of prices is not inconsistent with statistical evidence that speculation *on the average* stabilizes prices. While the view that speculation is generally destabilizing is insupportable when confronted with the statistical evidence, I find the opposite view that it is *never* destabilizing just as implausible when confronted with the occurrence of price bubbles.

Futures markets can be said to contribute to destabilizing speculation because of lower margin costs than are required in cash markets, but whether futures trading adds much to total speculation is an open question. In any event, the speculative price bubbles of commodity exchanges are far less characteristic of markets for financial securities, for which their anchor of a fixed-dollar value at maturity limits the price effects of interest-rate movements.

Defaults on Margin Loans

The concern over price volatility expressed in the Senate *Hearings* was that it increased the possibility of defaults on margin loans, with cascading repercussions on brokerage houses and financial institutions. The prime example cited in the *Hearings* of such dangers was not financial futures but the recent bubble in silver prices.[11] In January 1980 the

---

[10] This does not mean that cases of overshooting can be identified profitably. Overshooting is far less clear in foresight than by hindsight. If it is thought that the future rate of inflation, for example, will be higher than had previously been expected, stocks of physical assets such as gold will rise in price faster for a while, in anticipation of the higher future inflation rate, than will prices of noninvestment goods. Such a faster rise may appear at the time to be overshooting, but it could be justified by future developments.

[11] Senate *Hearings*, especially pp. 1-4.

price of silver reached $49 an ounce, five times its price four months earlier in September. Through increased position limits and margin requirements, the exchanges forced a liquidation of open positions, and the price collapsed. In April 1980 when a subsidiary of Placid Oil Co. assumed the silver margin debts of the Hunt brothers with a bank loan of $1.1 billion, the Hunts surrendered 63 million ounces of silver, over one-third of reported world stocks excluding government holdings and coin.[12] This did not include the additional positions of some major foreign buyers who appeared to have been buying in concert with the Hunts.

The final rapid collapse of silver prices in March 1980 produced several disquieting weeks for government officials who feared a financial crisis if there were major defaults on loans of banks or dealers. Although the Hunts were short of liquid funds for a few days and were unable to cover their debts until the Placid Oil loan was arranged, there was never any question of their ability to honor their debts. The only problem was whether a restructuring and extension of their debts might run up against the Federal Reserve's restrictions on bank loans for speculative purposes.[13] No defaults in fact occurred, though the forced liquidation of the Hunt holdings was accomplished at what must have been considerable loss to them and others and obliged the Federal Reserve to acquiesce in the consolidation of the Hunt debts by a consortium of banks. In the undisguised view of government officials the silver losses taken by the Hunts were well deserved. Whether that view is justified, the episode suggests the desirability of setting reasonable position limits at the beginning of trading on new contracts, taking into account the likely available deliverable supply on the contract, and of avoiding a change in the limits after positions have been taken.

Although no defaults resulted from the silver bubble, financial markets have experienced major defaults in recent years to provide evidence on the economic consequences. In 1970 the Penn Central went into bankruptcy, defaulting on a huge volume of outstanding commercial paper. The losses did not cascade, but the shock to the commercial paper market brought the Federal Reserve into action to support an expansion of bank loans to business borrowers until the commercial paper market revived. In 1974 the Franklin National had to close (due partly to unwise speculation in foreign exchange), and the Federal Reserve lent $1.7 billion to cover the Franklin's liquidity shortage until its assets could be sold. In neither case did the financial shock precipitate related defaults. Thus major isolated failures can and do occur without serious consequences for financial markets or the economy. The alarm expressed in the *Hearings* that the silver bubble carried potential dangers of large

---

[12] Senate *Hearings*, p. 622 (Hunts' silver position, but see also p. 161), p. 715 (world silver stocks in 1979), p. 318 (COMEX silver prices from September 1979 to March 1980).
[13] Senate *Hearings*, pp. 605, 617, 622, 623.

defaults and financial disorder appears exaggerated, but in any case a solution in terms of preannounced position limits seems adequate and is more attractive than the proposals for increased margin requirements.

Price Variability and Inflationary Pressures

The silver bubble was also seen by the *Hearings* as a source of inflationary pressure.[14] The bubble did disrupt certain industrial markets, passing a large price increase through users of silver to final products. The wholesale producer price index for photographic supplies, the only published component heavily dependent on silver, peaked in March 1980 with an increase of 74 percent over the preceding 12 months. It subsequently fell 12 percent and stabilized with an overall rise of 52 percent in the year and a half ending in September 1980. In September silver bars in the producer price index were 207 percent above their level at the beginning of 1979. It is doubtful that the overshooting of silver prices in early 1980 made photographic supply prices any higher permanently than they would have been if silver had risen 207 percent and stayed there without any overshooting. If the overshooting of silver prices had caused photographic supply prices to rise commensurately without falling back when silver prices receded, the photographic supply prices would have remained above unit costs of silver and other inputs, and profit margins would have expanded. This was unlikely. Profit margins may rise for many reasons, but typically not as a result of a rise in unit costs.

The main reason for these sharp price increases in late 1979 and early 1980 was that heightened fears of inflation bred investor panic, and the public rushed into real assets including precious metals. The price index for platinum and gold jewelry rose over 100 percent during this period, and neither the Hunts nor any other small group of speculators had anything to do with the extraordinary behavior of gold prices. Were the resulting price increases inflationary? Yes, in the sense that they added to the costs of production of products that use them as inputs. Can these price increases be considered a cause of inflation? Clearly not, since they were obviously only part of a general inflationary process and were themselves generated by expectations of overall inflationary pressures in the economy.

If speculation in silver and gold is to be viewed as inflationary, what of land and house prices in recent years? The rise in the latter, though less dramatic, dwarfed those in precious metals in quantitative significance. In recent years house price increases have produced a massive in-

---

[14] Senate *Hearings*, pp. 39, 49, 149.

crease in household real wealth[15] and have added more to the consumer price index than has any other major component except energy. But the increase in house prices also has been part of the public's response to the inflationary environment and not a cause. The view of speculation as inflationary is old and persistent, but it is a misleading confusion of particular with general effects. The implication of this view is that overall inflation in the economy would be perceptibly lower if speculation could somehow be eliminated. Such a view cannot be supported.

THE ABSORPTION OF CREDIT BY SPECULATION

Quite a different argument against speculation, also voiced in the Senate *Hearings*, is that it is largely financed by borrowed funds and thus absorbs credit from productive uses in the economy.[16] The relevance to futures markets, where margins are very low, is that the practice of marking to market passes funds from the losers, who may borrow to maintain their positions, to the gainers, who can use the funds to speculate further.

The notion that speculation absorbs credit is very old. It underlies the centuries-old "real bills doctrine" of banking, in which banks are to avoid any kind of loans for speculative purposes because they are thought to be inflationary (while in this view self-liquidating bank loans on goods in process are not). It was the rationale for the Federal Reserve's restrictive monetary policy in 1928 and 1929 undertaken to cut off credit for speculation in the stock market boom. It has resurfaced every time price increases are thought to reflect speculation, most recently as a result of the silver bubble.

The notion that speculation absorbs credit from "productive" economic uses has long since been discredited.[17] Trading in existing assets as distinct from the net purchase of newly issued assets does not absorb credit in any economically relevant sense. The amount of funds used to transact the trading on exchanges is miniscule compared with the total volume of trading. Consequently, if trading volume rises with speculative buying, the additional funds tied up are insignificant. Economic activity uses or "absorbs" credit when borrowed funds are spent on newly produced goods and services. A diversion of credit from capital investment

---

[15] Phillip Cagan and Robert E. Lipsey (1978): *The Financial Effects of Inflation* (Cambridge, MA, Ballinger Publishing Co. for the National Bureau of Economic Research), Tables 2-7, 2-10, 2-11.

[16] Senate *Hearings*, pp. 6, 34, 136, 618-623.

[17] It was also dismissed in the *Study*, pp. 12, 13.

means either that the funds are spent on consumer goods or not spent at all but are held as idle money balances. Neither outcome is the likely result of trading in existing assets. Credit that finances the purchase of existing assets passes through financial markets into the hands of net sellers who either are traders liquidating assets to hold money or to make consumption expenditures or are suppliers of new financial assets borrowing to invest in physical assets. For capital formation in the economy, the important distinction is the allocation of resources between consumption and investment expenditures. The effect of increased speculation on consumption is ambiguous (it may reflect an increase in saving and reduction in consumption or, if there are capital gains, it may lead to the purchase of luxury items), but in any case it is probably slight.

Credit controls directed to curtailing bank loans for speculative purposes have quite a different outcome and motivation. This was evident in the Federal Reserve's directive to member banks in October 1979 and again in March 1980 to curb lending for speculative activities. This directive may have contributed to the accompanying decline in open interest in bill futures. (See Appendix B for a discussion of the data.) Since small businesses and farming are dependent on banks for credit because bond or equity financing is not feasible for them, bank loans for speculation tend to channel funds through financial markets out of the reach of small businesses and farming. At times when banks are urged to curtail total credit growth, these borrowers will benefit if banks can be forced to concentrate lending on them as their traditional business customers. Whether such a reallocation of credit is the proper function of federal policy and regulation—and I doubt that it is—it is accomplished by regulating banks as the suppliers of the funds and not futures traders as the initial recipients.

THE PROTECTION OF TRADERS

A common argument for regulation of futures and spot trading is that amateur speculators foolishly overexpose themselves and suffer severe financial losses. Stiff margin requirements are often proposed to curtail these excesses and are defended, first, as good for the amateur speculators themselves and, second, as good for financial markets by reducing the effects of speculation on prices. The latter effect on financial markets is an externality that was discussed above. The first defense of regulation is not, barring major defaults, an externality, but is based on the presumed benefits from government protection of the financial position of speculators. This defense deserves close scrutiny, notwithstanding the superficial appeal of regulations intended to protect the public. The desirability of extending government control over private activities is less widely accepted today than it used to be.

A justification for protecting speculators might possibly be made on the grounds that a government service of providing information and preventing fraudulent practices is needed. The argument would be that only the government can provide this service efficiently and reliably because the exchangers and brokers cannot do so with disinterest. This might justify special regulations against fraud and a requirement that brokers prominently display the admonition made famous for cigarettes: "Warning: A government agency has determined that futures trading is dangerous to your pocketbook."

But, in the name of protecting individuals from their own imprudence, proposals to regulate futures markets go beyond dispensing information and friendly advice to an officious meddling in market activities. The regulatory approach to market control is illustrated by SEC proposals for options. As described in the Senate *Hearings*,[18]

> Many abuses arose in the options market from the failure of firms adequately to train their salesmen ... the self-regulatory organizations... are now engaged in substantially revising the examinations which registered representatives are required to pass ... These examinations ... will be administered in a controlled environment by independent examiners ...
>
> The Options Study also recommended ... rule changes to ... require every member firm to develop and implement a written program for the systematic review of customer accounts ... This program must be under the supervision of a "Senior Registered Options Principal" who must be an officer or general partner ... and also require[s] member firms to designate a senior supervisory officer to ... perform an audit function to determine that these activities are conducted in conformance with applicable laws, regulations and self-regulatory rules.

The SEC presents these regulatory initiatives with pride as evidence of its performance in protecting investors. I find them appalling. They are indicative of the regulatory morass that develops when an officious bureaucracy is charged with "reforming" behavior. No evidence of accomplishments is sought or presented other than the length of the list of new regulations, reports, and examinations. When these are revealed to fall short of the intended benefits, the next step, as indicated by the quotation above, is to appoint supervisors within firms to gain closer regulatory control over activities. The further regulation is again never more than marginally beneficial and, from the point of view of the regulators, always requires further control. The process is endless.

[18] Senate *Hearings*, pp. 127, 128.

Such regulation does not recognize a major difference in principle between closing a dangerous highway, in which heavy traffic itself magnifies the danger, and mandating seat belts, which are solely for the benefit of the belted individual. To restrict futures trading in order to reduce speculative losses is to mandate financial seat belts. Although the nation has moved hesitantly toward mandatory automobile seat belts. I question whether we want to tie down futures markets in order to try to guarantee the financial safety of individual speculators. Certainly it would not be justified to increase the costs of all hedging and to diminish the benefits of all futures trading in order to constrain certain forms of speculation.

SUMMARY AND CONCLUSIONS

The Treasury-Federal Reserve Study of Treasury Futures Markets was undertaken on the presumption of Treasury officials that futher regulation was needed. It was most concerned with squeezes of futures contracts due to manipulation that would affect cash market yields. Potential manipulation of futures trading in Treasury short term securities can be handled best by position limits, which can be set at some fraction of the expected deliverable supply or perhaps the existing number of contracts at time of purchase, and should be preannounced to avoid disruptive changes before contracts are terminated. Squeezes on bills that occur without manipulation could be a problem if trading volume continues to expand, but so far yields at delivery give no evidence of squeezes. They are most likely to result from the tax advantages of taking delivery on bill contracts, which could be eliminated by appropriate revisions of tax rules. The expansion of futures trading to notes, which greatly troubles the Treasury as interfering with its option of discontinuing their issue, is really a problem for the exchanges. They should be allowed to determine whether note contracts can survive and evolve in the face of a possible decision by the Treasury to discontinue these issues.

The evolution of new services and benefits is the basic advantage we gain from free markets, which regulation inevitably stifles. Since we generally do not know specifically what these benefits will be in the future or indeed whether there will be any benefits at all in particular cases, regulations intended to deal with the problems at hand appear to entail few identifiable costs. Although the costs are likely to be considerable, they will be indirect and difficult to demonstrate. The short term Treasury futures markets are particularly vulnerable to regulatory intervention, because the services of hedging and "price discovery" are not extensive, which makes it appear that regulatory constraints would not be very costly. The most forceful argument against regulation at the present time, therefore, is that it is not needed.

The important and controversial issues in the regulation of any market pertain to its externalities for other parts of the economy. Externalities here would be the dangers to the financial system and the economy from major defaults on margin loans and increased price variability. From experience we know that major defaults are not a problem, even though the Federal Reserve may occasionally be called upon to perform its traditional function of supporting the market in a short liquidity crisis. Moreover, such problems are most unlikely to develop from financial futures trading.

The problems attributed to speculative overshooting, aside from major defaults, are that it creates inflationary pressures and absorbs credit from productive uses. There is no validity to these contentions; moreover, they do not pertain to financial futures trading. A valid consideration that does pertain to financial futures is the difficulty for monetary policy of interest rate volatility. But the increased volatility in financial markets of recent years cannot be attributed to the accompanying expansion of futures trading. Actually, it is the other way around: the volatility resulting from escalating inflation has fostered active futures markets to provide the private sector with a means of hedging against the greater risks of large fluctuations in interest rates.

Most externality arguments favoring further regulation of futures markets boil down to the contention that they foster speculation because of low margin requirements, and that speculation is destabilizing. This contention about destabilization finds no empirical support in the data, however, probably for the good reason that it is generally untrue. Nevertheless, the occurrence of price bubbles indicates that speculation can be destabilizing at certain times, even though such episodes are too infrequent to affect the statistical evidence for a period of years. Price bubbles are not serious enough to warrant clamping restrictive regulations on the everyday activities of futures markets.

Financial futures markets are a product of our present inflationary environment. They reflect the attempt of financial markets to adjust to escalating inflation and sudden changes in interest rates. They could not have survived in the world of stable interest rates of earlier decades. It is clear that adjustments of financial markets and institutions have much further to go, if the high and escalating rates of inflation continue. Fixed-dollar financial instruments, developed in a stable era, will no longer meet the needs of investors. How it will all turn out is not clear, but, if present high inflation rates do not come down, financial markets and institutions will have to change radically. Financial futures markets need to be allowed to make their contribution to the evolving adjustments of financial practices to the high risk environment of inflation.

APPENDIX A

YIELDS ON DELIVERABLE CASH MARKET BILLS

A squeeze on cash bill yields owing to heavy delivery on futures contracts would be indicated by a rise in the price (fall in the yield) of deliverable bills prior to delivery, while after delivery the yields would no longer be subject to downward pressure. We may look for such pressures, therefore, on the yields of six-month bills deliverable on three-month bill contracts.

Table A shows the changes in yields on these bills for IMM contracts since 1976. To allow for other influences on yields, the changes are shown as differences from the average changes for corresponding six-month bills with maturities a week shorter and a week longer than the deliverable bill. Although the adjacent bill yields may tend to change in sympathy with the deliverable bill, there would be no squeeze on these bills and any abnormal demand for the deliverable bill would show up in the difference in yields. In the first column the differences are shown for the change in closing bid yields (average of five dealers) from the last day of trading on the futures contract to the day of delivery. The second column shows the change in an average of these differences from the five days before the delivery date to the five days after the end of trading on the futures contract. The third and fourth columns of Table A show the quantity of deliveries on the contract in millions of dollars and as a percentage of the potential supply of deliverable bills previously and newly issued outside of Federal Reserve Bank holdings. Deliveries have been less than 20 percent of the potential supply except for December 1979 when they were almost one-third.

A squeeze is indicated by a large positive difference. As can be seen in Table A, the differences are generally quite small, usually less than 5 basis points. A few larger differences appear to be aberrations in the yield curve rather than squeezes. The positive differences above 5 basis points in column 1, particularly that for March 20, 1980, pertained only to the last day of trading and the delivery date; the five-day averages show much smaller differences. Also, the differences are not uniformly positive after mid-1978 when the dollar volume of deliveries increased. The differences beginning in September 1978 are larger both in a positive and a negative direction, which is attributable to larger fluctuations in bill yields and greater disparities in the yield curve.

The only difference out of line with the others is for December 21, 1978, when the average difference of 9 basis points is about 5 points higher than the other largest positive differences, though that contract did not have an unusually large volume of deliveries. These data give no indication, therefore, of a systematic effect of squeezes on cash bill yields.

Table A Change in Discount Yields on Six-Month Bills Deliverable on IMM Contracts, Before and After Delivery Date, Relative to Adjacent Weekly Maturities (Basis Points)

Delivery Date of Contract	Change from Last Trading Day to Next Day of Delivery[a]	Change from Average of Five Days Before to Average of Five Days After Delivery Date[a]	Deliveries Millions of $	Deliveries Percent of Available Supply[b]
Sept. 18, 1980	− 8.0	−38.2	428	−
June 19, 1980	− 4.0	− 2.9	690	16
Mar. 20, 1980	+16.5	− 4.3	503	14
Dec. 20, 1979	+ 5.5	+ 4.1	1000	31
Sept. 20, 1979	0	− 4.2	661	19
June 21, 1979	+ 2.5	+ 3.4	706	17
Mar. 22, 1979	− 1.0	− 1.5	301	15
Dec. 21, 1978	+ 4.0	+ 8.9[c]	442	17
Sept. 21, 1978	− 3.5	− 4.2	293	15
June 22, 1978	+ 1.0	− 2.6	363	19
Mar. 23, 1978	+ 0.5	− 0.4	158	7
Dec. 22, 1977	+ 5.5	+ 2.2	172	6
Sept. 22, 1977	+ 3.0	+ 0.2	96	3
June 23, 1977	+ 0.5	− 2.4	127	5
Mar. 24, 1977	+ 2.0	− 0.7	76	3
Dec. 23, 1976	− 0.5	− 0.2	362	19
Sept. 23, 1976	+ 1.5	+ 0.4	210	10
June 24, 1976	+ 3.0	− 2.3	159	7
Mar. 18, 1976	+ 3.5	− 0.4	34	−

Source: Yields were compiled by the Federal Reserve (courtesy of Leigh Ribble of Board staff), deliveries are from the *Study*, Table 4, and the IMM, and available supplies are from the *Study*, Table 4, and Treasury public releases.

[a] A positive change means that the deliverable bill yield increased more from before to after the delivery date than did an average of the yields on the bills maturing one week earlier and later. The first yield after the delivery date is taken to be the closing bid on the day of delivery. Yields are closing bids, average of five dealers, on six-month bills deliverable on the contract and with one week shorter and longer maturities.

[b] Publicly held outside the Federal Reserve.

[c] Average of four days only.

APPENDIX B

BILL FUTURES OPEN INTEREST AND FEDERAL RESERVE LOAN RESTRICTIONS

The Federal Reserve directed member banks in October 1979 to avoid loans for speculative purposes and backed up the directive in March 1980 by monitoring banks' adherence. The evidence is not clear as to what extent these measures had an effect on the volume of futures trading.

Table B shows the open interest in three-month bill futures on the IMM at the end of each month since the beginning of 1979. The open interest reached a peak in May 1979 and then declined fairly steadily until February 1980, after which it had remained at roughly one-half the volume of early 1979 until November (not shown). The decline began well before the Federal Reserve's directive in October 1979, and, though continuing thereafter, had largely ended by the time the monitoring was introduced in March 1980. It appears, therefore, that, while the directive may have contributed to the decline in open interest, it was not the major cause.

The variation in bill rates, also shown in Table B, increased sharply after mid-1979 and, if anything, would have expanded the demand for bill futures. The cost of borrowing, as indicated by the average daily prime rate also shown in Table B, is likely to have been an important influence on open interest, since the prime rate rose to discourage borrowing during the latter part of 1979 and early 1980. The prime rate nevertheless does not provide a full explanation for the decline in open

Table B Bill Futures Open Interest, Yield Variability, and the Prime Rate

		End-of-Month Open Interest Three-Month Bill Futures IMM ($ Billions)	Variation in Three-Month Cash Bill Discount Yields (basis points) Monthly Range	Daily Std. Dev.	Average Prime Rate
1979	Jan.	54.2	23	7	11.75
	Feb.	54.2	30	9	11.75
	Mar.	52.7	19	6	11.75
	Apr.	56.4	77	23	11.75
	May	63.7	31	7	11.75
	June	61.2	77	25	11.65
	July	46.8	54	13	11.54
	Aug.	40.9	65	16	11.91
	Sept.	41.4	52	16	12.90
	Oct.	35.4	283	81	14.39
	Nov.	42.8	141	42	15.55
	Dec.	36.5	90	23	15.30
1980	Jan.	30.2	84	21	15.25
	Feb.	25.0	206	76	15.63
	Mar.	28.5	186	54	18.31
	Apr.	28.2	475	145	19.77
	May	24.7	292	80	16.57
	June	25.2	172	53	12.63
	July	22.9	148	28	11.48
	Aug.	23.1	192	64	11.12
	Sept.	21.4	170	44	12.23
	Oct.	24.2	190	56	13.48

Source: End-of-month open interest and daily discount yields are from IMM *Monthly Information Bulletin*, and average prime rate is from *Federal Reserve Bulletin*.

interest, which began earlier than the rise in the prime rate and was not reversed in mid-1980 despite the sharp fall in the prime rate.

A further and more extensive analysis of the volume of open interest is required to determine by statistical evidence the influence of the Federal Reserve's directive.

Living with Inflation: A Proposal for New Futures and Options Markets*

Louis H. Ederington[†]

The absence of a hedge against inflation is driving many investors away from financial assets toward real estate, gold and silver. Such a hedge could be provided by markets in which investors trade futures or options contracts whose values are tied to the Consumer Price Index.

In a CPI futures market, investors trade the right to purchase an amount in dollars equal to the CPI. The buyer of CPI futures effectively locks in, at the current price of the contract, the future cost of the market basket of real goods the Bureau of Labor Statistics uses to compute the CPI. He can use the contract to hedge purchasing power risk, not only in future wages, pensions, dividends, interest or alimony, but also in the ownership of financial assets.

In a CPI options market, the buyer obtains the right to purchase for a predetermined price an amount of dollars equal to the CPI. An options contract may appeal to those investors who wish to protect themselves from an unexpected increase in the rate of inflation without forfeiting the gains they might experience from an unexpected decrease.

The current price of the futures contract represents an equilibrium

---

*Reprinted from the *Financial Analysts Journal*, (January-February 1980). Reprinted by permission of the publisher.

[†]Louis Ederington is Professor of Economics at the College of Business Administration of Georgia State University, Atlanta. He thanks Fred Arditti, Pete Eisemann, Bruce Fielitz, Donald Rataczak and Ed Ulveling for their helpful comments and the Bureau of Business and Economic Research at Georgia State University for its research support.

price, in the sense that everyone who believes that inflation will be more rapid than implied by that price will tend to buy, whereas everyone who believes inflation will be less rapid will sell. The current price of the contract thus provides a continuous measure of consensus expectations regarding inflation.

Furthermore, because they shift risk to the speculator willing to bear it, futures and options markets may actually encourage inflation indexation. Life insurance companies and pension plans can offer policies with benefits linked to the inflation rate, hedging their commitments in the CPI markets. Most important, by replacing real goods as an inflation hedge, CPI futures and options markets discourage hoarding, hence encourage capital investment.

The race isn't even close: In one public opinion poll after another, inflation consistently heads the list of socioeconomic concerns. While we can continue to hope and search for a cure to this malady, there is none on the horizon. It is time we turned our attention to the symptoms of the malady—to alleviating the pain and suffering that inflation generates.

Inflation poses a particular problem for the investor. In economic and financial theory, saving is deferred consumption. Households forego buying goods today in order to accumulate financial assets that will stake them to claims against market baskets of goods in future periods. Because prices change over time, however, the quantity of real goods and services that an investor's accumulated wealth will be able to purchase is uncertain. This purchasing power uncertainty has led some investors to turn away from financial assets toward assets they hope will appreciate with prices in general—e.g., real estate, gold and silver. It has also led to proposals of new types of financial assets denominated in real terms—indexed bonds and (as presented in a previous issue of the *Journal*) the Purchasing Power Fund (PPF).[1]

This article proposes the establishment of special futures and options markets. Unlike indexed bonds or a Purchasing Power Fund, these futures and options markets would be supplements, rather than alternatives, to existing financial assets, hence would probably be accepted more readily than either index bonds or a PPF. Investors could buy or sell in these markets claims to future dollars that would be tied to the Consumer Price Index (CPI). An investor could thereby hedge any future interest, dividend or principal payment—and future wages or pensions—against a change in purchasing power due to unanticipated inflation.

While developing these proposals, I discovered that an idea for a CPI

---

[1] Nils H. Hakansson, "The Purchasing Power Fund: A New Kind of Financial Intermediary," *Financial Analysts Journal*, November/December 1976, pp. 49-59.

futures market had been advanced by Lovell and Vogel in 1973.[2] Perhaps their idea was too novel or unsuited for the time, for it has been ignored to date. Nonetheless, theirs is a practical idea that meets a serious need. Certainly there is universal concern with inflation, and the success of the new futures markets in GNMAs, Treasury bills and government bonds demonstrates that new, novel futures markets will be accepted if they fill an economic need.

ASSETS AND INFLATION

The *raison d'etre* for CPI futures and options markets is to provide a mechanism for hedging existing assets against unanticipated inflation. To understand the mechanism, it is necessary to examine the relation between financial assets—or, more specifically, the return on financial assets—and inflation.

The real return (r) on a financial asset is defined as the yield that a dollar invested today will earn *in terms of today's prices*. If one dollar invested in 1978 returns $(1 + i)$ in 1979, the real return in 1978 dollars would be calculated as:

$$(1 + r) = (1 + i) \frac{P(1978)}{P(1979)}, \tag{1}$$

or

$$(1 + r) = \frac{(1 + i)}{(1 + I)}, \tag{2}$$

where r equals the real rate of interest; i the market, or nominal, rate of interest; P(1978) the 1978 price level (e.g., the CPI in 1978); P(1979) the 1979 price level (the CPI in 1979); and I the rate of inflation from 1978 to 1979 (calculated as [P(1979) − P(1978)]/P(1978)).

According to Equation 2, the market rate (i) can be broken down into a real return and an inflation component. That is:

$$(1 + i) = (1 + r)(1 + I),$$

or

$$i = r + I + rI. \tag{3}$$

[2] See Michael C. Lovell and Robert C. Vogel, "A CPI-Futures Market," *Journal of Political Economy*, July/August 1973, pp. 1009-1012. A check of the *Social Science Citation Index* reveals that this article has not been cited in any of the economics, finance or business journals surveyed. The idea of a CPI futures market has also recently been suggested by Kurt Dew, who like the author was unaware of the Lovell and Vogel article. See Kurt Dew, "CPI Futures?" *Federal Reserve Bank of San Francisco Weekly Letter*, September 22, 1978.

The third term, rI, is usually so small that it is generally ignored and the market rate approximated as a real return plus the inflation rate:

$$i \simeq r + I. \qquad (4)$$

Investors in bonds, certificates of deposit and savings accounts know when they purchase these assets the market rate (i) they will earn if the asset does not default and is held to maturity. Since they do not know what the inflation rate (I) will be, however, they cannot know the real return they will actually realize. Nonetheless, investors will set the current market rate (i) according to their expectations of inflation (EI) and their required total return (rr)—that is, the minimum real return that will induce them to defer consumption. According to Fisherian interest rate theory:

$$i \simeq rr + EI. \qquad (5)$$

One argument in interest rate theory dating back to Irving Fisher is that the real return investors require is independent of the expected inflation rate. Consequently, the market rate completely incorporates expected inflation: If the market rate (i) is two per cent when the investors expect no inflation, it should be 12 per cent when they expect 10 per cent inflation, all other things equal. The point is, the present purchaser of financial assets is protected against *expected* inflation over the life of the asset. Investors will be hurt only if inflation proves to be more rapid than the general market expectation; in that case, their realized real return will be less than anticipated and may—as we have seen in recent years—even be negative.

Figure A graphs anticipated and unanticipated inflation over very short periods. The dotted line in the top part of the figure represents the average forecast (at an annual rate) for succeeding six-month periods, January through June or July through December.[3] The solid line in the top part of the figure represents the actual inflation rate, while the solid line in the bottom half shows the difference between actual and anticipated inflation—the surprise in the actual inflation rate. Investors have generally underestimated future inflation rates substantially, even though forecasting only two to eight months ahead; one can imagine how inaccurate the five and 10-year forecasts incorporated in five and 10-year securities will prove to be.

This purchasing power uncertainty has undoubtedly led some investors to turn to real goods such as real estate, art, gold and silver, which—

---

[3] These forecasts are from semi-annual surveys of economists conducted by Joseph Livingston of the *Philadelphia Inquirer* and are made about two months prior to each six-month period.

First Southeast's Service Area

these purchasers hope—will appreciate with prices in general, whatever the inflation rate turns out to be. Others have accelerated their purchases of consumer durables; surely this is one reason why personal savings in 1977 dropped to only 5.1 per cent of disposable, after-tax income—the lowest figure since 1963. By purchasing real goods, however, investors merely swap one type of uncertainty for another. Real estate, for example—one of the most popular inflation hedges—offers no assurance that it can match changes in the prices of other goods and services. Even if all real estate does appreciate enough to compensate for inflation, the price of any one particular parcel is unlikely to match the CPI. And purchasers of real estate incur taxes, insurance costs, supervisory costs and ralatively large brokerage fees.

Furthermore, when households hold as hedges against inflation goods they don't currently need or want, resources are misallocated. Savings that could be used to finance new plant and equipment are tied up financing inventories of gold, art, real estate and consumer durables. By providing markets in which investors can hedge against inflation without diverting their savings to non-productive assets, the proposed futures and options markets will free funds for more productive uses.

THE CPI FUTURES MARKET

Markets that offer investors protection against price erosion due to unexpected inflation do not exist at present. They can easily be provided, however, by futures and options markets in which investors can buy and sell claims or contingent claims to future market baskets of goods and services by trading claims to dollars, where the number of dollars represented by the claim is tied to the CPI (or some other price index).

In a CPI futures market, investors would trade the right to purchase—for the present futures price—an amount in dollars equal to the CPI. In October 1978, the CPI stood at 200.9—i.e., investors could buy a market basket of consumer goods and services that cost $100 in 1967 for $200.90 (or, to round, $200) in October of 1978. But suppose investors expect the CPI to rise at a rate of eight per cent a year over the next two years, so that in October 1980 it will be 233.28 ($1.08^2 \times 200$). The futures price should reflect this expectation, so that in October of 1978, October 1980 futures would sell for $233.28.

Suppose an investor purchases one of these contracts, but prices rise 12 per cent from October 1978 to October 1979 and 15 per cent from October 1979 to October 1980. By October of 1980, therefore, the actual CPI is 257.60 ($1.2 \times 1.15 \times 200$). The investor would then take delivery: He would pay $233.28 (the price to which he had agreed back in 1978) and would receive $257.60—a net gain of $24.32.[4] Of course, if inflation turns out to be less than expected, the investor will lose dollars and the seller of the futures will gain.

While it is dollars that actually change hands, the buyer of CPI futures effectively locks in at the futures price the future cost of the constant market basket of real goods that the Bureau of Labor Statistics (BLS) uses to compute the CPI. In our example, the buyer is assured

---

[4] Since October CPI figures are not released until November, settlement would have to wait one month.

Living with Inflation 469

Table I Hedging Against Unanticipated Inflation

October 1978	October 1980
Current CPI equals 200.	CPI equals 257.6.
Price of October 1980 CPI future equals $233.28.	
Action	*Actions*
Buy one October 1978 future at agreed price of $233.28.	Sell or accept delivery on October 1980 future:

Receive	$257.60
Pay	233.28
for a net gain of	$ 24.32
Buy $257.60 of real goods and services.	

The net cost of hedged purchase of goods and services equals one CPI market basket in October of 1980:

Purchase Price	$257.60
Net Gain on Futures	24.32
Net Cost	$233.28

that, in 1980, he will pay $233.28 for the market basket that cost $200 in 1978, regardless of what happens to prices over the period. Table I illustrates the transaction. In this manner, the hedger can lock in the purchasing power of any future dollar payment—be it wages, pensions, dividends, interest or alimony.

Investors in financial assets will be able to hedge their risks in the futures market. Assume, for example, that in October of 1978 an investor purchased a $100,000, two-year 10 per cent note or certificate of deposit that pays $10,000 at the end of the first year and returns $110,000 in principal and interest at the end of the second. The real return (r) is given by:

$$\$100,000 = \frac{\$10,000 \times \frac{P(1978)}{P(1979)}}{(1+r)} + \frac{\$110,000 \times \frac{P(1978)}{P(1980)}}{(1+r)^2}$$

or

$$\$100,000 = \frac{\frac{\$10,000}{(1+I)}}{(1+r)} + \frac{\frac{\$110,000}{(1+I_1)(1+I_2)}}{(1+r)^2},$$

where P(1978), P(1979) and P(1980) represent the price level in each year and I_1 and I_2 the rates of inflation from October 1978 to October 1979 and from October 1979 to October 1980, respectively.

If the expected rate of inflation, as reflected in the CPI futures price, is eight per cent, the expected real return (rr) on this two-year note will be 1.85 per cent:

$$\$100{,}000 = \frac{\frac{\$10{,}000}{1.08}}{(1+\text{rr})} + \frac{\frac{\$110{,}000}{1.08^2}}{(1+\text{rr})^2}.$$

If, however, the actual inflation turns out to be 12 per cent and 15 per cent in the two years, the realized real return will be a negative 3.01 per cent.

Assuming that the CPI futures market reflected the expected inflation of eight per cent in 1978, the investor could lock in the expected real return of 1.85 per cent by hedging the interest and principal payments. For each year, the dollar amount he owes at delivery of the corresponding futures contract will just equal the interest and principal to be received in that year:

$$\text{Amount of Year A Futures Purchased} = \frac{\text{Interest and Principal Received in Year A}}{\text{Price of Year A Futures}}$$

Table II illustrates this hedge.

The real return on the hedged security is calculated by finding the real rate that discounts back to the purchase price the net of both payments on the note and any futures market gains or losses (as shown in Table II). Since the investor cannot purchase fractional futures contracts, the real return on a hedged security will vary slightly, depending on the inflation rate, but not very much. Table III shows the realized real returns on our $100,000 note and our assumed 1978 futures prices for a series of possible inflation rates, given an expected rate of eight per cent.

In this example, the CPI futures market in 1978 reflects the general expectation of eight per cent inflation over the next two years, so that the October 1978 prices of October 1979 and October 1980 futures are $216 and $233.28, respectively. If the 1979 futures price were above $216, investors who expected eight per cent inflation could expect to gain by selling 1979 futures. If the CPI did rise eight per cent to $216, the seller would pay $216 and receive the higher futures price he contracted for in 1978. Such selling pressure would, of course, push the futures price down toward $216.

One might suppose that, since most hedgers in the market will be buying CPI futures, the resulting upward pressure on prices will cause the futures market to overestimate inflationary expectations. Nonetheless, any speculators who felt prices would rise more or less than predicted by the market could sell or buy futures and expect to profit. Consequently, the futures price is an equilibrium price, in the sense that everyone who wants to bet that inflation will be more rapid than pre-

Table II Hedging a Two-Year, 10 Per Cent Note (Brokerage Fees and Other Costs Not Included)

October 1978	*October 1979*	*October 1980*
CPI = 200	CPI = 224 (12 per cent inflation)	CPI = 257.60 (15 per cent above 1979)
Prices October 1979 Futures = $216.00 October 1980 Futures = $233.28	*Actions*	*Actions*
Actions (1) Buy $100,000 two-year note. (2) Buy 46 October 1979 futures*. (3) Buy 472 October 1980 futures*.	(1) Receive interest of $10,000. (2) Accept delivery (or sell) 46 October 1979 futures:	(1) Receive interest and principal of $110,000. (2) Accept delivery (or sell) 472 October 1980 futures:
	Pay $216 × 46 = $ 9,936 Receive $224 × 46 = 10,304 for a net gain of $ 368. Net receipt of interest and futures market gain of $10,368.	Pay $233.28 × 472 = $110,108.16 Receive $257.60 × 472 = 121,587.20 for a net gain of $ 11,479.04. Net receipt of interest, principal and futures market gain of $121,479.04.

Real Return Calculations

Unhedged

$$ \$100,000 = \frac{\$10,000 \times \frac{200}{224}}{(1+r)} + \frac{\$110 + \frac{200}{276.6}}{(1+r)^2} \text{, yields } r = -3.014\%. $$

Hedged

$$ \$100,000 = \frac{\$10,368 \times \frac{200}{224}}{(1+r)} + \frac{\$121,479 + \frac{200}{257.6}}{(1+r)^2} \text{, yields } r = 1.855\%. $$

*$10,000 in interest received in October 1979 would be just sufficient to pay for 46.3 futures ($10,000/216). This is rounded off to 46. The 472 for October 1980 was calculated by rounding off $110,000/233.28.

Table III Possible Real Returns on Hedged and Unhedged Two-Year, 10 Per Cent Notes when Eight Per Cent Inflation is Expected (Brokerage Fees and Other Costs not Included)

Actual Inflation Rates Year One	Year Two	Real Return on: Unhedged $100,000 Two-Year, 10 Per Cent Note	Hedged at Table II Futures Prices*
6%	2%	5.693%	1.849%
6%	6%	3.774%	1.851%
8%	8%	1.852%	1.852%
8%	12%	0.104%	1.854%
10%	10%	0	1.854%
12%	8%	−0.069%	1.852%
12%	15%	−3.014%	1.855%
15%	20%	−6.266%	1.857%

*The hedger buys 46 Year One futures at an assumed price of $224 each and 472 Year Two futures at $257.6 each. These are sample prices representing eight per cent inflation from a base CPI of 200.

dicted by the market is able to do so by buying futures, and everyone who wants to bet that inflation will be less rapid (or that prices will decline) is able to do so by selling.

As Lovell and Vogel have noted, one interesting aspect of the futures market is that it will provide a daily measure of price expectations. These data will allow researchers to test the many theories involving price expectations. Observers will also be able to gauge the market's evaluation of the inflationary impact of a new government program or a major wage settlement. Perhaps a CPI futures market will focus more attention on the inflationary impact of various programs and policies.

The CPI Options Market

A useful alternative or addition to the CPI futures market would be a CPI options market. In a CPI options market, investors would trade the right to purchase, for an agreed number of dollars, an amount in dollars equal to the CPI. Suppose, for instance, that the 1978 CPI were 200 and that an investor bought a December 1980 CPI option with an exercise price of $240. If the CPI rises to 260, he can exercise the option, pay $240 and receive $260. The investor buys the right to receive for the exercise price, $240, an amount of dollars equal to the CPI. In effect, he insures his ability to buy the market basket of goods that cost $200 in 1978 for no more than $240 in 1980.

This market might have more appeal than a futures market for those who wish to insure against extremely rapid inflation, and for holders of financial assets who do not wish to forego the gain they would realize from unexpected price decreases.

Options or futures markets using other price indexes could also serve a useful economic role. For example, a market using one of the construction cost indexes could allow prospective builders to protect themselves against unexpected increases in construction costs. Such a market might be more effective than the existing lumber and plywood futures markets as a hedging instrument against changes in total construction costs.

NEW COMPETITION FOR BOOKIES?

In discussion of these proposals, critics have frequently objected to the fact that, unlike existing futures markets, the proposed futures and options markets deliver dollars, not commodities. It is the delivery aspect of commodity futures markets that, for many, separates the corn futures market from the racetrack, or the commodities brokers from the neighborhood bookie.

This is a fallacious distinction. It makes no essential difference whether one delivers a bushel of corn or an amount in dollars just sufficient to buy that bushel. Indeed, most hedges are concluded in exactly this way: As the delivery date approaches, the hedger who bought corn futures doesn't normally take delivery, but sells his futures contract and uses the proceeds to buy corn. In the proposed futures market, investors are in effect trading claims to a constant market basket of real goods and services by trading claims to a quantity of dollars just sufficient to buy that market basket. The proper criterion for judging the economic appropriateness of new markets is not their delivery characteristics, but their potential for shifting risk, and the proposed CPI markets fill a real economic need in that regard.

The market basket of goods and services being traded on the futures market is that used by the BLS to compute the CPI. Since this is an average for all urban consumers, any one household's cost of living is unlikely to match it exactly. While futures markets in individual goods and services would allow each household to protect its particular consumption needs, this is clearly impractical. Right now, one can buy on the Chicago Mercantile Exchange 22,500 dozen fresh eggs—at a minimum—for delivery next June, but this of little use to the individual who wants two every morning for breakfast.

A single market in the CPI seems general enough to serve the needs of most households. Certainly it would tie more closely to an individual household's cost of living than present hedges such as real estate. Use of the CPI does, however, present some problems for the futures market mechanism. (Although, it should be noted, proposals for indexed bonds and Hakansson's Purchasing Power Fund also rely on the CPI, so any problems with this index are common to all extant proposals for protecting against inflation.)

Because the CPI for any given month is not announced until the latter part of the following month, settlement will be delayed. Our hedger who bought October 1979 and October 1980 futures to hedge interest payments received in those two months would either have to wait until November to take delivery on the futures contract or, more likely, sell the contract in October. But this is not a serious problem.

Revisions in the CPI are more serious. Since the BLS collects its own data and does not rely on respondents, the CPI fugures announced each month are final figures, not preliminary estimates. Nonetheless, revisions do occur on occasion. While it has happened only twice since World War II, both revisions occurred in the last 10 years.[5] A futures market contract might provide for settlement if revisions occur within a certain time.

From time to time, the BLS also updates the factors it uses to adjust for seasonal patterns in the CPI. Since adjustment could occur in the middle of a futures or option contract, it would probably be best to tie the contract to the unadjusted CPI. Finally, the contract would have to provide for any BLS adjustment to a new base for the CPI.[6]

Of course, many investors may be unwilling or unable to use the proposed futures or options markets. To the general populace, hedging will represent a new idea requiring some financial education. Furthermore, brokerage fees may make hedging uneconomical for the small investor. On the other hand, sophisticated investors have already gained some experience with hedging in existing futures and options markets, and the new futures markets in financial securities have been accepted.

CPI options and futures markets would be more readily understandable than Hakansson's Purchasing Power Fund. The costs of hedging would also be less than for a PPF. Investors wishing to lock in a real return to one specific date by using a PPF would have to purchase equal quantities of 111 different shares; under the futures and options market proposals, they have to purchase only one contract.

More important, it is not necessary that households participate in the futures and options markets directly. The existence of these markets will encourage indexation—the tying of future payments to the CPI. One reason why indexed securities have not been forthcoming despite much academic discussion is that indexation requires the borrower to

---

[5] In December 1971, an excise tax was repealed retroactively, affecting the August, September and October indexes. In November of 1974, an error was discovered in the used car data for the period April through October.

[6] Suppose that, in 1980, when the current index is at 250, the BLS replaces the current index for which 1967 equals 100 with a new index for which 1980 equals 100. The futures contract could provide that the CPI for settlement purposes would be calculated as (250/100) × the new CPI index.

bear all the risk of price changes, and borrowers may be no more willing than lenders to bear these risks.[7] Futures and options markets shift the risk to the speculator willing to bear it. For this reason, they might actually encourage indexation: Life insurance companies and pension plans could offer policies with benefits linked to the CPI, hedging these commitments in the futures and options markets. Likewise, banks could issue certificates of deposit at a fixed real rate and hedge their commitment in the proposed markets.

Most important, by replacing real goods as an inflation hedge, CPI futures and options markets would encourage saving, hence capital accumulation.

---

[7] See Nissan Liviatan and David Levhari, "Risk and the Theory of Indexed Bonds," *American Economic Review*, June 1977, pp. 366-375.

Market Index Futures Contracts[*]

Victor Niederhoffer and Richard Zeckhauser[†]

Investors may soon be able to trade futures contracts in stock market averages. The Chicago Mercantile Exchange plans a contract based on the Standard & Poor's 500 stock index. The Chicago Board of Trade has proposed several market index futures contracts, including one based on an index of its own construction. The Kansas City Board of Trade plans to trade a contract based on the Value Line Composite Index.

The Kansas City contract (VLF) based on the Value Line Composite Index (VLCI) is fairly typical. Each VLF contract would constitute a promise to buy or sell 500 units of the VLCI, measured in dollars. The underlying value of one VLF contract would be roughly $50,000, since the VLCI currently hovers around 100. Initial margin requirements would be $2,000 for hedgers and $4,000 for speculators. Six contracts will trade at any one time, with delivery in March, June, September and December.

Regular commissions on a round-trip transaction in one VLF contract are anticipated to be $60—only 13 percent of the cost of buying and selling a reasonably diversified stock portfolio of comparable value. Since the average monthly change in the VLCI is about 5.2 points, the

---

[*]Reprinted from the *Financial Analysts Journal*, (January-February 1980). Reprinted by permission of the publisher.

[†]Victor Niederhoffer is Chairman of Niederhoffer, Cross & Zeckhauser, Inc., New York. Richard Zeckhauser is Professor of Economics at the Kennedy School of Political Economy, Harvard University.

corresponding change in the value of a VLF contract would be $2,600 (500 × 5.2)—about 65 per cent of the initial investment of an investor speculating on margin.

Market index futures contracts will provide the margin speculator with a vehicle for participating in general market movements. He will enjoy both a high degree of leverage and low commission costs. In addition, he will know that the contract—being based on the prices of a large number of securities—will be difficult to manipulate and impossible to corner. But market index futures contracts will also be invaluable to investors (including institutions) who desire to protect themselves against such market movements; the contracts will allow them to take either a long or short position in the shares of a specific company without incurring the commensurate market-related risks.

Spurred on by the enormous success of the existing futures contracts in bonds and bills, various exchanges are promoting new market index futures contracts that offer a wide array of products of potential interest to anyone whose financial well being is affected by the performance of common stocks. The Kansas City Board of Trade has proposed a futures contract based on the Value Line Composite Index. The Chicago Mercantile Exchange has developed a contract based on the Standard & Poor's 500 stock index. The Chicago Board of Trade has prepared one contract based on an index of their own construction that reflects the stock market as a whole, and several others based on specific industry groups. Overseas, Pierson, Helding & Pierson, N.V., a Dutch investment banking firm, is actually trading a contract based on the Dow Jones Industrial Average. In Maryland, Computer Directions Advisors is developing a market for call option writing by pension funds and call option purchasing by speculators based on the Standard & Poor's 500 contract.

Naturally, the agencies, boards and commissions of the federal bureaucracy have been wrangling among themselves over jurisdiction of these contracts, and potential competitors, such as options exchanges, have raised substantial opposition. Thus, three years after the first contract was proposed, no definite date for the start of trading has yet been set. Because of the potential profitability of this market for both promoters and customers, however, it is hard to believe that that date is far off.

This article describes the mechanics of market index futures contracts and explores their potential uses and impact. For the sake of conciseness, it focuses on the Kansas City Board of Trade's contract based on the Value Line Composite Index, although most of what it says is applicable to the other contracts as well.†† This represents the oldest

---

††A comment by the present authors describing a DJIA contract appeared in *The Chicago MBA*, Volume 3, No. 1, and is available on request from the authors.

proposal, dating from 1976, and appears nearest to trading, having already been formally proposed to the Commodity Futures Trading Commission.

THE VLF CONTRACT

Each Value Line Futures (VLF) contract will represent a promise to buy or sell 500 units of the Value Line Composite Index (VLCI), measured in dollars. Since the VLCI hovers around 100, the underlying value of the stocks covered by the contract will be roughly $50,000. The initial margin requirements will be $2,000 for hedgers and $4,000 for speculators; as with any commodity contract, participants will be able to post this earnest money in cash or in interest-earning Treasury bills. There will be no daily trading limit.

The minimum fluctuation in the contract's value will be $5.00, which represents a change of 0.01 per cent of the value of the underlying stocks. The change in value of participants' positions will be credited or debited to their equity each day. In case of a profit, participants will be able to remove the increase in equity from their account. In case of a loss, they will have to put up additional capital.

Contracts of three, six, nine, 12, 15 and 18 months will trade, with delivery in March, June, September and December. If trading opened in March 1980, for example, the longest contract would be delivered at the end of September, 1981. As of July 1, 1980, the December 1981 contract would become available, and all buyers and sellers of March contracts who had not closed out their positions would settle with each other. The delivery mechanism calls for all open contracts to be settled at a price of 500 times the VLCI two days before the expiration of trading in the contract.

The average daily absolute fluctuation in the VLCI is approximately 0.6. Thus the mean change in the equity of a player long or short one contract will be $300 (500 × 0.6). This represents a profit or loss of 15 per cent ($300/$2,000) for a hedger posting minimum margins. But the change represents only 0.6 per cent of the value of the underlying stocks.

The contract's sponsors anticipate that regular commissions on a round-trip transaction will total $60.00. This represents a cost of only 0.12 per cent of the underlying value of the contract, or roughly 13 per cent of the cost of buying and selling a reasonably diversified stock portfolio of comparable value. It is also substantially less than an option commission. Even a 0.12 per cent commission can become substantial, however, if turnover over the course of a year rivals that of the typical commodity trader; while the average stock market investment may turn over once every few years, commodity speculators frequently look to a turnover of once every week.

Movements in the VLCI

Table I summarizes statistics on the distribution of changes in the VLCI for the 13 years from 1966 to 1978, inclusive. For all intervals except the yearly period, the distribution of changes is roughly symmetric about zero. Apparently, yearly rises tend to be more frequent than yearly declines, but the declines tend to be larger than the rises.

The mean daily change in the VLCI is 0.64 points. For a week of five trading days, the mean change is 1.93–roughly three times as great. The mean weekly change would be five times as great as the daily change if daily movements were always in the same direction, and only twice as great if consecutive daily movements were completely independent. Thus consecutive daily changes are positively correlated (a fact confirmed by the serial correlation coefficient of 0.16). With the passage of a month, the average change is about 5.2 points; the speculative investor in the contract, who "owns" 500 times the index, would thus incur an average monthly profit or loss of $2,600 (500 × 5.2), representing 65 per cent of his initial investment.

These swings, while precipitous, are comparable to swings in the actively traded grain futures contracts. Corn futures contracts, the most widely traded, experience an average daily change of approximately 0.6 per cent; the 0.64 point mean daily change in the VLCI represents

Table I Changes in Value Line Composite Index

	Each Day	Each Week	Each Month	Each Quarter	Each Year
Average Absolute Change in Points	0.64	1.93	5.22	10.66	24.74
Average Change on Rises	0.62	1.77	5.44	10.64	17.41
Average Change on Declines	−0.69	−2.09	−5.06	−10.69	−39.39
Percentage of All Rises	52.1	53.1	46.7	48.0	66.6
Percentiles of Changes					
5%	1.29*	3.54	9.76	19.41	23.5
25%	+0.51	+1.6	+4.53	+8.18	+11.17
50%	+0.05	+0.17	−0.64	−1.5	+0.19
75%	−0.47	−1.56	−3.93	−11.22	−17.348
95%	−1.54	−4.24	−12.1	−20.77	−56.8

*Five per cent of the daily closes in the VLCI were +1.29 points or more above the previous close.

Source: Based on all observations from January 3, 1966 to December 31, 1978. Between 1926 and 1966, Value Line computed its index only yearly.

Market Index Futures Contracts

about 0.6 per cent of its average value.

Table II illustrates another way of using historical data to gauge the likely rapidity of change in the VLCI: How long, on average, will it take a hedger to double or lose his initial stake of $2,000—that is, how many trading days will it take the VLCI to gain or lose a cumulative four points? During the period from June 30, 1976 to June 22, 1979, the VLCI gained 26.3 points, going from 87.83 to 114.14. It experienced six more cumulative rises of four points than cumulative losses. (In a period during which the index declined overall, of course, losses would be more frequent.)

Over the three-year period, a hedger could have doubled his stakes 21 times, with the average time for a cumulative change of plus or

Table II Past Duration of Doubling or Wipe-Out (Fully Levered Trading on Value Line Industrial Index Futures Market) Hedgers' Margin: $2,000

Dates From	To	No. of Days	VLCI From	To	Rise
\multicolumn{6}{c}{Gain of Money}
10/11/76	12/06/76	38	83.50-	87.98	+4.48
12/06/76	12/30/76	17	87.98-	92.53	+4.55
10/09/77	11/11/77	17	88.27-	92.34	+4.07
11/11/76	4/10/78	101	92.34-	96.45	+4.11
4/10/76	4/24/78	10	96.45-	100.92	+4.47
4/24/78	5/12/78	14	100.92-	105.15	+4.23
5/12/78	7/31/78	54	105.15-	109.73	+4.58
7/31/78	8/09/78	7	109.73-	113.85	+4.12
8/09/78	9/07/78	20	113.85-	118.00	+4.15
10/27/78	1/04/79	46	97.44-	102.00	+4.56
1/04/79	1/25/79	15	102.00-	106.20	+4.20
2/27/79	3/13/79	10	101.71-	105.94	+4.23
3/13/79	4/03/79	15	105.94-	110.08	+4.14
4/03/79	6/22/79	56	110.08-	114.14	+4.06
Average		30 Days			+4.28
\multicolumn{6}{c}{Loss of Money}
6/30/76	10/11/76	76	87.83-	83.50	−4.33
12/30/76	10/09/77	203	92.53-	88.27	−4.26
9/07/78	9/20/78	9	118.00-	113.54	−4.46
9/20/78	10/19/78	21	113.54-	108.00	−5.54
10/19/78	10/23/78	2	108.00-	103.70	−4.30
10/23/78	10/27/78	4	103.70-	97.44	−6.26
1/25/79	2/27/79	22	106.20-	101.71	−4.49
Average		48			−4.81

Note: The first transaction was considered to have started at the close on 6/30/76. Daily losses were noted until a closing price showed a change of at least 4.0 points from the opening transaction. At this point, the transaction was closed out and a new opening transaction undertaken at the current close.

minus four points being 36 trading days. The fastest doubling came in the seven trading days between July 31, 1978, when the VLCI closed at 109.73, and August 9, 1978, when it closed at 113.85. The fastest total losses took two and four days in October 1978. The longest period without a doubling was the nine and one-third month period between December 30, 1976 and October 9, 1977, when the index hovered around 90. On the other hand, during the five-month period between April 10, 1978 and September 7, 1978, a fully levered hedger buyer could have doubled his entire stake five consecutive times. But this period was followed by one and one-half months during which the hedger would have lost his entire stake on four consecutive occasions.

The major swings in the VLCI show considerable momentum. It also appears that volatility in the stock market, as reflected in the VLCI, is increasing. During the two years ending June 30, 1978, the futures hedger could have lost or doubled his money nine separate times. During the following year, there were 12 such occasions.

A speculator in the VLF contracts has to put up twice as much as a hedger: the VLCI must thus change a cumulative eight points to double his money or wipe him out. This futures contract would be substantially less volatile than most active futures contracts. The fluctuations in the VLCI have been such that speculators would have experienced only five doublings or wipe-outs during the entire three-year period. This lack of action for speculators may dampen their willingness to provide liquidity for those on the hedging side of the market.

While hourly figures on the VLCI are not available, the average absolute Dow Jones Industrial Average (DJIA) change has been running about 1.5 points an hour. This works out to an hourly profit or loss to the hedger of four per cent.

Features of the VLCI

Most averages and indexes of the stock market tend to move together, since all share many of the same individual stocks. Other things equal, the correlation between a part and the whole is positive. The correlation between two stock market averages is stronger still because the moves of the stocks included in only one average are highly correlated with the moves of the stocks contained in both averages. During the two-year period from December 31, 1976 to December 31, 1978, for example, the VLCI and the DJIA moved in opposite directions on only 69 days of the 500. Interestingly, for 45 of these 69 days, the DJIA moved down and the VLCI up. Over the same period, the two indexes moved in opposite directions in only 14 out of the 105 weeks.

Because of the high correlation between various averages, speculators and hedgers in market index futures should be able to achieve their goals regardless of the index used. Nevertheless, each average has certain unique features, and participants should be aware of them. The VLCI represents the most broadly based of the major security indexes. It now comprises 1,695 stocks—1,499 industrials, 177 utilities and 19 rails. These include 85 to 90 per cent of the stocks on the New York Stock Exchange and a significant sprinkling of American Stock Exchange, over-the-counter and Canadian offerings. The VLCI includes all of the Standard & Poor's (S&P) 500 and all 30 DJIA stocks.

The VLCI is computed geometrically relative to some base period. The percentages of base-period prices at which the different stocks now trade are first multiplied together. Then one finds the single factor, "A," that when multiplied by itself as many times as there are stocks in the index, comes to the same product. Say that a three-stock index was at one when its stocks were selling at 50, 100 and 200, and the stocks now sell at 40, 150 and 220, respectively. Multiplying the current to base percentages together yields 1.32 (0.8 × 1.5 × 1.1). Solving the equation A^3 equals 1.32 gives 1.097—the current value of the index.

Although less familiar than arithmetic indexes such as the DJIA or the S&P indexes, geometric indexes have some interesting properties. Each stock in each period, for instance, gets the same weighting regardless of its value. If the index consisted of two stocks, one at 10, which went up five per cent, and the other at 100, which went up 50 per cent, it would not matter for purposes of computing the index that the higher priced stock appreciated more. An arithmetic index would rise more if the higher priced stock appreciated more. (To increase the importance of a particular stock, of course, a geometric index could always include it more than once.) This equal-weighting feature of the VLCI, combined with its exceptional breadth, makes it a good indicator of overall market performance.

Performances of geometric and arithmetic indexes can be compared only if both indexes weight their stocks equally at the outset. If the geometric index includes each stock once, the arithmetic index must start with an equal investment in each stock. Surprisingly, so long as the stocks on each index do not go up or down by precisely the same percentage—in which case there will be no difference in performance—a geometric index will show less appreciation, or more depreciation, than an arithmetic index. The proof of this statement derives from the concavity of the logarithmic function, and is somewhat complex. As an example, consider two $100 stocks, with the index at one. One stock goes up to $160, the other drops to $40. While the arithmetic index will show a change of zero, the geometric average will be 0.8 (A × A = 0.4 × 1.6), representing a drop of 0.2.

Three factors determine how the VLCI will perform relative to the DJIA or the S&P 500—breadth of base, geometric versus arithmetic averaging and differences in content. Table III shows that the three

Table III Percentage Changes in Indexes

	Between Year-Ends 1965 and 1978	Between Year-Ends 1972 and 1974	Between Year-Ends 1974 and 1976
Dow Jones Industrials	−20%	−40%	+40%
Standard and Poor's 500	+ 2%	−43%	+43%
Value Line Composite	−30%	−52%	+80%

indexes can diverge considerably. The geometric VLCI shows a less favorable trend over the 13-year period. In the significant upswing of 1975-76, however, its inclusion of many small, more speculative stocks that had sizable gains, together with the greater relative weighting it assigned to low-priced stocks, enabled it to overcome the comparative downward bias of geometric averaging. Lower priced stocks offer a greater part of their return in the form of capital gains (as opposed to dividends) than higher priced stocks, hence will in general appreciate more (or depreciate less) than higher priced stocks. Thus the VLCI tends to appreciate faster than comparable arithmetic indexes. On the other hand, the more variability between the performances of individual stocks—i.e., some doing well while others do poorly—the more the VLCI will suffer relative to arithmetic indexes.

Given the relatively low margin requirements of all the proposed market index futures contracts, arbitrageurs should be fairly active across all of them. It would be surprising if, in most periods, the VLF contract did not sell at a lower price relative to present value than the contracts based on the arithmetic indexes. However, a belief that small companies will outperform large ones will give a boost to the VLCI relative to the S&P 500 and DJIA.

USES AND IMPACT OF MARKET INDEX FUTURES CONTRACT

Trading in market index futures contracts could prove beneficial to virtually everyone who invests in equities, for whatever purpose. Some traders—from the lowliest prospective pensioner to the highest flying seller of puts and calls or the corporation planning to issue additional stock—will use such contracts for hedging. These contracts also present speculators with a new opportunity that is particularly attractive because it offers significant leverage.

Hedging Against Market Declines

The commonest motive for hedging is to guard against a market decline that would diminish the value of stocks already held. Selling the

VLF contract short will prove a highly effective tool in this respect, since the value of the short position and the value of the stocks will move in opposite directions.

Consider the investor who feels that the market is entering a period of substantial volatility but is himself uncertain which way it will turn. (Haven't all investors found themselves in this situation at one time or another?) If the market is weak, he knows he cannot unload several thousand shares of individual stocks except at disastrous price concessions. He can reduce his risk, however, by selling a VLF contract short. He will thus insulate himself from both decreases and increases in the stocks' value, since a full hedge is roughly comparable to getting out of the market by selling one's stocks, except one retains title to the hedged stocks. When the period of uncertainty passes, the hedger may choose to buy the contract back.

Short sellers need not be sophisticated or wealthy institutions or hedgers who already own substantial pools of stock. Consider Professor Brown, who intends to retire in three months. His most significant assets are tied up in his retirement fund, the value of which is closely tied to the stock market. Professor Brown estimates the value of his nest egg at roughly $150,000 at current market prices. He wishes to purchase a condominium now under construction, and will be financially able to do so as long as his nest egg does not decline in value more than 10 per cent. Consulting the type of statistics presented in Table I, Professor Brown is understandably disturbed. The chance that the VLCI will decline more than 10 points—the critical 10 per cent—in the next three months is about one in four. He decides he must put off purchase of the condominium.

A market in VLF or other market index futures contracts will give Professor Brown a new option. He can sell three contracts short. While he may, of course, still lose his $6,000, it will take a 20 point swing to put him in a position where he can no longer afford the condominium. The chances of this happening in a three-month period are only one in 20.

Dr. Jones, a graduate school classmate of Brown's who pursued a more lucrative career, has just sold the stock of his closely held corporation to a major food company for 100,000 shares of stock currently valued at $2.5 million. Because of Securities and Exchange Commission registration and pooling of interest requirements, Jones must hold for a period of two years. He can hedge against a market decline, however, by selling a VLF contract short. In this way, he can ensure for his beneficiaries a sizable nest egg, provided the stock of the diversified food company moves with the market as a whole. Of course, if Jones did not take this precaution for his beneficiaries, they could make the investment themselves. Any person of moderate means with the expectation of a future windfall in stocks might take a similar tack.

A brokerage house with a net long position in a number of stocks, incurred perhaps to accommodate its customers, may also wish to protect itself, since a substantial decline in the overall market could prove disastrous. The VLF contract would offer an excellent and economical hedge. In fact, once such contracts begin to trade, brokerage houses should be more willing to accept long and short positions in connection with their market making.

Hedging Against Rises

Market index futures contracts, like most futures contracts, will initially be used to hedge against a decline in value more often than an increase. But some stock market participants, including those who have a current or future obligation to deliver stock or a product whose price is highly correlated with stocks, must also protect themselves against market rises. In the active grain markets, the volume of hedging against price increases frequently exceeds the volume of hedging against declines.

Many pension funds accrue contributions on a continuous basis, but receive the proceeds only periodically. A long investment in a VLF contract would assure that beneficiaries do not lose out if the market rises rapidly between the date of accrual and investment of the proceeds—an important advantage in an era when accountability in pension fund management is receiving considerably more attention.

For a firm that plans to grow by acquisition, a general market increase could carry target companies' stocks beyond the firm's ability to pay for them. But a firm that purchased a VLF contract could protect its acquisition potential. Similarly, the seller of a company whose deal is fixed in total dollars might wish to maintain future stock purchasing power by buying a VLF contract.

A firm that has committed to issue its shares on an installment basis, perhaps as part of a profit-sharing plan, might be happy to accept the risk that it will do well. But it may not want to get trapped into giving away excessive dollar value should the stock market as a whole have a favorable run. In that case, it should purchase a VLF or similar contract.

Foreign investors frequently plan to invest substantial funds in the U.S. but, for one reason or another, wish to defer action—perhaps because of restrictions against liberating their funds or because they expect the price of their currency to rise relative to the dollar. In the interim, they may wish to invest in the U.S. market, it simply looks more promising than anything at home. Purchase of a VLF contract would protect them against the loss of an attractive opportunity.

Another potential beneficiary of the VLF contract is Arnold Goldbug. Believing that excessive government intervention will ruin the U.S.

economy. Goldbug has purchased ample supplies of freeze-dried foods, secured his rural retreat, placed most of his funds in Swiss savings banks bearing negative real interest, and is long on hordes of gold and silver. He has only one worry: Disaster may not arrive as soon as his international advisers forecast. To maintain purchasing power until the advent or calamity, he could purchase a VLF contract, thereby also guarding against the possibility of massive inflation. On the other hand, if he believes the same set of circumstances will lead to a massive deflation similar to that of the 1930s, he could short the contract.

Speculators

In many cases, investors eager to go long or short market index futures contracts as hedges against the risks acquired in the course of their other investment activities will be accommodated by speculators in such contracts. The VLF and similar contracts are a splendid vehicle for individuals who like to bet that they can predict market movements.

Numerous speculators in the options market trade options for a lack of a better vehicle to play the market. The VLF contract will offer them the volatility they seek. As Table I shows, the VLCI changes 0.64 points per day on average. With the VLCI at 100, and a leverage factor of 12.5, a speculator who happens to be on the right side can achieve a return of eight per cent a day. Hourly rates of return from a correct prediction of direction should run about five per cent; exact figures are not available, since the VLCI is not tabulated on an hourly basis. Furthermore, in contrast to the options market, the market index futures market will always be thick, quotations will always be relatively easy to secure, and there will be no danger of a short squeeze.

The market index futures contract will also enable option traders and other speculators to hedge certain aspects of their other investments. Speculators will be able to create preferred portfolios that focus their stakes on the gambles they really wish to make and eliminate the risks that were previously unavoidable byproducts of investing. The ability of option traders to hedge against the risk of market movements should improve the liquidity of the options market, hence increase public participation in that market. Market index futures contracts may also encourage activity in other speculative vehicles, since they will free up capital for speculation elsewhere.

VLF contracts offer even small-scale speculators an easy and inexpensive way to put their predictions to the market test. Such speculators will be able to get into and out of $50,000 worth of the market for a small amount—$60, at a minimum—and should save on research costs, since they will not have to inform themselves about particular stocks. In this respect, the VLF contract offers the advantages of an index fund, plus the possibility of selling short. Because of the volatility of the VLF, however, small speculators who cannot face total loss with impunity would probably be foolhardy to establish a position with the minimum margin; some may purchase the contract directly, putting up the full margin.

Furthermore, only the most astute speculators should be encouraged to trade VLF and similar contracts if they intend to turn them over as frequently as they do other commodity futures contracts. Studies of the performance of the public in commodity markets show that between 70 and 90 per cent of speculators who are not brokers or dealers lose money. The main reason appears to be the high cost of commissions and bid-asked spreads relative to the absolute magnitude of gains and losses.

Tax Planning and Convenience

Ephraim Middleguy caught the market just right and has made a small killing. He would prefer to consolidate his gains by selling out now, but if he does, his tax penalties will be considerable. He wants to hold out until his profits qualify for favorable tax treatment as long-term capital gains; he would also like to hold his position until next year, thereby gaining some float from the IRS. But by doing so, he takes the chance that the value of his holdings will decline as he waits, and he is strongly risk-averse. He can protect himself by selling a VLF contract short.

Current commodities contracts offer some intrinsic tax advantages: While other capital assets must be held for a full year to qualify for long-term capital gains treatment, a long position in a futures contract requires only six months. The market index futures contract may thus offer stock market participants a unique opportunity to achieve long-term capital gains tax treatment. The potential in terms of more efficient tax planning for market participants is significant.

As noted, the market index futures contract also offers a convenient, readily monitored, readily marketable and potentially highly levered instrument for participating in market movements, and transaction costs will be relatively low. For example, an individual seeking diversification by purchasing and selling 100 shares of just 30 of the 1,700 odd companies comprising the VLCI would have to purchase 3,000 shares of stock at an average price of $45, for a total investment very close to the underlying value of three VLF contracts. In addition, the in-and-out commissions on the 30 round lots would total roughly $4,400; by contrast, the commissions on the VLF contracts would be about $180.

Even the largest institutional investors might find the purchase of a

VLF or similar contract a convenience. The time and brokerage commissions required to invest in individual stocks on a continuous basis are burdensome. Purchase of VLF contracts would reduce commissions paid, tighten spreads between bid and asked prices and save valued time of executive decision-makers. Mutual funds in particular will find that such contracts provide an economical and prudent hedge against risk; 85 per cent of the variability of the returns in individual mutual fund portfolios is explained by movements in the averages.

VLF contracts may also offer significant cash flow advantages. By purchasing the contract on a regular (say, weekly) basis, a cash-short company can remain current with the market, while investing only a small fraction of the funds that would be required to achieve comparable positions through outright stock purchases. When funds became available, the company could sell the contract and purchase equivalent amounts of securities.

CONCLUSION

We have discussed only the most direct and obvious advantages of market index futures contracts. They will offer many subtle and secondary benefits as well. From the standpoint of the investor, the contract's key advantages are its low transaction costs and the fact that it can be purchased with a considerable degree of leverage. This alone should lend market index futures markets exceptional liquidity, which may even eventually exceed the liquidity of the spectacularly successful interest rate futures market. Indeed, the market in such contracts may even have a favorable impact on the liquidity of the stock market itself.

Market index contracts could drain a great deal of speculative activity away from stocks that move strongly in concert with the market, hence represent a considerable risk that cannot be hedged. The net result may be much greater stability in the markets for these securities; a whole range of volatile stocks may be expected to act in a much more orderly fashion. Any sell-off or run-up associated with market index futures contracts would involve assets whose total value would be measured in the hundreds of billions of dollars; scared investors, or overcommitted investors, even by the thousands, could not drive these contracts into a speculative spin. The type of movements observed in the options expiration week of April 1978 and the Labor Day week of September 1978—attributed by many observers to the rush to cover by naked call writers—will not occur as frequently.

Of course, we must recognize that market index futures contracts may never realize their full potential. Continued regulatory intrusion or tie-ups due to unresolved jurisdictional disputes, for example, could keep these contracts from being traded as freely as would be desirable. It is even more difficult to predict which among the several contracts being offered will prove to be the most significant. The Kansas City contract in the VLCI has the advantage of being the broadest based and the most likely to be first on-line at a major stock or commodities exchange. The Chicago Board of Trade index, on the other hand, will enable hedgers and speculators to trade off risky positions in industries. And the Chicago Mercantile Exchange contract will use the more widely known and disseminated S&P 500 index. The DJIA contract, though limited in its availability, has the singular advantage of that venerable index as its base.

Despite seemingly interminable delays and dashed hopes, it appears likely that market index futures contracts will eventually trade. A futures contract in a market index represents an investment vehicle that can enable investors to neutralize the massive tidal movements of equities markets. Its potential economic benefits for speculators and hedgers, small and large, to those planning their taxes or securing their futures, are staggering. Most importantly, such contracts, by providing a sought-after investment vehicle with significant properties not now offered by other investment instruments, will further the primary aim of capital markets in our society—the efficient allocation of resources and risk. Significant economic benefit is not a force that can forever be denied, particularly if there are organizers who can expect fair recompense for their work. By the time you read this article, market index futures contracts may be a reality.

Bibliography

This bibliography does not attempt to include every article on interest rate futures that has been written. Nor is it restricted solely to articles just on interest rate futures. Rather, the attempt is to include a set of articles that would guarantee a comprehensive understanding of interest rate futures. For example, many articles on bond pricing and bond portfolio management are included. While some of these do not even mention interest rate futures, they provide a background very helpful to understanding the full range of uses for interest rate futures. We also apologize in advance for the unfortunate omissions that must have occurred.

Angell, G. 1977. "A Technical Approach to Trading Interest Rate Futures Markets." *Commodities*, Vol. 6, No. 6, June, pp. 46-48.
Angrist, S. 1976. "How to Hedge Interest Rate Risks." *Forbes*, December 15, p. 91.
Arak, M. 1980. "Taxes, Treasury Bills, and Treasury Bill Futures." Unpublished working paper, Federal Reserve Bank of New York.
—— and McCurdy, C. 1979-80. "Interest Rate Futures." *The Quarterly Review* of the Federal Reserve Bank of New York, Winter, pp. 33-46.
Arditti, F. 1978. "An Intermediate Stage Toward Efficient Risk Allocation." *Journal of Bank Research*, Vol. 9, No. 3, Autumn, pp. 146-150.
Arrow, K. 1981. "Futures Markets: A Theoretical Perspective." *Journal of Futures Markets*, Vol. 1, No. 2, Summer, pp. 107-115.
Arthur, H. B. 1971, *Commodity Futures as a Business Management Tool*. Boston: Harvard University.
Arthur Anderson and Co. 1980. "Interest Rate Futures Contracts: Federal Income Tax Implications." Chicago Mercantile Exchange.

Bacon, P. and Williams, R. 1976. "Interest Rate Futures: New Tool for the Financial Manager." *Financial Management*, Vol. 5, No. 1, Spring, pp. 32-37.

Baker, C. C. and Vignola, A. J. 1979. "Market Liquidity, Security Trading, and the Estimation of Empirical Yield Curves." *The Review of Economics and Statistics*, Vol. LXI, No. 1, February, pp. 131-135.

Barron's. 1980. Interview with Bill Kidder, "Strictly for Pros: Speculators Dominate the Trade in Interest Rate Futures." March 3, pp. 4, 5, 12, 16, 20.

Bench. 1978. "Computerized Analysis: An Aid to Competence in Financial Futures Markets," *The Money Manager*, May 1.

Benston. 1976. "Interest Rates are a Random Walk Too." *Fortune*, August, pp. 105, 108, 113.

Bettner, J. 1980. "Looking for a 1980 Loss in a "Tax Straddle?" There is a Time to Try it, but Risks are High." *Wall Street Journal*, December 22, p. 34.

Bierwag, G. O. 1980. "The Sensitivity of Immunization to Bond Portfolio Composition." Paper prepared for the meetings of the Western Economic Association. Center for Capital Market Research, University of Oregon.

———. 1979. "Dynamic Portfolio Immunization Policies." *Journal of Banking and Finance*, Vol. 3, No. 1, April, pp. 23-41.

———. 1978. "Measures of Duration." *Economic Inquiry*, Vol. 16, No. 4, October, pp. 497-507.

———. 1978. "Bond Portfolio Simulations: A Critique." *Journal of Financial and Quantitative Analysis*, Vol. 13, No. 3, September, pp. 519-525.

———. 1977. "Immunization, Duration, and the Term Structure of Interest Rates." *Journal of Financial and Quantitative Analysis*, Vol. 12, No. 5, December, pp. 725-742.

———, and Kaufman, G. G. 1977. "Coping with the Risk of Interest Rate Fluctuations: A Note." *Journal of Business*, Vol. 50, No. 3, July, pp. 364-370.

———, and Khang C. 1978. "Duration and Bond Portfolio Analysis: An Overview." *Journal of Financial and Quantitative Analysis*, Vol. 13, No. 4, November, pp. 671-681.

Bierwag, G. O., Kaufman, G. G., Schweitzer, R., and Toevs, A. "The Art of Risk Management in Bond Portfolios." *Journal of Portfolio Management*, Spring, pp. 27-36.

———, and Toevs, A. 1979. "Management Strategies for Savings and Loan Associations to Reduce Interest Rate Risk." *Proceedings of a Conference on New Sources of Capital for Savings and Loan Industry*, Federal Home Loan Bank, San Francisco, December.

———, and Khang C. 1979. "An Immunization Strategy is a Mini-Max Strategy." *Journal of Finance*, Vol. 34, No. 2, May, pp. 389-399.

Black, F. 1976. "The Pricing of Commodity Contracts." *Journal of Financial Economics*, Vol. 3, Nos. 1 and 2, January/March, pp. 167-179.

Bohnsack. 1978. "Financial Futures Markets: Hedging Convergence and Options Up Ahead." *The Money Manager*, June, 26.

Branch, B. 1978. "Testing the Unbiased Expectations Theory of Interest Rates." *Financial Review*, Vol. 13, No. 2, Fall, pp. 51-66.

Bibliography

Breeden. 1979. "Comments on Selected Articles Concerning the Variations in Spot Rates." Paper presented at the Columbia Futures Conference on Financial Futures.

Brennan, M. J. 1958. "The Supply of Storage." *American Economic Review*, March, pp. 50-72.

Brier. 1977. "A New Look at Tax Straddles." *Commodities*, December, pp. 38-40.

Brinegar, C. S. 1970. "A Statistical Analysis of Speculative Price Behavior." *Stanford Food Research Institute Studies*. Supplement to Vol. IX, pp. 1-58.

Buck, J. and Wardrep, B. 1981. "Time Series Characteristics of GNMA Financial Futures." Paper presented at the Mid-South meetings, February, Memphis.

Burger, A. E., Lang, R. and Rasche, R. 1977. "The Treasury Bill Futures Markets and Marekt Expectations of Interest Rates." *Federal Reserve Bank of St. Louis Review*, June, pp. 2-9.

Burton, J. and Toth, J. 1974. "Forecasting Long-Term Interest Rates." *Financial Analysts' Journal*, Vol. 30, No. 5, September, pp. 73-87.

Business Week. 1977. "Forward Trading that Vexes Treasury." August 22.

Cagan, P. 1981. "Financial Futures Markets: Is More Regulation Needed?" *The Journal of Futures Markets*, Vol. 1, No. 2.

Capozza, D. and Cornell, B. 1979. "Treasury Bill Pricing in the Spot and Futures Markets." *Review of Economics and Statistics*, November, pp. 513-20.

Cargill, T. C. 1975. "Temporal Price Behavior in Commodity Futures Markets." *The Journal of Finance*, Vol. 30, No. 4, Sept., pp. 1043-1053.

——— and Rausser, G. C. 1972. "Time and Frequency Domain Representation of Futures Prices as a Stochastic Process." *Journal of the American Statistical Association*, LXVII, pp. 23-30.

Chicago Board of Trade. 1977. "Hedging Interest Rate Risks."

———. 1980. *Commodity Trading Manual*. Chicago, Ill.: Board of Trade of the City of Chicago.

———. 1975. *Hedging in GNMA Mortgage Interest Rate Futures*. Chicago.

———. 1981. *An Introduction to Financial Futures*. Chicago.

———. 1975. *Origination and Delivery of Due Bills: GNMA Mortgage Interest Rate Futures*. Chicago.

———. 1978. "An Introduction to the Interest Rate Futures Market."

———. "Making and Taking Delivery on Interest Rate Futures Contracts."

———. "A Perspective on Yields."

———. 1981. "Understanding the Delivery Process in Financial Futures."

Chicago Mercantile Exchange. 1977. "Opportunities in Interest Rates: Treasury Bill Futures."

Chow, B. and Brophy, D. 1978. "The U.S. Treasury Bill Futures Market and Hypotheses Regarding the Term Structure of Interest Rates." *The Financial Review*, Vol. 13, No. 2, Fall, pp. 36-50.

Cleary. 1978. "Success in Futures Transaction Demands System and Caution." *The Mortgage Banker*, February, pp. 24-26.

Cohan, A. *The Risk Structure of Interest Rates*. General Learning Press.

Commodity Futures Trading Commission. 1978. "Financial Futures Markets and

Federal Regulation." December.

Cornell, B. 1980. "Taxes and the Pricing of Treasury Bill Future Contracts." Working Paper.

———. 1977. "Spot Rates, Forward Rates and Exchange Market Efficiency." *Journal of Financial Economics*, Vol. 5, No. 1, August, pp. 55-60.

——— and Reinganum, M. 1980. "Forward and Futures Prices: Evidence from the Foreign Markets." Unpublished working paper, UCLA.

Cox, J. C. 1978. "Shopping in the Futures Market: Risk and Returns on GNMA Contracts." *FHLBB Journal*, February, pp. 15-19.

———, Ingersoll, J. E., Jr., and Ross, S. A. 1980. "The Relationship Between Forward and Futures Prices." Unpublished working paper, University of Chicago.

———. 1980. "A Re-Examination of Traditional Hypotheses about the Term Structure of Interest Rates." No. 1, Chicago, University of Chicago.

———. 1979. "Duration and the Measurement of Basis Risk." *Journal of Business*, Vol. 52, No. 1, January, pp. 51-62.

———. 1978. "A Theory of the Term Structure of Interest Rates." Palo Alto: Stanford University. Mimeographed.

Cross. 1977. "Interest Rate Futures: Portfolio Managers Find a New Tool." *Money Manager*, June 25.

Culberton, J. M. 1957. "The Term Structure of Interest Rates." *Quarterly Journal of Economics*, November, pp. 485-517.

Daigler, R. and Houtakker, D. 1981. "Analyzing the Structure of T-Bill Future Prices." Paper presented at Eastern Finance Meetings, April.

Dale, C. 1981. "Brownian Motion in the T-Bill Futures Market." *Business Economics*, Vol. 16, No. 3, May, pp. 47-54.

——— and Workman, R. 1980. "The Arc Sine Law and the Treasury Bill Futures Market." *Financial Analysts' Journal*, Vol. 36, No. 6, November-December, pp. 71-74.

Dew, J. K. 1981. "Bank Regulations for Futures Accounting," *Issues in Bank Regulation*, Spring, pp. 16-23.

———. 1980. "The Synthetic Fixed Rate Loan: Covering the Risk of Rising Interest Rate Costs." Working paper, CMEX, June.

———. 1978. "CPI Futures?" Federal Reserve Bank of San Francisco Weekly Letter, September.

Duncan, W. H. 1977. "Treasury Bill Futures—Opportunities and Pitfalls." *Review* of the Federal Reserve Bank of Dallas, July.

Dusak, K. 1973. "Futures Trading and Investor Returns: An Investigation of Commodity Market Risk Premiums." *Journal of Political Economy*, Vol. 81, No. 6, November, pp. 1387-1406.

Ederington, L. H. 1980. "Living with Inflation: A Proposal for New Futures and Options Markets." *Financial Analysts Journal*, January/February, pp. 42-48.

———. 1979. "The Hedging Performance of the New Futures Markets." *Journal of Finance*, Vol. 34, March, pp. 157-170.

Edwards, F. 1981. "The Regulation of Futures and Forward Trading by Depository

Institutions: A Legal and Economic Analysis." *The Journal of Futures Markets*, Vol. 1, No. 2.

Emery, S. and Scott, R. 1978. "T-Bill Futures and the Term Structure of Interest Rates: A Means of Reconciling Market Forecasts and Values, Financial Assets." Paper presented to April Eastern Finance Association meetings.

———. 1977. "Evidence of Expected Yields Implied from Term Structure and the Futures Market." *Business Economics*, May.

Fama, E. F. 1976. "Forward Rates As Predictors of Future Spot Rates." *Journal of Financial Economics*, Vol. 3, No. 4, October, pp. 361-378.

———. 1976. "Inflation Uncertainty and Expected Returns on Treasury Bills." *Journal of Political Economy*, June, pp. 427-448.

———. 1975. "Short-Term Interest Rates As Predictors of Inflation." *American Economic Review*, Vol. 65, No. 3, June, pp. 269-283.

———. 1970. "Efficient Capital Markets: A Review of Theory and Empirical Works." *The Journal of Finance*, Vol. 3, No. 2, May, pp. 383-417.

Fisher, L. 1959. "Determinants of Risk Premiums on Corporate Bonds." *Journal of Political Economy*, Vol. 51, No. 3, June, pp. 217-237.

——— and Weil, R. L. 1971. "Coping with the Risk of Interest Rate Fluctuations: Returns to Bondholders from Naive and Optimal Strategies." *Journal of Business*, Vol. 44, No. 4, October, pp. 408-431.

Fong, G. H. Associates. 1979. "Immunization: Definition and Simulation Study." Santa Monica. Unpublished paper.

——— and Vasicek, O. 1980. "A Risk Minimizing Strategy for Multiple Liability Immunization." Working Paper.

Forbes. 1979. "Las Vegas in Chicago: Speculating on Interest Rate Futures." July 1, pp. 31-33.

Franckle, C. T. 1980. "The Hedging Performance of the New Futures Market: Comment." *Journal of Finance*, Vol. 35, No. 5, December, pp. 1273-1279.

——— and McCabe, G. M. 1980. "The Effectiveness of Rolling the Hedge Forward in the Interest Rate Futures Market." Working Paper.

——— and McCabe, G. M. 1979. "Hedging Mismatched Needs for Funds." Paper presented at the 1979 annual meeting of the Southwestern Finance Association.

——— and Senchack, A. 1980. "Economic Considerations in the Use of Interest Rate Futures." Working Paper.

——— and Wurtzebach, C. 1980. "Hedging Effectiveness of the GNMA Futures Market." Working Paper.

Friedman, B. 1979. "Interest Rate Expectations Versus Forward Rates: Evidence from an Expectations Survey." *Journal of Finance*, September, pp. 965-973.

Froewiss, K. 1978(a). "Futures and Taxes, Tax Spreads: Handle with Caution." *Commodities*, October, p. 27.

———. 1978(b). "GNMA Futures: Stabilizing or Destabilizing." *San Francisco Federal Reserve Bank Economic Review*, Spring, pp. 20-29.

——— and Gorham, M. 1978. "Everyman's Interest Rate Forecast." Federal Reserve Bank of San Francisco *Weekly Letter*, September, p. 1.

Gapay, L. 1976. "Two U.S. Agency Dispute Jurisdiction Over Treasury Bills, Ginnie Mae Futures." *Wall Street Journal*, June, p. 16.

Gardner, R. 1980. "The Effects of the T-Bill Futures Market on the Cash T-Bill Market." Paper presented at the Columbia Futures Conference.

Gay, G. and Kolb, R. "Interest Rate Futures: A New Perspective on Immunization," forthcoming, *The Journal of Portfolio Management*.

Gay, G., Kolb, R., and Chiang, R. 1981. "Interest Rate Hedging: An Empirical Test of Alternative Strategies." Working Paper.

Gotthelf. 1978. "A Systems Approach to Financial Futures Markets." *Commodities*, Vol. 7, No. 8, August, pp. 28-29.

Gray, R. W. 1972. "The Futures Market for Main Potatoes: An Appraisal." *Food Research Institute Studies*, Vol. XI, No. 3.

———. 1961. "The Search for a Risk Premium." *Journal of Political Economy*, June, pp. 250-260.

Greenbaum and Thaker. 1980. "Interest Rate Futures and Bank Credit Market." Paper Midwest Finance, March, Chicago.

Grove, M. A. 1974. "On 'Duration' and the Optimal Maturity Structure of the Balance Sheet." *The Bell Journal of Economics and Management Science*, Vol. 5, No. 2, Autumn, pp. 696-709.

———. 1966. "A Model of the Maturity Profile of the Balanced Sheet." *Metroeconomica*, Vol. 18, No. 1, April, pp. 40-55.

Hamburger, M. and Platt, E. 1975. "The Expectations Hypothesis and the Efficiency of the Treasury Bill Market." *Review of Economics and Statistics*, Vol. 57, No. 2, May, pp. 190-199.

Hegde, S. 1981. "Hedging in Financial Futures: Determinants of Hedge Ratio." Paper presented at Eastern Finance Association, Newport, RI, April.

Hicks, S. S. 1980. "The Hedging Performance of the New Futures Market: Additional Evidence." Unpublished Paper.

Hill, J. and Schneeweis, T. 1980. "Risk Reduction Potential of GNMA Futures for Issues and Holders of Corporate Bonds." Paper presented at International Research Seminar, Chicago Board of Trade, May.

———. 1980. "Risk Reduction Potential of Financial Futures for Corporate Bond Positions." Working Paper, University of Massachusetts.

Hobson, R. 1978. "Futures Trading in Financial Instruments." Commodity Futures Trading Commission, October.

Hoel, A. 1976. "A Primer on the Futures Markets for Treasury Bills." Research paper, Federal Reserve Bank of New York.

Holland, T. E. 1965. "A Note on the Traditional Theory of the Term Structure of Interest Rates on Three and Six Month Treasury Bills." *International Economic Review*, September, pp. 330-336.

Hopewell, M. and Kaufman, G. G. 1973. "Bond Price Volatility and Term to Maturity: A Generalized Respecification." *American Economic Review*, September, pp. 749-753.

Howard, C. 1980. "Forecasting Interest Rates and Implications for the T-Bill Futures Market." October, Paper presented at FMA, New Orleans.

Ingersoll, J., Skelton, J. and Weil, R. 1978. "Duration Forty Years Later." *Journal of Financial and Quantitative Analysis*, Vol. 13, No. 4, November, pp. 627-650.
International Monetary Market. 1977. "Treasury Bill Futures." Chicago.
——. "IMM Treasury Bill Futures Contract Specifications." Chicago.
——. "T-Bill Futures: Opportunities in Interest Rates." Chicago.
Jacobs, S. 1977(a). "Mortgage Bankers Must Develop Knowledge Strategy to Use GNMA Futures Market." *Mortgage Bankers*, April, pp. 53-57.
——. 1977(b). "The Short Hedge–Financial Boom for Mortgage Bankers." *Mortgage Bankers*, February.
—— and Kozach, J. R. 1975. "Is There A Future for a Mortgage Futures Market?" *Real Estate Review*, Spring.
Jaffe, N. and Hobson, R. 1979. "Survey of Interest Rate Futures Markets." December, Commodity Futures Trading Commission.
Johnson, L. L. 1960. "The Theory of Hedging and Speculation in Commodity Futures." *Review of Economic Studies*, Vol. 27, October, pp. 139-151.
Jones, F. 1981. "The Integration of Cash and Futures Markets and Holding Period Rates of Return." *The Journal of Futures Markets*, Vol. 1, No. 1, Spring, pp. 33-58.
Kane, E. J. 1980. "Market Incompleteness and Divergences between Forward and Futures Interest Rates." *Journal of Finance*, Vol. 35, No. 2, May, pp. 221-234.
Kaufman, G. G. 1980. "Duration, Planning Period, and Tests of the Capital Asset Pricing Model." *Journal of Financial Research*, Vol. 3, No. 1, Spring, pp. 1-9.
——. 1978. "Measuring Risk and Return for Bonds: A New Approach." *Journal of Bank Research*, Summer, pp. 82-90.
Khang, C. 1979. "Bond Immunization When Short-Term Rates Fluctuate More than Long-Term Rates." *Journal of Financial and Quantitative Analysis*, Vol. 14, No. 5, December, pp. 1085-1090.
Klapper, B. 1976. "New T-Bill Futures Market Has Light Volume–." *Wall Street Journal*, January 23, p. 24.
Kolb, R. 1981. *Interest Rate Futures: A Comprehensive Introduction.* Forthcoming, Robert F. Dame, Inc.
Kolb, R. and Chiang, R. 1981. "Duration, Immunization, and Hedging with Interest Rate Futures." Forthcoming, *Journal of Financial Research*.
—— and Chiang, R. 1981. "Improving Hedging Performance Using Interest Rate Futures." *Financial Management*, Autumn, pp. 72-9.
——, Corgel, J. and Chiang, R. 1981. "Effective Hedging of Mortgage Interest Rate Risk." Forthcoming, *Housing Finance Review*.
—— and Gay, G. 1981. "Immunizing Bond Portfolios with Interest Rate Futures." Working paper.
——, Gay, G., and Jordan, J. 1981. "The Efficiency of the Treasury Bond Futures Market." Working paper.
Lacey, J. 1979. "Why Interest Rate Futures Spreads Change." *Commodities*, April, p. 71.
Lang, R. and Rasche, R. 1978. "A Comparison of Yields on Futures Contracts and

Implied Forward Rates." *Federal Reserve Bank of St Louis Review*, December, pp. 21-30.

Lanstein, R. and Sharpe, W. F. 1978. "Duration and Security Risk." *Journal of Financial and Quantitative Analysis*, Vol. 13, No. 4, November, pp. 653-668.

Liro, J., Hill, J., and Schneeweis, T. 1981. "Risk Reduction of GNMA Futures for Issues of Mortgage Backed Bonds." Paper presented at Eastern Finance, Newport, RI, April.

Liviatan, N. and Levhari, D. 1977. "Risk and the Theory of Indexed Bonds." *American Economic Review*, June, pp. 366-375.

Loosigian, A. 1980. *Interest Rate Futures*. New Jersey: Dow Jones Books.

Lovell, M. C. and Vogel, R. C. 1973. "A CPI-Futures Market." *Journal of Political Economy*, July/August, pp. 1009-1112.

Lower, R. and Ryan, S. 1980. "Futures Trading by National Banks." *Banking Law Journal*, pp. 239-256.

Macaulay, F. R. 1938. *Some Theoretical Problems Suggested by the Movements of Interest Rates, Bond Yields, and Stock Prices in the United States Since 1856*. New York: Columbia University Press.

Mackie, V. 1976. "Interest Rate Futures Offer a New Hedging Alternative." *Pensions and Investments*, April 12, p. 17.

Madrick. 1977. "T-Bill Futures: The Loophole with Potential." *Business Week*, January 10, p. 71.

Malkiel, B. G. 1966. *The Term Structure of Interest Rates*. Princeton: Princeton University Press.

Maness. 1980. "Relationship Between the Hedge Duration and the Hedge Ratio in the T-Bill Futures Market." Paper presented at FMA, New Orleans, October.

——. "The Relationship Between "Ginnie Mae" and Treasury Bill Futures Rates." Unpublished Paper, Baylor University.

Marsh, T. and Webb, R. 1981. "Speculation, Differential Information and the Structure of Futures Markets." Paper presented at Eastern Finance, Newport, R.I., April.

Martell, T. F. 1976. "Adaptive Trading Rules for Commodity Futures." *Omega*, 4, pp. 407-415.

—— and Helms, B. P. 1978. "A Reexamination of Price Changes in the Commodity Futures Market." Chicago Board of Trade *International Research Seminar Proceedings*.

—— and Philippatos, G. C. 1974. "Adaptation Information and Dependence in Commodity Markets." *The Journal of Finance*, Vol. 29, No. 2, May, pp. 493-498.

Martin. 1979. "Hedging Interest Rate Volatility in Financial Futures." FMA paper, October, Boston.

McCabe, G. M. and Blackwell, J. M. 1978. "The Hedging Strategy: A New Approach to Spread Management Banking and Commercial Lending." Paper presented at 1978 annual meeting of the Financial Management Association.

—— and Franckle, C. 1980. "Cross Hedging in the Treasury Bills Futures Market: Is It Effective?" Working Paper.

—— and McLeod, R. W. "Regulating Commercial Bank Trading in Futures Markets." Forthcoming in *Issues in Bank Regulation*.

McEnally, R. 1977. "Duration as a Practical Tool for Bond Management." *Journal of Portfolio Management*, Vol. 3, No. 4, Summer, pp. 53-57.

—— and Rice, M. 1979. "Hedging Possibilities in the Flotation of Debt Securities." *Financial Management*, Vol. 8, No. 4, Winter, pp. 12-18.

McLeod, R. W. and McCabe, G. M. 1981. "Hedging for Better Spread Management." *Bankers Magazine*, pp. 47-52.

Miller, E. 1980. "Tax-Induced Bias in Markets for Futures Contracts." *Financial Review*, Vol. 15, No. 2, Spring, pp. 35-38.

——. 1978. "How to Win at the Loser's Game." *Journal of Portfolio Management*, Vol. 5, No. 1, Fall, pp. 17-24.

Moffett. 1978. "T-Bills and Taxes." *Wall Street Journal*, July 31.

——. 1978. "Futures Contracts in Treasury Bills Offer Gains and Tax Savings, to Some Investors." *Wall Street Journal*, July 3.

Morgan, G. E. 1980. "Forward and Futures Pricing of Treasury Bills." Forthcoming in *Journal of Banking and Finance*.

—— and Franckle, C. T. 1980. "The Error Learning Model and the Financial Futures Market." Paper presented for the annual meetings of the Financial Management Association, New Orleans, LA, October 23.

Morris, J. 1980. "Futures Markets Beckoning Hesitant Banks." *The American Banker*, October 12.

Oldfield, G. 1977. "The Relationship Between U.S. Treasury Bill Spot and Futures Prices." Working Paper.

Parker, J. and Daigler, R. 1981. "How Financial Futures Can Be Employed to Overcome Maturity Problems for Financial Institutions." Paper presented at Eastern Finance, Newport, R.I., April.

——. 1981. "The Pricing of Financial Futures Contracts." Paper presented at the Mid-South Academy of Economists, Memphis, February.

Peck, A. E. 1977. *Selected Writings on Futures Markets*. Chicago: Chicago Board of Trade.

Pesando, J. E. 1975. "Determinants of Term Premiums in the Market for Treasury Bills." *Journal of Finance*, Vol. 30, No. 3, June, pp. 761-771.

Poole, W. 1978. "Using T-Bill Futures to Gauge Interest Rate Expectations." *Federal Reserve Bank of San Francisco Economic Review*, Spring, pp. 7-15.

Powers, M. 1978. "Yield Curve: The Strip"; "Yield Curves." *Commodities*, Parts I and II, December, August, and September.

——. "Thin Markets—A Regulatory Perspective." Mimeograph.

—— and Vogel, D. 1981. *Inside the Financial Futures Markets*. New York: John Wiley and Sons.

Praetz, P. D. 1976. "On the Methodology of Testing for Independence in Futures Prices: Comment." *Journal of Finance*, Vol. 31, No. 3, June, pp. 977-979.

Puglisi, D. 1978. "Is the Futures Market for Treasury Bills Efficient?" *The Journal of Portfolio Management*, Vol. 4, No. 2, Winter, pp. 64-67.

Quint. 1977. "Interest Rate Futures Gain As Hedgers on CD Costs." *American Banker*, November 25.

Raleigh. 1979. "Mortgage Banker Marketing Study of GNMA Futures." *Mortgage Banker*, September, pp. 55-60.

Rendleman, R. and Carabini, C. 1979. "The Efficiency of the Treasury Bill Futures Market." *Journal of Finance*, Vol. 34, No. 4, September, pp. 895-914.

Rice, M. and Peterson, P. 1979. "Financial Contracts." *Proceedings International Futures Trading Seminar*, Vol. VI, May, CBT.

Roll, R. 1968. "The Efficient Market Model Applied to U.S. Treasury Bill Rates." Ph.D. dissertation, Graduate School of Business, University of Chicago.

Rosenbluth, G. 1975. "Trading Mortgage Interest Rate Futures." *Federal Home Loan Bank Board Journal*, September, pp. 2-9.

Ryan. 1978. "A Tax Shelter Where the IRS Fears to Tread?" *Medical Economics*, June 12.

Sandor, R. 1977. "Commercial Paper and Treasury Bonds: More Interest Rate Futures Innovation and How They'll Work." *Commodities*, Vol. 6, No. 10, October, pp. 22-25.

———. 1976. "The Interest Rate Futures Markets: An Introduction." *Commodities*, Vol. 5, No. 9, September, pp. 14-17.

———. 1976. "Comment (on a Paper by L. Ederington and L. Plumly)." *Futures Trading Seminar Proceeding*, Vol. 5. Chicago: Chicago Board of Trade.

———. 1975. "Trading Mortgage Interest Rate Futures." *Federal Home Loan Bank Board Journal*, September, pp. 2-9.

Scholes, M. 1981. "The Economics of Hedging and Spreading in Futures Markets." *Journal of Futures Markets*, Vol. 1, No. 2.

Schwartz, E. W. 1979. *How to Use Interest Rate Futures Contracts*. Homewood, Illinois: Dow Jones-Irwin.

Schweser, C., Cole, J., and D'Antonio, L. 1980. "Hedging Opportunities in Bank Risk Management Program." *The Journal of Commercial Bank Lending*, January, pp. 29-41.

Senchack, A. J. 1981. "Cross Hedging Performance Using Treasury Bill Futures." Paper Eastern Finance, April, Newport, R.I.

———. 1980. "Hedging Performance in the T-Bill Futures Market." Paper presented at FMA, New Orleans, October, working paper, The University of Texas.

——— and Easterwood, J. 1981. "Cross-Hedge Performance Using T-Bill Futures." Paper presented at Eastern Finance, Newport, R.I., April.

——— and Pearce, K. 1978. "Hedging Short-Term Interest Rate Risk in the Treasury Bill Futures Market." University of Texas working paper.

Shearson Hayden Stone, Inc. 1975. "Guide to Speculating and Hedging in Mortgage Futures." October 10.

Sherman, J. 1981. "Can Banks Successfully Hedge Their Municipal Bond Portfolio?" Paper presented at the Mid-South Academy of Economists, February, Memphis.

Silber, W. 1981. "Innovation, Competition, and New Contract Design in Futures Markets." *Journal of Futures Markets*, Vol. 1, No. 2.

Snyder, L. 1977. "How to Speculate in the World's Safest Investment." *Fortune*, July.
Stanley, K. L. 1981. "Elimination of Dual Trading on Futures Exchanges: An Analytical Framework." Paper presented at the Mid-South meetings, February.
Stein, J. L. 1961. "The Simultaneous Determination of Spot and Futures Prices." *American Economic Review*, Vol. 51, No. 1, December, pp. 1012-1025.
Stevens, N. A. 1976. "A Mortgage Futures Market: Its Development, Uses, Benefits, and Costs." *Federal Reserve Bank of St. Louis Review*, Vol. 58, No. 4, April, pp. 20-27.
Telser, L. G. 1981. "Margins and Futures Contracts." *Journal of Futures Markets*, Vol. 1, No. 2.
Teweles, R. J., Harlow, C. V., and Stone, H. L. 1974. *The Commodity Futures Game*. New York: McGraw Hill.
Vignola, A. and Dale, C. 1980. "The Efficiency of the Treasury Bill Futures Market: An Analysis of Alternative Specifications." *Journal of Financial Research*, Vol. 3, No. 2, Fall, pp. 169-188.
———. 1979. "Is the Futures Market for Treasury Bills Efficient?" *Journal of Portfolio Management*, Vol. 5, No. 2, Winter, pp. 78-81.
———. 1979. "Price Determination and the Treasury Bill Futures Market." Washington: U. S. Treasury Department. Mimeographed.
Wall Street Journal. 1978. "Interest Rate Futures Market Attracts Avid Interest, Diverse Trading Strategies." April 17.
Winsk, J. 1975. "Interest Rate Futures Trades Set Today; Mechanism May Help Mortgage Lenders." *Wall Street Journal*, October 20, p. 16.
Yardeni, E. 1978. "Hedged Rides in the T-Bill Futures Markets." *Commodities*, August, pp. 26-27.